· A

LIFE OF MEANING

Embracing Reform Judaism's Sacred Path

Edited by

RABBI DANA EVAN KAPLAN, PhD

Foreword by Rabbi Steven A. Fox

Central Conference of American Rabbis
5778   New York   2018

Library of Congress Cataloging-in-Publication Data

Names: Kaplan, Dana Evan, editor.

Title: A life of meaning : embracing Reform Judaism's sacred path / edited by
Rabbi Dana Evan Kaplan, PhD ; foreword by Rabbi Steven A. Fox.

Description: New York, NY : CCAR Press, [2018] | Includes bibliographical
references and index.

Identifiers: LCCN 2017048109 (print) | LCCN 2017049253 (ebook) | ISBN
9780881233148 | ISBN 9780881233131 (pbk. : alk. paper)

Subjects: LCSH: Reform Judaism. | Judaism--21st century.

Classification: LCC BM197 (ebook) | LCC BM197 .L563 2018 (print) | DDC
296.8/341--dc23

LC record available at https://lccn.loc.gov/2017048109

10 9 8 7 6 5 4 3 2 1

CCAR Press, 355 Lexington Avenue, New York, NY 10017 (212) 972-3636

www.ccarpress.org

Contents

Foreword

RABBI STEVEN A. FOX

Innovation anchored in Jewish tradition is the central motif that runs throughout the history of our people, and especially in the ongoing evolution of Reform Judaism. *A Life of Meaning* captures the spirit of that innovation: its creativity, inherent tensions, and roots in traditional Jewish life. As an anthology of essays written by rabbis, cantors, and other prominent scholars in the field of Jewish thought, *A Life of Meaning* presents an in-depth examination of Reform Judaism's practices, rituals, and beliefs, our relationship to Torah and halachah, the centrality of social justice in the Reform Movement, and issues such as conversion, interfaith families, and the relatively new Reform community in Israel.

The anthology you hold in your hands reflects conversations happening in the Reform Movement today. Importantly, the essays you will read often disagree, sometimes passionately, over what Reform Judaism could and should become as we look to the future. The diversity of thinking you will find in this book is, indeed, one of the great strengths of Reform Judaism. Robust discourse has become part and parcel of Reform practice, as it ensures that our Torah remains a living, breathing document that preserves Jewish tradition even as it informs and transforms it. The dialogue in the essays and among the essays, one to the other, will inspire and enrich larger conversations among Reform Jews and provide the insight into a Movement whose foundational tenets value debate, dialogue, and the ongoing evolution of thought.

While the earliest roots of Reform Judaism lay in Germany, students of American Jewish history (as I was, under the tutelage of Rabbi Dr. Jacob Rader Marcus, *z"l*) might ask what the visionary founder of today's Reform Judaism in North America, Rabbi Isaac Mayer Wise, would think of Reform Judaism today. It strikes me that Rabbi Wise would be quite proud of the accomplishments of the Reform Movement, which has nurtured and sustained a vibrant American Judaism while expanding its practice throughout North America and to other parts of the world. Ironically, he might not necessarily recognize that which he thought he had initiated. In the Talmudic scenario imagining Moses sitting in Rabbi Akiva's classroom and being confused by what he hears, it is not until Moses learns of the influence of the Oral Torah from the Mishnah and Talmud that he realizes the dynamic impact of subsequent generations on the meaning and experience of Judaism. Like Moses before him, Isaac Mayer Wise would understand that our innovations are built upon the foundation that he constructed, layered by the generations between our day and his. Wise would surely be pleased to find today's Reform Judaism built upon his core values and visions: making Judaism meaningful, compelling, and accessible for the contemporary Jew. At the same time, he would perhaps be somewhat perplexed and bewildered by current religious practices discussed in this book: the breadth of denominational and institutional Judaism, the depth of our connection to Israel, and our people's integration into general society. As he sought to balance the economic, cultural, and spiritual realities of his time, Wise would appreciate how we strive to do so today.

Some of the challenges that Wise faced in the late 1870s are also our challenges: technological advancement (railroad then, social media today), demographic shifts (European immigrants then, today's welcoming of community members raised in different faith or cultural traditions), and differences of opinion about issues of theology, the role of Jewish law, how to best use language in the prayer service, and religious observance, as well as how to engage the next generation in communal life.

I am proud that this collection is being published by the CCAR Press. As the rabbinic leadership organization founded by Rabbi Wise, the Central Conference of America Rabbis has, since the 1800s, led the ongoing conversation about who we are and what we believe as Reform Jews. In these essays, you will read of the platforms and positions promulgated by the CCAR that reflect the theology and ideology of Reform rabbis and the Reform Movement at particular points in time. The authors have succeeded in situating these platforms in a much greater historical context, relative to both the Reform responsa issued by the CCAR since 1906 and the resolutions of our organization and our sister organization, the Union for Reform

Judaism (originally founded by Wise as the Union of American Hebrew Congregations).

Another important contextual understanding comes from the writings in this book on Reform Jewish liturgy. Since we published the first *Union Prayer Book* in 1890, all the way through *Mishkan T'filah* (2006) and *Mishkan HaNefesh* (2015), the liturgical publications of the CCAR have contributed, on a macro level, to the unification of the Reform community and, on a micro level, to one Reform Jew feeling a sense of connection to the next. Yet, it is important to remember that this liturgy reflects our unity and not our uniformity. While *Mishkan HaNefesh* (the CCAR's newest liturgical publication for the High Holy Days) maintains the gorgeous, poetic, and often romantic language of prior prayer books, it also offers a range of theologies, ideologies, and traditions, allowing for individual intimacy and communal involvement.

Innovation anchored in Jewish tradition stands today as the focus of Reform rabbinic leadership. It enhances engagement and education in our congregations and community organizations and creates inclusive communities for Jews from all walks of life, as well as for those who wish to join us on a meaningful Jewish journey. Indeed, the essays in this collection, as well as the Reform Judaism of our people today, call to mind a teaching from Rav Abraham Isaac Kook (1865–1935): *Hayashan yitchadeish v'hechadash yitkadeish*, "The old shall be new and the new shall be holy."

Introduction

NOT IN THE HEAVENS,
NOT BEYOND THE SEA,
BUT CLOSE TO US

Rabbi Dana Evan Kaplan, PhD

In a Talmudic story, Rabbi Eliezer ben Hyrcanus disputed with
colleagues whether a clay oven that had become impure could be broken
up, reassembled with sand between the pieces, and thereby be made pure
again. Eliezer believed it could. All his arguments from Scripture, however,
were rejected. So Eliezer called on God to move a nearby carob tree if God
agreed with Eliezer. God indeed moved the tree. Eliezer was then able to
get God to perform more miracles, including making a stream flow uphill,
to show that God supported Eliezer's position.

Finally, still unable to convince his colleagues, Eliezer called on
God to speak directly. A heavenly voice declared, "The law should
be according to what my son Eliezer proposes." Upon hearing God,
Rabbi Yehoshua, speaking for most of those assembled, said that—
although, no doubt, they were awed and honored to hear directly from
heaven—nothing changed the fact that the Torah was *not* in the heavens!
(Babylonian Talmud, *Bava M'tzia* 59a-b).

Reform Judaism insists on responding to earthbound society and culture—to what is happening here in our world. Indeed, the Book of Deuteronomy declares:

> [The Torah] is not in the heavens, that you should say, "Who among
> us can go up to the heavens and get it for us and impart it to us, that we

may observe it?" Neither is it beyond the sea, that you should say, "Who among us can cross to the other side of the sea and get it for us and impart it to us, that we may observe it?" No, the thing is very close to you, in your mouth and in your heart, to observe it. (Deuteronomy 30:12–14)

Jews over the centuries have interpreted this to mean that the Torah is not just the Five Books of Moses, nor the Hebrew Bible, nor the oral tradition as understood by the Sages of the classical Rabbinic tradition. Instead, Torah is the process that sees each generation necessarily interpreting religion in the light of their own contemporary understanding of life.

The book you hold in your hands is a collection of essays written by rabbis, cantors, and other scholars interested in liberal Judaism's bold religious response to dramatic historical and sociological changes. Committed to their Jewish faith, the writers believe that it enriches our lives and merits all the time, energy, and emotional devotion we can put into it.

This is so even though we fundamentally disagree with each other on many core religious principles. Disagreement is the basis for discussion; we want you to talk about not only what you believe but how you feel about what others believe. We also want the essays to deliver not only information but new perspectives enriching the dialogue that is initiated.

The Reform Movement is filled with people who differ, sometimes passionately. They differ not just over what we should practice but over the entire premise for sustaining the Jewish religion, or indeed any religion. It can be difficult, then, to describe Reform Judaism and even more difficult to understand how Reform helps us build a life of meaning.

Within the Reform Movement, broad consensus exists on many social issues, and yet there is tremendous diversity in how we understand what we are doing and why. Whether considering different approaches to seeking God or examining Judaism's specific doctrines (chosenness, commandments, prayer, free will, life after death, and so forth), our writers want to give you a sense of how Reform thinkers today view religious practice, experience, and belief.

You should not expect definitive conclusions, however. As many of us are fond of saying, Judaism is better at asking questions than it is at providing answers. We claim a distinctive *discourse of disagreement* that makes our discussion about religion distinctly Jewish, and that discussion, rather than any particular or specific doctrine, is what characterizes our religious approach. There is an inherent tension in any discussion about what Reform

Judaism—or any type of Judaism—is and what it could and should become, precisely because we come to the question with conflicting visions.

For this reason, we thought the best approach would be to bring together a large number of writers to address the question of what is important about Reform Judaism for people today. Coming from a variety of perspectives, our contributors consider the most important parts of progressive Judaism, to help us all embrace a distinctively Jewish way of life. One of the hopes for this collection is that it can stimulate discussion, dialogue, analysis, and eventually action.

It is key that, in contrast to traditional Judaism, we accept religious autonomy as a core religious value. By that we mean that there is no religious authority laying down what we should and should not do. We do have a broad religious principle to help guide us: the Reform Movement speaks of *progressive revelation*, by which we mean that it is not that God communicated with human beings once, but rather that, with the proper spiritual preparation, we can have an ongoing mutual communicative experience with God. We open our ears to hear God speaking to us, however we envision that process. As Rabbi Maurice Eisendrath explained (in the non-gender-neutral language of his time), "God is a *living* God—not a God who revealed Himself and His word once and for all time at Sinai and speaks no more."[1]

If we see divine revelation as a long-term process, we can see our religion as an organic entity that breathes and grows over the course of time. If our relationship with God can grow, our religious experiences can consequently change and our Judaism be transformed. As a sociological report on the Reform Movement put it a generation ago, "Reform" is a verb. That is why the name is *Reform* Judaism rather than *Reformed* Judaism.

The American Reform Movement does have a central congregational organization, called the Union for Reform Judaism, which is a constituent of the World Union for Progressive Judaism. American Reform rabbis, cantors, educators, and communal professionals train at a central educational institution, the Hebrew Union College–Jewish Institute of Religion, with campuses in Cincinnati, New York, Los Angeles, and Jerusalem. The rabbis belong to a rabbinic organization called the Central Conference of American Rabbis, the cantors to the American Conference of Cantors, and the educators to the Association of Reform Jewish Educators. There are also various organizations associated with Reform, Liberal, and Progressive Judaism in different parts of the world. All of these organizations have leaders, whose role is to encourage vigorous inquiry and discussion—not to tell us what we must do religiously.

This is a tremendous deviation from historical norms. When people today think of traditional Judaism (or any other form of premodern religion), they think of obedience rather than choice. Colloquially, the word *mitzvah* today has come to mean a "good deed" one might choose to do. *Mitzvah's* true meaning, however, is "commandment." According to the Sages, God told the Israelites to fulfill the commandments as part of the covenant, which was obligatory for all time. Premodern religions, including Judaism, stressed obedience. And yet here we are talking about Judaism as a freely chosen spiritual path, not deriving from any obligation we feel to God, but because choosing it can help us to find meaning, build meaning, sustain meaning. It's a completely different approach to religion.

Reform Judaism has emphasized religious autonomy both of the individual and of the congregation. This means that we are charged with a tremendous responsibility. We have to take each and every commandment of the Torah and subject it to rigorous testing and analysis to determine how that particular mitzvah can be made meaningful in a contemporary context.

And if it cannot be made meaningful? Then we have the right and indeed the duty to abrogate it, moving on to other practices that are truly religiously significant. In short, how Reform Jews understand Judaism is something that evolves constantly, because we seek a faith that is in harmony with our actual beliefs and experiences. And *those* are shaped most directly by the society to which we belong—again, something that evolves constantly.

To fashion a Reform Jewish spirituality for twenty-first-century society requires a wide variety of sources of knowledge. One of those sources is Rabbinic literature, specifically its ideas about observing the commandments, something frequently ignored in Reform Jewish writings. That lacuna is closing, as this collection demonstrates.

Actually, one of this collection's core concerns is the commandments. *Mitzvah* is not a term that was used in earlier generations, because the early Reformers were not comfortable with the concept of God commanding us. The idea seemed to them to install Jewish law, halachah, as a binding system of practice as well as thought. Early Reform Jews may have disagreed on many things, but most considered Jewish law antiquated and purposeless.

That is no longer a universally accepted position. Some writers in this collection argue, implicitly or explicitly, that Jewish law can and should be Reform Jews' focus. Even the food laws come in for renewed attention, with one author explaining their religious meaning for her.

There's an oft-repeated expression that Judaism is much more about what you do than what you believe. Even so, we should remember that actions are typically predicated on beliefs. As you look through the various essays in this collection, you will find not only a variety of topics but also diverse theological assumptions. It will soon become clear that not all Reform Jews believe the same things. The collection does not try to affirm that any particular narrow belief system is the ultimate truth.

If we do not all believe the same things about the central mythic structure of the Jewish religion, how can we justify any observances? The key may be in seeing our observances as ceremonies rather than rituals. What is the difference? Ritual is stylized, repetitive religious behavior that is seen as being directly commanded by God. It is not only that God commands us to complete a particular act or series of acts, but we are commanded to perform them in a specific manner, time, and context. This is because ritual is potentially efficacious, meaning that if God is pleased by accurate obedience, there can and probably will be a positive divine response. In turn, if the ritual is not done exactly according to holy writ, then there likewise should be a response—but a potentially devastating, punishing one.

Unlike ritual, ceremony is a human effort to give concrete representation to abstract religious concepts. Participants do not believe that they are being directly commanded by God, and indeed they may or may not believe that God has anything to do with it. The important thing is that the ceremony express their search for meaning in a spiritually uplifting manner. The ceremony's purpose is to help us to connect with our spiritual self, however we define that, rather than to please God in objective terms that conform to biblical or Rabbinic texts.

Understanding Reform Jewish observances as ceremonies helps us make sense of what we might term "synagogue Judaism," meaning everything that is done in a Reform temple: worship, education, social events, and creative expressions of spirituality ranging from nature services to pet blessings. My experience in the congregations that I have led over the years is that some people find ceremonial practices deeply meaningful and are willing to drive long distances and brave the elements for the sake of the associated sanctifying moments. What motivates them to sacrifice so much to be there rain or shine? Clearly, the answer is that they derive spiritual meaning from their participation.

We do not need to understand all of our subconscious motivations. But if we want to embrace our religious faith with wholehearted devotion, we need to justify, convincingly, what we do and why. In an era when boundaries of all kinds are fading or gone, we must clarify our theology and convey our religious beliefs with conviction.

Books on Judaism abound today, but they tend to blur some quite real differences in the theological perspectives of various denominations. Perhaps their writers found these differences unimportant; perhaps they were positioning themselves to tap the broadest market. Whatever the case, this book takes a different approach, making the argument that Reform Judaism comprises distinct worldviews that deserve not to be blurred. Reform, we believe—more than some other forms of Judaism—is compelling for those who understand it and take it seriously. It is a belief system that is fulfilling admirably the spiritual needs of those who embrace it, even in a time when abandoning religion has become fashionable.

We hope that our collection will help situate some of Reform Judaism's long-held religious concepts in a contemporary context. We want to connect the Jewish communities throughout our country and elsewhere in the world to the God of Israel. We need to return to the beginning and try to imagine a God of Israel who can be a source for good in our world while also being believable. Our book offers a number of approaches to this religious quandary.

We want to stress that Reform Judaism is not just about ethnic identity and communal socializing. Reform's heart is an approach to God and religion. Conceptualized in whatever way, a vision of a divine presence is vital for developing a faith and expressing a mature spirituality. In Judaism, spirituality is of course an individual concern, but it is always framed in a communal context. After exploring some approaches to religious belief, this collection moves on to more-practical issues of observing commandments and building community. Community's prominent role here may surprise readers; we avoided strongly emphasizing individual spirituality, but not *just* because so many other books do.

Americans are looking for spiritual insight that can stimulate them on an individual, and indeed an individualistic, basis. This stands in dramatic contrast to Rabbinic Judaism's overwhelming concern with Judaism as communal system. According to the Sages, God made a covenant with the Children of Israel, who are collectively held responsible for upholding their end of the bargain. Traditional Judaism, then, holds the individual Jew responsible for conforming to the communal contract.

One of the most used terms in Rabbinic literature is *k'lal Yisrael*, meaning "the entirety of the community of Israel." What concerned the Sages of the classical Rabbinic tradition was the individual as part of the collective, not the individual alone. This is one difficulty in bringing Judaism forward into our contemporary society, one that is based on Christian notions of religion and, even more problematic, is steeped in individualism.

What drives our collection is this: Even though some laws set out in the Torah and the Talmud remain relevant, the laws—any law—are less important than the ethical motives underlying the entire Jewish tradition. We are free to select the aspects of the Bible and Rabbinic literature that we find spiritually meaningful and to expand on the insights they offer.

Once I talked about this freedom in an adult education course at my temple. A participant doubted our right to "cherry-picking," going into the cherry bushes to pick the plump, ripe, presumably tastiest fruit, leaving less appealing cherries on the branches. We discussed how "cherry-picking" means pointing out cases that confirm one's partisan position and ignoring all other cases. I felt that we were not in fact cherry-picking, because we were taking care to avoid biasing and ignoring part of the evidence to create a misleading conclusion. Instead, we were evaluating elements from religion's ancient sources, seeking a healthy, ethically sensitive twenty-first-century Judaism.

Within religions, changes happen, some unconscious and without deliberation, some conscious and deliberate. Conscious, deliberate changes within religion often reflect changing ethics. Fundamentalists quash change, warping the true intent of religion by emphasizing particular practices arising at a certain stage in a religion's development and ignoring earlier as well as later manifestations. We do not want to fall into the same trap.

There are those who argue that it would be much simpler to start over. We could gather a small group of like-minded individuals and create a new religion *ex nihilo*. We would cover all of the expected basic ethical precepts and create an emotionally gripping liturgy to recite once a week or once a month, whatever we felt best. Think of the energy that would save, not having to reconcile huge numbers of arcane rules written thousands of years ago in wildly different contexts.

But that is not the path that Reform Jews have chosen. We feel a loyalty to the Jewish past and an affinity with the Jewish historical experience. Our task is to reconcile our rich traditions with our contemporary values.

We do not, as we have said, try to minimize conflict and contradiction. On the contrary, we revel in our conflicts and contradictions, our inconsistencies and discrepancies. Religion is a messy business. We have ancient texts that were sewn together, figuratively as well as literally, by redactors who were unaware that they were molding a new whole out of disparate fragments. Maybe they had no idea they were radically changing the nature of Judaism; maybe they thought they could get away with creating documents that would be seen forever as unified, originating from a single source.

Modern textual analysis as well as a host of other academic disciplines that have existed for only a little over a hundred years have exposed the sinews as well as the bones, and if we look closely enough, we are left scratching our heads in wonder. What can we do with all of this material pushing and pulling in so many different ways? Can we hope to make it cohere sensibly and consistently to yield a religious system that is faithful to the past and spiritually meaningful in the present?

What the reader can easily see is that there is no coherent religious system that drives this collection. Classical Reform Jews look back wistfully at the 1885 Pittsburgh Platform, which presented eight principles to guide the entire American Reform Movement. For decades, there was a relatively high degree of theological agreement across the movement.

As early as the 1930s, however, factions started to diverge based not only on beliefs and practices but also on basic questions of core identity. Much of this was driven by external events, specifically the rise of the Nazis in Germany and later the creation of the State of Israel. We touch only lightly on these two central historical events, but they are present at least indirectly in all the essays. Indeed, much is left unsaid in this collection. Judaism is both a liturgical and a historical religion, and we have trod very lightly on a tremendous amount of helpful background, because the reader has limited time and cares most about the here and now.

One of our writers describes Reform as a "blatantly modern" rendition of Judaism. This is certainly true, and it comes with advantages as well as disadvantages. On the plus side, we can eliminate what we feel is obsolete, archaic, or ethically insensitive. This is a huge deviation from what our medieval predecessors did when they had to figure out ways to justify or explain away statements inconsistent, inappropriate, or downright unacceptable. It is a tremendous relief to be able to say, "I do not believe that," and then move quickly on to what we do believe.

There is much that we find compelling and inspiring in the Hebrew Scriptures, the Rabbinic writings, mystical works, even texts focusing on Jewish law. Unfortunately, it is usually mixed right in there with concepts and practices that, at best, we find irrelevant; at worst, offensive. That is our conundrum. How do you separate the wheat from the chaff?

That is a rhetorical question. Although systems designed to adapt Jewish law to Reform Judaism's needs have been proposed, none has been generally accepted. We have no sophisticated new machine into which we can throw everything but the kitchen sink, processing the good, the bad, and the ugly to produce all beauty and glory in five minutes. Rather, this is a manual process requiring each of us to get our hands dirty. It is a do-it-yourself approach to religion, and that messiness is reflected throughout this collection.

If it were simply deciding what to cut out and what to retain, the task would not be so complex, but our evaluation of Jewish tradition has to be nuanced. We are not so much looking to cut things out as we are to reinterpret, reappropriate, reposition. We want to embrace as much of Jewish tradition as possible, *fully recognizing* that we are living in an entirely different intellectual as well as social environment than existed centuries ago. Even in cases where we carry on exactly the same ritual, with exactly the same blessing, such as the lighting of the Shabbat candles on Friday night, we are doing so in a social context that differs from that of the women of Rashi's time who originated the blessing. Today, we understand both the acts we perform and the words we recite in new, and still-changing, ways.

How do we explore such a fluid tradition? There are no ready final answers. What we do know is that to be a devoted Reform Jew requires seriousness of purpose and a willingness to make a commitment to undertaking a journey of questioning. The term *halachah*, generally translated as "Jewish law," means "walking" (from the Hebrew root *h-l-ch*, source of the verb *holeich*, "to walk"). We do not know where that journey may lead us or even, precisely, the purpose of the journey. We must nevertheless get moving, with our hiking boots on our feet, water canteens clipped to our belts, and lightweight hats with visors firmly—but not too tightly—on our heads.

In essay after essay, we read how we can no longer see things the way our ancestors did. Whether we are talking about the fundamental beliefs of the tradition or about how we understand the core Rabbinic canon, or how we see the socioreligious institutions that form such a vital framework for our ceremonial practices, everything is different and has been for quite a long time.

To put it succinctly, our ancestors believed in an omnipotent, omniscient God, and we may not. Our ancestors believed that the Torah came from God, with the Written Torah having been written down letter-by-letter by Moses at Mount Sinai, accompanied by precise oral explanations, known now as the Oral Torah. These basic doctrines were not necessarily thought of as doctrines at the time, but that is what they became.

Is a changed religion a worthless religion? Many contemporaries believe so, but we would argue the opposite. Reinterpreting an ancient religion can be both creative and spiritual, and human beings endow both creativity and spirituality with intrinsic worth. I think it is a mistake to believe that because religion as it was five hundred or one thousand years ago is outmoded, religion as it is today is necessarily irrelevant. One of the motivations for this collection was the number of essays that I saw on the Internet that were attacking religion. In particular, I remember reading a blog entry written by a West Coast psychologist who had broken away from an evangelical group. She had a long list of ideas and practices she felt religion had brought to the world, to the world's detriment. At their best, these concepts promoted conflict; at their worst, they multiplied cruelty and evil.

The word "Judaism" was never mentioned in the blog entry, and I do not think the author had much exposure to the Jewish religion. If she was thinking about Judaism at various points in the post, she did her best to hide it. But much of her list certainly applied to Judaism, including Reform Judaism. I was pretty shocked, because for me, religion is a way of seeing that brings enlightenment and rational thought forward and encourages empathy and compassion.

But that is not how a lot of other people feel. Was she confusing fundamentalist religion with liberal religion, making gross generalizations? I certainly thought so, but it was clear that she felt that anyone who believed they were part of a chosen people who had been led to a promised land and might possess a soul that would return to God for eternity was making the world a terrible place filled with scarcity and suffering.

I also read that while the United States has traditionally been among the most religious countries in the world, each subsequent poll has shown further increases in the "none" category of religion. I knew that many of my former congregants, those whom I had met and those whom I had never met, now fit this category of religious "nones." Some had gradually lost interest in a religion they probably never invested much time or attention in, while others had been traumatized and dispirited by a traumatic event. Several had had children die suddenly in accidents or from rare, virulent diseases and either had found the temple community to lack interest in supporting them emotionally or could not feel the presence of God at a crucial time in their lives.

One of the most upsetting things, I found, was that critical thinkers were the most likely to lose their faith in God and cut their ties to religion. Many of the New Atheists, for example, were indisputably bright and intellectually passionate. That they used their mental energies *against* any and all types of religious faith alarmed me. As a rabbi, deep thought, sincere contemplation, and genuine commitment are my habits of mind. They are also what I hope for in those I would reach with my religious message. Religion has to be based on truth as truth is determined by such intellectual processes as the scientific method.

Entering a new century, it looked as if the group best equipped to pursue such processes was abandoning the religious search entirely, abandoning it to purveyors of simplistic ideas advocating blind devotion to an authority figure *du jour*. We do not need that. We need smart people to work at analytically solving logical problems. So when I saw social psychologists presenting evidence that analytic thinking tended to reduce religious belief, my warning lights went off.

This collection is not explicitly designed to refute accusations leveled against religion in recent years. Neither is it meant to further undermine the shaky intellectual foundations of absolute faith that can destroy religious commitment of any type. What we do hope to do is to present some of the most recent thinking on a variety of issues relevant to Reform Judaism today.

We want to explore why sensible and perhaps even intellectual persons might find enough in the Jewish tradition to make them willing to commit to such a faith with all their heart and all their soul. The authors in this collection share the conviction that religion, Reform Judaism in particular, can help us enrich our lives. We must only be willing to make the effort to confront where we have come from and where we could go, remembering too that religion is not just an intellectual exercise, but also needs to be felt deep in our *kishkes*, our gut. As the prophet Jeremiah put it, "You will search for Me and find Me, if only you seek Me wholeheartedly" (Jeremiah 29:13).

Over the past couple of generations, it has been mostly through our children that we have interacted with the Jewish tradition. People not only came to temple but founded temples in the first place so that there would be a way to educate the next generation. The implication is that children need Judaism to learn who they are and grow up with a solid background in their religious heritage. Of course, that obsessive focus on pediatric Judaism was not well thought out. When parents drop off children at the temple on the way to the tennis courts or Starbucks, children receive the message loud and clear. Rather than being practicing, believing Reform Jews, such parents embody alimony Judaism: "I'll pay for it, but I can't live with it." That's very far from the description of the Children of Israel in the Book of Exodus, where God declares to the Israelites that "although all the peoples of the world are Mine, if you obey My covenant it is you who shall be My kingdom of priests and a holy nation" (Exodus 19:5–6).

In Deuteronomy, this covenantal promise becomes a responsibility that requires the entire Jewish people, not just the priests, to live by a strict code of holiness (26:19, 28:9). Everyone would be obligated to live by God's commandments, thereby bringing divine knowledge and understanding to the entire world. In a classical Reform context, this was explained as the *mission of Israel*, which was to bring ethical monotheism to all peoples.

At the same time that we acknowledge that religion must change with the times, we also understand people's need for continuity. In Reform temples throughout the country, congregants still miss the *Union Prayer Book*, the little black book widely used in services from 1892 all the way up until 1975. For many reasons, they express a sense of loss over the replacement of their beloved prayer book, but I think one of the most important reasons is that it undermines their sense that religion is permanent.

Many take solace in the idea that in the midst of so much societal change, there is at least one thing that does not change—their religious experience in their house of worship: "In the midst of a congregation at prayer, God's presence will be found" (Babylonian Talmud, *B'rachot* 6a). In a time rife with redefining, re-explaining, and renegotiating, it can be nice to know something that is unchanging, permanent—to use a religious term, *eternal.* That is one appeal of fundamentalism, whether Jewish, Christian, Muslim, or Hindu fundamentalism. But that is not something that we can offer in this book or in this movement.

Implicit in our collection is the universalistic notion that Reform Judaism is for anyone who might find meaning in it. Here, too, you can find quite a variety of positions along a continuum. Certainly Judaism historically was closely intertwined with the experiences of an ethnic or national group, variously called the Children of Israel, the Israelites, the Judeans, the Jews. Many early Reformers stressed Judaism as a religion, trying to detach Judaism from Jewish ethnic identity. Rabbi Adolph Moses, one of my predecessors at the Springhill Avenue Temple in Mobile, Alabama, went so far as to suggest that Judaism should be renamed "Yahvism," but this ran counter to thousands of years of historical precedent as well as to how Jews felt about their own identities. Being Jewish is not just a religion, but it is not just an ethnicity, either. The question is how to balance a degree of universality with a level of particularism, in order to help as many people as possible to derive meaning from being Jewish.

One does not have to be born Jewish to embrace Judaism, a fact that was recognized and institutionalized by the Talmudic Sages and whose roots can be seen scattered throughout the Hebrew Bible as well. We are addressing this book, therefore, not only to Reform Jews curious about a religion to which they are already committed, but to anyone interested in what Judaism says about understanding existence and living in this world. Nevertheless, the writers here do favor treating Judaism as a spiritual path rather than an ethnic identity. We want to see Jewishness become an achieved, rather than an ascribed, status. By this I mean that to be a Jew, study and practice of

Jewish religion should matter more than ethnicity inherited at birth. This increasingly fits into how Americans see religion.

Reform Judaism responded to developments—principally, the Enlightenment and emancipation—of the eighteenth and nineteenth centuries in Europe. But we no longer live in the eighteenth or nineteenth century and we are not in Europe. What does that mean for American Reform Jews or anyone else asking, What do I believe? What can I believe? What might I believe? The core argument of Reform was that Jews could practice their faith according to traditional moral precepts *without* in fact following Jewish law. This was a radical concept for the time, and it continues to have important religious implications.

Society has moved on in new directions, however. If Reform is to stay relevant, we need to develop new responses to the new challenges that face us today and to the unknown ones that will face us tomorrow. Our guiding principle needs to be that the Torah is not in the heavens, it is not beyond the sea, but like our contemporary challenges, it is right here, close to us. It is our covenantal responsibility to undertake the task of interpreting the Jewish religion in the light of who we are today.

NOTE

1. Maurice N. Eisendrath, *Can Faith Survive: The Thoughts and Afterthoughts of an American Rabbi* (New York: McGraw-Hill, 1964), 243–44.

Part One

KNOWING GOD

L ike most major religions, Reform Judaism is based on belief in God. We quickly run into problems, however, concerning *exactly* what the belief is, which is why one essay in this section, by Rabbi Michael Marmur, is titled "Speaking Truthfully about God." We may accept that, as Reform Jews, we believe in God and yet lack a clear sense of what that means. This seems to lead many of us to say, when questioned, what we *think we should believe* about God, not what we actually believe about God. People can feel pressured to conform where religious belief is concerned, which discourages their beneficial, even necessary, analysis of what they might really believe. This leaves them unable to form a mature spirituality.

As long as religious thinkers have been thinking about God, they have debated what the nature of divine reality actually is. Reform Jews may hold quite a number of different conceptions of God, ranging from God as an authoritarian figure both engaged in the world and judgmental, to a benevolent force engaged in the world and not judgmental, to an immanent presence with us that connects us to all of reality.

As noted repeatedly by the writers in this section, "Knowing God," ancient Judaism did not have articles of faith. This was a medieval innovation. The Jewish philosopher Maimonides encapsulated the essential beliefs of our religion in just a few hundred words. This was long before the Internet pressured magazines to steadily reduce the number of words that one could write on a given subject. But the philosophers' audience was not all that more forgiving than ours is. People wanted to know who is God and what is God and to have answers in short, clear responses that spoke to their own worldview.

Michael A. Meyer, PhD, in his "Critical Thoughts on a Reform Jewish Theology," presents the triads "at the heart of Reform Jewish theology"—God, Torah, and Israel, and Creation, revelation, and redemption—and offers questions to consider about them for the reader who is seeking to formulate a sincere belief in God.

Rabbi Rachel Timoner opens "An Experiential Approach to God" with a nod to the challenges she encounters when, as a rational, moral person, she has to justify her belief in God and commitment to organized religion. To Timoner, belief is more of a knowing that we are part of a greater whole, based on paying attention to being alive.

According to Rabbi Suzanne Singer, in "My Fragmented Theology as a Reform Rabbi and Daughter of a Holocaust Survivor," we cannot separate how we think of God from our understanding of the relationships in our lives. Growing up as the daughter of a Holocaust survivor led to many years of "wandering in the wilderness" in terms of her faith and God's justice in the world, until she found her own intellectual and spiritual guides to Jewish tradition.

Rabbi Elyse Goldstein chronicles the history of the Reform Movement's thinking about gender in "Where God Meets Gender" and puts forth the idea that how and if we will continue to use gender as a Jewish identity marker—egalitarian and binary or not—will be this generation's leading Jewish question.

In "Speaking Truthfully about God," Rabbi Michael Marmur, PhD, explores how we can reconcile the two very different theological approaches of traditional commentators and today's Judaism.

In "The Persistence of Life after Life," Rabbi Paul Golomb discusses what we might believe, or not, about the soul's immortality and challenges the reader to think about it in terms of how we resolve the tension between our faith in divine will and human endeavor.

Rabbi Geoffrey A. Mitelman's "Science and Faith" discusses the implied conflict between religion and science in that many Jews erroneously believe that if they accept scientific knowledge as valid, they must therefore reject religious belief. Mitelman rejects the conflict model and presents alternative models through which scientific thought and religious faith can support one another.

The closing essay in Part One, by Rabbi David W. Nelson, PhD, "The God Thing," encourages readers to explore God language that uses new metaphors and different vocabularies that might be more accessible to modern, liberal Jews.

We offer the essays in Part One to open discussion in Reform communities and others interested in questions of how we can and might think about God, relate to God, and love God. It is not possible to describe all potential approaches to God likely to resonate with Reform Jews and with others seeking a non-fundamentalist form of Judaism. Our hope is that by having access to a number of thoughtful spiritual responses to the challenge of modernity, readers will find they can lead in other, equally fruitful directions as well.

1

CRITICAL THOUGHTS
ON A REFORM JEWISH THEOLOGY

MICHAEL A. MEYER, PhD

If you are at all thoughtful about your religious faith, then at some point in life, or perhaps even with great frequency, you ask yourself how that faith is to be understood and how it relates to traditional Judaism. If you are a Reform Jew, you may further ask: Where does it fit within the stated principles of Reform Judaism? And if you are a critical thinker, you cannot avoid taking into consideration all of the factors that would seem to stand in the way of sincere belief. Attempts at defending and structuring faith are theologies, and they are generally of great length and complexity. By contrast, and at the expense of nuance, I offer here a brief model of what a critical Reform Jewish theology might look like. It is, in fact, my own.

There are two triads in Judaism. The first, which has often been used as an organizing principle in Reform platforms, is God, Torah, and Israel. The second, which lies at the heart of any Jewish theology, is Creation, revelation, and redemption. The two triads are linked: God is the Creator, the Torah is God's revelation, and the people of Israel is either the object of God's redemption or is, together with God, an agent of redemption.

Each of the elements can be exemplified by a biblical text and by a passage in the current (1999) Reform platform. Each also presents problems to the critical mind, and to each the Reform Movement has offered a response.

First, the Creator: God. Here the relevant text is the very first in the Torah: "In the beginning God created the heaven and the earth" (Genesis 1:1). The reference in the 1999 Pittsburgh Platform is a bit oblique: "We regard with reverence all of God's creation and recognize our human responsibility for its preservation and protection." Although God as creator is not specifically mentioned, the implication arises from reference to "God's creation."

The notion of divine creation, however, raises multiple intellectual problems: the inability of human reason to prove the existence of a creator God; the eternality of matter as postulated by Aristotle and possibly also by Maimonides; the problem of a creation in six days; and the lack of a discernible divine purpose. Certain moral problems follow, as well: the apparently senseless destruction of human life by natural disasters, the animal universe of claw and fang, and God's non-interference in human evil, most devastatingly in the Holocaust.

What reasons can then be given for belief in a creator and sustainer God? For one, there is personal experience that seems to transcend the mundane, the inexplicable sense of amazement. In the words of the Reform platform: "We encounter God's presence in moments of awe and wonder, in acts of justice and compassion, in loving relationships and in the experiences of everyday life." Moreover, it is difficult to believe that our lives do not have some transcendent meaning anchored in a reality beyond ourselves. But is this sufficient? Although it traditionally stands at the beginning, for me Creation becomes a possibility only at the end, after revelation and redemption.

Second, the revealing God: Torah. The most relevant text introduces the Ten Commandments (Exodus 20:1): "And God spoke all these words, saying...." For Rabbi Isaac Mayer Wise, the organizational founder of American Reform Judaism, Sinai was a real event, and the current Reform prayer book, *Mishkan T'filah*, has the worshipers proclaim, "And this is the Torah that Moses placed before the Israelites, from the mouth of God, via the hand of Moses." The Reform platform affirms, "We cherish the truths revealed in Torah, God's ongoing revelation to our people and the record of our people's ongoing relationship with God."

This traditional conception of revelation is also problematic. Can we believe in a God who speaks in human language? And how can the notion of a Torah delivered to Moses be reconciled with biblical criticism, which insists on many sources authored over an extended period of time? Moreover, there are texts that we find morally abhorrent, such as, for example, utterly wiping out the nations living in Canaan, the toleration of slavery, and the subordinate status of women. Then too there is the primitive character of the ancient religion, with its bloody sacrifices. And finally, there are the commandments that seem, at least to us, both morally and religiously meaningless, such as the ordained separation of wool from linen. Penetrating to the level of philosophy, there is the additional problem of heteronomy in place of our valued autonomy: the Torah calls upon us to obey, not to choose.

How does one answer these objections? Since its origins in the nineteenth century, the Reform Movement has placed less emphasis upon ritual commandment, as reflected in the Five Books of Moses, and stressed instead the divinely inspired moral vision of the prophets. It has not seen revelation as a one-time event, but rather as ongoing and progressive, allowing for deeper understanding of "what God requires of us." It has, for the most part, limited commandment to moral imperatives while seeing ritual rather as an enhancement of the moral life. Most tellingly, it has come to see revelation not as dictation, but as divine inspiration documented by human understanding. This was tellingly stated by the principal Reform thinker of European Reform Judaism in its formative stage, Rabbi Abraham Geiger, who wrote, "Truly, Judaism originated with the people of the revelation. Why, then, should we not be allowed to use this term when we speak of penetration to the deepest foundation of an *illumination* emanating from the higher spirit, which cannot be explained and which, though subject to later evolution, was not evolutionary in its origin?" In other words, Geiger envisioned an influx of the divine that alone, to his mind, can explain human moral aspirations.

Finally, the redeeming God: Israel. The special position of the Jewish people in God's scheme of redemption is spelled out in Exodus 19:5–6: "Now then, if you will obey Me faithfully and keep My covenant, you shall be My treasured possession among all the peoples. Indeed all the earth is Mine, but you shall be to Me a kingdom of priests and a holy nation." Israel is chosen for a special relation to God, which the prophet Isaiah understood to mean bringing the light of God to the nations.

As it has been traditionally understood, this idea of redemption likewise raises difficulties. The goal of the covenant relationship is reached with the miraculous appearance of the Messiah, the redemptive return of all Jews to Zion, the rebuilding of the ancient Temple, and the reinstitution of the sacrificial service. Moreover, the chosen people concept, grounded in the noted biblical verse from Exodus, can and has been the source of a repellent chauvinism. One may also wish to challenge those in Israel who, seeing the state as representing the penultimate stage of the final redemption, have used the concept for questionable political purposes.

What response to these issues can the Reform Movement offer? The most current platform makes it clear that the necessary holiness has not yet been achieved, but we must continue to strive for its attainment. It states, "We are Israel, a people aspiring to holiness, singled out through our ancient covenant and our unique history among the nations to be witnesses to God's presence." For the personal Messiah, Reform Judaism has substituted a future-oriented messianism: a force aimed at the prophetic goal of amity among individuals and nations. We have directed it away from restoring the old in a single place to creating the new, a messianic age, in the entire world. We have understood chosenness to be for a moral purpose, not a reward for merit, but a destiny imposed by our history. And we have understood the State of Israel neither as representing the beginning of the end of time, nor as redemption achieved, but rather as a potentially redemptive force in the world.

Personally, my theology begins with revelation, with Torah. For Torah represents the sensed moral imperative, which, unlike most motivations, often runs against what seems to be my self-interest. From there it moves to redemption, the collective striving of Israel (the Jewish people), along with other persons and nations, for universal justice, human kindness, and world peace. Revelation—conscience—is the point of origin; redemption is the road taken. But there yet remains Creation. Is this all delusion, all of my own making? Or has the moral world and the physical world a single transcendent source, a Creator in whom my strivings are grounded? That is the question I ask myself each day, knowing that no final answer can be given.

2

AN EXPERIENTIAL APPROACH TO GOD

Rabbi Rachel Timoner

I often find myself in the strange position of defending God. As a rabbi, I encounter many people who think of God as a throwback to earlier times, a fantasy that sensible people gave up in the twentieth century. They are usually too polite to ask, "Don't you know about the big bang and evolution? Do you really believe there's a big man up there in the clouds controlling our world?"

In our era, when humanity has mastered so much of our world and can explain many previously mysterious phenomena, belief in God seems antiquated, I know. Many people do not trust organized religion for its contribution to human conflict and for the ways that religious institutions have placated suffering populations or promoted discrimination rather than changing unjust conditions. Some who are angry at religion think of belief in God not only as misleading but also as dangerous.

What's strange is that I too am a rational, critical-thinking, science-loving person. I too condemn the role that religious institutions have played in perpetuating human suffering and war, but I also know that religion has given profound meaning to countless lives, including my own. At its best, institutional religion demands that we reach for the holy within us and that we take action to create human societies grounded in justice, freedom, and peace.

I did not grow up with much belief in God, but as I grew I began to pay attention to the experience of being alive. When I practiced paying attention, I began to notice a reality beyond and within the material world. There was a camping trip in a Southwest canyon. Walking out by myself on the path, a stark blue sky colliding with the jagged edges of red rock cliffs, enormous black beetles scuttling across the road, trees rustling all around, birds swooping, and the motion of river nearby but out of sight. A sudden feeling of joy, of floating, of utter belonging. Sky and cloud and cliff and grass and river, tree and wind and leaf and rock and bird—all cousins, belonging to each other and to me from before time and again now. I saw that we are all part of a greater oneness. I felt it; I knew it beyond questions, beyond thinking.

There was the time after my father had a stroke. The physical therapy room of the hospital. Amputees, quadriplegics, stroke patients. He, down on a mat, paralyzed, afraid, trembling, unable to move his left arm. Me, age eleven, crushed, panicked, trying to help. And then the noise of the room went still; a softness came between us, in the lock of our eyes, a fearlessness. And he moved, reached out his paralyzed arm, and held my hand.

Each time I've sat in silence for extended periods of time I have felt this presence. My heart has swelled with love for all life, and I have known with utter clarity the interconnectedness of all being. I have, in those moments, felt determined to bring this consciousness to my every day, to infuse my every word and action with the utmost reverence.

Perhaps you too have looked at a night full of stars and seen yourself from the perspective of the dark and sparkling cosmos, suddenly so small as to be forgotten, so insignificant as to be a miracle. Perhaps you feel, you sense that there is something beyond us, running through us, pulling us, holding us. For me, this isn't belief. It's knowing. I use the word "God" as the label for the Ineffable that I know is there. The presence that we sense, perceive, intuit, feel beyond and within.

I would like to make the case that it is time for us to move beyond prescribed *ideas about God* toward real, lived *experiences of God*. When I ask the Jews I know whether they have ever had a spiritual experience, they speak of mountaintop hikes and the birth of a child. They tell me about a time when they felt that they were part of something larger than themselves. When the Jews I know tell me that they don't believe in God, the God they don't believe in is a big man in the sky. Why are we still stuck on the big man in the sky?

In the ancient cultures out of which Judaism grew, gods looked and acted like people. They had faces, arms, hands, and genitals. They were male and female, and they coupled with one another. They became angry and needed appeasement; they had loyalties, agendas, and dramas. They were superhumans, with human traits writ large.

In the Hebrew Bible, we can see the influence of these cultures on the descriptions of God with human attributes. God says, "Let us make human beings in our image" (Genesis 1:26). God walks through the Garden of Eden. God saves the Israelites with a strong hand and an outstretched arm. God becomes angry; God feels compassion. In the prophet Isaiah's vision, God is sitting on a throne. This anthropomorphic God concept continues in postbiblical Jewish tradition. In all Jewish blessings said to this day, God is referred to as *Melech haolam*, "Sovereign of the universe."

However, Judaism's primary innovation was its understanding that God cannot be reduced to any person or thing—not a body, an object, or a natural force. The *Tanach* (the Hebrew Bible) uses familiar imagery to appeal to people whose sole reference points were idols, but it does so to teach the very destruction of idolatry. The second of the Ten Commandments prohibits the creation of an image of God: "You shall have no other gods besides Me. You shall not make for yourself a sculptured image, or any likeness of what is in the heavens above, or on the earth below, or in the waters under the earth. You shall not bow down to them or serve them" (Exodus 20:3–5). How is it that the creation of an image of God was so offensive that it ranks in the top 10 of all 613 mitzvot that appear in Torah?

As we reach out for an invisible, unknowable Presence, it is human instinct to make images, to shape forms, to create intermediaries that enable us to imagine what God might look like or to evoke in us some feeling of affection or comprehension. This is the very danger that To-rah is warning against, for even if we know that the image or statue or fetish is not really God, we can easily become confused and transfer in our minds some measure of the Infinite to the image we have created. And in so doing, we risk the illusion that God is our creation.

The problem is not with the imagery in the mind's eye. Our minds will make images forever; and the shifting, changing imagery of our vibrant imaginations helps us to relate to the Ineffable. The problem is when we fix an image. When we shape God in stone or wood or paint, we exercise control over God's image and features, we tame God into something finite, as if the Infinite One were within our control. We reduce God in our imagination to a thing, which impoverishes our perception of who and what God is. It is the externalized, shared, fixed image that is dangerous because it falsely limits what is infinite.

Moses Maimonides, the twelfth-century rabbi-physician who was the greatest elucidator in Jewish history of the prohibition on idolatry, teaches that to worship any created thing or to make something a mediator between us and the Eternal One is idolatry. Even if the use of that intermediary is to direct one's heart to the Eternal, it concretizes the intangible and stands between us and God (*Mishneh Torah, Yesodei HaTorah* 1). This is why Judaism insists that God has no shape or form. This is why we must not attempt to represent God by what is found in the heavens, the earth, or the sea—for nothing that we find or know can adequately represent the unknowable One.

Since the days of Maimonides, all references to God's body are understood by Judaism as metaphor, as figurative language that enables us to relate to God. When a Jew reads of God's strong hand and outstretched arm bringing us out of Egypt, we understand the language to be poetic, describing God's might and saving power. When we remind ourselves that humanity was created in the image of God, we do not mean that God has a pinky finger, but that we have a sacred dignity about us and we should treat one another with that in mind. When we read of Moses speaking to God *panim el panim*, "face to face," we understand Torah to be describing an unrivaled intimacy between our great prophet and the Holy One.

If we were to shift our image-making minds from tangible to intangible metaphors for God, that might be progress. Ideas of God as spirit are one way. The Hebrew word most often translated as "spirit," *ruach*, appears 378 times throughout *Tanach*. Onomatopoeic (rhhuu-ahhh), *ruach* is life-giving breath, the wind, and the spirit that animates Creation. Each time our lungs fill and empty, it is *ruach* that enters and escapes. As we watch our sleeping children, it is *ruach* that lifts and lowers their resting bodies. It is *ruach* that rushes past us on a mountain crest, gently flutters the leaves of an aspen tree, and stings our faces on a blustery winter day. According to Torah, it is *ruach* that prompts ecstatic prophecy, endows us with understanding and skill, and girds us with courage and the strength to lead. *Ruach* is beyond us, around us, and within us. *Ruach*, the creative force present at the first moment of the formation of the world, is associated with God, with nature, and with humanity.

Unlike *ruach*, which is an impersonal, creative force, *n'shamah* belongs to the essence of God and the essence of humanity. *N'shimah* means "breath"; *n'shamah* means "soul." Our tradition teaches that our souls and our breaths are intertwined and interdependent, coming from God, dwelling in us for a short time, and returning to God each night and upon our death.

Given the Jewish evolution beyond God as body, it is easy to see why *ruach*—spirit, breath, wind—and *n'shamah*—breath, soul—are such immediate concepts in relation to God in Torah. Spirit is ungraspable, invisible, without shape or form. Wind is one of the few forces that we all feel, experience, and relate to even though we cannot see it and it has no shape. We feel breath every moment of every day; we live by it, but it has no image. For a religion bound by lack of imagery in description of God, these concepts are intuitive and fundamental.

It is therefore tempting to suggest that God in Judaism is all spirit, a universal spirit, the origin and aggregate of all spirit. But it is not that simple. To say that God is spirit would be another reduction of the mysterious Infinite One.

When Moses, the shepherd-in-exile, allows himself to be drawn off course by the bush that is all aflame but not consumed, when he turns aside and listens, the God he encounters does not define itself as spirit.

"Who should I say sent me?" the reluctant prophet asks of the One.

"*Ehyeh asher ehyeh*" is the response. "I am that I am" (Exodus 3:13–14).

God says: I am. You cannot comprehend Me, but I am real. The Jewish people's special name for God—the unpronounceable four-letter name, known as the Tetragrammaton, that appears throughout the Hebrew Bible—hints at breath, wind, and spirit but points to a mystery beyond them. If we could hear God's name, *yod-hei-vav-hei* (*YHVH*), expressed without vowels, it would be a deep, released breath, like wind moving through cliffs, like spirit hovering.

The four letters of the Tetragrammaton— *yod-hei-vav-hei*—are related to the verb "to be." The root of the word, *hei-vav-hei*, is the Hebrew word for "the present," as in the present tense. A *yod* before a Hebrew verb in Modern Hebrew brings that verb into the future, but in *Tanach* it generally shows continuing action, turning an action completed in the past into something ongoing. Therefore, it is possible to read the Tetragrammaton as the present becoming forever, from "what is" to "what always will be."

Human beings like to give others names, and we are good at it. When the first human being is created, God leads it around the Garden of Eden, inviting it to name all of the animals. When we know something's name and are able to speak that name, we gain some measure of power over it. We are able to objectify what we name. In contrast, "The Name," the four-letter name of God, is beyond our power of naming. Tradition has it that by the first century no one but the High Priest in Jerusalem knew how to say The Name. Rather than pronounce the Tetragrammaton, Jews developed a convention of saying *Adonai*, meaning "my Lord," to refer to God's name, but of course that's not what it means. Instead, the four-letter name of God retains a mystery and power that cannot be tamed with our speech. By remaining unpronounceable, The Name points to a magnitude beyond the limits of our capacity for expression.

When the Rabbis of the first century CE developed the fixed prayers that were said morning and evening, they identified three central themes of the Jew's relationship to God: Creation, revelation, and redemption. Morning and night in the liturgy, we express gratitude to God for the creation of the universe, for revelation through Torah and mitzvot, and for our liberation from Egypt, which serves as a symbol of our eternal hope for future redemption. These three themes shape the way that we experience God.

We look out across the vast sea, or we see the splash of purple in the center of a wild snapdragon, or we feel the sensations of our bodies—and we meet God. We exist, we experience, we stand in wonder at what we find here. We have a sense of origins, of coming from and belonging to something larger. We marvel at the intricacy, the harmony, and the balance in the biomes we encounter. The range and diversity of species dazzle us. This is the experience of Creation.

Human beings are not only a part of the unfolding drama of Creation, we are also conscious of it. We have flashes of insight, awareness, and understanding. The word *Torah* means "teaching" or "guidance." In study, in prayer, in silence, we feel the Presence that fills the world, we feel our interconnectedness with all life. We ask: What is our role in this world? What is a good way to live? We learn to restrain our desires to prevent harm to others. We learn that there is a middle path between excess and not enough. We see that we have obligations to others. We learn to balance between work and rest; we learn to find harmony with the earth. Sometimes, we have a sense of being called. Abraham heard a voice, followed it, and learned a way of life. Since then, Jews have understood ourselves to be in covenant with the Holy One, in a committed relationship of learning and action. This is the experience of revelation.

When we see the splendor of ongoing Creation and have insights about how to live in it, we become aware that the world is not only beautiful but also broken. When we look more carefully, we see suffering, injustice, and oppression. The experience of redemption is the pull we feel within ourselves to make the world whole. It is the sense that God is working through us to repair what's broken and to relieve suffering. It is the *emunah* (faith) that the world will be whole, that all will unite in a system of harmony and equality. It is knowing that this is the purpose of our lives—to wonder at the majesty of Creation, yes; to listen for how to live, yes; but ultimately to act in such a way that our lives are instruments to repair the broken world.

These experiences of God are not only available for kabbalists and mystics—they are accessible to all of us. When we engage in spiritual practice—paying close attention, noticing the details of our inner world and the world around us, devoting ourselves to prayer and study, spending time in silence—awe and wonder will become our companions, love and compassion will fill us, insight and understanding will flower within us, and we will hear ourselves called to action in service of the interconnectedness of all life. We will feel and know the Holy One within and beyond all that is.

3

MY FRAGMENTED THEOLOGY AS A REFORM RABBI AND DAUGHTER OF A HOLOCAUST SURVIVOR

RABBI SUZANNE SINGER

It is thanks to Reform Judaism that I was finally able to believe in God—because Reform Judaism allowed me to have a fragmented theology. You see, my mother was a survivor of Auschwitz; the rest of her family perished there. On a deep, cellular level, her trauma was transmitted to me, her eldest daughter, named after her murdered mother. Her nightmares became mine. Her mistrust of the world, her sense of ultimate vulnerability, her perception of ever-present danger, her anger and her rage, her depression—mine as well. The idea of a loving, caring, just God was as foreign to me as it was to her. She was even profoundly ambivalent about Judaism, having considered converting to Christianity, filled with a certain amount of self-loathing and of contempt for other Jews, yet comfortable only with Jewish friends and only with potential Jewish sons-in-law for her three daughters. Judaism was not practiced in our home; we had only the most tenuous connection to our classical Reform temple. Yet my mother never missed the service for *Yizkor* at the High Holy Days. This ambivalence became manifest in her children: I became a rabbi, and my sisters identify only slightly with Judaism. But my road to the rabbinate was a complicated one. After all, how could I be a rabbi if my only feeling toward God was outrage over God's injustice?

Outrage had led me to my first occupation, that of television journalist. I wanted to bring important issues to the public through news and public affairs programming. Deciding to become a journalist was my effort at *tikkun olam*, though I had never heard that expression. So I spent two decades as a producer and programming executive, primarily for public television. By some cosmic coincidence, the years that I worked for PBS were also the years that the children of Holocaust survivors (the Second Generation) produced documentaries about the Shoah, about their parents' experiences, about their own response, and about the rescuers. The vast majority of these programs came to me for my evaluation. And that is how I met filmmaker Aviva Kempner, producer of *Partisans of Vilna* and other seminal films. Aviva led me back to Judaism.

Aviva decided to have a bat mitzvah ceremony at the age of forty, having been deprived of that honor by being born female in an Orthodox community. She invited me to join her for a class in midrash and to accompany her to services, where rabbis, lawyers, and other professionals discussed the weekly Torah portion for forty-five minutes. I was enthralled. As someone who thrived on close textual analysis, it spoke to me. In my spare time, I began reading books such as *The Art of Biblical Narrative* by Robert Alter and *Who Wrote the Bible?* by Richard Elliott Friedman. I tried to share my excitement with the program directors of various public television stations. They looked at me as if I were an alien.

I read the Torah, the Five Books of Moses, and was amazed that human behavior seemed to have changed so little in several thousand years. Then I got the "call"—at least that is how Christians refer to what happened. I looked up, suddenly, and said to myself, "I am going to be a rabbi." I had no idea where the thought had come from; it was an eerie moment. I brushed it aside, but two days later, at lunch with a Catholic colleague, Clare Crawford-Mason, I ventured, "I think I might do something very different with my life." She looked me straight in the eye and said, "You are going to be a rabbi." I was blown away. It would be another six years, however, before I enrolled in the seminary.

I continued to work in television, occasionally allowing myself to contemplate a radical shift in my career. Shortly after my "call," I moved from Washington, DC, to Los Angeles and decided to check out Hebrew Union College–Jewish Institute of Religion (HUC-JIR). I met with Rabbi Shelly Marder, the dean of the School of Rabbinic Studies. He handed me Dr. Alfred Gottschalk's *To Learn and to Teach: Your Life as a Rabbi*, suggesting I check out a couple of classes. I was inspired by Tamara Eskenazi's session on the prophet Jeremiah and by David Ellenson's on medieval Jewish philosophy. But I walked out of the HUC-JIR building, talking myself out of following this path, again. Whom was I kidding? Dr. Gottschalk's powder-blue-covered book accompanied me as I moved from place to place; it would emerge as I packed and unpacked. I would glance at it, but never once did I read it. I finally threw it away, convinced this was not the place I would be going.

Determined though I was to ignore it, the pull to become a rabbi continued insistently. I took adult education classes in comparative religion, in *parshanut*, in Bible, in midrash. At first, I told no one about this crazy secret. When I finally shared it with close friends, they wondered why, since I loved Judaism so much, I wasn't making films about Judaism. That was not the point at all, of course. I was incredibly unhappy producing television. It was the wrong place for me, had always been wrong, did not speak to my deeper calling, and was a hornet's nest of ambitious backbiters. I had never known what I had wanted to do with my life except to try to address the world's injustices. And now I knew that television was not my medium. But what was? The rabbinate? How could I authentically become a rabbi when I was so angry at God? How could I serve a God who had allowed the Holocaust to occur and had also countenanced so much other suffering on the part of innocent people? Did the call to become a rabbi come to me from a God who had witnessed babies being tossed alive into the fires of the Shoah so that the Germans could save on Zyklon B?[1] How many genocides had followed the Shoah? How many people in the world, and in our own country, were living in dire poverty and deprivation? Why was God so silent about all this agony? Certainly my call could not be from this God or from the God I had learned about in Sunday school, an old man with a white beard, sitting on a throne in heaven, a King of kings running the world.

The questions about God and justice and life's purpose continued to plague me. I found myself drawn more and more to the study of Judaism, but I remained entrenched in the intellectual. It allowed me to explore what other people thought, to spend hours wrestling with texts and the issues they raised—and wrestling with God, although my anger and my intellectual stance kept me at a safe distance from both the tradition and from God. I could be angry all I wanted, but I never had to come to real terms with what Judaism was actually about or what it meant to me. I was never fully engaged.

Nor had I figured out what it meant in theological terms to hear and respond to Emil Fackenheim's 614th commandment to deny Hitler a posthumous victory by abandoning Judaism.[2] This had been driving me for many years. But what exactly was it that propelled me to remain engaged in the world? Certainly, it could not *just* be a desire to thwart Hitler. There was something higher that called me. For so long I had been grounded in the rational. It was logical to be angry with God. It made sense. And it allowed me to dismiss God, to subtract God from the equation of my commitment to *tikkun olam*. Certainly, calling the sense of awe and wonder that I occasionally experienced, or calling my profound sense of purpose, calling *that* God, did not resonate for me. I was comfortable wrestling with God, but not believing in God.

Still feeling comfortable approaching Judaism intellectually, I finally left television for good and enrolled in the Master of Arts Judaic Studies program at HUC-JIR, not in the rabbinic program—yet. I knew that deep inside there was more, but I was still unsure about where this urge that had tugged at me for so long would lead me. I have compared this plunge into Judaism to Abraham when he agreed to sacrifice his son. The story of the *Akeidah*, the Binding of Isaac, had impressed itself upon me from a young age. Ever since I could remember, I had been haunted by the image of Abraham raising a knife to kill his son. What kind of God could demand such a sacrifice? What kind of man is the Torah celebrating with such a demonstration of blind faith? Several people had helped me make sense of this awful and awe-filled tale. Leonard Cohen's "Song of Isaac" maintains that Abraham misunderstood God's command. In the song's words, "I thought I saw an eagle, but it may have been a vulture, I never could decide." Indeed, Rashi (on Genesis 22:12) cites a classic midrash based on a wordplay that suggests that Abraham misunderstood God: "I did not say, 'Slaughter him [i.e., offer him as a sacrifice (*olah*)],' but 'Bring him up [*alah*].' You have brought him up, now bring him down" (*B'reishit Rabbah* 56:8). I believe that Abraham failed the test. Eventually, he saw the ram caught in the thicket and understood that *this* was what he was meant to sacrifice, not his son. So I came to see the *Akeidah* as a cautionary tale, warning us against fanaticism. But there was more. Søren Kierkegaard teaches us that faith takes us beyond the realm of mundane certainty. This leap of faith entails plunging into the unknown, leaving behind simplistic morality. Kierkegaard sees the *Akeidah* as a metaphor for just such an awesome step, a measure not of blind faith, but of true faith. When I decided to leave my twenty-year television career and devote my life to the Jewish world, I felt like I myself had taken such a plunge into the unknown. It was a terrifying yet exhilarating experience, and at the same time, I felt like I had come home.

In the master's program, I took the same classes as the rabbinical students, secretly checking the school catalogue to see how many more classes I would need to fulfill the ordination requirements. But when people asked me if I was going to be a rabbi, I responded, "Absolutely not." After all, how could I be a rabbi if my only relationship with God was based on profound anger? Then I enrolled in David Ellenson's Modern Jewish Thought class. To my immense surprise, I discovered that Jewish thinkers throughout the ages had proffered very different ideas of God, different not only from the pediatric notion of the old man on the throne that I had been taught, but different from each other. There was a whole range of beliefs, from Spinoza's pantheistic view that God and Nature are one, to Maimonides's concept of God as the Active Intellect with no providential concern for humanity. And then there was Mordecai Kaplan, the founder of Reconstructionism, who believed that God is the power that allows us to become better people and to make the world a better place. Not a God in charge, not a Being we pray to and obey, not a personal God, not a supernatural God, not a God who intervened in the Exodus while staying silent during the Shoah, but a force through which we can be redeemed. "God is the Power that makes for salvation," he writes.[3] This was the God I could believe in; this was the God with whom I had no reason to be angry.

As satisfying as I found Kaplan to be, however, his theology could not sufficiently explain other stirrings of my heart and soul. What about my sense of being absolutely commanded by the ethical mitzvot? What about my sense of radical obligation to the other that is so clearly articulated by the French philosopher Emmanuel Levinas? Levinas believed that the self comes into being and can only be actualized in response to ethics, defined as the obligation to the one who commands me, the other whom I face. And this connects to his understanding of God: "The knowledge of God comes to us like a commandment, like a *Mitzvah*. To know God is to know what must be done."[4] This was not Kaplan's God. This was a very different God, a God that makes demands. How could I believe in both?

And then there was the problem of evil. Was God hiding from the world's suffering? The various theories explaining evil in a world ruled by a just and good God simply did not hold water for me. Eliezer Berkovits, for example, asks how one could be good if it were not possible to be bad.[5] This stunned me. In order for a person to be righteous, must the world be set up in such a way that unspeakable evil can befall the innocent? Is righteousness worth the price? Wouldn't it have been enough for humankind to have been created happy? Why must righteousness be measured against wickedness? Berkovits claims that God gives human beings freedom and, as a result, God cannot intervene when people use that freedom in ways that are offensive. Yet, did God not intervene in Egypt? If God, in the name of human freedom and responsibility, cannot be a savior in a situation as horrific as the Holocaust, what good is God?

Harold Kushner helped me grapple with the question of *theodicy*, the paradox resulting from a belief in an all-good and all-powerful God. In *When Bad Things Happen to Good People*, Kushner posits that God cannot be both these things or evil could not exist.[6] So we have to let go of one quality. Since we can't accept that God would be anything but all-good, we need to give up the idea of God being all-powerful. And there certainly are stories in the Bible to support this view, most notably the story of Job. Job suffers unjustly, demanding that God explain Godself. When God finally appears out of the whirlwind, it is clear that God can only do so much to keep the forces of chaos from overtaking the world. The image of God holding at bay both the land monster, Behemoth, and the sea monster, Leviathan, encapsulates this reality for me.

I found that I was drawn to a variety of theologies, not just to one, and that these theologies sometimes contradicted each other. To my surprise and relief, that was okay. While a good friend who was studying to be a Methodist minister had to defend her theology in order to be ordained, I was never asked to develop a consistent, systematic, defensible theology. Dr. Ellenson saw no problem when I called mine "fragmented theology." I could believe in Kaplan's God *and* feel commanded by the God of the Ten Commandments. I could believe that God was not providential—in other words, that God is not directly concerned with our lives and our actions—*and* believe that God would intervene were it possible to do so. This freed me from my guilt both over not believing in the traditional God of the Bible and over not having a coherent understanding of God. And I was released from my anger at God because *that* God was not the God I believed in. My developing relationship with God finally allowed me to enroll in the rabbinic program at HUC-JIR. I now felt that I could become an authentic rabbi.

Yet even with permission to view God in a prismatic way, and despite the beautiful articulations I have found in these learned rabbis' writings, I must admit that my theology is still tentative. There are moments when I resonate with Richard Rubinstein's view of "a cold, silent, unfeeling cosmos,"[7] moments when I feel adrift in an uncaring world, moments when I feel God can only be regarded as a "Holy Nothingness"[8] in light of the murder of the six million. I still get angry with God, even though I have rejected that kind of God. Rabbi Irving Greenberg identifies this as "moment faiths," explaining that "the difference between the skeptic and the believer is frequency of faith, and not certitude of position."[9]

Ultimately, what is so meaningful about Judaism for me is that whatever one's belief in God, the real measure of our faith is how we enact it in the world. Rabbi Harold Schulweis expresses this eloquently, writing, "The reality of God is proven behaviorally not theoretically. . . . God is authenticated not with our lips but with our limbs."[10] Or, as Arnold Jacob Wolf frames it, "The question 'What is a Jew?' is both un-Jewish and unproductive. I can think of many better questions, for example: 'What must I do?' 'What can I become?' . . . One of the greatest problems of modern Judaism is that we have the wrong problems: 'Is there a God?' instead of 'What does God want?' 'What is a Jew?' instead of 'How can I become a Jew?'"[11]

Rabbi Richard Levy, who was the director of HUC-JIR's School of Rabbinic Studies in Los Angeles when I attended, had a far more traditional view of God than I. Yet he embraced me and my theology when I finally made the decision to enter the rabbinate. I was very fortunate to receive his encouragement. I believe that many of my congregants have been on a path similar to mine, struggling to understand where God is in their own lives, so my own wandering in the wilderness has helped them feel that their questions are legitimate. Indeed, for each and every one of us, relationship to God is an ongoing enterprise, and I don't imagine that one ever reaches the Promised Land.

NOTES

1. See Irving Greenberg, "Cloud of Smoke, Pillar of Fire: Judaism, Christianity, and Modernity after the Holocaust," in *Auschwitz: Beginning of a New Era? Reflections on the Holocaust*, ed. Eva Fleischner (New York: KTAV, 1977).

2. Emil L. Fackenheim, *God's Presence in History: Jewish Affirmations and Philosophical Reflections* (New York: New York University Press, 1970), 84.

3. Mordecai M. Kaplan, *The Meaning of God in Modern Jewish Religion* (New York: Reconstructionist Press, 1962), 40.

4. Emmanuel Levinas, *Difficult Freedom: Essays on Judaism*, trans. Seán Hand (Baltimore: Johns Hopkins University Press, 1990), 17.

5. Eliezer Berkovits, *Faith after the Holocaust* (New York: KTAV, 1970), 89.

6. Harold S. Kushner, *When Bad Things Happen to Good People* (New York: Anchor Books, 1981).

7. Richard Rubinstein, *After Auschwitz: Radical Theology and Contemporary Judaism* (Baltimore: Johns Hopkins Press, 1966), 152.

8. Richard L. Rubinstein and John K. Roth, *Approaches to Auschwitz: The Holocaust and Its Legacy* (London: SCM Press, 1987), 315.

9. Greenberg, "Cloud of Smoke," 27.

10. Harold M. Schulweis, "The Uniqueness of Judaism," lecture 2, https://www.vbs.org/worship/meet-our-clergy/rabbi-harold-schulweis/sermons/keruv-search-oneness.

11. Arnold Jacob Wolf, *Unfinished Rabbi: Selected Writings of Arnold Jacob Wolf* (Lanham, MD: Ivan R. Dee, 2009), 20.

4

WHEN GOD MEETS GENDER

RABBI ELYSE GOLDSTEIN

At its inception, Reform Judaism promised equality for women. Now much later, could Reform have imagined how far the notion of "gender equality" would take us? The spectrum of gender identification in the twenty-first century is vast and complicated. How does Reform, which at its essence is egalitarian, deal with gender roles, gender fluidity, and the marking of gender so prevalent in traditional Judaism, Jewish history, and Jewish rituals? And how does our concept of gender inform our understanding of God, holiness, and spirituality—or does it anymore? The ordination of women— beginning with Sally Priesand in 1972—was a watershed moment not only for Reform Judaism but for the whole Jewish world. Of course it offered a new career opportunity to women from which they had been previously denied, but much more than that, in the years following, the sudden thrusting of women into a new kind of spotlight in the synagogue introduced the question of gender as a marker of Jewish identity. Until the question was raised as to whether women can be rabbis, our conversations about the role gender plays in our Jewish identity were mostly theoretical. Unlike in Orthodoxy, where gender roles define and delineate religious roles and determine one's whole religious set of obligations and responsibilities, in the

Reform Movement we hardly ever asked, "What can a woman do or not do?" We were not concerned with whether women could don tallitot or *t'fillin* (phylacteries), could sing at public events, or could count in a minyan. Those questions were answered early in the movement's history, when many of the ritual restrictions and taboos of traditional Judaism were lifted for both men and women. Yet, what brought us to the egalitarian and gender-sensitive moment in which we now find ourselves?

Early Reform thinkers in Germany not only argued *for* women's religious equality, but also argued *against* those laws and customs that differentiated women's religious roles from those of men. As the movement relocated to the United States in the late nineteenth century, practical innovations actively redefined the nature of women's participation in public worship. Most critical among Reform Judaism's innovations that changed the gender landscape was the elimination of the *m'chitzah*—the barrier separating the sexes in worship—together with the total elimination of a separate women's gallery within the architecture of the synagogue.

"Family pews" continued this physical manifestation of equality, although they may have arisen more as a matter of architecture than of ideology. Rabbi Isaac Mayer Wise's Anshe Emeth Congregation in Albany occupied a church building in 1851 and New York's Temple Emanu-El bought a former church in 1854, and both congregations decided to seat men and women together in those already extant pews, rather than build new galleries. The prominence of Temple Emanu-El and its cadre of well-known and influential congregants helped make mixed seating normative for Reform temples.

Along with the end of the *m'chitzah* and the normalization of mixed seating or family pews, the introduction of the confirmation service in place of bar mitzvah helped further embody Reform's commitment to equal Jewish education for both boys and girls. When the bar mitzvah ceremony regained popularity in Reform congregations, the bat mitzvah ceremony slowly joined its brother as a central expectation of a girl's religious upbringing. The equalizing of bat mitzvah ceremonies, to include similar if not identical requirements and rituals as bar mitz-vah, also contributed to early discussions of what role gender should play in the upbringing of Reform Jewish children.

Another important step in making gender a topic of discussion in the Reform Movement was the burgeoning of the Temple Sisterhood organization. Again, Temple Emanu-El led the way in providing a prototype for a women's organization, which was quickly copied in Jewish congregations throughout the country and eventually led to a confederation of Sisterhoods called the National Federation of Temple Sisterhoods (NFTS), much later renamed Women of Reform Judaism. It is true that early Sisterhood groups operated in circumscribed and stereotypical female ways, such as serving refreshments, aiding in religious schools, and being responsible for holiday and Shabbat decoration. Yet there is no doubt that these women's auxiliaries quickly became a place women could hone leadership skills, gain Jewish education, and begin to be seen as central players in synagogue life. More important, they could begin to imagine themselves as authority figures. At the synagogue Sisterhood Shabbat, women would be given public roles normally reserved only for the male rabbi, like delivering the sermon or conducting the service, and thus congregations would experience women in those kinds of public leadership roles, no matter how token it may have been at the time. Furthermore, the strength of Sisterhoods in the twentieth century was in merging new feminist sensitivities with traditional loyalty to temples, rabbis, and other auxiliary organizations. Because Sisterhoods were not seen as "threatening" to the status quo, it was often in these women's groups that relevant "women's topics" such as domestic abuse, women's health, and women's spirituality first surfaced. In fact, as early as 1963, the women of NFTS focused Reform attention on the question of women's roles by requesting that the then all-male governing bodies of Reform Judaism take up the question of women's ordination.

Ten years later the most decisive step—the ordination of women—finally served as a clear catalyst for us to begin asking the questions of gender that have, up until today, occupied a central and focal place in Reform Jewish thinking. Having women as clergy allowed us—in fact demanded of us—to begin to explore all the ways gender affects and influences our religious practice.

At first, those discussions focused around binary definitions of male and female, masculine and feminine. This revolution began with what I call "equal access feminism." It was simple: women wanted to have the same opportunities and the same religious responsibilities as men. Women wanted, in short, to be fully Jews out of a sense of being allowed to participate the way men did. We imagined women's religious equality to mean that women could practice those rituals that had been designated as historically men's rituals. In this stage the discussion around gender in Reform settings focused on women doing what men did.

Second-stage Jewish feminism went further, developing a thoughtful challenge to our theological language in describing God, and thus a shaking of our foundational assumptions about women, men, and the whole halachic system. We asked if women's spirituality was the same as men's, resting upon distinctions and separation into categories of difference like milk/meat, holy/profane, male/female. We didn't just have women rabbis—those rabbis made us rethink what a rabbi looks like, what a rabbi is, and what a rabbi does. My male colleagues will admit that with the admission of women to the rabbinic discussion, we all started to question work-life balance, parenting time, the hierarchies of synagogue life, the language of the prayer book, and the nature of the synagogue.

In this stage, as women redefined themselves and their place in Judaism, men were faced with the real and difficult task of redefining themselves as Jews. "The flight of men" from Reform synagogues was noted, and theories from busyness to boredom, from lack of privilege to lack of being needed have been offered. But, for the first time, exchanges around gender included considerations of male Jewish identity, not just female.

And now, in third-stage feminism, in the twenty-first century, the binary understanding of "men" and "women" itself has been challenged, and the conversation about male and female differences and similarities also takes into account the full spectrum of gender identification. Today's feminism leads the discussion into the less-clear waters of whether gender at all can, should, or will determine, define, or characterize the way we practice Jewish ritual. Twenty years ago we started the discussion about what a more "feminine" ritual would look like: tallit, *t'fillin*, *kippah*. We wondered if biology was spiritual destiny; if we should invent or establish rituals for the sacred moments in women's lives, like lactation, pregnancy, and menopause. Our God concepts changed, and with them, our concepts of ourselves as Jews.

With the ordination of openly gay, lesbian, and transgender rabbis in Reform Judaism; the movement's insistence on civil equality for gay couples; full welcoming of LGBTQ families, couples, and individuals into congregations; Reform rabbis performing wedding ceremonies for gay and lesbian couples; and the recent Union for Reform Judaism resolution against any and all forms of transphobia, our previous assumptions about gender, sexuality, and religion have once again been called into question. The Reform Movement began advocating gay and lesbian rights in 1965, when NFTS passed a resolution calling for the decriminalization of homosexuality. In 1977, the URJ (then Union of American Hebrew Congregations) and the Central Conference of American Rabbis passed their first resolutions calling for human rights for homosexuals. The CCAR, in its 1996 resolution on gay and lesbian partnerships, resolved to "oppose governmental efforts to ban gay and lesbian marriage." In March 2000, the CCAR made history by becoming the first major group of North American clergy, as an organization, to give its support to those in its ranks choosing to perform same-gender ceremonies. Since then, LGBTQ outreach and inclusion have been central in the Reform Movement.

A new generation of thinkers and their words have entered our vocabulary: transgender, intersex, transitioning, gender queer. This new generation of thinkers confirms that feminism, by definition, widens the conversation about gender. What is a gender? What does being "feminine" or "masculine" mean? Is spirituality something that includes our gender, ignores our gender, or is separate from our gender? Can all definitions of gender, and all expressions of sexuality, be considered "holy"? Do we indeed sanction—and sanctify—every way of being human? Every way of partnering? Does our biological sex or the genitalia with which we were born define us not only as people but specifically as Jews?

We now ask questions about transgender congregants and rabbis, about rituals for transitioning or for coming out; and we ask what gender *is*—as much as how and if gender informs us as Jews at all.

We have stopped thinking of ourselves as one of two possibilities, and we now realize the extent to which our conversation must shift to include the widest spectrums of ways to understand "gender."

Twenty years ago we imagined a new theological language with birth and moon and mothering imagery, and we began to wonder about what we looked like if we are "made" in that divine image. The biblical verse that "male and female God created them" (Genesis 1:27) was the basis for our earlier commitment to equality of men and women. Yet in the twenty-first century there is broadening beyond that binary understanding of gender that challenges us to rethink the whole theological enterprise of being made in God's image if that image is understood as gendered male and female.

The questions Jewish feminism once raised have so clearly entered our conversation that the tone and content of Jewish life have been forever altered. Today's Reform girls grow up fully expecting to celebrate becoming bat mitzvah. They regularly see women in tallitot at those services, and there are even some synagogues where the women on the bimah are required to wear one. People commonly talk of their rabbi as "she" without it being exotic or unusual, and the Conservative, Reform, and Reconstructionist prayer books all add the Matriarchs to the *Amidah* prayer. The "Jew" we had grown accustomed to identifying as the man with long sidecurls and a fur hat morphed into the woman with a pink tallit—and continues to morph into the androgynous or gender queer or transJew impossible to define. How and if we will continue to use gender as a Jewish identity marker—egalitarian and binary or not—remains to be seen and will be this generation's leading Jewish question.

5

SPEAKING TRUTHFULLY ABOUT GOD

RABBI MICHAEL MARMUR, PhD

I want to say something about God. Three boundaries set limits for my discussion: what I *should* say, what I *can* say, and what I *must* say.[1]

To be a person is to be limited. We live for a few years, see only what is within range, comprehend a small amount of what is taking place around us and within us. How can a person, essentially limited, hope to say something of meaning concerning that which reaches out beyond our limitations? One model of response to this perennial question is that of the disengaged thinker, sitting on top of a mountain pondering the great questions, untrammeled by conventions and doctrines. But for those of us who embrace being situated in a tradition, the response is different: when we grapple with the biggest questions, we look to those who have come before us. We are prepared to take the lead from a culture that was there before we were born and that will be there after we have gone.

The dichotomy between the abstract thinker and the one who is situated in tradition is a false one. Philosophers, even the most iconoclastic, are also part of a tradition. Their forerunners sat atop mountains before them. Even when they are kicking against a particular idea, they are paying homage to it. And those who study Jewish tradition know that innovation is an essential part of the tradition itself.

What is it that Jewish tradition tells us we ought to believe about God? The more one learns about Judaism, the more one appreciates that the notion of a single unchanging core of Jewish wisdom is bogus. The wisdom of Judaism is to be found in its dynamism. That said, those who argue that there is no such thing as an essential Jewish worldview would probably have been ridiculed by generations of Jews convinced they have espoused it.

Some have tried to spell out what it is a good Jew should believe about God. A particularly influential example is Maimonides (1135–1204), whose Thirteen Principles of Faith are directly concerned with this question. According to his formulation, a Jew should affirm that God exists and existed prior to all else, is One in an absolute and unparalleled way, has no body, is the only legitimate object of worship, gave us the Torah, knows the actions of humans and rewards the obedient, and more.

While it is true that many have undermined the validity of this or any other Jewish catechism, the fact that such dogmatic expressions of normative Jewish belief have had an impact on Jewish communities and individuals speaks to the power of the "ought," the pull of the "should." To be faithful to the tradition, so goes the argument, there are things I ought to believe about God.

Reform Judaism has often displayed a marked ambivalence to this normative dimension of the God conversation. Our sensitivity to the dimension of historical development reminds us that attempts to capture what every Jew is meant to think about God for all time are doomed to fail and have often been criticized from within the tradition. On the other hand, successive generations of Reform thinkers and leaders have come up with normative statements of their own. In 1918, Kaufmann Kohler, then president of the Hebrew Union College, published his *Jewish Theology*, in which he grappled with the question of whether Judaism has articles of faith. He notes that wherever one stands on this question, "the doctrine of the one and only God stands, as a matter of course, in the foreground."[2] This is both a historical claim and also an invitation for the contemporary Jew to continue the dynamic process of seeking to understand "what Judaism says" about God. In Kohler's words, "We must do as Maimonides did,—as Jews have always done,—point out anew the really fundamental doctrines, and discard those which have lost their holdup on the modern Jew, or which conflict directly with his religious consciousness."[3]

Here Kohler is tempering the "should" with the "can." He is arguing that the act of trawling our tradition for wisdom about ultimate meaning and reality is positive and necessary. This turning to tradition is an expression of humility—I do not assume that the search for meaning begins with me. It is an expression of fidelity and identity—as a Jew, I look to the riches of my own tradition (while staying open to wisdom wherever it is to be found). And it is also an agenda for continuity—I can educate the next generation, offering them a grounding in the key teachings of my tradition. The normative may also become formative.

For all its virtues, the notion that our search for God can begin and end in the transmission of someone else's formulation of traditional belief will not stand up to scrutiny. The ancient Rabbis already understood that as time and context changes, what can be stated in good conscience about our conception of God also changes. There is a remarkable tradition to be found both in the Babylonian Talmud (*Yoma* 69b) and in its parallel from the Land of Israel. It contains the suggestion that while Moses had described God as "the Great God, the Valiant and the Terrible" (Deuteronomy 10:17), in the wake of the destruction of the Temple Jeremiah omitted "the Terrible" (in Jeremiah 32). Then Daniel, in view of oppression and exile, omitted "the Valiant" (in Daniel 9). The Talmudic tradition embeds this teaching in an essentially conservative framework, lauding the Men of the Great Assembly who rehabilitated the abandoned epithets. But both versions include a justification of the actions of Jeremiah and Daniel. They acknowledged that God is a God of truth, and so deception and obsequiousness are not options. I can only say about God what can be said in honesty and integrity.

Many experience as a crisis the realization that they can no longer accept the idea of God presented to them from childhood. Having read Karl Marx (socialism) or Sigmund Freud (psychoanalysis) or Nietzsche (nihilistic philosophy) or Mary Daly (feminism) or Richard Dawkins (science-based atheism), or simply having listened to the world news, they must abandon the God of old. The "ought" of old, the "should" of tradition, is rejected.

This is not the only response. Some keep searching for a God they can believe in and relate to in good conscience. As the Talmudic teaching cited above notes, tradition itself recognizes that within Judaism the "can" is in conversation with the "should." One modern thinker who was prepared to face up to the radical implications of this encounter was Mordecai Kaplan (1881–1983), who declared:

> The fact that the nature of God is beyond our understanding does not mean that we can afford to think of Him in terms that are clearly not true in accordance with the highest standards of truth. Our conception of God must be self-consistent and consistent with whatever else we hold to be true. . . . We must insist that whatever we say or think about God shall be in harmony with all else that we hold to be true.[4]

Here Kaplan takes issue with the traditional notion of divine mystery. He refuses to interpret this to mean that we should accept living with a dissonance between what we believe about God and what we believe about the world in general. For Kaplan, one does not have to check in one's highest conception of truth at the door.

Many Reform thinkers predicated their search for a God concept on this same idea, the notion that it should be in complete harmony with one's highest conception of truth. Some have challenged this idea. In a 1957 essay, "The Idea of God," Eugene Borowitz suggests that any idea of God that keeps a Jew from acting in the world, observing festivals, committing acts of justice, and the like cannot be understood as a Jewish idea of God. In Borowitz's view, if your *can* leads to a weakening of Jewish life, something has gone wrong. "Any public idea of God in Judaism must stand not only before the test of intellectual coherence, but before the test of Jewish history as well."[5] One way of understanding the differences between traditionalists and progressives is to think about the emphasis each places on the "should" and the "can." A traditionalist will say that you can't just throw away the truths of tradition every time you are hit over the head by some new faddish notion. If the idea of a merciful God seems hard to reconcile with a world on fire, try harder. Meanwhile, the progressives respond by insisting that a tradition that requires us to give up on our credulity is not worth preserving.

A teaching usually attributed to the founder of the Chasidic movement, the Baal Shem Tov, notes that the *Amidah* prayer begins in a curious manner: "Our God and God of our ancestors. . . ." Why does it need to mention both ourselves and those who came before us? He concludes that there are two kinds of people in the world. The "God of our fathers" camp concentrates on the concept of God provided by tradition, while the "our God" people are engaged in their own search for a meaningful notion of God. We say both parts of the blessing because one sensibility without the other is weak. If all we have is tradition, we can become parrots repeating sentences we don't understand or believe in. And if we are constantly searching, we can be blown around by the winds of opinion, believing one thing today and another tomorrow. By combining the two approaches, we can have both firm roots and high aspirations.

So far I have described two ways of grappling with the truth of God. One is to delve within traditional discussions, learning from the wisdom of what has come before us. Another is to ask what our best understanding of morality, history, science, and society allows us to believe. The first approach scores high points for grandeur and mystery, and it is rooted in humility and identity. The second approach is all about honesty and integrity. If I cannot subscribe to the idea of a God who gives rewards based on the behavior of individuals, I have to look for a concept of God I can believe in without abandoning my principles. The second approach calls for a faith obtained in good faith.

There is a third dimension, which I am calling the "must" of God discourse. I may have an experience, sense a presence—or even an absence—that demands to be expressed. Abraham Joshua Heschel's account of the God whose name must be spoken includes a description of that moment when the spiritual fire breaks forth:

> A tremor seizes our limbs; our nerves are struck, quiver like strings; our whole being bursts into shudders. But then a cry, wrested from our very core, fills the world around us, as if a mountain were suddenly about to place itself in front of us. It is one word: GOD. Not an emotion, a stir within us, but a power, a marvel beyond us, tearing the world apart.[6]

It may happen that the experience of God "wrested from our very core" is at odds with the idea we profess in polite company. It certainly happens that exponents of old-fashioned religion find no inner resonance to their public pronouncements and that arch-rationalists are more emotive and experiential than their concepts should allow. It is also true that some who are convinced that nothing lies beyond the dimension of the immediately observable experience something in their heart that their head insists cannot be.

In a book with the deceptively simple title *Truth*, the philosopher Simon Blackburn describes the tension between the absolutist and the relativist. In many ways, the difference of approach and temperament between these two camps is more significant than the distinctions we usually identify between theists and atheists. He points out that absolutists, who are convinced that there is a Clear Answer to the Big Questions, and relativists, who believe that our answers are not The Answer, often talk past each other, rather than to each other: "The absolutist trumpets his plain vision; the relativist sees only someone who is unaware of his own spectacles."[7]

Progressive Jews are often accused of being and may often secretly think of themselves as relativists who don't want to admit it. The early Reformers were often absolutists, true believers in the power of reason and enlightenment to carry us on to the new dawn. Compared to them, I am a wishy-washy relativist. But in fact I am in search of a way of breaking out of this strangulating dichotomy. I want a third option.

Rather than subscribe to a comprehensive absolute Truth about the world—that it is run by a puppeteer God, or judged by a disciplinarian God, or that it is disenchanted and ruled only by physical laws—I find myself bounded on three axes. As a Jew, I get my language for the God conversation primarily (although not exclusively) from three thousand years of wrestling to be found in our tradition. As a person of my time and place, I bring Newton and Darwin and Einstein and the insights of this time to bear. Born in a century of apocalyptic inhumanity coupled with astonishing progress, I cannot subscribe to a God who kills the innocent as part of an unknowable plan. Even if I should, I cannot. And thirdly, I am compelled to acknowledge the urgent reality of the God I encounter.

That God calls out to me—and to everyone else too—to be better than I currently am, to speak out against injustice, to unsettle complacency. That God is not in competition with the claims of science, but rather it undermines all claims of superiority and authoritarianism, even when they are made in God's name.

As a child in Britain I used to watch a TV show called *Call My Bluff*. Three panelists would offer unlikely definitions of obscure words, and the other team had to decide who was telling the truth. The interesting truths, however, are not to be discerned by winnowing out falsehood and being left with the right answer. Rather, it is the tension between the truth claims—the space between the should, the can, and the ought—where truth is to be found. I reserve the right to reject some claims, but I don't believe that there can only be one winner in this game.

It is easy to declare that traditional representations of God—male, hierarchical, punitive—no longer work for me. In fact, though, it is more fruitful to consider how the God I experience today can be described in the language of my tradition.

I want to say something about God. It is my God and yet, I hope and believe, the God of my ancestors. It is a God calling out, demanding a response. Rather than me calling God's bluff, revealing truth and exposing falsehood, I am part of a more humbling, unsettling, and yet fulfilling process. The God in whom I believe is demanding of me to be better. The God in whom I believe is calling my bluff.

NOTES

1. Michael Marmur, "God of Language," in *Imagining the Jewish God*, ed. Leonard Kaplan and Ken Koltun-Fromm (Lanham MD: Lexington Books, 2016), 267–92.

2. Kaufmann Kohler, *Jewish Theology Systematically and Historically Considered* (New York: Macmillan, 1918), 21.

3. Kohler, *Jewish Theology*, 27.

4. Mordecai M. Kaplan, *The Meaning of God in Modern Jewish Religion* (Detroit: Wayne State University Press, 1994), 20–21.

5. Eugene B. Borowitz, "The Idea of God" [1957], in *Studies in the Meaning of Judaism* (Philadelphia: Jewish Publication Society, 2002), 40.

6. Abraham Joshua Heschel, *God in Search of Man* (New York: Farrar, Straus & Cudahy, 1955), 78.

7. Simon Blackburn, *Truth—A Guide for the Perplexed* (London: Penguin, 2006), xix.

6

THE PERSISTENCE OF LIFE AFTER LIFE

RABBI PAUL GOLOMB

In 1885, American Reform rabbis met for four days and worked out an eight-point "Declaration of Principles," commonly known as the Pittsburgh Platform. The seventh point proclaimed:

> We reassert the doctrine of Judaism that the soul is immortal, grounding the belief on the divine nature of human spirit, which forever finds bliss in righteousness and misery in wickedness. We reject as ideas not rooted in Judaism, the beliefs both in bodily resurrection and in Gehenna and Eden (Hell and Paradise) as abodes for everlasting punishment and reward.

For well over a century, this proclamation regarding life after death represented the dominant position of Reform Judaism. A much more fruitful and accessible source for determining the state of Reform Jewish belief, however, is in the liturgy. The prayer book (siddur) is, after all, an attempt to express what a congregation of Jews believes. It is little wonder that the prayer book has experienced development and change, particularly in subsequent editions by the Reform Movement. In this essay, I will examine assertions regarding afterlife in the three most recent North American Reform prayer books: the *Union Prayer Book* (*UPB*, published in 1940), *Gates of Prayer* (*GOP*, 1975) and *Mishkan T'filah* (*MT*, 2007).

There are two prominent locations in a worship service where the Jewish attitude toward afterlife is evident. They are in the second blessing of the central portion of the daily service—generally known as the Standing Prayer, or *Amidah*—and in the Mourner's *Kaddish*. With regard to the *Kaddish*, the three prayer books differ in only minor ways. We will take up its meaning and purpose later. The blessing in the *Amidah*, however, undergoes a significant and controversial change.

In traditional liturgy, the second blessing establishes God's unsurpassable might. The apotheosis of that power is to be found in the ability to revive the dead (*m'chayeih hameitim*). This power is stated four times in the prayer, especially in the concluding blessing: "Praised are You, Eternal, Reviver of the dead." Many non-Orthodox siddurim soften the specific assertion of resurrection by employing variations on "You give life eternal." The *UPB* goes further; it changes the Hebrew. *M'chayeih hameitim* becomes *m'chayeih hakol* and is rendered "Thou preservest all." The term is employed only once in the edited prayer, and the blessing concludes, "Praised . . . Who has implanted within us eternal life."

GOP restores the traditional prayer but replaces every instance of *hameitim* with *hakol*. The prayer book utilizes many paraphrases and creative reinterpretations of Hebrew prayers. They all convey the meaning of God as the Source of life and thus, unlike the *UPB*, eliminate any consideration in the prayer of what happens after death.

MT preserves the Hebrew of *GOP*, but with one critical change. Every instance of *m'chayeih hakol* is followed by *hameitim* in parentheses. The English furthermore does not soften the meaning, but rather states "revives the dead." (*M'chayeih hakol* is rendered "gives life to all.") The three prayer books therefore provide a conceptual development. The *UPB* affirms the immortality of the soul while also clearly implying a denial of resurrection. *GOP* is thoroughly neutral, removing any consideration of afterlife, either affirmation or rejection. *MT* restores the possibility, but avoids the affirmation, of resurrection. A meaningful personal existence following death, whose denial was once, in the words of one scholar in Jewish liturgy, a virtual article of faith, has now become a viable alternative belief.

The proposition that there is some sort of life after death occupies a liminal space in the human mind. It not only defies both verification and falsification, it also eludes any firm definition or description. The Reform Movement, as expressed in the statement from the Pittsburgh Platform, and echoed in the *UPB*, seemed to have cut through the uncertainty with a firm rejection. The traditional siddur is equally certain in its affirmation particularly of bodily resurrection. Assertions of clarity in both cases are overblown.

What are the strains and divisions that mark the entire Jewish tradition, including Reform? What compels one to either choose or reject a belief in a world-to-come? It is incontrovertibly true that *something* survives death. The fundamental law of conservation of matter is hardly overturned by the cessation of life. Nothing material is lost. Every atom and molecule remains. The poet Marge Piercy expresses the notion beautifully:

> We are given the body, that momentary kibbutz of elements
> that have belonged to frog and polar bear, corn and oak tree,
>   volcano and glacier.
> We are lent for a time these minerals in water. . . .

Most of us, however, would not consider the continuation of our physical elements as an afterlife. We expect something more personal. It is also incontrovertibly true that *we* may survive our death. My father once observed to me that "nobody dies anymore." We had just been viewing a set of home movies his father had made in the early 1930s. Not only were there the youthful images of my father and his kid brother doing home movie antics with my grandparents, there were also shots of my great-grandparents self-consciously standing before the camera. Audio and video preserve individuals long since passed away. And even without the electronic aids, our memories and the stories we choose to tell over and over assure that the dead are preserved alive and vital.

Once again, most of us would object. This preservation in memory is not what we mean as a life after death. It is not living in someone else's mind, but rather retaining a consciousness of one's own survival. Afterlife is therefore the continuity of *self* following the death of the body. Here is the heart of the matter.

Is afterlife meaningful? The question is purely philosophical. The prospect of an afterlife does not require any theological affirmation; that is, God need not have anything to do with whether we somehow survive death or not. Moreover, it need not be factually true in order to be meaningful. Indeed, matters of fact require some sort of confirmation. What confirmation is there that there is afterlife? What, conversely, disconfirms it? Facts have nothing to do with it! Meaningfulness is just what it connotes: does the assertion make sense; is it possible to accept the soundness of the argument, even if you disagree with it?

For there to be continuity of self, we must have an understanding of what self is. What makes you, you; what makes anyone, anyone? As each of us thinks about ourselves, we can sense that which we call the self is distinguished from the material elements of our body. We are born and grow. Over time, every cell is replaced, and yet we retain the notion of self. Certainly, one can make the argument that each individual's uniqueness (one's selfhood) derives from the singular combination of genetic properties that make up our genome. Thus, self is an emerging property of biochemical combinations. This notion, a materialist attitude, while sound, is not exhaustive. It is hardly the only meaningful way of describing the self. It is based on the firm, but untestable notion that only the material exists.

Yet even if the self is immaterial, is it meaningful to assert that it can survive death? Self requires some means for identification. Even as our body undergoes change over the course of our lives, there is always continuity. It is always uniquely our body! What is the means by which the self can retain identity even after the body is gone?

Let me propose this analogy. I grew up on the north shore of Long Island, New York. For over one hundred years, my hometown has been served by a commuter railroad. One of the trains leaves each morning at two minutes after six for the trip into New York City. Since inaugurated decades ago, it has been known as the 6:02 to Penn Station. Over that time, the line was electrified and the locomotive was replaced, the cars were updated, and the entire personnel—engineer, conductors, and passengers—have changed many times over. There is absolutely nothing that has remained the same, except the name. Identity can be twisted and buried, and yet it can find a way to emerge. If something survives the material death of a body, is it so unlikely that it can retain identity as well?

The biblical attitude of toward life after death is best expressed in the Book of Job. The book is a series of dialogues framed by a short and powerful story. Job, who is described from the start as a righteous man, is beset by a series of calamities that have taken away his wealth, health, and sense of well-being. Readers are informed that Job's ill fortune is due to a challenge brought by God's adversary, who suggests that people are good only because they fear God's retributive anger. The adversary expects that Job, if afflicted, will bargain with God for restoration.

A series of acquaintances come to comfort Job, but also to argue that Job should beg forgiveness for some unspecified wrongs he must have committed. Job is steadfast in refusing to do so, demanding rather that he wants his day in court and to learn what charges are being set against him. At the end, he receives his wished-for encounter with God. For his steadfastness, Job is rewarded with a double portion of what he had lost. The final verses of book state, "Job lived 140 years to see four generations of children and grandchildren. So Job died old and contented."

Throughout the book, Job is presented with basically two choices: repent or die. He refuses to do either. With respect to the latter, he repeatedly avers that death can be no solution: "As a cloud fades away, so whoever goes down to Sheol does not come up; he returns no more to his home, his place does not know him" (Job 7:9–10). In all, the book affirms that there is an afterlife, and it is to be found in some mysterious subterranean place called Sheol. This afterlife, however, is totally cut off from God. By dying, Job can no longer receive his day in the divine court. (Psalm 6:6 echoes this sentiment: "For there is no praise of You among the dead; in Sheol, who can acclaim You?") Moreover, the Book of Job asserts in its final verses that the ultimate reward for righteousness is in life itself.

Thus, Hebrew Scripture affirms an afterlife—Sheol—but also affirms that it is the place of all the dead, irrevocably cut off from God's goodness. The reward of a good life is to be found exclusively in this life, and in nothing that would be experienced after death. The *Tanach* is not, however, wholly consistent on this matter. Even Job contains a cryptic comment: "So one lies down never to rise; to awake only when the heavens are no more" (14:12). Perhaps the alienation from God brought on by death is not permanent.

The cracks in a neutral and virtually superfluous afterlife deepen in postbiblical literature, culminating in the affirmation we find in Talmud, "All Israel has a place in the world-to-come," followed by a listing of those who do not have a place (*Mishnah Sanhedrin* 10:1). No longer merely a place where all dead reside, afterlife is associated with reward.

What is a "place in the world-to-come"? There are two principal concepts. One is an emphasis on the word "place." When the deserving die, they go somewhere befitting their reward. Conventionally, that place is called "heaven" or "paradise." Jewish literature prefers "the Garden," as in Eden. The name is not as important as the very notion that death is a spatial portal to somewhere else. A second concept stresses the phrase "to come." The world-to-come does not exist now, but rather in the future. And the world is not somewhere else, but rather this world. Afterlife is therefore conceived as resurrection— a return in bodily form to a messianic and redeemed earth. In Jewish writings, it is called *t'chiyat hameitim*, "revival of the dead." There is a third concept, principally limited to mystic literature and folklore: reincarnation, in which a finite number of eternal souls are recycled in material bodies.

Each concept fulfills the notion of a place in the world-to-come. Each concept, moreover, is fully established in Jewish writing. It is very important to realize that Judaism definitively affirmed a faith in an afterlife that would differentiate the deserving and the undeserving, but could not settle on just what form that life takes. The siddur is no help.

Every worship service includes the *Amidah*. It also includes a Mourner's *Kaddish*. The *Kaddish* is a very ancient prayer, composed no later than the early first century CE. It is a pure doxology, only praising God and betraying no hint of having a purpose with respect to the departed. Indeed, its role as a prayer to be recited by mourners only begins to appear in the early thirteenth century. This repurposing is nowhere explained in the liturgy itself, but attending literature and a well-known midrash make clear that the *Kaddish* is intended to provide a measure of comfort to the dead (*korat ruach*) as they transition into the next world. The imagery is unmistakably spatial—our prayer on behalf of a soul that has been transported elsewhere for purposes of reward or punishment. Traditional Jewish liturgy promotes *both* resurrection and heaven/hell!

Reform Judaism has consistently maintained the *Kaddish* as a prayer for mourning the death of loved ones. Meditations that have been placed in the *UPB*, *GOP*, and *MT* all tend to highlight the mystery of death and the power of memory, but they only mask the underlying purpose of the prayer that remains essentially unchanged for over eight hundred years—that is, for the sake of the immortal soul.

The Pittsburgh Platform strove to dispel notions of heaven/hell and of resurrection as products of a pre-scientific and more superstitious past and, further, as not inherent in authentic Jewish thought. Yet, it also reasserted an immortal soul "that finds bliss in righteousness and misery in wickedness." Just how does this work? In the final analysis, Judaism, whether Reform or traditional, has an uncertain understanding of what comprises the world-to-come.

The Mishnah—the same foundational document that asserts that all Israel has a place in the world-to-come—states, "Those who put their minds to these matters, it would have been better if they were never born: what is above; what is below; what is beyond; what is before" (*Mishnah Chagigah* 2:1). "What is beyond" implies any speculation about life after death. Afterlife exists, the Rabbis averred, but it is all a big mystery.

The outstanding medieval Jewish thinker Maimonides (Rabbi Moses ben Maimon) fully agreed. In his commentary on the Mishnah, he asserts, in accord with numerous biblical and Rabbinic statements, that doing good is its own reward. Such inherent saintliness in a human being, however, is rare. Most of us are not so inner-directed. Thus, paradise or resurrection, Maimonides argued, is given as an inducement to strive to be righteous. It is not dissimilar from offering young children a cookie if they finish the vegetables on their plate.

Maimonides and classical Reform Judaism are in accord. Visions of a world-to-come are considerably less important than the way one acts in this world. Both the medieval sage and the late nineteenth-century Reformers quoted a passage in *Pirkei Avot* (a tractate of the Mishnah filled with Rabbinic wisdom): "Do not be like those who would serve a master on the condition that they would receive a reward" (*Pirkei Avot* 1:3). What is truly important in Jewish thought—traditional and modern—is one's conduct in this life.

Nineteenth-century Reformers chose to suppress consideration of the world-to-come, and for good reason. They were responding to the magical and otherworldly concepts inherent in premodern images of afterlife. Scientifically oriented Jews were increasingly repulsed by such notions. Afterlife, however, has not been completely eliminated.

Franz Rosenzweig, an influential early twentieth-century Jewish thinker, taught that we human beings are quite aware of our mortality. Even if we are privileged to live into our nineties or past one hundred, it is only a small sliver in a span of human existence that reaches both backward and forward for millennia. What gives such an inconsequential span of years any meaningfulness? It is, Rosenzweig reminds us, the possibility that our lives have transcendence. They make a difference, not only during the span of life itself, but for eternity. While classical Reform felt the obligation to combat the fantasy associated with traditional and folkloristic images of afterlife, the challenge for liberal religious Jews today is to combat a hyper-scientism that denies anything outside the material. If human existence is nothing more than chemical protoplasm, then assigning it meaningfulness is virtually absurd.

Reinserting "reviving the dead" into contemporary Reform Jewish liturgy is controversial. The issue is not a matter of knowledge or faith. The idea of resurrection or any other form of afterlife is absolutely untestable. It defies scientific investigation but nonetheless has philosophic coherence. Further, the issue is not a matter of deviating from Reform Jewish principles. At no time has Reform Judaism denied the notion of the individual soul's immortality. The fundamental question is how or whether one calls attention to the possibility of a world-to-come without also devaluing the supreme Jewish value of focusing on how to live this life.

Mishkan T'filah includes an aphorism, whose origin is uncertain, prior to the Shabbat evening *Amidah*: "Pray as if everything depended upon God. Act as if everything depended upon you." It is a pithy saying but also an irreducible paradox. Which is it that sustains our existence: divine will or human endeavor? Rabbi Abraham Heschel, who is quoted liberally throughout *MT*, teaches us not to be unduly bothered by the apparent contradiction. He wrote, "Most high religions make an effort to present the world and life as a unified whole, and to regard all discord and incongruities as provisional or illusory. . . . To Jewish tradition . . . paradox is an essential understanding of the world. . . . Tension, contrast, contradiction characterize all of reality." He then adds, "There is a polarity in everything except God. For all tension ends in God. The Eternal is beyond all dichotomies."

So it is with the Reform Jewish approach to afterlife. We pray that our immortal souls are worthy of everlasting bliss. And we try to act as if this life—and only this life—is fundamentally important.

7

SCIENCE AND FAITH

RABBI GEOFFREY A. MITELMAN

Today, the public discourse about the role of religion in our scientific age is almost never productive, because two main reactions are filling the airwaves and the blogosphere.

On one side are religious fundamentalists, who argue that religion should be the primary, if not the only, source for ultimate truth and morality. As a result, they often either ignore or even actively try to shut down scientific inquiry. On the other side are adamant atheists, who claim that religion is the source for much of the evil in this world and is based on outdated superstitions. As a result, they have come to believe that religion has no value in this world at all and often strive to eliminate religion entirely.

Yet while both sides are arguing, few people are truly listening—their arguments are creating a lot of heat, but they are producing very little light. Indeed, both of these perspectives are major contributors to the increased polarization of our society. But in this public conversation about religion and science, there is a large population in the middle that has not found a way to express its voice.

This is particularly the case in the Jewish community. When a study done by the American Association for the Advancement of Science and Rice University asked people how they perceived the relationship between science and religion, several potential responses were offered. One was "in collaboration," one was "independent," and two were "in conflict"—one "on the side of religion" and the other "on the side of science." About 25 percent of the American populace chose one of the two conflict options, which, interestingly, was the same percentage as the Jewish population. But while most of the Christians who saw religion and science in opposition viewed themselves as on the side of religion, those Jews who saw science and religion in conflict came down on the side of science—and by a huge margin. For the "conflicted Christians," three out of four opted for religion, and one out of four chose science. But for the 25 percent of conflicted Jews, fifteen out of sixteen saw themselves on the side of science and, therefore, anti-religion.

This finding implies that it's often less of a challenge to get Jews to embrace science than it is to get them to embrace Judaism. Perhaps because Judaism has long celebrated questioning and challenging authority or perhaps because theology is rarely emphasized in Reform Judaism, many Jews erroneously think that if they accept science, they need to reject their Judaism.

These numbers, then, reflect not only the challenge of making Judaism relevant and meaningful in our scientific world today. They represent a larger question: how to present a worldview that gives purpose to people's lives and lets them make a positive impact on societal and global issues and, at the same time, embraces critical thinking and scientific inquiry. Indeed, the biggest questions we face aren't religious and aren't scientific. They are human, and we need wisdom from both sources in order to truly flourish, and so I want to highlight a few topics where both Judaism and science can enhance the conversation.

Let's start with the question of morality, which traditionally was categorized as a subject of religious exploration. However, morality is now also a subject of scientific inquiry. Books such as *The Moral Arc* by Michael Shermer and *The Blank Slate* by evolutionary psychologist Steven Pinker show scientifically how our deepest moral convictions, such as altruism, empathy, and justice, are all products of human evolution.

Pinker explains, for instance, that as humans evolved on the African savanna, they had to continually balance two competing needs to survive and pass their genes on to the next generation: taking care of themselves and aiding others. Tens of thousands of years later, the emotions associated with those two needs continue to drive our social mores. "Contempt, anger, and disgust . . . prompt [us] to punish cheaters. Gratitude . . . [prompts us] to reward altruists. . . . Sympathy, compassion, and empathy prompt [us] to help a needy beneficiary. . . . And guilt, shame, and embarrassment . . . prompt [us] to avoid cheating or to repair its effects."[1] Indeed, a classic experiment done by biologist Robert Trivers showed that treating others fairly by striking the right balance between justice and mercy is an ideal evolutionary strategy.

This also explains why some version of the Golden Rule has appeared in almost every culture and forms the basis of almost every religion, and which we Jews see in Hillel's dictum "What is hateful to you, do not do to another: that is the whole Torah. The rest is commentary; now go and learn it" (Babylonian Talmud, *Shabbat* 31a). The central tenet—"What is hateful to you, do not do to another"—is easy to understand. But its application in real life is much harder. Should we lie to prevent someone embarrassment? What's our financial responsibility to both ourselves and our community? What should we do if we discover a friend has done something unethical?

That's why the second part—"The rest is commentary; now go and learn it"—is so crucial. It's how we manifest that guideline in specific situations. It allows us to understand the unique situation we're in, to find appropriate Talmudic texts or moral guidelines, and to help us navigate competing values. While evolution has trained us to intuitively know that we shouldn't hurt someone, religion can guide exactly *how* to get through that challenge.

Or consider the flip side of hurting someone, namely, showing compassion. "The world stands on three things," *Pirkei Avot* 1:2 says. "On Torah, on prayer, and on acts of loving-kindness." Can science help us better understand what generates compassion and even engender more of it? That's the focus of the work of Professor David DeSteno, director of the Social Emotion Group at Northeastern University. He conducted an experiment on the human motivation for kindness, which he described in a 2012 *New York Times* article:

> We paired up participants in teams: one real participant and one confederate. First, they had to tap their hands on sensors to tones played over earphones. In some cases the tones led them to tap their hands in synchrony; in other cases . . . to tap in a random mismatching manner. We next had the participants watch their tapping partner get cheated by another confederate, which resulted in the partner's being assigned to complete a stack of onerous word problems. As participants were leaving, they were informed by an automated message that if they desired, they could help complete some of the work assigned to their partners. If they did so, we timed how long they spent working on the task.
>
> The results were striking: the simple act of tapping one's hands in synchrony with another caused participants to report feeling more similar to their partners and to have greater compassion for their plight; it increased the number of people who helped their partner by 31 percent and increased the average time spent helping from one minute to more than seven.
>
> These results suggest that if our minds draw an association between a victim and ourselves—even a relatively trivial one—the compassion we feel for his or her suffering is amplified greatly.[2]

DeSteno notes that there is often tension between our religious *beliefs* and our religious *identities*—between our religious teachings that tell us to be compassionate to all people and the way religious groups can create an "us" and "them" mentality. And he shows that if we are looking to encourage more compassion toward others, we don't always need religious teachings to get us there—a sense of commonality can also pave the way. There is nothing special about tapping in synchrony; any such commonality will do. Increased compassion for one's neighbor, for instance, can come from something as easy as encouraging yourself to think of him as, say, a fan of the same local restaurant.

This insight, however, can help religious communities link ethical action with ritual life. After all, singing together, praying together, or reading together—the heart of almost every service—creates synchrony. And developing a sense of connection to the Jewish community or a deeper sense of Jewish identity can advance our compassionate impulse, since we would find unexpected commonality. Too often, we separate ethical mitzvot and ritual mitzvot. DeSteno's research suggests that we should be striving to join them more intentionally, since they create more of each other.

Another example is the field of memory. Most of us wish we had a greater capacity for memory. Why can we remember some things well and other things poorly? The writer Joshua Foer was inspired to train for the 2006 USA Memory Championship because, he writes, "among the things I regularly forgot [were] where I put my car keys (where I put my car, for that matter), my girlfriend's birthday, our anniversary, [and] Valentine's Day . . . why I just opened the fridge . . . [and] to put the toilet seat down."[3]

Recent scientific discoveries show that the most crucial reason we remember some things and not others is because we tend to remember the things we think about most frequently. When we learn something new, it takes a while for the synaptic connections to strengthen in our brains. The operative phrase in neuroscience is "Cells that wire together fire together." Cognitive scientist Daniel Willingham explains it this way: "Your memory lays its bets this way: if you think about something carefully, you'll probably have to think about it again, so it should be stored. Thus your memory is not a product of what you want to remember or what you try to remember—it's a product of what you think about."[4]

Notably, this is essentially the same message found in the Torah. We Jews are commanded to remember through acts of repetition. We are instructed to participate in the Passover ritual ("Remember that you were slaves in Egypt"; Deuteronomy 5:15 et al.). We are reminded to observe Shabbat each week ("Remember Shabbat and keep it holy"; Exodus 20:8). We are obliged to remember our loved ones by observing their *yahrzeits*, the anniversary of their death (*Shulchan Aruch, Yoreh Dei-ah* 402:12).

Thus, Jews are enjoined to take action in ways that become constant reminders of what is most important. Rabbi Arnold Jacob Wolf points out that "uniquely Jewish is the idea of memory as will. Memory is not something that befalls a passive consciousness. It is something purposefully appropriated in awe and love."[5]

The Baal Shem Tov, founder of Chasidism, taught that "redemption lies in remembering." We remember the good and the bad so that we can make tomorrow better than today and yesterday. We honor Jewish tradition, our past, not for its own sake, but for the future. Embodied in Judaism is the hope that despite inevitable setbacks and missteps, we can become the people we want to be and help create the world we wish to see.

From both the Jewish and scientific perspectives, the more frequently we think about our heritage, the more likely it is to become a permanent fixture of our memory and to influence our thoughts and actions. As neuroscientist Antonio Damasio explains, "Memory is responsible for ceaselessly placing the self . . . between a thoroughly-lived past and an anticipated future."[6]

Finally, what can scientists teach us about "self-control"—specifically, why we often ignore our better judgment to pursue immediate pleasure? Evolutionary psychologist Douglas Kenrick argues that we have many "modular subselves," with different parts of our brain advocating for different goals. For example, in his book *Sex, Murder and the Meaning of Life*, Kenrick calls these different subselves

> the team player (concerned with the goal of making friends), the go-getter (concerned with getting ahead), the night watchman (concerned with protecting us from the bad guys), the compulsive (concerned with protecting us from disease), the swinging single (concerned with finding mates), the good spouse (concerned with the very different problem of keeping those mates), and the parent (concerned with taking care of our kin, especially any children we might have).[7]

All these modular subselves have their own specific role and own specific purpose, so when we feel like different parts of our "self" are at war, it's really because our different subselves are trying to get us to act in conflicting ways.

Our Rabbinic sages explored the concept of the *yetzer hara*—the impulse to evil, or, alternatively, the part of ourselves that seeks immediate pleasurable gratification. Generally, the *yetzer hara* is viewed as dangerous. Not only does it yearn only for what is forbidden (Jerusalem Talmud, *Yoma* 6:4), it is a powerful force that can quickly grow if left unchecked. We are told: "Who is mighty? The one who subdues his *yetzer hara*" (*Pirkei Avot* 4:1). Most troublingly, it's what leads us to transgressions like sexual impropriety or an unchecked desire for power. However, without this impulse, we are taught, "no man would engage in business, build homes, marry, or have children" (*B'reishit Rabbah* 9:7). Sex and power are basic human drives and are crucial for maintaining and improving our world. After all, sex is what creates the next generation, and power is how we make an impact to better our world.

The problem, then, is not sex or power per se, but rather letting our impulses run rampant and having our animal nature overrun our humanity.

That's where both science and religion can help us in gaining mastery over our impulses. We can learn, for example, from the strategies children employed in the classic scientific "Marshmallow Experiment" conducted by Walter Mischel at Stanford University in the late 1960s. A group of four-year-olds were told that if they waited while the experimenter ran a fifteen-minute errand, they would receive two marshmallows when he returned. If they ate the one marshmallow in front of them, they wouldn't receive a second one. The children who controlled their desire for immediate gratification employed various strategies—covering their eyes, talking to themselves, singing, playing games, trying to sleep—to block out the temptation.

Mischel recently wrote a book about the test (called, unsurprisingly, *The Marshmallow Test*), and as he notes in an interview in the *New Yorker*: "We've found a way to really improve human choice and freedom. If we have the skills to allow us to make discriminations about when we do or don't do something, when we do or don't drink something, and when we do and when we don't wait for something, we are no longer victims of our desires."[8] And as Professor Roy Baumeister describes it, in many ways, self-control is a muscle—it can get exhausted, but it can also be strengthened with practice.[9]

Similarly, rather than avoiding temptation altogether, the Jewish tradition of Mussar offers a path to personal spiritual development that includes developing the soul trait of patience. Rabbi Yisrael Salanter, who founded and led the Mussar movement in the nineteenth century, spoke of three stages of practice: (1) *hergesh*, meaning "sensitivity," in which we pay attention to traits in our inner world that are at varying degrees of balance and wholeness; (2) *kibush*, literally "conquer," in which we use our intelligence and will to stretch ourselves toward the ideal expression of the traits in which we're challenged; and (3) *tikkun*, usually translated as "repair" but better understood as "transformation," whereby we aim to transform the impulse itself and thereby reach our highest spiritual potential. (To learn more, see reformjudaismag.org/fall_2008 and the website for the Mussar Institute, mussarinstitute.org.)

While these examples show how we might integrate science and religion to improve our lives and our world, they do not address a fundamental religious question: the existence of God. If we cannot "prove" the existence of God, how can science be part of the conversation?

Reframing our understanding of what constitutes "science" can help. What we believe to be true can change at any given time as a result of new data, instruments, analysis, and/or interpretations. In this sense, a scientific discovery may be better seen as temporal and historical than as an eternal, unchanging truth.

In fact Steven Goldman, co-founder of the National Association of Science, Technology, and Society Studies, suggests that viewing everything around us as "scientific objects . . . is a useful way of eliminating much of the controversy [surrounding] the [imperfect and temporal] status of scientific knowledge and truth claims."[10]

We can apply the same metaphor to God—yes, even conceiving of God as a "scientific object." This does not mean that God can be studied scientifically or that if we find enough evidence we can prove or disprove God's existence. It simply means that our understanding of God can change with new knowledge and insights. It means that we are willing to rethink or reexamine what we believe about the Divine.

I have regular discussions about science and religion with a friend who is a self-described atheist. "We need to have a clear definition of 'God,'" he tells me. "Otherwise, we don't know what we're talking about." I reply that what we really need is a "working definition of 'God,'" a theology that can adapt when new knowledge or experiences arise. Rather than saying either "This is what God is, and I know that I am right" or "There is no omnipotent, omnipresent, benevolent God that created the universe and directly impacts the world today," we can instead say, "Given what I know now, this is what I believe God is and how God acts in this world. But I might later need to change my understanding."

Even people who do not believe in God have different perspectives about the Divine. A recently published study about atheists at the University of Tennessee at Chattanooga identified six types of non-believers: intellectual atheist/agnostics (who enjoy engaging in discussions of science, philosophy, and epistemology); activist atheist/agnostics (who pursue social justice work); seeker agnostics (who don't avow a clear ideological stance because they recognize the complexity of theological questions); antitheists (who actively try to convince people that religion is harmful); non-theists (who are generally apathetic about religion and its role in society); and ritual atheist/agnostics (who find inspiration in ceremonies, meditation, yoga classes, holiday traditions, and the like). Many Reform Jews appear to fall into this last category.

Even Reform Jews who believe in God have a diversity of perspectives. Women, for example, tend to view God more in terms of relationship and interdependence, and men conceive of God in more abstract, autonomous ways. And Reform Jews often change their beliefs about God during the course of their lives. Younger Jews, for instance, are much more likely to God-wrestle than middle-aged adults, and seniors encountering illness and death return to question God's presence.[11]

For all these reasons, just as scientists have (more or less) been willing to broaden what is known about the universe to include metaphysical questions, so too we should be willing to embrace a "working definition" of God, approached metaphorically as a "scientific object," that changes with what we come to understand about the metaphysical world.

Ultimately, instead of trying to "reconcile" religion and science, let us continue to find the ways in which they support one another. When we apply the lessons of both science and religion to learn more about our morality or to help us become more compassionate or more aware of what is most important, we not only better ourselves and our relationships with others, we maximize what we have to contribute to *tikkun hanefesh* and *tikkun haolam*—a repair of ourselves and repair of our world.

NOTES

1. Steven Pinker, *The Blank Slate: The Modern Denial of Human Nature* (New York: Penguin, 2002), 271.

2. David DeSteno, "Compassion Made Easy," New York Times, July 14, 2012, http://www.nytimes.com/2012/07/15/opinion/sunday/the-science-of-compassion.html?mcubz=0

3. Jonathan Foer, *Moonwalking with Einstein: The Art and Science of Remembering Everything* (New York: Penguin Books, 2011), 6.

4. Daniel T. Willingham, *Why Don't Students Like School?* (San Francisco: Jossey-Bass, 2009), 53.

5. Arnold Jacob Wolf, "Remember to Remember," *Tradition* 15, no.3 (Fall 1975): 40.

6. Antonio Damasio, *Self Comes to Mind* (New York: Pantheon Books, 2010), 297.

7. Douglas T. Kenrick, *Sex, Murder and the Meaning of Life* (New York: Basic Books, 2011), x–xi.

8. Maria Konnikova, "The Struggles of a Psychologist Studying Self-Control," *New Yorker*, October 9, 2014, http://www.newyorker.com/science/maria-konnikova/struggles-psychologist-studying-self-control.

9. See, for example, http://www.apa.org/monitor/2012/01/self-control.aspx

10. Steven L. Goldman, "Science Wars: What Scientists Know and How They Know it," course no. 1235, lecture no. 24, available at thegreatcourses.com.

11. Leah Hochman, "Theology: How Reform Jews Picture God," *Reform Judaism*, Spring 2013, http://reformjudaismmag.org/past-issues/spring2013/picture-god.

8

THE GOD THING

RABBI DAVID W. NELSON, PHD

Some time ago I taught a monthly Torah study group. I would meet with six or eight adult learners, and we would read the English translation of the Torah text carefully and discuss what we thought it meant. There was one fellow in the group who participated enthusiastically. He was always eager to suggest interpretations of text and to argue with me and the other students, in a positive way. After a few months, as we were settling down to study one evening, he said, "David, I love discussing this stuff. But I just don't get the God thing." When I probed, he said, essentially, that the book was fascinating, that it raised wonderful questions about Jewish values and ethics and history, but that he just could not find any meaning in its portrayal(s) of God.

The fact is that I too have a hard time with "the God thing," if by that is meant the way God is portrayed in our ancient texts. God as Shepherd, King, Father—these lovely, picturesque metaphors hold little attraction for me. Their attributes are too human. They are too gendered. They simply do not speak to me. But they are only metaphors, impressionistic descriptions by which we attempt to suggest some of the qualities that we would like to see in God. I have come to believe that many—perhaps most—people who say that they do not believe in God actually mean that they do not accept many (or any) of the traditional metaphors that we use when describing and discussing God.

In response to this insight, I set out in the late 1990s to explore new metaphors, new descriptions using different vocabularies, that might be more accessible to modern, liberal Jews. I mined the vocabulary of modern physics to find my new metaphors. Using the language of big bang cosmology, quantum theory, chaos theory, general and special relativity and string theory, I explored a number of different ways to think about God that would maintain a sense of God as Creator without resorting to the anthropomorphisms that cause many people such discomfort. In the end, I concluded that when I say "God" I mean something like "the enormous, complex set of natural forces and laws that brought the universe into being and continue to govern its evolution on every scale, from the intergalactic to the subatomic." As such, God clearly fills every space and time of the universe (in the words of Isaiah 6:3, "The whole earth is full of His glory"), since the entire universe is an expression of the laws and principles that govern it. In that respect, depending on how picky you want to be, I may be fairly characterized as a pantheist ("God *is* everything") or a panentheist ("God is *in* everything"), perhaps in the tradition of the seventeenth-century Dutch Jewish philosopher Baruch Spinoza. Described in this way, God is also omnipotent, literally, for nothing can violate the laws of nature. They are absolute. I used the language of fractal geometry, according to which a fractal shape looks roughly the same no matter the scale at which one examines it, to show how, in fact, we are indeed created in the image of God. I explored the (biblical) image of God as light and pointed out that light has a constant, measurable speed that is not infinite. This led me to argue that God may be seen as tremendously powerful without being infinitely so. These are just a few examples of how I "riffed" on the language of physics to explore some fairly traditional Jewish beliefs. And in the end I concluded that God is the complex set of laws that determine, quite literally, the shape of reality.

There is, however, a problem with this model of thinking about God. The problem is that it provides no room for the God who appears on virtually every page of our ancient sacred texts, in every chapter of our cherished tales. There, whether in *Tanach* or midrash or Talmud, we see a God who interacts with us, enters into relationships with us, loves us, gets angry at us, forgives us, instructs and commands us. It is a God to whom our ancient ancestors brought gifts of sacrificial animals, fruit, grain, incense, and oil. Later on, when the destruction of the Temple made the bringing of gifts impossible, we substituted words for sacrificial offerings and prayed to God in shul, or, like our highly fictionalized ancestor Tevye the Milkman, we poured out our hearts about the tsuris that threatens to overwhelm us. Like Rabbi Levi Yitzchak of Berdichev, we sometimes complained to and argued with God, and in the aftermath of the greatest of all Jewish traumas, the Holocaust, we were outraged and confused and troubled by God's ability to remain silent. In short, the God of all of Jewish tradition is a God who behaves very much like a person, which is what we mean when we say it is a "personal God." By contrast, the God I described through the language of physics was a non-personal God. The laws of gravity, the principles of quantum theory, and the intricacies of chaos theory do not care about or even know me. It would make no sense to speak to them. They neither hear nor respond. They are not aware. I found this problem too large to simply dismiss. A Judaism without a personal God would be so totally foreign to all previous generations of Jews as to be essentially a new phenomenon rather than an evolved continuation of the old system. And I am simply too much in love with the old system to give it up.

In response to this dilemma, I searched for a way to develop the model further to include a rational way of imagining God as conscious, aware, and thus open to interaction. My requirement, however, was that any theory of "personal God" would have to make sense to me. It could not depend on a "leap of faith" or a non-rational intuition. It would have to stand up to scrutiny by someone who "didn't get the God thing."

I started the search by reading widely in the fields of science and philosophy that are trying (with only very limited success, it is important to note) to understand how human consciousness works. If I need my God to be conscious, I reasoned, there would have to be some analogy, however imprecise, between what the word "conscious" means when applied to us and what the same word means when applied to God. (Note: This line of reasoning is quite contrary to the teachings of Moses Maimonides [1135–1204] who insisted that God's utter uniqueness must mean that no word, when applied to God, could have any similarity in meaning to the same word as applied to any other thing. I reject Maimonides's view in this regard.) My reading soon revealed that there is nothing even vaguely resembling a consensus among neuroscientists and philosophers regarding how our consciousness works. The theory that makes the most sense to me, however, is the one rooted in *emergence theory*.

Emergence theory is a way of thinking about science, art, culture, or almost any complex system. Although its roots are ancient, most of the important developments in the field have occurred in the last forty years or so. It is enormously complicated but can be simply put as follows: An emergent system is one that comes about when a large number of units (e.g., things, entities) interact with one another in a highly complex way that leads to the appearance of a new phenomenon. This new phenomenon is said to be *emergent* because it emerges from the interaction of the original things. The emergent phenomenon exhibits features that are not found in the original, underlying units and obeys rules that are different from the rules that govern the underlying units. In its strongest form, the emergent phenomenon exerts causal influences on the individual units; it can change their behavior. The definition sounds mysterious but can be more easily understood by seeing how it works with an everyday example. Water is made up of molecules, each of which consists of one oxygen atom and two hydrogen atoms. That's all water is. But the features that we normally associate with water are only seen in the emergent phenomenon that comes into existence when a very large number of water molecules interact in a complex way. Water flows, but individual water molecules do not flow. Water is wet, but individual water molecules are not wet. Water occurs in three basic forms (a solid called ice, a liquid called liquid water, and a gas called water vapor), but water molecules do not exhibit these three forms. Furthermore, ordinary water (the emergent phenomenon that occurs when a large number of molecules interact) behaves according to clear rules with respect to temperature, pressure, turbulence, and so on. These rules are completely different from those that govern the behavior of one water molecule. Finally, water, as we know, flows. In its fluid state it does all sorts of things, including forming droplets and becoming turbulent. When these things occur, the water in the glass or the pail or the river is forcing its constituent molecules to behave in certain ways. It is controlling them.

Similar principles of emergence can be seen when we look at the emergent theory of consciousness. Our brains are made up of nerve cells called neurons. Each neuron is a nerve cell with an input end that looks sort of treelike, called the dendrites, and an output end called an axon. A neuron is pretty simple. It receives electrochemical signals from the axons of other neurons through its dendrites, and if it receives a sufficient amount of input, it "fires" a signal through its axon to the dendrites of whatever other neuron(s) it is attached to. (To be more precise, axons are never "attached" to dendrites. Rather, they signal to them across tiny empty connective spaces called synapses.) That's all that happens in the brain. But there are many billions of neurons in each of our brains (neuroscientists cannot agree as to even an approximate number), and they are connected in many trillions of networks, subnetworks, loops, feedback loops, local complexes, and more, to create what many believe is the single most complex "thing" in our universe, namely, the human brain. No neuron knows anything. No neuron is aware of anything. No neuron has memories, feelings, thoughts, or fears. No neuron likes chocolate or worries about global warming. But when you put billions of them together and connect them in trillions of ways, the result is something that can call itself "Me" and can do all the marvelous things that we humans do—including thinking about what it means to be conscious—with hardly any effort at all. The human "mind" or "consciousness" is thus the emergent result of the interconnection of all those billions of neurons. It is a new phenomenon that cannot be anticipated by examining one neuron (or ten or twenty or a thousand). It exhibits features (anger, hope, love, creativity, and fear, to name just a few) that neurons do not exhibit, and it operates according to rules that mean nothing to neurons. It can also have profound causal influence on the neurons that underlie it, as is the case when we drink alcohol or use drugs (thereby damaging neurons) or when we study a new skill or participate in psychotherapy (thereby creating new synaptic connections among our neurons). Understood in this way, consciousness is emergent.

Armed with this theoretical sketch of human consciousness, I propose a model of God as follows: One of the most common behaviors we humans engage in is interaction with other humans. Whether it is low-level interaction (e.g., nodding a polite hello to the bus driver or exchanging a pleasantry with a retail clerk) or a higher level (e.g., helping a son or daughter think through the future or engaging a close friend in a deep, extended conversation about religion or politics or art), we engage one another all the time. When we read, we engage authors—people who are in different places and perhaps even different times (as is the case when we read the work of an author who is no longer alive). The very existence of "society" requires that we engage and interact and communicate many times every day. The huge number and complexity of human interactions, not only at any one moment but across all periods of human history, *must* be generating an emergent phenomenon, a new, higher-order reality that is as different from the reality of any given human being as a bucket of water is from a water molecule or as the reality of a human mind is different from the reality of any single neuron in a human brain. This emergent reality that arises from the massive interaction of human consciousnesses must exhibit features, like any emergent phenomenon, that are not exhibited by the lower-level things (humans) that generate it. Like any emergent phenomenon, it must operate by rules that are utterly different from the rules that govern the units (humans) that give rise to its existence. And like many emergent phenomena, it certainly has causal influence on its lower-level entities. It guides and shapes their behavior. This emergent entity is what I have come to identify as the conscious part of God.

In *Pirkei Avot* 3:6 we read, "When ten sit and engage in Torah, the *Shechinah* is present among them." The model proposed here is essentially a contemporary reframing of this ancient Rabbinic view. God's presence (the *Shechinah*), or God's consciousness, emerges when humans beings interact—in study, in prayer, or in community activities of almost any sort. God's Self emerges as a result of the interaction among human consciousnesses. By contrast, in a situation in which there is no human interaction, no conscious exchange, God's conscious presence would be absent. God's influence understood as the complex set of physical laws and principles by which the reality of our universe is governed would still exist in such a situation. Gravity and entropy and the electromagnetic forces that animate the universe would still function, but the conscious part of God would not. This may be compared to a human being who is under general anesthesia. The body of such an individual continues to exist and function, but the conscious part is not present.

Is this a different model from the one suggested earlier that sees God as a label we use to signify the complex of physical laws, forces, and principles that brought our universe into being and govern its continuing evolution? No, this is not a different model, but rather a different *stage* of that model. For the first roughly fourteen billion years of the universe's life to date, we are not aware that there was any consciousness in the universe (at least not in our neighborhood). In fact, consciousness as we know it seems to be no more than a million or so years old—the blink of any eye in cosmological terms. For those first fourteen billion or so years, the universe had no consciousness, and God may rightly have been thought of as the forces and laws that govern it—gravity, quantum mechanics, entropy, and so on. In the last little bit of time, however, the evolution of the universe, in its ever-increasing complexity, has created consciousness, and with that new phase of the life of the universe, there came a new phase in the life of God, a phase of emergent consciousness that arose from the increasing interaction among conscious beings in the universe. Note that here again I reject a major tenet of much of traditional Jewish thought. Many traditional theologians are adamant that God does not ever change. God always was and always will be the same, eternally unchanging. I disagree profoundly with this claim. In a universe characterized at every single level and scale of its existence by dynamism and constant becoming, it makes no sense to me to imagine a God who is static and unchanging.

The ramifications of this model of God are many. If God's consciousness emerges from the interactions among humans, then the long-standing debate over whether the Torah and the mitzvot were revealed by God or written by humans fades into the background, as the clear dichotomy between what is divine and what is the product of human interaction (i.e., study, argument, and legislation) becomes fuzzy. On the other hand, the ages-old certainty among religious thinkers that God is completely just, always good, and totally righteous also begins to dissolve, as we are acutely aware that human behavior, whether exhibited by a single human actor or by a group whose members interact, is often less than just, good, and righteous. Perhaps most importantly, if God's consciousness, the divine Self, is generated as the emergent result of interacting human consciousnesses, then the existence and strength of *community* become the most important elements of Jewish life. In fact, I would suggest that in the long tradition (going back to the Talmud) of arguing about which mitzvah is most crucial to Jewish life, these new models of understanding God lead inexorably to the conclusion that anything that creates, strengthens, or enriches Jewish community is the most important mitzvah of all.

These models do not represent either the historical development of Reform thinking about God or the current consensus of any group in the Reform Jewish world. My only claims are these: (1) some prominent role for God is crucial in any authentic system of Jewish thought and belief; (2) many contemporary Jews have a great deal of difficulty accepting such a role for God when God is defined and described only in terms of the language of our ancient sacred texts; and (3) therefore, the proposed models may provide access to God for many, currently "theistically disaffected" Jews. Based on these claims I would argue that it is crucial to the intellectual depth and spiritual health of contemporary Jews that we engage in, ponder, and discuss the questions of what we *really* believe about God and how those beliefs affect our Jewish lives.

· Part Two ·

CHOOSING COVENANT

In the Torah, the Jews are called "a people apart," chosen to live in a unique covenant with God. This doctrine of chosenness is difficult for many of us moderns to accept. It seems religiously elitist, completely contrary to modern notions of egalitarianism. And yet there it is, front and center in many of our most important prayers, including the Torah blessings. In this section, we look carefully at the concept of God's election of the Jews as a chosen people, discussing chosenness in a context of Jewish religious pluralism both within and beyond Judaism.

In "Chosen for Torah," Rabbi Ammiel Hirsch speaks metaphorically of how Jews are the Torah. We are the spiritual descendants of Abraham and Sarah, whether or not we are biologically descended from them, and by virtue of that religious relationship, we are meant to bring benefit to the entire world.

Rabbi Rachel Sabath Beit-Halachmi, PhD, in "Refining the Covenant," explores the concept of Jewish chosenness and the tremendous promise it holds as the centerpiece of Jewish religious thought.

In "Is Reform Judaism Authentic Judaism?" Rabbi Kari Hofmaister Tuling, PhD, examines the ways in which we as Reform Jews, who do not look to tradition as the source of our authenticity, can construct our theological positions in a liberal context.

In her carefully argued essay "Jewish Religious Pluralism," Rabbi Joan S. Friedman, PhD, offers a definition of Judaism that includes even the most orthodox sectarian Jews as "Jews responding to God by living a life rooted in the teachings of the Torah."

In "Freedom within Limits," Rabbi Jan Katzew, PhD, looks at religion and science to ask how we can reconcile belief in God with the idea of free will, of actions chosen freely.

In "Let Every Blade of Grass Sing a Song of Praise," Rabbi Shoshanah Conover brings the wisdom of classic texts to bear as she identifies the environment as a necessary, central feature of any contemporary spiritual approach.

Historian Robert M. Seltzer, PhD, in "What Is Modern about Reform Judaism?" discusses the concept of the Axial Age, referring to intellectual, cultural, social, and religious developments that took place millennia ago, followed by a modern Axial Age in which Reform Judaism has emerged as "one of the most recent manifestations of the repeated re-forming of Judaism."

Rabbi Stanley M. Davids ("A Zionism of the Soul") and Rabbi Gilad Kariv ("The Role of Reform Judaism in Israel") discuss today's Israel and the challenges that the State of Israel's rejection of Reform Judaism poses for the future.

Reform Judaism developed out of the Enlightenment and the Emancipation, two historical processes occurring in Europe over a long period. But we are not writing a history book, nor are we necessarily writing for people convinced of the importance of Reform Judaism to their own lives. So the underlying question in "Choosing Covenant" is how we can understand Reform Judaism in a historical context that helps people grasp its religious importance and its spiritual meaning.

Some have argued that the doctrine of chosenness becomes more pronounced in times when the Jews are being persecuted. There is an obvious logic to this theory. The more you express your hatred for me, the more I need to justify my unique religious identity. The question is, what happens when anti-Semitism declines? Is there a way to understand the religious category of a chosen nation that will resonate within the hearts of fully emancipated Americans who do not experience prejudice or discrimination? If Reform Judaism can develop such an understanding, we have the potential to bring new vitality to our ritual as we reinforce our religious identity.

9

CHOSEN FOR TORAH

Rabbi Ammiel Hirsch

The heart of Judaism is the concept of *am*, the Jewish people. This heart pumps ideological energy to the entire body of Jewish thought.

We have never considered ourselves a mere faith community. We do not impose a faith-based test to determine Jewish status. A Jew is a member of the Jewish people. Most of us become Jewish by birth; the rest of us, through a voluntary process of joining the Jewish people.

From the moment we encounter the first Jew, Abraham, the thrust of *Tanach* is clear: "I will make of you a great people" (Genesis 12:2). After the first eleven chapters of Genesis, the entire remainder of *Tanach*, at its most basic level, is about the unfolding destiny of the Jewish people. It is about the descendants of Abraham, defined first and foremost in a physical (not spiritual) manner. And even the first eleven chapters of universal creation are included, *inter alia*, in order to establish the legitimacy of God's granting the Land of Israel to the people of Israel (Rashi, comment to Genesis 1:1).

Of course, the Jewish people developed profound ideas, values, and articles of faith, many of which are explored in this volume, but none of them, on their own or all together, determine Jewish status. We do not have a gospel of theological principles that determines who is a

Jew. We do not have a centralized authority that defines and imposes an infallible religious doctrine.

There have been attempts by Jewish thinkers to deduce core principles that all Jews should embrace, as, for example, Maimonides's Thirteen Principles of Faith. But Jews always differed on matters of belief and welcomed argumentation and intellectual and practical diversity. Authority to interpret sacred texts was granted to many, who throughout Jewish history disagreed with each other. And in any case, for us it was always "your people shall be my people," even before "your God shall be my God" (Ruth 1:16).

The Jewish people, not the individual leader, formed a covenant with God. "I bore you on eagles' wings and brought you to Me. . . . You shall be My treasured possession among all the peoples . . . a kingdom of priests and a holy nation" (Exodus 19:4–6). This relationship was voluntarily embraced by the Jewish people: "All the people answered as one saying, 'All that the Eternal has spoken we will do!'" (Exodus 19:8). According to the Sages of the Talmud, the covenant was reaffirmed in the days of Ahasuerus (Babylonian Talmud, *Shabbat* 88b).

Once entered into, the covenant was for all time. It could not be severed. There would be sanctions imposed on the Jewish people for failure to live up to its terms, but God would never utterly destroy the Jewish people. "I will not wholly wipe out the House of Jacob" (Amos 9:8). "You will search for Me and find Me, if only you seek Me wholeheartedly . . . and I will restore your fortunes . . . and I will bring you back to the place from which I have exiled you" (Jeremiah 29:13–14).

The centrality of the people of Israel and its covenant with God was so obvious and so enshrined in Jewish thought that it was never seriously questioned by any group of Jews from early Christianity until modern times. Indeed, it was the evolving understanding of early Christian thinkers that all nations dissolve into one universal family and that salvation is available to the individual, qua individual, that contributed to Christianity's separation from Judaism.

If Jewish peoplehood constitutes the heart of Judaism, and the covenant of the Jewish people with God its primary mode of religious expression, then it is possible to understand the radical nature of nine-teenth-century Reform Judaism: "We consider ourselves no longer a nation but a religious community," stated the Pittsburgh Platform (1885). This was the essence of what later generations termed "classical" Reform Judaism: a rejection of Jewish particularism. In the history of Judaism, no previous group of rabbis ever proclaimed the death of Jewish nationhood. It was a revolution in Jewish thought.

The revolution lasted less than a century. Reform Jews, themselves, rejected it. As Rabbi Abba Hillel Silver pointed out, Judaism absent the centrality of peoplehood is not Judaism: it is something else, more resembling Pauline Christianity.[1]

Eventually, even most Reform Jews did not buy the argument that particularism was a less-advanced vestige of our pre-Enlightenment past and that universal brotherhood and bliss were within our grasp. They simply looked at the world and saw the evidence themselves. As the twentieth century advanced, the classical Reformers' optimism in the coming of a universal era of peace and unity seemed not only un-realistic, but increasingly delusional.

By the middle of the twentieth century, the Reform Movement even came to embrace Zionism. The early Reformers had bitterly opposed Zionism because it is premised on the very principle that the Pittsburgh Platform rejected—Jewish nationhood. But by the end of World War II, the restoration of Jewish sovereignty in the Jewish people's ancient homeland seemed a much more realistic solution to the Jewish prob-lem than the "approach of the . . . kingdom of truth, justice and peace among men" (Pittsburgh Platform).

There was always a healthy tension in Jewish thought between the centrality of the Jewish people and Jewish interactions with, and obliga-tions to, the world at large. Judaism was both particular and universal. But by rejecting the Jewish particular, the Reform Movement ripped Judaism's universal aspirations from their particularistic moorings, and what was left was not Jewish universalism, but simply universalism. For this reason, even the emphasis on prophetic values in the Reform Movement was, and remains, misleading.

The Hebrew prophets were, of course, deeply concerned about what we may term "universal" values. They preached peace, justice, righteousness, mercy, law, and compassion. Their insistence on personal and collective morality changed the world. But at no time did they abandon the Jewish particular in favor of the universal. To the contrary: the universal was a function—a product—of the particular. Universal aspirations emerged from, and were a result of, Jewish particularism. The impetus and urgency of prophetic morality were an outcome of the centrality of the Jewish people, not its negation.

Thus, the very Amos who thundered, "Let justice roll down as water and righteousness as a mighty stream" (Amos 5:24) was the same prophet who insisted, "I will restore My people Israel. They shall rebuild ruined cities and inhabit them; they shall plant their vineyards and drink their wine; they shall till gardens and eat their fruits. And I will plant them upon their soil, nevermore to be uprooted from the soil I have given them" (Amos 9:14–15).

The very Isaiah who insisted, "The poor and the needy seek water, and there is none; their tongue is parched with thirst. . . . I will not forsake them" (Isaiah 41:17) was the same prophet who insisted, "But you, Israel, My servant Jacob, whom I have chosen, Seed of Abraham My friend . . . I chose you, I have not rejected you—fear not, for I am with you" (Isaiah 41:8–9). "I have grasped you by the hand, I created you, and appointed you a covenant people, a light of nations, opening eyes deprived of light" (Isaiah 42:6).

The very Micah who declared, "What does the Eternal desire? Only this: to do justice, love mercy, and walk humbly with your God" (Micah 6:8) was the same prophet who declared, "God will take us back in love" (Micah 7:19).

The very Zechariah who preached, "Execute true justice; deal loyally and compassionately with one another. Do not defraud the widow, the orphan, the stranger, and the poor, and do not plot evil against one another" (Zechariah 7:9–10) was the same prophet who preached, "I have returned to Zion, and I will dwell in Jerusalem" (Zechariah 8:3).

The very Malachi who said, "Have we not all one Father? Did not one God create us?" (Malachi 2:10) was the same prophet who said, "They shall be My treasured possession" (Malachi 3:17).

The propensity of nineteenth-century Reform thinkers to emphasize prophetic values over all else and to interpret the prophets as Kantian universalists who cared little for the Jewish particular remains in the Reform Movement. It has grown stronger in the past generation.

Many Reform Jews still consider Micah's vision of "they shall beat their swords into plowshares and their spears into pruning hooks; nation shall not live up sword against nation and they shall never again know war" (Micah 4:3) to be more compelling, more "Jewish," and more enlightened than Micah's final words, "You will keep faith with Jacob, loyalty to Abraham, as You promised on oath to our fathers in days gone by" (Micah 7:20).

To uphold only the universal and negate the particular is to distort the prophetic message. Hosea was not Hegel. Micah was not Mill. Jeremiah was not John Locke. All of the Hebrew prophets were of the Jewish people, by the Jewish people, and for the Jewish people. All of them spoke of the *b'rit*—the covenant and chosenness of the Jewish people. It is the source of their universal power.

The concept of chosenness—the idea that God can have a special relationship with one people—is both intellectually and morally challenging for contemporary liberal Jews. It is often seen as offensive and exclusionary. As Jewish history unfolds in North America, and as the impact of the Holocaust and the creation of the State of Israel recedes; as younger Jews incline against what they consider narrow tribalism and morally troubling actions of the Jewish state, in practice, if not philosophy, there has developed a movement back to universalism—not as a function of, but at the expense of, Jewish peoplehood. It is consistent with the spirit of the times. Contemporary liberalism has launched a compelling critique against religion in general that undermines our confidence.

Individual, communal, and national distinctiveness—separations between people—is among the most basic of human realities. It is why progressives emphasize the value of pluralism. Pluralism assumes that people are different and cherishes these differences. It assumes that freedom and unity can be maintained—and social progress can be advanced—through diversity and that diversity is not a blemish on human progress but, to the contrary, is a social good.

This was the biblical approach. The Bible is a book about a particular people, Abraham and Sarah's descendants. It has universal aspirations, but the way to achieve universal goals is through particular actions. One language, one culture, one mode of thinking is incompatible with the human personality, and as we see in the Tower of Babel narrative, attempts to impose uniformity often lead to destruction.

That a group sees itself as special or unique, by itself, should not be offensive to progressives. Many peoples of the world, including Americans, consider themselves "exceptional." One wonders why, of all the peoples of the earth, it is only the distinctive existence of the Jewish people that troubles some of us. The classical Reformers, too, were patriots and nationalists of every country where they lived. They were German nationalists and American nationalists of the highest order. Jewish nationalism was the only nationalism they opposed.

Nations and groups have different proclivities and talents. The unique vocation of the Jewish people is Torah. We are chosen for, and choose, Torah. The religious term for this is *b'rit*, "covenant." We are bound by sacred agreement to God, all living Jews, and all past and future Jewish generations.

Why should this be offensive to anyone? Why do some of the very people who uphold the value of diversity as a social good find the distinctiveness of the Jewish people intellectually challenging? The midrash points out that all the other nations of the world were offered Torah and rejected it (*Sifrei* on Deuteronomy 33:2). That offer, extended during the days of the Exodus, always was and still remains open to any individual who wants to join the Jewish people. Moreover, the special relationship with the Jewish people was never considered to be an exclusive relationship. From the beginning, Judaism emphasized that God has a general covenant with humanity

(Genesis 9). The "God of Israel" (Jeremiah 30:2) is the "God of all flesh" (32:27).

The covenant with the Jewish people does not replace the covenant with humanity. To the contrary, the specific covenant with the Jewish people enhances the human covenant. Its purpose is not self-aggrandizement, elitism, superiority, or special privilege. The Bible tells us over and over again that we were the lowest of nations; we were slaves. The purpose of the *b'rit* is explained in Genesis 18:19: "I have selected [Abraham], so that he may teach his children and those who come after him to keep the way of the Eternal, doing what is right and just." Why would liberals, most especially, reject these values? Liberalism is all about doing what is just and right and upholding the dignity of human difference. If others also see themselves as exceptional; if they, too, define a distinctive relationship with God, by and large, Judaism regards these as positive examples of yearning to understand and execute God's will: "The righteous of all nations have a share in the world-to-come" is a central Jewish value (see Babylonian Talmud, *Sanhedrin* 105a).

To be Jewish is not to separate from society; the opposite, it is to be part of society—to influence society: "Whoever can influence the people of his city to stop sinning, but does not, is punished for the sins of the people of his city. If he can stop the whole world from sinning and does not, he is punished for the sins of the world" (Babylonian Talmud, *Shabbat* 54b).

But we believe that the path to universalism lies through the collective efforts of peoples and nations. The collectivity is the key force of history, not the individual. The collectivity, more than the individual, will determine the destiny of the human race. Nations, not individuals, are the most powerful force of universal redemption. Nations develop special talents that contribute to human progress and social repair. The special talent, and gift, of the Jewish nation is Torah. The Jewish people has contributed disproportionately to the welfare of the world. The world is a better place because of the Jewish people.

The Reform Movement possesses many of the strengths of contemporary liberalism: openness to change; willingness to innovate; an emphasis on reason, science, and evidence; a general optimism about human progress; a belief in the universality of the human condition; a yearning for peace; and confidence in and a desire for the resolution of disputes short of coercion and war.

But we also possess many of the weaknesses of contemporary liberalism, including an over-reliance on the capacities of science, technology, and reason to resolve human problems. It is easier for us to recognize goodness in the human heart than to acknowledge the implacable evil lurking there. We tend to under-appreciate what matters most to most people: religion, God, personal and national interests, patriotism, group pride, custom, and tradition.

The growing inclination in the Reform Movement to de-emphasize Jewish particularism is the gravest threat to the future of Reform Judaism in North America. For what are the prospects of the continuity of the people if the people is not committed to its own distinctive continuity and does not even agree philosophically that it is a legitimate objective and a social good? Is it possible to sustain the Jewish people without being committed to the Jewish people? Can Judaism exist without Jews?

It is the will to Jewish distinctiveness that ensures Jewish distinctiveness. It is the will to continue that has led to continuity. There is a ferocity to Jewish survival instincts, an indomitable sense of Jewish destiny. When these are lost, the future is lost. In the modern world, where assimilatory pressures are as strong as they have ever been, those who are not committed to Jewish survival will not survive as Jews.

NOTE

1. *CCAR Yearbook*, 1935, 312–42.

10

REFINING THE COVENANT

RABBI RACHEL SABATH BEIT-HALACHMI, PhD

At the core of all human existence are universal questions. How should we live? What will sustain us? What will be the source of our values? What rituals will we practice? And in the case of the Jewish people, we have long asked: What does it mean to be a Jew? To live in relationship to God? All of these questions and more confront us anew as human beings and as Jews in each new phase of history. The central feature of Jewish thought and life since Abraham first responded to God's call is the idea of covenant. A covenant—in religious terms—is a sacred agreement, a contract between two parties committed to agreed-upon outcomes. In the case of the Jewish people and God, the covenant has meant a commitment to a binding relationship: we will be God's people, and *Adonai* will be our God.

Living out the covenant, however, is a much more complicated matter. Over time and space there have been many different interpretations of what it means to fulfill the covenant between God and the Jewish people. Different texts and different periods of Jewish life have emphasized different aspects of the covenant. At times it is clear what behaviors and rituals must be upheld in order to sustain the covenant, and at other times, given utter failures on both sides, it appears that the covenant is eternal and unconditional. Must we uphold all of God's

commandments in order to sustain the covenant, or if we fail to do so—
or even sin—will the covenant be broken? And if the sacred covenant
between God and the Jewish people is broken by either party, can it
ever be restored? Renewed? How?

This chapter will trace the development and transformation of the
idea of covenant and the development of covenant theology. We will
trace the idea from the biblical period to early modern and postmodern Jewish thought. Ultimately we will ask: How has Reform Judaism
understood the idea of covenant? And: How might it be understood in
our time? Indeed, since its emergence, Reform Judaism has sought to
transform core beliefs and practices in ways that would ensure their relevance in the modern world while often redefining what they meant for
the individual. If the single most significant idea in Judaism is the idea
of the covenant between the Jewish people and God, Reform thinkers
sought to redefine it so that it would have meaning beyond its original
context and become no less significant in our Jewish lives and the lives
of our descendants.

Throughout Jewish history—regardless of varying cultural and political contexts, textual interpretations, ideologies, or ritual practices—
the foundation of what it means to be a Jew is to uphold the covenant.
For some this has meant being part of a civiliaztion and a people, while
for many it has also meant fulfilling a religious covenant with God. Similarly, there is also a covenant between and among the Jewish people, and
certain absolute obligations that Jews have toward each other. Modern and postmodern thinkers, like Eugene B. Borowitz (1924–2016),
even argue that there is a multifaceted covenant: the covenant between
God and the Jewish person, the covenant with the Jewish people, past,
present, and future, as well as a covenant with one's self. As Borowitz
explains, it is only as an "autonomous Jewish self" that a modern or
postmodern Jew can stand before God and with community.[1]

More than we are the "people of the book"—or any interpretation
thereof—we are the people of the covenant. The covenant was initially a sacred commitment declared by God to Abraham in the Book
of Genesis (12:1–3; 17:1–9). While it was initially established between

God and Abram, it was immediately extended to his family and to his descendants for eternity. The early biblical form of the covenant took on many characteristics of an ancient contract. Each party was bound to the other in ways that could and should be behaviorally demonstrated. And—as in such contracts—there were consequences for the failure to fulfill one's part of such a covenant. For the ancient Israelites, such consequences ranged from suffering life-threatening droughts to destruction to expulsion from the Promised Land.

While the Book of Genesis chronicles a covenant passed down from father to son for several generations of faithful descendants of Abraham (renamed so in Genesis 17:5), the covenant is not fully actualized for the people of Israel until the Exodus from Egypt. It gains form and extensive content with the revelation at Sinai (Exodus 14–21). In Jewish life and practice, *the covenant* generally refers to that which flows from the revelation at Sinai. The giving and receiving of the Torah at Sinai expands possibilities for the fulfillment of its content, which forms the basis for Israel's fulfillment of the covenant. "Then he took the record of the covenant and read it aloud to the people. And they said, 'All that the Eternal has spoken we will faithfully do!'" (Exodus 24:7). The terms of the covenant between God and the people of Israel are given form and specific content through the giving of Torah. A wide range of biblical texts depict and clarify the significance of the covenant, including Genesis 15:18, 17:4; Exodus 19:20; and Deuteronomy 4:13, 28:69.

Scholars have noted that, while the covenant is in most instances an unconditional covenant, other texts emphasize the conditional nature of the commitment. The covenant between God and Israel can indeed be broken, which could lead to drastic consequences. But later biblical books such as those of prophets like Isaiah and Hosea, which decry the shattering of the covenant, also call for a repair of it, a return of the people to God and to God's demands and love (Hosea 3:5, 6:5–7, 14:2–7). The establishment of the covenant with the people of Israel not only bestows upon Israel a unique relationship with God and among Jews, but it also sets forth a unique role with regard to other nations of the world. Being chosen to be God's precious and unique people, to bear witness to God's miracles and to uphold God's Torah, was an election that brought with it a hyper-particularism. Scholars have argued about the particular and universal significance of the "election of Israel" for hundreds of years. Were only the people of Israel elected to be God's chosen people? Or do the people of Israel have a chosen role to play, in their particular covenantal relationship with God? Some Jewish thinkers have entirely repudiated the idea of the Jews as the chosen people fulfilling a unique covenant with God.

Many liberal Jewish thinkers continue to debate the idea of chosennesss and the complications with regard to Israel's unique mission. While some contemporary thinkers seeking to emphasize Judaism's universalism may reject the notion that the Jewish people are superior to all others by virtue of being chosen according to biblical texts, the idea of a unique covenant remains. Reform thinkers have rejected and challenged other core ideas of Judaism, but no major thinkers ever rejected the notion that the Jewish people are chosen in the sense of Israel's distinctive covenantal relationship with God. The Jewish people play a unique and necessary role in the world. In short, writes the contemporary scholar David Novak, "Israel enlightens the nations when God and Israel demonstrate their faithfulness to each other."[2]

The covenant evolved and was characterized by a mutual commitment. God would protect Abraham and his descendants, and they in turn would maintain their faith in God and observe God's commandments. From a biblical perspective, being "chosen" by God to be God's treasured people (see, in particular, Deuteronomy 7:6–8) also meant being obligated to perform specific commandments. Fulfilling those commandments, like prayer and charity and service to God, results in receiving rewards such as rain for the crops in the right seasons, food from the harvest, and protection from one's enemies. The biblical texts are strikingly clear about the reward and punishment for heeding or failing to heed God's instructions. Exodus 19:5 most succinctly determines the relationship formed anew at the revelation at Sinai: "Now then, if you will obey Me faithfully and keep My covenant, you shall be My treasured possession among all the peoples. Indeed, all the earth is Mine, but you shall be to Me a kingdom of priests and a holy nation" (Exodus 19:5–6).

Several Rabbinic passages in the Talmud question the biblical idea of the establishment of the covenant with the Israelite former slaves, who didn't have the opportunity to first understand its laws and implications before committing to observing them. Did they truly enter into the covenant voluntarily? Were they freely able to choose to be part of it? Is a covenant established under duress valid? If established by coercion, then what is the status of its authority? One famous Talmudic text interprets in a radical way a verse about the Israelites gathering at Sinai to receive the Torah. For the verse in Exodus "And they took their places *at the foot* of the mountain" (Exodus 19:17), the Talmud offers the following remarkable set of possibilities:

> Said Rabbi Avdimi bar Chama bar Chasa: This teaches that God held the mountain over their heads and said, "If you accept My Torah, all will be well. But if not, here will be your graves!" Said Rabbi Acha bar Yaakov: Thus we learn an important thing about the Torah. Said Rava: Nevertheless [it is binding] for they accepted it again in the days of Ahasuerus, as it is written, *"The Jews upheld that which had been accepted"* (Esther 9:27); they agreed to uphold that which they had already accepted. (Babylonian Talmud, *Shabbat* 88a)

While the Sages of the Talmud knew well the problems of identifying the possibility that the covenant was established without free will, they were also quick to establish that later generations—in the Book of Esther—did in fact reconfirm the covenant and dedicate themselves to upholding what they had accepted originally at Sinai. In many ways this is a radical text for the ancient Sages, and yet it also serves to answer many theological questions about the possibilities of the establishment of the covenant resolving that regardless of what had happened then at Sinai, now here for us, we know that it is accepted and it is to be upheld finally and freely.

Appreciating the Rabbis' diverse views, and emboldened by modernity's spirit of human independence and autonomy, early modern thinkers asked: What kind of covenantal relationship does God now demand of us? Early modern Jewish thinkers like the Enlightenment philosopher Moses Mendelssohn (1729–86) knew that for Judaism to engage with modern ideas, it would have to embrace the idea of free will already inherent in it. Mendelssohn also knew that Jews must understand their religious obligation to serve the modern state as *citizens*. True religion, argued Mendelssohn, persuades adherents that the worship of God is good in and of itself, because God's power and God's beneficence attract our free assent.[3] This notion of the ethical truth inherent in Judaism merged with rationalist philosophy to form the basis of modern Jewish thought. Mendelssohn and early modern philosopher Immanuel Kant had a deep, lasting impact on how emerging liberal Judaism would understand religion, obligation, and ethics, in that universalism became a core feature of liberal Judaism.

How has Reform thinking about covenant changed over time? It might be helpful to think of the theological development of the idea of covenant in Reform thought in three distinct phases, or eras. The initial phase is what Hermann Cohen (1843–1918) called "ethical monotheism," followed by a modern "social action/justice phase," and finally, what Eugene B. Borowitz called a postmodern spiritual phase. In each of these eras Reform thinkers emphasized different approaches to the sacred, or ways of being pious or religious as Reform Jews. One of the most important elements of Reform Judaism is its understanding of the relationship between God and the Jewish people: What authority does God have, and what authority do the community and the individual have? Reform Jewish thought has always seen itself as a natural development originating out of the revelation at Sinai. As the Bible itself and certainly later Rabbinic literature make clear, how the human role in revelation is understood determines how a particular community understands its relationship to God. In Reform Judaism, as in the premodern forms of Judaism that preceded it, the community also plays a significant role in how individuals understand their obligations as Jews. These phases are accompanied by three major periods of Reform Jewish thought, each of which is reflected in the core teachings, liturgy, and documents of the Reform Movement.

Early Reform thinkers, who characterize the first era of Reform theology, embraced core ideas originating in the Bible and Rabbinic literature about human involvement in revelation and interpretation. They also embraced Enlightenment-influenced ideas about God, such as the divine demand for ethics and equality, and emphasized the role of the human being in determining best practices to bring people closer to God. They held, however, that the interpretive process must always be based clearly on what God demands of us.

Breaking from traditionalist notions of commandment and observance as a fulfillment of the covenant, and influenced by Kant and his peers, early Reform thinkers' radical new understanding of God and commandment contended that, ultimately, the individual's moral conscience must determine what is true about God and what constitutes an appropriate response to religious demands. They laid the groundwork for a liberal religious denomination in which autonomy—the authority of the individual to decide his or her own religious practice—would become an essential feature. Judaism was regarded as the source of ethics, not as a religion in conflict with ethics.

Leading Reform thinker Abraham Geiger (1810–74) pointed out the ways in which Judaism embodied notions of equality, ethics, human progress, and the universal value of perfecting human society. For Geiger, Judaism's nationalistic and particularistic aspects were developmental states in its progress toward universalism. The covenant no longer required Hebrew language as a form of prayer, or a rebuilt ancient Temple for sacrifice, much less hope for Jews' collective return to a particular land, Zion. Instead, the fulfillment of the covenant is the mission of integrating Jewish ethics among all humankind. Geiger also believed in the idea of the Chosen People, in that Jews had been especially "gifted with the powerful religious sense" that resulted in the emergence of the universal idea of ethical monotheism.

If Judaism shared the core values of modernity and its values could in fact serve modernity itself, then the broader society could and should fully embrace Judaism and the Jewish people. Thus the covenant was no longer a covenant that could only be lived out in Jewish community totally apart from any particular polity or apart from the nations of the world, but rather it could be extended to a life committed to the nation-states in which the Jews lived. This direct linkage between the particulars of Jewish commitment with universal values of the early modern era constituted the first era of Reform piety.

Neo-Kantian philosopher Hermann Cohen similarly embraced modern ideas of universalism and focused on the core universal ethics within ancient Jewish texts. Cohen developed ideas such as "the ethical and monotheistic core of Judaism" and interpreted the idea of obligation anew. For the early Reform thinkers, Judaism's foundational commitment toward perfecting society through the application of the universal and particular ethical ideas of Judaism met the urgent need for a Judaism that could flourish in the modern world. If fulfilling one's Jewish commitment meant—among other things—fulfilling one's commitment as a citizen and as a person of ethics, then Judaism and modernity could be mutually reinforcing. Hence Cohen called Judaism's core teaching "ethical monotheism," a term that characterized Reform Judaism well into the next phase of its theology.

Reform Jewish thinkers of the early twentieth century deepened and expanded on many of these ideas. Leo Baeck (1873–1956) expanded on Hermann Cohen's work and emphasized God as the source of the moral law that was developed by rationally autonomous human nature.[4] With ethics at its core, this second stage of Reform theology focused on the living out of those ethical ideas in the world, both among Jews and non-Jews. Universal in its breadth, much of the next phase was focused on Judaism's ethical message and the focus on practices and social campaigns that allowed the individual to engage in social action or social justice, thus perfecting the world through *tikkun olam*.

A third phase also confirmed the primacy of the ethical core—often falsely understood only in universalist terms—as essential but also encouraged individuals and communities to reflect on God's role and the extent to which an Absolute God demanded a certain kind of relationship. Grounding ethics in God was at the foundation of the theology of Eugene B. Borowitz. His new theology was called "covenant theology," a term he coined in the early 1960s, which characterizes the theology of this third phase.

As explained here, covenant was an idea that already existed among ancient and modern Jewish thinkers, but in this new late-modern/early-postmodern era covenant theology gained significantly new and different interpretations. One should note that the idea of covenant theology was developed in different ways by several Jewish thinkers in the postwar period across the Orthodox-liberal spectrum, including but not limited to Eugene B. Borowitz. Modern Orthodox thinkers such as Yitz (Irving) Greenberg and David Hartman (*z"l*) also dedicated much of their work to developing a covenant theology. For Hartman it meant developing a Modern Orthodox theology of a "living covenant," and for Greenberg it meant developing a radical post-Holocaust notion of a "voluntary covenant."

Borowitz defined covenant theology initially in 1961, teaching about its development until his death in 2016. He argued that in contrast to a focus on halachah or on universal ethics, covenant theology is the only theological foundation that can continue to serve as the centerpiece of Jewish life and thought in a postmodern age. Only covenant theology can allow for the complex roles of authority and autonomy in modern Jewish theology and practice. Over the course of more than fifty years of writing on God, tradition, authority, ethics, individualism, and society in modern and postmodern Jewish theology and practice, Borowitz continued to develop his thinking on the postmodern Jewish self, the individual autonomous self, whose Jewishness causes him or her to have limited autonomy while living in covenant with God and with the Jewish people, past, present, and future. He titled his summary theology *Renewing the Covenant: A Theology for the Postmodern Jew* (1991). A cumulative and apologetic theological statement, the work presents ideas, such as the "autonomous Jewish self," that he published in the two prior decades. Borowitz described his book as an attempt "to speak intellectually of Judaism as 'Covenant,' not as law, ethics, ethnicity, or nationality."[5] He insisted on a capital "C" to distinguish the special relationship between God and the Jewish people from the covenant God had established with all of humanity.

Through the force of his teaching, writing, and personality, Borowitz compelled Reform Jews to take seriously the conception of a religious covenant, and he taught about the "false messiah" of modernity and its false promises in which the worship of humanity served as substitute deities for the traditional God of Israel. Borowitz wrote, "People who had lost the only god whom they had truly worshiped, the god of human competence, now began an intense, widespread search for a more worthy faith. Nothing in our secularized culture directly prepared us for the passion, depth, diversity, and endurance of the religious quest of the late twentieth century."[6]

In the 1961 article "Crisis Theology and the Jewish Community," Borowitz describes both the ancient meaning of the term as well as his new application of the idea and the kind of relationship with God it entails in a new context. "This system," he wrote, "might be called 'Covenant Theology,' for it rests upon a reaffirmation, in contemporary terms, of the Covenant of Sinai and its renewal."[7] Borowitz, along with several contemporaries who would also become major Jewish thinkers and leaders—including Arnold Jacob Wolf, Steven Schwarzchild, Emil Fackenheim, Yitz Greenberg, and David Hartman—rightly perceived a radically altered world and the urgent need for new Jewish theology. Each knew and attempted to respond to a post-Holocaust reality—a world that saw the rebirth of the nation-state of the Jewish people and the successful integration of Jews into every aspect of American and other Western societies and a world that would be forced to deal with unprecedented human power to destroy and to save. What would be the foundation for meaning and ethics if one could no longer naively count on the notions of the Enlightenment and modernity to lead us toward a more redeemed world?

From 1960 to 2015 Borowitz taught several generations of rabbis and other Jewish leaders a covenant theology that understands Judaism "as a way of living one's life based on a relationship with God, a relationship in which the whole self is involved." Covenant theology appreciated the core modern commitment to autonomy of non-Orthodox Jews but also understood that no fully Jewish self is simply an individual self but rather lives in covenant with other Jews. A Jew's faith is "not simply the private faith of an individual. The Jew is the [person] who shares the common faith in the mutual promise existing between God and Israel—that is, the Jewish people as a whole."[8]

Borowitz's term "covenant theology" seemed to many of his colleagues and generations of students particularly fitting for a new way of trying to understand Jewish faith in the second half of the twentieth century, an age in which American Jews were both increasingly extraordinarily at home in America and also struggling to determine the meaning of their uniqueness and what kind of religious activity it might engender. Borowitz, along with several liberal Jewish thinkers in the 1950s, affirmed the intrinsic truth of Jewish particularity. They knew "it had to do with our peopled response to God's 'commanding,' which prompted us to more fully Judaize the non-Orthodox theology of Jewish duty. Though the term was not yet in common use, 'covenant' seemed to me to point to our commitment to an actional piety of mitzvah."[9] The kind of piety that characterizes this third phase of Reform thinking on covenant embraces a large degree of autonomy and yet retains and even renews a significant degree of being commanded, of being in covenant with that which limits one's autonomy. As Borowitz pertinently encapsulates it: *The result is a dialectical autonomy, a life of freedom-exercised-in-Covenant.*"[10]

At the core of Borowitz's more developed covenant theology is the idea of a threefold covenant: a Jewish self lives in covenant with God, with the Jewish people (past, present, and future), and with one's self, because of the absolute aspect of autonomy for the modern/postmodern Jew. First and foremost, Borowitz emphasizes that "the Jewish self lives personally and primarily in involvement with the one God of the universe." Borowitz knew that the realities of postmodernity ought to teach us "a more realistic view of our human capacities and a determination not to confuse the junior with the senior partner." Secondly, the Jewish self lives in a relationship with God that inextricably binds selfhood and ethnicity, with its multiple ties of land, language, history, traditions, fate, and faith. "For the Jewish self," Borowitz wrote, "Covenant means Covenant-with-all-other-Jews past, present and future." Thus it always requires conscientious "self-examination" in the light of community standards and in relation to God.

What made Borowitz both radical and traditional at the same time was his conclusion that while the Jewish self lives in covenant—with God and the Jewish people, present, past, and future—"it is as a single soul in its full individuality that the Jewish self exists in Covenant." For the Jewish self, "Covenant means Covenant-with-one's-self." The self, the other, and God are all inextricably bound up in what postmodern Jewish covenant theology must be. While Borowitz gave contemporary Reform Judaism the thinking and the language to live out this third phase of Reform Jewish piety, he was decidedly and intentionally less clear about the specifics of the Jewish practice such theology should embody. He was more interested in the seriousness of the thinking and believing and praying and doing of the theology and believed that if all these were based on significant learning, the practice resulting would be worthy of being a member of the people of the covenant. He concludes toward the end of *Renewing the Covenant*, "If Jews could confront their Judaism as Jewish selves and not as autonomous persons-in-general, I contend that they would find Jewish law and lore the single best source of guidance as to how they ought to live. Rooted in Israel's corporate faithfulness to God, they would want their lives substantially structured by their people's understanding of how our past, present, and future should shape their daily existence."[11]

Ultimately the idea of covenant in Reform Jewish thought has come full circle. To live as a Jew means to live in relationship with God. While ideas of God and notions of the individuality of the self may shift in different periods of Jewish life and thought, the idea of the covenant remains remarkably stable. Covenant in Reform life and practice is the relationship or relationships that have such a compelling voice in our lives that it is as though the voice is commanding. What God asked of our ancestors God still asks of us today: to live a life in which the highest ethical values guide our daily lives and shape who we are and who we strive to become as Jews, as individual human beings, as a Jewish community, and as a civilization.

NOTES

1. Eugene B. Borowitz, *Renewing the Covenant: A Theology for the Postmodern Jew* (Philadelphia: Jewish Publication Society, 1991), 280ff.

2. David Novak, *The Jewish Social Contract: An Essay in Political Theology* (Princeton, NJ: Princeton University Press, 2005), 51.

3. Moses Mendelssohn, *Jerusalem*, trans. A. Arkush (Hanover, NH: University Press of New England, 1983), 43 (German), 118–19.

4. Leo Baeck, *The Essence of Judaism* (London: Macmillan, 1936), 59–72.

5. Borowitz, *Renewing the Covenant*, ix.

6. Borowitz, *Renewing the Covenant*, 24.

7. Eugene B. Borowitz, "Crisis Theology and the Jewish Community," *Commentary*, July 1, 1961, https://www.commentarymagazine.com/articles/crisis-theology-the-jewish-community/.

8. Borowitz, "Crisis Theology and the Jewish Community," 39–40.

9. Borowitz, *Renewing the Covenant*, 207.

10. Borowitz, *Renewing the Covenant*, 288.

11. Borowitz, *Renewing the Covenant*, 288–89.

11

IS REFORM JUDAISM AUTHENTIC JUDAISM?

RABBI KARI HOFMAISTER TULING, PhD

Some years ago, while I was standing at the library circulation desk at the Hebrew Union College–Jewish Institute of Religion, I had a conversation with a young Orthodox man. He told me that he believed that the Reform Movement should bow to the sensitivities of the Orthodox and accept their demand that only males be involved in leading the Jewish Community Center (JCC) prayer vigil for Israel. He was particularly upset by a suggestion that a female cantor sing at the vigil.

"A large number of this area's rabbis are female," I countered, "including the rabbi of the congregation housed in the new JCC site. Why shouldn't ordained rabbis and invested cantors participate?"

"But they're not *really* rabbis," he insisted. I gave him a raised eyebrow, the one that asked, "You didn't really just say that, did you?" After all, he and I have talked before; he knew that I am a rabbi. He hesitated for a moment but then continued undaunted. "I mean, I know that Reform ordains women and that's fine for Reform, but even so everyone agrees that Orthodoxy is *authentic* Judaism."

The young man's assumption was that a single continuous chain of Jewish practice extends from Moses on Mount Sinai to the present day, having been articulated over time through the medium of Jewish law. Further, he assumed that contemporary Orthodoxy is the truest, most authentic expression of this chain of tradition. To his way of thinking, Reform stepped away from authenticity when it began to negotiate with the ways of modernity.

From this individual's perspective, authenticity rests upon being true to the essence of Judaism, which exists without any interference from the outside world. To listen to the rest of the world, to heed what "they" say, is to fall away from authenticity. It is a line of thought that Reform Jews also unconsciously believe; we assume that Orthodox practice is the most authentic form of Jewish observance. Thus, as we become more knowledgeable or more pious, we tend to adopt outward forms of Jewish practice that particularly mark Orthodoxy: wearing a tallit and yarmulke, adding to our prayers references to the revival of the dead, substituting *HaShem* or "G-d" for the name of God when we write.

The implicit assumption we make is that what is absolutely particular to Judaism must be Judaism's most authentic expression of Judaism, whereas what is universal must necessarily be some kind of compromise or attempt at assimilation. The problem with authenticity, though, is that no such thing as a singular, exclusively authentic form of Judaism exists.

The concept of authenticity as it is used in this context has its roots in Martin Heidegger's thought, particularly the idea that authenticity requires rejection of the outside world. In *Being and Time*, for example, Heidegger argues that engaging in multiculturalism is an inauthentic mode of being, since multiculturalism pulls us away from our direct experience of being-in-the-world into the realm of accepting what others say about the matter.

So why should that concern us? Well, for one thing, Heidegger was a member of the Nazi Party, and his thought on authenticity has certain affinities with the *volkisch* ideas current in Germany at the turn of the last century, reaching as far back as the anti-Jewish "Hep! Hep!" riots and Hitler's rise to power.

Specifically, I refer here to the idea that each kind of folk should strive for its most authentic mode of being, to the exclusion of all foreign elements. As we are painfully aware, the German folk took that line of thought to its most deadly logical conclusion, excluding Jews from all aspects of German society, purifying the folk of foreign elements to the point of committing genocide.

Of course, the search for authenticity does not necessarily lead to fascism and Nazism. But there does seem to be something amiss in the premises of such a search. It has the power to perpetuate the exclusion of those who are different.

We need to reject this notion of authenticity. This concept of authenticity presupposes a whole host of seriously objectionable assumptions. That is to say, our adaptability as Jews is actually a strength. Look at Jewish cooking, for example: every kind of cuisine has been adapted to the laws of kashrut (the Jewish dietary laws) and to the food preferences of Jews worldwide. There is Polish-derived babka and Moroccan-derived carrot salad, both of which are fully, authentically Jewish. How could it be possible to claim that one is more authentic than the other?

To return to the complaint of my Orthodox friend at the college library about the proposed vigil, I explained to him that Reform and Conservative congregations in my town find the exclusion of women from a prayer service just as offensive as the Orthodox find it to include them. If the two could not find common ground, then, I suggested, we should conduct a relevant event, but not a prayer service, such as a joint program in the neutral meeting rooms of the JCC, which is in fact what happened.

What I hoped to convey to the young man as I explained myself was that we Reform Jews are just as committed to our principles as the Orthodox are to theirs. We have in fact the same claim to authenticity. We are both the continuation of the same tradition, and it would be a violation of our integrity as Reform Jews to give in to pressure on this issue.

How did it come to pass that Orthodox and Reform are so different? The image I have used to answer this when teaching introductory undergraduate courses on Judaism is that of a prism. Prior to the

Enlightenment, the various strands of Judaism were all joined together, like white light, for there were few options for stratification or variation within Jewish society. With the Enlightenment, however, came choice: participation in the community was no longer enforced from outside but rather chosen from within. So the community stratified into all of the colors of the rainbow.

If we asked which color most *authentically* expresses the original white light, the answer would be *all of them.* What's more, to suppress any of the colors would be to destroy the original content of the white light. On this basis, therefore, I contend that there is no such thing as a singular authentic Judaism; instead, the fullest expression of post-Enlightenment Judaism is its plurality of forms. No one color by itself conveys the fullness of Jewish experience.

Nonetheless, as Reform Jews, we are still stuck with a very basic question: how do we construct our theological positions in a liberal context? If we cannot make an appeal to this notion of authenticity wrapped in the trappings of traditional practice, how then do we make decisions about our Jewish lives? Looking to the traditional sources poses difficulties. The medieval Jewish philosopher Moses Maimonides believed that the Torah was brought to Israel directly from God by the hand of Moses, the greatest of the prophets. From Maimonides's perspective, then, the Torah is indeed perfect (as perfect as it can be, given that it is written in the language of humanity), and that is why it may not be changed. As he wrote in *Guide of the Perplexed* 1:40, "You must know that this divine guidance comes from Him, may He be exalted, and that this Law is divine."

It is fairly common for Orthodox philosophers to think of the tradition in Maimonides's terms. For example, Joseph Soloveitchik held that the halachah—that is, Jewish law—is actually a science. It can be derived logically, much in the way of certain branches of mathematics. In Soloveitchik's mind, there was no negotiating with the absolute that is Torah. It is possible to accept the insights of science and employ the critical thinking of academia, but at the same time, some topics are off-limits. The Torah enjoys a special place, to that way of thinking.

But one difficulty I face with Soloveitchik and Orthodox thinkers like him is the fact that he is untroubled by the gender inequality inherent in traditional Judaism. It views as a feature of the natural world that women are not as important as men, just as Jews are more important than non-Jews. I find this position very troubling.

I am influenced by the philosopher John Rawls, who argues that the role each of us is assigned is somewhat arbitrary, an accident of birth. A genuinely ethical system, therefore, would not disproportionately reward some people for their merely accidental status at birth. My objection to traditional Judaism's gender inequality is also grounded in genuine religious commitment: if we are all created in the image of God, how can it be that some of us are considered to be *more equal* (to borrow George Orwell's phrase) than others?

In contrast, Abraham Joshua Heschel wrote a series of moving books about what genuine faith should look like. In the wake of translating his doctoral work on the prophetic literature, he came to realize that the prophets emphasized how all people are equal in the eyes of God. This awareness persuaded him to march in Selma with Martin Luther King, Jr.; it led him to engage in interfaith dialogue with the Catholic Church; and it convinced him to protest the Vietnam War. He argued strenuously for the idea that all of humanity is created equal. I find Heschel's work much more compelling than Soloveitchik's, for that reason. He affirms the value of all of humanity, without arguing that some are more worthy than others on account of their birth.

As a Jew and a rabbi, when I am thinking theologically, I read the traditional literature, especially Maimonides. And I read the works of thinkers with whom I do not usually agree, such as Soloveitchik. But I am sure to be most strongly influenced by thinkers like Heschel, for whom the basic humanity of the other person is a consideration more important than considerations of ritual or tradition. He was indeed a most traditional Jew, but Heschel would not let that fact be a barrier to his recognition of needs of the other.

Recent years have seen the Reform Movement extend its understanding of human rights, starting from the ideas that we are all created in the image of God and that we have responsibilities with regard to the stranger in our midst. These new areas of growth and change (for instance, the recognition that respecting human rights encompasses protecting the rights of transgender individuals) sometimes can discomfit those who easily conform to the normative expectations of Jewish participation. Those who have not felt the pain of exclusion might be prompted to ask whether we have not gone beyond what is (authentically) Jewish, in changing so much. I would say no, we have not.

My certainty is rooted in the work of the neo-Kantian philosopher (and German Reform Jew) Hermann Cohen. According to Cohen, what makes the expansion of human rights a Jewish project is the Jewish roots of human rights. The instruction to "love your neighbor as yourself," he argued, is the basis of all ethics. Once you recognize that your neighbor hurts just like you do, that your neighbor is a fully realized human being just like you are, then you are not able to willfully hurt him or her. Cohen argued that our criticism of the tradition, when we criticize from the meta-perspective of human rights, is grounded in the tradition itself. It draws upon such examples as the argument Abraham made for saving ten righteous souls from Sodom and Gomorrah. In other words, it is grounded in the sense that we face an urgent religious imperative.

In a liberal context, then, what might it mean to be commanded? We are not literalists, after all, for the grand imagery of Moses on Mount Sinai is taken as a metaphor. What if the Bible looks to us like the heritage of a people rather than the word of God? Is it possible to build a sense of awe on that basis? Is it possible to feel commanded in a real sense if the rules are not handed down from the mouth of God?

First, the language of autonomy that has dominated the Reform Movement's discussion has been a distraction from our core principles, from the driving force of our religious self-understanding. Yes, to be sure, we allow and should continue to allow for individual choice. It is not the sum total of our religious commitments, however. Somehow we have put the emphasis on the least important part when a more important part is that we are indeed commanded, in the fullest religious sense.

Specifically, we are commanded to respect human dignity in all its forms. And this commandment amounts to something much deeper, grander, and more pervasive than Immanuel Kant's philosophical ethics. Kant teaches, "Treat everyone as an end rather than as a means to an end." But where his ethics falls short—and where Judaism fundamentally parts ways with Kant—is the question of feeding the poor.

In Kant's view, if you have done what is right and attended to all of your moral duties, it is possible to walk without a thought past someone who is hungry. A sense of pity is, in fact, a moral weakness, for it might distract you from the rational calculation of your duties. As long as you yourself have not, by doing something immoral, directly caused that person's poverty, you have met your moral obligations.

We Jews say no. To the contrary, a hungry person is yet a person, and to ignore the hunger is to profane the name of God. A Jew must act. A Jew is commanded to act. The commandment to practice *tzedakah* (meaning "righteousness"), to engage in righteous living, is a pillar of Jewish practice and belief. Across the movements and across the political spectrum we find genuine differences of opinion about the best way to accomplish *tzedakah*, but we agree on the need to act. That commandment is a point of agreement across all streams of Judaism.

Where Reform Judaism parts ways with the other streams is in extending its reach. When the Torah says, "Do not oppress the stranger," Reform Jews take that to mean something more than just providing food. We believe that we are commanded to treat persons with dignity in all other areas of life, which means (among other things) offering an equal opportunity to participate meaningfully in our community. In other words, the Reform Movement's willingness to pay attention to the needs of the stranger is precisely the reason why we are willing to rethink how we approach the issues of gender in Jewish life. We do so because it enables us to fulfill the commandment more fully.

So, then, what does it mean to be commanded in a liberal congregation? It means to recognize that you may not profane the name of

God through sexism or xenophobia, but rather, you must reach beyond yourself to respect and protect the basic human dignity of the stranger, the orphan, and the widow. It means to set a place and invite the stranger, the widow, and the orphan to dine at your table. That is what it means to be commanded; that is what it means to glorify the name of God.

12

JEWISH RELIGIOUS PLURALISM

RABBI JOAN S. FRIEDMAN, PhD

"Pluralism: 1. A condition or system in which two or more states, groups, principles, sources of authority, etc., coexist."[1]

Today there exist multiple ways of being a Jew, each of which claims to be *a* correct or *the* correct way. What is the Reform Jewish perspective on this reality? Do Reform Jews think that Judaism can legitimately be conceptualized and lived in multiple ways? If so, do Reform Jews think that there are limits to the ways Judaism can be legitimately conceptualized and lived? Or do Reform Jews think that there is, in fact, one right way and that pluralism exists only because it is impossible to suppress or eliminate the wrong ways?

It may seem paradoxical that a movement grounded in a universalist approach to religion ("We recognize in every religion an attempt to grasp the infinite, and in every mode, source or book of revelation held sacred in any religious system the consciousness of the indwelling of God in man"[2]) should care about which forms of Judaism are, or are not, correct. But, of course, any group must define itself both by who it is and by who it is not, who belongs and who does not. *Religion* is a human creation. A religious community is a group of people who all implicitly or explicitly share a worldview and a way of life rooted in something—text, story, whatever—that they regard as authoritative. *Pluralism* becomes a religious issue when, for any number of reasons, members of the community develop some variations in the shared understanding. This raises questions: How much variation is legitimate? At what point does a variant differ so greatly from the original that it has become something else? And who determines that?

A historical perspective on Judaism shows us how Jews have dealt with pluralism in the past. All Jewish religious expression rests on one fundamental premise: that God and the people Israel made a formal agreement (a *b'rit*, "covenant") at Mount Sinai, in which God gave them a set of laws by which to live, embodied in the Torah, and promised blessing and protection in return. Jews are *b'nei b'rit*, "members of the covenant," and Jewish life is lived out within a covenantal nexus of God, Torah, and Israel. Everything else is contingent and mutable. Even the very definitions of "God," "Torah," and "Israel" are dynamic, to a degree. Determining what is Judaism and what is not Judaism is not a new endeavor, and it has never been a simple one.

Sometimes mutability is due to historical contingency, those fascinating "what ifs": What if the Romans had not destroyed the Temple in 70 CE? What if, in the eighth century, the caliph in Baghdad had not granted authority over Jewish life in the vast Muslim empire to the rabbis, thus ensuring that the Babylonian Talmud would acquire its authoritative status? What if the Shoah had not taken place? Historical contingency, however, does not reduce the importance of intra-Jewish dynamics—not only spirited polemical and ideological debates, but also trends created out of myriads of individual decisions. What constitutes a "Jewish" worldview in any era is the result of a constant sifting of possibilities—a dynamic interaction, evident only in hindsight, among Jews, their inherited authoritative tradition, and their cultural "now." In any given time and place Jews consciously and unconsciously gravitate toward ideas and concepts that cohere with or build upon their existing worldview. Thus the vast majority of first- and second-century Jews rejected the religious view of the small group that created the theological innovation that eventually became Christianity because it did not cohere with their existing understanding of Jewish life. Conversely, when the *Zohar*, the central text of Kabbalah (Jewish mysticism), was printed in the sixteenth century, Kabbalah spread like wildfire among Jews everywhere because it did cohere, that is, it "made sense" to them as a way to add meaning to their lives.

"Rabbinic Judaism" became the Jewish norm through the complex interaction, over centuries, of historical contingency and Jews gravitating toward what made sense to them and gravitating away from what didn't. The Rabbinic interpretation of the God-Torah-Israel covenantal nexus held that God had revealed at Sinai not only the Written Torah (i.e., the Pentateuch) but also the Oral Torah, the way of interpreting the written commandments and applying them to daily life. At Sinai God had also designated Moses as the first *rabbi*, the original arbiter and interpreter of Torah law; the rabbis of every generation were his authoritative successors in the "chain of tradition" (*Pirkei Avot* 1:1; see also Babylonian Talmud, *Bava M'tzia* 59b). Covenantal life, therefore, was what the Rabbis determined it to be, and for them it meant fulfilling the commandments of the Written Torah as expounded in the Oral Torah. "Oral Torah" eventually became a vast written corpus comprising the Mishnah, the Talmud, the medieval codes of Jewish law, and much more, all of which make up the halachah (literally, "way," but commonly used to mean "law").

In some ways premodern Jewish society was pluralistic. There are distinctive regional liturgical customs, for example. There were controversies among rabbis over the use of philosophy to interpret Torah and controversies over mystical theologies and practices, but ultimately most of these were judged to fall within acceptable ranges of the God-Torah-Israel nexus. The halachic practices of Ashkenazic (Northern and Eastern European) Jews and Sephardic (Spanish and Portuguese) Jews diverged enough that Rabbi Moses Isserles of Cracow had to add copious annotations to the *Shulchan Aruch*, the great digest of law published by Sephardic rabbi Joseph Karo in 1575, to adapt it for use by Polish Jewry. Even Chasidism, the eighteenth-century mystical-pietist movement, and its opponents reached a *modus vivendi* despite the disruptive force of the former.

However, this pluralism had a definite limit: all these Jews accepted the Rabbinic way of interpreting Torah as normative. One Jew might conceive of God as the Aristotelian First Cause and another insist that God was the mystical unknowable Infinite; but as long as they were not violating the halachah (e.g., eating pork, doing business on Shabbat, failing to circumcise a son, marrying and divorcing in ways not in accordance with Jewish law), they remained members in good standing of the covenant community. State recognition of a separate Jewish community reinforced this normative Jewish life. The Jewish, Christian, and Muslim legal systems all recognized "Jew" as a legal category, and Jewish communities enjoyed varying degrees of internal self-government, for which halachah was essential.

Modernization, however, called into question every aspect of traditional Jewish life, including the very nature of the covenantal community; the meanings of God, Torah, and Israel; and their hitherto unbreakable linkage. Enlightenment intellectuals advanced the idea of a state in which religion was irrelevant to citizenship. The state's law governed citizens' behavior, but citizens' consciences were free to believe what they wanted in matters of "faith." Wherever Jews were emancipated, the separate Jewish community came to an end and Judaism was reconceptualized as a "religion" in the model of Protestantism.[3] Reconceptualized Judaism's function was to offer ethical guidance and spiritual uplift—not to regulate either the individual body or the social body.

Many emancipated Jews simply abandoned Judaism, like immigrants to a new country who come to see their native culture as backward and unattractive. Others tried to find some way of maintaining a Jewish life, but again, like immigrants in a completely new environment, much of that life seemed to make no sense or clashed with the values and mores of the new society. Acculturated laypeople who desired a style of worship appropriate to modern sensibilities created new houses of Jewish worship, which they called "temples" to distinguish them from traditional synagogues. These laypeople did not think about the theological implications of their rejection of most of the commandments.

However, when a critical mass of traditionally educated rabbis acquired university educations and realized the extent of the intellectual gap between their beloved tradition and modern knowledge, they created *Reform Judaism*, an intentional reinterpretation of the God-Torah-Israel covenantal nexus.

Jews entered the mainstream of European society precisely at the time and in the places where new ideas about truth were upending centuries of received wisdom. Nineteenth-century Europeans were certain that virtually all elements of human culture evolved over time in a linear progression, from "lower" to "higher," from less advanced to more advanced, from primitive and superstitious to enlightened and rational; and that their own time, place, and civilization constituted the pinnacle of human achievement. Universities studied the natural and the social worlds "scientifically," that is, critically, rather than accepting the truths of the past. Scholars particularly valued the "scientific" study of history, certain that it would reveal truths about the present. Documents were a crucial element of this process, with the result that texts handed down from the past and hitherto revered as divinely revealed were now regarded as human artifacts subject to critical analysis.

Jewish scholars applied this critical approach to the study of Jewish texts, calling it *Wissenschaft des Judentums*, the "science of Judaism." Rabbis like Abraham Geiger (1810–74), the main intellectual progenitor of Reform, were certain that the disconnect between Judaism and rational, progressive modernity was the result of the centuries of oppression. Ghettoization had distorted Judaism's natural evolution, but now the critical study of the history of Judaism would reveal the principles according to which Judaism should be properly reformed in the present.[4]

Other academically trained rabbis shared Geiger's commitment to modern scholarship but not his willingness to see all of Judaism's sacred texts as historical artifacts. The differences among these rabbis—over how much of Judaism was divinely revealed, and over which laws could be changed and how—led to the emergence of three strands of modern Judaism in the nineteenth century: Reform, Positive-Historical (later known as Conservative), and Neo-Orthodoxy (later called Modern Orthodoxy). Though they were very different, they all differed from the "traditionalists" who completely rejected all elements of modern thought.

To Geiger and his fellow Reformers, however, *all* the other approaches were merely varieties of "Orthodoxy"—all equally unwilling to allow Judaism to evolve as it should. Geiger and his reforming colleagues did not think they were creating an alternative form of Judaism that would coexist with Orthodoxy, because they were certain that their studies proved that all forms of Orthodoxy would naturally disappear as modernity progressed. As Isaac Mayer Wise (1819–1900) explained, Orthodoxy was incompatible with "the understanding and consciousness of the nineteenth century" because "the orthodox principle [is] that religion must be in conflict with reason."[5]

Wise was the great organizer and popularizer of Reform in the United States, but the radical Kaufmann Kohler (1843–1926), who drafted the Pittsburgh Platform, was largely responsible for the intellectual core of American Reform Judaism until the 1920s. Kohler insisted that Reform was not a movement within Judaism but rather its inevitable, scientifically verifiable next stage: "Reform is no principle in itself; *progress* is. . . . There is no such thing as an Orthodox or a Reform Jewish science. Science has neither color nor party. Historical study is the study of *progress*."[6] In other words, the founding generations of Reform Judaism believed that their form of Judaism was *the* correct one and that history would bring about the inevitable switch to Reform among all Jews.

This sense of historical certainty had a geographical aspect as well. Western Europeans looked down on the backward, "oriental" peoples to the east and south of them. Even as Western European Jews tried to defend Russian, Romanian, and Ottoman Jewry from persecution, they shared this Western contempt for these "oriental" varieties of Judaism. American triumphalism reinforced this perspective. Just as Americans in general viewed their country as a higher stage of nationhood than the states of old Europe, so American Reform leaders viewed America as the place where Judaism would evolve into its highest form. They were certain that America's environment would lead Eastern Europeans to abandon traditionalism and embrace Reform. As American Reform rabbi Max Landsberg confidently assured his rabbinical colleagues in 1894, "To our Jewish brethren who are not yet redeemed from the influence of medieval persecutions, and believe, that Judaism must necessarily be clothed in oriental garments, we are the pioneers who carve the way which, sooner or later, they will all surely follow; we are their torch-bearers."[7]

Reality, however, did not conform to expectations. Yes, modernity led more and more Jews to doubt that God had commanded them at Mount Sinai not to eat bacon cheeseburgers or lobster salad; but joining a Reform temple was not the inevitable next step. Many Jews found that other ways of being Jewish—Conservative Judaism, or various forms of cultural identity—made more sense to them. And some chose to remain Orthodox. Nevertheless, most twentieth-century Reform Jews shared the conviction that Orthodoxy was incompatible with modernity and would inevitably disappear.[8] In the meantime, however, Reform had never denied that Orthodoxy was a *valid* form of Judaism, so Reform Jews readily cooperated with Orthodox and Conservative rabbis in all sorts of institutional settings.

Orthodoxy, however, has had a lot of difficulty cooperating with Reform, because it never accepted Reform as a valid form of covenantal living. Reform rejects the Orthodox insistence that "Torah" in the God-Torah-Israel nexus must mean that all the laws of the Torah were divinely revealed and still in force and that they must be interpreted only according to the views of Orthodox rabbis down to this very day. From an Orthodox perspective, Reform (and Conservatism, as well) went too far in revising the God-Torah-Israel covenantal nexus.

Historical contingency has influenced how this intra-Jewish conflict of ideas plays out today. Orthodoxy has experienced a resurgence since the Shoah, greatly facilitated by its privileged position in the State of Israel, where the state gives the Orthodox rabbinate control over all Jewish religious affairs. The Israeli rabbinate has used its political power for years to try to stop the spread of Reform Judaism in the Jewish state and in struggling Diaspora communities where Israeli assistance comes with Orthodox strings attached.[9] Only in the United States do the majority of religiously identified Jews declare an identification with Reform or Conservative Judaism.[10] The size and influence of the American Jewish community gives Reform Jews a seat at the transnational Jewish table, but Reform is increasingly compelled to use that seat to fight for recognition as a legitimate form of Judaism, as evidenced by the struggle over space for non-Orthodox prayer at the Western Wall.[11]

Jewish religious pluralism, however, is about more than the Reform/Orthodox struggle. It is also about how Reform defines the boundaries of what constitutes Judaism. Reform makes distinctions and draws boundaries based on an informed and critically reflective understanding of the continuity of Jews and Judaism through history—in other words, by applying the process we described at the beginning of this essay: reflecting on what coheres with what has been the Jewish understanding of the God-Torah-Israel covenantal nexus.

From a Reform perspective, any form of Judaism that is about *Jews* responding to *God* by living a life rooted in the teachings of the *Torah* is a legitimate form of Judaism. We do not read even the most extreme anti-Reform traditionalist out of the Jewish community. Ultra-Orthodox, Orthodox, Conservative, Reconstructionist, Renewal—each in its own way agrees with the Reform Movement's 1937 statement that "Judaism is the historical religious experience of the Jewish people."[12] Crucially, we no longer hold to the simplistic nineteenth-century view that there is a single "scientifically" correct form of Judaism.

We do, however, exclude variations that are at odds with the historical Jewish religious experience. We categorically reject all the so-called "messianic Jewish" groups, because their belief in Jesus as divine and as savior places them utterly beyond the boundaries of Judaism.[13] The Reform Movement also rejects Humanistic Judaism. While many individual Reform Jews may hold views similar to those of the Humanists, the Reform Movement itself does not embrace this form of

Judaism, because it dismantles the God-Torah-Israel covenantal nexus by eliminating God.[14]

It is important to underscore that Reform also adheres to the historic Jewish legal principle that Jewish status is permanent and cannot be revoked or lost. A Jew who abjures Judaism and adopts another religion is a "transgressor," but still a Jew.[15] In the premodern world apostate Jews were "banned"—excluded from the Jewish community. In the modern world, when identities—including religious identities—are increasingly fluid, individual Jews sometimes choose to adopt spiritual practices or beliefs from other traditions. Ethical Culture, Christian Science, Unitarian-Universalism, and Zen Buddhism have all attracted modern Jews over the last 150 years. Reform rabbis are saddened when Jews neglect or disdain their own spiritual heritage while looking elsewhere, but they prefer to decide on an individual basis whether a person has crossed the line from interest to a formal commitment that would lead to their exclusion from Jewish religious life, usually after consultation with the Responsa Committee, the committee of Reform rabbis that offers guidance on questions of Jewish practice on the basis of precedents in traditional rabbinic sources.[16]

In conclusion, then, we can say that Reform Judaism exists comfortably within the reality of a pluralistic Jewish world and is confident that in both its openness to religious pluralism and its recognition of limits to that pluralism, it is consistent with historic Jewish tradition.

NOTES

1. *Oxford English Dictionary*, s.v. "pluralism," accessed September 22, 2016, https://en.oxforddictionaries.com/definition/pluralism.

2. "The Pittsburgh Platform" (1885), http://ccarnet.org/rabbis-speak/platforms /declaration-principles/. This 1885 document was an attempt by nineteen American rabbis to define the essential principles and beliefs of Reform Judaism and was accepted as such by most Reform Jews until the 1930s.

3. See Leora Batnitzky, *How Judaism Became a Religion: An Introduction to Modern Jewish Thought* (Princeton, NJ: Princeton University Press, 2011), especially the introduction and chapter 1.

4. Abraham Geiger, "A General Introduction to the Science of Judaism," in *Abraham Geiger and Liberal Judaism: The Challenge of the Nineteenth Century*, by Max Wiener (Philadelphia: Jewish Publication Society, 1962). See also Michael A. Meyer, "Abraham Geiger's Historical Judaism," in *New Perspectives on Abraham Geiger*, ed. Jakob J. Petuchowski (Cincinnati: Hebrew Union College Press, 1975); and Meyer, "Religious Ideology," in *German-Jewish History in Modern Times*, ed. Michael A. Meyer (New York: Columbia University Press, 1997), 2:138–51.

5. Isaac Mayer Wise, *American Israelite* 15, no. 4 (April 30, 1869): 4, and quoted in James G. Heller, *As Yesterday When It Is Past: A History of the Isaac M. Wise Temple* (Cincinnati, 1942), 3; both cited in Heller, *Isaac M. Wise: His Life, Work and Thought* (New York: Union of American Hebrew Congregations, 1965), 553–55. See also Kaufmann Kohler, "The Concordance of Judaism and Americanism (1911)," in *The Jew in the Modern World: A Documentary History*, ed. Paul Mendes-Flohr and Jehuda Reinharz, 3rd ed. (New York: Oxford University Press, 2011), 525–26, originally published as "American Judaism," in *Hebrew Union College and Other Addresses* (Cincinnati: Ark Publishing, 1916).

6. Kaufmann Kohler, "A United Israel," *CCAR Yearbook* 8 (1898): 87, 89–90.

7. Max Landsberg, "The Duties of the Rabbi in the Present Time," *CCAR Yearbook* 5 (1894): 122.

8. See Solomon B. Freehof, introduction to *Reform Jewish Practice and Its Rabbinic Background* (Cincinnati: Hebrew Union College Press, 1944); see also Joan S. Friedman, *"Guidance, Not Governance": Rabbi Solomon B. Freehof and Reform Responsa* (Cincinnati: Hebrew Union College Press, 2013), 187ff.

9. See these resolutions of the Central Conference of American Rabbis: "Disestablishment of the Chief Rabbinate of Israel" (1981), http://ccarnet.org/rabbis-speak /resolutions/all/chief-rabbinate-disestablishment-of-1981/; "Support for Religious Freedom in Israel" (2000), http://ccarnet.org/rabbis-speak/resolutions/all/freedom-in-israel-support-for-religious/; "The Israel Supreme Court's Affirmation of Non-Orthodox Conversions in Israel" (2002), http://ccarnet.org/rabbis-speak/resolutions /all/israel-supreme-court-s-affirmation-of-non-orthodox-conversions-in-israel/; and numerous other resolutions on "Religious Freedom" and "Religious Pluralism" in Israel, http://ccarnet.org/rabbis-speak/resolutions/all/.

10. Pew Research Center's Religion and Public Life Project, *A Portrait of Jewish Americans: Findings from a Pew Research Center Survey of U.S. Jews* (Washington, DC: Pew Research Center, 2013), 10, http://www.pewforum.org/2013/10/01 /jewish-american-beliefs-attitudes-culture-survey/.

11. See, for example, Judy Maltz and Barak Ravid, "Unprecedented Clashes as Non-Orthodox Rabbis Bring Torah Scrolls into Western Wall," *Haaretz*, English ed., November 2, 2016, http://www.haaretz. com/israel-news/1.750459. See also Helen Chernikoff and Naomi Zeveloff, "Western Wall Prayer Deal Crumbling as Rivals Stage Dueling 'Provocations,'" *Forward*, June 16, 2016, http://forward.com/news/israel/342783 /western-wall-prayer-deal-crumbling-as-rivals-stage-dueling-provocations/.

12. "The Guiding Principles of Reform Judaism" (1937), http://ccarnet.org /rabbis-speak/platforms/guiding-principles-reform-judaism/.

13. "Deceptive Proselytization of Jews," *CCAR Yearbook* 96 (1985): 241. See also Responsum #5759.2, "Baptism and Jewish Status," and Responsum #5758.11, "On

Patrilineal Descent, Apostasy, and Synagogue Honors," in *Reform Responsa for the Twenty-First Century*, ed. Mark Washofsky, vol. 1 (New York: CCAR Press, 2010), e-book. In the early twentieth century many Reform Jews were attracted to Christian Science; in 1912 the CCAR declared that formal affiliation with that church also put a Jew outside the pale of Judaism; *CCAR Yearbook* 22 (1912): 229–36.

14. For an overview of the matter, see Dana Evan Kaplan, *American Reform Judaism: An Introduction* (New Brunswick, NJ: Rutgers University Press, 2003), 54–55; and Friedman, *"Guidance, Not Governance,"* 251–52. See also Eugene Mihaly, *Qualifications for Membership in the Union of American Hebrew Congregations: A Responsum* (Cincinnati: Beth Adam, 1990); and "Responsum #5751.4, "Humanistic Congregation," in *Teshuvot for the Nineties*, ed. W. Gunther Plaut and Mark Washofsky (New York: CCAR Press, 1997).

15. *Yisrael af al pi shechata Yisrael hu*, "A Jew who has sinned nevertheless remains a Jew." Babylonian Talmud, *Y'vamot* 47b and Rashi, s.v. *de'i hadar be*; Babylonian Talmud, *Sanhedrin* 44a; Maimonides, *Mishneh Torah, Hilchot Isurei Biah* 13:17; *Shulchan Aruch, Yoreh Dei-ah* 268:2; *Maggid Mishneh* to *Mishneh Torah, Hilchot Yibum V'chalitzah* 1:6, s.v. *mi sheyesh; Mishneh Torah, Hilchot Ishut* 4:16.

16. See the numerous relevant references at http://www.ccarnet.org/rabbis-speak/reform-responsa/index/, accessed October 10, 2016.

13

FREEDOM WITHIN LIMITS

Rabbi Jan Katzew, PhD

"All is foreseen and free will is given" (*Mishnah Avot* 3:15), a teaching attributed to Rabbi Akiva (first century CE), acknowledges a paradox that is as timeless as it is timely. One does not need to be a philosopher to wonder about to what degree we govern our thoughts and our actions. All any of us needs to do is look inside and around us, locally and globally, to question our freedom to live the lives we choose. From the first time we ask "why?" until we die, we struggle to understand the causes of events in our lifetime. Because of this, we will consider, in this chapter, multiple Jewish voices in the frequently dissonant chorus composed of thinkers who have contributed to the perpetual, perhaps eternal conversation that is framed by the subject "free will and determinism."

Free will is not an absolute. At best, we are free to choose from a limited range of options. For some people, the menu of options is severely limited by factors that are entirely beyond their control. They may be victims of a crime or discrimination or genetic predisposition. They may suffer from a disease or live with a disability that prevents them from participating in a communal activity. In extreme cases, a person can be enslaved and consequently have her or his free will severely restricted. Victims have few, if any, choices. They have had their already limited free will stolen from them. Victims cannot be held accountable for their actions. Free will is anything but free. Indeed, it is a prize that comes at great existential cost. Isaiah Berlin, in a magisterial essay entitled "Two Concepts of Liberty," wrote compellingly about a distinction between negative liberty—freedom *from*—and positive liberty—freedom *to*.[1] In Jewish thought, this profound distinction can be seen in a phrase that underscored a repeated phrase by Moses to Pharaoh, "Let My people go [negative liberty] so that they may serve Me [positive liberty]" (e.g., Exodus 4:23, 7:16). Freedom and responsibility are philosophical Siamese twins. They live and die in tandem. Our freedoms are constrained by factors of nature and nurture, culture and custom, choice and chance.

Determinism, the claim that all events are preordained and necessary, comes in many forms—theological, psychological, biological, and social. God (or the devil) made me do it. I was conditioned to act in a certain way. It is part of my DNA. It is a communal norm and expectation. Each of these explanations for an action takes its cue from an expression of determinism, which takes responsibility away from the actor and places it elsewhere—on God, on conditioning, on genetics, and on tradition. In a predetermined state, there is no oxygen for freedom to breathe. Where there is no freedom, there can be no responsibility. Each of the forms of determinism is a philosophical force with which to be reckoned, and each deserves its exploration. However, this chapter will focus on the theological—the relationship between God and humanity, especially the covenantal relationship between God and the Jewish people.

How can free will and determinism coexist? That is the question prompted by "and." That is a question that has preoccupied philosophers, and that is the question whose anatomy we will trace through Jewish time and whose meaning we will consider here and now.

We humans are finite beings; we are mortal. We are also empowered beings; we are moral. Ever since the primordial myth of Adam and Eve eating from the Tree of Knowledge of Good and Evil, mortality and morality have been inextricably intertwined. Endowed with a *yetzer hara* (evil impulse) and a *yetzer hatov* (good impulse), human beings continually make choices by deciding to which impulse to yield. For the sake of moral complexity, the Sages were careful to note that "the *good* impulse" is not always good and "the *evil* impulse" is not always evil.[2] It is noteworthy that the link between morality and mortality was forged between God and Adam and Eve rather than Abraham and Sarah, because the questions at hand—"Are we free to make choices?" and "Are our lives predetermined?"—are *universal human* questions rather than *particular Jewish* questions. Each one of us makes decisions based in part on whether we believe we are self-determining creatures.

Political climate and culture have had a profound impact on Jewish thought generally and on the matter of free will and determinism in particular. When the Children of Israel were enslaved in Egypt, God was described repeatedly as "hardening Pharaoh's heart" (e.g., Exodus 7:3) in response to the first several plagues inflicted on the Egyptians. On its surface, the biblical narrative describes a Pharaoh whose free will had been usurped by divine prerogative. Indeed, this episode is the subject of significant rabbinic interpretation because of the moral problem involved in punishing not only a person, but also an entire people, for behavior that was determined by fate rather than choice.[3]

The Book of Deuteronomy recounts Moses's valedictory address in words that reverberate through time. "I have put before you life and death, blessing and curse. *Choose* life—if you and your offspring would live—by loving the Eternal your God, heeding God's commands, and holding fast to [God]" (Deuteronomy 30:19–20). When the Children of Israel were on the cusp of realizing their hope of finding a spiritual and physical home, God empowered them. After having been victims of slavery, they achieved the victory of freedom. The chosen people had become the choosing people. But that empowered status proved to be evanescent.

The Babylonian Talmud weighs in on the subject of free will and determinism through diverse narratives. One that is especially important to look at addresses the free will and determinism dialectic based on a verse that precedes the revelation at Sinai. "Moses led the people out of the camp toward God, and they stood under the mountain" (Exodus 19:17). The Rabbinic sage Rava teaches that God overturned the mountain upon the people like an inverted cask and said to them, "If you accept the Torah, fine; if not, there shall be your burial" (Babylonian Talmud, *Shabbat* 88a). In this reading of Torah, free will is hanging by the thinnest of threads. However, commenting on the same verse, Rabbi Acha ben Yaakov observed that if this is true, then the covenant was entered into under duress, which would render it invalid. According to Rava, however, the people re-accepted it in the days of Ahasuerus, as it is written, "The Jews confirmed, and accepted" (Esther 9:27)—on that occasion they confirmed what they had accepted long before. The thinnest of threads had been transformed into the strongest of ties. The Talmudic sages argued with each other because they refused to sacrifice human freedom on the altar of God's sovereignty. We stand on their shoulders and continue their conversation.

The zenith of Jewish thought, especially on the subject of free will, was reached under Muslim hegemony in Spain. The works of Plato and Aristotle had only recently become accessible in Arabic and Hebrew. The Jews on the Iberian Peninsula resembled pawns in a chess game played by warring factions of Christians and Muslims, subject to sacrifice as well as capable of becoming valuable pieces to help achieve strategic victories. Jews were also beneficiaries of profound philosophy and sublime poetry. Arguably the three leading Jewish thinkers of their times, Moses ben Maimon (Maimonides) (1135–1204), Levi ben Gershom (Ralbag) (1288–1344), and Chasdai Crescas (1340–1411), represented three distinctly different perspectives on the subject of free will and determinism.

1. Maimonides, in *Moreih N'vuchim* (*Guide of the Perplexed*), endeavored to harmonize free will and divine providence, by claiming that human knowledge and God's knowledge cannot be compared, only contrasted, and therefore free will and determinism can coexist.

2. Ralbag's most famous work, *Milchamot HaShem* (*Wars of the Lord*), was known by his critics as "Wars against the Lord" because he argued for maximal free will and a constrained Deity.

3. In *Or Adonai* (*The Light of God*), Crescas claimed that God was the ultimate cause of every human action. He argued for a maximum of divine providence and a minimum of human autonomy, severely limiting, if not eliminating, free will.

There are timeless lessons in this philosophical version of "three Jews, three opinions," a sacred principle codified in the Mishnah as a *machloket l'shem shamayim* (a controversy for the sake of heaven): (1) conflicting ideas are an integral element of Jewish thought; (2) Judaism can thrive on passionate, principled disagreement; (3) there are some arguments that are meant to endure; and finally, (4) differing beliefs in Judaism can be tolerated, if not celebrated.

Baruch Spinoza (seventeenth-century Dutch philosopher), the radical herald of modern biblical criticism,[4] was a powerful advocate for determinism, who claimed, "Everything that exists, necessarily exists." Some of his critics claimed he was an atheist; others have called him a pantheist and a God-intoxicated person. I understand him to have espoused neither theological extreme, but rather a version of panentheism, that is, someone who claims that God is *in* everything and yet God is *greater than* everything. Spinoza flouted fundamental understandings of Jewish thought, such as claiming that the Torah is not of divine origin and therefore no longer binding on Jews to practice. Consequently, Spinoza's rabbinical authorities labeled him a heretic and excommunicated him. He was a harbinger of political democracy, arguing that the state is necessary because most people are ruled by their passions, whereas a person driven by reason would seek a rational benevolence. On the subject of free will and determinism he came down unequivocally on the side of the latter, which would put him in the distinct minority of Jews who have addressed the topic throughout time, and most especially in contemporary Jewish life.

Moses Mendelssohn (eighteenth century) supported critics of Spinoza such as Leibnitz and Wolff, who claimed that his doctrine of necessity was tantamount to atheism. A staunch theist, Mendelssohn nevertheless endeavored to prove the validity of determinism—that all human volitions are products of fate. Mendelssohn's personal and private religious practice was consistent with halachah; yet his public persona advocated interaction with the surrounding culture, such as embracing use of the German language rather than speaking Yiddish as an expression of Jewish particularism. Mendelssohn was a rationalist and a universalist, two of the fundamental elements that led to the birth and growth of Reform Judaism. In his time and place, Mendelssohn was regarded as an "exception Jew," a Jew who was tolerated, although not fully accepted, by his contemporaries in Germany.[5] Moses Mendelssohn constituted an existence proof that it was possible for a Jew to also be a German. Nevertheless, he proved to represent an ominous portent for what would become the most virulent expression of anti-Semitism in Jewish history.

This concern about Jewish identity and loyalty has proved to be a recurring theme in Jewish life that has transcended time and place. At the turn of the nineteenth century in France, Napoleon convened a Sanhedrin, a Jewish court, asking for clarity on the question of Jewish identity and loyalty. One of the twelve questions put to the Sanhedrin was "Do the Jews born in France, and treated by the law as French citizens, acknowledge France as their country? Are they bound to defend it? Are they bound to obey the laws and follow the directions of the civil code?"[6] The persistence of variations on this question is remarkable, painful, and telling. The charge of Jewish dual loyalties (to the state and to God and/or Israel) did not die in nineteenth-century France. In the United States since the birth of the State of Israel in 1948, Jewish Americans who have served in leading political positions have had their loyalties questioned when the interests of the United States and Israel have come into perceived tension or conflict.

Choice has not always been perceived of as a virtue by Jewish thinkers. The Babylonian Talmud (*Kiddushin* 31a) states explicitly that the performance of a mitzvah, a commanded act, is more meritorious than an autonomous act.[7] The twentieth-century French Jewish thinker Emmanuel Levinas wrote that each person has an innate ethical obligation to care for and about each other, the primacy of responsibility.

Levinas served as the principal of a Jewish high school in Paris, where he translated theoretical ideas into educational practice. His unwavering commitment to ethical responsibility stands out as a modern challenge to the champions of unbridled choice.[8]

One of the deep sources of ethical tension in a society that prizes inalienable rights is a culture that argues for inalienable responsibilities. Prior to the advent of Reform Judaism, when Jewish thinkers argued for free will, they did so in the Kantian sense. They applied the categorical imperative, which states that anyone who was in the same circumstances would make the same choice. That is autonomy in the purest sense, the ideal of a self-legislating person whose choices would be universal. Contrary to popular culture, autonomy does not sanction doing whatever one wishes. Reform Jewish thinkers have yet to make this case convincing for large numbers of Reform Jews.

Eugene Borowitz, the leading Reform Jewish thinker of the latter half of the twentieth century, developed a covenantal theology that insisted on a place for the voice of God in a context of human autonomy. In 1975, when the Central Conference of American Rabbis celebrated its centennial, there was a concerted effort to articulate the evolving principles of Reform Judaism. That attempt was thwarted by an inability of the assembled leaders to arrive at a shared vision, the result being a decision to yield the responsibility to Dr. Borowitz, thereby making him the arbiter of Reform Jewish thought. There is a profound irony in the reality that a movement predicated on democratic principles ceded to one person the responsibility to define Reform Judaism. "In the realm of Jewish experience, the strong rational validation of universal ethics makes the rest of Jewish practice seem optional in a time when Jewish ties badly need strengthening. . . . How rationally to mandate an ethical system and how to justify group authority against individual autonomy remain utterly troublesome philosophic issues."[9] He aimed to preserve the dialectical relationship between free will and determinism, insisting that not only is there room for both, but also that both were sacred aspects of Jewish life. Borowitz names the problem and acknowledges its tenacity. Reform Jews tend to prize autonomy and resist authority, respect the universal and be wary of the particular, revere the individual and question the communal. Given these perceived tendencies, it is no wonder that Reform Jews gravitate toward free will and away from determinism.

Every one of the Jewish thinkers I have mentioned to this point is male, and I am mindful of this fact. I am also deeply troubled by it. When the history of Jewish thought in the twentieth century is written, I am among those who would claim that its greatest innovation has been the increased involvement of women in the subject. Judith Plaskow, Rachel Adler, Judith Hauptman, and Tamar Ross are but four of the luminaries whose contributions have already challenged previously held articulations of Jewish ideas and ideals. They represent voices in a choir that has heretofore been composed solely of tenors and basses. Women's Torah commentaries and an evolving women's commentary on the Babylonian Talmud are but two examples of the first fruits of women's Jewish scholarship. Perhaps there will come a time when gender will no longer need to be asserted boldly as a component of Jewish thought, but that time has not yet come. Feminist theologians reject strong determinism and affirm human responsibility.

Feminist theologians also tend to advocate for a relational rather than an individual ethic, claiming that human beings are more interdependent than independent. Perhaps due to the relatively few Jewish women's theological voices that have been recorded across Jewish time, even when they disagree on the cogency of Jewish law, for example, they disagree agreeably. They engage one another. Perhaps on this and other points, they will teach men who have more hardened positions how it is possible to cross boundaries and engage in arguments that shed more light than heat.[10] The androcentric nature of Jewish thought is both a historical fact and a moral burden, which slowly but surely is being lifted. The future deliberations about the nature of free will and determinism will be shaped in no small measure by a majority of Jews who have largely been a silent majority until now—women. I add only "Amen!"

The Holocaust brought the matter of free will and determinism into sharp focus. Was the genocidal murder of European Jewry ultimately attributed to a divine mandate? Was the unmitigated evil purely reducible to human action? What kind of a God and/or what kind of human beings could be responsible for such monstrous atrocities? If only these were theoretical questions. Most of a century has passed since the end of World War II and we are witnesses to multiple genocidal acts. It is painfully obvious that we have yet to come to any conclusion about the source of unalloyed evil. On a global scale we seem powerless to diagnose the moral disease that perpetrates evil and to treat it.

The State of Israel represents a compelling response to the issue of free will and determinism in Jewish thought. There are multiple, diverse, and conflicting narratives that led to the creation of the State of Israel, narratives that continue to unfold. There were and are Jewish opponents to Zionism because of a phenomenon termed in Hebrew, *d'chikat hakeitz*, "pushing the end of history," asserting human autonomy rather than accepting divine authority. Rather than waiting for God to return the people of Israel to the Land of Israel, Jews took the matter into their own hands and conquered the Land. The State of Israel continues to struggle in its search for a balance of political sovereignty and moral integrity. On an individual as well as a collective basis, it is much more difficult to be ethical and powerful than it is to be ethical and powerless. The State of Israel is a living case in point. In the three weeks during which Israel's Declaration of Independence was written, several versions were proposed.[11] One of them based Israel's existence on land that had been given by God. However, the one that was eventually accepted did not include a divine mandate. Rather the Declaration of Independence asserts that the Land of Israel was the place where the people of Israel were born. Historically, this is not an accurate statement, as a case could be made for the Jewish people having been born in Egypt or, even better, in the desert. Nevertheless, as in many other instances, memory trumps history. The narrative account of Israel's Declaration of Independence claims the history and the destiny of the people of Israel to be inextricably tied to the Land of Israel, the place where faith met fate, where Jews had once been chosen and were now choosing.

On balance, Jewish thinkers have opted for the existence of relative free will, claiming that without some amount of free will, morality is a cruel myth, an illusion if not a delusion. For us to be moral beings, we must have the ability to act in accordance with our own will. Instead of simplifying a complexity and regarding free will and determinism as binary opposites, Jews have repeatedly insisted on the holistic "and," arguing for a complementarity that defies and transcends logic by asserting that free will and determinism can and do coexist. Rather than answer the question "Do we have free will *or* is our fate predetermined?" Jews have kept the question alive by rejecting the "or" and replacing it with "and," thereby giving us reason to address it as an enduring dilemma.

A personal reflection: I am adopted. The first book read to me and the first book I read myself was *The Chosen Baby*.[12] Our children are adopted. The first book I read to them was *The Chosen Baby*. My parents did not choose to be infertile nor did we. They and we did choose to pursue adoption. Was God involved in these events? I choose to believe "yes." Would I have believed that God was involved if I had not been adopted and/or if we had been unable to adopt children? I do not know. I do know that nearly every day I say the following prayer: "God, teach me to count my blessings and to appreciate them as well as to prolong them." It is my way of integrating free will and determinism. I hope you find your way.

NOTES

1. Isaiah Berlin, *The Proper Study of Mankind* (New York: Farrar, Straus and Giroux, 1998), 191–242.

2. See Genesis 2:7. In the creation of a human being, the letter *yod* is written twice (וייצר), leading the Rabbinic imagination to conclude that there are two impulses (יצרים), good and evil. See *B'reishit Rabbah* 9:7: Without the *yetzer hara* (evil

impulse) human beings would not marry or procreate or build a house or engage in trade. The evil impulse, therefore, is necessary, although it is not necessarily evil.

3. Nehama Leibowitz, *Studies in Shemot* (Jerusalem: World Zionist Organization, 1978), 149–59.

4. Abraham ibn Ezra (twelfth century CE) already anticipated some of Spinoza's challenges to the divine authorship and, therefore, divine authority of the Torah, Prophets, and Writings. For example, the last twelve verses of the Torah record Moses's death and its aftermath, thereby raising questions about Moses's ability to record God's teaching after he, Moses, was deceased.

5. Alexander Altmann, *Moses Mendelssohn: A Biographical Study* (Tuscaloosa, AL: University of Alabama Press, 1973).

6. Grand Sanhedrin Convened by Napoleon in 1806. Question #6.

7. Babylonian Talmud, *Kiddushin* 31a: Rabbi Chanina: "Someone who is not commanded to honor his father received such a reward. One who is commanded will receive even more! One who is commanded and fulfills is greater than one who is not commanded and fulfills."

8. See Emmanuel Levinas, *Humanism of the Other* (1972), trans. Nidra Poller (Urbana: University of Illinois Press, 2006).

9. Eugene B. Borowitz, *Renewing the Covenant* (Philadelphia: Jewish Publication Society, 1991).

10. I shared a first draft of this essay with Rachel Adler, author of *Engendering Judaism* (Boston: Beacon Press, 1999), who graciously expanded my understanding of feminist theologians on the subject of free will and determinism. I stand in Dr. Adler's debt, yet I remain solely responsible for any misrepresentation.

11. Rabbis for Human Rights, *Masekhet Atzmaut*: Tractate Independence (English version), 2013–14, pp. 13ff.

12. Valentina Wasson, *The Chosen Baby*, ill. Hildegard Woodward (Lippincott, 1950).

14

LET EVERY BLADE OF GRASS
SING A SONG OF PRAISE

Rabbi Shoshanah Conover

Ever since Adam and Eve were born into the natural environs of *Gan Eden*, the Hebrew Bible has documented our people's quest for meaning by connecting with nature. Before meeting his beloved, Isaac went out into the open fields to meditate. Alone and afraid, Jacob wrestled with a divine figure near the River Jabbok. At the farthest end of the desert near Mount Horeb, Moses encountered God through the burning bush. And the Israelites became a people guided by God in the wilderness of Sinai. Our history, our people's sense of purpose and connection with the Divine, intimately connects us to the natural world. No wonder, then, that Reform Jews have taken to heart the need to perpetuate the environment and its bountiful resources. Its preservation has become our religious mandate. As the midrash teaches:

> When the Blessed Holy One created the first human, God took him and led him round all the trees of the Garden of Eden and said, "Look at My works, how beautiful and praiseworthy they are! And all that I have created, it was for you that I created it. Pay attention that you do not corrupt and destroy My world; if you corrupt it, there is no one to repair it after you." (*Kohelet Rabbah* 7:13)

The Reform Jewish Movement has accepted this responsibility with relish. Its Religious Action Center of Reform Judaism (RAC) and its Kibbutz Lotan, its URJ camps, its NFTY initiatives, the resolutions written by every major body of the Reform Movement—all speak to Reform's commitment to these tasks. From encouraging sustainable habits in our synagogues to inculcating green values at URJ camps, from making movement-wide environmentally minded resolutions to supporting important legislation, the Reform Movement has an important role in global environmental efforts. This type of engagement with the environment has led to living a meaningful life in pursuit of perpetuating a healthy planet for future generations to enjoy. Its success is due to the interplay between grass-tops and grassroots efforts.

The Reform Movement's impact on environmental issues built slowly. While individual Reform Jews found a unique expression of their faith through preservation of the natural world, it took time to become a touch point of our movement. The Pittsburgh Platform of 1885 and the Columbus Platform of 1937 both addressed Reform Jews' obligation to help solve social justice problems, but the environment was not named as a social justice issue until the 1999 "A Statement of Principles for Reform Judaism." The first movement-wide resolution on the environment—the "Resolution on Conservation and Development of Natural Resources"—was not issued until 1965 (it came from the organization now called the Union for Reform Judaism, or URJ, but then known as the Union of American Hebrew Congregations, or UAHC).

This tardiness is due, in part, to the fact that the Reform Movement took root in the United States at a time when very few American Jews lived an agrarian lifestyle. Some of the biblical guidelines for how to care for the earth—allowing the land to rest during the *Sh'mitah* (Sabbatical) year (e.g., Exodus 23:10–11; Leviticus 25:1–7, 20–22), offering *bikurim* (first fruits) to God instead of using them for human gain (Deuteronomy 26:2), and building a one-thousand-cubit public parkland, or *migrash*, around Levitical cities (Numbers

35:2–5)—neither applied to them nor pervaded their consciousness. As a relatively small immigrant community caught in the throes of the Industrial Revolution, U.S. Reform Jews did not act on the Jewish values of *bal tashchit*, a biblical edict that forbade destroying fruit trees in war (Deuteronomy 20:19–20), which Maimonides extended to forbidding destructive acts against anything in nature (*Mishneh Torah*, *Hilchot M'lachim* 6:10); and *hamafkir nezakav hayav*, or taking responsibility for dangerous objects (including pollutants) left in a public space (Babylonian Talmud, *Bava Kama* 29b). It was as though they had read the mitzvah of subduing the earth, in Genesis 1, without taking into account the mitigating mitzvot in the rest of Jewish tradition. Yet, slowly, slowly, individual members of the Reform Jewish community and then the community as a whole came to manifest environmental values in creative, impactful, and sometimes distinctly Jewish ways.

As North America emerged from the Industrial Revolution, individual Reform Jews moved the American environmental agenda forward. Reform Jewish leaders Louis Marshall and his son Bob Marshall became instrumental in preserving wilderness in the United States in the first decades of the twentieth century. *Silent Spring*, Rachel Carson's clarion call for environmental protection, directly influenced the 1965 UAHC "Resolution on Conservation and Development of Natural Resources."

A pioneer in linking the Reform Movement to environmental action is Rabbi Everett Gendler. For him, the Russian-born Hebrew poet Shaul Tchernikovsky expressed Gendler's own connection to and motivation for preservation of the natural world. As Tchernikovsky wrote:

And if you ask me of God, my God,
"Where is He that in joy we may worship Him?"
Here on earth too He lives, not in heaven alone,
    And this earth He has given to man.
A striking fir, a rich furrow, in them you will find His likeness,
    His image incarnate in every high mountain.

Wherever the feeling of life flows—in animal, plants,
In stones—there you will find Him embodied . . .
No God disembodied, mere spirit—He is God-In-Nature!

(Translation by Robert Cover,
Everett Gendler, and A. Porat)

Influenced by Helen and Scott Nearing's 1954 book *Living the Good Life*, by the psalms' depiction of the natural world, and by his own awe-inspiring experiences in nature, Rabbi Gendler has striven to infuse Reform Jewish communities with an appreciation for the environment and sustainability. He made headlines in 1978 when he installed solar panels to fuel the *ner tamid* (eternal light) in the sanctuary of his Lowell, Massachusetts, synagogue.

As evidenced by these actions, Reform Jews found greater meaning and purpose in their lives by communing with God through the natural world. Yet they feared that our environment was in great peril. They understood that to preserve it, more people in our country and in our movement must act. Thankfully, the Religious Action Center of Reform Judaism helped lead that charge.

The same year that Rabbi Gendler saw the installation of his solar *ner tamid*, the Religious Action Center's advocacy on the environment came into stark focus. The oil embargo during the Carter years had created a real sense of crisis concerning the country's general energy policy, and the Clean Air Act and Clean Water Act were up for reauthorization. Under the direction of Rabbi David Saperstein, the RAC's first generation of efforts on the environment was focused on conservation. The RAC and the Council of Jewish Federations hosted the first Jewish conference on energy conservation, attended by three hundred registrants from synagogues, Jewish community centers, and camps. Playing to its strength at building interfaith cooperation, the RAC worked with several Protestant groups to found the Interfaith Coalition on Energy, a national coalition of religious groups.

Yet, the RAC realized that they needed to engage members of congregations in meaningful grassroots work and personal action. Therefore, in the early 1980s, the center published an environmental manual for synagogues called *To Till and to Tend*. The manual enabled Reform congregations to find meaningful ways to incorporate environmental consciousness into their local communities. In 1984, a first group of high school students went to the RAC in Washington, DC, for a brand-new program called L'Taken (the Hebrew word means "to repair"). The students learned about social issues, including environmental concerns, and ultimately lobbied senators and congressmen on issues that mattered to the movement. In this first cohort of high school students from the Village Temple was Jonah Pesner, the current director of the Religious Action Center of Reform Judaism.

This small experiment has grown into a robust program drawing nearly two thousand high school students every year. At a time in their lives when our youth begin to grapple with how to find a purpose that transcends the daily grind of social and academic pressures, L'Taken helps teens find meaning as they use their voices to speak out on issues of social concern from a Jewish perspective. As one L'Taken participant told a congressional staffer, "It is never too early or too late to stand up for your beliefs."

In a quest to engage meaningfully with this burgeoning environmental movement, Reform Jews charged forward with a series of resolutions and actions throughout the 1990s. Reform rabbis formed an Environment Committee around the twentieth anniversary of Earth Day. They brought several environmental resolutions that passed the CCAR at various conventions and inspired movement-wide resolutions. Additionally, some Reform rabbis represented the CCAR at international gatherings on climate change.

The formation of the Coalition on the Environment and Jewish Life (COEJL) and the National Religious Partnership for the Environment in the early 1990s brought a new wave of environmental effort to the Reform Movement. COEJL convened a group of major Jewish leaders to discuss a Jewish response to environmental challenges. Representing the Reform Movement were the president of the UAHC, Rabbi Alexander Schindler; president of the CCAR, Rabbi Walter Jacob; and president of Hebrew Union College–Jewish Institute of Religion (the Reform seminary), Dr. Alfred Gottschalk. They joined with Jewish U.S. senators and heads of additional influential Jewish institutions and movements to sign COEJL's founding statement, which declared, "We, American Jews of every denomination, from diverse organizations and differing political perspectives, are united in deep concern that the quality of human life and the earth we inhabit are in danger, afflicted by rapidly increasing ecological threats."

These environmental organizations proved to be powerful forces in the national environmental movement. Rabbi David Saperstein recalls one memorable meeting of religious leaders with Virginia senator John Warner. At the time, he was a ranking member on the Environment and Public Works Subcommittee on Private Sector and Consumer Solutions to Global Warming and Wildlife Protection. This gathering that was to last fifteen minutes turned into an hour-long theological discussion on the environment that entirely turned Senator Warner around on the issue of protections for the poor in climate-change legislation.

Scientific discoveries about climate change and the repercussions of environmental destruction led Jewish activists in the 1990s to speak to the urgency of the environmental movement. Whereas *Kohelet Rabbah* and the psalms highlighted the wonder of Creation as an invitation to join God in stewardship of the earth, Jews of this decade highlighted the burning need for Jews to act for the sake of the survival of the planet and its inhabitants. As COEJL cited in its founding charter:

> Among the most pressing of these threats are: depletion of the ozone layer, global warming, massive deforestation, the extinction of species and loss of biodiversity, poisonous deposits of toxic chemicals and nuclear wastes, and exponential population growth. We here affirm our responsibility to address this planetary crisis in our personal and communal lives.

They could not have foreseen the ways in which the science of climate change would be questioned in our own day.

As American Reform Jews continued to make impact on the environment from their global vantage point, Israeli Reform Jews began making impact from theirs. One of the great ongoing success stories of the Reform Movement's commitment to the environment is Israel's Kibbutz Lotan. It began in 1983 as, essentially, the fifth "congregation" within Israel for Progressive Judaism, which is Israel's equivalent of the Union for Reform Judaism. Its young founders, many of whom were barely beyond age twenty, wanted to create a progressive youth movement to be a bridge between North American and Israeli youth.

They found great meaning in their role as pioneers. While the idea of living in the foothills of Sinai, bringing life to a desert wilderness, excited the youth, they seemed little aware of sustainability and other environmental concerns. Instead, they passionately pursued building a Jewish culture—writing their own Pesach Haggadah, combining Sephardic and Ashkenazic traditions at a time when Prime Minister Menachem Begin was undermining the kibbutz movement. This pioneering group in the middle of nowhere created a sanctuary free of politics, embodying what egalitarian Reform Jewish life could be.

It took a decade for the kibbutz to become active in environmental issues. And the environmental piece was an unintended consequence of putting Jewish values into action. In the words of Alex Cicelsky, one of Kibbutz Lotan's founders, "We were not Jews with social justice values, but Jews who have Jewish values that require social justice responses." The reading of psalms proclaiming God's wisdom in creating the earth's riches—mountains, valleys, and creatures—obligated these Jews to protect the environment around them.

As air pollution from the Hiriya garbage dump near Ben Gurion Airport threatened migratory birds and the safety of airplane passengers in the early 1990s, members of Kibbutz Lotan sprang into action. They significantly reduced and recycled the waste the kibbutz generated and built a sanctuary for the migrating birds. In a few years' time, they reduced waste by 70 percent, becoming the regional model of

waste reduction education. The sanctuary has become a global destination for birders and eco-tourists.

Additionally, kibbutz members found Jewish inspiration for their
organic farming efforts. Most high-tech agricultural efforts depend on
pesticides, herbicides, and chemical fertilizers to protect a monoculture
crop. Kibbutz member Leah Zigmond urged her fellow kibbutzniks
to mimic nature, planting and harvesting according to seasonal cycles
and following the biblical symbolism of the seven species by planting
a large variety. She helped them understand that a greater assortment
of microsystems leads to greater sustainability. As the years go by, the
soil of Kibbutz Lotan farmland enriches itself; more bees and but-
terflies are coming and staying. Obviously, Kibbutz Lotan is doing
something right.

Soon, the goals of the kibbutz included education. From immersive
educational farming experiences to its intensive Green Apprenticeship
program, Kibbutz Lotan has taught thousands of global citizens. Many
have stayed in the EcoCampus Domes (what members of the kibbutz colloquially call the Domatory), simple handmade earth-plastered
straw bale domes that are air-conditioned and offer Wi-Fi. All have
learned the principles of permaculture, which is, as Center for Creative
Ecology co-creator Mike Kaplin explained for *Reform Judaism* magazine, "a culture, philosophy, and design method that teaches us to look
at a whole system or problem, to observe how the parts relate, and to
mend what needs fixing by applying time-tested sustainable practices."

Many North American institutions of the Reform Movement have
learned the principles of permaculture from Kibbutz Lotan. Summer
camps throughout the United States have incorporated Jewish teaching on the environment into the informal education that our camps do
best. Hence, at a time when youth learn the values of self-reliance and
resilience, the incorporation of learning how to protect the environment has been seamless.

While the American Jewish camping system began in immigrant
communities in the 1880s as a way to get out of the city and into nature, a self-conscious concern for ecology and the well-being of our

planet did not take root in Jewish camps until several decades later. In the late 1960s, thanks to the rising environmental consciousness of the day, counselors and other staff began to voice *sh'mirat hateva* (protecting the environment) as a Jewish value to be taught to campers through experiential learning. For example, in Reform Judaism's first camp, Olin-Sang-Ruby Union Institute Camp (opened in 1952), campers began learning about Jewish points of view on the environment in an "Ecology *Chug*" (an interest group). They planted trees on the sprawling campgrounds and read related texts from Judaism's vast literary tradition.

As the second millennium approached, camping's environmental efforts flourished. Summer camps throughout North America began cultivating organic gardens and orchards, composting, and developing educational tools in an effort to better connect youth to the natural world and to "green" Jewish camps. The key has been for campers to make a meaningful connection to their Jewish faith through ecological action. Through hands-on experiences, they learn what it means to be God's partners in *sh'mirat hateva*.

An especially robust example is the URJ Greene Family Camp. In 2012, this camp established the Wise Academy Eco-Village for ninth-grade campers in its Kibbutz Machar program. In the eco-village, campers live in earth-friendly, energy-efficient concrete domes and learn through several means to be intentional about their relationship with the environment. They produce and prepare their own food; measure, reduce, and use the waste they generate in growing organic produce; and monitor the energy they consume, much of it from solar panels atop camp buildings. Creative lesson plans and a dedicated staff ensure that campers connect the green way of living with their Jewish values, preparing them to continue living by green principles at home in more urban settings. Thanks to greening efforts at Reform synagogues across North America, campers can act on these values easily and often in their local communities.

The Deepwater Horizon oil spill in 2010 spurred religious groups to build a reinvigorated faith-based environmental movement. Out of this disaster was born a relationship between the Religious Action Center and GreenFaith Interfaith Partners for the Environment. Green-Faith had become, as Isaac Nuell of the RAC explained, "the leading faith voice and convener of all things faith and environment." In partnership with the RAC, GreenFaith recruited several Reform congregations to participate in the intensive, two-year GreenFaith Certification Program. From 2010 to 2015, sixteen Reform synagogues participated in the program, "greening" their synagogues and learning how to be environmental activists in conjunction with other religious communities. In 2016, the RAC appointed a full-time program coordinator to work exclusively on projects with GreenFaith. Instead of working hard to engage three to four congregations per year to become GreenFaith certified, they decided to recruit fifty congregations in a year to the less-intensive, month-long GreenFaith Shield program. By broadening their reach, they felt that they could make a larger impact on environmental issues over time.

The Religious Action Center has also broadened their reach by engaging Reform Jewish institutions in Travel Justly. Introduced to the entire Reform Jewish community leading up to the 2009 URJ North American Biennial in Toronto, Travel Justly is the Reform Movement's environmental sustainability fund. Mimicking carbon offset funds in the secular world, Travel Justly supports projects that help to green Reform institutions through education, advocacy, and building projects. Since 2008, every major gathering of the Reform Movement has included an opportunity for participants to donate to the fund. To date, Travel Justly has allocated thousands of dollars to dozens of Reform congregations, local communities, camps, and kibbutzim, funding everything from improving energy efficiency to creating community gardens, from composting to hosting faith-and-environment symposiums.

Some congregations have been pioneers in greening their communities. In these cases, a passion for making the environment core to the synagogue's mission makes these initiatives a success. As Rabbi Warren Stone of Temple Emanuel in Kensington, Maryland, described in an interview with the online magazine Grist in 2007, "I've been truly fortunate. My early love of both the outdoors and the values and traditions I learned in my observant Jewish home came together seamlessly in my life's work as an environmentalist rabbi!" This love is perpetuated by green initiatives at Temple Emanuel including energy audits, passage of environmental policies by their board, using wind and solar power, maintaining a biblical garden, and involving students in numerous cleanups and other environmental projects and trips.

When Congregation Ahavath Beth Israel in Boise, Idaho, moved to a four-acre campus near a community of refugees from around the world, it worked with the Idaho Office of Refugees and built a community garden. Members of the congregation tend the garden shoulder to shoulder with the new Americans. Similarly, Chicago's KAM Isaiah Israel Congregation broke ground on a community garden in 2009. Members of the congregation's Food Justice and Sustainability Committee and others have grown more than twenty thousand pounds of organic produce and distributed it to soup kitchens and shelters.

People of all ages have been the builders and benefactors of these transformative experiences, putting Jewish values into ecological action. If Reform Jewish environmental activism is to be sustained, our youth must be educated and trained to take their place in the generations doing this work.

The National Federation of Temple Youth (NFTY) has made community service and social action signatures of its identity. In 1971 the Social Action Committee of City Region, Federation of Temple Youth (CRaFTY, now known as NFTY-NYC) produced "Ecology Action: A Guide for Jewish Groups in Combatting Pollution." This exhaustive manual on taking environmentally conscious action included such varied activities as reading Rachel Carson's *Silent Spring*, reducing use of plastics, promoting vocational high school training in environmental occupations, and checking the neighborhood for illegal furnace and incinerator emissions.

But environmentalism seemed too abstract a concept for most teens to rally around. Often, it took an urgent human need to move them to meaningful engagement with the environment through their faith. In the wake of natural disasters that devastated human beings and human-made disasters that devastated the environment, our youth have responded time and again with meaningful social action and impactful educational programs. The youth response to Hurricane Katrina illustrates this well. While many individual youth groups around the country led service trips to New Orleans in the wake of this terrible storm, the disaster brought about a new way of thinking of the URJ's Mitzvah Corps, a major youth program in the Reform Movement.

For five decades the Mitzvah Corps has given Jewish teens opportunities to take meaningful action on the issues of their time. It began in New Brunswick, New Jersey, as a short summer program during which teens participated in the civil rights movement. Its first expansion beyond New Jersey happened after Hurricane Katrina in 2006. By 2013, the Mitzvah Corps offered several summer programs in far-flung locations, including one in Costa Rica focusing on environmental justice.

Around this time, the focus shifted from volunteering over a summer to using the summer to transform the teens' consciousness. Instead of coming and "helping" others by giving them the answers, Mitzvah Corps leaders realized that volunteers could do more for the world in the long run by learning to ask better questions. The emphasis moved from service to engagement. The corps has learned the value of *tzimtzum*, the contraction of the ego in order to walk more gently in this world. This Jewish value bodes well for the environment. Volunteers continue to develop this essential Jewish value through Mitzvah Corps summer experiences in Costa Rica's alternative energy corridor and even in Seattle, where the emphasis is urban ecology.

There is reason to cheer the many ways in which Reform Judaism has advanced the environmental movement in North America and Israel. However, to better embody Jewish ecological values, we must integrate this ethic into everything we do as a movement—every gathering, every institution, every individual. This requires a healthy amount of another Jewish value: *kavod*, or respect. We must build and renovate structures to give *kavod* to the earth upon which they are built and to the natural beauty that surrounds them. All members of Reform Jewish communities should be given and should take *tiyulim* (trips) in nature on a regular basis. Avenues for environmental advocacy from Reform Jewish perspectives must continue to widen. Communal gardens and orchards should surround every Reform Jewish institution as *migrashim* once surrounded Levitical cities, giving young and old the opportunity to hear that "every blade of grass sings a song of praise to God."[1]

If we live this kind of environmental *kavod*, as Reform Jews and as citizens of this earth, then the wilderness and the land shall rejoice and blossom abundantly,[2] and we shall celebrate with it.

NOTES

1. *Magid Sichot*, p. 48.
2. Based on Isaiah 35:1–2.

15

WHAT IS MODERN ABOUT REFORM JUDAISM?

ROBERT M. SELTZER, PHD

Reform Judaism, a blatantly modern rendition of Judaism, is a relatively recent reformulation of the Jewish heritage in response to issues and circumstances that also confronted other traditional religions in modern times. The history of Judaism can be best depicted as a lengthy tapestry—a weaving, through at least three thousand years, of threads of different colors, textures, widths, and lengths, a fabric in which some of the elements persist while others come into prominence, change shape, disappear, or even run off the edge to be woven into other traditions.

Judaism has repeatedly re-formed itself. It originated out of older, "archaic" ideas and practices, so a brief account of Reform Judaism must start with observations on how early Judaism rejected certain practices and assumptions, morphing into one of the formal, historic religions now often labeled "Abrahamic" (Judaism, Christianity, and Islam) religions, which trace their historical origins to the biblical patriarch Abraham and which have much in common.

Each religion tends to have an official, fixed conception of how it came into being and developed, but reconstructing its history using the methods of modern scholarship often affords a different view from the long-accepted, hallowed account. The past may be over and gone, but understanding what took place in the past repeatedly changes.

To place Judaism in the context of world history, the concept of an "Axial Age" in ancient history is helpful. The German philosopher Karl Jaspers coined the term for developments that took place from 800 BCE to 200 BCE in what were then the most advanced areas of the world.[1] According to Jaspers, during the Axial Age new conceptualizations were developed in the most advanced civilized regions of that time: around the Aegean Sea (Greece), in Canaan (Israel, Palestine), the Indian subcontinent, and East Asia (China). These new ways of thinking were manifested in such diverse forms as Greek philosophy and literature, the Hindu Upanishads and early Buddhist writings, the Chinese literary classics, and the Hebrew texts eventually canonized in our Bible. According to Jaspers, the thought and writings of the Axial Age embodied novel and different structures of religious thinking, "breakthroughs" that built on archaic concepts and myths but transformed them drastically. What made them "axial" (that is, pivotal) was that they were new modes of thinking about spiritual matters that posited in quite different ways a transcendent cosmic or divine realm beyond mundane, tangible reality. Greek philosophers, especially Plato and Aristotle, lay the groundwork for a rational understanding of nature and the polity as reflecting a realm of eternal ideas. Hindu and Buddhist sages explored the spirituality of the core of the self in relation to Being-as-such. Chinese sages defined a peaceful and balanced world as a society in harmony with "Heaven," the underlying level of the whole universe. In the prophetic books of the Hebrew Bible, justice was God's demand to the people as well as the moral behavior expected of the individual delineated in biblical codes such as the Ten Commandments in the Books of Exodus and Deuteronomy. For the biblical writers, Israel was to exemplify justice and other supreme moral qualities that exemplified the ultimate meaning of human history. The prophets were re-forming earlier Israelite beliefs about divinity, facilitating the transition from monolatry to monotheism, that is, from an earlier insistence that the people worship only one god (*YHVH*, the name of the God of the ancient Israelites) to the principle that there *is* only one God and that all other gods were idols (human fictions).

According to the Hebrew Bible, which resulted from the Axial Age concepts of these ancient Israelites, the people of Israel was central to the history of the world. The biblical thinkers borrowed from other cultures the concept of a covenant (*b'rit*) between a ruler and his subjects to represent the relationship between *YHVH* and the whole people from the top to the bottom of the social ladder. The biblical account ties together in an overarching epic, stories about patriarchs and matriarchs who were the earliest direct ancestors of Israel, the descent of their progeny to Egypt and their descendants' exodus from slavery under Moses, the settlement of the twelve tribes and formation of the kingdoms of Israel and Judah, the destruction of these states by the Assyrian and then the Babylonian Empires, return of the exiles from Babylonian captivity, and Judaism's renewal in the Holy Land under Ezra and Nehemiah. No other ancient people produced such a saga.

According to passages in the prophetic and other books of the Bible, God demanded ethical behavior of the particular people of Israel as a collectivity in a historical process moving toward an end of days of the cessation of oppression and war, peace and justice on earth, and a flourishing of all humanity under the supreme king of kings, *YHVH*, the only God. We will see that the biblical concept of God who formed the heavens, the seas, the earth, and everything in them—especially humankind—was eventually to be crucial in the history of thought. According to the biblical worldview, natural forces were not in themselves divine or by-products of a variety of divine beings, as in the ancient Near East, nor were nature and history illusions from which one can and should escape, as in India, nor a system of pure ideas that had far greater reality than the objects of the ordinary world, as in some forms of Greek philosophy.

The various Axial Age conceptions of a transcendent reality became a key feature of all "traditional" or "organized" religions. What is usually called a historical religion was built on conceptions derived from the ancient Axial Age, so these traditions can be considered to some extent a second stage of the Axial "breakthrough" that took place in later ancient times.

The resulting formal religions had at least four components: beliefs, practices, texts, and social institutions. The first component was the ideational dimension: evocative symbols, terms, depictions, and assumptions about living a holy life. The second was a body of religious practices: daily, weekly, or yearly observances, life-cycle rituals, charitable acts, other duties to infuse the lives of the individual and the group with its holiness. The third component was holy writings, variously applied to new situations and issues. The last was a formal institutional structure, concrete social arrangements in which adherents regularly gathered for prayer and study (churches, mosques, synagogues, monasteries, assemblies, yeshivot) under the direction of authoritative religious leaders (rabbis, Christian priests and bishops, Muslim *ulema*). Moreover, traditional religions came to have a recognized place in an encompassing political order; even if they sought to separate themselves from it as much as possible, they were related to the power structure of society, directly or indirectly, and therefore affected by it.

As just noted, each traditional religion that emerged out of the ancient Axial Age had a group of holy texts. In Judaism the Hebrew Bible was considered a summary of the creation of everything, the unfolding of their identity in their past and a guide to the future. A means of reforming the religion was to reinterpret these texts in light of changing circumstances. In the last few centuries BCE and the first centuries CE, this gave rise to several streams of Judaism. Prominent for a while were Jewish apocalyptics who expected that the climactic goal and therefore the final end of world history were imminent, so that the most important task one could undertake was to purify oneself in preparation for its coming. Apocalypticism was a factor in the ideology of the Dead Sea Scrolls community and in early Christianity. Another stream of thought developed out of the Jewish encounter with Greek culture, especially in Alexandria in Egypt, where certain writers interpreted the Bible symbolically according to Hellenistic philosophical concepts, a synthesis of biblical and other ideas that would be repeated in later Jewish intellectual history and that was very influential in Christianity. (By the way, it was in the Hellenistic era that the religion of the people of Judea came to be termed Juda-ism.)

A third stream involved the emergence, mainly in Judea, of Jewish sages who eventually replaced the Temple priests as the religious authorities in Judaism. These sages were precursors of the Rabbis, a title that came into use in the later first century CE. Exactly when and how the sages gained such authority is an issue in modern Jewish historical scholarship, but their arrival on center stage represents one of the most important of Judaism's periodic reforms. The survival of Judaism in the long run was largely tied to "Rabbinic Judaism," a body of teachings and actions grounded in the Hebrew Bible, reinterpreted according to such postbiblical concepts as Written Torah / Oral Torah, this world / the world-to-come, the good impulse / the bad impulse in human nature, and above all, the "mitzvah system" of duties incumbent on Jews. (The word *mitzvah* literally means "commandment" but has come to include good deeds as defined in Rabbinic discussion and debate on the inner meaning of biblical injunctions and other considerations.) Unlike Christianity, Rabbinic Judaism did not produce dogmatic creeds. Differences of opinion, within certain limits, were considered legitimate. The Rabbis considered themselves collectively the authorized interpreters of God's Torah, with due deference paid to a few great figures among them. In subsequent Jewish history the Rabbis were the crucial channel for adapting Judaism to new circumstances. Rabbinic Judaism involved the principle that a wide range of individual rabbinic opinions should be acknowledged, a principle that turned out to be apt in the creation of modern Reform Judaism.

Despite the brutal repression of Jewish revolts against the Romans that resulted in the destruction of the Jerusalem Temple in 70 CE and repression of Judaism for a while after 135 CE, a post-Temple re-formed Judaism flourished in the early centuries CE, the period that also saw the rise of Christianity. (How Christianity arose out of Judaism, separated itself, and defined itself somewhat differently but retained much from Judaism is of course a major subject in the history of religion of that era.) In the fourth century CE, the Roman emperors, up to then "pagan" in that they revered the gods and goddesses of ancient Rome, adopted Christianity as the sole official religion of the empire. This development had major implications for Jewry. Jesus and the apostles had been Jews, but the church was largely antagonistic to it progenitor. The Christian Roman emperors severely limited the legal status of the Jews. In the seventh century Islam's rise and dissemination provided yet another channel for the spread of ideas that originated in Judaism, such as monotheism, prophecy, connections to a specific people (the Arabs, considered by Islam descendants of Abraham and Hagar's son Ishmael), a divine plan for history, practices such as circumcision and the prohibition of eating pork (which Christianity had rejected), and eventually a Muslim scholar class, the *ulema*, somewhat like the rabbis. Arguably the success of the newer Abrahamic faiths served to affirm key features of the Jewish story and viewed the universe as the creation of the one God, although Christianity's God was triune and Islam's supreme prophet was Muhammad.

A condition of Jewish survival in Christian and Islamic lands thenceforth was a narrowly restricted status. Jews could not participate in many aspects of society, but there were some areas in which they were able to retain their distinctive identity, such as trade. Anti-Jewish persecutions repeatedly erupted in Christendom and sometimes in Islamic realms. In what came to be called the Middle Ages, the Jewish Diaspora expanded in Central Asia, China, North Africa, the Iberian Peninsula, Western Europe north of the Alps, Central and Eastern Europe, and more. Judaism became even more variegated in various Jewish sub-cultures (Arabic, Greek, Italian, Sephardic, Ashkenazic, Ethiopic, and so forth).

Medieval Judaism to some extent was yet another re-form of Jewish thinking. New modes of Jewish expression emerged in Jewish poetry, rabbinic legal treatises, commentaries, chronicles, and ethical texts. Like the early Islamic philosophers and medieval Christian scholastic thinkers, Jewish thinkers sought to reconcile the theological ideas of their religion with the metaphysics and natural science originating in ancient Greece. Jewish philosophers, such as Moses Maimonides, probed the reconciliation of ethical monotheism with natural philosophy (God as the First Cause of all the causes in nature, the Prime Mover of all forces in nature, and so forth). To be sure, concerned with such matters were a relatively small number of Jews, such as physicians seeking to reconcile science and religion. In addition and by way of contrast, there were works of Jewish piety (*chasidut*) and ethical instruction (*mussar*) explicating how Judaism could infuse the religious life of the individual and shape one's soul in one's lifetime and in preparation for judgment by God after physical death. A medieval version of the Jewish mystical stream, the Kabbalah, drew on ancient esoteric teachings to conceptualize the human spiritual nature via a structure of divine principles (the *s'firot*) that connected the endless, infinite God (the *Ein Sof*) to lower levels of reality, especially the human.

The theosophical spirituality of the Kabbalah became especially important during what has come to be called the early modern period (ca. 1492–1789). And Kabbalah played a role in various movements culminating in the emergence in eighteenth-century Eastern Europe of a new Chasidism, a diverse and widespread folk movement. Chasidism's legacy of teachings and practices took on great meaning in later Jewish literature and in the writings of some religious thinkers, such as Martin Buber, who was an influence in later twentieth-century Reform Judaism. Medieval Jewish philosophical writings would also be studied by later Jewish philosophers, including those associated with Reform Judaism, such as Hermann Cohen.

As for modernity, some of its aspects can be traced back to the Renaissance and the Protestant Reformation. However, it derived to a great extent out of the "new science" of Copernicus, Galileo, Newton, and others who rejected the medieval theological-scientific synthesis of biblical and Greek principles. This new critical mentality challenged long-standing religious and other beliefs that had been basic to religion since the ancient Axial Age. The new scientists dismissed as unnecessary such hallowed concepts as a divine Prime Mover explaining the dynamics of nature; they rejected the assumption that all truths could reliably be found in the reinterpretation of Scripture rightly understood. Their conclusions about such matters as the earth's revolving around the sun (not vice versa) and Newton's laws of universal gravitation discredited ancient astronomy and physics. This emerging modern mentality can be considered the beginning of a new, modern Axial Age in which belief in the transcendent realm of religion has become increasingly problematic.

The eighteenth-century European Enlightenment writers in France, England, Scotland, and a few figures elsewhere were heavily indebted to the legacy of the Scientific Revolution of the preceding century, not just on scientific matters but through the development of the critical frame of mind that was to drive modernity onward, repeatedly expanding its purview. Thus biblical and other holy writings became subject to criticism, as ancient documents were said to be no longer easily applicable to modern times or at all, leading to new theories as to their historical composition and redaction. This modern Axial Age was quite different in content and in some ways to the old, ancient Axial Age in that it spurred religious doubt rather than reinforced religious faith. This complex of attitudes to the past and the universe resulted in a rethinking of the place of humanity in the cosmos and the organization of society. A dynamic modern frame of mind led to undermining the venerable belief that kings, nobles, and churchmen were the apex of a "great chain of being" authorized by God. Eighteenth-century Enlightenment thinkers rejected the idea of a society divided into "estates," each with delimited rights and duties.

Such revolutionary changes required a redefinition of the place of Jews in society and of the image of Judaism in general culture. When did Judaism first confront modernity? A controversial early figure was the philosopher Baruch/Benedict Spinoza, who was expelled from the Jewish community of Amsterdam; he rejected the Mosaic authorship of the Torah and its modern relevance, and his thinking on metaphysical and ethics issues was indicative of the issues posed by the new rationalism. But it was in the late eighteenth and early nineteenth centuries that a modernizing tendency developed in European Judaism, the Haskalah (Hebrew Enlightenment) associated with the Jewish philosopher Moses Mendelssohn and drawing on the general European Enlightenment movement. The encounter between Judaism and modern ideas that began to take center stage in certain parts of the Diaspora affected not just Jewish religious thought but the way Jewish peoplehood was situated in the larger society (the two dimensions were closely related). The status of Jewry as a barely tolerated but semi-autonomous group allowed to reside in a few lands with many restrictions was absurd in view of Enlightenment-inspired political ideologies of representative government and the inherent rights of the individual. The situation of the Jews was about to be totally transformed, although the struggle to do so took considerable time in some lands.

Modernity supported the idea of intellectual freedom for the individual (and other freedoms compatible with a functioning society) and a complex of issues with profound political ramifications. One of the first new religious movements in Judaism responding to this complex situation was the reform Judaism that emerged mainly in German-speaking lands in the first decades of the nineteenth century among Jews who sought civil and legal rights as citizens without having to convert to Christianity. (This reform is "lowercase" at this point because it was not a separate movement or denomination but a tendency among German Jews who no longer wanted to pray only in Hebrew and so forth.) In German-speaking lands Jewish emancipation was a long-drawn-out process, because most of Central Europe was a conglomeration of political entities in which the Jews had not attained anything like the emancipation achieved in France, England, and Holland by the end of the eighteenth century. (Frustrated, many young German Jews immigrated to America in the middle decades of the nineteenth century, where they were accepted as citizens.) Early German Reform Judaism was to some extent a continuation of the Haskalah, rationalistic and critical of certain aspects of traditional Judaism, using a modernizing Hebrew and new forms of literature (new to Judaism) as the main vehicle for expression. Reform-minded Jews set out to modernize Judaism appropriately, that is, in relation to their time and place, motivated by the strong desire to show that their Judaism was neither obsolete nor alien, but eminently deserving of respect: that the Jews should be considered Germans of the Jewish persuasion.

A complicating factor was that in the late eighteenth and in the nineteenth centuries the Enlightenment gave way to new movements such as romanticism, nationalism, philosophical Idealism (especially that of Immanuel Kant), and later tendencies. Modernity entailed a continual series of novel scientific, cultural, artistic, and political ideologies spurred by its core attitude of skepticism about the inherited beliefs; a willingness, even eagerness, to criticize them; belief in progress; and the legitimation of personal autonomy in political, religious, and other matters. The modern Axial Age has involved repeated change.[2] To be sure, some movements in modern times have responded to these principles with a "circle the wagons" resistance to changing what they consider any and all fundamental religious beliefs and practices. Twentieth-century totalitarianism (fascism, communism) may have been modern in certain regards, such as a pseudo-scientism and advocacy of mass political mobilization, but showed itself to be far more repressive of individual freedoms than traditional hierarchical regimes. As one scholar notes, there have been multiple modernities—and therefore multiple new understandings of Judaism.

In Reform Judaism the liberal religious response to modernity was not merely cutting out what was felt to be obsolete but reappropriating elements of the Jewish heritage meaningful under the changed Jewish social situation and adding new prayers and ceremonies in light of new ideas. We recall that the ancient Axial Age had drawn on earlier aspects of archaic myth and worship but re-formed them in light of new ideas; the biblical god had a history even before *YHVH* became the one and only God for Judaism and later for the other Abrahamic religions. Likewise, the Jewish response to the modern Axial Age drew on still-valid elements of premodern Judaism not just to maintain Jewish continuity, essential as that is for identity; it also looked to the past for abiding aspects of religion that make human life meaningful, that sustained the significance of the moral life, and that affirmed the place of human creativity in the universe. The modern historical consciousness was a challenge and a resource. Nineteenth-century Reform rabbis were influenced by the new *Wissenschaft des Judentums* (academic study of Jewish history and literature) as well as philosophical Idealism, which made "the moral law" central (especially Immanuel Kant). Because so much of premodern Judaism was out-of-date in light of the end of the semi-autonomous legal status of the Jewish community and the hoped-for political emancipation of the Jews, traditional Jewish law as such (halachah) was to a great extent abandoned by Reform Jews, although some of its moral values were deemed worthy of respect. According to nineteenth-century advocates of the reform of Judaism, the "essence of Judaism" was found in prophetic ethics, Rabbinic interpretations, and medieval rationalism as long as they were compatible with modern science and historiography. What they called the "mission of Israel" (the meaningful presence of Jewish people throughout the world) involved a vision of the future of humanity in a messianic age of justice and peace. Jewish "particularism" was a rational means to this universal goal. Prayers and other synagogue and life-cycle ceremonies could be reformed accordingly.

Reform Judaism was brought to America largely by German-Jewish immigrants in the middle of the nineteenth century and found a hospitable home here. The parameters of "classical Reform Judaism" were articulated in the Pittsburgh Platform of American Reform Judaism of 1885. Classical Reform did not deny continuity with premodern Judaism, it reconceived it. By way of contrast, the Ethical Culture movement, founded by Rabbi Felix Adler of Temple Emanu-El of New York, affirmed the ethics but rejected the particularism and underlying theology of Judaism. That Reform Judaism did not follow Adler's path testifies to its underlying commitment to perpetuate the distinctive Jewish heritage. Jewish law as such may have been obsolete, but halachah preserved moral and theological ideas of great importance. In this regard, Reform took a somewhat different tack than Conservative and Orthodox Judaism, which maintained, each in their own way, a commitment to the centrality of halachah.

The 1880s can be seen as a turning point in the progress of Jewish integration and therefore modernized Jewish identities. There were new ideologies to contend with (especially Darwinism), but by far the most conspicuous factor and dark side of modernism was reformulation of the old Jew-hatred and anti-Judaism in a pseudo-scientific racism that was cultural and political rather than mainly religious.

At that point in time the sociopolitical situation of the Jews in Eastern Europe was different from those to the west. The authoritarian tsarist regime had never contemplated the emancipation of Jews, so the struggle for equal rights for Jews in the way it had taken place in Germany was not viable in the Russian Empire. Moreover, in large areas inhabited by the Eastern European Diaspora there was an explosion of chauvinistic nationalist movements that made a focus on Jewish peoplehood far more urgent than Jewish theology. The upsurge of socialist movements made religion appear obsolete in certain quarters. For the most dynamic sectors of Jewish intelligentsia, the social/ethnic/national elements of the Jewish tradition took center stage, leading to a proliferation of nonreligious (sometimes anti-religious) Jewish movements. Secular Jewish ideologies, liberal or socialist, Zionist or Diaspora-centered, sought to redefine and defend Jews in ways that made the ethnic dimension of Jewish identity primary, often reasserting the Jewish values of social justice and drawing on the transformation of Hebrew and Yiddish into modern languages and the creation of a modern Jewish literature in them.

This shift within Jewry had an impact on religious Judaism elsewhere; sometimes secularist Jewishness was rejected, but more often some of its approach was absorbed into the orientations of the modernized Jewish religious movements, although a sizeable traditional community continued to exist. This shift in modern religious Judaism took place especially in America, where a large percentage of Diaspora Jews came to live in the second half of the nineteenth and the early decades of the twentieth centuries. The reorientation had a growing impact on

Reform Judaism, drawing attention to the other primary dimension (besides religion) on which Judaism was based—that is, peoplehood. A new generation of Reform rabbis, including the eminent Stephen Wise, the founder of the Jewish Institute of Religion, were positive toward Jewish peoplehood. The Columbus Platform of Reform Judaism adopted by the Central Conference of American Rabbis in 1937 reflects Reform Judaism's acknowledgment of its connection to all Jews in the present and in the past.

Anti-Semitism had a tragic climax during World War II. Modern Jew-hatred was used to justify the Nazi determination to exterminate the whole Jewish people. The Holocaust was a caesura—a hiatus, a fissure—in Jewish history on the order of the destruction of the First Temple by the Babylonians, the revolt against the Roman Empire that led to the destruction of the Second Temple, the massacres during the First Crusade, the expulsion of Jews from Spain and Portugal, the 1648 massacres in the Ukraine, and other murderously disastrous episodes in the Jewish past.

The aftermath of the Holocaust—rescue of survivors, honoring the memory of those murdered, the healing effects of the establishment of the State of Israel—preoccupied Jewish religious and other movements in the second half of the twentieth century. Much has been accomplished since by way of revitalizing Judaism by Conservative, Reconstructionist, Modern Orthodox, and Reform Judaism, as well as some traditionalist groups. Post–World War II Reform Judaism had a new cadre of leaders from German-Jewish immigrants of the 1930s, the National Federation of Temple Youth, and other involved synagogue members. The postwar decades brought the merger of the Hebrew Union College, founded in 1875 in Cincinnati, with the Jewish Institute of Religion of New York—now Hebrew Union College–Jewish Institute of Religion (HUC-JIR), with new branches in Los Angeles and Jerusalem. Reform worship came to move away from the emphasis on dignity and decorum toward less passive worship, often in Hebrew and involving communal singing. The role of the Reform rabbi expanded to include civic leadership and increased pastoral functions.

Reform Judaism committed to the equality of women in Jewish life, recognizing women as synagogue leaders, cantors, and rabbis and addressing institutional discrimination against them. Appropriate to the modern status of Judaism, Reform directed attention to general social justice issues and related constructively to the State of Israel, establishing programs there. The surge in the intermarriage rate has both brought non-Jews into Judaism, through formal conversion, and resulted in the growth of interreligious familes. Newer intellectual tendencies, such as existentialism and process theology, were used to explain the continued relevance of Jewish ideas.

The effects of the modern Axial Age continue to unfold. By the turn of the millennium Judaism had become even more variegated and challenged. Concern about an increasing secularization of American culture and the growth of Jewish assimilation led to programs to convey Judaism to marginal Jews or non-Jews interested in Judaism. New orientations include "Humanistic Judaism," an anti-theological offshoot of Reform, and, at the other end of the modern religious spectrum, a Jewish spiritualism that expresses a yearning for personal moments of cosmic awareness through meditation practices, using as a model Westernized Asian traditions, such as Buddhism. As a result of the incorporation of Jewish studies in colleges and universities in addition to the modern Jewish rabbinical seminaries, there has been a flourishing of academic scholarship in Judaica. A cohort of researchers, many with Reform rabbinic training, are researching Jewish history and probing its dynamics. We are in some regards far more aware of the evolution of Judaism than previous generations. A modern conception of Jewish cultural, literary, and ideational history is integral to modern Jewish identity. In one way or another Jewish history as such has become a central part of modern Jewish identity in ways not envisioned in the premodern Jewish past. We know more and more about the Jewish past, but what to do with this knowledge?

The changing role of religion in American and similar societies and the problematics of relating Jewish beliefs to Jewish peoplehood have made the borders and contents of "Jewish identity" less sharply defined, more fluid, and easily transitory. Some observers speak of a present-day "big tent" of Judaism embracing the widening range of ways to expressing one's Jewishness. Electronic means of communication offer new ways of bringing information about Judaism to wide circles. In a cultural environment increasingly affected by this technology and in light of such fields as neurological psychology, the religious basis of personhood and moral responsibility are issues to be wrestled with in new ways. Because we know so much more about how ideas, practices, and institutions emerged and developed, we see differently how Judaism furthered itself in many different contexts, but how to ground Jewish religious thought in a universe increasingly viewed only or mainly in scientific and technological terms that deny the reality of God and other aspects of meaningful spirituality? Modernity liberates but does not by itself generate values and discover meaning.

In sum, Reform Judaism is one of the most recent manifestations of the repeated re-forming of Judaism, an exemplar of the principle of change while maintaining continuity, thus showing how an ancient heritage has remained vital and meaningful in the lives of its adherents.

NOTES

1. Karl Jaspers, *The Origin and Goal of History* (1949, English translation 1953). A few other books on the subject: Robert N. Bellah and Hans Joas, editors, *The Axial Age and Its Consequences* (Cambridge, MA: Harvard University Press, 2012); Robert N. Bellah, *Religion in Human Evolution from the Paleolithic to the Axial Age* (Cambridge, MA: Harvard University Press, 2011); S. N. Eisenstadt, ed., *The Origins and Diversity of Axial Age Civilizations* (Albany: State University of New York Press, 1968).

2. The new complex of attitudes eventually spread to other cultures, such as those of South and East Asia, producing what some scholars call "multiple modernities." Shmuel N. Eisenstadt, ed., *Multiple Modernities* (New Brunswick, NJ: Transaction Books, 2002). Also Zygmunt Bauman, *Liquid Modernity* (Cambridge: Polity Press, 2000); and Charles Taylor, *A Secular Age* (Cambridge, MA: Harvard University Press, 2007).

16

A ZIONISM OF THE SOUL

RABBI STANLEY M. DAVIDS

There was no State of Israel when I began my studies at the Cleveland Hebrew Schools. But in 1948, when I was nine years old, my Hebrew school teacher brought into our classroom a shiny new coin. It was a fantastic thing to see! This coin actually had Hebrew writing on it. That same Hebrew language that I had associated with ancient times now had a place of honor on a real currency, like those Indian Heads atop the pennies that I loved to collect.

My teacher explained to the class that there is a new Jewish state, the State of Israel, a place where the Hebrew language is spoken and written, just like our English. Hebrew is no longer just an antique to be admired or a doorway through which to explore ancestral beliefs and practices. M'dinat Yisrael is real and tangible. It is a nation among nations. It has a flag of its own and a national anthem that we would then sing in assemblies. It is valuable in its own right. It is *today*, younger even than I was, with a vibrant new literature and art forms—and with a strong army as well! And that State of Israel was somehow mine. It belonged to me and to every Jew in the world. I was somehow doubly normal, doubly blessed, doubly enriched. Even as my American identity had a geographical base, so now did my Jewish identity. Even as my American identity rooted me in the world and gave my life meaning, so did my Jewish identity.

I wasn't brought to Zionism by logical argumentation or by intellectual discourse. I wasn't brought to Zionism by the twice yearly recitation of "Next year in Jerusalem." I wasn't brought to Zionism by studying midrashic expositions about why Jerusalem has nine-tenths of all of the beauty found in the world. Rather, Jerusalem itself called out to me at that moment. And it still does so now. My soul was transformed long before I could begin to articulate any of the multitudes of definitions of Zionism, long before I could care to parse the differences between the Zionism of Herzl and the Zionism of Achad HaAm. My Zionism was born in my *n'shamah*, in my soul.

I have never forgotten that event, now some sixty-eight years ago. That teacher, that coin, that moment in time created a perfect emotional storm that permanently shaped a huge part of my identity. I am a Jew; I am an American. I am attached both to the State of Israel and to the United States by powerful forces that are not in conflict with each other. They don't negate each other. Today I am as much at ease in Zion as I am in the United States, and I cannot imagine my world without either. There are two chambers to my soul, and they function interdependently and in tandem.

I am a citizen of the United States. I served in its army as a chaplain during the Vietnam War. My wife and I are also citizens of the State of Israel. We lived there for some twelve years following my retirement. But even prior to our *aliyah* (when we "went up" to Israel to establish citizenship) in 2004, we and our children had visited Israel dozens and dozens of times. And yes, our gravesites await us in the Jerusalem hills.

As an American Jew, I am a passionate advocate for *tikkun olam*. I regularly participated in civil rights marches as well as in feverish efforts to end our participation in that misbegotten war in Southeast Asia. As an American Jew, I helped to lead rallies on behalf of Soviet Jewry, and I visited the Soviet Union several times to offer both moral and practical support to the Prisoners of Conscience. As an American Jew and as an Israeli citizen, I was privileged to serve for many years as national chair of the Association of Reform Zionists of America (ARZA), as a member of the Board of Governors of the Jewish Agency, and on the Executive Board of the World Zionist Organization. As an Israeli American Jew, I am a passionate advocate for *tikkun olam*. I was active in Israeli politics. I marched on behalf of LGBTQ rights in Jerusalem. I protested the destruction of Bedouin villages in the Negev. I still try to stoke the fires of hope that a two-state solution can be achieved. And no matter where I live, I still battle the ossified institutions of the chief rabbinate and its destructive impact on Israeli society.

It is my intention to argue in this essay that the most enduring foundation for liberal Zionism is shaped by the interactions of our emotions, our memories, and our values. No amount of *hasbarah* (propaganda) emanating from the Israeli government or from the multitude of American Jewish institutions that claim to have found a magical way to convince the unattached that Zionism is important to them will have much of a lasting impact. No amount of on-campus training sessions on how to combat the BDS (Boycott, Divestment, Sanctions) movement, no matter how important and how well intentioned, can suffice to kindle a love for Israel. We must begin with the soul.

Many of the current so-called leaders of the American Jewish community have had experiences similar to mine. But rather than emerging out of an encounter with a coin, their embrace of a soul-centered Zionism usually began with those profoundly traumatic days of the 1967 Six-Day War or, to a lesser extent, during the Yom Kippur War of 1973. Their unshakeable attachment to Israel, their total identification with Israel, blossomed in a cascade of fear and hope and love and joy. Only later would many of them participate in intensive study programs such as those offered through Melton or the various Wexner initiatives. Only later, in meaningful encounters with Israeli intellectuals and thought leaders (such as Rabbi David Hartman, Amos Oz, and Yossi Klein Halevi), would they begin the process of trying to comprehend the meaning of their commitments. First came the soul, and then the mind.

In 2017 those wars and their complex consequences no longer suffice to counter the sense of separation and of indifference that mark so many in the American Jewish community. And neither can holding a beautiful ten-shekel coin in one's hands. And therein lies one of Zionism's greatest opportunities and challenges.

In today's America, finding significance and purpose through belonging to large, undifferentiated organizations, institutions, and movements is no longer normative nor considered desirable. Our major religious denominations, Jewish and Christian alike, are experiencing severe difficulty in retaining membership. Religious institutions are still extraordinarily powerful in the United States, but voting with their feet as well as with their wallets, increasing numbers of people are looking for smaller, more intimate, more profoundly personal ways to express their spiritual identities.

The fastest-growing religious movement in America is "Unaffiliated." The fastest-growing political party is "Independent." It is not that "unaffiliated" or "independent" people do not care about the core purposes of larger groups. But anonymously paying dues or membership fees or automatically responding to quadrennial calls to vote just are not experienced as personally satisfying or meaningful. And this is most obviously true for that cohort referred to as millennials. Whatever else they are, they are not lemmings milling about looking for a cliff to collectively jump off of. In their own way, even as many of us did in our own way, they are seeking a personal means to give a unique value added to their lives.

Proverbs 29:18 reminds us that "without a vision, a people dies." The search for a significant source of spiritual meaning is rapidly moving people beyond the impersonal organizational and formally structured settings that used to anchor their lives. People still need and search for the transcendent, but they very often prefer to do so alone or in smaller groups.

Individuals still go bowling in the twenty-first century, but as Robert Putnam points out, fewer belong to bowling leagues.

Additionally, especially among young Jews today, to enthusiastically embrace a particular ethnicity is often derided as narrow-minded and self-limiting. To declare allegiance to a particular nationality is seen by many to deny the universality of the human experience, to be opting for those kinds of barriers that only sow the seeds for endless conflicts and confrontations.

The Pew Research Center reports, by now quite well known in our midst, show beyond reasonable question that there is a weariness and a wariness among many younger American Jews of having to continually defend Israel, especially when American society itself is so deeply involved in problems that demand our attention and our active concern. It has become acceptable in many circles to distance oneself from Israel. It has become acceptable to admit that one just doesn't care about Israel.

Many younger American Jews see no attraction in labels such as "Reform" or "Zionist" or "liberal." Our millennials are seeking to redefine the terms and change the rules that hold our collective together. Described by some as narcissists with a powerful sense of entitlement, these millennials are also optimists and idealists who see themselves as unconstrained by the givens of traditional social structure.

The America of today is going through a powerful shift in how it views those who in the past have been dismissed as "the other." Gender identities are coming to be understood as fluid. Religious identities in all sectors of the population continue to evolve. In some places it is accepted that ethnic and racial identities exist on a spectrum, rather than being frozen at a single point. It is counterintuitive if not downright countercultural in the twenty-first century to choose to emphasize national differences.

Yet at its heart Zionism is precisely an expression of Jewish nationalism, of a desire to assert the attachment of a particular people to a particular land and to view that attachment as redemptive, even if not every member of that people lives on that particular piece of ground. As multifaceted as Zionism is—with liberal and religious and secular and socialist and ultra-nationalist and isolationist forms competing ideologically across the globe, and with political (disciples of Herzl) and cultural (disciples of Achad HaAm) Zionists constantly denying each other's authenticity—what binds all Zionists together is a singular identification with a particular nation-state.

Lib'yot am chofshi b'artzeinu, in the words of *HaTikvah*: to be a free people in our own land. These are the words, these are the ideas, that can still penetrate the most obdurate of souls. Freedom. Independence. Shared community. Shared visions. A purposeful existence. A life of caring for something far larger than ourselves. A chance to build a model of existence that can transform our world. A love of Israel that can bring about *tikkun* (repair or perfecting). What are souls for if not to dream such dreams? What then is a Zionism of the soul?

I am a Reform Zionist—by choice. "Reform" modifies my Zionism, even as "Zionism" modifies my Reform Judaism. I see no inherent contradictions between "Reform" and "Zionist." As a Reform Zionist, I feel impelled to be a warrior in the struggle to strengthen the State of Israel as both a Jewish and a democratic state. All those things that are deeply troubling about the State of Israel to so many are for me a compelling appeal to be involved, not a reason to turn away. As a Reform Zionist, I feel called to do everything in my power to make certain that the Third Jewish Commonwealth will be more than just another nation-state *k'chol hagoyim* (like any other country). I feel driven to help the State of Israel to live up to the highest ethical and moral standards of our tradition, even as it protects its borders and its citizens. My soul makes that demand—not a political treatise, not residual anguish over the Holocaust, and not words echoing from Sinai.

Israel is no longer the brave little David that confounded the world during the Six-Day War of 1967 by defeating enemies that threatened her by land, by sea, and in the air. Israel today is a regional military and economic superpower, a start-up nation, which is besieged by her neighbors and is the target of escalating anti-Zionist and anti-Semitic rhetoric and actions across the globe.

The Jewish state of which I dream my Reform Zionist dreams will do everything in its power to nurture a two-state solution leading to a viable, secure, and just peace with the Palestinians. It can do this only by embracing not only the ancient biblical and prophetic moral imperatives, but by embracing as well the solidity of the American-Israeli partnership, without which reasonable risks for peace will never be taken. The commitment of American Jews to Israel must be perceived as unshakeable, and our role must be that of an active partner in shaping American and Israeli political decisions and public opinion.

Reform Zionists do not desire that anyone should conceal or even mute any of our critiques of Israel, nor back off from efforts to convince influencers in Israeli society to advocate changes in policy and practice. Reform Zionists do insist, however, that any perceived ambivalence (or even neutrality), no matter how principled, assigned to our commitment to a militarily and diplomatically secure Israel can only be counterproductive.

A Zionism of the soul is marked by empathy. Therefore most Reform Zionists do not believe that settlement expansion beyond the major blocs displays concern for the humanity of the Palestinians. Such expansion is far too often a disruptive and dangerous ransom paid over and over again by dysfunctional coalition governments. Most Reform Zionists hold that Palestinian violence against Israeli civilians, rockets and tunnels from Gaza, and the threats from Iran and Hezbollah reflect intensifying Muslim religious extremism in some segments of Arab society around the Middle East just as much as they express the endemic desire of some to destroy the Jewish state. Most Reform Zionists hold that despite the truth that two thousand years of Western history explain some or perhaps much of the animus, today's Israel is far from powerless to change the calculus of conflict.

The Jewish state of which my soul dreams will swiftly do away with the ultra-Orthodox monopoly over all matters of personal status. The chief rabbinate's official role as an arm of the state must be ended, though it may retain significance for those choosing freely to live under its control. Rabbis of all streams must be acknowledged as Jewish religious functionaries for all Israelis who choose to embrace their leadership. Conversions by such rabbis must be fully accepted by the state apparatus. Completely secular Israelis must have the freedom to live their secularity—especially in all matters touching upon marriage, divorce, burial, and conversion.

At the same time, most Reform Zionists insist that within a Jewish state, Jewishness needs to be celebrated and privileged. The church-state separation so uniquely American does not fit the paradigm of a contemporary Jewish and democratic state. Reform Zionism will be invaluable to the process of deciding internally how Shabbat can be a source of humane and spiritual value without imposing a "one size fits all" approach. So, too, other aspects of the Jewish calendar must be allowed to bring their messages of hope and faith and ethical challenge to Israeli society and government operations, even as they must be present in a way that grants flexibility and choice to all Israelis.

My Reform Zionism demands of me a high level of respect for "the other," those whose ethnicity or nationality or gender are other than my own and those living with disability in one form or another. We once were strangers in the land of Egypt, so we must be attuned to the cries of refugees who cross Israel's borders. We have been singled out for merciless persecution because of our faith. As Reform Zionists, then, how can we not be profoundly responsive to the just demands of the Beta Israel Jewish community of Ethiopia, the Bene Israel Jews and the B'ne Menashe Jews of India, still suffering unacceptable discrimination in Israel because of their ethnicity? How can we not fight on behalf of LGBTQ rights in Jerusalem? My Reform Zionism responds to the challenge: You shall not be silent.

So much attention has recently been paid to the activities of the Women of the Wall that one might think all that stands between Israel and full gender equality is a top-notch prayer space at the Kotel, the Western Wall. This is far from the truth. Even as Reform Jews worldwide battle for full egalitarian rights for women to worship at the wall, Reform Zionists should not be deceived into thinking that that particular battle is the sum and substance of the problem; gender equality must be addressed with far more depth and seriousness. Within North American communities and elsewhere in the world, Reform Jews have embraced egalitarianism at high levels.

Reform Zionism sees each of us *b'tzelem Elohim*, "in the image of God," so we need to make full gender equality a banner for Reform Zionism as it addresses Israel.

No true democracy exists in Israel if any segment of the community is marginalized either by statute or in practice.

Zionism of the soul can ignite passionate commitment from many aspects of our community. Think back to the post-'67 euphoria and to the post-'73 relief. Inspired by a heroic State of Israel, emboldened by the Jewish community's rising up as one to support Israel in a truly dire time, American Jews created innovative, substantive institutions serving to transmit the richness of Jewish life and Jewish values to new generations. Today we stand on the shoulders of those who rose to full Jewish consciousness in that era.

Reform Zionism, with its unshakeable commitment to *tikkun olam* (repairing the world), can offer a new generation of American Jews a serious opportunity to transform the world, by helping Israel embrace what the prophets once demanded of us: to become *l'or goyim* (a light unto the nations). Reform Zionism declares that the Zionist vision has not yet been fulfilled. Reform Zionism insists that a Jewish state can and must become the model to which other nations in the democratic world aspire.

Further, Reform Zionism can and should be a two-way bridge between the finest aspects of American culture and the finest aspects of Israeli culture. American Jews need to experience the incredible spiritual and religious revolutions that many parts of Israeli society are experiencing today. We need to be able to read the works of Israel's world-class authors, to participate in all aspects of the encounter between a living, breathing, contemporary Jewish state and the finest ideas of world culture. We need to understand what early Zionists meant by *Anu banu artza, livnot u-l'hibanot bah*, "We have come to the Land to build and to be rebuilt by it."

American Jews, one by one and collectively, need a strong, healthy, secure, culturally rich Jewish democratic State of Israel. In turn, Israel needs access to our passionate embrace of the benefits of an

American-style democracy. When our souls are inflamed by the noblest of dreams, we can change an entire world.

We need each other. That is why Reform Zionism is an unshakeable part of who I am, and has been since that liminal day in 1948 when I first held a shiny coin in my hand. Zionism of the soul is a worthy pathway for all who dream of making this world a better place.

17

THE ROLE OF REFORM JUDAISM IN ISRAEL

Rabbi Gilad Kariv

The radio that sat on the coffee table in the living room of my grandparents' home was old and broken; however, from the days we first learned to speak and understand stories, we knew that this was the radio with which my grandparents listened to the historic United Nations General Assembly announcement on November 29, 1947, issuing the decision to establish a Jewish state in Eretz Yisrael. Having learned of the historic decision, my grandmother, like so many others, ran out to dance in the streets. I grew up as a secular child in an Israeli Zionist household. When I am asked what I found as a secular teenager in a synagogue, many times I share the story about that radio. The synagogue, for me, was that place where I could go and dance freely—just as my grandmother did on that historic day.

In recent years, Israel is experiencing a significant phenomenon of cultural and communal Jewish renewal. We have become aware of the growing interest of Israelis in Jewish culture, in traditional sources of Judaism, and in communal and spiritual experiences. While this phenomenon may not encompass the majority of non-Orthodox Israeli society, we cannot deny that secular Israeli society is dealing more than ever before with questions of Jewish identity and culture.

I first entered Kehillat Beit Daniel, the original Reform congregation in central Tel Aviv, during my final year of high school. At that
time, over twenty years ago, there were twelve Reform congregations
across the country; by 2004, the Israel Reform Movement had grown
to twenty-two congregations. Today, forty-five congregations, groups,
and community initiatives in Israel are affiliated with our movement, and
we believe we will soon cross the fifty-congregation mark. Major studies
conducted in Israel in recent years indicate that one in three Israelis has
already participated in a Reform or Conservative prayer service, study
session, or life-cycle event.[1] That means no less than 250,000 Israelis
identify as Reform Jews when it comes to religious identity.

For a long time the central challenge the Israel Reform Movement
faced was establishing a target audience for our values and activities. In
recent years our central challenge has become providing for the needs
of an Israeli audience that already exists and is awaiting us. If in the
past the Judaism of secular Israelis was expressed through their Israeli
identity and native Hebrew, today a framework is slowly developing
for richer dialogue based on expressions of Jewish tradition intertwined
with democratic values of social justice and *tikkun olam* (repairing the
world), shared by Jews in Israel and around the world.

Almost seventy years after the State of Israel was established, we
are ready—in many ways we are required and obligated—to write new
chapters in the moving story that is the connection of the Jewish people
to the State of Israel. For several decades, millions of Jews' identification with Israel, and the story of its establishment, was their basis for
Jewish identity and the practical expression of such identity. This has
surely been the case in Israel itself, and it could also be said of many
Jews around the world.

The goal of Zionism then was to ensure the future of the Jewish
people and Judaism in the modern age. Today Reform Judaism and Zionism, which recognize the legitimacy of Jewish life in every place and
site, must include the belief that the cultural, spiritual, and intellectual
fruits of Jewish sovereignty can enrich the lives of Jewish families and
Jewish communities around the world.

One well-known Talmudic saying reminds us that *kol Yisrael areivim zeh lazeh*, "all of the Jewish people are responsible for one another" (Babylonian Talmud, *Sanhedrin* 27b). The Jewish world is changing before our eyes. Many of the narratives that informed the identities of our parents and grandparents are becoming less and less relevant. But we must remember that a changing reality also brings with it new and exciting opportunities, including everything having to do with the connection between Israeli society and a renewed sense of Jewish identity and, in turn, the relationship between Jews all around the world. Hand in hand with this notion is Reform Judaism's renewed obligation in the twenty-first century to ensure the democratic character of the State of Israel, alongside its Jewish identity. People in Israel today tend to hold one of two views. The first is that in order to secure its democratic character, Israel should abandon its Jewish identity; the second is that in order to ensure its Jewish uniqueness, Israel has no choice but to put democratic values aside. Reform Judaism, however, is strongly committed to democratic values, religious tolerance, and equality and unwaveringly loves Israel. As a result, the Reform Movement stands firm in its will to protect both the Jewish and democratic character of Israel.

The Israel Reform Movement and Israel Religious Action Center (the movement's legal and public advocacy arm) have stood at the forefront of Knesset committee deliberations over the writing and implementation of an Israeli constitution. Reform leaders were the only ones to present a progressive constitutional vision of the State of Israel as the national homeland of the Jewish people and a state ensuring equal treatment of all its citizens across religious, gender, linguistic, and ethnic lines.

The relationship between Israeli and Diaspora Jewry can no longer be taken for granted. We can no longer expect young Jews of the world to get excited (let alone dance) in response to a past century's defining moments. The same is true of Israeli millennials. Therefore, a true relationship between the up-and-coming generations in Israel and the Diaspora can only be based on the knowledge and feeling that young Israelis share similar values and worldviews as their Jewish counterparts around the world. Reform Zionism is based on the idea that the fruits of modern Jewish sovereignty can assist in strengthening Jewish life in Israel and outside Israel. The precondition for the fulfillment of Reform Zionism is ensuring that progressive Diaspora Jewry have significant numbers of Israeli partners who exert meaningful influence in the development of the State of Israel.

A few years ago I spoke with a leading Israeli journalist, an avid secular Israeli. In a sort of apology, he told me he does not feel comfortable in Reform congregations because—as he put it—he cannot "smell" his grandfather's smell in them. I responded that my grandfather had never, as an Israeli adult, visited a synagogue—which means that, unlike the journalist, I am not particularly prompted to remember my grandfather when I am at a synagogue. I explained to the journalist that when I go to synagogue, what I care about most is taking in the fragrance of my children and dreaming of the day when I will take my grandchildren to the same synagogue or to another of many spread across the world.

This encounter reminded me that we must continue to strengthen our awareness of *k'lal Israel*, Jewish peoplehood and Jewish solidarity. The Reform Movement's greatest task is nurturing the sense in the individual that Judaism has something to add to personal and family life. As it nurtures that sense, it also strives to emphasize and highlight Jewish tradition's universal and humanistic foundations. We are called upon at the same time to think of exactly those cultural and spiritual mechanisms through which we can fortify both the sense of global Jewish cooperation and all of us being part of one extended family.

Special thanks to Yonatan Melamed for his contribution in translating and editing this work.

NOTE

1. Tamar Hermann and Chanan Cohen, *The Reform and Conservative Movements in Israel: A Profile and Attitudes* (Jerusalem: Israel Democracy Institute, 2013), http://www.reform.org.il/Assets/07%202013/idi%20poll%202013%20reform%20and%20conservative%20movements%20in%20israel.pdf.

Part Three

CONNECTING TO THE DIVINE

In this section, "Connecting to the Divine," we offer a number of challenging approaches to the question of how we connect to God through Jewish religious practice. There is a long tradition of Talmudic discourse that produced hundreds of years of halachic analysis. How can Reform Jews plug into this extensive literature in order to draw out those aspects that seem to provide us with religious meaning? What role can the concept of commandments play in enriching our lives, not only in making us more spiritually aware and helping us contribute to the world?

In "The Power and Pitfalls of Personal Religious Autonomy," Rabbi Ben Zeidman points out that religious autonomy is, at the same time, both the greatest advance over previous Jewish religious systems and the biggest weakness of Reform Judaism.

In "The Jewish Path," Rabbi Mark Washofsky, PhD, makes the case for increasing halachah's role in the Reform Movement, as it is a rich source for guidelines related to rituals and for spiritual enlightenment.

Rabbi Carole B. Balin takes up the topic of the commandments in "Mitzvah/Mitzvot." What do Reform Judaism's principles, those that obligate us to observe only those commandments aligned with our ethics, mean for us today?

In "Eating Our Values," Rabbi Mary L. Zamore proposes that observing the laws of kashrut (keeping kosher), a practice historically rejected by classical Reform, can have great spiritual meaning in today's world. Not only might it deepen our ritual practice, it can sensitize us to ethical concerns.

Rabbi Lisa L. Goldstein, in "Shabbat as a Spiritual Practice," inspires readers to practice intention as we prepare to receive the "extraordinary gift" of Shabbat and shows us how to open our hearts and to invite our souls to emerge in all its beauty.

In "Take Back Your Time," Rabbi Mark Dov Shapiro gives us practical ways to celebrate Shabbat, balancing contemporary Reform practice with traditional observance.

In "Ceremony versus Ritual," Rabbi Stephanie M. Alexander shows us how to manage the conflict between religious spontaneity (*kavanah*) and religious obligation (*keva*).

In "Seeking a Wild Heart in Wilderness," Rabbi Mike Comins looks at why so many people feel closer to God when they are out in nature.

Rabbi Ted Falcon's essay, "Toward a Reform Jewish Mysticism," explores how Jewish mysticism has influenced Reform Judaism, including how the *Sh'ma* can form the basis for a Jewish meditative practice of mindfulness.

One can see from these essays that we advocate a Reform Judaism that is rational, scholarly, experiential, and mystical. While this is in dramatic contrast to the way founding generations understood the task of reforming Judaism, whose aim was to remove non-rational elements from the Jewish religious experience altogether, we understand that universal principles can be applied to all of our mitzvot, for they serve as our way of connecting to God.

18

THE POWER AND PITFALLS OF PERSONAL RELIGIOUS AUTONOMY

RABBI BEN ZEIDMAN

When many people think of "religion," they think of a faith tradition based on archaic notions of the world that tells them what to do and how to do it. But, there is an alternative. There is such a thing as religious experience without fundamentalism. That means an individual's engagement with their religious tradition on their own terms.

Until the Enlightenment period in Europe (which began in the eighteenth century), most of history saw the Jewish people defined both from without and from within by their religious heritage for the sake of all things political and social. Jews were not French, for example; they were Jews who happened to live within French borders. Things could be better or worse depending on the time and the political landscape, but the Jewish community was often set to handle most of its own affairs. This meant that a typical individual's social and commercial destiny was bound up with the rest of his or her Jewish community. Especially true in Europe, a ghetto or shtetl-like life was all one knew and all one needed. Because of this reality, an individual was beholden to his or her Jewish community and its practices. To go against the grain too much, to wonder about how to adapt "tradition" to fit into the modern world, to question core Jewish principles and practices too publicly, was to risk being formally expelled.

One of the most famous cases of expulsion, or *cherem*, was that of Baruch Spinoza in 1656 in Amsterdam. Schooled in the classic philosophy, he was perhaps a century or a century and a half before his time.[1] His views of God as Nature, rather than as a force of Will and Creation, may very well have given impetus to some early Reform thinkers. Even if they disagreed with his ideas, he served as just one example of the possibilities of Judaism and Jewish theology when engaged from a different perspective.

Though the early thinkers who would establish the Reform Movement disagreed with significant pieces of Spinoza's theology, this case of expulsion is well known and helps to serve as an example. This is how the Jewish community would exercise authority to ensure that Jewish thinking and behavior stayed within a certain traditional framework. His expulsion meant that the Jewish community was not permitted to have any interaction with Spinoza, neither in person nor in writing, financial or personal. For the typical Jew, *cherem* would have been ruinous to a person's livelihood and family.

By the latter half of the eighteenth century, most notably in Germany, a desire to apply contemporary ideas and philosophies while at the same time preserving Judaism's heritage and unique tradition brought about a surge of new thinking around what Judaism could be in the modern world. That excitement in some circles of the Jewish world first required the right situation in the broader non-Jewish world as well—a readiness to accept Jews as part of the broader national community. This was shown famously through the French emancipation of 1790–91. Emancipation meant (in theory) equal rights for Jews under broader, national law. At the same time, it allowed new ways of thinking about Judaism to enter into the hearts and minds of Jews who had previously been reliant upon maintaining the status quo within their segregated communities for generations.

Historian Michael A. Meyer tells the story of the free city of Hamburg leading up to the founding of a temple there in 1818 that incorporated reforms in worship, including an organ and choir and the omission of a partition separating men from women (though they still sat separately). Already in 1799 the rabbi of Hamburg resigned because the government withdrew "his right to excommunicate Jews who violated the ceremonial law." This is just one example of the political-social situation that led to a portion of the community becoming relatively secular, but imagine what that meant for someone who found traditional ritual practices to be cumbersome and less than meaningful. "What scores of Hamburg Jews were now seeking was a means to express religious feelings within an acceptable setting that would reestablish their Jewish roots while compromising neither their aesthetic and moral sensibilities nor their social relationships with non-Jews."[2] This was one of the first temples to incorporate reforms, and it was only possible with the right mix of both internal and external factors.

As the world around them was changing in new ways, the Jews of the modern age were seen (theoretically) as potential citizens no matter their religious tradition. So, the foundation of Jewish community began to shift. The more Jews were allowed into public life, the less a Jewish individual's financial or social stability relied upon the Jewish community. This meant that one could reflect upon *personal meaning* within Jewish tradition with less fear. Unfortunately, for some the doors that opened in broader society led them down a path toward complete secularization or even a different religion entirely. But thankfully, reforms taking place at synagogues and in schools where adults were given the opportunity to take a more *scientific* or *critical* approach to Jewish text and history captured the hearts and inspired the minds of many who were interested in engaging in Judaism from this new, modern context.

This renewed interest in the study of Judaism with a rational approach would inspire scholars to ask questions about Jewish history, texts, traditions, and heritage without fear of punishment or expulsion—questions like: Who wrote the Torah and how was it compiled? What really happened during the Maccabean revolt, and what are the authors of the Rabbinic literature trying to teach us by adding on layers of tradition to that ancient story? How do we engage meaningfully with Shabbat without being required to participate in its observance with irrational ritual practices and behaviors (like not being permitted to light a light, but allowing a non-Jew to do it for us)?

Admittedly for some, the questions (and the permission to question) had a polarizing effect. Many felt that this line of thinking was extremely inappropriate (to say the least), and Orthodox Jewish groups were born. Others were overwhelmed by the process of investigation and saw no purpose to Jewish religious practice any longer, and secularism (along with conversion to Christianity) similarly grew. But for others, the reflection on core Jewish values and allowing traditional practices to inform belief and behavior yielded a great deal of spiritual meaning. The question became, for example, not whether to celebrate Shabbat (an all-or-nothing approach), but how to honor Shabbat in a meaningful and relevant way for a new era. Rote ritual was dismissed. Superstitious practices and authoritative hierarchies were eliminated, and the individual pursuit for Jewish meaning in a modern context flowered. Early reform thinkers were spurred especially by the desire to respond to Immanuel Kant's dismissal of Judaism. They sought to establish a rational religion, both morally inspired and grounded in reinterpreted Jewish text and tradition. The endeavor to reform Judaism was born.

Whereas for most of Jewish history the tradition and local communal practices, as taught by its rabbinic leadership, served as the authority for the Jewish people, this was no longer the case. The political reality brought about the opportunity for a new scenario in which the authority lay with the individual. Personal religious autonomy is the foundation stone of Reform Judaism.

That the Reform Movement allows the individual to be the religious authority is at once liberating and challenging. As we've seen, the process to bring about the Reform Movement was long and complicated (as things involving human beings usually are), winding its way through Europe and coming to America as Jews immigrated. It is in the United States that Reform Judaism was arranged as a formal movement. As early as 1885 the Pittsburgh Platform formally announced a denomination of Judaism that intended to establish itself as *the* modern approach to the religion.

Clearly this was liberating in a variety of ways. No longer bound to traditional Jewish law (halachah) and customs, an individual could make decisions for him- or herself about theology and practice. For example, the Pittsburgh Platform declares, among other things:

> We hold that the modern discoveries of scientific researches in the domain of nature and history are not antagonistic to the doctrines of Judaism, the Bible reflecting the primitive ideas of its own age, and at times clothing its conception of divine Providence and Justice dealing with men in miraculous narratives.
>
> . . . Today we accept as binding only [the Mosaic legislation's] moral laws, and maintain only such ceremonies as elevate and sanctify our lives, but reject all such as are not adapted to the views and habits of modern civilization.
>
> We consider ourselves no longer a nation, but a religious community. . . .
>
> We recognize in Judaism a progressive religion, ever striving to be in accord with the postulates of reason.

With an obligation toward only "moral laws" and toward choosing only those "ceremonies" that elevate and sanctify one's life (and the life of a community), the roles of the rabbi as judge and of the community as punisher for failing to practice Judaism to a certain standard become moot. And with the elevation of reason over tradition, the "reasonable" individual realizes that he or she is the one responsible for making his or her own Jewish decisions. With a focus on being out in the world, no longer a separate nation within a nation, and with a desire to engage in the study of our own tradition and history through a critical lens, we each have the power to decide what our Judaism looks like.

However, this was also challenging. Because not only *could* a person make his or her own decisions about how to engage in Judaism, but the principles of the Reform Movement *relied* on the individual actually doing just that!

Today, the obligation to make choices about how to engage in one's personal and communal Jewish life has left open the possibility that some will avoid making any choices at all. Those who utilize their personal autonomy to connect to Judaism, who engage in the Reform Jewish endeavor, find deep and powerful connection to Jewish life and within the Jewish community.

However, the difficulty, the pitfall, of personal religious autonomy is a dangerous one. Many generations removed from traditional, communal "obligations," and living in a postmodern world, for many the energy and effort of engaging in the process of making meaningful Jewish decisions has lost its priority. The freedom to make choices means one has the ability to walk away from one's community and heritage. The freedom now exists to simply not make any choices at all, to not exercise one's autonomy and authority in one's personal Jewish life.

This is especially because many lack the knowledge of Judaism that was front and center for the original reformers. While they were often very well learned in traditional Judaism, they became interested and even passionate about reforming their religion *because* of their knowledge and experience. Today, descendants of Reform Jews often have very little understanding of the origins of the movement or of the traditions that are being reformed in the first place. Minimal Jewish education post–bar or bat mitzvah and a general American (perhaps even Western) cultural attitude that religion is only for fundamentalists and children have led to a misunderstanding about the complexity and the relevance of Jewish tradition in today's world.

With personal religious autonomy, Reform Judaism expects individuals to be learned and thoughtful enough to make decisions about how to engage tradition meaningfully in their own lives. While many misinterpret Reform Judaism to be a Judaism for doing what you want when you feel like it, it in fact *requires* one to engage in this endeavor of exercising personal religious autonomy, and to do so responsibly (with learning and with thoughtfulness). In this way, there are "expectations" and "obligations" for Reform Jews—not with regard to specific ritual practices, but with regard to learning and making personal

Jewish decisions. This is extremely difficult, and it takes a gargantuan effort. It's tempting to succumb to the challenge and avoid it entirely.

"I only go to services for the High Holy Days, so I am Reform." "I grew up keeping kosher, but I sometimes eat shrimp, so I am a Reform Jew." "I respect the halachah, the Jewish law, as a guideline, but not as a requirement more important than ethics and morals. I am informed by my Jewish heritage and through my studies of Jewish theologians and am in a constant state of self-reflection and examination as I search for meaning and holiness." One of these things is not like the others.

Sometimes people misunderstand and take Reform Judaism to be the "easy way out." Nothing about Reform Judaism is for the lazy. A few years ago I was talking with a young man, seventeen years old, who grew up in Orthodoxy. We had just concluded services, his first inter-action with Reform Judaism beyond whatever rumors he had heard within his own community. He was trying to understand the Reform approach to Judaism, and it was very difficult for him to grasp.

"What do you mean you believe God didn't write the Torah? If that's the case, why follow it at all? How can it possibly be holy?" I tried to explain. "But if that's the case, what happened at Mount Sinai?" I tried to explain. "If God didn't give the Torah at Mount Sinai, and if God didn't write the Torah in the first place, what about the Creation?" I tried to explain. "I don't understand this 'metaphor' concept, how can that be? Science is the absence of religion; they can't possibly be understood together." I tried to explain. "This is too hard, you only make it harder for yourselves, it's so much easier to believe that God wrote the Torah and that we have to abide by its laws and the laws God gave in the Oral Torah too." Aha!

In a world where fundamentalism and fanaticism are the first thing people think of when they think of religion, it is no wonder that many turn away. But the response in Judaism to the issue of fundamental-ism is not easy. The obligation of participating in the Reform Jewish endeavor—exercising the right to personal religious autonomy—is a challenge. Ongoing study, reflection, and self-assessment, with a con-tinued willingness to adapt and change as the world around us changes, can be exhausting—mentally, emotionally, spiritually. But Reform Judaism is also a Judaism that focuses on how we make our lives meaningful and our relationships with one another more precious. It is the attempt to find holiness in this world, not via rote ritual acts and blind following, but by engaging our own intellect and examining our own spiritual selves as we look into Jewish history and tradition to decide what Judaism means to us.

NOTES

1. For more on Spinoza, see Rifat Sonsino and Daniel B. Syme, *Finding God: Selected Responses*, rev. ed. (New York: URJ Press, 2002).

2. Michael A. Meyer, *Response to Modernity: A History of the Reform Movement in Judaism* (Detroit: Wayne State University Press, 1998), 53–61.

19

THE JEWISH PATH

RABBI MARK WASHOFSKY, PhD

What role does halachah, the Jewish legal tradition, play in Reform
Jewish life?

Some readers might respond to that question with a question
of their own: what role *could* it play? After all, we sometimes hear
Reform Judaism described as a "non-halachic movement." That description is mistaken, but it's an understandable mistake. Our movement originated in the early nineteenth century as an effort to *reform*
the inherited religious practice that had characterized Judaism since
medieval times. And ever since, Reform Jews have not hesitated to
eliminate ritual observances that they no longer find meaningful. As
the Pittsburgh Platform of 1885 so memorably put the point, "We
recognize in the Mosaic legislation a system of training the Jewish
people for its mission during its national life in Palestine, and today
we accept as binding only its moral laws, and maintain only such
ceremonies as elevate and sanctify our lives, but reject all such as
are not adapted to the views and habits of modern civilization." In
our own time, the rhetoric of Reform stresses the importance of
creativity and personal freedom of religious choice ("autonomy"),
and these values conflict with the notion of legal discipline, which
is apparently what halachah is all about.

Still, the description of Reform as a non-halachic movement is mistaken, for two reasons. First, there is no such thing as a non-halachic Judaism. Second, our own Reform religious practice is based in halachah and would be incoherent without it. There is no such thing as a non-halachic Judaism because "Jewish religious life" could not exist in the absence of halachah. Judaism has historically expressed itself largely through mitzvah (religious duty) and *maaseh* (sacred action). We Jews have interpreted the covenant (*b'rit*) of Sinai as a call to action, and we have responded to it in the form of *praxis*, a system of concrete acts that covers almost every aspect of human existence and functions as a mechanism by which to sanctify our world and our lives. Halachah is the *substance* of that praxis, and the halachic texts, the Talmud and the massive body of commentary, codes, and rabbinical responsa that flow from it, are its literary source. It is in the halachic literature that Jewish tradition works out its understandings of the covenant; it is there that all Jewish observance, ritual and ethical, takes its shape.

Put differently, if the question is one of practice—"What does God or Torah or Judaism teach us to *do*?"—the answers are to be found in the halachic literature. Halachah is also the *discourse* of Jewish praxis, the language with which students of Torah create the world of Jewish religious observance in all its structure, content, and detail. Like all languages, this discourse has its unique style and manner of expression. Its predominant characteristic is *argument*; the pages of the halachic literature are chock-full of dispute (*machloket*) and debate (*shakla v'tarya*). This is because the texts of halachah allow for a plurality of readings and interpretations and because no halachic authority, not even the most eminent rabbi, possesses the authority to decide the correct interpretation for all Jews. Students of halachah must therefore *argue* for their conclusions, in order to persuade their colleagues and community that theirs is the best interpretation of Torah's message on any particular issue. This two-thousand-year-old tradition of substance and argument is what we mean by "halachah," and no religious expression that defines itself with any sincerity as "Jewish" can do without it.

Reform Judaism certainly does not do without it. Both the substance and the discourse of halachah are deeply embedded in its history and religious life. The proof of this lies, first of all, in our doctrinal statements. The 1885 Pittsburgh Platform, which as we have seen takes a somewhat dim view of the meaning of "the Mosaic legislation" for modern Jews,[1] has been superseded three times by platforms that display a much more accepting attitude toward traditional observance. The Columbus Platform of 1937, for example, declares that "Judaism as a way of life requires in addition to its moral and spiritual demands, the preservation of the Sabbath, festivals and Holy Days, the retention and development of such customs, symbols and ceremonies as possess inspirational value, the cultivation of distinctive forms of religious art and music and the use of Hebrew, together with the vernacular, in our worship and instruction."[2] The Centenary Perspective (San Francisco, 1976) speaks a great deal about individual autonomy, but it also calls upon Reform Jews to give heed to our "religious obligations." And while previous generations recognized these primarily as ethical duties, they now "extend to many other aspects of Jewish living, including: creating a Jewish home centered on family devotion: lifelong study; private prayer and public worship; daily religious observance; keeping the Sabbath and the holy days; celebrating the major events of life; involvement with the synagogues and community; and other activities which promote the survival of the Jewish people and enhance its existence."[3] By 1999, the "Statement of Principles" adopted in Pittsburgh could say, "Throughout our history, we Jews have remained firmly rooted in Jewish tradition, even as we have learned much from our encounters with other cultures." And to be rooted in the tradition implies that "we are committed to the ongoing study of the whole array of *mitzvot* and to the fulfillment of those that address us as individuals and as a community. Some of these *mitzvot*, sacred obligations, have long been observed by Reform Jews; others, both ancient and modern, demand renewed attention as the result of the unique context of our own times."[4] While each of these platforms differs in its emphasis, they are united in the belief that ritual and religious practice—the very stuff of the halachah—is an essential rather than secondary aspect of Reform religious life and expression.

The second proof of halachah's continued role in Reform Judaism is the fact that over our two centuries of existence, we have produced a considerable halachic literature of our own. During our early decades, Reform-leaning rabbis and scholars wrote halachic responsa in defense of the changes that the movement introduced into the liturgy of the synagogue. Halachic texts featured prominently in the nineteenth-century Reform rabbinical conferences and synods in Germany and in North America, as the movement's leaders debated their stances on Shabbat and festival observance, marriage and divorce, conversion, cremation, and other issues. The records of those arguments are preserved in such sources as the yearbooks of the Central Conference of American Rabbis (CCAR), the rabbinical association of the North American Reform Movement. The CCAR has published rabbis' manuals that, alongside liturgies for life-cycle ceremonies, contain sections entitled "Halachic Notes" that explain and support the CCAR's stances on these issues. Both the CCAR and the Union for Reform Judaism, the association of Reform Jewish congregations in North America, have published a number of guides to Reform Jewish religious practice (*Gates of Mitzvah*, *Mishkan Moeid: A Guide to the Jewish Seasons*, and *Jewish Living*, among others) that, as measured by their endnotes, rely extensively for their material upon the literature of Talmud and Jewish law. And, above all, there are the responsa, rabbinical answers to questions on observance posed by rabbis and laypersons, a genre intentionally patterned after the traditional halachic literature of *sh'eilot ut'shuvot*, "questions and answers." The Responsa Committee of the CCAR was established in 1906 and since has produced over thirteen hundred individual responsa, making this literature by far the single largest body of Reform writing on Jewish religious practice. These responsa, like all responsa, are halachic texts, supporting their decisions by citing Jewish legal sources and arguing their meaning.

How did a supposedly non-halachic movement end up producing such a considerable halachic literature? The answer, of course, is that Reform Judaism is more complex than it is sometimes portrayed. Yes, we emphasize creativity and innovation. Yes, we love our personal freedom of choice. But we have also understood our movement to be *authentically* Jewish, rooted deeply in the soil of the Rabbinic tradition from which it developed. Though we have set aside any number of traditional observances that no longer speak to us, and though we have reimagined many of those that we retain, the basic forms, patterns, and structure of our ritual practice—the synagogue liturgy, Shabbat and festival observance, life-cycle ceremonies—are *Rabbinic*—which is to say *halachic*—in nature. These *Reform* rituals all originate in the Talmudic literature. It is the texts of halachah that define such observances as the reading of the Torah, *Kiddush*, the Passover seder, the sukkah, Chanukah, *b'rit milah*, the marriage ceremony (*chuppah v'kiddushin*), the *Kaddish*, and so many others. The same applies to our ethical practice. Indeed, if there is such a thing as a "Jewish position" on issues of social action, bioethics, business ethics, economic policy, war and peace, and the like, that position will be based somewhere in the halachic literature, for as we have seen, that literature is where Judaism has historically argued and developed its conception of sacred action. Thus, when we Reform Jews talk about our observance, when we seek to identify just what is *Jewish* in our ritual and ethical practice, we necessarily turn for guidance to the halachic literature. We study its texts, debate them, construct arguments with them, and in response to them create halachic texts of our own. Precisely because we see ourselves as an authentically *Jewish* movement, one that for all its openness to change wishes to describe itself in *Jewish* language, the halachic literature is an indispensable element in the substance and discourse of our Reform religious life.

Why then do some people call Reform Judaism a "non-halachic movement"? Perhaps what they really mean is that we are a *non-Orthodox* movement. That is, while Reform Judaism engages with halachah, Jewish law functions differently in our movement than it does in Orthodoxy or in other segments of the Jewish world. One major difference is that the halachic literature functions for us as "guidance, not governance,"[5] exerting no binding constraint upon the religious decisions of a Reform Jewish individual or community. We emphasize pluralism, a variety of approaches to religious practice, over uniformity, so that while our halachic writings offer information and argument, they do not constitute authoritative legal rulings in the traditional sense. Let's illustrate the difference with an example: Imagine that a pregnant Jewish woman asks her Orthodox rabbi whether she is permitted to undergo an abortion to terminate the pregnancy. And let's presume that the rabbi takes his pastoral role seriously, so that he will truly listen to this woman and offer his guidance with all possible empathy and sensitivity. Still, in the Orthodox setting, the rabbi's role is primarily to issue a *p'sak*, a binding halachic ruling. He will consider the circumstances of the case—the medical, psychological, social, and other factors that have led this woman to make her request—in light of his understanding of the halachah on abortion, an understanding drawn from the Talmud, the codes, and the other texts of Jewish law. He will then issue his ruling, either permitting or forbidding the abortion in this case, and the woman is considered morally bound to accept that ruling and to act accordingly. Now imagine that this woman were to present her question to a Reform rabbi. In addition to pastoral counsel, the rabbi may respond with her or his understanding of the teachings of Jewish tradition on abortion. There are a number of Reform responsa that speak to the subject, and they draw upon the same Rabbinic and halachic sources as do Orthodox responsa. Reform halachic writings tend to take a more permissive stance on abortion, approving the procedure in a wider variety of circumstances than do most contemporary Orthodox authorities. But however the Reform rabbi understands the tradition, he or she will not communicate it in the form of a *p'sak*. The Reform Jewish individual, not the rabbi, decides; the woman herself, with the help of the guidance that her rabbi can provide, must ultimately choose for or against the abortion. Another way of saying this is that our halachic writings are "authoritative" only to the extent that they are *persuasive*, that their readers accept their argumentation as presenting the best reading of the message of Torah on any specific topic. This last detail suggests another unique feature of Reform halachah: our legal literature is written by Reform Jews, it is intended for a Reform Jewish audience, and it reflects a consciously Reform perspective. This means, first and foremost, that we interpret halachah through Reform Jewish eyes, on the basis of certain affirmations that we regard as fundamental but that are not necessarily shared by all other Jews; these include our commitments to gender equality, to the moral equality of all humankind, and to the value of diversity and creative expression in religious observance. It also means that our halachic texts, unlike those of other Jews, draw upon the writings of our own Reform predecessors, the teachers to whom we turn for guidance (if not governance) and whose words serve us as persuasive (though not binding) precedents. These features ensure that ours is an unmistakably *Reform* halachic literature, one that enables us to make our own unique contribution to the interpretation of Jewish law, to add our own voice and our own insights to the tradition of argument that is the halachah.

Reform Judaism, in other words, is very much a halachic movement. The texts of the Talmud and the halachah are the foundation of our own religious practice, and the discourse of halachah figures prominently in the way we talk and argue about that practice. Since this is the case, we ought to embrace it and accept our role as the latest link in the chain of the halachic tradition. For if we do not take our part in the study of Jewish law, other voices will by default gain a monopoly over the interpretation of its texts. Let it be our challenge to make sure that doesn't happen, to make sure that *our* interpretations are represented in the argument. In that way we can continue to create—and to bequeath to future generations—a halachah that is truly engaged with the values by which we understand and live our Torah.

NOTES

1. "The Pittsburgh Platform" (1885), http://ccarnet.org/rabbis-speak/platforms/declaration-principles/.

2. "The Guiding Principles of Reform Judaism" (1937), http://ccarnet.org/rabbis-speak/platforms/guiding-principles-reform-judaism/.

3. "Reform Judaism: A Centenary Perspective" (1976), http://ccarnet.org/rabbis-speak/platforms/reform-judaism-centenary-perspective/.

4. "A Statement of Principles for Reform Judaism" (1999), https://ccarnet.org/rabbis-speak/platforms/statement-principles-reform-judaism/.

5. See Joan S. Friedman, *Guidance, Not Governance: Solomon B. Freehof and Reform Responsa* (Cincinnati: Hebrew Union College Press, 2013).

20

MITZVAH/MITZVOT

RABBI CAROLE B. BALIN, PHD

Historically, obedience lay at the heart of Jewish practice. Since the time of the Bible, Jews have understood themselves as commanded (Hebrew root: *tzadi-vav-hei*) by the divine Commander (*m'tzaveh*) to fulfill commandments (*mitzvah*, singular; *mitzvot*, plural) as part of the covenant (*b'rit*) between them and God. In fact, even before the Israelites converged at the base of Mount Sinai to enter into the divine covenant and obligate themselves to practices that would distinguish them as "a kingdom of priests and a holy nation" (Exodus 19:6), God issues an imperative to the entirety of the human species. "Be fertile and increase," the Almighty charges Adam and Eve in the Garden of Eden, "fill the earth and tame it; hold sway over the fish of the sea and the birds of the sky, and over every animal that creeps on earth" (Genesis 1:28). The mandate to procreate and dominate lesser forms of life is incumbent upon all humanity, as are the Seven Noahide Laws, a universal moral code established after the Flood (Genesis 9:8–11). In the Talmud, it is taught that "descendants of Noah" are obligated to seven commandments: (1) to establish courts of justice, (2) to refrain from blaspheming the God of Israel, as well as from (3) idolatry, (4) sexual perversion, (5) bloodshed, and (6) robbery, and (7) not to eat meat cut from a living animal (Babylonian Talmud, *Sanhedrin* 56a).

Whereas Jews have hundreds of commandments in addition to these seven (traditionally, 613 altogether), those of other faith communities who observe the "seven commandments of the descendants of Noah" can meet with God's approval.

It is also the Talmud that introduces the notion that exactly 613 commandments were given to Moses at Mount Sinai. In a pivotal passage credited to Rabbi Simlai, who was active in the Land of Israel at the end of the third and beginning of the fourth century CE, it states:

> Six hundred thirteen commandments were said to Moses, 365 negative commandments paralleling the number of days of the solar year, and 248 positive commandments paralleling the number of discrete segments in the [body of a] human being. (Babylonian Talmud, *Makot* 23b)

While it is debatable as to whether all 613 are explicitly articulated in the five books of Written Torah (*Torah Shebichtav*), after the historical era described in the Bible came to a close, generations of rabbis continued to update, adapt, and generate new commandments—all understood as derived from the original 613 in the Torah.

These legal renderings were initially handed down from rabbi to disciple and memorized, and thus became known as the Oral Law (*Torah Sheb'al Peh*). And they continue to be known as such though their renderings were eventually written down in the Mishnah (200 CE) and then commented on and analyzed by multiple generations of rabbis in the Gemara, which with the Mishnah appears in the Talmuds (Babylonian, ca. 600; Jerusalem, ca. 400). With the increased ritual obligations imposed by the Rabbis, the mitzvot were further divided into two main categories: biblical commandments (*mitzvot d'oraita*) and Rabbinic commandments (*mitzvot d'rabanan*), though both the Written and Oral Law are traditionally understood as divinely ordained and thus equally valent. Later compositions, namely codes and responsa, are further guides for practicing Jews. As is well known and variously interpreted today, once a boy comes of age at thirteen years and a day, it becomes incumbent upon him to fulfill all mitzvot. At twelve years and a day, girls become obligated to negative mitzvot ("thou shall not") but exempt from those affirmative mitzvot ("thou shall") contingent on a particular time or season (*mitzvot aseh shehaz'man g'ramah*), such as thrice-daily worship.

Jewish law (halachah) held sway over most of the Jewish community until the rise of modernity in nineteenth-century Western Europe and America and the concomitant beginnings of Reform Judaism. As Jews and others asserted their individual autonomy, religion came under increasing scrutiny, including especially its presumption of divine revelation. No longer could rabbis assume that adherents to Judaism would abide by religious law because "God said so." Jews instead sought rational and/or provable explanations for practices both inside the synagogue and at home. This new mind-set led to irrevocable changes in the meaning and performance of mitzvot.

In 1885, the Reform Movement in America codified its novel interpretation of mitzvot in the document that became known as the Pittsburgh Platform. In a forthright sleight of hand, the authors overturned the classical Jewish understanding of commanded-ness by obligating Reform Jews only to those mitzvot that either (a) bring about ethical behavior or (b) enhance the spirituality of human existence. In a statement whose reverberations are felt in liberal Jewish circles today, Reform rabbis asserted:

> We recognize in the Mosaic legislation a system of training the Jewish people for its mission during its national life in Palestine, and today **accept as binding only its moral laws, and maintain only such ceremonies as elevate and sanctify our lives**, but reject all such as are not adapted to the views and habits of modern civilization.[1] (emphasis added)

In no uncertain terms, the early Reformers relegated biblical law to a bygone age while elevating moral conduct to the plane of religious duty. This audacious shift from obligatory observance of all mitzvot to a mandate to carry out moral laws represents nothing less than a revolution in Jewish practice and theology. By denying the claim that halachah represents the revealed will of God, Reform Jews were in effect asserting that divine revelation is progressive, akin to inspiration and ultimately concerned with ethics.

The theological underpinnings of such a claim is known as ethical monotheism, the concept that the single incorporeal God's greatest desire is for human beings to act toward one another with justice and mercy. In a phrase: God demands goodness. Thus, for early Reform Jews, if a Jewish ritual enhanced that ethical imperative, it was to be retained; if it appeared to contradict the ethics of religion, it was to be rejected. In many ways, these Reform Jews regarded themselves as having taken a quantum leap from the time of the prophets—in whose call for social morality they saw God's revelation most clearly embodied—to their own time. They looked to the prophetic tradition of the Bible as Judaism's essence and imagined, in the mentalité of the optimistic era in which they lived, that enlightenment and reform would lead to progress and the ever-increasing improvement of the "commonweal," to employ the language of the day.

In addition to utilizing mitzvot as a vehicle for ethical living, the early Reformers, as stated in the Pittsburgh Platform, obligated themselves to "such ceremonies" that would "elevate and sanctify [their] lives." They sought to make their existence holy, to elevate the human spirit from a mere animal nature to one created and reflected in God's image. Deciding which mitzvot to observe became for Reform Jews an exercise in individual autonomy rather than obeisance to halachic renderings of communal authorities (*poskim*). They were full citizens and as such could be champions of the Enlightenment, meaning the individual was the protagonist of his or her life and destiny, and the rational human mind to be the final arbiter of religious decision-making, women and men equally obligated to this pursuit (at least in theory).

At the same time, Reform Jews drew on the aesthetic sensibilities of their surroundings to determine the ways in which they would worship and behave. As full-fledged members of the societies in which they lived, they took their cultural cues from trends in their midst, adapting their sacred practices to cohere with the local ambience and context of their lives. This meant jettisoning particularistic practices, such as the dietary laws of kashrut (they held that it served to separate Jew from others), and the wearing of tallitot and *t'fillin*. They explained that these "originated in ages and under the influence of ideas entirely foreign to our present mental and spiritual state." For them, observance of such mitzvot would "obstruct [rather] than . . . further modern spiritual elevation."

Even as the three revised rabbinical statements of principles issued since 1885 have sought to expand the scope of mitzvot Reform Jews might consider observing (Columbus Platform, 1937; Centenary Perspective, San Francisco, 1976; "A Statement of Principles," Pittsburgh, 1999), the premise of autonomy and regard for spiritual elevation established in the Pittsburgh Platform are very much on display. In the latest iteration of 1999, Reform rabbis call on individuals to commit "to the ongoing study of the whole array of mitzvot and to the fulfillment of those that address us as individuals and as a community." They seek "renewed attention" toward "both ancient and modern" mitzvot. Outright rejection has made way for experimentation, if not out-and-out adoption, of practices formerly regarded as outmoded. Take ritual garb as the most obvious example. Where a century ago, heads and shoulders remained uncovered during prayer, now most men and some women in the pews of Reform temples are wearing *kippot*, and a healthy minority don tallitot. However, while many more Reform Jews are embracing many more practices, and seemingly more traditional ones at that, what is guiding those choices remains the same as a century ago. As enunciated in "A Statement of Principles," "mitzvot [are] the means by which we make our lives holy." Indeed, the entire document is shot through with "the hope to transform . . . lives through holiness (*kedushah*)." Whether prescriptive or descriptive, the most recent promulgation of Reform principles spells out the conduct that elevates a life: "We bring Torah into the world when we seek to sanctify the times and places of our lives through regular home and congregational observance."[2]

At the same time, aesthetics remains the bar by which ritual practices are judged to be meaningful and thus worthy of taking on. As
sensibilities change due to the zeitgeist, so too does the sense of what
is thought to enhance or obstruct spirituality. (Even the currency of
the term "spirituality" among contemporary Jews is an outgrowth of
the period in which we now live.) For sure, the organ of classical Reform Judaism has gone the way of the intellectualized notion of the
God-idea expressed in the Pittsburgh Platform. It has been replaced
with the American musical traditions of folk guitar and African-infused
drumming, or even the strains of the Eastern European klezmer clari-
net, often heard now in less formal worship spaces designed to evoke
a God who will listen closely to our prayers even among the silences
borrowed from Buddhist meditation. Culture and religion have always
been inextricably linked, and Jews are among the greatest consumers
of civilization's accoutrements; they are keenly attuned to and in some
cases the very creators of the spirit of the age. Couple that with general
acceptance, and even unabashed admiration, of Jews by the majority
population, and we can understand why Reform Jews have picked up
practices previously discarded and grown increasingly comfortable with
the idiosyncrasies of their religious traditions.

There are multiple, if not infinite, ways of "doing Jewish" today.
That was not always the case. After the destruction of the Temple in
Jerusalem in 70 CE and before the rise of modernity, Jews were largely
covenantal and performed their Jewishness through regular and steadfast observance of practices and rituals. Emancipation of Jews in the
West led to a new response to identity, including for many a *hyphenated existence*. So Jewish-Americans or Germans-of-the-Mosaic-faith,
to take two examples, along with new citizens of every other emerging,
secular nation-state of the modern era, could elect (or not) to be a part
of a religious community. At least theoretically, the state would no
longer regard the Jews as a corporate body or "nation within a nation"
with specific privileges and obligations owing to that status. Rather,
each individual Jew could decide for him- or herself whether to affiliate voluntarily with a synagogue or follow the mandates of a particular

rabbi. For some Jews, this has meant cordoning off Jewish practice to the private sphere or, in the words of the Hebrew poet Yehudah Leib Gordon, becoming "a man in the streets and a Jew at home." Others still, under the sway of modern nationalism, express Judaism through the ineffable bonds and heartfelt *solidarity* they feel with all Jews world-wide, while Jews of a *universal* orientation, hearkening to the biblical prohibition against "oppress[ing] a stranger, for you know the feelings of the stranger" (Exodus 23:9), act Jewishly by striving toward justice and equality on behalf of all humanity. Jews today stretch the elasticity of Jewish practice in all the above directions and more, far more. Does one "do Jewish" by listening to an online podcast devoted to study of the ethical underpinnings of eco-kashrut? Does Shirah Yoga count? What about marching with Black Lives Matter?

If you were to ask Jews today to define *mitzvah*, most would respond "good deed"—as in "Go visit your aunt in the hospital; it's a mitzvah." While it is true that already in the Talmud the Rabbis provide a secondary definition of *mitzvah* as "an act worthy of praise" in contrast to "commandment" (Babylonian Talmud, *Chulin* 106a), few in our day would interpret calling on one's sick relative as fulfilling the commandment of visiting the sick (*bikur cholim*), and even fewer would regard such an obligation as divinely ordained. This might lead us to ask whether God has become such an abstraction in our time that mitzvah has become devoid of its theological implications. Even in the urgent and worthwhile quest to repair the world (*tikkun olam*)—likely the most widely observed mitzvah among Reform Jews—do we avow a hubris so great that it threatens to overshadow the divine-human partnership inherent in this doctrine? Whatever the case, there can be no doubt that Reform Jews' unassailable right to autonomy has spread to the liberal Jewish community at large. Most allow their own conscience to guide their decisions about how to be and do Jewish. At the end of the day, for most liberal Jews in the twenty-first century, the observance of mitzvot quite literally stands to (human) reason.

According to the Mishnah, in order that the Jews will be granted abundant merit, God gives them copious laws and commandments

(*Mishnah Makot* 3:16). Imagine then God's pleasure in witnessing the Jews of today engaging Jewishly in God-only-knows how many myriad ways.

NOTES

1. "The Pittsburgh Platform" (1885), http://ccarnet.org/rabbis-speak/platforms/declaration-principles/.
2. "A Statement of Principles for Reform Judaism" (May 1999), https://ccarnet.org/rabbis-speak/platforms/statement-principles-reform-judaism/.

21

EATING OUR VALUES

Rabbi Mary L. Zamore

Food sustains us, yet our interaction with our sustenance transcends mere biological practicality. Rather, our food choices reflect our values and identity, express our ethics, and shape our greater society. While liberal Jews may be identified with secular food ways, Reform Judaism offers an accessible path for integrating Jewish identity, ethics, ritual, and spirituality into daily living through kashrut, Jewish dietary practice. In fact, Reform Judaism, with its emphasis on educated individual choice, opens infinite paths for creating a Jewish relationship with food and its production that bridges Judaism and modern living.

Reform Judaism and kashrut may seem an unlikely combination. In fact, Reform is considered to be a movement that does not uphold archaic ritualistic commandments. Such an understanding tempts one to think Reform Jews *should not* keep kosher. After all, if this movement celebrates free will, pluralism, multiculturalism, assimilation, and rationalism, then ancient dietary laws that restrict diets and social interactions are not compatible with Reform's foundational approach to Judaism. However, this analysis does not recognize the power of Reform Judaism to live in both the ancient and modern worlds. While Reform Jews freely explore other parts of Judaism, studying and adopting old Jewish practices, they frequently write off kashrut, taught to believe it is a one-size-fits-all regimen governed by the Orthodox establishment. A better approach to kashrut is to look to this subset of Jewish laws and teachings as the answer to this question: "What is your Jewish relationship with food and its production?" Reframing the understanding of kashrut and its relationship to liberal Judaism multiplies daily opportunities to engage in Jewish practice, drawing one closer to Jewish heritage, identity, mission in the world, and God.

Keeping kosher is often mistaken for an all-or-nothing endeavor. It is that, of course, for those who take an orthopraxy approach to dietary practice. However, Reform Judaism values studying tradition to discover and adopt practices meaningful for our own lives. This picking and choosing, moreover, is ongoing; each of us must return regularly to the study of tradition, to educate ourselves more deeply and consider the state of our lives, which, of course, continually evolve. What feels cumbersome at one stage of life may offer comfort and meaning in another. Regarding Reform Jewish dietary practice, Rabbi Richard Levy points out, "Just as we have set forth models of Shabbat observance for our people, so we can create models of dietary practice, and just as they are free to follow our Shabbat examples, reject them, or find models of their own, so, of course, are they free to do the same with kashrut."[1] As Rabbi Levy notes, Reform Jews celebrate Shabbat every week, observing it in a myriad of permutations. For some, Shabbat means no driving or spending money or using electricity; it is a day of rest, spent at services and within community. For others, the day is marked with prayers, special meals, and such modes of restoration as hiking, attending museums, or social service. For others still, Shabbat dinner may be followed by errands or work on Saturday. All of these are considered to be ways to observe Shabbat, and the term *Shabbat* would never be removed from these various Reform religious practices. Why not the same for kashrut? Reform ideology invites us to a buffet of choices, offering us the opportunity to explore ritual, ethical, and spiritual expressions of Judaism through the food we grow, buy, eat, and serve to each other.

Embodying the essence of Reform, "A Statement of Principles for Reform Judaism," adopted at the 1999 Pittsburgh Convention by the Central Conference of American Rabbis, states:

> We are committed to ongoing study of the whole array of mitzvot and to the fulfillment of those that address us as individuals and as a community. Some of these mitzvot, sacred obligations, have long been observed by Reform Jews others, both ancient and modern, demand renewed attention as the result of the unique context of our own times.[2]

Human beings interact with food at least three times a day. Kashrut, in whatever form embraced as Reform Jews, allows us to encounter and express our Jewish identity and values whenever making choices about food. Thus, food selections become a full expression of Judaism as a living, daily practice. In many ways, there is no better venue than food for Reform Jews to apply the above statement of Reform Jewish belief, as dietary practice can be highly customized, linking traditional Jewish values with modern knowledge, science, and priorities.

The Reform Jewish practice of studying Jewish law and then selecting ritual laws to follow outright or even adapt is not born of laziness or hypocrisy. Rather, it is rooted in the understanding that Jewish law may have a God-given or inspired foundation, but the bulk of Jewish tradition is shaped by history and humanity. With this approach, Jewish laws and teachings (those outside of the ethical laws) retain their sacred nature, but they are not immutable. In considering which laws to practice, it is incumbent upon Reform Jews to preserve their individual and communal connection to the greater community of Jews, as well as their relationship to the non-Jewish world, realizing that personal autonomy needs to be exercised within the context of community.

While some Reform Jews may feel distant from Jewish dietary law, the reality is that many are already engaging in food choices rooted in kashrut or broader Jewish food teachings. When the idea of kashrut as a one-size-fits-all template is removed and individuals are empowered to make Jewish value-based choices regarding food and its production,

Jews are given the freedom to reclaim kashrut in their lives and communities. The following list offers food practices commonly observed by liberal Jews. Each practice is followed by Jewish ritual and ethical values found within the approach to food and its production. The values suggested are not exhaustive, but well illustrate how one practice embodies multiple values. An individual may choose a particular practice because she finds meaning in one of the values it exemplifies. At the same time, she may not even be aware of or drawn to the other values found within the practice.

Eating challah on Shabbat or holidays:
   Continuity with past generations; connection to community; Jewish identity

Reciting *HaMotzi*, the blessing for bread, before eating challah or a meal:
   Ritual observance; recognizing God as the source of food; Jewish identity; community; mindfulness; taking stock of food before eating

Concern about the impact of food production on the environment:
   Bal tashchit, environmental ethics; *sh'mirat haguf*, guarding human health

Refraining from eating pork, either at home or away from home:
   Ritual observance; Jewish identity; community

Practicing vegetarianism or veganism:
   Tzaar baalei chayim, kindness to animals; *bal tashchit*, environmental ethics; *sh'mirat haguf*, guarding human health

Reducing meat consumption:
   Sh'mirat haguf, guarding human health; *tzaar baalei chayim*, kindness to animals; *bal tashchit*, environmental ethics

Promoting better treatment of animals for meat production:
   Tzaar baalei chayim, kindness to animals; *bal tashchit*, environmental ethics; *sh'mirat haguf*, guarding human health

Creating holiday meals using family recipes:
Continuity with past generations, connection to community, Jewish identity

Fasting on Yom Kippur:
Ritual observance; connection with God; repentance for wrongdoings; empathy with those who are food insecure; connection to community; Jewish identity

Observing Passover by eating matzah:
Ritual observance; continuity with past generations; connection to community; Jewish identity

Observance of Passover by refraining from eating *chameitz*, leavened foods like bread, pasta, or cake:
Ritual observance; continuity with past generations; connection to community; Jewish identity

Concern for the rights of the workers who produce our food:
Oshek, preventing oppression of workers; *sh'mirat haguf*, guarding human health; *tzedek*, justice

Eating healthy food:
Sh'mirat haguf, guarding human health; *bal tashchit*; environmental ethics; *tzedek*, justice

Eating organic food:
Sh'mirat haguf, guarding human health; *bal tashchit*, environmental ethics; *oshek*, preventing oppression of workers

Purchasing food at a farm or farmer's market:
Tzaar baalei chayim, kindness to animals; *bal tashchit*, environmental ethics; *sh'mirat haguf*, guarding human health; *tzedek*, justice; connection to community

Contribute money or food to help feed the hungry:
Sh'mirat haguf, guarding human health; *tzedek*, justice; connection to community

Reform Jews, living in a society that features a burgeoning food culture, are likely to engage in quite a few of these practices already. While some clearly reflect aspects of kashrut, others may be a surprising link to ritual law. For example, references to pork or eating matzah on Passover obviously connect to ritual observances. In contrast, fasting on Yom Kippur is a ritual practice, albeit one not usually included when teaching dietary law. However, when "kashrut" is used as a synonym for our Jewish relationship with food and its production, fasting becomes part of the discussion. The choice to refrain from all food as a limited ritual practice is as important in the buffet of kosher choices as what specific foods are or are not eaten on a daily basis.

Including practices of ritual kashrut in our dietary choices can be extremely meaningful for Reform Jews, as they can connect us to God, Jewish identity, and the greater Jewish community. Some may feel comfortable with the 24/7 structure of traditional kashrut, removing the forbidden animals (e.g., pork, shellfish) from their diets and separating milk and meat. These Jews honor God and Jewish tradition by living the commandments daily. Others may choose to follow the tenets of kosher eating only at home, in order to sanctify their home as specifically Jewish, a *mikdash m'at*. However, these Jews may want the freedom to eat unfettered outside their homes. Having this flexibility allows them to retain a connection to Judaism while not completely dictating their eating. Still others may only include kosher practices at uniquely Jewish occasions, such as Shabbat, holidays, and life-cycle events. Each Reform Jew, household, and institution has the joy and privilege of exploring the ritual part of the buffet of choices to select what is meaningful and practical for them. In doing so, liberal Jews connect to Jewish tradition, the greater Jewish community, Jewish identity, and God.

Many of the food practices listed above are informed by ethical values. Our food choices affect the environment, the animals we eat, the welfare of the workers who produce our food, the health of people who live near farms and food factories, and the wellness of people who eat the food, just to name a few. Judaism has always grappled with the ethical values that address these issues. Established in the Torah (Deuteronomy 20:19–20) and then expanded in the Rabbinic laws, the value of *bal tashchit*, environmentalism, has deep roots in Judaism. Literally meaning "do not destroy," *bal tashchit* is frequently associated with the term *shomrei adamah*, "guardians of the earth," referring to the role of humans as described in the Genesis Creation narrative. A concern with environmentalism deeply shapes our food choices as we confront complicated issues like pesticides, monocultures, farm runoff (especially fertilizer) with its impact on our waterways, factory farming's effect on the environment, the carbon footprint of meat production and of global food sourcing, and the role of food packaging in landfills and recycling operations. The applications of Jewish environmental teachings to modern food production are limitless.

Many people in our greater society are finding meaning and value in not eating meat (either red meat or all meat) or in reducing meat consumption. Some of this interest is driven by a concern for personal health. This goal is supported by the value of *sh'mirat haguf*, caring for our bodies, which is rooted in the Jewish teaching that we are all created *b'tzelem Elohim*, "in the image of God" (Genesis 1:27). Upholding this value need not lead to self-preservation in a self-centered manner. Rather, taking good care of ourselves and each other honors God, our Creator. Of course, caring for ourselves or loved ones must not come at the expense of others, since each human being is *b'tzelem Elohim*. For example, although reducing the consumption of factory-farmed red meat to improve cardiovascular health may be supported by Jewish values, patronizing a local farm selling grass-fed beef, but at the expense of polluting neighbors' water wells, is not supported by the same values.

Many people are exploring diets that are meat minimalist, vegetarian, pescatarian, and vegan. Some are motivated by health concerns; some by environmental; some by animal welfare. Of course, human behavior is complex, and rarely does one pick a diet for just one reason. In addition, picking a culinary habit may have positive effects in multiple venues, even if one is drawn to that choice for only one sole cause.

Rooted in the Torah (Exodus 23:5), *tzaar baalei chayim*, the prevention of suffering to animals, commands thought about the treatment of animals in our food production. Whether one is choosing to reduce, eliminate, or ameliorate the impact of animal food sources in one's diet, Jewish teachings can guide these choices. The ritual law of separating milk and meat in kosher eating and food preparation is based on the commandment "You shall not boil a kid [young goat] in its mother's milk" (Exodus 23:19, 34:26; Deuteronomy 14:21). This law, along with two other commandments, teaches humans to have compassion for the animals they will eat. The first additional commandment is "No animal from the herd or from the flock shall be slaughtered on the same day with its young" (Leviticus 22:28). The second is "If, along the road, you chance upon a bird's nest, in any tree or on the ground, with fledglings or eggs and the mother sitting over the fledglings or on the eggs, do not take the mother together with her young. Let the mother go, and take only the young, in order that you may fare well and have a long life" (Deuteronomy 22:6–7). These three biblical commandments together create a powerful foundation for food laws related to *tzaar baalei chayim*. Reflecting these, the kosher slaughter of animals calls for the *shochet*, the person trained to perform kosher butchering, to check the knife he will use to ensure it is perfectly sharp, without dent or imperfection, recite a blessing, and then cut the neck of the animal in one smooth action to ensure a quick death. Whether or not individual Jews choose to adhere to the ritual commandments of separating milk and meat or eating only Jewishly butchered meat, all Jews can learn from the ethical value of *tzaar baalei chayim* and apply it to their food choices.

Fair trade issues have rapidly come to the attention of modern North American consumers, as many NGOs (nongovernmental organizations) have thankfully shed light on the abuse of workers within and beyond our continent. The food industry is unfortunately filled with such abuses. The Torah explicitly forbids *oshek*, the oppression of a worker, commanding, "You shall not defraud your fellow. You shall not commit robbery. The wages of a laborer shall not remain with you until morning" (Leviticus 19:13–14). In addition, "You shall not abuse a needy and destitute laborer, whether a fellow Israelite or a stranger. . . . You must pay out the wages due on the same day" (Deuteronomy 24:14–15). Today, grocery stores offer fair trade choices, most commonly for chocolate, tea, and coffee, and less frequently for nuts and bananas. While these food industries are notorious for their abusive labor practices, they are hardly alone. It is easy to mistake a fork as solely an eating implement, but it is also a tool for social change. When one grabs a meal or snack, it is easy to forget that your daily food choices drive an entire global economic industry. Demanding transparency and ethical treatment of food workers can greatly reduce *oshek* in food production.

When the nutritional and ethical quality of food increases, the cost of that food usually goes up, too. Food that is devoid of these qualities is cheaper because the costs brought upon human health, environment, animals, and society are externalized, meaning that the cost of the food is deferred to other places, like health care, global warming, and impoverished families. Listening to the ancient Jewish teachings and demanding a more ethical production of food will inevitably cause food costs to increase. While some in our society may be able to devote more of their household income to food expenses, it is vital to recognize this is not an option for many in our communities. The value of *tzedek*, social justice, is intrinsic to Judaism, and Reform Judaism has adopted the charge of *tikkun olam*, fixing the brokenness of its world, as its informal motto. Demanding better-quality food and food production for ourselves must include advocating to make high-quality food available to all. This must be combined with *tzedakah* (charity), giving money and food donations to feeding programs. Nutritious, plentiful food is a right, not a privilege.

Judaism teaches a wonderful spiritual practice of gratitude: to say a blessing before eating. The best-known food blessing is *HaMotzi*, which declares, "Blessed are You, Adonai our God, Ruler of the universe, who brings forth bread from the earth." Long before there were low-carb diets, most meals included bread, meaning bread defined the meal and *HaMotzi* was the predominant food blessing. However,

Judaism provides six food blessings, corresponding to the six different categories of food consumed: bread, wine and grape juice, fruits, vegetables, grains, miscellaneous/composite foods. The ritual of blessing food, whether or not adopted on a daily basis, teaches a great deal. Acknowledging God as Creator and Source of sustenance, blessing food requires the practitioner to pause, recognize what he or she is eating, then select the correct food blessing, recite it, and then, finally, eat. This is the point of all of kashrut—pausing and thinking before buying, preparing, and eating food. It is easy to see that this sequence alone could transform our interaction with food, and with the world, into one of meaning and purpose. Reform Judaism provides a beautiful buffet of ritual, ethical, and spiritual choices to shape our interaction with our food and its production. When kashrut defines our Jewish relationship with food, our Jewish traditions, laws, spirituality, and values give meaning to our lives every time we shop, cook, or eat.

NOTES

1. Richard N. Levy, "Kashrut: A New Freedom for Reform Jews," in *The Sacred Table: Creating a Jewish Food Ethic*, ed. Mary L. Zamore (New York: CCAR Press, 2011), 69.

2. "A Statement of Principles for Reform Judaism" (May 1999), https://ccarnet.org/rabbis-speak/platforms/statement-principles-reform-judaism/.

22

SHABBAT AS A SPIRITUAL PRACTICE

Rabbi Lisa L. Goldstein

Jewish tradition offers us an extraordinary gift. Every week we receive a day, Shabbat, that is surrounded with words like "love," "rest," "pleasure," "blessed." It is a day that is filled with rituals that have the potential to become a deep and sustaining spiritual practice.

For a ritual to be elevated to spiritual practice, we begin with setting an intention. What inner transformation are we seeking by engaging in this ritual? What are we hoping for when we begin observing Shabbat?

Our tradition offers two suggestions for an intention. We are commanded in regard to Shabbat in the Ten Commandments. But when we look at the fourth commandment, the commandment about Shabbat, in the two versions of the Ten Commandments in the Torah, we notice they are not exactly the same. In Exodus (20:8–11) we are told to remember Shabbat because God created the world in six days and then rested on the seventh day, blessing it and making it holy. In Deuteronomy (5:12–14) we are told to keep the Sabbath because God liberated us from Egypt with a strong hand and an outstretched arm.

One intention for Shabbat could be to remember it in such a way that we are re-created, refreshed, renewed. As the Torah tells us (Exodus 31:17), God rested on the seventh day and *vayinafash*—was re-ensouled. Our practices on Shabbat can be for the sake of feeling anew the soul within us.

Another intention for Shabbat could be to keep it in such a way that we feel liberated. There are classically thirty-nine main categories of work from which the Rabbis determined we should refrain on Shabbat. Dr. Michael Chernick once pointed out that you can sort these categories as being every task necessary to do three things: bake a loaf of bread (e.g., plowing the ground, harvesting, threshing, mixing, lighting the fire), make an article of clothing out of wool or linen (e.g., shearing, carding, weaving, sewing, dying), and build a structure (e.g., sawing, carrying, hammering). In other words, the categories of work are the tasks required to provide for our food, clothing, and shelter, our basic survival. For one day we are free to put down those tasks and investigate: What are we surviving for?

We can explore some of the rituals of Shabbat through the lens of these intentions—renewal and liberation—to see how we might observe Shabbat as a practice and how it can help us remember to remember.

Light. We usher in Shabbat by kindling candles. Just as the sunlight is fading and the darkness is beginning to thicken, we deliberately and intentionally kindle light.

It's not that we are trying to banish the darkness. After all, darkness is where beginnings begin—the darkness of the womb, the darkness of the new day that begins with nightfall, the darkness of the new month with the new moon. God is the one who creates both light and darkness, each in its own season. So why do we kindle light?

Perhaps it is to remind us of the mystical myth of Creation in which before the world came into being, Divine Presence was all that there was. In order to create the sense of separateness that is necessary for relationship, God contracted (*tzimtzem*) divine light into vessels so that there could be space for time and space and things as we know it. But something went terribly wrong and the vessels shattered, like very hot water poured into a delicate glass. The Divine Light went scattering out, and the shards of the vessels did too.

This story is one way that we can explain why we sometimes don't feel Divine Presence, why we feel stuck. It's not that the divine light isn't there; it is just that a fragment of the broken vessel is hiding it. If we were able to peek under or around the fragment that is blocking it, we would see the light shining, just as the clouds might obscure the moon or the stars.

I often arrive at Shabbat with the fragments piled up all around me—the things I didn't finish at work, the rush of preparing the meal, hoping it will be tasty, the accumulated weariness of the week. When I light the Shabbat candles, I strike the match and light appears where it was not just a moment before. I heighten the experience. I increase the darkness; I close my eyes to say the blessing. I pause to bring into my consciousness my family members, near and far, others I am thinking about, those in need of blessing. I feel my heart begin to open and lighten. Then I open my eyes. And there is light!

Prayer—*L'chah Dodi*. The contemporary master teacher Parker Palmer has described the soul as a tough, resilient, but shy wild animal. It wants to communicate to us about what is most important, but it doesn't show itself unless we sit quietly and wait for it to emerge. The Chasidic master Kalonymus Kalman Shapira taught something similar. The soul cries out to us to be heard, but we have a hard time listening. We confuse the stirrings of the soul with hunger or desire for other distractions and turn away to eat or drink or play video games.

Either way the soul can't quite find the right environment in which to be appreciated.

The tradition teaches that we receive a second soul on Shabbat, but Rabbi Arthur Green suggests that perhaps it's not that we actually get something extra. Instead, we have the opportunity to fully welcome the soul we have to fully show herself, because Shabbat is the time we have the space and the inclination to listen.

L'chah Dodi is the liturgical invitation for the soul to emerge. Traditionally there are six psalms that precede *L'chah Dodi* in the Friday night liturgy. I love singing them, because the melodies speak directly to the soul in ways that words don't always. Then, as we begin singing

L'chah Dodi, I direct the beautiful words to my soul, my own secret self, that part that wants to be seen and appreciated just for who she is. "You don't have to sit in the valley of tears any longer. Arise from the dust, put on your most splendid garments," I urge her. "Awake, awake, your light has arrived! You can sing!"

By the time we get to "Enter, O bride, enter, O bride," I can feel the light shining in my face. She has arrived. I have been re-ensouled.

Prayer—Gratitude. Perhaps the practice that best contains both Shabbat intentions of renewal and liberation is engaging with the liturgy, the prayers that are specific for Shabbat. There are many small differences between the weekday prayers and those we say on Shabbat, but the one glaring distinction is in the *Amidah*, the "standing prayer," the heart of both the morning and evening liturgy and, indeed, of almost the entirety of the afternoon service.

During the week, the *Amidah* is made up of nineteen prayers. There are three introductory prayers and three to conclude. The middle thirteen prayers are all petitions. We open up to God and say: This is what we need. We need wisdom and forgiveness; we need a decent livelihood and a government based in law; we need leaders who are righteous and a vision of better days. We need our needs to be heard.

But on Shabbat, these thirteen prayers are missing. Instead we have one that reminds us of the holiness of Shabbat.

It's not that we don't have needs on Shabbat. But on Shabbat we are cultivating a different orientation, one of gratitude, one in which we already have everything we need. The Rabbis called this a "taste of the world-to-come."

On Shabbat we hearken back to that moment of Creation when everything was finished. Nothing else needed to be added. It was all "very good" (Genesis 1:31). And we remember that we are free. We can set down the burden of providing for ourselves and others. Instead of feeding the anxiety of what we do not have, we luxuriate in what we do have: a day of rest, the opportunity to pursue holiness, the ability to give thanks.

The Sages taught that during the weekdays, we should be specific when we get to the petitions. We should name the people we seek healing for; we should add personal prayers, if necessary, if our livelihood is not what we need it to be. On Shabbat, we can do this with gratitude. During the concluding prayers of the *Amidah*, there is one specifically for giving thanks. I usually stop at that point and add my own words: "Here are five things I am grateful for on this Shabbat." I try not to repeat what I said last time; I am very specific. It is my own gratitude journal, spoken in prayer with a grateful heart.

Food. Hillel and Shammai, the sages of the early Rabbinic period, had different philosophies in how they shopped for Shabbat. When Shammai went to the market, he kept his eyes open for something special, something particularly fine and delicious, that he could bring home for Shabbat. It was his way of honoring the day. Hillel, on the other hand, enjoyed delicacies whenever he found them. That way every day can be special; every day can be holy (*M'chilta* on Exodus 20:7).

Even though Hillel's and Shammai's approaches, as usual, seem diametrically opposed to each other, they are both wise. Eating on Shabbat is not like eating on other days of the week. It is not (only) for the sake of satisfying our physical hunger; after all, Shabbat is the day we pause to consider what survival is for. So how do we set this meal apart?

Shammai's answer is to focus on the pleasure of eating itself. What an extraordinary gift that the act of eating, which gives us the nutritional energy we need to get through our day, can actually be an act of such pleasure, involving all our senses: the delightful colors, the mouth-watering fragrances, the smooth and crunchy textures, the varied tastes! Most of the time we eat without paying any attention to these things at all. By choosing special food, we can pay special attention and marvel at the joy of nourishing our bodies.

Hillel's response is that we can actually pay attention all the time, if we are so inclined. What makes a Shabbat meal special is more than what is on our plates. It is the leisurely pace, the warm company, the possibility of conversation that is different, slower, deeper. Perhaps it is singing. Those are the things that are harder to replicate on the busy workdays. It is not what we eat but how we eat that makes Shabbat meals an act of liberation.

When we sit down to a Shabbat meal, we can take care to eat food that is tasty, healthy, special. We can pause to really taste it, to marvel at all the factors that had to align in order for this food to end up on our plate. We can express gratitude through a blessing to the One and also in our own words to those who helped make the meal possible. And we can bring awareness to all the other things that contribute to the holiness of the meal in addition to the food. What joy to eat together on Shabbat!

Community. It is, of course, possible to observe Shabbat alone, and many of us do, whether by choice or not. However, celebrating Shabbat in community is a powerful practice.

According to Genesis, Creation took place through a series of separations: light from darkness, sea from dry ground, all the different living things, each kind separate. And yet, the Sages sensed it wasn't quite that simple. They noted that God did not say, "It is good," on the second day and suggested that it was because on the second day, God divided the waters into upper waters and lower waters. The lower waters wept at being separated from the upper waters and from God, and in deference to their grief, God refrained from the utterance of approval (*B'reishit Rabbah* 5:4).

Separation is a necessary—and important—part of this world, and yet, it is also the first, and perhaps primary, source of suffering. During the week we go about in our unique roles and our distinct lives. Hopefully we have created good things in our separateness through our words and our actions.

When we come together with our community on Shabbat, we reenact the Creation story. We can come together as one community in prayer and song. That is not to say that each of us gives up our unique perspective and stories. But it is often what kids love most about camp: the Shabbat song sessions, when everyone is in white and all the unique voices join together into something that is greater than the individual parts. It's not about losing our selves, but instead about rediscovering the deep interconnectedness between us. It can lead us to say with conviction, "It is very good."

Torah. There is no rule that we may study Torah only on Shabbat; in fact, traditionally we read Torah publicly at least three times a week and are encouraged to study every day. But on Shabbat, we have the longest and most formal Torah reading and often unique opportunities to study and learn. Why?

On Shabbat we have a special opportunity to dip into the joy of learning and of recognizing anew the freshness that is in our Torah. It is another way of being both re-created and liberated, all at the same time. On Shabbat, we don't have to achieve; we don't have to prove anything to anyone. We don't even have to know. We can explore what we don't know, and this can lead us to the actual joy of learning.

Melvin Konner, in his seminal book *The Tangled Wing*, suggests that one of the greatest sources of human joy is resolving cognitive dissonance, when we see things suddenly in a new and fresh way and think, Aha! Rabbi Levi Yitzchak of Berdichev, the great Chasidic master, took it a step further in a sermon on Rosh HaShanah. He taught that we are created anew with every breath. He agreed that there is no joy in the world of routine. When we forget that things are new every moment, we may lose our enthusiasm for spiritual service, for the wonder of life itself. But as our morning prayers remind us, God, in great goodness, renews the work of Creation every day continually, moment to moment. Our Torah study on Shabbat reminds us as well.

Studying Torah on Shabbat is a practice for remembering that we can always learn, that things are always new, that there can be great joy in new things. One way I engage in that practice is to look for the passage that sparkles to me, not because I already know it, but because I never noticed it before. I make a list of questions about things I truly don't understand—and may never understand. If we focus on every-thing we already know in what the Torah teaches, we may experience less joy. Sometimes astonishing new insights arise. I feel the joy rise with them.

Rest. Rabbi Kalonymus Kalman Shapira, a great Chasidic master who died during the Holocaust, wrote that one reason we are not aware of divinity around us all the time is that we are too distracted. He wrote this in Poland almost one hundred years ago; imagine what he would think about our lives now!

We often wedge in Shabbat amid all the other things in our lives we are balancing—soccer games, travel, yoga classes. Even a traditional Shabbat can be filled with rushing and distractions. Quick—finish preparations, rush to synagogue, get the meal on the table, hurry to Torah study, when is *Havdalah*? But the beauty of Shabbat can be found in rest.

Rest can be a nap. Rest can be a walk in nature. Rest can be a quiet conversation or meditation or a good book. Rest is intentionally setting aside, just for now, the distractions so that the heart can open, the mind relax, and a different awareness emerge.

Yearning. There is a Shabbat practice that is not part of many Reform communities, but that is a beautiful and important offering. Before *Havdalah*, the ceremony with wine, fragrant spices, and candlelight that brings Shabbat to a close, in some communities there is a custom of coming together for *s'udah sh'lishit*, a "third meal," the other two being Shabbat dinner and lunch.

But this meal is not about the food. It takes place in the tender hours toward the end of the day, when the light is fading, the sun is setting. There is a softness, a quietness, and a kind of sadness even that enter the room. Shabbat is coming to a close, but it's not gone yet.

These moments are like the ones just before saying goodbye to a beloved when you wish you didn't have to say goodbye, even if you know you will see each other again. They awaken tremendous yearning. So often in our spiritual life we cultivate the capacity for gratitude. We usually shy away from yearning, and yet, when the heart is fully open, yearning is often what comes to the surface.

Yearning is different from desire. Desire is usually focused on an object, human or otherwise, that we may or may not acquire. Desire demands to be satisfied. But alas, it rarely leads to happiness. We often get bored with what we possess—and we experience great suffering when we do not get what we desire.

Yearning, however, is a spiritual stance, an orientation of longing to connect with the fundamental love that underlies everything. It is not about obtaining anything or getting any answer. In fact, yearning is its own answer. Shabbat can be that time when we have experienced the connection to love. When we cultivate yearning, we cultivate our capacity to be open to finding that love everywhere, even during the days of the week that lie ahead.

To practice yearning toward the end of Shabbat, we might sit as the light is fading and not turn on the lights. We might watch as the light dims. We might sing simple sweet songs that touch the heart. We might simply sit quietly. We might notice what thoughts arise, welcoming each one as Shabbat comes to an end.

Shabbat is such a counterintuitive offering. It is an invitation to slow down, open up, reconnect with each other and with God and with our own beautiful souls. These practices are all invitations, bundled or separately, and of course, there are many others as well. May they help us make Shabbat truly holy and a transformational source of meaning and joy.

23

TAKE BACK YOUR TIME

RABBI MARK DOV SHAPIRO

Do you "run" through life so quickly that you sometimes feel breathless? Are you always busy?

If so, Judaism offers you an alternative. Instead of noise, think quiet. Instead of 24/7, think 1 in 7. Consider the possibility that at least one day in seven, you give yourself permission to pause.

Or to put the matter in more traditional terms, try Shabbat. That is the gift that Judaism offers you. Shabbat means stepping outside the demands of our everyday schedules to take a break. If electricity drives our world with bright lights that make night into day and replenish our electronics with never-ending power, Shabbat suggests stepping away from those speeding electrons. Shabbat is about unplugging. You light candles Friday evening to declare that sometimes a beautiful flame is all we need—especially if the flame comes with friends, family, and something good to eat.

But, you may say, here's the challenge. Although Shabbat the way you describe it sounds tempting, the real Shabbat I have heard about is much more severe. It's full of dos and don'ts to complicate my already busy life.

Here is where Reform Judaism offers us a way to be observant without losing our sense of self. It is true that there is an extensive legal tradition surrounding Shabbat. The halachah (Jewish legal tradition) pays great attention to the rules of Shabbat observance. But the rules aren't meant to obscure the purpose of Shabbat. In fact, because Reform Jews recognize that many of the rules developed over time, we believe that they can continue to change in our time. What we are after is the soul of Judaism's seventh day. Capture that soul and you have something that is as contemporary and personal as you could want.

To do that, let's start by reading two passages from the Torah.

The first comes from the Shabbat commandment in Deuteronomy 5:15: "Remember that you were a slave in the land of Egypt and the Eternal your God freed you from there . . . therefore the Eternal your God has commanded you to observe Shabbat."

The second text teaches that the Jewish people are called to observe Shabbat because "in six days the Eternal made heaven and earth, and on the seventh day [God] ceased from work and was refreshed" (Exodus 31:17).

Take these two texts together and you begin to define the core of Shabbat. From the Book of Deuteronomy we learn that Shabbat is observed by calling to mind the end of Egyptian slavery and the gift of freedom that came with it. From the Book of Exodus we learn that Shabbat rest has to do with feeling refreshed. Combine freedom, rest, and refreshment, and you learn that Shabbat is a day to feel liberated from weekday obligations. Shabbat is for activities that bring a sense of renewal.

That is why Shabbat is so perfectly associated with the light of candles. After all, Shabbat could quite literally be a "dark" experience. The Torah actually says that fires are not to be lit on Shabbat (Exodus 35:3), which could have meant that when the sun set on Friday, Jewish homes had to settle into a shadowy seventh day. But the Rabbis, who gave shape to Judaism around the turn of the eras, had a more positive idea of Shabbat. If it was to be a day for liberation and replenishment, they taught that Shabbat had to be welcomed with light.

Shabbat, you might say, was to begin with a smile.

And celebrating Shabbat with a sense for the blessings it might bring could involve activities like some of the following. They are written in the first person because they are comments from Reform Jews describing their personal approach to Shabbat.

I don't open mail on Shabbat so that I can be free of bills and expectations.

Not wearing a watch on Shabbat reminds me that Shabbat is an island in time.

I listen to Shabbat music while driving home from work on Friday afternoon.

I use different dishes on Shabbat. Even if we're eating pizza, the dishes tell me this day is different.

When we do the blessings around the Friday evening table, we often make a FaceTime or Skype connection with family who live elsewhere.

I like writing a letter (with real ink and paper!) to someone with whom I've lost contact.

I like to go to a museum on Shabbat. Museums are places that touch something other than the "weekday" part of me. They lift me up.

But now we return to that question above: As sweet as these Shabbat activities are, can they truly be considered appropriate ways to observe the "real" Shabbat? Aren't activities like writing a letter or going to the museum the kind of "work" forbidden on Shabbat?

It all depends on what Jewish tradition means by "work" on Shabbat. Once again, we go back to Torah, where we are told, "Six days you shall labor and do all your work, but the seventh day is a Sabbath of the Eternal your God: you shall not do any work" (Exodus 20:9–10; Deuteronomy 5:13–14).

Although the meaning of this commandment seems clear, the Rabbis of the Mishnah and Talmud (first to fifth centuries CE) felt that neither Exodus 20 nor Deuteronomy 5 were specific enough about the kinds of work forbidden on Shabbat.

Elsewhere in the Torah and the rest of the Bible the Rabbis did find prohibitions against certain activities. For example, baking and cooking (Exodus 16:23), buying, selling (Nehemiah 13:15–17), and pursuing your occupation (Isaiah 58:13) are not to be done on Shabbat.

Despite that, the Rabbis felt that a broader definition of "work" was required. To that end, they developed a system consisting of no fewer than thirty-nine categories of work plus innumerable sub-categories (*Mishnah Shabbat* 7:2).

Basing itself on the Talmud, later Jewish legal literature continued to define the meaning of work on Shabbat. In modern times, for example, this has involved dealing with such matters as the use of electricity and the automobile. (Both require "kindling a flame" either with a spark for the flow of the current or a spark that ignites the car's gasoline. Consequently, both are not permissible according to the halachah.)

These don'ts regarding Shabbat are voluminous. But if the soul of Shabbat has to do with joy and refreshment, why does the halachah restrict rather than encourage so many behaviors?

The Rabbis very simply devoted so much effort toward defining work on Shabbat because it is not easy to define what rest on Shabbat is supposed to be. The Rabbis knew resting on Shabbat couldn't involve merely taking the day off or sleeping late. The absence of activity alone couldn't create Shabbat. On the contrary, Shabbat is very much associated with involvement in friendship and community plus prayer and study in the synagogue. That spirit of Shabbat is lively and full of stimulation.

To ensure, however, that weekday activities didn't overwhelm the seventh day's rest, the Rabbis devoted attention to prohibiting activities that might intrude on Shabbat. Like foresters who want to clear an opening in the forest, the Rabbis used the Torah's injunction against work on Shabbat to build a fence that held back anything resembling weekday occupations and diversions.

Shabbat became the protected clearing when whatever was not work could blossom. That would be rest.

If the week is for the business of life—for making our mark on the world—Shabbat is the opposite. We step back from the world to let it be.

Imagine a seesaw going up and down all week. Imagine the same device when left alone. It slows down. It reaches equilibrium. That is Shabbat rest.

As Harvey Cox, professor at Harvard University, puts it, "[The Sabbath] means being fully aware of the apple tree but having no judgments, plans, or prospects for it."

If this is what the halachah is all about, why not follow it?

You can do so. Reform Judaism invites Jews to explore the fullness of our historic tradition. At the same time, most Reform Jews depart from traditional definitions of Shabbat work and rest because we believe that they do not represent the final word on Jewish practice. We maintain that our Sages only developed definitions of work and rest in response to the historical circumstances of the Jews they knew. The Sages themselves even acknowledged that much of their Shabbat legislation was loosely related to the Torah (*Mishnah Chagigah* 1:8). Nevertheless, they continued refining their ideas of Shabbat because the biblical Shabbat had to be clarified if it was to be followed in their postbiblical world.

Reform Jews believe that the same holds true for us today. We are "commanded," as it were, to continue what Jews have done for centuries. We need to develop definitions of work and rest that draw on the spirit of Shabbat while still resonating with contemporary life.

Thus a Reform Jew might Skype with family and friends on Shabbat because the seventh day is about who we humans are at heart. We live at our fullest in relationships. By the same token, another Reform Jew might use pen and paper to write a letter because the core of Shabbat involves human connectedness. Another Reform Jew could also go to the museum (even if he needs to drive there) because the museum is so clearly not a workday proposition. No benefit accrues. Art sets the mind free. In a way, art is Shabbat.

This is Reform Judaism when it comes to the seventh day—with one major caveat. Reform Jews do not function in a vacuum. Although we may depart from ancient practices, we live with a sense of responsibility to the continuum of Jewish experience.

Therefore, we try to balance our creativity in practice with the desire to conserve and adapt what speaks to us from the past. We are free to be novel, but proud as well to maintain our connections with the best of the Jewish past.

In fact, this essay is not suggesting that visiting the museum and setting aside your watch are in and of themselves Shabbat activities. Yes, they do make Shabbat sense if you want to tap into the spirit of the day. But for these and other new "rituals" to be more than pleasant ways for stepping away from the busyness of life, they need to be part of something larger. They should be part of the Shabbat whole that takes its shape from the home and synagogue ceremonies to which we now turn our attention. What might otherwise merely be a leisure activity becomes an expression of Shabbat when it complements the sacred acts that are part of Jewish tradition—from Friday evening's candle lighting to Saturday evening's *Havdalah*/concluding service.

Fear not.

If you and your spouse are too busy for fixed ceremonies at fixed times, if you're spouse isn't Jewish, if you're single, if you're retired and more or less "free" every day, if you don't feel religious, Shabbat can still be yours.

The call for awareness of the classic Shabbat rituals is not meant to squelch your soul. Because Jews and Jewish households come in so many different shapes, Reform Judaism acknowledges that one size doesn't fit all.

Nevertheless if something about Shabbat intrigues you, then you ought to become familiar with the historic customs that have sustained Shabbat over the centuries.

Consider these ten steps (among many) that can make your seventh day unique. Try one. Try five. Choose your order.

Be there. If you are just beginning to approach Shabbat, being home for dinner may constitute a major accomplishment on your part. Leaving work in time to prepare the Friday evening meal or at least being present when the others in your household sit down to eat may mean thinking about Friday's schedule one day or possibly several days in advance. It may mean breaking old work habits to make space for a new Jewish commitment.

Candles. We've spoken about the symbolism of candles on Friday evening. To make Shabbat, then, light candles in your home. Try it once. Or better still, to help yourself create a new custom, try an experiment. Commit yourself to candles for perhaps four weeks. Promise yourself to light candles under almost all circumstances (before or even after sunset). This discipline might be just what you need to begin to make candles (and Shabbat) a habit.

You can learn the blessing and its history by consulting the book *Gates of Shabbat,* which is the Reform Movement's guide to all facets of Shabbat.

Wine and bread. Friday evening's blessings also include the *Kiddush* (the blessing over wine) and *HaMotzi* (the blessing over bread). *Gates of Shabbat* will give you the details. You'll find the blessings there in Hebrew, in transliteration, and in English.

Tzedakah. It is customary to make charitable donations when Shabbat arrives. That usually means placing change into a collection box, although you may want to broaden the moment by inviting the people at your table to discuss where to give the *tzedekah.* Some people save the charitable requests they receive in the mail and bring them to the table for just this kind of conversation.

Conversation. Before or after dinner, you might invite whoever is present to complete this statement: "Something good happened to me this week. It was. . . ." Alternatively, each person could be invited to complete the following: "I'm proud this week that . . ." or "I'm grateful this week that. . . ."

Children will enjoy this opportunity. The prompts can also help adults cultivate a sense of mindfulness about their week.

Synagogue/temple. Where your "home" celebration is private, the synagogue enlarges the focus to include the community. The synagogue is the place where Jews of all kinds can pray together, study together, and simply be together. That is why Shabbat ought to involve finding a place for yourself at the synagogue.

If you are someone who wants to pray, you'll discover that different synagogues offer services on both Friday evenings and Saturday mornings. Worship styles vary in fascinating ways. Experiment and you may find a match for your soul.

On the other hand, you may be someone who tends toward study. Most synagogues offer Torah study on Shabbat. Find a setting you like. Go weekly. Go monthly. Do the same with services. Go weekly if you can. Otherwise, find your own pattern and try to attend with some regularity.

Most of all, consider the synagogue from the perspective of community. Shabbat means placing yourself among Jews. Be with them. Community is good for the soul.

Making Shabbat different. If you want to create an aura around your Shabbat, it helps to avoid certain activities that are part of your everyday experience. Thus, some Reform Jews choose not to spend money on Shabbat. They might purchase the entrance ticket to a museum but would fill up the gas tank on Friday so that they don't have to buy gas on Shabbat. For others, Shabbat means a day when the computer is turned off. Some avoid errands and housework.

Shabbat becomes a no-chore day when you "rest" by taking a break from the world of demands.

Friends and family. All week you may be at work. You pass your days with acquaintances. Make Shabbat a day for something deeper. Use it to connect with family and friends—the people who are truly central to your life.

Havdalah. Shabbat lasts through Saturday, and *Havdalah* is the brief service that draws on candles, wine, and spices to conclude the day. Although *Havdalah* may be unfamiliar to many people, it is a very accessible service you can do at home or anywhere you choose. It also highlights Judaism's focus on repairing the world and hoping for a messianic time.

Learn. Perhaps Shabbat can find its way into your heart via learning. Consider Saturday afternoon for that purpose. Delve into Jewish literature—nonfiction, fiction, or poetry. Explore the weekly Torah portion using *The Torah: A Modern Commentary* or *The Torah: A Women's Commentary*. Or make a choice to use your computer on Shabbat and access the Reform Movement's website (www.reformjudaism.org) for a collection of commentaries on Torah.

Take back your time. That is one way to understand Shabbat in our running, hurried, jostled world. Shabbat is the antidote to our speed. It slows us down and offers the possibility of making us healthier in both body and soul.

On the other hand, Shabbat is also specifically Jewish. It draws on Jewish symbols, prayers, and values. When you observe Shabbat, you are not merely talking about Judaism in theory. You encounter it in reality. You chant blessings, study Torah, and meet other Jews. On a weekly basis, you experience life as a Jew. You can grow as a Jew.

You can even come to understand what the early Zionist thinker Achad HaAm meant when he taught, "More than [the people of] Israel has kept Shabbat, Shabbat has kept [the people of] Israel."

In other words, Shabbat has been good for the Jews over time, and it can be good for you as a Jew today.

24

CEREMONY VERSUS RITUAL

RABBI STEPHANIE M. ALEXANDER

A Chasidic tale is told of two sages, Rabbi Elimelech and Rabbi Zusiya, who wondered as to what the holiness one feels on Shabbat should be attributed. Is it a function of the day itself—are the twenty-five hours of Shabbat intrinsically holy? Or is it a function of what one does on Shabbat—the rituals and intentionality with which one observes the day?

So they derived an experiment: They would "make Shabbat" on a weeknight, a regular old Wednesday for instance, and see what happened. All day Wednesday they went about their preparations. They set the table with a beautiful white cloth and all of their finest silver. They cooked an elaborate feast of their favorite Shabbat foods. They put on their Shabbat clothes and *shtreimels* (fur hats). And when the sun set that Wednesday evening, they lit the Shabbat candles, blessed the Shabbat wine, sang Shabbat songs.

So what happened? Well, there are two different endings. According to one account, after they concluded their "Shabbat," Elimelech and Zusiya looked at each other with trepidation—for they had indeed experienced holiness on this weekday, and they were frightened. It appeared that it was not the Sabbath day that held the secret to holiness at all. Anxious about their findings, they immediately set off to consult with a wise teacher and told him of their experiment. "Do not fear," he said. "The preparation of the heart has the true power to draw the light of Sabbath holiness down to earth." Shabbat is more than chronology; it's a matter of intentionality.

Yet, a second account of the same story tells that Elimelech and Zusiya were unsuccessful in their bid to bring the holiness of Shabbat to a weekday. In this version, they recognize that Shabbat—and all of the holidays—are not merely the sum total of the rituals that we perform and the prayers we recite. Only when combined with the auspicious nature of the set days themselves do rituals give Jewish observances their true beauty and power—only then do they bring holiness.

These two alternative endings to the story reflect an ancient debate in Jewish thought and practice between *keva*, the prescribed times and parameters set for rituals, and *kavanah*, approaching ritual with intentionality and, to a degree, spontaneity. The tension between the two continues to the present day. Tradition prescribes that a baby boy be entered into the covenant of the Jewish people with the ritual of circumcision on the eighth day; but the boy's grandparents live hundreds of miles away and could be included in the celebration if it were delayed by a week or two. A congregation would like to plan a festive, family-oriented service for Simchat Torah, but the holiday falls on a Wednesday night and Thursday; if they moved the service to the weekend, far more families would be likely to attend.

Reform Judaism has been sensitive to the rhythms and routines of the modern calendar, and certainly when spontaneous occasions for worship and ritual arise, we encourage religious creativity. It's this innovative spirit of *kavanah* that has led to the recognition of new milestone moments, such as leaving for camp, beginning to drive, transitioning gender, or saying goodbye after a visit with a loved one in long-term care. The creative spirit of *kavanah* allows us to utilize existing rituals for new purposes—incorporating *Tashlich* into a recovery program, performing *Havdalah* during the proceedings of a divorce, visiting a mikveh on the journey to healing. And it is the embrace and value of *kavanah* that have led us to look at our siddurim, our prayer books, with fresh eyes and produce new liturgy that seeks to speak to and for diverse spirits in a modern age.

However, Reform Judaism has also understood that embracing *kavanah* cannot come at the expense of *keva*, for it is the fixed routine of prayer and ritual that teaches us their value and trains us in their practice. As Dr. Eugene Borowitz (*z"l*) taught, "The man who objects that he cannot pray on schedule often does not pray at all." A child who learns to recite the *Sh'ma* or sing *Hashkiveinu* before she goes to sleep each night learns that words can dispel the fears and anxieties of darkness. A boy who learns to say *Shehecheyanu* on the first day of school, when he loses his first tooth, and when he learns to ride a bike knows that no milestone should go unnoticed. A family that celebrates the festivals that marked the ancient harvests of spring, summer, and fall will be more attuned to the ways nature and the seasons signal the passage of time all year long.

So perhaps, in the evolving, yet rooted, spirit of Reform Judaism, we might suggest a third ending to the Chasidic tale: Following the conclusion of their Wednesday evening "Shabbat," Elimelech and Zusiya looked at each other and were truly astonished—for they had indeed experienced holiness on this otherwise ordinary day. They went to the wise teacher and told him of their experience. "Do not fear," he said. "The preparation of the heart has the true power to draw the light of Sabbath holiness down to earth." But this time he continued and instructed them further. "Go home and, with my permission, treat this Friday night and Saturday as any other. Do not light candles, do not recite the Shabbat prayers or sing Shabbat songs—act as if this Shabbat is any other weekday."

The two rabbis did as they were instructed, and when the sun set on Friday night they simply sat down as they would to any other meal. Elimelech began to say the prayers over the table's candles, and Zusiya had to silence him with the reminder that tonight the candles were only for light. Zusiya began to sanctify the day with his glass of wine, and Elimelech had to remind him that tonight wine was nothing more than drink. And so it continued throughout the day—with each act, it was as though something called to each of their souls to do a little more.

Immediately after the sun set on Saturday night, the two men ran back to their teacher and described the frustration of their experience. The sage listened and responded, "On Wednesday, your self-proclaimed Shabbat, you experienced holiness by drawing the light of Shabbat down to you. But on the Shabbat appointed by God, the holiness of Shabbat draws each one of us up. And so it is on each of the festivals established and fixed by God: if we strive to elevate ourselves through observance at the appointed time, *keva*, and bring to it the devotion of our hearts, *kavanah*, the fullness of our experience lifts us higher and higher."

25

SEEKING A WILD HEART IN WILDERNESS

RABBI MIKE COMINS

Wherever I go in wild, remote corners of the world, I run into Jews. Like their peers throughout the first world, more and more Jews recreate outdoors. More and more are moving to places like Montana and Colorado, even Utah and Wyoming. What is surprising, perhaps, is that when they discover I am a rabbi, they love to tell me that nature is their synagogue. They feel transcendence in the mountains, speak with reverence about the stars, and unabashedly call the rivers and forests sacred. They describe themselves as spiritual-not-religious, spiritual but not into organized religion.

While the idea that Judaism is "organized" always makes me chuckle, I understand what they mean. The experiences that led me to think that there really might be a God usually happened outdoors, and rarely in a synagogue. Aside from the redwood grove at Camp Swig, my beloved Reform summer camp, I experienced Judaism and nature as separate domains.

When I approached ordination in the Israeli Reform rabbinical program, I had a problem. I was a wannabe when it came to truly believing in God. I loved Judaism for the study, the values, the community, even the prayer life. But I had no real sense of God. Fortunately, a friend showed me how to backpack in the Judean desert, and everything changed. After years of yeshivah and university study, I was back in nature, where I had spent much of my formative years. As I like to put it, God kicked in. I had actually been experiencing God in nature all my life but did not have the vocabulary to articulate it.

Why do people feel close to the Divine in nature? I set out to answer that question when I became an Israeli desert guide. I walked Israel's deserts and the Sinai mountains with Bible in hand. Since there were no Jewish teachers of spiritual practice in nature, I studied with Buddhists, Taoists, and Native Americans. Little did I know that I would find the best information at home. The two most influential, liberal Jewish thinkers of the last century, Martin Buber and Abraham Joshua Heschel, both begin their paradigm-shifting thought by reflecting on the relationship between God, humans, and the rest of creation.

Shortly after World War I, Martin Buber (1878–1965) introduced the terms "I-Thou" and "I-It" to describe the primary modes in which, he claimed, we engage the world. Whereas I-It relations between people are utilitarian and functional, I-Thou describes moments of communion. I-Thou moments—sometimes called "genuine" or "authentic" dialogue—are characterized by respect, undivided attention on the other, and active listening. In I-Thou, we move beyond our own dramas and pettiness. The usual subject-object dichotomy is replaced by a subject-subject unity that Buber called the "Between."

Two additional characteristics of I-Thou are important to our discussion. First, Buber locates the source of ethics in I-Thou relation. Imagine a crying baby in your arms as you try to discern what is wrong. What the toddler needs is not optional; it is an ethical command directed specifically to you. So, too, in any I-Thou relation. The Thou's need is the I's command. The religious tradition, as well as the reasoned, rational thinking that we bring to moral situations, is an extension and commentary on what is revealed to us in moments of genuine relationship.

This leads to perhaps Buber's most controversial point. Revelation takes place in I-Thou moments because God is present in every I-Thou encounter. I-It interactions take place on the matrix of time and space, but I-Thou moments in the Between are eternal and reveal to us the Absolute, that is, God.

While a defense-less, honest, and open Socratic dialogue is the paradigmatic example of genuine dialogue, I-Thou does not require a common language or equal status between the interlocutors. A teacher may have an I-Thou moment with a student, or a parent with a child, even though they do not share equal power or intellect. Nor is genuine dialogue limited to humans or human language. The first experience of I-Thou described in Buber's "Autobiographical Fragments" is between the young Buber and a horse on his grandfather's estate.[1] The first I-Thou moment Buber relates in his book *I and Thou* is with a tree.

Here are some of the expressions that I would use to describe my best moments in the natural world: mysterious, awesome, sacred, paradigm-shifting, inspiring, and no less important, ethically demanding. After experiencing moments of I-Thou in the natural world, I know that protecting endangered species and fighting human-driven climate change are not optional.

One can debate Buber's metaphysics and psychology. But Buber's depiction of the experience of I-Thou accurately describes and explains why I feel most spiritual in the most material of places, the wilderness, and most human when I am in deep relationship with other beings, including my relations in the natural world.

A prodigy in traditional Jewish learning in Poland and university educated in Germany, Abraham Joshua Heschel (1907–72) became the most important liberal Jewish writer on American soil. Voicing early opposition to the Vietnam War and walking into Selma shoulder to shoulder with Martin Luther King, Jr., he is remembered as the conscience of American Jewry. Among his writings, it is his groundbreaking theology and spiritual writings of the 1950s, particularly his book *The Sabbath*, that first established him on the national stage.

Heschel's magnum opus is *God in Search of Man*, a four-hundred-page treatise that covers the major topics of Jewish practice and belief: revelation, commandments, evil. Its first pages are dedicated to God and the universal experience of transcendence that provokes religious thinking and living. In particular, he devotes chapters to wonder and awe.

Heschel discusses wonder by contrasting it with curiosity. Curiosity leads to questions that have answers. Once we discover the mechanisms that cause photosynthesis, for instance, we take on a new set of questions. Wonder, on the other hand, can never be satisfied by knowledge.

> Wonder or radical amazement is the chief characteristic of the religious man's attitude toward history and nature. . . . As civilization advances, the sense of wonder declines. Such decline is an alarming symptom of our state of mind. Mankind will not perish for want of information; but only for want of appreciation. The beginning of our happiness lies in the understanding that life without wonder is not worth living. What we lack is not a will to believe but a will to wonder.[2]

Wonder, then, describes a way of relating to the world that evokes amazement and gratitude. The last line is a direct reference to William James's lecture "A Will to Believe." James was a leading intellectual voice in the late nineteenth century. Among his many accomplishments, he contributed to the new American philosophy, pragmatism, that advocated "radical empiricism." He was also a practicing Christian. The essay responded to those who criticized Christianity as false and irrelevant in light of modern science.

Science, wrote James, has inherent limits. It cannot, for instance, replace poetry or decide ethical questions. To live well, it is neither irrational nor irresponsible to seek the fruits of religious wisdom, prayer, and ritual. On the contrary, religion enables human flourishing.

But in the end, the problem still remained. How does one avow required dogmas that are counterintuitive or seem unlikely in light of current science? James responded that one must cultivate "a will to believe," echoing Søren Kierkegaard's claim that modern Christians must take a "leap of faith" across the "abyss of the absurd" to uphold Christian dogma.

Heschel, of course, affirmed many beliefs from his religious tradition, but he has no quarter for a faith that requires belief *despite* our best information about the world. The issue is how one relates to knowledge. For him, the more science teaches us, the stronger our "radical amazement" and thus the stronger our faith.

Equally important, Heschel does not ask his readers to accept Judaism's core beliefs simply because the tradition asserts them or because we can reason that they are true. This may have been enough in the Middle Ages, but not for modern Jews. Rather, he wants us to find God through our direct experience of the world. The key is to educate our perception.

"To the prophets wonder is a form of thinking . . . it is an attitude that never ceases."[3] Before I read this line, I thought of awesome moments in nature as a *reaction*. Heschel taught that we can *cultivate* "eyes of wonder." Just as we can consciously nurture compassion or become more sensitive to injustice, we can train ourselves to experience more and more moments of radical amazement. In fact, this is a central goal of Jewish prayer.

> Every evening we recite: "He creates light and makes the dark." Twice a day we say: "He is One." What is the meaning of such repetition? A scientific theory, once it is announced and accepted, does not have to be repeated twice a day. The insights of wonder must be constantly kept alive. Since there is a need for daily wonder, there is a need for daily worship.[4]

For Heschel, wonder is critical because wonder leads to awe, and awe leads to God. "Awe is a sense for the transcendence, for the reference everywhere to Him who is beyond all things."[5]

Wonder is but one of the many components of awe. Take childbirth, for instance, a paradigmatic example of an awesome event. Childbirth evokes wonder, beauty, possibility, humility, danger, death, and more. The mysteries of life concretely confront us. Whatever life means, we are often moved to look for it in awe-filled moments. The question of God is not contrived.

> The meaning of awe is to realize that life takes place under wide horizons, horizons that range beyond the span of an individual life

or even the life of a nation, a generation, or an era. Awe enables us to perceive in the world intimations of the divine, to sense in small things the beginning of infinite significance, to sense the ultimate in the common and the simple; to feel in the rush of the passing the stillness of the eternal.[6]

The beliefs and values we inherit from our ancestors are important and true, says Heschel, but they are not the source of Hebrew faith. "*Awe precedes faith;* it is *at the root of faith.* We must grow in awe in order to reach faith. We must be guided by awe to be worthy of faith. Awe rather than faith is the cardinal attitude of the religious Jew" (italics in the original).[7] And there is no easier or more reliable place to experience awe than the natural world. Heschel was famous for beginning evening lectures or sermons by exclaiming, "I've just seen a miracle. I've seen the sunset."

In late antiquity and the Middle Ages, Jewish thinkers looked away from the earth. Following Greeks and Gnostics, and later Christians and Muslims, most Jewish medieval mystics and philosophers found meaning in non-earthly, spiritual realms and denigrated material existence as the place of sin and temptation.

But the Hebrew Bible, particularly the Torah, displays a different attitude to our physical world. The first generations were predominantly shepherds. In the later Israelite nations, farming joined animal husbandry as the main occupations. Unlike their neighbors along the Nile or the Euphrates, Israelite farmers lacked a reliable source to irrigate their crops. Drought brought suffering and death. The Temple cult in Jerusalem was designed to address their most pressing needs: the continued fertility of the soil and the timely coming of the rains. The sacrificial rites featured agricultural yields and domesticated animals. The Israelites offered their first fruits to God.

We know the major holidays as retelling our mythic history. Pesach, Shavuot, and Sukkot commemorate the Exodus, the revelation at Sinai, and wandering in the desert, respectively. Originally, however, the pilgrimage holidays celebrated the three harvests in the Land of Israel (barley on Passover, wheat on Shavuot, and fruit on Sukkot).

The Sabbatical and Jubilee years, in which the land was left fallow, protected the fertility of the soil and sought to preserve an egalitarian society by periodically abolishing debt, freeing slaves, and preventing the concentration of land in the hands of the few.

So many of the formative events of the biblical period did not take place in the Temple or at shrines, the ancient equivalent of seminaries and synagogues. We remember Abraham on the mountain and digging wells, Isaac's fields returning a hundred-fold yield, Jacob at the well, Joseph in the pit, Moses at the Burning Bush, the people crossing the Red Sea, Miriam, Aaron, Korach, and the spies during forty years in the desert, Joshua conquering the land, Elijah on Mount Carmel, God answering Job out of the whirlwind, Jonah in the belly of a fish, and of course, the giving of Torah on a mountain in the heart of wilderness. The Patriarchs build their altars on mountaintops or next to wells or revered trees.

Ancient Israelite practice was intimately connected with the natural world. They looked for God's action in the land just as much as in historical events.

Biblical scholars have long speculated on the possible connection between the desert and the rise of monotheism. The debate has not been resolved, but all agree that the desert played a leading role in shaping Israelite history and culture.

The desert is constantly presented as an enemy in the Hebrew Bible. In times of plenty, the farmers extend their fields into the wastelands. In times of drought and calamity, the desert takes them back. But in our earlier, mythic history, the Israelites coalesce during the forty-year sojourn in the wild, which Hosea (chapter 2) describes as a love story.

The slaves who left Egypt are the generation of miracles. They experience the ten plagues, the crossing of the Red Sea, and the revelation at Mount Sinai. And yet, all but two of them, Joshua and Caleb, die early deaths in the desert. Time after time, the generation of miracles fails the test of faith and suffers divine retribution.

Who does merit the Land of Israel and establishes the Israelite presence in Canaan? The generation of the desert, people who left Egypt as children or were born in the wild. What did the Sinai wilderness give them?

I am solo backpacking in the Sierra Nevada mountains, where my parents took me every summer of my childhood. I love the challenge and the adventure, and best of all, I am free. Food and shelter are on my back, water flows in the endless lakes and streams. I can go anywhere. Joyfully working my body, I see unspeakable beauty in every direction. It's all there for the taking. Sweet freedom!

Until I think about it. In reality, the only thing I can "take" is taking nothing for granted. If I get caught in a storm, lose my backpack while crossing a rapid, or leave a well-traveled trail and break my leg, the consequences are real. I must plan my route carefully, weigh my food down to the ounce, and avoid poison oak, rattlesnakes, and loose boulders. Most important, I can never lose track of the weather. Mistakes are not forgiven here.

In wilderness, I heighten my senses, focus my mind, and listen to the world around me. The terrain, the weather, and my body tell me where I can safely go. If I don't obey, I might die. Wilderness demands heightened awareness and informed surrender. Freedom, I learn, is less about imposing my will and more about attuning myself to my surroundings, less about independence and more about finding a healthy dependence.

To be here I must clearly recognize the dangers. I must develop the courage to face them and the awareness to avoid them. Unlike in civilization, I see dead trees, rotting plants, and unburied animal bones as I hike. I am constantly reminded of my mortality. Wilderness is where one learns to live with fear without succumbing to anxiety.

I also see the sunset and the flowers, the birds and the rivers.

A subtle realization evolves and ripens over the years; a voice emerges from within with a clear message. This world is good. This world is meant for good. I am here to experience the beauty and wonders that humans have evolved to see, touch, and hear. I am meant to be here.

As I summit a peak, I feel my strength. As I watch the sunrise, I am smitten by beauty. As I catch my dinner from the lake, I am filled with gratitude. It dawns on me that I feel more at home here than at home. I feel safer here than in civilization. (Statistically, I am.) I am in a sea of God's love—awestruck, inspired, wholly alive.

It is just as Genesis states it. This world was created for good, and I am part of that goodness. It is as Heschel described it. To be in awe is to be attracted not only to the mystery of existence, but to hear God's call for justice and compassion. My potential is as wide as the horizon.

Emunah, the Hebrew word rendered as "faith" in English, means "trust." As mentioned above regarding James and Kierkegaard, "faith" in Christianity-rooted, Western society has come to mean belief despite evidence. Some Jews agree, particularly the ultra-Orthodox. But in biblical times, *emunah* was about loyalty and trust. It had nothing to do with dogma, and everything to do with relationships.

Despite the mosquitos and the lightning storms, I come to trust in this raw, beautiful, dangerous world. In wilderness, in the embrace of God's creation, a naïve, organic faith arises. I recognize the divinity in God's good world. I believe I can live in holiness. No leaps required.

What did the Israelites learn in the Sinai desert? I imagine they discovered that miracles come not only in the form of manna, but in the sunrise and sunset, in the existence of a spring in the desert, in the form of a desert plant, in the beauty of the mountains. They learned to live at risk without anxiety. Unlike their parents, who pined for the onions and watermelons they ate as slaves, the generation of the desert could understand the basic goodness of their harsh environment. And while they saw that their fate primarily rested on their skill and effort in navigating life in the wilderness, they knew, every day, that their situation would be futile without the loving grace of God.

Settling the land would bring many hardships. The Sinai wilderness prepared them well. The desert taught them courage, resourcefulness, and faith.

We are the People of the Book, a fact I love. But intellectual inquiry is not the only way, or even the primary way, that we learn.

Consider Jacob and his famous wrestling match with the *ish*, the man who wrestles him until the dawn and then names him Israel. Jacob has spent the last twenty years running from Esau, and now he runs back to Canaan from Laban. When Esau comes to greet him with four hundred men, an army, his worst fears are realized. As the literal meaning of *Yaakov* (he will circumvent) indicates, he has managed life through cleverness and guile. He is no match for Esau in a fight, not as a boy, and certainly not now.

Jacob prays, splits his camp into two, sends seven sets of gifts, and eventually crosses his family over the Jabbok river—everything to avoid a physical confrontation. But as he is left alone on the riverbank, the *ish* attacks him. Jacob is out of options. He has no choice but to fight. And to our surprise, he prevails. Jacob earns the name Israel, "God-wrestler."

The Hebrew word that conveys his victory, *vatuchal*, is usually translated "and he prevailed." Literally, it means "and you were able." To my mind, herein lies the meaning of the wrestling match. Jacob's transformation does not result from an insight gained through study or philosophical reasoning. Rather, Jacob discovers his abilities, his own capabilities. He discovers what he needs to learn—courage, strength, and resilience—through his body.

The physical leads to the spiritual, the body to the heart. *Yisrael* means "He will wrestle with God." But the Torah has no vowels, and another plausible reading of the same consonants is *Yashar El*, "the straight one of God." *Yashar* also means "honest." Jacob, who enters the wrestling match as the circumventer, the clever manipulator of others in stealth or deceit, exits as the honest man of God. After the wrestling match, despite the risk to his life, he walks straight to his brother, and the two reconcile.

The role of our bodies in spiritual life is as important today as it was for Jacob.

Nothing is harder for Jewish educators to teach than the subjects of God and prayer. Many have noticed that the same prayer service or theological discussion that students resist in a classroom is welcomed next to a lake or on a trail. I have often wondered why. Is it simply the beauty of nature?

Current neuroscience sheds light on the question. We know today that when we speak, compute a math equation, or think conceptually, more neurons are firing on the left side of the brain. Artistic, intuitive, emotional, physical, non-linguistic activity is associated with the right side of the brain. Most people would agree that spiritual experience, when it is powerful, is primarily a right-brain phenomenon (even if one starts in left-brain activities like Torah study).

We also know that the body is connected to the heart, to right-brain experience. Unless one is a great actor, emotions express themselves in the body. When you want to know how someone is feeling, do you put more weight on their words or the expression on their face? The mind-body connection is real, and it is reciprocal. When we are angry, our bodies tense. If we can turn our thoughts from anger, the body relaxes. Conversely, we can go for a run or take a hot shower, relax the body, and the anger in our minds recedes.

Putting these truths together, we receive important guidance. If we want to facilitate emotional, intuitive, heartfelt moments of prayer and ritual, we should create the conditions that activate the right side of the brain. Unfortunately, we can't just think the thought "I don't want to be in my left-brain, thinking mind now" and have it happen. As those who practice yoga, make music, play a sport, dance, or sing know so well, the way to get out of the thinking mind is to engage the senses.

These factors guide our synagogue services. What do we do when we begin a service? We open a book and begin to read. We immediately go left brain. Fortunately, we know the antidote. We engage our bodies through music. Sensual experience brings the right brain into play. Music is central in Reform worship because it literally "moves" us, that is, it touches our emotions and opens the heart by stimulating our bodies.

The same dynamic is at play anytime we venture into the natural world. When our eyes and ears are engaged, when we activate our senses, we are creating the conditions to open our hearts as well. We are more likely to feel wonder and awe or find ourselves in I-Thou. We are more likely to speak from our souls in prayer, more likely to listen deeply, and more likely to find God—in our hearts and in the world around us.

We in the Reform Movement have long been aware of the positive role of nature in Jewish education. What many call our most successful educational project, the extensive network of URJ camps, integrates the natural world into Jewish life daily. URJ Israel programs spend significant time in nature. It is no coincidence that the two American rabbis who have created innovative, outdoor programs and devoted their careers to Jewish education in the wild, Jaime Korngold (Adventure Rabbi) and myself (TorahTrek), are Reform rabbis.

But our current efforts are not nearly enough. When we fail to recognize that there is no greater classroom to teach God and prayer than the natural world, we lose a precious opportunity. Reform educators are renowned for their ability to think out-of-the-box. We also need to think out-of-the-building.

Judaism needs nature. Our Jewish way of life has God at the center, yet so many people struggle with questions of faith. Where is there a more reliable place than the natural world to experience awe, the gateway to God? Where better than wilderness to seek a visceral, direct connection to the Divine? Where better than nature to cultivate one's prayer voice?

And nature needs Judaism. Endangered species and polluted lands need their human protectors. So does a warming planet. When Jewish educators facilitate I-Thou moments in wilderness, we help to create them.

Our spiritual-not-religious friends need Judaism, too. If one's spiritual life ends when one leaves the mountains, it is not much of a spiritual life at all. Judaism is a conduit for bringing the experience of transcendence in nature to all of one's life everywhere. Judaism offers a vision of an ethically infused, balanced relationship between humans and the earth's animate and inanimate beings. It has the power to integrate individuals and society, and the earth that sustains them, in ways that inspire the flourishing of all.

Shortly after dawn, six souls return to camp with tired bodies and gracious smiles. I think of Moses coming down from Mount Sinai. His face was so radiant after meeting God, he had to wear a veil. In the morning light, these faces are also radiant—happy and humble in the afterglow of standing face-to-face with the Divine within and the Divine without.

They are among the thirty or so people, about a third of them rabbis, whose wilderness solos I was privileged to facilitate. They have just completed seventy-two hours alone in the wild, dwelling within a space the size of a bedroom. They prayed, chanted, danced, meditated, reflected, and journaled; they spoke, sang, cried, and laughed. They came to know stars, trees, plants, and animals. They discovered depths in themselves they did not know.

Each called out to God. And listened.

None will tell the same story of their solo, but each will say that they are not the person they were before. Each experienced a part of reality they did not know was accessible. Each will tell you that words are not adequate to describe the experience. No matter. Their glowing faces say more than words can convey.

Just like the ancient Israelites in the Sinai desert or Jacob on the riverbank, we too can discover our abilities and cultivate our virtues when we leave the illusive safety of civilization and trust in the wild. The wilderness is our *ish*, a place where we might discover our wild hearts, where we might learn to walk straight and see with eyes of wonder, where we might behold this awesome world and wrestle with God.

NOTES

1. Martin Buber, "Autobiographical Fragments," in *The Philosophy of Martin Buber*, ed. Paul Arthur Schlipp and Maurice S. Friedman (La Salle, IL: Open Court, 1967), 24.

2. Abraham Joshua Heschel, *God in Search of Man* (New York: Farrar, Straus and Giroux, 1955), 46.

3. Heschel, *God in Search of Man*, 46.

4. Heschel, *God in Search of Man*, 48.
5. Heschel, *God in Search of Man*, 75.
6. Heschel, *God in Search of Man*, 75.
7. Heschel, *God in Search of Man*, 77.

26

TOWARD A REFORM JEWISH MYSTICISM

RABBI TED FALCON, PhD

Reform Judaism embraces the whole of the human adventure, honoring the ways in which evolving knowledge of the human condition allows us to discover and to celebrate more profound wisdom within Jewish tradition. In the realm of spirituality, sometimes we learn from contemporary teachings to appreciate more profound levels of ancient wisdom. For many of us, this learning reveals a rich Jewish spiritual heritage that has often been neglected.

Because spirituality is far more than a cognitive pursuit, this chapter invites a more meditative participation. We live in a time that urgently needs the wisdom springing from the spiritual depths of human consciousness and reflected in Jewish tradition.

The Jewish spiritual path grabbed me by surprise some forty-six years ago, during a time when I was practicing meditation from the Zen Buddhist and Hindu traditions. Until then, my exposure to Jewish spirituality had been solely an intellectual one. That intellectual approach was the veil through which Jewish spiritual teachings emerged.

One day, as was my custom, I opened a traditional prayer book to discover what passage would randomly emerge. The page I opened to contained the words of the *Sh'ma*. I almost closed the book to try for a different passage, because those six Hebrew words, "Listen, Israel, the Eternal is our God, the Eternal is One" (Deuteronomy 6:4), are perhaps the most central and well-known in Jewish tradition, and my first thought was they could offer me nothing new. But something told me to take time to contemplate those words as if I was meeting them for the first time.

The words immediately following those six words proclaim that "these words [the *Sh'ma*] shall be upon your heart" (Deuteronomy 6:6). I recalled that "heart," in the biblical idiom, was not the organ associated with feeling—it was the organ associated with thought, with the mind. It was as if the sentence said, these words shall be upon your *mind*. The text then says that the six words are to be repeated "when you sit in your house, when you walk by the way, when you lie down, and when you rise up" (6:7). That's all the time! It suddenly struck me that these were clear instructions for a meditation practice—a *Jewish* meditation practice—the first that I had found. There was much spiritual wisdom in the other traditions that I had been learning, but there was a special joy in finding this in my own tradition. I began the practice of silently reciting the *Sh'ma* as my focus for meditation, my mantra, and as time went on, I started to discover and study a richness of Jewish spiritual teachings of which I had been unaware.

Jewish mysticism and a Jewish spiritual path stopped being intellectual exercises for me and became my Way. I do not pretend to be an awakened being. I still walk the earth and often stumble. But I know that the One proclaimed in the *Sh'ma* includes it all—everything and nothing. I appreciate that this One is shared with love, met with acceptance, and expressed with kindness. Although this is part of all authentic spiritual teachings, there is unique wisdom to be found on Jewish spiritual paths. I have come to believe that Jewish spiritual practices, supporting a more inclusive awareness, are part of the healing most needed in our deeply polarized world today.

I often share the story of a rabbi who, before beginning his daily teaching, spent some moments alone in his private office. His students noticed he had a greater clarity about him when he emerged. As the rabbi aged, he became less careful about closing the door, and the most adventurous students would sneak a glimpse of what their teacher was doing. Each day, he studied a book he kept in the lower left-hand drawer of his desk.

When this teacher died, students returned to pay him honor. Following the funeral, many hurried to the old classroom. The quickest pulled open the door to the office and sat down at the desk. As that former student opened the drawer and pulled out the book, those closest could see that every page was blank—except one. And on that one page, to which the book opened naturally, was a single sentence: "Remember the difference between the container and that which it contains."

Remember the difference between the container and that which it contains. Spiritual teaching and practice comprise paths that helps us explore the "contents" for which our individual and separate identities serve as unique containers. Spiritual practices help us quiet ourselves enough to pursue those paths. Mysticism is the moment of meeting beyond all particular paths, at the heart of awareness.

Hillel the Elder, one of the most famous Jewish sages of the first century, combined ethical and spiritual wisdom. One of his central teachings appears in Ethics of the Fathers (*Pirkei Avot* 1:14):

Im ein ani li, mi li?
Uch'she-ani l'atzmi, mah ani?
V'im lo achshav, eimatai?

If I am not for myself, who [will be] for me?
But if I am for myself [only], what am I?
And if not now, when?

On its surface, the injunction encourages us to take good care of ourselves. Of course, the "self" referred to here is our own personal self, our personality that Jewish tradition calls the *nefesh*. This is our individuality, the definition of how we are different and distinct from others. Hillel urges us to be responsible for ourselves.

Hillel's second question warns us of the consequences of limiting our identity to our separate self alone. It's one thing to take responsibility for our individual identity, but it's another to imagine that this exclusive individuality comprises the whole of our being. Hillel very specifically refers to that separate self with the word *atzmi*, which means "bone" and points to the physical essence of our body-self. And so he asks, "When we limit that *I* to this body-self alone, what have we done to our *I*?" The question implies the answer: We are far more than an individual identity. We are more than our persona, our personality, our *nefesh*.

The third line of Hillel's teaching, "And if not now, when?" is frequently interpreted to simply say that this is something we need to do right now. But the *nefesh*, the consciousness associated with our separate self, has trouble simply staying with the "now." Our ordinary mind seems always to be yearning for something more; it is always judging, and it cannot rest in the completeness of *now*. Only a more inclusive level of self can transcend the limitations of our mind. One way we meet this aspect of self is through spiritual practice.

Spiritual learning differs from all other forms of learning. Usually, when we wish to learn something, we seek information outside ourselves, finding a teacher, a text, or a class. Most of us who become interested in spirituality probably first pursued spiritual learning that way, as well. It soon becomes clear, though, that the spiritual learning we seek is not to be found "out there." No one can "give" us spiritual awareness because spiritual awareness is something we need to *remember*. It is part of who we *are*. Hillel's final question calls us to attend to the fullness of the present moment, where what we seek spiritually is always to be found. Throughout history, those who have awakened to the mystical moment have acknowledged that it is always right here, and right now.

So we turn to the practice of meditation to reclaim dimensions of our own being that exist behind the ego. Many who begin this practice have the initial experience of their thoughts speeding up. Too often, this leads them to stop meditating. What they do not understand is that when we begin to relax, our minds actually slow down enough for us to become more conscious of that voice "talking" to us inside our heads.

Most of the time, that voice is going so fast—constantly judging things and commenting on our environment and ourselves—that we are not consciously aware of it. And as we do begin to listen, we often notice that our harshest judgments are reserved for ourselves.

The most popular and most researched meditative technique today is mindfulness, a deceptively simple practice. The instructions are, indeed, simple: Accept everything that arises in the mind, in the body, and in the emotions. Accept what presents itself, the negative as well as the positive judgments the mind makes. Here is an opportunity to explore an increased inner focus even as you read:

1. Get as comfortable as you can, making sure that your back is supported so that you can breathe easily. Consciously take time to breathe: take a full breath, hold it for just a moment, and then release it fully. Do this another time or two before moving on to the next step.

2. Allow yourself to become more consciously aware of your body. Notice any places of discomfort as you do a gentle body scan. There is no need to change anything. You can begin at your feet and slowly move your attention up through your legs, your hips, your back, your belly, and into your breath. Then move your focus to your fingers and your hands. Gently move your attention up your arms, through your shoulders, your chest, and into your breath. Finally, focus on your head, starting on the top, then moving your attention to your forehead, eyes, mouth, and jaw, down through your neck, and, again, into your breath. Your body scan naturally brings you to the area of your breath, which can serve as your center.

3. Gently become aware of the commentary that your mind continually provides. Notice that as the body calms, the activities of the mind become more apparent. The voice of the mind comments on, and has opinions about, just about everything you experience. Perhaps you will meet judgments about this calming process itself. Can you simply allow the mind to do whatever it

is doing now? Even negative judgments can simply be accepted as they are.

4. Merely witnessing the activities of the mind, noticing how we comment on our sensations, feelings, and thoughts, begins the process of mindfulness meditation. An attitude of simple acceptance does not mean that all the thoughts are positive—far from it. It simply means we accept all our thoughts exactly as they are. There is no need to change anything.

   Often we believe that if we accept everything as it is in this moment, nothing will ever be any different. And there is much in current reality that we would wish to change. But, rather than keeping things the same, unconditional acceptance actually allows change to occur. Carl Jung's teaching that "what you resist persists" reminds us that acceptance is the path to letting go.

5. If you are following along in this process, you are probably now more aware of the activities of your mind than usual. It is also likely that you feel less identified with the specific thoughts and more aware of the part of you that is witnessing, the part of you that is listening. You may have begun to realize that the listening part is *not* the part of you that does the talking. As you observe the activities of your mind, you might begin to wonder, "Who is the one who is listening?" You can continue this gentle inquiry as you allow yourself to simply witness your sensations, your thoughts, and your feelings.

6. Each time you read over these steps you may find that your experience is different. In the presence of unconditional acceptance, change is the one constant. As our awareness becomes more inclusive, the moment we call "now" expands.

Becoming available for more inclusive aspects of our identity sets the stage for appreciating spiritual teachings from Jewish tradition that may have eluded us before. Spirituality can be measured as the degree to which our awareness is inclusive rather than exclusive. The more we experience our interconnectedness with others and with our world, the more spiritual our awareness. The more separate we experience ourselves, the more fragmented our reality, the less spiritual our awareness. Moving from the more exclusive to the more inclusive is the work of spiritual practice. Consider, for example, how the beginning of ancestor Abraham's journey provides a universal paradigm for the spiritual journey:

> *Lech l'cha mei-artz'cha, umimoladet'cha, umibeit avicha, el haaretz asher areka.*

> Get you out from your land, from the place of your birth, and from the house of your father, to the land that I shall show you. (Genesis 12:1)

An important way that Jewish tradition points to different layers of meaning in biblical texts is with the acronym *pardes*. The word is translated as "orchard," but the consonants, *PRDS*, represent the four levels of meaning a text can convey. The *P* stands for *p'shat*, indicating the surface, literal meaning. The *R* stands for *remez*, which means "hint," and points to a more general allegorical meaning extending beyond the specific moment being described. Where the *p'shat* describes a particular event at a particular time and place, *remez* extends that description to something others can experience. The *D* stands for *d'rash*, meaning "exposition," and points toward a metaphorical or metaphysical level at which the text speaks of inner rather than outer events. The stories and the characters are all experienced as parts of one's own being. Finally, the *S* stands for *sod*, or "secret," acknowledging the mystical level, the pathless path, beyond the capacity of words to describe. Each level of understanding a text moves from the more specific to the more universal.

In the verse in Genesis, Abram (his name will be changed to the more familiar Abraham a little later on) is told emphatically to leave his home and trust that he will discover his destination as he goes along. This is the *p'shat* level, at which the text communicates the surface events being described.

Appreciating the *remez* level invites us beyond the specific to the general nature of a life-changing journey. We may not be able at the beginning to know exactly where our journey will end, but we feel the need to move beyond where we are now. When we take the first steps, we need to trust that the path will emerge only as we progress, just as Abram heard that he would be shown the destination only after he had begun. When we venture beyond the life we have known, a considerable level of trust is required. We cannot know exactly where we are headed until we fully release where we have been.

When we move to a more metaphorical level of those words Abram heard, the level of *d'rash* invites us to find the call within ourselves. We are no longer observers, we are participants in a journey. So let us consider the words of the text more carefully.

The biblical injunction *Lech l'cha*, while clearly a biblical Hebrew emphatic form for "Go you!" also means "Go to *yourself*." This additional, rather literal translation ushers us into the spiritual dimension of the call to Abram. "Go to yourself from your [external] land, from the place of your birth, and from your father's [parents'] house," Abram is instructed, "[in order to see] the land that I shall show you." Our separate identity is shaped by our responses to our "land," the "place of our birth," and our "parents' house." We each fashion a personality in response to our inborn proclivities (our birthplace), the physical place where we are (our land), and the nature of those from whom we seek attention, nurturing, sustenance, and love (our parents or other caregivers).

Each of us constructed a self, an ego, from the available internal and external raw materials. We came into this life naked in a number of ways, devoid of a separate personal identity. In our earliest days, we knew no distinction between self and other. But soon, the nipple we sought proved to be "not us," and the fingers we sucked proved to be "us." We began to define ourselves as distinct entities. As we grew, our self-definitions grew increasingly clear, usually influenced by the judgments of significant others. For example, some of us became compliant, in order to get the nurturing and the care that we needed. Others became troublemakers, in order to get attention that way. We grew our own self, our distinct and separate identity in the world.

But this self, this discrete identity, reinforces separation and keeps us bound in a matrix of conditioned responses. We have developed our "story," and although there are subplots, the character we play frequently remains pretty much the same. In a spiritual sense, this traps us in a separateness from which we cannot know the greater picture, and we cannot know our fuller and more inclusive identity.

The command given to Abram and to those available to listen, *Lech l'cha*, "Go to yourself!" is a radical call to move behind our separate self and be open to our more inclusive identity. After all, it is this more inclusive identity that creatively formed our personality in the first place. Spiritual "awakening" is a remembering of aspects of our more inclusive identity that have always been present.

But if fuller dimensions of our own identity have always been present, what has kept them so hidden? Perhaps it has something to do with the very nature of the consciousness associated with our separate identity. For example, most of us would like lives with less pain; we often desire relationships with less conflict. Along with our culture, we might seek continual—and even instant—happiness. But these desires wind up increasing the very frustration, anger, and sense of separation that we are attempting to heal. This is because the world known by the senses, through the mind and through the body, will always reveal a world of contrasts.

In this material world, we cannot know *up* without knowing *down*; we cannot know *easy* without knowing *difficult*; we cannot know *sweet* without knowing *bitter*. Seeking a life free of difficulty is like seeking a coin with one side. To deny our own shadow side—the aspects of ourselves that we want to hide from others and even from ourselves—breeds lives of pretense and greater separation. We cannot escape such polarizations by pretending or projecting them away. The path to inner and outer peace follows from unconditional acceptance, and this is a spiritual pursuit.

Jewish meditation often focuses on specific verses of the Hebrew Bible to support us in various stages of our journey, and one verse that invites us to move beyond the polarization of the separate self is called the *Shiviti* (Psalm 16:8):

Shiviti Adonai [YHVH] l'negdi tamid.
I set the Eternal before me always.

The Hebrew word *Adonai* is a replacement word standing in for the four-letter name of God that is not to be pronounced. That name, written but not spoken, is composed of the Hebrew letters *yod-hei-vav-hei* (*YHVH*) and is a form of the Hebrew verb that means "to be." The four-letter name signifies Being without limit of space or time: Infinite and Eternal Being. The *Shiviti*, then, encourages us to place Infinite Being before our individual identity. We affirm that we are part of something far greater than our separate self.

The Baal Shem Tov, the great Chasidic master of the eighteenth century, suggested that the word *shiviti*, usually translated as "I set," can also mean "to make equal." He taught that when we are able to respond equally to applause and to criticism, we have the equanimity needed to know that the Eternal One is "before me always." To know this greater Reality, we need to transcend the limitation of our polarizing ego minds.

We transcend our individual identity when we step behind the perceived polarities and enter a consciousness of equanimity. You might take a few moments right now to take this verse as a focus for meditation. Repeat it either in Hebrew or English, allowing it to be your focus. After some minutes, when you open your eyes, continue the recitation silently. Consider that everyone and everything before you is a manifestation of an Eternal Being.

In Jewish tradition, the weekly observance of Shabbat is a time to practice unconditional acceptance, an acceptance that includes even our resistances, our negative judgments, and our current challenges. Reflecting the original Creation myth, we have the opportunity to radically accept all that is. Blessing all Creation helps us reclaim the wholeness of our own beings. In such a moment of acceptance, we finally meet the moment Hillel directed us toward when he taught, "And if not now, when?"

The *Now* moment is always a surprise, cutting through the veils of our conditioning, our expectations, and our personal judgments. *Now* is an awakening to the absolute interconnectedness of all Being. *Now* we are whole and Creation is complete.

Part Four

LIVING THE TEXTS

The Jews have been called *the people of the book*. However, we face many challenges in reading, interpreting, and connecting emotionally with the texts of our tradition. In this section, we look at these challenges. How can we understand our current religious situation in the context of history? How should we study the wisdom of our sacred writings? How do we study them in their original languages and in translation? What is the meaning of Written and Oral Torah to a Reform Jew? And what role does the prayer book play in our self-understanding? These are just a few of the questions that arise.

In "Four Exiles and Four Spiritual Revolutions," Joel M. Hoffman, PhD, presents a framework for understanding Jewish history in the context of Jewish texts. Our spiritual revolutions have all started with exile, after which we created new types of religious literature and paradigms of thought.

Rabbi Amy Scheinerman's "Our Tree of Life" highlights the foundational value of Torah study for every congregation and community organization and shows us that "Reform Judaism is uniquely positioned to extend Torah learning in new directions."

In "Reform Approaches to Our Sacred Texts," Rabbi Geoffrey W. Dennis argues that since we do not read Jewish sacred literature in the way people did long ago, we must reinterpret the meaning of the Torah to unlock the texts for our generation.

Rabbi Hillel Gamoran, in "Hebrew in the Reform Movement," challenges American Jews to learn Hebrew as a living language, seeing it as the only way we will succeed in transmitting a vibrant Reform Judaism from generation to generation.

To Rabbi Dvora E. Weisberg, PhD, Talmud is a key part of our inheritance as Jews. In "Why Reform Jews Should Study Talmud," the author teaches Talmudic reasoning as she demonstrates the clear benefits that result from an investment of time and energy in learning this essential text.

In "Reflections on Prayer," Rabbi Peter S. Knobel introduces the book's essays on prayer, worship, and liturgy, while he presents a personal perspective on prayer and the centrality of it in his own belief and practice.

The prayer book is the most frequently utilized Jewish religious text, and it reflects both personal and collective hopes and dreams. Reform Jews consider prayer-book editing and publishing to be an essential part of our religious lives. Rabbi Richard S. Sarason, PhD, in "Worship and the Prayer Book," and Rabbi Dalia Marx, PhD, in "Reform Liturgy: Then and Now," illuminate the choices made in the creation of those texts and what those choices say about who we are as a movement.

To Cantor Rosalie Boxt ("Music and Worship"), the centrality of music in the Reform worship experience "provides us with rich opportunities for growth of soul and spirit" and is the key to entry for many in our diverse community. She takes the reader on a journey through the marvelous landscape that is our diverse worldwide Jewish community, and shows how our music can help us all to feel like we belong.

The Torah is our tree of life, and studying it intensively unlocks the riches of our tradition. Today, we have unprecedented opportunities to develop new approaches through which we can draw sustenance and inspiration from the essential wisdom of our sacred texts.

27

FOUR EXILES AND
FOUR SPIRITUAL REVOLUTIONS

JOEL M. HOFFMAN, PHD

Some three thousand years ago, according to historical and archaeological evidence, a Semitic group in Jerusalem who would later be called "the Jews" began an experiment in what they thought was a better way of living. Their experiment is ongoing and still thriving today, despite four potentially devastating exiles, because each exile was followed by a period of spiritual revolution that reinvented Judaism.

Though the early Jews (or, technically, Israelites) are primarily known now for advocating monotheism, they actually gave four things to the world: monotheism, the weekend (Shabbat), the alphabet, and the concept of human rights. These have all worked in tandem and continue to do so to this day.

Shabbat seems like an obvious way to end a week, but that's actually looking at it backwards. The only reason for the week is to have the weekend, to have Shabbat. That is, unlike other common calendrical units, the week was invented for social purposes: A day is one rotation of the earth, a month one revolution of the moon around the earth, and a year one revolution of the earth around the sun. A week, though, doesn't correspond to anything in nature. Its purpose is not to mark a natural phenomenon but to create a social one based in a belief that people shouldn't spend their whole lives working.

Next is the alphabet, which the Jews created by modifying a pre-alphabetic consonantal system used by the Phoenicians. It proved so popular that three thousand years later it still forms the basis of almost all of the world's communication, whether the Roman alphabet used in the Americas and Western Europe or the Cyrillic alphabet used in Eastern Europe, whether the Middle East's Hebrew and Arabic or the writing from the subcontinent of India; Chinese is written with a non-alphabetic system, but even it is often entered into a computer using an alphabet.

The Jews needed their alphabet for two important reasons. First, they hoped to record and thus preserve the guidelines of their experiment for future generations, in the form of written Scriptures. (Writing had never been used this way before, so its success was not guaranteed, though we now know, of course, that it worked.) Second, the alphabet was crucial to making sure that all Jews could stay abreast of what was going on. The Jews were all expected to learn to read and write. (Archaeological confirmation of widespread Jewish literacy surfaced in 2016.)

So the alphabet was a distribution system for transmitting information to Jews of the day and to Jews of future generations. And the information that was transmitted included the novel idea that people should not spend their whole lives working ("Shabbat"). The reason people should not spend their whole lives working, the early Jews said, is that every person has value. Though this outlook lies at the core of Western thought, it is rare across the world and throughout history. The more widespread pattern is for people to be the property of a local monarch, whether a king, some other king-like ruler, or a dictatorial government. In antiquity, certainly, most people belonged to the king.

By contrast, the Jews decided that every person—rich or poor, man or woman, peasant or aristocrat, inept or talented, local denizen or visitor—was more than mere property and had certain basic human rights.

Among these was the right to a day off every so often. Also among these was the right to due process of law. This is why the Torah commands that neither the rich nor the poor be favored in courts, and why the Torah specifically legislates that the rich cannot buy their way out of a death sentence.

To emphasize this new way of looking at humanity, the Jews re-framed a familiar motif. Whereas in other cultures people belonged to the king, in the Jewish communities both the people and the king belonged to God. And this is where monotheism comes in.

Indeed, Genesis bravely declares that Adam and Eve—meant to represent all of humankind—were created in the image of God. And lest there be any confusion, the text is clear that both men and women are in God's image. Every person, then, is godlike and God's property, not to be co-opted by human masters.

Taken in whole, then, we find an early Jewish agenda focused on universal human rights, including rights to due process, equality before the law, and a day off from work at least every seven days. The details of the day off from work were encoded in Shabbat, for which the Jews needed the week. The details of human rights more generally were tied to a single God, who was master over every human. And to let people know about the new program of human rights, the Jews needed mass communication: the alphabet.

The whole endeavor relied on various other institutions for support. A professional class of priests was tasked with maintaining the system. Because their job demanded their full-time attention, others had to provide for their sustenance. Sacrifices filled that need. To house those sacrifices as well as promote the centrality of God, the Jews built the impressive First Temple in Jerusalem.

Before long, the Temple and its city came to represent the valid-ity and success of the Jewish experiment. This is why the traumatic exile of 586 BCE, when Nebuchadnezzar sent the Jews to Babylon (or Babylonia—roughly modern Iraq), might have marked the end of Juda-ism. For nearly half a millennium, Jerusalem had served as the center of Judaism, while the great Temple had served both as the physical manifestation of the people's connection to God and as the home for the priests who oversaw Judaism.

These most visible symbols of God's approval were more than mere aspects of Judaism. They were the embodiment of Judaism. Serving God meant sacrificing at the Temple, and God showed approval of the sacrifices—and approval more generally—by granting the Jews ongoing prosperity in Jerusalem.

A year or two of drought could be dismissed as a temporary sign that the Jews had made some minor error or be discounted as a minor setback in a larger pattern of success. Exile, though, from the very land that had birthed and then sustained Judaism for hundreds of years pointed to one terrifying, tragic conclusion: there was no God.

The Bible even records the misery and confusion of exile, for example, in Psalm 137: "By the waters of Babylon, we sat down and wept," because "how can we sing God's song in a foreign land?"

In the midst of this potentially devastating exile, the prophets step in and save Judaism. Facing a population increasingly worried that there was no God, the great prophets turn things around, pointing to the exile itself as proof that God exists. "Who do you think exiled you?" the prophets ask rhetorically. God, they say.

And the prophets explain that God exiled the Jews because they weren't taking good enough care of other peoples.

"You are just like the Ethiopians to me," Amos (9:7) quotes God as saying. The point is that Israel is no better than any other nation, and no more deserving of God's grace. Isaiah, for his part, demands equitable behavior in addition to ritual observance: "Is this the fast that I have chosen?" (Isaiah 58:6). Isaiah also opens Judaism to foreigners: "For My house shall be called a house of prayer for all peoples" (56:7). Micah goes so far as to reject sacrifice: "Will God be pleased with thousands of rams? . . . Shall I offer my first-born?" The implicit answer, Micah writes, is no, because "God has shown you" what is necessary; it is necessary to "act justly" (Micah 6:7–8). In other words, what God really wants isn't sacrifice but equitable behavior.

That is, the prophets explain that God demands more than ritual service. God has charged the Jews with taking care of other nations, a task at which the Jews have failed, bringing about their own exile.

What's amazing is that the prophets made this up. Not one line in the Five Books of Moses demands that the Jews do anything outside their own communities. While the Jews have a responsibility to foreigners visiting among them, they have no obligation to those same foreigners when they are in their own lands (with the possible exception of treating them equitably during war).

It is difficult now to appreciate just how revolutionary the prophets' revisionist understanding was, because it has become part of mainstream Judaism. It was this prophetic vision that, generations on, led Rabbi Stephen Wise to co-found the NAACP in 1914, for instance. More generally, it has led to our modern notion of *tikkun olam* and to the host of Jewish social-action projects that come with it. At the time, however, the prophets were completely reinventing Judaism—a fact all the more remarkable considering the prophets' relatively minor role before the exile.

This is a pattern we will see four times: a previously marginalized group steps in after an exile and remakes Judaism as part of a spiritual revolution. In this initial case, the prophets turn the Jewish eye outward, whereas formerly it had focused strictly inward on the Jews' own communities.

The next case will come about more than five hundred years later, after the Second Exile (in 70 CE), when the Rabbis change Judaism even more.

The Second Exile was the culmination of a series of cascading events that began not too long after the First Exile ended. Around 515 BCE, the Temple was rededicated as some Jews returned to Jerusalem. (Contrary to popular conception, most exiled Jews probably stayed in Babylonia.)

For a while, the Jews again thrived in Jerusalem. Ezra started teaching Torah in 458, and in 445 Nehemiah built new city walls. But 120 years later, Alexander the Great died, having conquered his known world but having neglected to put in place a plan of succession. This unfortunate combination led to an ongoing pattern that mixed chaos, temporary stability, and infighting among the families that took over the territories Alexander had conquered. Jerusalem found herself at the center of much of that turmoil.

One family that rose to power after Alexander died was named Seleucid. And one Seleucid ruler in Syria, Antiochus IV (dubbed Antiochus the Insane), is well known as the regent who sullied the Second Temple around 168 BCE. It's equally well known that a family called the Maccabees repelled Antiochus IV a few years later—events that are still commemorated by the holiday of Chanukah. Less well known is the fact that the Maccabees were better at fighting than ruling, which is why Jerusalem quickly descended into chaos in the final decades of the first millennium BCE. Before long, Rome would take over, the wicked Herod finding himself in charge of Jerusalem. (It's ironic, perhaps, that Herod was eligible to rule the Jewish city only because the Maccabees had forcibly converted his grandfather to Judaism.)

Herod bequeathed Jerusalem to his son Archelaus, who took over in the year 4 BCE. The younger ruler shared his father's cruelty but lacked his father's ability, which is why the Roman ruler Augustus had to intervene in the year 6 CE, reorganizing the region of Jerusalem into a Roman province like any other. Jerusalem, now a walking corpse, lasted only a few decades longer. Two years after Nero's death in the year 68 CE, Roman troops sacked the city and razed the great Temple that had stood in one form or another for a thousand years. And the Jews were exiled from their homeland for a second time.

Even more than Nebuchadnezzar's earlier banishment of the Jews in 586 BCE, this new exile could have spelled the end of Judaism.

Instead, we find our pattern again: a previously marginalized group of people stepped in to reinvent Judaism. This time it was the Rabbis, who would go on to write the Talmud and the Midrash and generally give us most of what we now think of as Judaism: worship services, Shabbat candle lighting, fasting on Yom Kippur, the laws of kashrut, and other mainstays of Jewish practice.

Amazingly, the Rabbis changed things even more than the prophets had. The prophets advocated interest in and compassion for all peoples. But they didn't eliminate any core aspects of Judaism. By contrast the Rabbis did nothing less than abandon the most central Jewish practice: sacrifice itself. And this after sacrifice had been the backbone of Judaism for fully one thousand years.

A persistent rumor holds that sacrifice was impossible away from the great Temple in Jerusalem and that, once exiled, the Jews had no choice but to abandon sacrifice. But we know that is not true. We know from the Dead Sea Scrolls that sacrifice was possible anywhere, with only the provision that people within a three-day walk of Jerusalem were supposed to sacrifice at the Temple. We also know that the First Exile to Babylonia didn't end sacrifice. Moreover, it surely would have been easiest, upon being exiled, to temporarily suspend any restrictions limiting sacrifice to the Temple.

The Second Exile, then, did not force an end to sacrifice. Rather, the Rabbis wanted an end to sacrifice, finding the practice to have outlived its usefulness. They wanted something new.

In place of sacrifice, the Rabbis instituted worship services, offering God words instead of food. And the Rabbis created an order for those words—what we now know as the liturgy—and rules for almost everything else, too.

We now call those rules halachah, or Jewish law. And though it currently lies at the heart of Judaism, the Rabbis' set of laws, like the prophetic innovation, was in its time a radical invention.

The Rabbis are the ones who give us, for instance, not just the tradition of putting Chanukah candles into a Chanukah menorah, but a proper and improper way to do so (the proper way is right to left). There's also a proper way to light those candles (left to right).

Similarly, there are rules about building a sukkah. The sukkah must have four, three, or two and a half walls. It must be temporary, according to a wide variety of criteria. It must offer a partial view of the sky. It must be at least ten hand-breadths high (some three feet) but not more than about ten yards. These and other regulations are found in a book of the Talmud called *Sukkah*, and they were codified by the Rabbis in the centuries that followed the Second Exile.

Concerning the sukkah, the Talmud next asks whether an elephant can be used for one wall! The answer is no, because the elephant might walk away. What about a dead elephant? Yes, so long as the deceased pachyderm is at least ten hand-breadths tall.

This part of the discussion was obviously humorously intended. It highlights the way in which the Rabbis enjoyed being Jewish through the Judaism they were developing—something often lost in the modern quest merely to follow the laws.

At any rate, the Jews headed north, south, and east in the aftermath of the Second Exile (the Mediterranean Sea prevented direct movement west). Many Jews settled in Babylonia—modern-day Iraq—because of their ongoing connection to that area dating from the First Exile. "The" Talmud was in fact written by the Rabbis living in Babylonia. (There's also a lesser Talmud written by the Rabbis living in Jerusalem.) Other Jews moved south to Africa, then west across northern Africa, often settling somewhere on the way. Those who didn't stop eventually made their way to Morocco and, from there, across the Strait of Gibraltar to the Iberian Peninsula, southern Spain, where that locale's magic paved the way for what is now called the Golden Age of Spain.

Jews in the Iberian Peninsula were integrated into the newly formed Muslim empire, which had conquered the area in the eighth century. This fertile environment yielded such Jewish scholars as Abraham ibn Ezra, the famed Bible commentator; Rabbi Yosef Karo, author of the authoritative *Shulchan Aruch*; Y'hudah HaLevi, a gifted poet, physician, and philosopher and possibly the first to write secular Hebrew poetry; Maimonides (Rambam), whose works seem to have come, Abraham Joshua Heschel once said, from an entire university rather than one man; and many more.

The Jews thrived there in nonreligious ways, too, practicing law, medicine, and finance and rising to positions of power in government. They spoke local languages (primarily Arabic) and assumed local names, as, for example, Hasdai Abu Yusuf ben Isaac ben Ezra ibn Shaprut, a tenth-century Jew who served as court physician to the powerful caliph Abd al-Rachman III.

In fact, many twenty-first-century Jews living in the West will see their own circumstances mirrored in the Golden Age of Spain: success, general acceptance, and a balance between religious and secular life.

As it refers to the Jews, the term "Golden Age of Spain" is both ambiguous and contested. Some scholars date its start as early as the eighth century's first decades, others two hundred years later. Similarly, while its end is often pegged to eleventh-century political upheavals, it was in 1492 that Jewish life in Spain came to a final end, a few months after the Christian Spanish army defeated the last remnants of Muslim power there. In March 1492, their Majesties Ferdinand and Isabella ordered every Jew to convert to Christianity or to leave by July 30. By July 1492 the Golden Age of Spanish Jewry was over.

And this is the third time we find our recurring pattern of exile and spiritual revolution, again led by a previously marginalized group. In this case, however, the exile is not from Israel but rather to it. Among other destinations, the Spanish Jews arrived in a backwater city on a hill in northern Israel: Safed.

Not surprisingly, the Jews fled to many spots, but the destinations in which they would be most successful were those in the Ottoman Empire, including Safed. For unclear reasons, it was there that the previously marginalized adherents of a book called the *Zohar* thrived.

The *Zohar* was written in the thirteenth century in Spain by a man named Moses de Leon, though sacred myth attributes the book to Shimon ben Yochai of the second century. According to the myth—promulgated by Moses de Leon himself—Moses's only involvement was as copyist. He only copied and distributed Shimon ben Yochai's much older original work, he said. But though the *Zohar* may incorporate older themes, all of the evidence points unequivocally in the direction of it being a thirteenth-century creation. Still, it's quite a creation.

The modern scholar and mystic Arthur Green aptly describes the *Zohar* as a work of "sacred fantasy" to "be considered the highest

280 · A LIFE OF MEANING

expression of Jewish literary imagination in the Middle Ages" and "one of the most important bodies of religious text of all times and places." He adds that it is "a lush garden of sacred eros." The work's "secret universe" is the center of Jewish mystical faith, or Kabbalah.[1]

The *Zohar*'s nearly unparalleled appeal in a context of practically fraudulent distribution meant that it met with immediate controversy and with only partial acceptance. Many Jews in thirteenth-century Spain loved it. Others hated it. The majority of Jews outside of Spain didn't care one way or the other.

Initially, followers of the *Zohar*'s teachings—the Jewish mystics, or as they came to be known, the kabbalists—were like the prophets before the First Exile and like the Rabbis before the Second Exile, in that they envisioned great changes for Judaism, but their message fell largely on deaf ears. Then, after the fifteenth century, amid the upheavals in the aftermath of the Spanish exile, the kabbalists both thrived and managed to become mainstream.

The kabbalists were the ones who insisted that Friday night services ought to differ significantly from services held on other nights, not just through the minor additions and changes that had previously marked the start of the Sabbath, but with new texts of joy and celebration. Friday night should be a wedding! Friday night was when God—separated during the week into male and female parts—came together in marriage to form a unified God, even consummating the marriage in ecstatic joy.

To mark these new ceremonial aspects of welcoming Shabbat, a man named Rabbi Shlomo HaLevi wrote a poem in iambic tetrameter (a meter popular in classical Arabic) that may be the most perfect poem in our liturgy, perhaps in all of Judaism. He called it *L'chah Dodi*. With text based almost entirely in Scripture, it is metrically perfect, brilliant in its imagery, and masterful in its kabbalistic allusions.

The poem's opening line, "Go forth my lover to meet the bride," reflects the revisioning of Shabbat as a wedding. (The line is often wrongly translated as "Go forth my beloved," perhaps in an effort to downplay the sexual content.) The ten verses of the poem mirror a central organizing principle of Kabbalah, that of ten emanations of God—*s'firot*, in Hebrew.

The poem is among the most well-known texts in Judaism, and there is hardly a Jewish community that does not incorporate it into Friday evening worship services.

Yet for all its merit and ubiquity, *L'chah Dodi* is simply a poem that some guy wrote. It enjoys no halachic importance or mandate; the Talmud, obviously, doesn't mention it. More generally, mysticism in its broadest sense had never been part of mainstream Judaism.

But the kabbalists of Safed—though once marginalized in Spain—changed all this. Like the prophets who turned the Jewish eye outward after the First Exile, and like the Rabbis who substituted prayer and halachah for sacrifice after the Second Exile, the kabbalists in the aftermath of the Spanish exile gave Judaism mysticism and the Friday evening *Kabbalat Shabbat* service.

We have one more exile and spiritual revolution. This last exile to date is much more modern and, therefore, more immediately painful to modern readers, so it is harder to analyze with any sense of detachment. But it follows the same pattern of producing a spiritual revolution.

It is, of course, the Holocaust, or Shoah. During the 1940s, the Jews in Europe were slaughtered en masse, only the lucky ones escaping. A population of about 9.5 million European Jews—more than half of the world's total Jewish population—was cut to less than 4 million. By 1945, Europe was home to only about a third of the world's Jews (a number that has dropped to about 10 percent at the time of this writing).

And although Germany is most closely associated with the Holocaust, most of Europe's Jews in 1939—some 85 percent, in fact—lived in Eastern Europe (Poland, the former Soviet Union, and so on). Only about two hundred thousand, or roughly 2 percent, lived in Germany. Or to put things in global context, about half of the world's Jews in 1939 lived in Eastern Europe; about 1 percent lived in Germany.

Yet it was Germany's Jews—once again, a previously marginalized group—who would lead the post-Holocaust spiritual revolution. In the early part of the 1800s, largely in response to Napoleon's message of an enlightened, modern Europe with emancipated Jews, some Jews in what would later become Germany started experimenting with an enlightened, modern Judaism. They wanted to leave the Jewish ghettos and live (then-)modern lives.

As early as the eighteenth century, Moses Mendelssohn (1729–86) worked to integrate the Enlightenment into Judaism, even translating the Torah into German. He argued for a rational, tolerant, modern, ethical religion. (Moses Mendelssohn's grandson, Felix Mendelssohn, is the famous composer.)

In response to this kind of thinking, a Hungarian rabbi named Moses Sofer, widely known as the Chatam Sofer, began to argue that nothing in Judaism could be changed. He claimed that the Torah itself prohibits anything new. Ironically, though, the Chatam Sofer's argument was itself a new interpretation of an old text. He argued that "the new is forbidden by the Torah," quoting *Kiddushin* 38b in the Talmud. But in that phrase in the Talmud, "the new" specifically refers to "new" grain in certain circumstances. Sofer used the word "new" instead to denote the kind of new practices that Mendelssohn favored.

After reading Mendelssohn's writings, a man named Israel Jacobson (1768–1828) similarly began working to modernize Judaism. And having married the granddaughter of Philip Samson, founder of the prestigious center of Jewish education known as the Samson School, Jacobson was in a position of influence. He was also in a position to meet other influential people, including another future advocate for reforming Judaism, Leopold Zunz (1794–1886), who similarly attended the Samson School.

Likewise, a man named Abraham Geiger (1810–74) sought to create a Judaism that welcomed secular fields like history, archaeology, and, more generally, the then-new and growing *Wissenschaft* approach to the world that mirrors our modern notion of "science."

Geiger studied at the University of Bonn, where he met Samson Raphael Hirsch (1808–88). Friends at first, Hirsch and Geiger became vehement opponents. Hirsch ended up founding a movement now called *Trennungsorthodoxy*, literally "Separation Orthodoxy," akin to today's Modern Orthodoxy. Hirsch disagreed with modernizers like Zunz and Geiger, but he also disagreed with the Chatam Sofer's radical opposition to change.

In many ways, Geiger is the founder of Reform Judaism, and Hirsch is the founder of Orthodox Judaism. Judaism's Conservative Movement was born in the United States in response to Eastern European immigration, but it traces much of its theology and approach to yet another German thinker, Zacharias Frankel (1801–75). So the Reform and Orthodox Movements began in nineteenth-century Germany as responses to modernity, and in a roundabout way the Conservative Movement did, too.

In the first half of the nineteenth century, these and other Jewish leaders, and their respective followers and supporters, battled over pivotal issues like organ music and sermonizing as part of a broader philosophical disagreement about the nature of Judaism in the face of modernity.

The fighting was both bitter and public. But the fights were largely limited to Germany. A few congregations beyond Germany—in the United States, for example—had been established in the spirit of the German movements. For the most part, though, the world's Jews were still in Eastern Europe, where they did not adhere to the schools of Jacobson, Geiger, Zunz, Hirsch, or the Chatam Sofer because they had never left the ghetto, Napoleon never having conquered Eastern Europe. And certainly the Sephardic Jews of the Arab world (Yemen and Iraq, for example) didn't care about the German religious debates.

So as late as the start of the Holocaust, the vast majority of Jews were not Reform, Conservative, or Orthodox. Those three were minority movements limited to Germany and a handful of other congregations.

Then, in the aftermath of the Holocaust—our fourth exile—we find the pattern we now recognize. A previously marginalized group reinvents Judaism in a fourth spiritual revolution. We naturally tend to focus on that group's internal divisions, because we ourselves are still in the fourth revolution. For instance, we devote attention to how

Reform differs from Orthodoxy, to liturgical styles, and to cell phone use on Shabbat.

But such divisions mask the larger pattern. There was no Reform, no Conservative, and no Orthodox until eighteenth-century Germany, and only in the twentieth century did any of the three become mainstream.

For political reasons, Orthodoxy's public platform emphasizes continuity, while Reform's emphasizes change. That difference makes it easy to imagine that only Reform was the product of a minority movement in Germany. But even a cursory look at history reveals a different story. We've already seen how even the most vehement opponent to new thinking based his argument in new thinking. More importantly, current Reform, Conservative, and Orthodox practices all evidence revolution.

For instance, one modern battle line is over the use of cell phones on Shabbat. Reform congregations allow it; Orthodox congregations do not. It is abundantly obvious, though, that the Jews of the 1800s, to say nothing of the Jews in the second century, had no policy regarding cell phones, just as they didn't have one for electricity.

Certain halachic considerations do rein in particular uses of electricity on Shabbat. For example, the Talmud suggests that heating metal to the point that it glows is forbidden on Shabbat, and Maimonides explicitly says so. Since that is exactly how incandescent light bulbs work, there's good reason to think that turning on an incandescent light bulb should be considered a halachic violation of Shabbat. But that reasoning doesn't extend directly to fluorescent or LED lights.

What halachah might say about cell phones is even more tenuous and is based primarily on the (obviously modern) prohibition against using electricity in general on Shabbat. And here halachah is anything but clear. What we seem to find is a desire among certain communities to prohibit electricity, and therefore cell phones and non-incandescent lights. But disagreement is rampant about how to achieve that prohibition. The earliest opinion—no longer highly regarded—was that using electricity, like spraying fragrance onto cloth, is creating something new (technically, *molid*), and that is a category of actions prohibited on Shabbat. Using electricity was later compared to other forbidden Shabbat activities: building, completing a project, creating sparks, burning (because additional fuel has to be burned at a power station to create the electricity), and more. The prominent Rabbi Shlomo Zalman Auerbach even wrote (*Minchat Shlomo* 74, 84) that there's no halachic reason not to use electricity on Shabbat, but Jews still shouldn't do it!

So both the Reform practice of allowing cell phones on Shabbat and the Orthodox practice of disallowing them are modern innovations.

A second modern battle line is drawn over wearing a *kippah*. Through happenstance, the generally progressive practice of donning a *kippah* only for services has the most historical support. That's what Maimonides did in the thirteenth century. It was the post–Spanish exile kabbalists who first suggested that Jews should always wear a *kippah*. So in this case, Reform and Orthodox practices draw on different historical opinions.

A third modern battle line concerns kashrut and shows again how modernity challenges old ritual laws in surprising ways. In the case of kashrut, this is because the laws were created long before modern chemistry became involved in processing food. For example, is maltodextrin kosher for Passover? On one hand, maltodextrin is simply a polysaccharide, that is, a chain of glucose units. Glucose is kosher for Passover, so why wouldn't a chain of glucose units be kosher? On the other hand, maltodextrin can be made from corn (as is common in the United States) or wheat (the usual practice in Europe). The prevailing Orthodox opinion on wheat-based maltodextrin is that it is forbidden, because wheat is forbidden unless specially handled to avoid any rising, and to the extent that corn is forbidden, so too is corn-based maltodextrin. That's certainly reasonable. But it is not the only reasonable approach. Equally reasonable is the argument that two identical molecules ought to have the same kashrut status, wherever they might have come from.

Similarly, why should honey be kosher (though it is)? After all, honey comes from bees, bees are not kosher, and according to the

Talmud (*B'chorot* 1a), anything that emerges from a nonkosher animal is not kosher. Camel milk, for instance, is forbidden because it comes from the nonkosher camel. So why is honey okay? The Talmudic answer (*B'chorot* 7b) is that bees don't produce honey the way camels produce milk. Bees only store honey, between the time they collect it from blossoms and the time they regurgitate it. But the Talmud was wrong. While bees do store nectar (in a special extra stomach, or crop), they also process the nectar while they are storing it. There are bee enzymes in honey. The most common approach here is to ignore the (uncontested) modern scientific objections to the Rabbis, but an equally reasonable approach would be to introduce a long-overdue correction.

Our final example of kashrut comes from New York City tap water, which was discovered some years ago to contain tiny crustaceans related to shrimp called copepods. Crustaceans are not kosher. And it's not just New York. Many public water supplies contain copepods. How can such water be kosher? Some rabbis ruled that it isn't. Others ruled that the laws of kashrut apply only to what we can see without a microscope. Once again, these are reasonable interpretations, but not the only reasonable interpretations.

In sum, the general pattern we see—with cell phones, with the *kippah*, with maltodextrin, and in many other instances—is that Reform Judaism tends toward less stringent practice while Orthodox Judaism tends toward more stringent practice, and both tendencies are modern reactions to the modern world. Modern Jews tend to focus on the different outcomes, but these hide the common pattern: we are all re-creating Judaism.

That is, we are living through only the fourth major spiritual revolution since the days of King David and our ancestors' original experiment in human rights and in a better way to live. We follow the pattern of the prophets, who moved from the periphery to the center and turned our eyes outward toward other peoples; the pattern of the Rabbis, who moved from the periphery to the center and created halachah even as they rejected traditional sacrifice; and the pattern of the kabbalists, who moved from the periphery to the center and gave Judaism Kabbalah and *Kabbalat Shabbat.*

As participants in the revolution, we don't know how it will end. We don't know if the moderation of Reform or the intensification of Orthodoxy will ultimately triumph, though certainly the evidence so far suggests it will be a mixture heavily weighted toward moderation.

We do know that we are living through an extraordinary era. We are the modern guardians of an ancient dream of human dignity, joy, and honor. And we are the ones who will define Judaism not just for the coming decades, but for centuries and millennia. We are voicing the new prophetic vision, writing the new Talmud, living the new Kabbalah.

And what a privilege it is.

NOTE

1. Arthur Green, introduction to *The Zohar*, Pritzker ed., trans. and commentary by Daniel C. Matt, vol. 1 (Stanford, CA: Stanford University Press, 2004), xxxi.

28

OUR TREE OF LIFE

Rabbi Amy Scheinerman

We are all searchers. As we travel through life, we seek purpose and meaning, a sense of deep belonging, a path to lives of integrity and decency, and a way to leave a positive mark on the world. Jewish tradition has always held that the key to purpose, meaning, belonging, wisdom, morality, and immortality is our sacred books. The precious teachings of Torah are unlocked by study. This is reflected in the many dynamic, exciting, and inspiring Torah study groups fostered by Reform congregations. Study requires intellectual skills and emotional openness, and preferably a social venue (with one partner or as a member of a class), but it is, fundamentally, the quintessential Jewish spiritual practice. Happily, Jewish tradition is brimming with literary gems.

Torah is our *Eitz Chayim*, our Tree of Life. Lying at the core of Jewish identity, Torah roots us historically and religiously. It is the glue that binds Jews together across time and space. Our customs and traditions vary significantly from place to place and from century to century, but we all hold sacred a set of texts that we identify as "holy books." Studying, interpreting, and reinterpreting Torah (both the Written Torah, the Five Books of Moses, and the Oral Torah, the Talmud)—complete with disagreements, debates, and differing interpretations—have been the mainstay of Jewish life throughout the centuries. What is more, Torah has served as the sounding board and reflective window for Jews to examine their own lives and situations; Torah study has been a means of examining the big, thorny questions of life, something off which to bounce new, even radical ideas, in the quest for insight. Through Torah study, each generation has found wisdom and meaning in our sacred texts. As an outgrowth of study, each generation has promulgated its own understandings and interpretations of Torah, adding new branches to the growing, life-giving tree that sustains the Jewish people. The understandings we glean are gifts we give our contemporaries and a heritage we leave the generations to come. The *Eitz Chayim* is not so much one tree as it is an ever-expanding forest.

Talmud, which tradition holds is Oral Torah, affirms this in a teaching that inspired one of our morning prayers:

> These are the obligations without measure, whose reward, too, is without measure: To honor father and mother; to perform acts of love and kindness; to attend the house of study daily; to welcome the stranger; to visit the sick; to rejoice with bride and groom; to console the bereaved; to pray with sincerity; to make peace where there is strife. And the study of Torah is equal to them all, because it leads to them all. (*Mishnah Pei-ah* 1:1; Babylonian Talmud, *Shabbat* 127a)

Talmud Torah—Torah study—surpasses other mitzvot (Jewish obligations, practices, and traditions) because it teaches the student of Torah how to live as a Jew and inspires him or her to become immersed in Jewish life and live by the moral values cherished throughout our generations. Torah study, more than any other aspect of Jewish life and practice, combines our spiritual and intellectual proclivities and our obligations to better ourselves, nurture our families, improve our communities, and repair the world.

Reform Judaism has always affirmed the value and centrality of Torah study, no less now than at any time in the past, and perhaps more in recent decades as we rekindle our relationship with a wider sense of what constitutes Torah: Talmud, midrash, Kabbalah, Mussar literature, and *chasidut* are all the products of Torah study that are thus Torah themselves. From the 1885 Pittsburgh Platform to the Pittsburgh Platform of 1999, we have acknowledged Torah as our guide and Torah study as a fundamental obligation of committed Jewish living. In 1885, the leaders of Reform Judaism asserted the centrality of our *Eitz Chayim* to our essential purpose as a people: "We recognize in the Bible the record of the consecration of the Jewish people to its mission as the priest of the one God, and value it as the most potent instrument of religious and moral instruction."[1]

In time, our vision of Torah grew. In 1999, the second Pittsburgh Platform stated:

> We affirm that Torah is the foundation of Jewish life. We cherish the truths revealed in Torah, God's ongoing revelation to our people and the record of our people's ongoing relationship with God. We affirm that Torah is a manifestation of *ahavat olam*, God's eternal love for the Jewish people and for all humanity. . . . We are called by Torah to lifelong study in the home, in the synagogue and in every place where Jews gather to learn and teach.[2]

With time, our horizons have been broadened, and we are rewarded when we engage with sparkling, spiritual texts that speak to the mind, the heart, and the soul. What is more, Torah study brings us together with other Jews, forming communities of learning and forging relationships we might not otherwise enjoy.

Reform Judaism is uniquely positioned to extend Torah learning in new directions, due to its historical respect for the full spectrum of academic and intellectual fields and methods the secular world offers. (These range from sciences such as physical cosmology and quantum physics, to social sciences such as anthropology, psychology, and economics, to the gifts of the humanities, including comparative literature, philosophy, and semiotics.) The tools and insights of the many academic disciplines help us shed light on the contextual meaning of our sacred texts. They also offer new ways to read traditional texts and extract their wisdom and meaning, obtaining direction for our lives.

Where the academic wishes to understand the author's intent—and that can help us appreciate the text in new ways—the goal of Torah study as a spiritual practice is to find interpretations that speak to us not only on an intellectual level, but on a religious and spiritual level. We prize the spiritual meaning our sacred texts impart when we allow them to speak to us and the lives we live. As liberal Jews, we appreciate both the historical, rational view of the texts, as well as the spiritual nurturing and succor we derive from the texts.

Bridging the worlds of the modern intellectual study of our sacred texts and traditional spiritual searching for wisdom and meaning can be challenging. What is "true"? What is "real"? Here, I have found the spiritual development theory of philosopher Paul Ricoeur helpful. Ricoeur describes three steps of spiritual interpretation. The first, which he terms "the first naiveté," is the literal interpretation of Scripture, accepting it on faith, at face value. Once rationalism (the second stage) entered the world, Scripture was subjected to rational scrutiny and analysis, and the narratives and laws once accepted as "true" came to be regarded as "myth." In the third stage, "the second naiveté," we learn how to engage the text without insisting upon a literal reading and without jettisoning rationalism. In the third stage, we recognize symbolism and metaphorical constructs that bespeak values dear to us, uplift us, and address the core questions of life. For Reform Jews, Ricoeur offers the best of all possible worlds: we retain our sacred texts as bridges to the Divine and view them through all the intellectual and spiritual lenses that help us draw out their wisdom.

As much as Reform Judaism respects the choices of the individual concerning religious and spiritual life, we nonetheless affirm that Torah study is an obligation. I would hope that all Reform Jews would recognize the value of committing ourselves to Torah learning for our own sake, to the benefit of our children (for whom we are behavioral role models), toward the strengthening of the broader community, who will benefit from our insights and ideas, and as a gift to future generations, who will look to those who came before them for insight.

We should aim to make Torah study a central facet of our communal life, with opportunity for a wide variety of learners. Paraphrasing the cultural Zionist Achad HaAm, who wrote about Shabbat observance, as much as the Jews preserve Torah, Torah study preserves the Jews. Rabbi Shlomo Ephraim (1550–1619) of Lunschitz, Poland, in his popular commentary on Torah, *Kli Yakar*, identifies Torah study as the *minchah chadashah* ("*new* meal offering") of Leviticus 23:15–16. He writes, "The Torah must be new for each person every day as the day that it was received on Mount Sinai. . . . For, in truth, you are commanded to derive novelty each and every day."

The only way for Torah to be new is for us to explore it through study so that we might find new interpretations that speak to us concerning the lives we are living. Rabbi Lunschitz goes beyond inviting us in to learn; he considers study and the generation of new interpretations to be an obligation. I am in total agreement. Torah, our *Eitz Chayim*, emits life-sustaining oxygen, but we must actively breathe it in deeply. Scholar Gerald Bruns put it this way: "What is at stake with respect to the Scripture is not what lies behind the text in the form of an original meaning, but what lies in front of it where the interpreter stands. The Bible always addresses itself to the time of interpretation: one cannot understand it except by appropriating it anew."[3]

Talmud tells an intriguing tale about Moses at the moment God gave him the Torah. Standing atop Mount Sinai, Moses is eager and impatient for God to reveal the Torah to him. He sees that God is busily tying *tagin* (decorative crowns) on some of the Hebrew letters of the text. Impatiently, Moses asks why God delays giving the Torah in order to finish what seem inconsequential aesthetic flourishes. God responds that these *tagin* will help ensure that novel interpretations of Torah enter the world when Rabbi Akiva learns and teaches Torah. Moses is astonished. If God has someone like Rabbi Akiva who can interpret Torah with such skill and virtuosity, what need has God for Moses? God's response is to transport Moses some fourteen centuries into the future. Moses finds himself sitting in the back row of Rabbi Akiva's classroom. He listens and comprehends nothing Rabbi Akiva says. Finally, another student asks the source of the law Rabbi Akiva is expounding, and Moses hears him say, *Halachah l'Moshe mi-Sinai*, "It is a law transmitted to Moses at Sinai." Moses's Torah is the Torah of the words on the scroll; Rabbi Akiva's Torah includes the myriad laws and lessons he derives from the *tagin*. The Rabbis who craft this story are keenly aware that the historical Rabbi Akiva's hermeneutics and halachic exegesis form the foundation of Rabbinic Judaism. Moses gave Israel the Written Torah (the Five Books of Moses), but Rabbi Akiva made possible and thereby *gave* to Israel the Oral Torah (Talmud). We, too, can join the interpretive conversation. The Rabbis view Rabbi Akiva as a second Moses, giver of the Oral Torah.

We can find another layer to the story: It is not that Moses is incapable of grasping the ideas propounded by Rabbi Akiva. Rather, Torah is a living, breathing text tradition, and it will grow and change with each generation in ways that we cannot foresee. There will be extraordinary minds whose imprint on Torah tradition is groundbreaking, formative, and eternal—Rabbi Akiva is a prime example—but each generation will generate a wealth of novel interpretations, *Kli Yakar's minchah chadashah* (new meal offering).

When we come together to study Torah, to share our insights and interpretations, we will not always agree with one another. That, too, is Torah. Talmud is filled with disagreement and arguments. One of the most valuable outcomes of learning Torah with others is learning how to agree to disagree—and remain civil and friendly. Our Sages sometimes found this challenging, no less than we do today. Mishnah teaches:

> An argument that is in the name of heaven shall in the end lead to a permanent result; but every controversy that is not in the name of heaven, shall not lead to a permanent result. Which controversy was that which was in the name of heaven? Such was the controversy of Hillel and Shammai. And that which was not in the name of heaven? Such was the controversy of Korach and all his company. (*Pirkei Avot* 5:17)

This teaching is more than about how to hold a civil argument. It's about what builds community and what destroys community. The mishnah references Numbers 16–17. Korach and his minions attempt to undermine Moses's leadership. Korach, jealous of Moses's authority and seeking Moses's power, equipped with an appealing ideology and supported by followers, foments a self-aggrandizing rebellion. He does not have the needs of the entire community in mind, but only his own narrow interests.

The Rabbis contrasted Korach with our feisty and spirited sages Hillel and Shammai, who agreed on very little and disputed virtually every morsel of Jewish practice, theology, and philosophy. They did not argue for their narrow interests or reputations, however, but rather for religious and spiritual truth as they understood it. During one of their disputes, recounted in the Babylonian Talmud (*Eiruvin* 13b), we are told that Beit Hillel (the School of Hillel) and Beit Shammai (the School of Shammai) were so deeply divided that heaven intervened. A *bat kol* (heavenly voice) declared in the hearing of all, *Eilu v'eilu divrei Elohim chayim*, "Both the words of the one and the words of the other are the words of the living God." The story of their vociferous disagreement and God's assertion that differing opinions can both hold divine valence is valuable enough, but the story doesn't end there. It goes on to say that nonetheless, the halachah more often follows the opinions of Beit Hillel. But neither is that the end of the story. The climax concerns *why* Beit Hillel was given predominance. Talmud explains: it is because they were *nochin v'aluvin* (kind and humble), they would study the teachings of their rival, Beit Shammai, and what is more, they would mention the opinions of Beit Shammai before their own. The medieval Talmudist Rabbi Menachem Meiri elucidates the Talmud's intention even further: a *machloket l'shem shamayim* is a dispute in which one party challenges the other not merely to provoke or to seek victory but rather out of a sincere desire to know truth. This is a profound lesson about managing a *machloket l'shem shamayim*, a conflict for the sake of heaven. The Sages are teaching us that Torah study rests on a foundation of respecting the views of others when their intentions are noble, a value that transcends the hours we spend studying Torah and informs our relationships and interactions with others on every level. At the same time that the Talmud affirms the legitimacy of diverse views concerning Jewish practice and interpretation, it elevates kindness and humility to the level of crowning moral achievements. Torah study not only brings us together in the common pursuit of wisdom and meaning, but teaches us—nay, demands of us—civility and mutual respect.

Torah study is a lifelong process. As a community, we read Torah (the Five Books of Moses) annually, and those who dive into its waters know that although we return to it year after year, it is never the same twice, because each time we come to the text we are different. This is why, when we finish a book, we acknowledge its power to support and strengthen us by reciting together, *Chazak chazak v'nitchazeik,* "Strengthen us, strengthen us, and we will be strong."

A parable from the Chasidic master Rebbe Nachman of Bratzlav is as germane to our lives as it was to his followers' lives in the Ukraine early in the nineteenth century: A Jewish man named Isaac dreamed that priceless treasure lay buried under a bridge far from his home. He set out and traveled for many days to uncover and lay claim to the treasure. When he reached the bridge that had appeared in his dream, he began to dig. A soldier approached him and asked, "What are you doing?" He described his dream to the soldier, who laughed heartily and replied, "What a crazy old man you are! Why, if I believed my dreams, I would travel at once to the town you come from and dig in the cellar of somebody named Isaac, where a great treasure is to be found." Isaac quietly put away his shovel, returned home, and climbed down into his cellar, where he found a great treasure.

We have a wonderful treasure right here at home. We are blessed with a wide variety of jewels, holy books to challenge our intellect and refine our *n'shamah,* rewarding both mind and soul. And we are fortunate to have such a rich and bountiful library of choices so each of us can follow our interests and inclinations, nourished, enlarged, and enriched by the traditional Jewish spiritual practice of Jewish learning.

NOTES

1. "The Pittsburgh Platform" (1885), http://ccarnet.org/rabbis-speak/platforms/declaration-principles/.

2. "A Statement of Principles for Reform Judaism" (May 1999), https://ccarnet.org/rabbis-speak/platforms/statement-principles-reform-judaism/.

3. Gerald L. Bruns, "Midrash and Allegory: The Beginnings of Scriptural Interpretation," in *The Literary Guide to the Bible*, ed. Robert Alter and Frank Kermode (Cambridge, MA: Harvard University Press, 1987), 627–28.

29

REFORM APPROACHES
TO OUR SACRED TEXTS

Rabbi Geoffrey W. Dennis

We can no longer read Jewish sacred literature in the same way our ancestors did. Reform Judaism celebrates the freedom and creativity ancient and medieval Jews brought to the reading, interpretation, and application of Torah to their lives. But it is also true that they labored diligently to find meaning in Torah while operating under certain axioms that Reform Judaism has, by and large, abandoned: the belief that the Written Torah comes directly from the divine mind; that it is—factually, literally—God's words; that the Torah is without error or superfluous detail; that even seeming errors in spelling, grammar, and syntax are actually divine disclosures. The Sages were less occupied with fact and historicity than with the text's ability to point them toward contemporary consolations, future hopes, and eternal truths.

Today, we don't have such confidence. It is evident now that our sacred texts are human in composition, with all the biases and flaws that entails. They are also human in transmission, a process that results in an evolving text that has undergone changes over the long course of its history.

Two hundred years ago, the earliest reformers in Europe had already started to put aside the doctrine of the divine origins of the

Torah and sacred books. By 1828, for example, Abraham Geiger, the leading rabbi-scholar of our nascent movement, was publishing his theories of the human composition, editing, and canonization of the Hebrew Bible.[1] In this he offered one of the earliest modern rationales for the modern relevance of Torah, though a human document: it has unique aesthetic and moral value. Geiger wrote, "The Talmud must go; the Bible, that collection of mostly beautiful and exalted—perhaps the most exalted—human books, as a Divine work must also go."[2] This was not a universal position among reformers. Through most of the nineteenth century, there were many Reform rabbis and thinkers[3] who held to the notion that the Bible was the "word(s) of God," often to the frustration of a modern-minded Jewish laity.[4]

By the end of the nineteenth century, however, the Reform commitment to enlightenment and modern critical thinking proved decisive. As products of the best European universities and their own modern seminaries, Reform laypeople and rabbis came to recognize the validity of modern biblical criticism and its claims. The Bible was a human-made collection of texts shaped by different political, social, and moral agendas, rather than being the uniform perspective of a single, transcendent mind.[5]

Given this knowledge, the fundamental move by most Reform thinkers was to historicize revelation. Thus the Written Torah was expression of divine revelation *in its time*, but human understanding of the divine continues to advance. The prophets, in particular, radically advanced humanity through the revelation that God's primary concern is morality (as opposed to say, ritual), yet the insights of the prophetic writings were still often bound to their own historical context.[6] And so it continued, with Talmud, midrash, and medieval Jewish philosophy, each a link in a process of *progressive revelation*, each advancing our understanding of divine will. Thus Reform educator Maurice Eisendrath would state, "God is a living God, not a God who revealed Himself and His word once at Sinai and speaks no more."[7]

This theology of progressive revelation worked well with the Reform sense of progressive improvement in history, and while the theologian Kaufmann Kohler insisted that this process continues "without ever placing the old and new in opposition," it has often had the unintended effect of undermining the continuing relevance of Torah as a whole. It implies that the older the teaching, the more likely it has been superseded by a superior, more advanced inspiration,[8] so why should these ancient documents still be at the center of our communal life? Why should the *sefer Torah* (Torah scroll), as opposed to the writing of Maimonides or Kaufmann Kohler, forever occupy the holy ark in a Reform synagogue?

Yet while this may logically follow, intuitively this seems wrong on its face. If Torah is important, then surely *the Torah* is still the essence of the essential. Reform thinkers have offered a variety of answers over the past century in order to affirm the continued centrality of the Torah. We have already noted the appeal to the sublimity of the Bible, its artistic worth.

Perhaps the most enduring arguments are exemplified by two great Reform rabbis of the mid-twentieth century: Jakob Petuchowski, a professor of liturgy and Jewish thought at Hebrew Union College (Cincinnati), and Bernard Bamberger, a pulpit rabbi and biblical scholar.

Dr. Petuchowski argues that our sacred Scriptures have a dual nature—they are the human-made by-product of our encounter with God: they are God-given in that God manifests in experiences, and human-made in that they express our efforts to make sense of those experiences.[9]

Dr. Bamberger's argument for Torah's relevance is, effectively, secular. He does not even explicitly claim divine inspiration for it, though at places he hints that this is what he believes.[10] Rather, his argument approaches being a tautology: the reason the Bible is relevant for us is because it remains relevant. It remains, he observes, "the book of life in this world," the primary template from which contemporary Westerners draw guidance. It confronts us and comforts us with stories and inspiration for our most pressing concerns—family and community, death and grieving, illness and suffering, anxiety and consolation. It gives us the language of our lives. Its ethics inspire us to confront our own ethical conundrums, even if we discover our own values push us beyond those set out in Torah. Like the fining used to clarify wine, our sacred texts help us crystalize our thinking, even though the fining itself must then be, at the end of the process, set aside. Torah is still the enzyme that refines our human nature.

More recently, Reform thinkers have emphasized the social role of Torah in creating and sustaining not just human development, but *Jewish* identity. Rather than either divine revelation or moral history, Torah is essential to being Jewish. Reform rabbi and biblical scholar David Aaron, for example, characterizes the Bible as a persuasive tract that "fuses fiction with allegory" intended to ensure "a culture, an identity, a peoplehood, a faith, might survive and thrive against all odds."[11]

Regardless of where one stands on divine influence or historicity, the idea that Torah is essential to Jewish identity is one that seems the most irrefutable, and thereby most essential. Torah is actually more important, in some sense, than "Judaism." Consider the very word "Judaism." Or the German *Judentum*. Or even the Hebrew, *Yachadut*. Whatever the language, these words are only a few hundred years old. The word, and therefore the concept, of Jewish religion is of recent coinage. In fact, the very word for "religion" in Hebrew, *dat*, is adopted from Farsi—Hebrew lacks a native word for "religion"! Does this imply that Jews don't have religion? Well, historically Jews made no great distinction between spiritual traditions and cultural ones. Only with the advent of modernity did the word "Judaism," distinguished from "Jew," come into usage. Many religious groups in America today like to distance themselves from the word "religion" because of its negative connotations, but Jews alone, among all the brand-name faiths in the world, have the strongest claim to not being an actual religion.

But if so, what term did past Jews use for the distinctly spiritual dimension of Jewish civilization? It was *Torah*. Torah was and is the wellspring of Jewish identity. From it we derived our ethics, our transcendent beliefs, and our rituals, but also our music, norms, customs, food preferences, stories, cultural habits—our very lifestyle as Jews. Historically, Jews don't have religion; what we have is Torah.

But what, precisely, do we mean by *Torah*? The Written Torah is the Five Books of Moses, the *sefer Torah*, and the *Chumash*—hence the definite article. *Torah*, on the other hand, has been the traditional Jewish shorthand for the entirety of Jewish tradition: *Tanach*, Talmud, and midrash; Jewish philosophy and Jewish mysticism; halachah (law) and aggadah (lore). But Torah also encompasses our distinctive customs and habits, from the words we use to the way we argue, and now includes the wisdom and instruction we take from Internet blogs and Jewish Facebook groups. So broadly speaking, the totality of Yiddishkeit, Jewish culture, from Bible to bagels, *gam zu Torah*—this too is Torah.

Bagels aside, there is no denying that the bulk of Torah is both literary and spiritual. This is a special challenge for Reform Jews because our movement is, in the Western idiom, a "religious" movement, although many of us no longer easily identify with religion. And as people inclined toward universalist thinking and multiculturalism, we struggle with why we should grant a special place to any sacred literature, even our own, when we no longer believe that literature came from the hand of God, at Sinai. We know that our literature is very much like other sacred literatures of other peoples. Why, then, should it command a unique, or even special, place in our lives?

Because Torah, the full scope of our sacred texts, has proved essential to Jewish identity and culture. Reformers have always understood this, and for the past two hundred years, as Jews have been buffeted by the forces of modernity, we have had Torah, and it has been our lifeline.

How, then, can contemporary Jews study and apply our sacred texts to their life in a way that is both modern and authentic, one that values Torah to instruct us without us having to compromise the integrity of our modern and critical beliefs? Paradoxically, though we may reject the axioms of our ancestors, many of their premodern modes of interpretation are still useful. To partially refute my own opening sentence, there *are* some ways we can still read our sacred literature as our ancestors did.

Even if we cannot read Scriptures as divine anthropology (an account of what God knows we can and should be) or as history, Torah can still be relevant and meaningful in the life of a modern Reform Jew. I propose that there are (at least) three fundamental—but non-fundamentalist—ways we can fruitfully interpret Torah in a Reform context: as analogy, as allegory, and as myth. All of these are venerable strategies of hoary Jewish antiquity, but each remains a vibrant and valid method for us today.

Analogy is the most frequently used approach, and indeed analogies are important in all verbal communication. They allow us to contextualize something unknown through the lens of known and familiar ideas or experience. Anyone who has listened to a sermon or attended Torah study has witnessed someone draw an analogy from a biblical or Talmudic story that made the story applicable to their own life. Analogy is a very traditional method of interpretation; it combines *p'shat*, which accepts the narrative at face value, with an added analogical maxim: *Maasei avot siman b'neichem*, "The actions of the ancestors are signs for their descendants." Thus, we can read these narratives and draw parallels as to how we should (or shouldn't) behave in a similar situation. Perhaps the most important analogy made in Scripture is the one that says we are made in the likeness of God. This is a profound message about human capacity and human responsibility. Yet, while analogies are common, they are hardly simple. It is easy to make facile and even false analogies if one makes them without discernment. So, for instance, while our abilities sometimes approach the godlike, our wisdom remains limited, whereas God's knowledge is unlimited. Because of these differences, we can easily misjudge a matter through false analogy, with potentially disastrous results. I would call this the modern analogue of idolatry, for what is idolatry, but the granting of ultimate value and authority to something that doesn't deserve it?

Reading the Scriptures for analogies to our contemporary condition is easy, but reading it as allegory—as a narrative that requires interpretation to reveal a hidden meaning—typically an abstract moral or theological one, is harder for us. Our tradition calls this interpretive strategy *remez*, "hint." It is hard to do because we have been conditioned by modern habits of contextual reading to read each description, claim, or statement that appears in any text in the most literal fashion. When Torah records, for example, that humanity's violence corrupted the earth, leading God to bring forth a devastating flood, we are inclined to embrace or dismiss that narrative on its face value. We falsely think if we cannot embrace the story as factual, we must necessarily reject the story as useless.

But knowing that something is not factual does not mean it is not still true in another sense. Take, for example, the uncultured country cousin of allegory, the parable. We know when we hear a parable "Once there was a woman who met a prince . . ." that it is not a factual account of people and things that actually once occurred, but through its intentional obliqueness, it can provide valuable insight. It can be said that a parable actually avoids the *truth* in order to make a *real* point. Thus, to use a modern parable:

> A group of people are standing at a river bank and hear the cries of a baby. They see an infant floating—drowning—in the water. One person immediately dives in to rescue the child. But as this happens, yet another baby comes floating down the river, and then another! People jump in to save the babies, but see that one person has started to walk away from the riverside. Accusingly they shout, "Where are you going?" The response: "I'm going upstream to stop whoever's throwing babies into the river."

The story is certainly not factual; it is absurd on its face, but the point is far from absurd: it is smarter to figure out the cause of a problem than merely treat the symptom.

Returning to our biblical example—the Flood story—if read as a factual account of the past, I would agree it deserves to be dismissed. But if read allegorically, as a tale of how human violence and callousness will inevitably lead to catastrophic results for all creatures on the planet, well, I can hardly think of a more relevant story to reflect upon in the twenty-first century.

Moreover, reading Torah as allegory is not a modern evasion, but one of the most authentic Jewish approaches to our sacred teachings. The very idea that we have to read the Bible for its plain meaning, and therefore primarily factual and scientifically descriptive, is largely an invention of sixteenth-century Protestantism.[12] Reading it as allegory allows us to find real and instructive applicability in Torah, even when the plain sense of the text does not seem relevant or useful.

For moderns, the most challenging of the three categories is myth— the many and obvious mythological features of the Bible.[13] The Enlightenment framed myth as akin to fairy tales, fantastic stories of the gods and heroes that never happened, without useful application and preserved purely for entertainment value. Properly understood, however, the myths of Torah serve and sustain the community and the people of Israel, just as allegory may serve and sustain us as individual Jews. Myth is part of the interpretive strategy of *sod*, a deeply embedded message, one could say a concealed lesson, in Torah. It is a way of reading that Reform Jews would do well to embrace, because these fact-free, yet truth-telling stories define us as a *people*.

We may never find historical support for our founding myth, our story of slavery and liberation from Egypt. Still, it is one of the most powerful narratives ever told. Thinking of the Exodus not as a fiction that never happened, but as an experience that can repeat itself again and again in human history makes it a potent, timeless tale. Its lessons—the superiority of freedom over servitude, the importance of moral resistance to oppression, the possibility of new birth or rebirth out of tribulation—all these resonate with peoples across the world. This particular myth has inspired us to not settle for the world as is, but to constantly strive to make it better. And that's how really good myths have always worked. Even a myth that makes most modern Jews uncomfortable, the myth of being a chosen people, has nonetheless driven our small community to be fierce in its extraordinary contributions to the world.

Perhaps my favorite myth in the Torah is the giving of the Ten Commandments. Understanding this Israelite myth requires us to understand its ancient Near East context. In Babylonian myth, the gods possess a mighty book—a set of stones called the *Tup Shimti*, the "Tablets of Destiny." Whichever god holds these tablets "holds the reins of heaven." Knowing this, we realize that the Torah's story of God presenting us with the divine tablets makes an extraordinary claim for human empowerment. Humanity, it says, has the power to take charge of the very world itself, but we must learn, often painfully, to use that power with wisdom and discernment. I find this a very powerful—and truthful—insight from Torah, and it is only one among many we can gain from embracing and understanding our ancient heritage of myths and sacred stories.

One last myth. This one comes from the great compilation of Jewish mystical teachings, the *Zohar*:

> Rabbi Shimon said: Woe to this man who says that the Torah came to simply relate stories in an ordinary language, because if this is so, even in these times we could make a Torah from ordinary tales, and one even nicer than from those [ordinary tales]. If the Torah came to explain worldly subjects, even the rulers of the [present] world have books of even greater merit. If so, we could emulate what they [those stories] say and use them to compile some such torah of our own. But really, of all that the Torah says, it holds supernal truths and sublime secrets. . . .
>
> Therefore, the stories related in the Torah is simply her outer garments. . . . Come and see, in a man the garment is visible to all; those without understanding see a man well dressed and judge him by his clothing. In reality the clothing represents the pride of the body of the man and his soul constitutes the pride of the body.
>
> Likewise is the Torah; it has a body which are the commandments called "the body of the Torah." This body is dressed with garments which are the stories of the present world; the ignorant only looks at this garment which is the stories in the Torah, not any further, and not at what is under this garment. The ones that know more do not look at the garment but rather at the body under this garment. The wise, the servants of the Lord, the ones that stood at Mount Sinai, only look at the soul of the Torah, which is the essential of all, the real Torah. . . . Just as wine must be contained in a jug to keep; similarly the Torah must be contained in

an outer garment; consequently it is necessary to look also at what is contained within.[14]

For Jewish mystics, the stories of the Written Torah are merely God's "garment," and its commandments the "body" of God, as it were, the aspects of divinity that we can directly interact with on a day-to-day basis. They also understood that if we read the Torah purely for its obvious meaning, if we perform its rituals as an end to themselves, the greater possibilities of Torah as a source of inspiration and instruction are obscured.

So they claim there is a higher Torah, one that is the source from which the Torah as we know it—Jewish law and Jewish lore—flows. In this myth, the *Zohar* does not specify what precisely that "soul of the Torah" is, but I like to regard the "soul of the Torah" as the entire universe. If we think of the whole world as a text, then the sum total of our knowledge about it and ourselves that we have accumulated—the physics, chemistry, biology, psychology, sociology—the totality of what we have learned about reality, *gam zu Torah*, this too is Torah, and we as Reform Jews, the Jewish movement of modernity, have the greatest access to Torah in all its manifestations and, by implication, to the mind of God. We can use the world to inform our view of Torah, and Torah to enrich our perspectives on the world around us.

NOTES

1. Max Weiner, *Abraham Geiger & Liberal Judaism: The Challenge of the Nineteenth Century* (Cincinnati: HUC Press, 1981), 216–22.
2. Michael Meyer, *Response to Modernity: A History of the Reform Movement in Judaism* (New York: Oxford University Press, 1988), 91.
3. *Protokolle und Aktenstucke der zweiten Rabbiner Versammlung* (1845), 182–87.
4. Meyer, *Response to Modernity*, 122.
5. Kaufmann Kohler, *A Jewish Theology* (New York: Macmillan, 1928), 23–24.
6. Kohler, *A Jewish Theology*, 34–39.
7. Daniel Cohn-Sherbok, *The Future of Judaism* (London: T. & T. Clark, 2000), 111.

8. The Pittsburgh Platform (1885), section 2, http://ccarnet.org/rabbis-speak/platforms/declaration-principles/.

9. Jakob Petuchowski, *Heir to the Pharisees* (Lanham: University Press of America, 1986), 116–29.

10. Bernard Bamberger, *The Bible: A Modern Jewish Interpretation* (New York: Schocken Books, 1963), 74–76, 84.

11. "Some Current Intellectual Trends Potentially Important to the Reform Rabbinate," a lecture given at the HUC-JIR's President's Rabbinic Council Chicago Kallah, October 19, 2015.

12. Roughly two thousand years ago, some Sages already regarded the Book of Job and Song of Songs to be allegories (Babylonian Talmud, *Bava Batra* 15b; *M'chilta*, Shirata, B'shalach 3). Twelve-hundred years ago, Saadyah Gaon argued that a biblical passage should not be interpreted literally if that made a passage mean something contrary to the senses or reason (*Emunot V'Dei-ot*, chapter 7).

13. Jon Levenson, *Creation and the Persistence of Evil: The Drama of Divine Omnipotence* (Princeton, NJ: Princeton University Press, 2000).

14. *Sefer HaZohar, Bamidbar, B'haalot'cha* 58–64, Soncino edition.

30

HEBREW IN THE REFORM MOVEMENT

RABBI HILLEL GAMORAN

It reads backwards. It has a whole different alphabet. It is strange and distant from the language spoken by American Reform Jews, but it is our people's language, and it must be preserved. It is Hebrew. When a Reform Jew enters the synagogue, he hears the Hebrew prayers. When the Torah is taken from the ark, it is the Hebrew scroll that is read. The Hebrew language binds us to our people from ancient times to our own day. As Mordecai Kaplan once said, "A Jew who knows Hebrew will never ask, 'Why am I a Jew?'"[1]

Most American Reform Jews know little Hebrew. They may have gone to Hebrew school in their youth, but they have forgotten what they learned. They have heard the Torah read in their temple, but they don't understand it. They may know some Hebrew songs, but they don't know the meaning of the lyrics. They may have traveled to Israel, but they didn't speak the language of the people of Israel. Most Reform Jews are far removed from the Hebrew language.

Our ancestors probably learned Hebrew from the Canaanites, the people among whom they lived in the Land of Israel/Canaan. Hebrew was the language spoken by our ancestors during the First Temple period (ca. 1000–586 BCE). However, during the Second Temple period, Aramaic replaced Hebrew as the spoken tongue of the people in the

Galilee, while Hebrew remained in use only in Judea. After the fall of the Second Temple in 70 CE, Hebrew fell into disuse as a spoken language altogether.

However, the sounds of Hebrew were not forgotten by the Jewish people, for they still prayed and studied in Hebrew. They read and sang from the prayer book, and they listened to the words of the Torah and the prophets as they were chanted in the synagogue. From early childhood, they learned to understand the Bible and the Mishnah. And when Jews, in a wide variety of countries using many different languages, sought answers to questions of Jewish law and practice, they wrote to their rabbis in Hebrew, and the rabbinic authorities responded in kind.

For close to two thousand years Hebrew was not the language spoken by the Jewish people in day-to-day conversation, but it was not forgotten. In the middle of the fifth century BCE, Nehemiah, the governor of the province of Judea, pointed to the fact that a large number of Jews had abandoned Hebrew as their spoken language. He urged the people to reclaim their native tongue (Nehemiah 13:24).

All through the Middle Ages, rabbis stressed that it was a religious duty to use Hebrew as the language of study and prayer. But Rabbi Baruch Epstein (1860–1942), author of *Torah T'mimah*, went a step further. He was a strong supporter of using the Hebrew language in secular conversation. He said, "Whoever has a hand and heart of faith, whose spirit and soul are faithful to his people, his religion and his language, and wants to build a loyal household in Israel, should try hard to ensure that his sons and daughters, from the time they are being nursed by their mothers, hear Hebrew spoken and are encouraged to emote in Hebrew. . . . In all their daily activities, including their play, from the time they wake up until they go to sleep, children should speak Hebrew."[2]

In the second half of the nineteenth century, Hebrew as a spoken tongue was reborn. In 1879, prior to his coming to Palestine, Eliezer ben Yehudah published his first article on the revival of the Hebrew language. Arriving in Palestine two years later, he brought with him the idea that speaking Hebrew was essential to the building of a new Jewish nation. On his arrival in Palestine as a twenty-three-year-old, he pledged that only Hebrew words would come from his mouth in the Holy Land. He kept that promise. His wife learned Hebrew. His children learned Hebrew. He brought Hebrew into the school classrooms. He published a Hebrew newspaper. He wrote a Hebrew dictionary. He even invented Hebrew words, many of which are still used by Israelis today.

Today Hebrew is the official language of the State of Israel. It is the glue binding Jews to their people and their faith.

There are certain basic elements of Judaism that matter most to Reform Jews: God, Torah, the Jewish people, the Land of Israel, and the Hebrew language. Our devotion to these concepts help us to maintain our commitment to be Jewish.

When we say the Hebrew words in our services *Sh'ma Yisrael* ("Hear, O Israel"), *Mi chamochah* ("Who is like You"), *V'ahavta et Adonai Elohecha* ("You shall love Adonai your God"), *Bayom hahu yih'yeh Adonai echad* ("On that day Adonai will be one"), it is terribly important that we know the meaning of these words, the context in which they were written, and their meaning in our lives. We Reform Jews are not automatons. We don't want to repeat syllables in the synagogue whose meaning we do not know. We want to say or sing the ancient words with understanding. And when we do so, we tie ourselves to our faith and our people in the strongest of bonds.

And likewise with the Torah. When the rabbi reads *V'ahavta l'rei-acha kamocha* ("Love your neighbor as yourself"; Leviticus 19:18), *Ukratem d'ror baaretz* ("Proclaim liberty throughout the land"; Leviticus 25:10), *B'tzelem Elohim bara oto* ("He created him in God's image"; Genesis 1:27) from the scroll, if we know the meaning of those words, if they tell us that our highest obligation is to care for our neighbor, if the words that Moses spoke to Israel still speak to us today in the same language, then our Judaism is a powerful part of our being.

A Reform Jew who says *shehecheyanu* ("who has given us life") when she celebrates a festival or *likboa m'zuzah* ("to attach the mezuzah") when affixing a mezuzah to a new home, who says *Harei at m'kudeshet li* ("Behold, you are consecrated to me") as he places a ring on his bride's finger, who exclaims *Baruch haba* ("Welcome"—to a boy) or *B'ruchah habaah* (to a girl) when she welcomes a new child into the family, one who can say these holy words with understanding and conviction will never waiver from a commitment to Judaism.

It is not just that our knowledge of Hebrew will allow us to communicate with a Jew in far-off parts of the world, it is not just that Hebrew is the spoken tongue in Israel, it is not just that knowing Hebrew will open to us the Bible and the Mishnah, works of poetry and law composed through the ages. It is that Hebrew is *our* language, the language of the Jewish people.

It has been said, mistakenly, that the Orthodox are the most Jewish, the Conservative less so, and the Reform the least Jewish. The truth is, however, that a Reform Jew who understands his prayers and seeks to instill Judaism's principles into her life is likely to be the most Jewish of all.

But what is happening in the Reform Movement today? It used to be that the goal of Hebrew educators was to teach the Hebrew language. In 1923 the Union of American Hebrew Congregations engaged my father, Emanuel Gamoran, a PhD graduate of Columbia University, to come to Cincinnati to bring modern educational principles to Jewish education. In 1932 he, together with H. A. Friedland, published the first volume of *Gilenu: The Play Way to Hebrew*. In 1936 he spoke to the members of the Central Conference of American Rabbis about teaching Hebrew in the Reform religious schools. He told them that Hebrew ought to be taught through jingles, stories, poems, games, songs, activities of all sorts. Hebrew language classes could be, should be, can be fun. For more than fifty years the Reform Movement aimed at teaching its students Hebrew as a language.

But, this is no longer the case. Hebrew education is largely devoted to reading the letters and vowels and saying the prayers. As the bar mitzvah or the bat mitzvah approaches, more and more emphasis is placed on the correct pronunciation of the prayers and an accurate reading of one's Torah portion. Whether one understands the meaning of the Hebrew words takes a back seat in the educational program.

The vast majority of Reform temples no longer teach Hebrew as a living language. The Hebrew schools seek to teach the meaning of the Hebrew prayers but not the words used in daily conversation. Whereas Hebrew language learning can be exciting and fun, learning Hebrew prayers is dull. The students do not understand the relevance of the words, and the teachers are themselves bored.

There is, of course, a goal, that goal being bar or bat mitzvah. So the students slog along. They learn their blessings and their Torah portion. The parents and grandparents are proud; the Hebrew is forgotten and life goes on.

Though the Hebrew language, as a rule, is not being taught in our congregational schools, there are other places where it is being taught. One is in the public schools. Public high schools with a significant Jewish population are now offering Hebrew as a foreign language. Some of these schools offer classes in Hebrew language five days a week for four years of high school. The students who take these classes accomplish much in Hebrew reading, writing, and speech. Even those who study for only two or three years usually achieve quite a bit of fluency.

A second avenue for Hebrew language learning is in day schools. There are now twelve Hebrew day schools in the United States that operate under Reform auspices and even more community day schools (multidenominational). These schools have immersion programs for kindergarten and first-grade students and build on them, so that by the sixth, seventh, and eighth grades students can read and understand biblical and Rabbinic texts. Many of the classes in the upper grades are conducted in Hebrew, and the students feel comfortable conversing in Hebrew.

Another area where Reform teenagers are successfully learning Hebrew is in the Chalutzim program at Olin Sang Ruby Union Institute, a Reform summer camp in Wisconsin. The seven-week Hebrew learning program finds campers spending the morning hours in language classes conducted in Hebrew. They are also encouraged to speak Hebrew throughout the day. The counselors, many of whom are Israelis, speak to the campers only in Hebrew. Camp announcements are made in Hebrew, and many of the daily activities including art, dance, music, and sports are conducted in Hebrew. In previous years campers were encouraged to attend Chalutzim for two summers, but now, with the very large enrollment, the camp can accommodate Chalutzim for only one summer. Even so, a camper who completes a Chalutzim summer can usually carry on a simple conversation in Hebrew and has acquired a love for the Hebrew language. Many of the Chalutzim campers continue their Hebrew studies in college.

One more way that Hebrew is acquired by Reform youth is through Israel programs. The Union for Reform Judaism sponsors the Eisendrath International Experience, which brings American high school students to Israel for a semester. The students learn in Hebrew in the morning and are exposed to Hebrew in many other settings during their time in Israel. Many EIE graduates have returned to Israel for longer periods, where their Hebrew knowledge and skills have continued to grow.

A survey of Reform rabbis shows that in spite of the decline in Hebrew language learning in the religious schools, most Reform rabbis still believe that Hebrew should be a higher priority in the Reform Movement.[3] But what can be done to actuate this conviction? Some have increased the amount of Hebrew in the synagogue services. Many have instituted Hebrew classes for adults. But what can be done about the decline in Hebrew language learning in the Reform religious schools? Perhaps the best way to use our Hebrew schools is to develop a positive attitude among the children toward Hebrew and encourage the students to pursue Hebrew learning in one of the four avenues we have described. Some temples have been successful in encouraging students to sign up for the Hebrew classes in their public high schools, where offered. Other communities can take advantage of intensive Hebrew learning provided at Hebrew day schools.

Two avenues are more broadly available. Not just Midwestern teens but any student from a Reform temple is eligible to attend the

Hebrew-speaking camp in Wisconsin and spend seven weeks in a Hebrew environment. And the EIE four-month program in Israel is a great opportunity for our Reform youth to improve their Hebrew literacy.

The foreign language summer programs at Middlebury College in Vermont have, for many years, included Hebrew among the languages offered. This means that a student can attend Middlebury for a summer and hear and speak only Hebrew for eight weeks. To participate in the Middlebury program one must sign the following pledge: "In signing this Language Pledge, I agree to use Hebrew as my only language of communication while attending the Middlebury Language Schools. I understand that failure to comply with this Pledge may result in my expulsion from the School without credit or refund." Anecdotal reports on the Middlebury program tell of students who have been ousted from the program because they were found speaking in English during the summer session. The strict system seems to have worked, and students who have completed a summer at Middlebury have made great progress in speaking, reading, and understanding Hebrew.

To conclude, Hebrew language learning is at its lowest point among Reform Jews. The Hebrew schools have generally given up on their efforts to teach Hebrew. They teach how to read but not to understand, and what understanding is taught deals with the prayers. Students can attend Hebrew classes for four or five years and barely say a few words in Hebrew. And their bar or bat mitzvah may serve as their graduation from Hebrew learning for the rest of their lives.

There is still hope that Jews, literate in Hebrew, will emerge from the Reform Movement. If the temple can make Hebrew learning fun, if it can inspire students to take Hebrew in public high school (where it is offered), to attend the Chalutzim program in Oconomowoc, or to go to a Hebrew learning program in Israel, then Hebrew can survive and flourish. Hebrew day schools can also serve as a strong beginning. Even if Hebrew is not acquired by a large number of Jews, it can live through those who make the effort to study and read and speak.

In the days of Eliezer ben Yehudah, there were those who said that Hebrew was a dead language and that it could not be revived. But he and others proved them wrong. If we make the effort, we can keep Hebrew alive among our Reform Jewish families.

NOTES

1. In Morristown, NJ, 1958.
2. Alvin Schiff, *The Mystique of Hebrew* (New York: Academic Press, 1998), 16.
3. Jeffrey Wildstein, "Hebrew in the Reform Movement," *CCAR Journal*, Winter 2005, 83–84.

31

WHY REFORM JEWS SHOULD STUDY TALMUD

RABBI DVORA E. WEISBERG, PHD

Fifteen years ago, soon after I accepted a job teaching Rabbinic literature on the Los Angeles campus of Hebrew Union College–Jewish Institute of Religion, I participated in a conference call with two of my new colleagues. They wanted to help me think about what I would teach during my first semester of the introductory Talmud course required of all rabbinical students. The Talmud is a massive compilation that has been at the center of Jewish study and has served as one of the bases for Jewish law and practice since the early Middle Ages; it is characterized by debate and rhetorical discussions. I could not expect my students to be enthusiastic about studying Talmud, my colleagues told me. They recommended that I teach only passages about festival observance—fasting on Yom Kippur, lighting Chanukah candles, the Passover seder—since the more "relevant" the material, the more likely my students would respond positively.

Fast-forward ten or twelve years. I am teaching an adult education class at a Reform congregation in Southern California where the rabbi is one of my former students. The topic for my session is "Why Reform Jews Should Study Talmud." After the session, a woman comes up to me. She introduces herself as the daughter of a Reform rabbi and a regular participant in the temple's adult education program. "I wasn't sure about coming today," she said, "because I didn't think Talmud was important for Reform Jews."

These stories have what we would call happy endings. My HUC-JIR students over the years have, for the most part, enjoyed their study of Talmud, and the woman assured me that she had enjoyed the class. At the same time, these occurrences underscore the challenge of arguing that Talmud study should be part of Reform Judaism. Reform Jews, be they committed laypeople or future Jewish professionals, do not take it for granted that Talmud study fits into their self-understanding. We tend to associate Talmud with halachah, traditional Jewish law, and with Orthodox Judaism. Even as adult education programs have flourished in our congregations, Reform Jews avoid studying Talmud. There are several reasons for this.

We are, as our platform statements and history remind us, a prophetic movement. Our vision of the world is built on the Bible, specifically that portion of the Hebrew Bible known as *N'vi-im*, Prophets. Reform Jews have traditionally defined themselves by their commitment to the ethical ideals of Isaiah and Amos, two of the biblical prophets whose calls for justice continue to inspire us today, not the laws of either Moses or the Rabbis. Even our sustained study of Torah, now a regular feature of many Reform congregations, is a relatively new feature. But Torah study seems a natural step for us to take. After all, the Torah is the text that resides in the ark in our sanctuary. It is read every week during our Shabbat services. It is, together with the other sections of the *Tanach*, the Hebrew Bible, the basis of Judaism. And, of course, Torah is an accessible text. It is available in beautiful English translations and with excellent commentaries. The narrative parts are great, and the legal sections are usually thought-provoking.

Contrasted with the Torah, the Talmud feels alien. Its language is terse, its use of technical and legal terminology unfamiliar to the novice. While there are now English translations of the Talmud, they cannot be easily picked up and read the way the Torah can, for the Talmud is a highly edited and stylized document, and some students find it difficult at first to make sense of its structure. The Rabbis' thinking, while undoubtedly logical to them, often seems less reasonable to us: why give the weakest answer first, why ask so many questions about a subject and then offer no definitive answer, why spend all this time on a ritual no longer practiced?

The inaccessibility of the Talmud is an issue for many Jews—Reform, Conservative, and even Orthodox. In the past two decades, two new English translations of the Talmud have been published, largely to make Talmud accessible to a wider readership. But as Reform Jews, we face another obstacle when we try to imagine ourselves studying Talmud. We are the heirs of a movement that, on some level, dismissed Rabbinic Judaism and turned for its guidance and inspiration back to the prophets. In its early phases, our movement also expressed minimal interest in—and even distaste for—ritual. We are often told or assume that the Talmud is first and foremost a legal text, the early Rabbis' expansion on the laws of the Torah. Therefore for us, the possibility of Talmud study raises the question of relevance or applicability. Why should we, as modern, liberal Jews, spend any time on Talmud, particularly those parts of the Talmud that deal with law?

So why should Reform Jews study Talmud? I could argue that all forms of Judaism build on earlier Judaisms. When you read early documents of Reform Judaism, you can see that the founders of Reform were struggling with Rabbinic Judaism, the Judaism represented in and shaped by the Talmud. Today, as we explore the role of ritual in Reform Judaism, we are considering the role Rabbinic practice and theology will have in shaping our Judaism. As important as the Bible is to Jewish tradition, we are Rabbinic Jews in our practice and in the way we approach the Bible.

Consider, for instance, our celebration of Jewish holidays. One of the holidays most commonly observed by Reform Jews is Chanukah. But Chanukah is not a biblical festival. It has its origins in the second century BCE, when the Jews of Judea rebelled against religious persecution and triumphed, rededicating the Temple in Jerusalem. If you read the books written closest to the Maccabean Revolt, their descriptions of Chanukah focus on battles and on cleansing and dedicating the Jerusalem Temple; the eight-day observance that we now know as Chanukah commemorates the rededication of the Temple or the belated observance of Sukkot that occurred after the Temple was rededicated. Observance of Chanukah through kindling lights and our common explanation of the reason for the holiday are first set forth in the Talmud.

> What is [the reason for the festival of] Chanukah? Our rabbis taught: From the twenty-fifth day of Kislev are the days of Chanukah, which are eight, on which eulogies and fasting are forbidden. When the Greeks entered the sanctuary, they defiled all the oil in it. But when the Hasmonean house grew strong and defeated them, they searched and found but a single cruse of oil that was sealed with the seal of the high priest. It contained sufficient oil for only one day. A miracle occurred, and they lit [the menorah] from it for eight days. The next year, they established them and made them festival days with *Hallel* and thanksgiving. (Babylonian Talmud, *Shabbat* 21b)

So when we celebrate Chanukah today, we are following the practice set forth in the Talmud.

When we look at the discussion of Chanukah that precedes the story of the miracle, we learn something else that makes the Talmud a valuable resource for Reform Jews. The Talmud is *not* a code of Jewish law, but discussion of ritual practice is a major feature of the Talmud. The Talmudic discussion of lighting Chanukah candles underscores both the ways that Judaism today reflects the Judaism of centuries before and the ways that it has evolved.

> Our rabbis taught: The commandment of Chanukah is [to light] one [lamp] per household. Those who are more exacting [light] one [lamp] for each and every person [in the house]. And those who are the most exacting—the House of Shammai say: On the first day one should light eight; from then on, he reduces [the number of lights] as the holiday progresses. But the House of Hillel say: On the first day one should light one; from then on, he adds [to the number of lights] as the holiday progresses. (Babylonian Talmud, *Shabbat* 21b)

This passage reflects something about Judaism that is crucial to the project of the Reform Movement: Judaism is not static. Between the Maccabean Revolt and the institution of Chanukah in the second century BCE and the compilation of the Talmud seven hundred years later, there were several stages in the development of the ritual created to mark the holiday. First, every household lit a single lamp to commemorate the miracle. Then some people decided they wanted to make a bigger deal over Chanukah (and I suspect they were also people with money to burn—pardon the pun), so each person in the household had his or her own Chanukah lamp. Then others decided to go a step further and light multiple lamps on a given night. This version of the ritual became the focus of a debate between the followers of Shammai and the followers of Hillel. Our current practice reflects the view of the Hillelites, with some of us also honoring the practice of the first set of "exacting" folks by giving each member of the family his or her own *chanukiyah*.

Another passage that teaches us about the evolution of Jewish practice, while also offering us an insight into Rabbinic disputes and leadership, deals with sounding the shofar, the ram's horn, on a Rosh HaShanah that coincides with Shabbat.

> When Rosh HaShanah fell on Shabbat, the shofar was sounded in the Temple but not around the country. When the Temple was destroyed, Rabban Yochanan ben Zakkai decreed that the shofar could be sounded [on Shabbat] any place where there was a court.
>
> Our rabbis taught: It once happened that Rosh HaShanah fell on the Sabbath. Everyone came together. Rabban Yochanan ben Zakkai said to the sons of Beterah, "Let us sound the shofar." They said to him, "Let us discuss the matter." He said to them, "Let us first sound the shofar and then discuss the matter." After they sounded the shofar, they said to him, "Now let us discuss the matter." He said to them, "The shofar has already been sounded in Yavneh, and one does not undo that which has been done." (Babylonian Talmud, *Rosh HaShanah* 29b)

Again, we see a ritual evolving, this time in response to external events. According to the Mishnah, the earliest compilation of Rabbinic law (third century CE) and the starting point for the Talmud, when Rosh HaShanah fell on Shabbat, the shofar was sounded only in the Jerusalem Temple. We learn from Talmudic discussions on sounding the shofar that the Rabbis believed it was forbidden to sound the shofar on Shabbat due to concern that a person might carry the shofar through the streets to reach the synagogue (Rabbinic tradition forbids carrying objects more than a few feet through public spaces on the Sabbath). This type of secondary prohibition did not apply to the Temple, so the shofar could be sounded there. After the destruction of the Temple, Yochanan ben Zakkai wanted to allow the sounding of the shofar on Shabbat in many places.

The Talmud's story offers the backstory for Yochanan ben Zakkai's decree. It asks us to imagine what might have been the first time after the destruction of the Temple that Rosh HaShanah fell on Shabbat. According to some readings of the Talmud, many people gathered together in Yavneh, presumably hoping to hear the shofar. Yochanan is prepared to sound the shofar, but his colleagues want to debate the subject first. Unwilling to wait—or perhaps unwilling to risk losing the argument— Yochanan tricks his colleagues. After sounding the shofar, he argues that a discussion would be counterproductive, insofar as it might lead the Sages to undermine something that they had already done.

At first glance, this passage validates contemporary Reform practice. But a look at other Talmudic passages about shofar indicates that Yochanan ben Zakkai's ruse did not lead to ongoing sounding of shofar on Shabbat. The Talmud simultaneously provides a basis for our ritual practice while indicating that another practice, the custom of not sounding the shofar on Shabbat, remained the norm.

Beyond teaching about the evolution of a ritual practice, this story asks us to consider the way we make decisions. We might ask ourselves: Why did Yochanan's view carry the day but fail to pass the test of time? Was the reason for his Pyrrhic victory his disregard for process or his treatment of his colleagues?

A third example of the evolution of ritual over time can be found in Tractate *P'sachim*, which focuses on the observance of Passover. The tenth chapter of *Mishnah P'sachim* discusses the seder; parts of this text appear word for word in the Haggadah. Early Rabbinic literature— Mishnah, Babylonian Talmud, and Jerusalem Talmud—reveal multiple versions of what we know as the Four Questions. Study of this material indicates that during late antiquity, the number of questions grew from three to four, and several of the questions underwent changes, with one falling into disuse as another came into existence. In this way, the study of Talmud allows us not only to see the connections between our liturgy and the liturgy of Jews who lived close to two thousand years ago, but to see how liturgy and ritual first came into being, then changed in response to changing circumstances.

While the passages I cited above focus on ritual, the Talmud is also a repository for Jewish ethics. The rabbis whose words fill the Talmud saw no distinction between ritual and ethical imperatives; both derived from Torah and expressed the will of God for the people of Israel. The Talmud teaches us how to treat each other in a complex world. Through a combination of law and story, the Talmud offers guidance for human and humane interactions.

> Some porters broke wine jars belonging to Rabbah bar bar Chana. He confiscated their cloaks [to pay for the damage they had caused]. They went and complained to Rav. Rav said to Rabbah bar bar Chana, "Give them their cloaks." Rabbah bar bar Chana said to Rav, "Is this the law?" Rav said to him, "[Yes,] 'Follow the way of the good' (Proverbs 2:20)." So he gave them their cloaks. They said to him, "We are poor men, and we worked hard all day and we have nothing to show for our labor." Rav said to him, "Give them their wages." Rabbah bar bar Chana said to him, "Is this the law?" He said to him, "[Yes,] 'And keep to the paths of the just' (Proverbs 2:20)." (Babylonian Talmud, *Bava M'tzia* 83a)

This story comes at the end of a discussion of the laws regulating the conduct of employers and employees. The law teaches that workers, if they are negligent, are responsible for damage to goods they had been hired to convey from one place to another, a ruling that anyone who has ever hired a long-distance moving company can appreciate.

The story speaks of just such a case; Rabbah bar bar Chana hires porters to transport wine, and the wine is lost through their carelessness.
Yet when Rabbah seeks compensation for his loss by confiscating the
porters' outer garments—perhaps hoping to hold them until he receives payment for the damages—the porters sue him! Moreover, his
colleague Rav rules in favor of the porters, not only forcing Rabbah to
return their cloaks, but also compelling him to pay their wages. Rabbah is understandably annoyed and also surprised, since he thought the
law supported him. He asks Rav, "Is this the law?" and Rav responds
with a quote from Proverbs. The verse from Proverbs says nothing
about employer-employee law; rather it counsels us to do what is right
and just. Some versions of the Talmud add the word "Yes" to Rav's
response, while other versions omit the word. In either case, it seems
clear that what Rav is telling Rabbah is that even with the law on his
side, in this situation he should not use the law against the workers. Rav
calls upon Rabbah to go beyond the letter of the law and forgo his legal
rights, in consideration of the porters' poverty. In placing this story at
the end of the legal discussion about workers, the Talmud reminds us
that a just society is not only a society based on law; it must be a society
that refuses to use the law to harm others.

So far, I have made a case for studying material from the Talmud.
In this day and age, English translations and online resources make
it very easy to extract material on almost any topic from the Talmud.
Because of this, Jews with no background in Talmud study and with
no knowledge of Aramaic can be exposed to what we might call "the
wisdom of the Talmud." However, I want to make a more sweeping
argument, namely that Reform Jews should consider studying Talmud
itself, rather than being satisfied with snippets of Talmud.

Why should Reform Jews study Talmud? I actually believe the question should be: Why *wouldn't* Reform Jews study Talmud? Although
the study of Talmud is most widely embraced by Orthodox Jews, it is
liberal Jews who ought to most appreciate the Talmud. Almost every
page of the Babylonian Talmud contains disputes. One of the most
noticeable (and, for the beginning student, often the most frustrating)

characteristics of a Talmudic discussion is a high degree of tolerance for difference of opinion. In fact, the Talmud delights in debate and is eager to consider every side of an argument. The editors of the Talmud were willing to devote considerable space and energy considering the most "preposterous" solutions to a problem. Answers—especially definitive halachic answers—are secondary or even irrelevant to many Talmudic discussions. One of the hallmarks of Reform Judaism is its adherence to the principle of informed choice, the belief that every Jew should learn about Judaism in order to decide which aspects of Jewish ritual could guide and enrich his or her life. And so, Talmud models for us what it means to be a liberal Jew, a Jew who engages in study not to find a particular "right" answer, but to think deeply about the enterprise of constructing a Judaism that speaks to us.

It is important to acknowledge that we will not like everything that we encounter in the Talmud. The Talmud is a product of a different world, of rabbis whose worldview and cultural assumptions are often foreign to us. The Talmud takes for granted the existence of slavery, the absence of women from the house of study and the synagogue, and the superiority of the Jewish people. Some of its theological positions are disturbing to many modern Jews. But to be Jewish is to engage with Torah in its broad sense, to struggle to find new meaning in old traditions, and sometimes to acknowledge that what spoke to Jews centuries ago does not speak to us with the same force. It is with that understanding that we can study Talmud and find value in much of what it offers.

I would argue that the best reason to study Talmud is that Talmud is our *y'rushah*, our inheritance as Jews. If we are going to transmit any kind of Judaism, we need to be firmly rooted in Judaism. We are entitled to react to any Talmudic passage with enthusiasm or amazement or even horror, but we need to be in dialogue with these texts if our Judaism is to be part of the tradition stretching back to Sinai. In the years that I have studied Talmud, I have found it a deeply satisfying endeavor, both intellectually and spiritually. When we turn to the classic texts of Jewish tradition, we find more than instructions on the proper way to put Chanukah candles into the menorah or drink four cups of wine at a seder. We find the words of individuals who were deeply committed to living full Jewish lives, infusing the values of the Torah and the prophets into every moment of the day. Additionally, we enter into a conversation that has been going on for thousands of years and become active participants in that conversation about what it means to be Jewish. The study of Talmud, then, is not simply an intellectual or educational project. It is a religious activity through which we not only explore the Jewish past but become part of shaping the Jewish present and future.

32

REFLECTIONS ON PRAYER

Rabbi Peter S. Knobel, PhD

While the two essays on prayer that follow, written by Rabbi Richard S. Sarason, PhD, and Rabbi Dalia Marx, PhD, examine the historical changes that have occurred in the Reform community's liturgical texts, this chapter offers a personal approach to prayer, my own. It is a multilayered approach, for in addition to using our prayer books, I compose my own prayers spontaneously as the need arises or turn to the many collections of contemporary poems and prayers that are available in print or on the Internet. These are treasure troves of beautiful and deeply meaningful sources for reflection, meditation, and contemplation.

I want to distinguish among three terms: liturgy, worship, and prayer. *Liturgy* refers to the texts that we find in our prayer books. These texts have a prescribed structure, are hallowed by tradition, and are often enhanced with additional material. The texts at the core of the Reform prayer books connect us to the whole of Jewish history and the whole of the Jewish people. They are the most important statement of our values and our obligations. We use them whenever we gather together for communal worship.

Liturgy becomes *worship* when performed in a communal setting accompanied by song and chant. At its heart, worship is a communal experience. The presence of others can enhance the ways we are supported in difficult moments, the ways we celebrate joyous moments, and inspire us to translate the words of the prayer books and Torah into action.

Prayer is an experience of profound connection to something beyond ourselves. During the worship service, there are often moments when I feel deeply connected to an entity greater than myself. God? The Source of Being? The *Shechinah*? The Soul of the universe? The Rock of Israel? Divine Friend? Sacred Partner? I cannot really name what I mean, but I feel connected. At these moments I am not rationally examining my theology, but experiencing something important and meaningful that speaks to the deepest aspects of my being. Prayer is an experience inspired by words addressed to God, but it is more than just the words. This connectedness does not occur all of the time or even as frequently as I would like, but it can occur amid community in a worship service or even when I'm alone. When it happens, it feels real and it feels important—both as a moment in my spiritual life and related to my membership in the Jewish community and the Jewish people.

Liturgy, worship, and prayer enable me to regard myself as part of a great tradition. They set forth my responsibilities to myself, to the Jewish people, and to the whole of humanity. Taken together, they create an opening for me to express my greatest concerns. The texts of the siddur and *machzor* provide focus for my personal prayers, as well as guidance and inspiration for living. For example, in the morning service we recite:

These are things that are limitless,
of which a person enjoys the fruits of this world
while the principal remains in the world to come.
They are: honoring one's father and mother,
engaging in deeds of compassion,
arriving early for study, morning and evening,
dealing graciously with guests, visiting the sick,

providing for the wedding couple,
accompanying the dead for burial,
being devoted in prayer,
and making peace among people.
But the study of Torah encompasses them all.

(*Mishkhan T'filah*, page 44)

These words drawn from the Mishnah, by emphasizing certain important mitzvot, create an agenda for daily Jewish living. In a similar manner, in a world where violence and chaos are daily occurrences, the recitation of *Shalom Rav* or *Sim Shalom*, our prayers for peace, is not merely an expression of pious hope, but a clarion call to get involved in resolving the many conflicts. Speaking the words out loud or silently reinforces our values and strengthens our commitments.

For many years I ran five miles every morning. Now that running is out of the question, I walk that same distance instead. This alone time has become, for me, a vehicle for engaging in extended prayer. Most important to me is a part of the *Amidah*: *Sh'ma Koleinu*, "God, hear our voice." Traditionally when this prayer is recited, one pauses to add one's personal petitions. When I recite this prayer during my morning exercise, I often engage in an extended conversation with God. I address God in an intimate and personal way. It is like having a conversation with a trusted friend or advisor who listens but does not speak. These conversations have helped me through many a personal crisis and aided me in clarifying my thinking and goals. At the end, although I have no explicit response, I feel that that there is a "listening ear," and I can discern with greater clarity the path that I must take.

One of my most profound prayer experiences emerged as a result of the reintroduction of a liturgy for healing into the Reform Movement. Debbie Freidman's *Mi Shebeirach*, which became the anthem for a growing spirituality within the Jewish community, infused our worship with profound moments of communal and personal caring. Because of the *Mi Shebeirach*, for years I carried a list of names of the people for whom I had been asked to pray. Each day I would pause for a moment, take out the list, and recite silently each name and then offer Debbie's powerful combination of words: Hebrew and English, old and new. Its beautiful melody carries this petition for healing and reminds me that I need to be engaged in acts of caring. It calls upon me to make contact with the ill and their loved ones, to follow up on those whose acute phase of illness has passed but to let them know that they have not been forgotten, and to help those for whom there is no cure to find healing. This *Mi Shebeirach* also led to the creation of a healing service in my own synagogue, one that included not only prayer but text study and that reinforced the congregation as a caring community.

A simple act of prayer can truly surprise us. Twice in my rabbinate I have entered the hospital room of a comatose patient, taken hold of the person's hand to recite the *Sh'ma*, and the person awoke. In one case the person completed the words of the *Sh'ma* with me. These occurrences seemed miraculous and were remarkably powerful.

Prayer can be equally powerful even when the hoped-for event does not occur. I remember being in the hospital completing my rounds of visiting congregants when I ran into a person whose husband was in a coma in the intensive care unit. I offered to go into the ICU with her and pray for him. The man died. But my presence and prayers led to a connection that allowed me to help a family through a difficult moment and to comfort them through the funeral and mourning process. I am never sure why things work out the way they do, and I remain agnostic about God's role, but I do know that prayer is a very significant part of my life.

My day begins and ends with the recitation of the *Sh'ma*. In the morning I recite *Modeh Ani*, thanking God for the opportunity of a new day. At night I add a simple petition for God to take care of my family and help us make a difference in the world. The efficacy of petitionary prayer is a matter of great theological discussion. I have found that two quotations that appear in our siddur have helped me to understand the spiritual value of petitionary prayer without truly solving the theological dilemmas.

The first is from Rabbi Ferdinand Isserman: "Pray as if everything depended on God. Act as if everything depended on you" (*Mishkhan T'filah*, page 165). And the second is from Abraham Joshua Heschel:

Prayer invites
God's Presence to suffuse our spirits,
God's will to prevail in our lives.
Prayer may not bring water to parched fields,
nor mend a broken bridge,
nor rebuild a ruined city.
But prayer can water an arid soul,
mend a broken heart,
rebuild a weakened will.

(*Mishkhan T'filah*, page 165)

Our liturgy is the *keva*, the fixed text, of our people and our community. It is the greatest source for personal prayer. Yet personal prayer, as does any worthwhile activity, requires regular practice. Frequent repetition can become mindless ritual, or it can be a mantra that helps take us to a new spiritual dimension. Our tradition says that we should recite our prayers with *kavanah*, with intention. When we concentrate on the meaning and intent of the words, we can experience deep connection to transcendence—the God out there in the universe—and to immanence—the God who dwells within us. Liturgy, worship, and prayer, along with Torah study and deeds of loving-kindness, constitute a full Jewish life. Liturgy, worship, and prayer are important components of my Jewish practice. They continue to inspire and sustain me. I hope that these reflections will enable others to find an approach to prayer that will be as significant for them as my approach has been for me.

33

WORSHIP AND THE PRAYER BOOK

Rabbi Richard S. Sarason, PhD

Judaism's most basic textbook, it is often remarked, is neither the Bible nor the Talmud. It is rather the siddur, the Jewish prayer book, with which all traditionally practicing Jews interact at least three times every day. As the script for liturgical performance, the prayer book gives expression to the most fundamental Jewish communal aspirations, needs, beliefs, and values. By voicing its words and ritually enacting them in a communal liturgical space, each individual Jew ideally becomes energized to live out Jewish values in daily life: this is how worship, at its best, "works."

If this holds true of the traditional siddur, it is even truer of the Reform prayer book. The prayer book is effectively the Reform Movement's calling card. The prayer book is thus one of the best sources from which to learn about both contemporary and historical Reform Jewish values, sensibilities, and commitments; these are literally on display in its pages and practices.

Nonetheless, the prayer book is not the same thing as the worship service; it is only the script for that service, which can be, and has been, performed in a variety of ways. So the prayer book by itself gives us only part of the picture. The Reform Movement from its beginnings has been most visible through its reforms of the worship service—with regard to music, decorum, patterns of speech, movement, and gesture: all matters of aesthetics, public symbolism, and social convention.

Yet another factor contributing to the prominence of both the prayer book and the worship service in the Reform Movement historically is the fact that the project of modernizing (that is to say, Westernizing) Jewish religion, of which the Reform Movement has always been the most prominent expression, began and took root primarily in Protestant Christian countries—the northern German states, England, the United States. In these countries, the public religious space was understood to be the individual congregation, since the civic space had to be sufficiently neutral to tolerate (if only that) other Christian denominations as well as Jews. The most public, communal form of religious expression and piety in these countries was the weekly worship service, the script for which was the denominational prayer book. So modernizing Judaism would also be most noticeable in the act of communal synagogue worship—where the state recognized and sanctioned difference. Indeed, the felt need to reform the traditional Jewish prayer book and worship service derived, at the outset, from the equally felt need to incorporate into Jewish worship the aesthetic tastes and styles (particularly regarding music, movement, gesture, and decorum) and the enlightened ideas that were experienced as the essence of modernity and modern religiosity.

Because of the Reform Movement's historical commitment to the project of modernity, and because of its openness in responding to both local cultural contexts and cultural changes, it is easy—and crucial—to view changes in both Reform worship and prayer books over time as reflecting their various local cultural contexts and the changes in those contexts. This point cannot be overstressed. There is nothing intrinsically "Jewish" about accompanying synagogue worship with either an organ or a guitar once one admits instrumental music into the service; nothing intrinsically "Jewish" about either four-part choral music and congregational hymn singing in the vernacular or setting Hebrew liturgy to American folk-pop-rock-style tunes. Like the definition of Jewish food as the kosher version of what your neighbors are eating, Jewish worship styles in the modern era have reflected, and continue to reflect, the integration of Jews into their local societies and cultures—and the aesthetic preferences and tastes of those cultures (often at the particular socioeconomic levels to which Jews have aspired). The bottom line, therefore, is that Reform worship is, and has always been, the product of its time and place; our contemporary stylistic-aesthetic judgments about worship styles therefore can only be relative and never absolute.

Leonard Fein coined the phrase "Reform is a verb" to underscore just this point: that what has been, and remains, constant in the Reform Movement is its openness in responding to an ever-changing world. "The future," noted Fein, "is not something we discover just around the next corner. It is something we shape, we create, we invent." This chapter will illustrate the validity of this insight in the area of Jewish worship and prayer book styles, while leaving room for my colleague Dalia Marx's more detailed discussion in the next chapter.

Reform worship and prayer books, since their nineteenth-century beginnings, above all have sought to be accessible to the average Jew in the pew (and to those Jews whom we would like to invite into the pews). With the decline in Hebrew literacy among Jews integrating into modern Western society in the late eighteenth and nineteenth centuries, it was important to supply full vernacular translations of the Hebrew portions of the service, as well as new prayers in the vernacular that would express contemporary religious longings and concerns. Many early Reform prayer books also provided transliterations of those Hebrew sentences (such as *Bar'chu*, *Sh'ma*, *Mi Chamochah*, and the *K'dushah* verses) that were intended as congregational responses. *Mishkan T'filah*, the current North American Reform prayer book, valuing inclusiveness, provides transliterations of the entire Hebrew text in every service, so that everyone in attendance can follow along irrespective of their ability to read Hebrew.

Concern for accessibility also dictated early on that the traditional service be abbreviated. The traditional liturgy had grown since its inception through the inclusion of new prayers, hymns, and customs, but nothing had ever been removed. If Reform worship was to be conducted with *kavanah* (intentionality, inward concentration, conviction) and reverence at a decorous modern pace and with sufficient time for an inspiring sermon, the liturgy would have to be shortened. This was done by removing repetitions (such as multiple recitations of the *Kaddish* throughout the service and the twofold recitation of the *Amidah*, first individually by all worshipers and then by the prayer leader), compressing those portions of the service that were deemed less essential (such as the preliminary morning prayers and psalms before *Bar'chu*), shortening the Torah readings on Shabbat and the Festivals, and removing those prayers and kabbalistic additions that were deemed to be late, superstitious/magical, or otherwise offensive to contemporary Western sensibilities. In recent years, some of these materials have been restored in order to provide a richer exposure to the historic Jewish liturgical tradition as well as a greater variety of options for use in services. The traditional liturgy is still abbreviated, but not as radically as it had been.

The issue of broad accessibility ultimately lies as well behind the aesthetic choices that have been made in Reform worship services over the past two centuries. European Jews who had been socialized into Western cultural and aesthetic sensibilities in the nineteenth century and, more recently, American Jews who are fully and primarily American in their sensibilities found the traditional mode of conducting services foreign and inaccessible. During much of the nineteenth century, European Jews were made to feel that they constantly needed to prove themselves to be good citizens and not "foreigners." When Christians disparaged traditional Jewish services and service music as "oriental" (i.e., non-Western) and unaesthetic, modernizing Jews responded by reforming and Westernizing the performance style of both the services (introducing, for example, decorum, responsive readings, and the prominent role of the service leader) and their music (reducing the amount of traditional chant, the inclusion of more orderly unison hymn singing and choral responses accompanied by an organ). This, of course, provoked the criticism of "aping the gentiles" from more traditional Jews. But it is important to remember, when considering the early Reform Movement from a distance of two centuries, that these innovations were not intended to be a station on the way to the baptismal font. Rather their aim was to provide Jews with a third—and Jewish—option between traditional, premodern Judaism and modern Christianity. That third option was a modern Judaism, so that Jews could be full members of Western society as Jews.

Similarly, in the past half-century in the United States, the importation into the Reform synagogue (as well as into Christian churches) of contemporary folk, pop, and rock musical idioms is best understood as yet another way of making services accessible to Jews whose "native language" is that of American popular culture. That way, both the language of the text and the language of the music are familiar.

But this is only part of the picture. In the past half century in the United States, as the pressures of the melting-pot approach to assimilating immigrant populations receded and hyphenated identities became more and more central to how we see ourselves, many American Jews (parallel to Blacks, women, Latinos, and so on) have found in Jewish identity a kind of counterculture, in which precisely the non-Western and non-rational elements provide a sense of both exotic fascination and authenticity. As Israel came to the fore of American Jewish consciousness in the wake of the Six-Day War in 1967, more American Jews visited and studied there, generating more interest in Hebrew and Jewish traditions. All of this has been part of the American context for a revaluation of more traditional prayers and practices, and their reintroduction into Reform worship—specifically, more Hebrew, more traditional chanting of prayers and of scriptural readings, more embodied rituals (e.g., processions with the Torah scrolls, waving the *lulav*). Both of these tendencies can be seen in North American Reform worship today, and both are on display in *Mishkan T'filah*. Rather than competing, they actually complement each other.

Yet a further, formal and symbolic, aspect of the concern for accessibility can be seen in the physical layout of Reform prayer books—whether they open from right to left (in the direction of the traditional Hebrew siddur) or left to right (in the direction of vernacular prayer books). The first congregational Reform prayer book (Hamburg, 1819) opened from left to right and integrated Hebrew and German texts on the same page. The first American Reform prayer book (Temple Emanu-El, New York, 1855) opened from right to left, with facing pages of Hebrew and English. The first prayer books edited and published by the Central Conference of American Rabbis (*Union Prayer Book*, 1892, 1894–95, and subsequent revised editions in 1918–22 and 1940–45) opened from left to right, integrating Hebrew and English texts on the same page. The CCAR's 1975 publication of *Gates of Prayer* allowed congregations a choice between the two directional formats (with Hebrew and English texts integrated on the same page), while *Mishkan T'filah* (2007) is published only in the right-to-left format, using a two-page spread with Hebrew and English translation integrated on the right page and interpretive readings (mostly English, but some Hebrew) on the left page. There are also attractive graphics, sidebar menus, brief interpretive materials below the text, and much white space in place of the earlier "square block" style of layout. The two-page spreads are self-consciously designed to resemble a webpage. This publication history of CCAR prayer books conveys a great deal about the shifting sensibilities of American Reform Jews regarding the symbolism of directionality and layout.

So far we have been dealing with the larger issue of accessibility as it has been expressed in the stylistics of worship and the physical look of the prayer book. We turn now to changes made in the content of the prayers, which also reflect a concern for intellectual accessibility: to what extent do the prayers reflect what modern Jews actually have believed over the past two centuries and believe today?

The first significant change that was made to the content of the liturgy in all nineteenth-century Reform prayer books was the elimination of petitions for the restoration of the Temple and its rituals, as well as petitions for the return to the Land of Israel. Bloody sacrifices played no role in an enlightened modern spirituality; that continues to this day. (Even the Conservative prayer books in the United States from their earliest editions have eliminated petitions for the restoration of the Temple sacrifices.) The traditional petitions for a return to the Land always bore a political dimension (as was recognized and acknowledged by the modern Zionist movement). This political dimension became highly charged during the era of Jewish emancipation in Europe. Citizenship rights were extended to Jews with the expectation of complete loyalty to the European nation-state; no dual loyalty would be allowed. One French legislator at the time put it this way: "To the Jews as individuals, everything; to the Jews as a people, nothing!" Anxiety about the charge of dual loyalty, warranted or not, became ingrained in Western Jews (it occasionally surfaces even today in some American Jews' ambivalence about supporting Israel); this is what lies behind the elimination of the prayers for the return to Zion in virtually all Reform prayer books before the rise of Nazi Germany in the 1930s. Since 1967, that reticence has diminished, and Reform prayer books have restored prayers for "a Zion renewed."

Similarly, the traditional hope for a Messiah ("anointed redeemer"), who would lead the Jews back to their land and restore the Davidic monarchy, was politically unacceptable to nineteenth-century Western Jews for the same reasons. Their messianic expectations were decidedly this-worldly, embodied in the hope for continual social and political amelioration in Europe and America. And that is how Reform prayer books transformed the traditional messianic hope. The prayers now asked not for the coming of a mythic redeemer (*go-eil*), but for an age of this-worldly redemption (*g'ulah*).

Moreover, as we shall discuss at greater length below, in some Reform prayer books the Jewish people itself became a kind of messianic figure for the whole world, charged with the universal mission of spreading the teachings of an enlightened ethical monotheism and of leading all peoples in the fight for social justice. The ethical concern for social justice and social action certainly continues to this day in the Reform Movement and may be seen in many of the creative and interpretive passages in *Mishkan T'filah*.

As just noted, a further consequence of Jewish integration into European and American society was a commitment to the welfare and

342 · A LIFE OF MEANING

betterment of all people, and not just of fellow Jews. Those prayers in the traditional liturgy that disparaged or expressed animosity toward non-Jews (as a result of gentile persecution of Jews), therefore, were eliminated, and prayers that were deemed to be too particular in their language were universalized. Thus, the first paragraph of *Aleinu*, which describes Jewish destiny as "not like that of other peoples," was either eliminated or reworded. (*Mishkan T'filah* provides both the traditional text and several more universalizing options.) Phrases like that in the *Amidah* asking God to bless "His people Israel with peace" were often replaced with more generic language, such as "Maker of peace." (*Mishkan T'filah* provides both versions.)

The Reform commitment to universalism ("One God over all; / One brotherhood of all," in the words of the *Union Prayer Book*) ironically generated a thorny paradox: if the Jew's ultimate concern should be to work for the good of all humanity, pure and simple, why should he or she remain Jewish? Beyond the very real social fact that ongoing discrimination against Jews would continue to promote Jewish social cohesion until well after the Second World War, a necessary theological rationale for Jewish continuity came to be articulated forcefully in the nineteenth century by Rabbi David Einhorn (1809–79). This rationale transmuted the traditional tenet of Israel as God's chosen people into the idea of the mission of Israel. The Jewish people, in Einhorn's classic formulation, had a world-historical role to play as God's vanguard in the religious and social progress of humanity. The prophets of ancient Israel had held up a beacon of social justice, ethical behavior, and compassion that shone forth for all peoples, just as Jewish ethical monotheism (more pure than Christian trinitarianism or bi-theism) was to serve as the template and model for universal religion. The dispersion of Israel among the nations, therefore, was not to be understood as a catastrophe or a divine punishment, but as a necessary part of Israel's mission, like Abraham's, to be a blessing to humanity. Jews were to be moral and religious exemplars to the larger world. This became the lynchpin of classical Reform theology and appears prominently in all editions of the *Union Prayer Book*.

Further changes in the content of the prayers were due to the fact that the nineteenth-century Reformers were enlightened rationalists. Anything that smacked of the miraculous, superstitious, or mythological in the prayers was to be eliminated. So the elaborate descriptions of the angelic choirs praising God in the *K'dushah* were deleted, as was the extended description of angels and the angelic *K'dushah* in the first blessing before the morning recitation of the *Sh'ma*. The latter, and most of the former, remain absent from *Mishkan T'filah*. Deleted, too, were kabbalistic prayers and meditations that had entered the traditional prayer book over the centuries—including the ritual of *Kabbalat Shabbat* and the hymn *L'chah Dodi*. With the increased interest today in the non-rational aspects of religion, some of this material has been restored in *Mishkan T'filah*. (*Kabbalat Shabbat* already had been restored in the 1975 *Gates of Prayer*, and an abbreviated version of *L'chah Dodi* appeared in the 1940 revision of the *Union Prayer Book*.)

Early Reformers also found the idea of physical resurrection after death to be incredible and unscientific. In this, they also followed many enlightened Christians of the period. But both groups continued to believe in a spiritual continuation after death, an immortality of the soul. In the early Reform prayer books, the phrase *m'chayeih hameitim* (resurrecting the dead) was retained, but paraphrased in the vernacular to indicate rather a belief in spiritual immortality. In later Reform prayer books, the phrase was eliminated or changed. In recent years, both a greater appreciation for the metaphorical, as opposed to the literal, meaning of this phrase and a willingness to entertain non-rational aspirations has led to its restoration as an option in *Mishkan T'filah*.

Another theological change involved curtailing the penitential tone of some parts of the traditional liturgy, since the stance of constantly acknowledging human imperfection, inadequacy, and guilt before an all-powerful and all-righteous Deity did not (and does not) comport with a modern sense of human capacity and self-worth. Hence, the daily *Tachanun* prayers—penitential supplications—were (and remain) deleted from most North American, and some other, Reform prayer books. Similarly, the penitential tone of the Yom Kippur liturgy has been muted somewhat by omitting most of the traditional *piyutim*—liturgical poems—that give it pervasive expression. (*Piyutim* were also omitted because of their difficult language, largely unintelligible to most worshipers and heavily reliant on deep familiarity with traditional Rabbinic interpretation of Scripture.)

Most characteristic have been the original prayers and meditations composed specifically for individual Reform prayer books. Here is where contemporary concerns are most visible. For example, while social justice has always been a concern of the Reform Movement, the particular social needs and their expressions have often been highly topical. For example, the revised *Union Prayer Book*, volume 2 (1922) used the occasion of Yom Kippur to address the issues of income disparity and capital versus labor in the United States, in the presence of wealthy businessmen in the pews. The newly revised *Union Prayer Book*, volume 1 (1940) famously alluded in a Shabbat evening prayer to the 1930s-era struggles of coal miners for better wages and working conditions. A creative meditation to be recited before lighting the *Havdalah* candle in *Gates of Prayer* (1975) makes an oblique reference to the Vietnam War (as well as, perhaps, to the fire-bombings of European cities during the Second World War) and to the problem of industrial pollution. Finally, *Mishkan T'filah* (2007) includes a creative ecological interpretation of the second paragraph (Deuteronomy 11:13–21) of the *Sh'ma*, although the traditional text remains deleted from the book.

It is also important to note that most Reform prayer books have sought to strike a balance between innovation and tradition, between contemporary expression and the historic markers of Jewish prayer. Virtually all Reform prayer books retain the traditional order of the service and the traditional elements (however abbreviated) of that service. The structure and major contents have almost always been recognizably Jewish. As we noted above, the style of worship performance has varied, allowing worshipers to feel both Jewish and a part of their larger society at the same time.

We conclude with some observations about the present and about Reform worship using *Mishkan T'filah*. The American Jewish community today is fully Americanized; it is therefore more willing publicly to explore "Jewish difference" in the context of an American culture that itself is more open to such difference. In the worship context, Reform Jews seek meaningful ways to affirm and to enact through ritual a distinctive Jewish identity that is also accessible to all (including non-Jewish family members and service attendees). More Hebrew appears in the service today; it is fully transliterated in order to be inclusive. There is greater freedom to experiment with traditional forms and styles of worship, including appropriations from the Jewish mystical tradition and the use of Chasidic *nigunim* (wordless melodies) and teachings, though all of this is filtered through contemporary sensibilities. At the same time, there continues to be great openness to religious and spiritual wisdom from all sources. There is also some appropriation of Eastern forms of meditation and mindfulness training in the pursuit of personal spirituality. (The Yom Kippur *Yizkor* service published in *Mishkan HaNefesh*, the newest North American Reform High Holy Day prayer book, for example, includes a two-page spread devoted entirely to a visually arresting guided meditation about our deceased loved ones.)

The current prayer books of the North American Jewish community, *Mishkan T'filah* and *Mishkan HaNefesh*, are also deeply informed by the insights of contemporary psychology and anthropology, as well as postmodernist philosophy. From Sigmund Freud comes the recognition that there are deeply irrational (or non-rational) and emotive wellsprings to the human personality that must be given their due as much as rationality. In response, contemporary Reform worship has affirmed the importance of incorporating music, gesture, movement, and social interaction within the service as shared modes of expression and experience that enact and reinforce shared values and identity. The very first of the stated goals of *Mishkan HaNefesh* is phrased in emotive terms: to "inspire participation in the multi-faceted experience of the High Holy Days—from feelings of awe to moments of solace, from the solitude of contemplation to the solidarity of song and worship." Indeed, many of the creative texts in both prayer books are allusive, emotive, and attempt to evoke a sense of transcendence.

Similarly appropriated are contemporary insights on the importance of myth, ritual, symbolism, and metaphor in human activity and meaning-making—all figurative and allusive, rather than literal, in their significance. Contemporary Reform worship affirms that traditional mythic language, imagery, and metaphor (including resurrection of the dead and angelology) can be reclaimed and reimagined through individual and contemporary lenses and promotes the creation of additional life-cycle ceremonies, rites of passage, and rituals (particularly, but not exclusively, for girls and women), such as those for healing of both body and spirit.

Postmodern thought calls into question the singularity and universality of truth, affirming instead the value of complexity and of multiple perspectives and lenses. The postmodern turn honors the particular, local truths of many diverse cultures and religious traditions (such as Judaism in its multiple forms), as well as the differing perspectives of individuals. This also supports the presence in the prayer book of multiple theological perspectives, reflecting the actual diversity within the Reform Movement and promoting inclusivity.

Finally, these contemporary prayer books have thoughtfully responded to the challenges and insights of modern feminism—substituting gender-neutral for gendered language (including language for God) and eliminating hierarchical language (including such metaphors for God as "King" and "Father"), but also at times supplying feminine metaphors and language to equalize the gender-consciousness.

The newest Reform prayer books provide many texts—both contemporary and traditional—as options for individual or communal meditation, study, and prayer. These texts run the whole gamut of religious emotion and belief: affirming and questioning, theistic and nontheistic, supportive and challenging, ecstatic and grieving, but above all, supporting and inspiring the quest for a life of holiness and social responsibility.

The contemporary Reform Movement is a "big tent"; the prayer books aspire, through inclusiveness and variety (including more tradition), to reach out and, in some sacred moment, to touch a deep, resonant chord in each person within that tent. In such a moment, it is hoped, the personal and the collective; the human and the Jewish; the present, past, and future may come together and mutually inform each other. And in that moment, Jewish worship will be able, once more, to perform its work.

34

REFORM LITURGY:
THEN AND NOW

Rabbi Dalia Marx, PhD

Even more than it was a theological or halachic revolution, Reform Judaism was a liturgical one. From its earliest days, its mark was most clearly apparent in the orders and prayers of synagogue life. Exponents and opponents alike focus first and foremost on its prayer, and despite the many transformations Reform has known over some two centuries, liturgy continues to occupy a central place in the movement.

It can be said that the history of Reform prayer is the history of Reform Judaism. Jewish prayer books, in general—as the vessels that have, for generations, embodied the hopes and fears of the Jewish people, its aspirations, and contemporary challenges—offer informative insights into Jewish history. Traditional prayer books have always reflected theological and ideological perceptions, and on occasions even political positions, but for the most part this theology was not conscious. One of the innovations brought by the Reform Movement is ideological and theological expressions in prayer books that are the products of explicit and conscious choice.

Over the past two centuries, the editors of Reform prayer books have repeatedly striven to find the proper balance between local and contemporary needs and the desire to maintain permanent foundations

and the connection to *k'lal Israel* (Jewish peoplehood). The editors of
Reform prayer books have constantly and carefully weighed the considerations involved in making changes, and refraining from change.
The question at hand has never been *whether* to pay a given price for
the omission, amendment, or deletion of any particular liturgical unit
that raises ideological, theological, or aesthetic difficulties, but rather
what price the editors (and the worship communities) are willing to
pay, and what benefits of faith or aesthetics this offers the community.[1]

From the earliest days of Reform Judaism, its leaders argued that
liturgy was not only a manifestation of faith and poetry, but also a revelation of theology and ideology (albeit not necessarily in the systematic sense of the two). However, the changes made by the editors of the
early Reform prayer books were in many ways moderate by comparison
to the views those editors presented in their theological writings.[2] This
is particularly true in the case of the German prayer books, which were
intended to meet the complex and sometimes contradictory religious
and cultural needs of the entire community. It should be noted that
the editors of the first Reform prayer books, the Berlin (1817) and the
Hamburg prayer book (1819),[3] were not rabbis but laypeople. Only
in later decades did ordained rabbis with academic backgrounds take
their place. The liturgical changes in the printed prayer books generally reflected a mood that had already become prevalent among the
public for which they were intended. It can be suggested that, for the
most part, the progressive prayer book accompanied developments in
worship and in greater Jewish society rather than creating them. It has
been shown that all the American Reform prayer books were published
in close proximity to the publication of the movement's platforms,
thereby realizing the directions adopted in these platforms.[4]

The editors of the Reform prayer books (many of whom head a
committee comprising rabbis, experts, and laypeople) are aware that
their innovations in prayer form part of a chain of liturgical creativity.[5]
They are also aware of the educational and communal aspects of their
task, since in many cases the prayer book will become its users' principal Jewish text. Because of this, the editors often detail their editorial

considerations in the introductions to the prayer books, in statements or accompanying booklets, and more recently on the Internet.

In order to examine the principles that governed the creation of the classical Reform prayer books, we will first look at the ten characteristics of Reform prayer proposed by liturgy scholar Jakob J. Petuchowski in 1967. We will seek to examine to what extent these characteristics are present in contemporary Reform prayer.[6]

1. **Shortening the traditional prayer:** This reflects the principle that "better a little with intention [*kavanah*] than much without intention."[7] In addition to omitting many liturgical passages, poems, meditations, and reflections were added, and a sermon given by the rabbi came to occupy a central place in the synagogue worship.

2. **Use of the vernacular:** The translation of the prayer book into German (printed in Hebrew letters to facilitate reading) by David Friedlander in 1786 was perceived as a relatively revolutionary innovation. Several decades later, the use of the vernacular in the sermon and in various parts of the service became commonplace in Western Europe, and later also in the United States. In classical Reform prayer books, most of the traditional prayers were translated, and prayers and poems composed in the vernacular were also added.

3. **Omission of angelology:** Classical Reform emphasized the importance of scientific truth in religious expression and was opposed to the manifestation of angelology (and demonology) in prayer,[8] arguing that belief in angels and demons was incompatible with the intellectual honesty that was so important to the Reformers.

The following four characteristics reflect the manner in which the Reform prayer books grappled with the *redemption narrative* in prayer: the concept of the chosen nature of the Jewish people; petitions for the return to Zion; and belief in the coming of the Messiah and the

352 · A Life of Meaning

resurrection of the dead. The ambivalence and hostility toward the redemption narrative that characterized most of the classical Reform prayer books reflected a perception that saw Judaism as a religion whose role was to act among the nations as "a kingdom of priests and a holy nation" (Exodus 19:6) and a tendency to refrain as far as possible from regarding Judaism as a national or ethnic group.

The first platform adopted by the Reform Movement in the United States (Pittsburgh, 1885) reflects the principal characteristics of early and classical Reform liturgy:

> We consider ourselves no longer a nation, but a religious community, and therefore expect neither a return to Palestine, nor a sacrificial worship under the sons of Aaron, nor the restoration of any of the laws concerning the Jewish state.[9]

Different prayer books reflected different approaches to the perception of Judaism as a nation and the affinity of that nation to its historical homeland. All of these approaches manifest belief in the imminence of Jewish redemption, with an emphasis on the moral mission of Judaism among the nations. Exile is perceived as more a task than a punishment.

4. **The weakening of particularism and the idea of the Chosen People:** The Reform Movement was founded in Western Europe during the emancipation, an era when Jews had begun to hope that they could be accepted as legitimate members of the nations among which they lived, enjoying equal rights. This explains the emphasis on the universal components in the Reform vision and, accordingly, on an approach that sees the Jews as a religious community rather than an ethnic or national group.

5. **The omission of the petitions for the ingathering of the exiles and the return to Zion:** Based on the abovementioned perception of Judaism as a religious community rather than an ethnic or national group, the classical Reform prayer books in the Diaspora omitted petitions for the ingathering and return

to Zion and further muted references to Zion as the spiritual home of the Jewish people.[10] In contrast, Israeli Reform liturgy has, since its early days, embraced Zionism, and so it contains all the references to Zion and modern-day Israel.[11]

6. **The omission of prayers for the reinstatement of the sacrifices:** As noted, early and classical Reform toned down the affinity between Judaism and Zion to a varying extent. However, they were unanimous in their rejection of the petitions for the reestablishment of the Temple and the reinstatement of the sacrifices.

7. **The concepts of a "messianic era" and redemption, rather than references to the Messiah:** Reform generally rejected the classical concept of an individual messiah (as it relates to the return to Zion and the rebuilding of the Temple). However, they believed that we are on the verge of a time of peace and equality for all.

8. **Substitution of spiritual immortality for belief in physical resurrection:** As noted, opposition to the concept of an individual messiah appears in the earliest Reform writings in Europe. By contrast, opposition to the concept of physical resurrection only appears in an explicit form in Geiger's statement of 1869, where he proposed that the principle of the spiritual immortality be adopted in place of belief in resurrection.[12]

9. **Provision of variety:** Psalms and prayers used in traditional liturgy on a single occasion are distributed over many occasions. Different services are made available for the same occasion.

10. **The addition of new prayers expressing contemporary aspirations:** These prayers, which were usually composed in the vernacular, reflect hopes for a new era of friendship between the nations and the acceptance of the Jews as equal citizens in their countries of dispersion. Caesar Seligmann notes the principles that guided him as he composed new prayers:

> In creating new prayers, my ideal was to introduce into the liturgy, and win the right of domicile in the synagogue

for, the new elements and problems arising out of the new conditions and circumstances, the new moods and sentiments, cares and hopes, which have found no expression in the old prayerbook and *mahzor*. I have tried to give to those prayers all the religious sincerity and a solemn mood, all the verve and artistic expression, of which I was capable—in order to kindle them a new religious enthusiasm, and to warm, for the holy religion of the fathers, the hearts of those who have become estranged from it.[13]

As noted, the early and classical periods of Reform were not monolithic. If we compare Petuchowski's list from the 1960s to that proposed by ethnomusicologist Avraham Zvi Idelsohn some three and a half decades earlier,[14] it is apparent that Petuchowski adopts a less decisive tone than his predecessor. Idelsohn was writing during the heyday of classical Reform, before the clouds of Nazism had overshadowed Europe, shattering the hope that we are at the verge of a new and better world and the idea of a Jewish message to the world, and before the movement had recognized the achievements of Zionism and the need for a national home. Petuchowski's far more moderate tone reflects the zeitgeist when they were written. Differences in the manifestations of German Reform were "at most ones of degree rather than type."[15] This was due in part to the form of organization of the Jewish communities in Germany, where Orthodox and Liberal congregations existed under the same umbrella of the *Einheitsgemeinde* (the unified community). In the United States, by contrast, where community affiliation was voluntary, Reform Judaism developed separately from Orthodoxy.[16]

We now turn to discussing Reform prayer books published since the beginning of the current century: *Mishkan T'filah*[17] and *Mishkan HaNefesh*[18] in the United States, *Forms of Prayer*[19] in the United Kingdom, and *HaSimcha SheBaLev*[20] in Israel. Time will tell what character will be adopted by the prayer books and *machzorim* currently in process and how these will be accepted by their communities. By way of example, it remains to be seen what directions will be taken by the new Israeli Reform prayer book and new British Liberal and Reform prayer books currently in the editing process.

In many ways, contemporary prayer broadly continues the liturgical trends seen during the early and classical periods. Now, too, the focus is on the search for honesty of expression and concern for the validity of the prayers in the contemporary context, on the one hand, combined with maintaining the tradition and the relationship with the past, on the other. Nevertheless, the patterns of new prayer in the Reform Movement are breaking new ground. In a lecture in 2000, Rabbi Peter Knobel, the head of the CCAR's Liturgy Committee at the time, maintained that the challenge facing contemporary Reform liturgy should be framed as multidirectional *to tradition* and *from tradition*, simultaneously. Both approaches—the desire to return to a more traditional Judaism and the radical approach to the liturgical canon— coexist, albeit with a certain tension and in differing degrees, in the various centers of the Reform Movement.

Mishkan T'filah offers a clear illustration of the changes that have occurred in the American Reform approach. The process of preparing the prayer book took a relatively long time (almost twenty-five years) and was undertaken by both rabbis and laypeople. In the early 1980s, the need arose to make changes to prayer and to the possibilities for expression it provides. In 1985 the Siddur Discussion Group was established, headed by Rabbi Leonard Poller. In 1994 the Editorial Committee was formed, headed by Rabbi Peter Knobel. In 1999 Rabbis Elyse Frishman and Judith Abrams were initially chosen to serve as co-editors, with Judith Abrams eventually becoming a consulting editor and Elyse Frishman serving as sole editor. Various drafts were circulated to some three hundred communities and at movement events. The work on the prayer book entailed more than a few dramatic episodes in terms of both organization and content before it was finally published in 2007.[21]

Thus the preparation of *Mishkan T'filah* was a public process extending over a generation, and one that was unprecedented in terms of its use of technological knowledge and advances.[22] Its editors did not recoil from the challenges of the age. The pages of the prayer book, for example, were designed somewhat as Internet pages. The text includes different alternatives for every prayer: the Hebrew prayer on the right, together with an English translation and transliteration, and on the left, alternative prayers and readings illuminating various aspects of the traditional prayer. In addition, the lower part of each page provides explanations on aspects of history, faith, and commentary.[23] This juxtaposition of traditional and new liturgical passages had been employed prior to *Gates of Prayer* (1975), as for example in the youth prayer book of the Israeli Reform Movement, *HaChavaya SheBaLev* (2000).[24] In the British Reform prayer book *Forms of Prayer*, each page presents both the Hebrew prayer and its English translation. This prayer book also includes numerous explanations regarding the history of the prayers, choices made by the editors, as well as guidelines for the worship regarding the choreography of prayer. Reflective pieces, poems, and selected readings are confined to the opening and ending sections.

The following are the characteristics of new Reform prayer as manifested in its prayer books. The list constitutes a revised version of the characteristics proposed by Petuchowski.

1. Abridging and Expanding Prayer

Contemporary Reform liturgy also reflects the principle that shorter prayer is preferable. Nevertheless, most of the prayer books being published by the Reform Movement include the fuller format of the prayer. This approach embodies two goals: that those leading services can enjoy autonomy in the selection of prayer texts, and that most of the content of the prayer is presented to the readers, even if it will not be recited in full.[25]

Unlike its predecessor, *Gates of Prayer* (1975), which included no fewer than ten services for Friday night, each reflecting distinct theologies and styles, the new prayer books *Mishkan T'filah* and *Mishkan HaNefesh* present a single option for each service, combining diverse liturgical, theological, and stylistic components. The editors' objective for this generation with its own diverse religious needs was to make it easier for worshipers to orient themselves on the page and to deepen their identification with the prayer in accordance with their own style and faith.[26] The new service is relatively long, although many synagogues do some parts only, and some rabbis distribute prayer sheets to their communities. This phenomenon began in the Reform summer camps and reached its peak in the mid-1970s, prior to the publication of *Gates of Prayer*. It was sometimes argued that the new prayer book impaired the creative character of liturgical action.

In recent years, the integration of technology into every aspect of life, specifically mobile phone apps and online resources, has led to the expansion of this phenomenon, whereby community members, students, and youth movement participants prepare their own aesthetic prayer sheets.[27]

2. The Use of the Vernacular alongside a Return to Hebrew

As mentioned above, *Mishkan T'filah* is the first prayer book in the history of the American Reform Movement to include the full Hebrew version of the prayers alongside the English as well as transliteration in Latin letters. The change is also apparent in symbolic aspects: the prayer book opens from right to left, in Hebrew fashion, and has only a Hebrew name. It should be noted that alongside the return of Hebrew to the prayers, importance continues to be attached to the use of the vernacular in Reform prayer. This is consistent with the principles of the new Pittsburgh Platform ("A Statement of Principles," 1999), which called for the deepening of Hebrew studies among the movement's congregations. Increasing use of Hebrew in prayer does not necessarily imply knowledge of the language and may instead be associated with the sense of authenticity and mystery that the language evokes among the worshipers.[28] In any case, the change marks the importance attached to this aspect by rabbis and prayer leaders.

According to scholar of liturgy Richard Sarason, the change regarding Hebrew can be seen as indicative of the change in the social status of Jews in the United States (and earlier in Europe). The Jews who emigrated to the United States in the nineteenth and early twentieth centuries sought to assimilate into American society and did not wish to be perceived as aliens. Accordingly, they introduced English in their prayers in place of Hebrew (and Yiddish). Conversely, Jews who grew up in the generation following the Second World War felt entirely American. The challenge they faced was refashioning their Jewish identity. Identification with Zionism and with the Hebrew language became a type of positive counteraction on their part.

In Israel, where Hebrew is also the vernacular, the challenges are different. The affinity with the liturgical text is immediate and unmediated. But precisely because of that, theological and ideological difficulties that emerge from the traditional language are emphatically felt and cannot be circumvented by means of a moderating translation. The use of Hebrew requires a more special attention to prayer, to the concepts it represents, and to the system of images and symbols it contains. This explains both the relative conservatism of the liturgy of the Israeli Reform Movement and the profound need for a creative approach in this respect. The liturgical language itself is traditional, and in Israel, the use of a language that is understood by everyone demands explicit attention, both on the textual level and in interpretative contexts—aspects that can be resolved overseas through the use of a "user-friendly" translation.

3. Gendered Prayer

One of the central aspects of contemporary Reform prayer is the selective use of gendered language. This change is a relatively new one on the Reform agenda and has been credited to the ordination of women as rabbis and cantors.

The change in the gender language of prayer is manifested mainly in the following:[29] the inclusion of the voice of women worshipers, and thus adding feminine grammatical gender alongside the male voice (it is interesting to note that some of these discussions have infiltrated Modern Orthodoxy in recent years);[30] mentioning female figures from Jewish heritage, such as the addition of the Matriarchs alongside the Patriarchs in the *Amidah*; the creation of new rituals and ceremonies and the revival of old ones, particularly life-cycle-related ceremonies marking female experiences (e.g., pregnancy, birth, menopause, miscarriage, healing from illness or abuse); and God language—that is, the forms used to address God. While on the first three issues there is relatively broad consensus, the last issue is the subject of considerable debate and controversy. The demand to adapt the gender of prayer reflects the perception that language is a powerful tool through which humans understand the world. It is a powerful and manipulative tool, and yet also a covert one. As the Christian theologian Sallie McFague remarked, "Whoever names the world owns the world."[31] Feminist theoreticians argue that God cannot be understood or described in human language, but merely through metaphors. Naturally, this awareness was not born with feminism and was noted by Maimonides, among others. The innovation feminism has brought is the perception that metaphors are tools through which humans order their world; accordingly, religious language should be enriched, and as far as possible, the exclusive use of male descriptions of God should be avoided. The prayer book *Mishkan T'filah* replaces the pronoun "he" with "God," and references such as "our Father" and "our King" were removed.

The situation in Israel regarding gender discourse is more complex. While the first edition of *HaAvodah SheBaLev* (1982) shows no interest in gender matters, the second edition of the prayer book (1991) made some isolated changes in this respect, such as adding the names of the Matriarchs in the *Amidah*, as an alternative version to the traditional one. Newer liturgies, such as the youth prayer book *HaChavaya SheBaLev* (2000), include the Matriarchs in the standard text, and not by way of an alternative, and since then it has become the rule. However, gender-neutral language is impossible in Hebrew, since every noun, verb, and adjective is either feminine or masculine. Moreover, the use of the feminine to refer to God is still perceived by many as alien. Accordingly, a moderate approach can be seen in the new Israeli Reform prayer book in the making with regard to the use of feminine "God language" and the symbolic importance of the languages of prayer.

4. A Symbolic Reading of Prayer

In contrast to classical Reform, which took the literal meaning of prayer extremely seriously and accordingly changed liturgical usages that were incompatible with the speakers' beliefs and opinions, this was a very intellectual cognitive version of Judaism—every word that was uttered in prayer had to be "true." In contemporary Reform, by contrast, there is a lesser commitment to "speak truth" and more interest in finding meaningful words. The prayer books refrain whenever possible from the wholesale deletion of prayers and instead look to attach symbolic meaning to the traditional forms.

Earlier American Reform prayer books refrained from using the concluding *chatimah* (concluding formula) of the second blessing in the *Amidah*, "revives the dead," expressing belief in physical resurrection, and instead preferred more general phrases, such as "who revives all" or "who revives every living thing." The drafts of the *Mishkan T'filah* reflect a theological back-and-forth on this aspect, exposing the disagreements that have emerged within American Reform on this question. The disagreements were so virulent at some points that it seemed they might lead to a split in the movement or at least prevent the publication of the new prayer book. It was ultimately decided to leave the Reform wording and to present the traditional form "revives the dead" in parentheses.[32]

5. The Attitude to the Return to Zion

From as early as the 1930s, a gradual change occurred in the attitude of the Reform Movement toward Zionism. The horrors of the Holocaust coupled with the establishment of the State of Israel formed the background to this fundamental change. Above all, however, it was the anxiety surrounding the future of the young State of Israel during the period preceding the Six-Day War in 1967, and the sense of relief that followed, that led to the most significant changes in prayer. Many liturgical sections that have to do with Zion and Zionism, previously deleted, were restored to the prayer book.

The Reform Movement in Israel never questioned the importance of Zion and Zionism and never omitted from its prayer books references to the centrality of Zion. In some respects, as we will see, the Reform version is even more explicit than traditional prayer books regarding the centrality of Israel.[33]

6. The Attitude toward the State of Israel

While the reinstatement of expressions of prayer referring to Zion is a restorative act, the introduction of prayers concerning the State of Israel is an act of liturgical creativity. *Mishkan T'filah*, largely the product of the same spirit that characterized the second Pittsburgh Platform (1999), shows a warm and sympathetic approach to Zionism while recognizing the importance of Diaspora Jewry. Like *Gates of Prayer*, this prayer book also includes a service for Israel Independence Day and for Memorial Day,[34] a prayer for the State of Israel, and a selection of Israeli Hebrew poetry in English translation.

In Israel, of course, there have never been any reservations regarding Jewish nationhood. Our prayer books have a clear Zionist orientation. In *HaAvodah SheBaLev*, the petition "and bring us peacefully from the four corners of the earth" was replaced by "and bring in our exiles from the four corners of the earth." And one example that reflects our recognition that Jerusalem is indeed being built as the capital of the State of Israel and that it is the city we yearn for, not the dwelling place of the Temple, is reflected in the changing of the petition "build Jerusalem, the holy city" in *Birkat HaMazon* to "complete the building of Jerusalem."

HaAvodah SheBaLev ascribed a central role to aspects of Israeli reality. The prayers for the State of Israel and for IDF soldiers are recited every Shabbat, there are services for the Memorial Day for Fallen IDF Soldiers, Independence Day, and Jerusalem Day. In recent years, the movement's communities have held creative services on the Memorial Day for the Late Yitzhak Rabin. The new prayer book currently in preparation devotes much attention to the diverse Jewish groups and ethnic communities in

Israel, including their prayer customs and *piyutim*. For example, it always includes the Sephardic *Kaddish* alongside the Ashkenazic one.

7. The Attitude toward the Concept of the Chosenness of the Jewish People

The new British prayer books adopt a universalist tone. For example, The Liberal prayer book *Lev Chadash* ends the *Kaddish* as follows: "May God who makes peace in the heavens make peace for us and for the whole world, and let us say: Amen." The newest American High Holy Day prayer book, *Mishkan HaNefesh*, adds the words "and all who dwell on earth."[35] A universalist approach no longer needs to stand in contrast with the unique character of Jewish peoplehood.

8. Inclusive and Yet Individualistic Approach

The editors of the contemporary Reform prayer books seek to emphasize the inclusive aspects of the prayer book in order to encompass the range of opinions and beliefs found among worshipers. Users of the prayer books include well-educated Hebrew readers as well as those who have little familiarity with the language; those looking for poetic beauty and those grappling with questions of faith; and those who have a strong Jewish background and newcomers. Moreover, the format of the prayers also seeks to serve such diverse groups as LGBTQ people, interfaith families, converts, single-parent families, people with special needs, and people living alone. The inclusive approach of the Reform Movement as manifested in the new prayer books reflects not only its longstanding support for social justice concerns,[36] but also postmodern values, as adopted by Reform in its new format.[37]

A key change is the new emphasis on the experience of the individual, rather than the people, including the individual search for meaning and spirituality. Thus, for example, the *Mi Shebeirach* prayer, which had traditionally been no more than a minor petition, became imbued with a central status in emotional and experiential terms when the composition by Debbie Friedman (z"l) was adopted for use by the Reform Movement.[38] Many ceremonies marking transitional life events have been added or enriched to celebrate personal experiences and emphasize individual autonomy.

9. Pluralism in Prayer

Rabbi Richard Sarason, PhD, one of the editors of *Mishkan T'filah*, saw the editing process as a product of the counterculture of the 1960s, combining the following characteristics:

> Romantic—feeling versus ideas, experience, relationship, mystical, spirituality unregimented, decentralized, participatory, stress on individual seeker in supportive community, multi-daven, splitting the difference in theological conflicts, user-friendly, inclusive, gender-neutral, PC, Eastern European (through a romantic haze).[39]

Just as the counterculture movement was formative to communities all over North America and Israel, *Mishkan T'filah* incorporates the ethos of a generation that will stretch into the future, as it seeks to meet the constantly evolving needs of worshipers, while also reflecting the movement's belief in pluralism.

In this respect, the sources of Reform liturgy in Israel are even more diverse. The editors of the prayer books integrate texts from Hebrew literature of all ages: the Bible and the Qumran scrolls, medieval poetry, classical and modern philosophy, modern Israeli poetry, liturgical texts of different Jewish communities, and so forth. The children's siddur *HaChavaya SheBaLev* includes prayers written by members of the youth movement. The explicitly inclusive and intertextual approach is intended to reflect in the prayer book the words, hopes, and pains of Jews of all generations, thereby expanding the historical canvas of prayer. As noted, the new prayer book currently in preparation seems to reflect this approach even more strongly.

The new prayer books also seek to be more organic and to address diverse life experiences. Accordingly, the prayers are not intended solely for recital in the synagogue, but also for use at home, in nature, and in various family and social contexts.

10. New-Wave Influence: Spirituality and Corporeality

In recent years, various new religious practices have been adopted by the Reform Movement, including meditation, drum circles, breathing exercises, and the mantra-like use of God's name or of single verses of prayer. Such elements are acquiring an increasingly important status within individual and public religious practice. Eastern cultures (albeit in a Western version), the Kabbalah, and the teachings of Chasidism (though not always its systemic study), as well as New Age culture, are all making their mark on contemporary Reform liturgy.

Classical Reform often showed a marked reluctance to include the body in worship, consistent with its reservations about other "physical" aspects of Judaism, such as ritual objects (e.g., *kippah*, tallit, *t'fillin*, mezuzah), and indeed the "physical" dimension of nationhood—the people and its land. There is now a growing awareness of the importance of the physical dimension, including bodily gestures as part of the experience of prayer. The renewed liturgical attention to the "national body," with its territorial dimensions, can be seen as part of the corporeal revolution of the contemporary Reform Movement.

Sarason suggests that this attitude to the body is a generational and cultural matter. For classical Reform, reticence regarding physicality reflected a desire to be "Western" and "bourgeois," and accordingly the synagogue emphasized decency and decorum. The traditional body language of Jewish prayer was perceived as alien. Conversely, the generation that followed the Second World War rediscovered their grandparents' Eastern European popular enthusiasm and unrestrained physicality in prayer and opposed the restrained atmosphere of Western culture, particularly among the upper-middle classes.[40]

An example of the changing attitude to physicality is the blessing *Asher Yatzar*, which alludes to physical functions, actions, and excretions ("Blessed . . . who formed the human body with skill, creating the body's many pathways and openings"). Classical Reform found this content inappropriate for prayer, and it was omitted from many prayer books, left untranslated, or translated in a periphrastic manner. Contemporary Reform prayer books have reintroduced this prayer in Hebrew, with a literal translation. The engagement with the physical does not contradict the spiritual search; on the contrary, the two are regarded as mutually compatible.[41]

Just as the early Reformers sought to fashion an authentic religious language that seeks truth, so do today's Reform Jews. However, considerable changes can be seen in the character and quality of this search. The classical style of Reform prayer largely took the form of the ceremonial expression of a manifesto of faith or perhaps even that of a legal contract embodying rational perceptions. Today, Reform Jews today do not seek *truth* in prayer, but rather *meaning*—the connection to God and to the community to which they belong.[42]

The dominant mood in Reform today is one that is highly open to facing contemporary challenges, yet reluctant to decisively deal with theological matters, and overly influenced by a desire for comfort and feeling good.[43] Contemporary Reform prayer books are more traditional in terms of their attitude toward the Hebrew language and the Return to Zion, and more innovative in terms of the issue of gender, the inclusion of diverse Jewish sources, and multiple prayer formats and styles. Only time will tell what fruits will be yielded by the trends and developments described above.[44]

NOTES

I would like to thank Professor Michael Meyer and Rabbi Professor Richard Sarason for their important comments on this article and to Shaul Vardi, who translated it into English.

1. Traditional prayer books also manifest differing versions, although the origins of these variations are usually ancient and obscure. The grounds quoted in

halachic literature for or against any particular version often seek to justify an existing liturgical reality. In many cases, the editors of traditional prayer books declare that they have striven to provide a refined version free of "errors." The situation is different in the case of the non-Orthodox prayer books, and particularly in Reform ones, where changes reflect an awareness of philosophical, theological, literary, and educational questions.

2. David H. Ellenson, *After Emancipation: Jewish Religious Responses to Modernity* (Cincinnati: Hebrew Union College Press, 2004), 203–14. Avraham-Meir Goldschmidt made the following comments in his introduction to the Leipzig prayer book (1876): "We all know from personal experience how hard it is, in the religious realm, to act according to purely theoretical principles. Religion is life; but life goes its own way, not caring about the theories of the scholars—be they ever so ingenious and penetrating" (Jakob J. Petuchowski, *Prayerbook Reform in Europe: The Liturgy of European Liberal and Reform Judaism* [New York: World Union for Progressive Judaism, 1968], 177).

3. *Seder HaAvodah: Ordnung der Öffentlichen Andacht für die Sabbath und Festtage des ganzen Jahres* (Hamburg: S. Fränkel & M. Bresselau, 1919).

4. H. Bronstein, "Platforms and Prayer Books: From Exclusivity to Inclusivity in Reform Judaism," in *Platforms and Prayer Books: Theological and Liturgical Perspectives on Reform Judaism*, ed. Dana E. Kaplan (Lanham, MD: Rowman & Littlefield, 2002), 25–39.

5. The editors of the British Liberal prayer book *Lev Chadash* expressed this perception in explicit terms: "We have no doubt at all that the present one will prove to be only a phase in the ongoing history of Jewish liturgy. But we hope that it will be regarded as a serious and responsible attempt" (John Rayner and Chaim Stern, eds., *Siddur Lev Chadash: Services and Prayers for Weekdays and Shabbat, Festivals and Various Occasions* [London: Union of Liberal and Progressive Synagogues, 1995], xxii).

6. This chapter will examine the textual aspects of Reform prayer. It is also important to address nonverbal aspects, such as the prayer arrangements, the structure of the synagogue, music, and aspects relating to the implementation of prayer.

7. Yaakov ben Asher, *Arbaah Turim, Orach Chayim*, 1.

8. In the traditional context, too, reservations are apparent regarding angelology in prayer, and particularly regarding explicit appeals to the angels. See Simcha Emanuel, "On the Recitation of the *Piyut 'Machnisei Rachamim'*" [in Hebrew], *Hamaayan* 38, no. 1 (5758): 5–11; Shlomo Sprecher, "A Debate on the Reciting of *'Machnisei Rachamim'*" [in Hebrew], *Yeshurun* 3 (5757): 706–19.

9. "The Pittsburgh Platform" (1885), ccarnet.org/rabbis-speak/platforms/declaration-principles/.

10. Dalia Marx, "Zion and Zionism in Reform Prayer Books," in *The Fragile Dialogue: New Voices of Liberal Zionism*, ed. Stanley M. Davids and Lawrence A. Englander (New York: CCAR Press, 2017), 155–74.

11. Dalia Marx, "When L'shon HaKodesh Is Also the Vernacular: The Development of Israeli Reform Liturgy," *CCAR Journal*, Fall 2009, 31–62.

12. Petuchowski, *Prayerbook Reform*, 166.

13. Petuchowski, *Prayerbook Reform*, 199–200.

14. Abraham Z. Idelsohn, *Jewish Liturgy and Its Development* (New York: Dover Publications, 1932), 277–78.

15. Ellenson, *After Emancipation*, 220.

16. Michael A. Meyer, "Our Collective Identity as Reform Jews," in Kaplan, *Platforms and Prayer Books*, 93–94; idem, *Response*, 225–95.

17. Elyse D. Frishman, ed., *Mishkan Tefilah: A Reform Siddur* (New York: CCAR Press, 2007).

18. Edwin Goldberg, Janet Marder, Sheldon Marder, and Leon Morris, eds., *Mishkan HaNefesh: Machzor for the Days of Awe* (New York: CCAR Press, 2015).

19. Jonathan Magonet, ed., *Forms of Prayer: Daily, Sabbath and Occasional Prayers* (London: Movement for Reform Judaism, 2008).

20. Oded Mazor and Levy Weiman-Kelman, eds., *HaSimcha SheBaLev: Machzor for the Pilgrimage Festivals and Their Shabbatot* (Jerusalem: MARAM and Kehillat Kol HaNeshama, 5775).

21. Elliot L. Stevens, "The Prayer Books, They Are A'Changin'," *Reform Judaism*, Summer 2006. In addition, Rabbi Carmit Harari wrote her thesis on this subject.

22. Peter Knobel, "The Challenges of a Single Prayer Book," in Kaplan, *Platforms and Prayer Books*, 157–58. The online version of *Mishkan T'filah* was published in 2011.

23. The early drafts included an even larger number of alternatives, but some felt that this was liable to cause confusion.

24. *HaChavaya SheBaLev: Youth Prayer Book of the Israel Movement for Progressive Judaism* (Jerusalem: IMPJ, 5760).

25. However, the second passage of the reading of the *Sh'ma* (Deuteronomy 11:13–21) is prominent in its absence. This passage has been omitted from many Reform prayer books due to its focus on reward and punishment, the centrality of Israel, and the fact that in part it repeats the content of the first section. The *Mishkan HaNefesh machzor* reinstated the second passage.

26. In an online article, Sarason determines that *Mishkan T'filah* ironically represents "the institutionalization of the anti-institutional 60's boomer culture, for better and for worse."

27. Lawrence A. Hoffman, "Creative Liturgy," *Jewish Spectator* 40, no. 4 (1975): 42–50. In an article written approximately one-quarter of a century after that quoted here, Hoffman describes the circumstances and ramifications of this process.

28. Peter S. Knobel and Daniel S. Schechter, "What Congregants Want in Worship," *CCAR Journal*, Winter 2006, 46; Knobel, "Challenges of a Single Prayer Book," 163–64.

29. Dalia Marx, "Influences of the Feminist Movement on Jewish Liturgy: The Case of Israeli Reform Prayer," *Sociological Papers* 14 (2009): 69–79.

30. An example is the proposal to replace the blessing thanking God "that did not make me a woman" with an egalitarian alternative. See Joseph Tabory, "The Benedictions of Self-Identity and the Changing Status of Women and Orthodoxy," *Studies of Kenishta: The Synagogue World 1* (2001): 107–138.

31. Sallie McFague, *Metaphorical Theology* (Philadelphia: Fortress Press, 1982), 8. And see the classical work of Rachel Adler, *Engendering Judaism: An Inclusive Theology and Ethics* (Philadelphia: Jewish Publication Society, 1988); and Judith Plaskow, *Standing Again at Sinai: Judaism from a Feminist Perspective* (New York: Harper & Row, 1990).

32. Judith Z. Abrams, "The Continuity of Change in Jewish Liturgy," in Kaplan, *Platforms and Prayer Books*, 125–28; Daniel S. Alexander, "Is God Stronger than Death? *Tehiyyat Hametim* Reconsidered," *CCAR Journal*, Winter, 1997, 47–53; Richard N. Levy, "Upon Arising: An Affirmation of *Techiyyat Hameitim*," *Journal of Reform Judaism*, Fall 1982, 12–20.

33. Marx, "Zion and Zionism."

34. In contrast to *Gates of Prayer*, Independence Day and Memorial Day are marked not by services but by ceremonies or seder formats.

35. Recently the inclusive addition made headlines in Israel, when Dr. Zvia Valden added at the end of the *Kaddish* recited for her late father, the former Israeli president Shimon Peres: "and all the human beings."

36. This is consistent with the 1995 Pittsburgh Platform, which emphasizes the importance of an inclusive approach to prayer.

37. Peter Margolis, "Postmodern American Judaism: Origins and Symptoms," *CCAR Journal*, Spring 2001, 31–50.

38. Lawrence A. Hoffman, "Re-imagining Jewish Worship," *CCAR Journal* 49, no. 1 (2002): 77.

39. Sarason's comments convey a palpably critical tone regarding these phenomena. The comment is quoted from a lecture he gave on the subject of *Mishkan T'filah*. I thank Dr. Sarason for sharing the remarks with me.

40. Quoted from personal correspondence with Dr. Sarason.

41. Abrams, "Continuity of Change," 128.

42. Hoffman, "Re-imagining Jewish Worship."

43. In 1993 Stefan Reif writes, "This new prayer-book [*Ha'avodah Sheba-lev*] and its later equivalent *Kavvanat Ha-lev* demonstrated that the movement that produced them had come a long way, in every sense, from Berlin 1819 to Jerusalem almost a century and three quarters later" (*Judaism and Hebrew Prayer* [Cambridge: Cambridge University Press, 1993], 331).

44. This chapter has focused mainly on the liturgical aspects of theology, and less on its theoretical dimensions; on the literary, rather than halachic, aspects of prayer books; and on liturgical creativity itself, rather than the manner in which it was received. Further attention is needed in these three dimensions in order to appreciate the multiple aspects of prayer in the Reform Movement, as well as with close and detailed discussion, which couldn't be provided here, of the variety of the Reform prayer books and liturgical tastes and styles within it for the last two hundred years.

35

MUSIC AND WORSHIP

CANTOR ROSALIE BOXT

It must certainly be the case that a Jewish worship service has existed—
somewhere in time—without music. But we would be hard-pressed
to imagine it. Every part of the service—even breathing, meditation,
and reflection—is couched in music. The way Jews pray, even with
an inexperienced musical leader or even someone who does not have
an "ear" or "voice," almost always has chanting, davening, a singsong
way of engaging the prayers of the liturgy. On any given Shabbat one
can attend two different congregations and hear different melodies at
each one or be part of the same congregation week after week and hear
significant variations in the repertoire. This musical diversity in our
prayer service is truly a gift to us as a praying people, for it provides us
with rich opportunities for growth of soul and spirit.

New compositions, not just in current days, but through all time,
are really a reflection of people who have had unique experiences of
prayer and worship. They felt that the current repertory didn't express their own response to a given liturgical text. As a result, there
are hundreds of settings to every liturgy, as well as psalms, wedding
ceremonies, biblical and Talmudic sayings, and more. Just as with texts
it makes intellectual sense to have so many different books on political
leaders or on child-rearing, why not express our deep yearnings when

we seek to connect with the Divine in multiple ways? As humans and individuals we each have "unique" experiences, viewpoints, and ways of identifying with the world around us. Why not even more so for prayer, which is challenging on just about every level for most people? We are challenged in prayer if we aren't sure to What (if Anything) we are praying. Hebrew is not the native language for many Jews, and so we wonder what it all means or how the historical events described in worship fit in with our daily lives. Does it surprise us that Jews (and people of other faith backgrounds) have tried for generations to express their own prayer questions and feelings through new musical settings? Music has always been a natural response to deep questioning—a form of expression when conventional methods of inquisition are insufficient. Classical composers, folk singers, and pop performers frequently have the deep questions of life and the universe, of love and war at the center of their compositional motivation, if not actually articulated in a text. The creation of liturgical music is similar. If we can't imagine what the Exodus might have felt like, because it actually seems beyond our grasp, musical settings can express what we hope the experience might have felt like, which may be easier than explaining our theology of redemption. The spoken word can lock us into a commitment of belief, whereas music is more nuanced in the way it expresses the way we may or may not be feeling. When we sing or experience music set to prayers or texts that are challenging, the ideas become more palatable, more relatable. This is not to say that music should become a cover for theological questioning. Rather, our liturgy is often set to music because just as the music is diverse, so too is the invitation that our theologies, our yearnings, our confusion, our hopes can be diverse.

New settings are written not to replace, but to add, and thereby acknowledge that every person's experience is unique. Yes, it is true that in a given service we all sing along to one melody at a given moment, but sometimes the shifts that occur, the diversity of musical settings over repeated attendance, tap into more possible expressions of a prayer that speaks to us, that we didn't know we felt, until a particular music setting opens that part of our spirit-self that hadn't been opened before. To be sure, we cannot sing every setting of a single prayer in a given service, but the beauty of music in worship is that it expresses an experience that might not be ours alone in a given moment but that might be someone else's. This kind of openness can be powerful—someone else's experience can in fact be our own. The richness of these settings allows us a window into the soul of others with whom we walk the journey of Jewish life.

While this constant evolution of repertoire and an ever-growing canon is not unique to Reform Judaism, it is in and of itself in line with the essence of Reform Judaism. For part of the richness of this way of living a Jewish life is how it connects us to the history and traditions and weaves them into our search for meaningful expression. Therefore, when we share a liturgical text that is part of our canon, one that Jews in other communities also recite but with a different melody, we are articulating this unique idea that there is not a singular expression, path, doorway into a religious life. Cantors are constantly asked if there are so many melodies because the cantor is bored; but if you ask any members of a worshiping community which setting of a certain powerful text (a prayer for peace, the joy of celebrating Shabbat) they are drawn to, all will have a different opinion—and perhaps a different idea depending on how they felt on the given Shabbat at which they attended services. Each melody provides a window into a possible liturgical experience—be it a connection to the Divine, or to the community, or to joy, or through hope. The desire is that new melodies continue to help each person in our communities move even deeper into their own sense of prayer and spirit through worship.

The music that comes from different parts of the world, as well as repertoire that is rooted in different musical genres, helps people already rooted in a given community appreciate the diversity of the Jewish world at large and perhaps even the diversity within our own communal midst. Much of this music has reached us from across the Diaspora, when Jews from other lands have immigrated to America. These styles are specific to the cultures in which those Jews lived previous to their move to North America and cultural relationships created in those countries of origin (such as Mizrachi, or Middle Eastern sounds, influenced by North Africa and Iraq; Latin American sounds and rhythms). Melodies like "Ein K'Eloheinu—Non Komo Muestro Dio" (with Hebrew and Ladino) and "Et Dodim" from Israel, brought by many Argentinian and Israeli cantors and musicians, or "Elohei Oz" (a healing song), from Baghdad via Calcutta, have opened our ears and our bodies to new syncopations, non-Western counting forms, and different harmonization. By expressing this international diversity in the liturgical selections within worship, we are reminded that the story of the Jewish people is not linear, monolithic, and singular of experience, but instead one that has traveled many streams and offshoots, becoming part of the tapestry of who we (all) are. When texts that we often imagine must be *miSinai* (from Sinai itself) are paired with a melody that seems wholly foreign, it might seem surprising in the moment, but at the same time, it illuminates and connects us to the generations of Jews all over the world who sang the same songs of freedom, of yearning, of Torah but with utterly different tonality, rhythm, and sensibility. We are no longer a completely Ashkenazic Jewry, here in North America—we may know this intellectually to be sure. To be faced with it, or, more specifically, to hear it in the words and music of our liturgy, we are reminded anew of our brethren from all corners of the globe.

The Jews and Jewish music that have influenced our repertory have not only come from lands across the seas, they have come from within these North American borders as well. Jews of color, Jews-by-choice, and non-Jews alike who have rich musical and prayer traditions to share have brought the soundtracks of their lives into our synagogues and communities, adding to the rich tapestry of the music we have to choose from for worship moments.

All this music opens doorways to those who are just beginning to step over the threshold. As many seekers or those searching for a spiritual home usually attend worship in order to figure out what a given congregation is about, the music in worship can say a lot about who prays there and what prayer means to that group. Music that expresses the richness of different cultures and different styles serves to welcome and invite those who maybe do not see themselves as the antiquated, stereotypical model of "Jewish." This growing cohort includes Jews of color, Jews from the Middle East, as well as those who were not born Jewish. When people hear the music of their ancestors or their upbringing in the context of worship and prayer, which is already very challenging, perhaps they are more willing to take further steps to learn and explore their own spirituality. But if the service and music do not remind them of their own experience or do not seem to say "you are part of the story that we are telling," they are less likely to want to continue to write their story with us.

Our synagogue communities encourage participation from all kinds of individuals. For decades we have invited, encouraged, even sought families where one partner is not Jewish, and as other authors in this volume have noted, this has had a real positive impact on our Reform community. And yet, if the music, chanting, expression of our prayers was held firm in all Hebrew or in a musical mode that was familiar or accessible only to those raised Jewish and who grew up attending synagogue, I suspect a significant portion of our communities would truly struggle. Rabbi Rick Jacobs, the president of the Union for Reform Judaism, has shown time and time again, when gathering a group of synagogue presidents, that the majority of them were *not* Reform Jews before adulthood. They were from other faith backgrounds or came from Conservative, Orthodox, or unaffiliated congregations. If our presidents, the most active and committed members of our synagogues, did not grow up knowing the same "traditional" (read, 1950s melody) tunes, why would we imagine that our congregations are made up solely of folks who come from similar "traditionally Reform" upbringing?

The challenge for our congregations and worship leaders is of making a connection between the changing nature of the members of our community with the changing nature of the music they might experience in worship. The influence of rhythm instruments, of English, of melodies that come from a hymnal or an African American spiritual of freedom is not the invention of music leaders! Instead, it is a response to, and influence of, the growing diversity of our Reform community. There is something very powerful in witnessing the relaxing of features or slight movement of bodily engagement when a member of the congregation recognizes a melody of *his* childhood. When someone hears the story of *her* people being expressed in the musical style of a prayer that until then she couldn't quite understand or find her way into, the communal worship is made richer and the individual's prayer life made more meaningful.

New melodies are being written every day. Composers, pray-ers, members of congregations are continually inspired by our texts and by their experiences to create new settings to share new ideas. The more Jewish music is seen as integral to the worship experience, the more people who experience it are subsequently moved to compose. In the last decade plus, hundreds of people, young and old, have been setting liturgy in new ways. We have new compositions that blend Hebrew and new English interpretations, or storytelling, or spoken word/rap within. Some music is composed with oud or mandolin or slide guitar. We have acapella groups writing liturgy and teens finding their voice through the expression of new music, to "old" prayers. With access to technology, new music can be recorded and shared instantly—which creates fast access and sometimes an overwhelming volume of new music. Only twenty years ago we had to wait for a publishing company to make a CD or a songbook to learn what the new sounds were. Now we have instant access. Some melodies may move one person and never move another. Some melodies may move all of us at one time or another, but never at the same moment. Liturgical music can evolve as we evolve—as each of us experiences prayer anew each day, each week—so too can the melodies of those prayers express those ever-shifting emotions.

At the core of this discussion of music and worship is the prayer service. The values of the community, why members of a given group pray the way they do, and how the worship leaders and community agree to embark on this prayer business together are central. Decisions about music used for liturgical expression, to elevate a moment, or to highlight a text have to be based in a clear vision of what the point of a given prayer moment is at a given time in a service.

Communicating values and ideas is central to Reform Judaism and our religious practice. We have shown a passionate commitment, most significantly through the publication of new prayer books, to being intentional (and constantly growing, making mistakes, and growing again) about language and inclusion, about engaging our sacred texts in living dialogue. How much the more so should our music do the same! Why would our texts evolve and our liturgy adapt as we recognize an ever-changing communal makeup, and our music not grow and struggle right along with it?

Some worship leaders may consider "diversity" of music style to mean the creating of intentionally "eclectic" services, which show in their attention to many modalities (Cantor Benjie Ellen Schiller taught us to consider the four M's of prayer: meditation, majesty, memory, meeting) that prayer can and should express multiple yearnings of the soul. For example, music of meeting will allow the congregation to connect to each other, through communal singing accessible to all, whereas music of majesty takes our hearts away from the interpersonal and toward the Universe beyond our knowing, which we might experience with a soaring piece of music or a spoken word/music underscore moment. Music of memory may be the "traditional" or "old warhorse" tunes, and music of meditation inspires moments that lend themselves to quieting the breath, reflection, and peace. And these moments should all find their place in the prayer life of a community. But perhaps each form might not need to exist in every service. We run the risk of getting stuck in a fragmented worship experience if we attempt to ensure that the Jew from abroad, the Jew of color, the person of another faith background, and the Orthodox-raised Jew all have a "moment" in the service. This serves neither the worship nor the worshiper. While as individuals we might hope that every moment speaks to us personally, the joy and tension of communal prayer are giving over some of the desire for expected comfort in all moments to the knowledge that those around us are moved by what they are experiencing.

The need for an expansive sense of how our Jewish musical repertory can be used need not be prescriptive; each community will create
its own soundtrack to prayer. The richness of our musical tradition is
that there are so many settings to evoke so many aspects of prayer. We
can intentionally widen our understanding of Jewish music and prayer
to include the sounds of our community that we may not have always
considered, particularly as some within our community still consider
themselves (if not intentionally, in language) "Ashkenazi." Our worship
music repertoire now contains the rhythms and sounds of Argentinian
Jews (part of our story for many years), Yemenite Jews, and Jews of
color, as well as the influences they bring from cultural or communal
pieces of their identity, melodies rooted in the secular or Christian
musical traditions, Ladino, contemporary Israeli . . . the list goes on.
Worship leaders are now able to create an environment where not only
can their community be exposed to and enriched by the prayer expression from other communities or new voices, but those within our own
communities, and also perhaps those who stand in the doorway peeking
in, can hear, feel, and sense that they too belong.

Part Five

BUILDING COMMUNITY

A *community* is a group of people who are linked by social ties, share common perspectives, and engage in joint action. In a Reform Jewish context, we are not just trying to build a social community composed of people from similar backgrounds with similar interests. Rather, what is central for our holy task is to build a religious community devoted to fulfilling the divine covenant with the Children of Israel. Our aim is to be inclusive, embracing all those who seek a house of prayer and a center for spiritual reflection. At the same time, we want to nurture our particularistic roots and reinforce the links that bind generation to generation. As you will see in the essays that follow, tradition is a cherished value but one that needs to be malleable in a rapidly changing society.

Rabbi Charles A. Kroloff opens this section with "Community: The Vehicle for Fulfilling the Jewish Dream," reminding readers that our synagogue is meant to be a house of study, a house of prayer, and a house of gathering.

According to Joshua Holo, PhD, the creative aspects of Reform Judaism allow us to find religious meaning in our "connectedness across the generations." To the author, Jewish civilization is a tree, with our stories as the roots, and the trunk our common heritage.

In "Tradition! Transition!" Rabbi Lisa Edwards, PhD, discusses what we used to call "the life cycle" in the context of the many social and economic changes that have marked the past several decades, inspiring us to envision the future.

In "Family," Rabbi Sue Levi Elwell, PhD, places the concept of family—the first group that we feel a part of—in a religious context and guides the reader in exploring the myriad ways that Reform Judaism changes along with us.

In "Contemporary Jewish Sex Ethics," Rabbi David A. Teutsch, PhD, presents a number of universal ethical values for us to consider in our sexual decision-making, giving the reader guidelines for living morally and religiously.

Rabbi Dana Evan Kaplan, PhD, explores the theological as well as the practical implications of embracing the Jewish religion in his essay "Converting to Judaism." The author explains that because a person becoming Jewish is not only converting to a religion but joining a group that is almost like a family, becoming a Jew-by-choice has wide-ranging impact on one's personal as well as communal life.

In "A Personal Comment by a Reform Rabbi on Conversion," Rabbi David Ellenson, PhD, advocates an inclusive policy concerning intermarried Jews and their spouses, to welcome as many people as possible into our community, regardless of whether the partner of another faith or cultural background chooses to convert.

In "Interfaith Families," Rabbi Rachel Gurevitz, PhD, shares stories of her work with interfaith families within her community and envisions, in a contemporary interpretation of classic texts, new ways of welcoming families of Jews-by-choice, as well as families in which each partner is of a different faith background and their relationship to Judaism is one of convergence rather than conversion.

Evan Traylor introduces us to the millennials and the role they are playing in building the future of Reform Judaism. As members of this generation are finding out how Judaism may fit into their lives, identifying how they may need to adapt, the Jewish community will need to adapt also in order to make that happen.

Rabbi Neal Gold looks at how a life of meaning can be created simply by caring for others. The author emphasizes two ways in which we can do this: *tzedakah* and *g'milut chasadim*, in which we give time or resources.

In the final contribution to Part Five, "Sacred Aging," Rabbi Richard F. Address, DMin, reflects on how we can respond religiously to the gifts and the challenges of longevity and interprets three Jewish wisdom texts that can guide us as we think within that framework.

36

COMMUNITY: THE VEHICLE FOR FULFILLING THE JEWISH DREAM

RABBI CHARLES A. KROLOFF

A longtime member of our synagogue—let's call her Sylvia—reminded us year after year that she was an atheist. At age ninety-five, during a Shabbat service at which she was honored, Sylvia asked if she might ascend the bimah to make a statement. Smiling broadly, she announced to the congregation, "I want you all to know that I am now a believer. Not in God, but in each of you, my community."

What happened to our sometimes-atheist–sometimes-agnostic Sylvia during her fifty-plus years of synagogue membership that would cause her to affirm publicly that community—specifically her synagogue community—had become central to her Jewish life? What was the personal growth she had experienced and the support she received that prompted her to declare to her synagogue family that they had become part of her evolving belief system? And what does it mean to "believe" in a community?

Sylvia studied Torah with our rabbis every Tuesday morning. There she learned in Exodus 19 how the Israelites prepared to receive the Ten Commandments. They accepted the commandments not as individuals, but as a people, *am Yisrael*. This term, which acquired deep meaning in the Torah, continues to this day to resonate among Jews who feel strong connections with their fellow Jews in North America, Israel, and worldwide.

Indeed, in chapter 19 of Exodus alone, the word *am* occurs not less than sixteen times. Already in biblical times we were more than a mere collection of individuals, each developing her or his relationship with God. In Exodus 19:5 and later in Deuteronomy (7:6, 14:2, 26:18), the text states that if the Children of Israel will follow God's commandments, they will become not just any *am*, but an *am s'gulah*, a "treasured people" of God. From our earliest beginnings, our relationship with God was not only individual, but tribal and then communal.

As Jewish history proceeded, institutions emerged that helped to create a robust community: synagogues, schools, burial societies, mikvehs (ritual immersion pool), loan societies, soup kitchens and social welfare agencies, and courts of law. Without these community institutions, it would have been very difficult for Jews to fulfill most central commandments of Judaism such as helping the poor, teaching the children, gathering regularly for prayer, and accompanying the dead for burial. For even one deceased Jew, consecrated ground was required for burial. For that function alone, community was needed.

Jews are expected to say the *Kaddish* prayer for their loved ones who are deceased. According to tradition, that prayer should be said in the presence of a minyan of ten Jewish adults. The minyan functions, in effect, as a small community lending support to the mourner.

The synagogue is often referred to as a *k'hilah k'doshah*, a "holy community," denoting that it has a significant role in the socialization of the Jewish people. It is traditionally referred to as a house of study, prayer, and gathering. In this threefold description, its role as a gathering place for community is given equal importance as study and prayer.

Another form of community-based support were landsmanshaftn, mutual aid societies that were organized by immigrants on the basis of their communities of origin. According to Gerald Sorin, "As early as 1892 there were eighty-seven eastern European landsmanshaftn in New York. By 1910, there were more than two thousand, representing over nine hundred European cities and towns, embracing every Jewish family in New York."[1]

Without community, the Torah could not have emerged as the blueprint for our Jewish lives. It was the people living in community who became the vehicle that spread the idea of the one God, the God who expects us to live by the tenets of justice and mercy. It was this people who transformed dream into reality, experience into tradition, through centuries of community building in Canaan and Babylonia, Spain and Poland, Ethiopia and North America. In our own time, when Jews are asked in what ways they identify as Jews, they often respond, "I'm not sure about God, but I do feel part of the Jewish people."

Fast-forward to 1963, when Sylvia and her husband traveled to Washington, DC, along with a quarter million other Americans to be part of the historic and transformative March on Washington. Sylvia's pilgrimage was motivated by two powerful factors: her passionate belief in the cause of civil rights and her supportive synagogue community.

What if her synagogue community had not chartered a bus to Washington? They might have traveled as individuals, but their participation became far more meaningful because their rabbi and members of their Jewish community were right alongside them in Washington and, on return, collaborated with them on turning dream into reality.

Hers was also a community that took its marching orders from the Hebrew prophets Amos, Micah, and Isaiah, who helped shape the Jewish dream: to share our bread with the hungry, to bring the homeless poor to our house, and when we see the naked to cover them (Isaiah 58:5–7). Her vision of justice and fairness was nurtured by the community that recalls every weekday and Shabbat in our liturgy that we are required to befriend the stranger because our people were strangers in the land of Egypt (Deuteronomy 10:18–19).

Sylvia is not an ardent Zionist, but she supports Israel as the Jewish homeland, convinced that it is indispensable to the Jewish future. When Israel was threatened in May 1967 by Egypt's blockade of the Straits of Tiran, Sylvia's community gathered a thousand strong in our sanctuary to hear Abba Eban's impassioned address to the United

Nations. We were inspired to open our pocketbooks for the belea-
guered Jewish state. Sylvia was there advocating for Israel's security
because her community and its leaders had summoned her to action
to fulfill the Zionist dream of Israel as the Jewish homeland. Sylvia
understood, as she headed to that rally, that she would not be one of a
handful of isolated individuals, but part of an empowered community.
And it was the powerful communal spirit that emanated from that large
gathering that propelled us into action.

Sylvia attended Shabbat services at our synagogue without fail. I
once asked, "Sylvia, since you don't believe in God, why do you come
to temple every Friday evening?" She responded, "I come to temple to
learn, to think about life's deepest questions, and . . . to be with other
Jews." Yes, she was reluctant to acknowledge any belief in God, and
yes, she reminded us that she knew very little Hebrew. But on Shabbat
she sang the songs of our people with fervor, including *Sh'ma Yisrael*,
Adonai Eloheinu, Adonai Echad, "Hear, O Israel, Adonai is our God,
Adonai is One!"

"Why," I asked, "would you sing about God's existence?" Her response rang clear, as always: "Rabbi, this is my community and if I'm
going to be part of it, I'm going to sing with them, even if I have to
stretch a bit." Sometimes it takes a little stretching to fit into a community, but the strength and support we receive make it worthwhile.

In the 1970s and '80s, as our synagogue membership grew to over
a thousand families, it became clear that the close relationships fostered by our once smaller congregation were becoming more difficult
to achieve. Having heard about the *chavurah* movement launched by
Rabbi Harold Schulweis of Encino, California, we decided to undertake that initiative. A *chavurah* consists of ten to twenty individuals
(often families, frequently singles, and sometimes a mix of demographics) who gather in each other's homes or at a synagogue to celebrate
holidays, study, welcome Shabbat, and engage in acts of *tzedakah*. Sylvia was one of hundreds who found friendship and spiritual sustenance from the mini-community, the intimate *chavurah*. Once again,
community worked!

Adopting the *chavurah* was moreover an example of the cross-denominational openness of Reform Judaism. Rabbi Schulweis was an esteemed colleague in the Conservative Movement of Judaism. We Reform Jews, being committed to religious pluralism, recognize that we can learn from our fellow Jews of all stripes. We are part of the larger Jewish community, to which we contribute our spiritual resources and through which we ourselves grow. This larger community extends not only to the religious branches of Judaism—Orthodox, Conservative, and Reconstructionist—but also to local Jewish Federations and to Jewish organizations large and small. Jews often find co-religionists who share their values and interests in groups such as B'nai B'rith, American Jewish Committee, Hadassah, National Council of Jewish Women, American Israel Public Affairs Committee (AIPAC), and J Street, a pro-Israel, pro-peace organization.

As Sylvia grew older and more limited in what she could do, she was assisted with daily tasks by members of our Caring Community taskforce, which provides food, counsel, and help with doctors' visits, and by our *Bikur Cholim* team, which visits the sick and shut-ins and provides spiritual support. These supportive calls on Sylvia would not have been possible without the connections and services that emerge from a dynamic community.

Like so many Reform Jews, Sylvia cherishes her individuality and her personal autonomy. She is an independent thinker, *sui generis*, in a class of her own, when it comes to the power of her intellect and her willingness to express disagreement, whether it be with her rabbi's sermon or our synagogue's ritual practices.

Independent thinkers are sometimes skittish about identifying with community. They fear that their autonomy will be circumscribed and that "instructions from on high" will force them to compromise. For Sylvia, and many like her, being part of a strong community never once restrained her from expressing her principled opinions and her unique religious philosophy. On the contrary, community provided a robust forum where she was able to express her iconoclastic thoughts and impact the thinking of her fellow Jews.

Personal autonomy is a central tenet of Reform Judaism. It was forcefully expressed in the Centenary Perspective of the Central Conference of American Rabbis:

> Reform Jews respond to change in various ways according to the Reform principle of the autonomy of the individual. However, Reform Judaism does more than tolerate diversity; it engenders it. . . . How we shall live with diversity without stifling dissent and without paralyzing our ability to take positive action will test our character and our principles. We stand open to any position thoughtfully and conscientiously advocated in the spirit of Reform Jewish belief. . . . We accept such differences as precious and see in them Judaism's best hope for confronting whatever the future holds for us.[2]

Reform Jews have historically engaged in a dialectic, a conversation, between those who cherish the sovereign self, as Sylvia does, and those who are primarily committed to community, which Sylvia also embraces. Reform Jewish communities are somewhat unique in being able to foster diversity and dissent while still providing the communal vehicle for effective action in areas as wide-ranging as economic justice, innovative prayer, and gender equality.

An example of this dialectic is the struggle for gender equality. When Sally Priesand, the first female rabbi in the North American Reform Movement, was ordained by Hebrew Union College–Jewish Institute of Religion in 1972, she was greeted with support by many and opposition from some. Among the latter were congregants who asserted their independence and objected to engaging a woman as assistant or senior rabbi. Even in synagogues where a female rabbi had been appointed, congregants occasionally requested that a male rabbi be available for a life-cycle event. Thanks to our communal structure—reflected in the Union for Reform Judaism and the Central Conference of American Rabbis—and thanks to the ethical standards that our community fostered, our religious movement overcame that bias. Today, hundreds of female rabbis lead synagogues throughout the world with extraordinary success.

In previous times, the organized Jewish community often had legal authority delegated to it by the secular ruling power, which enabled it to impose its will on the individual. In Western Europe, the title "rabbi of such-and-such community" was frequently used, emphasizing the communal-centered, top-down structure of the Jewish society. Jewish courts had authority to impose penalties for not adhering to established standards. Not so today! With rare exception, voluntarism is a defining characteristic of Jewish identity in the modern world. The barriers to individual free choice have largely disappeared.

Reform Judaism not only respects free choice, it encourages it. It recognizes that communal institutions are not automatically "entitled" to a Jew's participation and support. They must earn it. The nature of the Jewish community is changing. The allocation of charitable dollars is increasingly donor driven, rather than determined by a board of trustees. The programmatic agendas of synagogues and Jewish organizations are shaped by the needs of diverse demographic groups (young families, singles, empty-nesters, boomers, LGBTQ, and seniors).

Sylvia helped to make this happen. Her dream was that intellectual honesty and social justice would power her Jewish religious life. She discovered a synagogue community that embraced that mission. She helped to shape that community in a way that preserved her autonomy, but which, in the process, yielded supportive relationships that enriched her life.

The result? The ever-questioning Sylvia became a believer in her fellow human beings, in her Jewish community, and in the unlimited possibilities of the human spirit.

NOTES

1. Gerald Sorin, *The Jewish People in America: A Time for Building, the Third Migration 1880–1920* (Baltimore: Johns Hopkins University Press, 1992), 97.

2. Central Conference of American Rabbis, "Reform Judaism: A Centenary Perspective," *CCAR Yearbook*, 1976, 174–78; http://ccarnet.org/rabbis-speak/platforms/reform-judaism-centenary-perspective/.

37

FINDING MEANING IN OUR
CONNECTEDNESS ACROSS THE GENERATIONS

JOSHUA HOLO, PhD

The *reform* component of Reform Judaism invites us to *make* meaning—to fashion our destiny looking forward. This bold element in our approach to religion and culture inspires action and creativity. To it we owe much of the unique vibrancy of modern Judaism, including how we influence Judaism beyond our movement.

In very different fashion, the *Judaism* component of Reform Judaism calls us to *discover* meaning—to root around the past and unearth this three-thousand-year-old experience that exists of its own accord, which we can study and interpret, but which we cannot change. The *Judaism* part of Reform Judaism is intrinsically conservative, drawing from notions such as tradition, text, trans-generational covenant, and antiquity. In it, we grasp our religion and culture as we have inherited it from our forebears—a process of discovery we commonly call "history." In that ancient, venerable, and unique history that we Jews alone can claim, we find one particularly compelling and renewing source of meaning, which spans millennia and crisscrosses the Jewish world: connectedness.

This connectedness of Judaism, or of being Jewish, derives from our solidarity across a global dispersion of three millennia, as embodied in our shared story. Admittedly, Jewish history resists easy generalizations; varieties of Judaism evolved naturally in that vast span of time and space. But at the same time, certain consistent themes emerge, through which we can relate to Jewish history—not merely to connect to it but also to "own" it and, from that ownership, to derive a sense of meaning and purpose.

In the world of Reform Judaism, many of us readily relate to sophisticated notions of metaphorical meaning, current in circles of high culture. One routinely hears about non-literal truth: "It doesn't matter if it really happened; the story itself relates deeper truths." Often enough, this is very much the case. For instance, there is no historical evidence for the Exodus from Egypt, much less for its miraculous elements as described in Torah. Nevertheless, as the metaphorical reading affords, this paradigmatic story of freedom from slavery clearly conveys enduring truths.

Equally often, however, this allegorized work of meaning-making overlooks the raw power of literal historical truth, which we find in the stories of our Jewish past. Israelite tribes of the late second millennium BCE really did reside in the Land of Israel as reticulated clans, united by a common language (Hebrew), a religious covenant, an invested priesthood, and (like us, their descendants) a shared story. Moreover, these tribes did in fact coalesce under Kings David and Solomon, around the turn of the first millennium BCE. And the stories in the books of the prophets, for all their patent allegory and bias, also relate to a flesh-and-blood world of politics, religion, war, and literature.

Even more than that, those people are indeed our literal ancestors, and that specific familial connection matters, because it helps define who we are today. *Peoplehood*—call it ethnic, tribal, clan-based, or national—constitutes an essential ingredient in Jewishness and in our tensile connectedness to the Jewish story. So thoroughly is our identity embedded in the notion of the *people Israel* that we even apply it when we embrace new people from the outside. In its wisdom and at the outset—from the Book of Ruth (which may not have literally happened!) to the much later Rabbinic rules for conversion—Judaism has opened itself to the presence of others. But crucially, a mere confession of religious faith to the covenant of Israel does not suffice; a kind of naturalization must occur, whereby one is effectively adopted by, or grafted onto the trunk of, the people Israel.

Ultimately, Judaism conveys a very direct message: No matter if you are born Jewish or convert to Judaism, you belong to a living, breathing people. Our identity does not rest simply on shared values, but also on solidarity with one another. At its heart, this common destiny of the Jews derives directly from our connectedness to our people's unique and very real past and to our collective decisions about how we define ourselves in relation to that past.

Judaism stakes a firm claim to a specific kind of meaning-making, grounded in our meaning-discovery. We argue that our sense of direction and purpose arises from our history, which we rehearse and celebrate all the time. It is no accident that Jews around the world, of all stripes and types of observance and identification, focus heavily on the Passover seder. No event or holiday better expresses our connectedness to the past than the Passover meal, which boils down to, of all things, the telling of our story.

In claiming this specific drama of slavery and redemption as *our story*, we define ourselves not only as free people, but more remarkably as a people who clings to the encumbrance of slavery as a reminder of freedom's deeper value. Ultimately, it is solely against the backdrop of this storytelling that we can understand Torah's multiple exhortations to empathy: "Welcome the stranger, for you were a stranger in the land of Egypt." Thus, our past becomes our moral mandate for the future.

However, if the Exodus did not necessarily take place, then its message, though essential, becomes one of memory and storytelling, rather than history. What of factual events? Most of all, what emerges when we combine factual events with our deep tradition of storytelling and meaning-making?

Many of us may instinctively resort to the most recent historical events, such as the Holocaust and the founding of the State of Israel, to find our most compelling sources of meaning. To be sure, those events deservedly loom large, and their proximity in time means that they are in living memory. But if we do the work of meaning-discovery in the annals of our more distant history, we will find some other tremendously powerful sources of connectedness, together with some of our most enduring moral and cultural commitments.

One could argue that Jewish civilization has cultivated its identity, most of all, out of the Roman destruction of the Temple in Jerusalem, in the year 70 CE. The facts are not too complicated. Inspired by a sense of oppression and recognizing the creeping imposition of evermore direct Roman rule, the Jews of Palestine rebelled in 66 CE and suffered devastating defeat. The general Titus, later to be emperor, destroyed the Temple in Jerusalem, which had functioned as the economic, ritual, political, and symbolic center of the Jewish people and imagination.

Out of the ashes of that defeat a new class of leaders arose to replace the priestly stewards of the Temple: the Rabbis. These scholar-statesmen refashioned Judaism as a religion of prayer and study, instead of Temple sacrifice. In our myths about this actual defeat, the Romans imposed mass exile on the Jews from Jerusalem and Palestine, whereby our forebears scattered to the four winds and the four corners of the world. In fact, however, the Jews had already been living abroad for decades and even centuries, across the Mediterranean and into Mesopotamia.

What really took place was not a radical relocation of the Jews but of Judaism. The Rabbis' reformulation of religious duty, from Temple sacrifice to prayer and study, freed the Jews from geographical limitations of a ritual that took place in a single location, that is, Jerusalem. Rabbinic Judaism allowed Jews to carry their religion wherever they could carry themselves and their books (or, more properly, their scrolls). Out of these tragedies the synagogue and the academy evolved as our organizational centerpieces, and Jews began to socialize in the midst of their non-Jewish majorities in a different way, now that they lacked a formally recognized political home.

In a nutshell, the destruction of the Temple and the Rabbinic re-creation of Judaism seeded the Diasporic consciousness that some call the Jewish genius. If we define *acculturation* as the ability to be fluent in a second culture, and *assimilation* as the abandonment of one's culture for the sake of that second culture, then the Rabbis made it possible to acculturate without assimilating. Jews need not fear that by adopting Greek, Arabic, German, Yiddish, Ladino, or English as their native languages, they are betraying their heritage. And Rabbinic custom promoted a geographical flexibility of Jewish expression that remained rooted in Jewish faith, Jewish peoplehood, and Jewish connection to the Land of Israel, despite global distances that might separate us from one another.

The Rabbis made it kosher to be Jewish in Diaspora, which is the reality that American Judaism (as one example) does not merely enjoy but affirmatively celebrates and enriches, in both its Americanism and its Jewishness. Our values of philanthropy and tradition, of Zionism and American patriotism, of Jewish and secular education, to name a few, all owe their seamless non-competition to the Rabbis prescient, wise, and creative response to tragedy. We inherited this generative outlook from our ancient leaders, and we rely on it with every step forward.

If we imagine Jewish civilization as a tree, our stories are the roots, the nourishing experiences that emerge from our kaleidoscopically complex past. Through the trunk, they become the common heritage of all Jews and communities, who in turn recombine and ramify, as represented by the branches atop the tree. And even though it seems as if each individual branch and sprout exists apart from the other branches or lacks connection to the root system, the entire system relies on all the parts—both that which represents variety and that which represents unity.

So, let us not forget our stories, represented by the humble roots in this image. They are invisible; the work they do is subterranean, and for that reason we often overlook them. But the capacity of a tree's branch system to reach high and spread wide depends on the breadth and depth of the root system. In this way, our potential mirrors our past.

38

TRADITION! TRANSITION!

RABBI LISA EDWARDS, PHD

In 2014, in celebration of the fiftieth anniversary of the musical *Fiddler on the Roof*, members of our congregation wrote and performed a Purim-spiel (skit) entitled *Fiddler on the BCC Roof*. BCC stands for Beth Chayim Chadashim (meaning "House of New Life") in Los Angeles, which was the first synagogue founded by gay men and lesbians (1972). It was voted in as a member congregation of the Reform Movement in 1974, making Reform Judaism the first mainstream religious organization to officially accept a gay and lesbian community into membership.

The Jewish holiday of Purim is itself a relative latecomer to the Jewish calendar, and its custom of a spiel (comic skit), which often comments on politics and social mores of the day, evolved much later than the holiday itself. Some say the story of the Bible's Book of Esther, the reading of which is the centerpiece of Purim, is itself a commentary on the politics and social mores of the time in which it was written and gave rise to the customs of the holiday that evolved later.[1] In the manner of a Shakespearean comedy—the more weddings the better—the closing scene of our rollicking Purim celebration saw four couples marry under a rainbow chuppah, with a lesbian rabbi officiating. The couples, including several characters from the Book of Esther, were two lesbians, one of whom was Esther; a gay man, Mordecai, and a gay transman; a straight couple, Ahasuerus and Vashti, remarrying each other, newly in love after a bitter divorce; and the Muppets Bert and Ernie (finally, after all these years).

What Reform Jewish values brought about this particular happy ending in a 2014 Purim-spiel at an LGBTQS synagogue? How does this scene reflect or speak to the ways Reform Jews mark events in their lives and how those events have changed in the last few decades?

Rituals like marriage mark the *life cycle*, a term that may often conjure up the stationary bicycle at the local gym, but which clergy often apply to a standard list of transitional moments in life, traditionally marked by rituals. Perhaps *life spiral* would better describe them, in that these rituals mark unique moments in a person's or a family's life over time, rather than cyclical events that come along each year. These unique, traditional rituals include baby namings, circumcision, bar/bat mitzvah, weddings, and funerals. In our time, liberal Jews in general and the Reform Movement in particular continue to devise new rituals marking other transformational moments in our lives. The ritual of confirmation (of allegiance to Judaism) for teenagers was devised in 1810 in Seesen, Germany, during the Reform Movement's early years, and has been a widespread Reform practice since at least 1927 when the Central Conference of American Rabbis (CCAR), the professional organization of American Reform rabbis, recommended that confirmation become a Reform Movement practice. American rabbis adapted confirmation to encourage the celebration of the often overlooked holy day of Shavuot, which itself had evolved long ago from an agricultural festival described in Torah (Exodus 23:16, 34:22; Leviticus 23:15–16; Numbers 28:26; Deuteronomy 16:10) into a commemoration of the revelation at Sinai and God's gift of the Ten Commandments—and law itself—to the Jewish people.[2]

Confirmation was a Reform addition to the "life spiral" of the Reform Jew, but Reform Movement innovations also influence long-held Jewish traditions. In the 1990s Rabbi Lewis Barth, a Los Angeles faculty member at Hebrew Union College–Jewish Institute of Religion, developed the Reform mohalim/*mohalot* program that trains Jewish medical professionals already expert in the circumcision of infants to become practitioners of the ritual of *b'rit milah* (the covenant of circumcision). The presence of a physician explaining and performing the circumcision makes the ritual more accessible and more comfortable for Reform and secular Jews, as well as non-Jewish family and friends, unfamiliar with the Hebrew prayers and unexplained practices of Orthodox mohalim (those trained in the religious practice of circumcision). Even as the *b'rit milah* ceremony was being transformed, Reform Jews in the late twentieth century began to design new rituals of welcome for baby girls. These days many Reform Jews go even further, opting for a gender-neutral ritual for children new to a family (not all of whom are babies), leaving circumcision to private spaces and moments or bypassing it altogether, while publicly giving Hebrew names and blessings in a ceremony of welcome.

Other notable newer rituals are also taking root among more liberal Jews. Author Savina Teubal and singer/songwriter Debbie Friedman created in 1986 a *simchat chochmah*, "joy of wisdom" or "coming into wisdom," ceremony in celebration of Savina's sixtieth birthday. It was for that ritual that together they wrote the now familiar song "L'chi Lach," based on God's first call to Avram in Genesis 12:1–2: *Lech l'cha*, "Go forth . . . to the land that I will show you. I will make of you a great nation, and I will bless you; I will make your name great, and it shall be a blessing." Inventions such as a *simchat chochmah* also helped inspire ceremonies for other life moments. Liberal Jews have created public ceremonies marking someone's embrace of the covenant (conversion to Judaism), rituals of transition for transgender people, adoption rituals (becoming a "forever" family, or children becoming Jewish upon their adoption by foster parents), name changes including taking a Hebrew name, new rituals within traditional frameworks (such as weddings between people of the same gender and blessings for blending families when children's parents enter a new marriage), even rituals of divorce that invite equal participation of the ex-spouses in a gentle, respectful parting including, if possible, sincere wishes for a happy future for each (and with a promise, where relevant, to put their children's welfare ahead of all else). Often influenced by other Jewish rituals, these newer life-change rituals typically stand firmly grounded in traditional texts and teachings of Judaism. For example, opportunities to enter a mikveh (ritual bath) with a ritual devised for the occasion have become commonplace in recent years, not only for traditional reasons like becoming a Jew or before one's wedding, but also for new reasons like helping individuals through grief or trauma (such as a miscarriage or rape). In her 1998 book *Engendering Judaism: An Inclusive Theology and Ethics*, Dr. Rachel Adler created a widely adopted *b'rit ahuvim* (covenant of lovers) ceremony, changing the basis of a wedding from ancient symbols implying ownership of the bride by the husband to an egalitarian ceremony derived from a Talmudic ritual for business partners creating an "equal partnership."[3] And Reform rabbis, at least since the 1980s, incorporated a ritual for divorce in their guides for rabbis but created an egalitarian ritual and document of separation, rather than the Jewish tradition that allows only husbands to grant divorces.

Designing or even desiring such new ceremonies doesn't come easily to every Jew, however, let alone to family members who did not grow up with Judaism.

"Rabbi, my father didn't belong to a synagogue or go to services, and neither do I. But when he went on hospice recently he asked me to please find a rabbi to officiate at his funeral. Would you?"

"I didn't think being Jewish was important to me until our wedding planner suggested we stand beneath an arch of flowers instead of a chuppah. No way, I thought to myself, we're having a chuppah and breaking a glass! So then we thought, why not a rabbi too? Rabbi, could you?"

"I wasn't interested in Judaism until we had kids. Now we both think it's important that our son become bar mitzvah. What's the easiest way to make that happen, Rabbi?"

"My wife doesn't want us to circumcise our new baby, but that just feels wrong to me. Rabbi, can you talk her into it?"

I'm certainly not the only rabbi, Reform or otherwise, who has entertained such questions from strangers or acquaintances, whether by appointment in the Rabbi's study or in casual conversation at, for example, someone else's wedding.

I usually smile and use the opportunity to explore what's drawing this person to a change of heart or newfound interest in aspects of Jewish tradition. My evidence may be anecdotal, but after a couple of decades as a rabbi and many conversations with colleagues, it does seem that life-cycle rituals, especially ones designed to be accessible and understandable to all, tug at the heartstrings even of ambivalent Jews and, increasingly, those of people brand-new to Judaism. And for many reasons: a desire to honor the wishes of family members, such as a long-ago promise to a grandmother; the pull of history or romantic notions of history—consider how frequently the song "Sunrise, Sunset" from *Fiddler on the Roof* is sung at wedding parties; an unarticulated identification—a sense that this is what Jews do.

Perhaps a stronger, if less conscious, motivation to ritualize a life-cycle moment is the anchoring that the ritual offers during a time of transition. Even the most welcome and eagerly anticipated of such transitions can be an emotionally scary time of change. A yearning for holiness, even if it's an unconscious inclination, or the seeking of blessing when approaching a significant change seems to come naturally. Whether the change is within—becoming a parent or spouse or Jew or different gender—or less internal—welcoming another's new baby into the world or helping bring another's life to a close (a body laid to rest, a life tenderly remembered)—ritual during significant life moments can bring participants closer to each other and to their sense of a presence of God.

In Jewish tradition historically and still today, life-cycle ceremonies highlight the way an individual's life is woven with love and embrace into the life of a community or a family. How better create such a ceremony than to sit with an officiant (rabbi, cantor, or other guide to Judaism) to learn about traditions and the variations on traditions, weaving in your own desires in order to design a ritual that speaks to you and your loved ones about your life and the meaning of this moment. A wedding stands out as the best example, but all life-cycle moments are like that—even death, for it is the relationships, the love, built during a life that ensure a person will be remembered as a blessing. Marking transitions in our individual lives by inviting family, friends, and community to witness us, to take part in our ceremony, to celebrate with us, teaches and reminds us that few people choose to live lives of isolation, without love. And when our celebrations and commemorations take on a Jewish focus, we remind ourselves that Judaism itself, that living as a Jew, emphasizes the human impulse to live life with others rather than alone.

Our congregation's Purim celebration in 2014 was a tribute not only to a significant cultural phenomenon, *Fiddler on the Roof*, but as well a sign of a huge culture shift in the United States, a shift that Reform Judaism helped to bring about. For although in the summer of 2013 marriage equality had again become law in the state of California, marriage between same-gender couples would not be legalized throughout the United States until June 2015. It remains to be seen whether the U.S. Supreme Court decisions legalizing marriage between two women or two men (Windsor v. United States and Hollingsworth v. Perry, both in 2013, and Obergefell v. Hodges in 2015) will continue to be a strong enough foundation to maintain marriage equality as the law of the land without further legislation (or reversal of legislation). Regardless, it's inspiring to realize that Reform Judaism's road to the support of marriage equality predates the Supreme Court decisions by more than two decades. In 1996 and 1997 resolutions by the CCAR and the Union for Reform Judaism supported civil marriage for same-sex couples. In 2000 the CCAR gave its full support to Reform rabbis who choose to officiate same-sex marriages.[4] On the cusp of a monumental change, our congregation used the tradition of parody and merriment at Purim to celebrate the diversity of love under a rainbow chuppah.

And why *Fiddler on the Roof*? Fifty-plus years after its premiere, *Fiddler* remains a vehicle for amusingly and movingly examining the tension in American Jewish life between tradition and change. It's not just Golde and Tevye's daughters and their singular, yet familiar, choices diverging from the norm. The story is a portent that, arguably, helped set the stage for ever more radical changes as Jewish life evolves in America. Each new generation of performers and audiences finds in *Fiddler*'s story not only an American Jewish journey but, familiar to immigrants and native-born alike, journeys to new lands, to assimilation and/or acculturation, to feminism and women's rights, to an incipient shift away from the old patriarchal family structure. The setting of *Fiddler* foreshadowed not only waves of Jewish migration to the United States, as well as the catastrophe of the Shoah, but also much that American Jews have been exploring in the decades since the musical first appeared on a Broadway stage. It foreshadowed marriage for love, marriage to someone of one's own choosing, intermarriage, conversion into and out of Judaism, a woman's right to choose her own life and partner. And it gave rise as well to a kind of nostalgia for a Judaism that may or may not ever really have existed, for analyses and questioning of the historical accuracy of the setting and Judaism portrayed in *Fiddler on the Roof* continue well past the musical's fiftieth anniversary.

Following the Purim tradition of comedy and social satire, the couples under the chuppah at our congregation's Purim-spiel sequel to *Fiddler* mirrored political and personal and religious changes that Jews and liberal Judaism have helped bring about. Within the framework of Reform Judaism, life-cycle ceremonies old and new have, as the CCAR "Statement of Principles" put it in 1999, enabled "the Jewish people to introduce innovation while preserving tradition, to embrace diversity while asserting commonality, to affirm beliefs without rejecting those who doubt, and to bring faith to sacred texts without sacrificing critical scholarship."[5]

To some Jews it may seem like yesterday that life-cycle rituals were "by the book," officiated by rabbis reciting prayers in a language few people in the room understood. Happily, change has come, with participants and their officiants designing rituals together as they learn about each other and the tradition that sprang generations and generations ago from a yearning so many of us today also feel: a yearning to be part of and not apart from each other, Judaism, and the presence of something or Someone beyond ourselves.

NOTES

1. For more on the origins and purpose of Purim traditions, see article and bibliography: "Purimspiels and Where to Find Them," Jewish Agency for Israel, http:// www.jewishagency.org/purim/content/24414.

2. See Daniel Syme, *The Jewish Home*, rev. ed. (New York: URJ Press, 2003); and "What Is a Confirmation?," ReformJudaism.org, http://www.reformjudaism .org/what-confirmation.

3. Rachel Adler, *Engendering Judaism: An Inclusive Theology and Ethics* (Boston: Beacon Press, 1998).

4. "Stances of Faith on LGBT Issues: Reform Judaism," Human Rights Campaign, http://www.hrc.org/resources/stances-of-faiths-on-lgbt-issues-reform-judaism.

5. Preamble to "A Statement of Principles for Reform Judaism" (1999), https:// ccarnet.org/rabbis-speak/platforms/statement-principles-reform-judaism/.

39

FAMILY

Rabbi Sue Levi Elwell, PhD

Family is the first crucible of our identity.

But what is family? For some of us, family seems to begin with the randomness of birth, as we push our way from the shimmering waters of the womb into the glare of the world. Who catches us, welcomes us, sings to us? Are we wrapped in love and care as we take our first breaths? Some of us are born under fluorescence that makes day and night indistinguishable. Some of us are immediately handed into arms that promise care and nurturance that those who create and birth us cannot provide.

For all of us, family begins long before we are born, with dreams and fears and hopes that are often unarticulated, unspoken, hidden from awareness but pulsating and potent. Martin Buber taught that each of us comes into the world because no one else can fulfill our destiny; we are created precisely because there is a place—and a job—waiting for us.[1] We are born into families as unique as we are, each framed by time and place and circumstances that underscore our individuality.

To speak of Jewish families in this second decade of this twenty-first century is challenging, because our world and our sense and understanding of Jews and Judaism have evolved significantly. At the beginning of the twentieth century, many families sat for a "family portrait," which became an essential part of the decoration of many Jewish homes. These monochrome gray or brown photos gathered family members who lived in the same house or neighborhood, most probably in an enclave of Jews in similar socioeconomic circumstances, with shared political and religious convictions. Three generations of biologically related individuals sat stiffly in their "Sabbath best." Bewigged or bejeweled, the grandmother, next to the black-suited grandfather, sat in front, anchoring the family. They were flanked by one or more of their adult children, who stood awkwardly next to their spouses. Grandchildren sat on laps or stools, unsmiling or even scowling. These photos became the iconography of the Jewish family, especially as American culture challenged and changed both the ideal and the reality of the family unit. The historian Jenna Weissman Joselit writes, "As the nineteenth century gave way to the twentieth, the home acquired new meaning, becoming the 'nursery' of identity, religious expression, and culture. Long admired as a safe haven for its inhabitants in an often hostile world, the Jewish home was now placed at the core of modern Jewish identity, often become indistinguishable from Jewishness itself."[2]

For many, those portraits became a final remnant of a bygone world, where roles and expectations of each member of the group had been clear and circumscribed. The grandparents were the bridge from the old world to the new, the bulwark against changes that threatened to undermine tradition or fervently held sociopolitical commitments. Their adult children were tasked with navigating America and providing for the family's economic well-being, while somehow passing down the values inherited from their parents. The journey from Europe to America, whether in the late nineteenth century or in the first decades of the twentieth, challenged and changed Jewish families.

The postwar generation built grand synagogues across America and a network of Jewish communal agencies and institutions to nurture a generation who, it was hoped, would become proud synagogue members and committed to Jewish community. Yet too often Jewish Community Centers and Jewish day and overnight camps for children and youth focused on the social connection between Jews without teaching the basics of Jewish culture or tradition. The 1960s were a time when many accepted norms were challenged. What did this mean for individual families, and for individual Jews?

Throughout my childhood, as my family gathered around the Shabbat table, my father read these words from a slim green volume subtitled *Sabbath Sentiment*: "At this hour, God's messenger of peace comes and turns the hearts of the parents to the children, and the hearts of the children to the parents; strengthening the bonds of devotion to that pure and lofty ideal of the home pictured in sacred writ (Prov. 31:10)."[3] Never mind that I later discovered that there was no single "ideal of home pictured in sacred writ." Our Torah begins with a tale of competition for God's attention that ends in fratricide and continues with a competition for Abraham's attention that ends in a misunderstanding between brothers that has informed the bloodshed between his heirs for five thousand years. What, then, was the prayer referencing? This prayer evoked an idealized notion of home that, even without being "pictured in sacred writ," was a model of how our home should be. The message I received was that this "messenger of peace" (probably Elijah, for similar words are used when Jews gather around the Passover table), this individual who has been sent by God, was making sure that "the hearts of the parents" and the "hearts of the children" were turned toward one another, at least for that "hour," or the minutes it took my father to read those words.

Three generations of my family gathered around a table that, week after week, was set with a white tablecloth and matching napkins, even for the young children, for paper napkins were not yet ubiquitous. The ritual began when my mother kindled the elegant white tapers that perfectly fit into twin brass candlesticks. In her clear, strong voice, she began to sing the prayer that ushers in the Sabbath. We joined her, three generations strong. Then my dad announced the arrival of the divine messenger who entered the room, unseen but felt, unnamed but powerfully present for me and for each of my four siblings. Every week, no matter what angers or jealousies or conflicts had erupted, regardless, or because of, our arguments and frustrations with one another and with our parents, the Sabbath arrived. And with it, the promise of a cessation, however momentary, of pinching or kicking under the table, a brief truce of snide or cruel words, a ceasefire of the looks or half-whispers between siblings that are often the prelude to physical or verbal entanglements that escalate.

Somehow, in those few moments, I glimpsed that "parents and children" was a multigenerational concept: until they died, my grandparents were present at the Shabbat table, so I saw my parents as children and, conversely, could imagine myself as, someday, a parent with children of my own. In those moments when my father read those words, even when someone was absent—even after my grandparents, and my brother, died—that messenger arrived and turned our hearts to one another. For a moment, Shabbat, our precious Sabbath, was an island in time.

The historian Paula Hyman wrote that "Jews entered the modern era with a powerful myth about the strength and stability of the traditional Jewish family throughout the ages."[4] Professor of Talmud and Rabbinics at the Jewish Theological Seminary David Kraemer reminds us that our understanding of Jewish families has changed over the ages:

> "Jewish families" through the ages have assumed multiple and varied forms. And, inevitably, they have looked more or less like other families in the society around them. . . . As societies changed, and Jews were forced to make homes in new cultures, they had no choice but to create families in the image of the culture in which they made their home. It was by virtue of this adaptability that they were able to survive.[5]

My 1950s family reflected both the myth and the reality of many American Jewish families of that time. My dad worked, but until her youngest was in school full-time, my mom did not have a job outside the home, devoting her considerable energies to her five children, the first four of whom were born in a five-year span. Both my parents had been born and had grown up in the city in which we lived, so our family was multigenerational, with grandparents, uncles, aunts, and multiple cousins. Both of my parent's parents were longtime members of our Reform temple; one of my grandmothers was in an early confirmation class there. When I was confirmed in the early 1960s, ten of the one hundred confirmands were related to me.

My parents' and my grandparents' social circles were part of the orbit of our temple. My siblings and I were expected to attend religious and Hebrew school, to be active in the temple's youth group, and to create our own versions of the connections and friendships that had nurtured and supported our family for generations.

The years from 1950 through 1980 saw the dismantling of many barriers that had kept Jews and women out of elite schools and a range of professions. Many who went "away" to college did not return "home." Some, following in the footsteps of parents who had returned "home" after serving in World War II, "returned" to build lives and families that looked very much like their parents' (and grandparents') homogeneous circles of common history and assumed shared values. Today, many contemporary Reform Jews find themselves in cities and towns and neighborhoods that may be philosophically, politically, and/or geographically distant from where they began their journeys. And many of us are living in family situations that those who nurtured us in childhood would have found unimaginable, foreign, disconcerting, or even troubling.

So what do today's Reform Jewish families look like? I worked for the Reform Movement for nearly two decades, traveling from community to community, attending temple board meetings and Shabbat and festival services, and meeting with a wide range of individuals and families who belong to Reform synagogues and identify with Reform Judaism. Through those connections and the privilege of being in many homes across the country, and having served as rabbi for many life-cycle celebrations, I have listened to many stories and reflections. Jewish families continue to be crucibles of identity and value formation.

And, as Kraemer observes, our families reflect the societies, and even the very specific locales, in which we live. The processes of acculturation that shaped American Jewish life a century ago continue into the twenty-first century, albeit in some new and perhaps surprising ways. Jews today are choosing a wide range of partners as they seek shared values and aspirations, compatibility, a complementarity of interests and backgrounds, and shared dreams of what can be. I have officiated at more than one Jewish wedding during which the couple both "jump the broom" (often the only marriage ritual available during slavery in the American South) and follow the Jewish tradition of smashing a glass under the marriage canopy. I have also spoken with couples who want to have a marriage ceremony but, for various reasons, choose a non-clergy friend or family member to "officiate" at their ceremony, a choice that few Jews, or other Americans, would have made in previous decades. (Of course, there have always been couples who elect private, civil ceremonies, and there are those who continue to make that choice, even though many Jewish clergy are delighted to officiate at ceremonies that were, at one time, unlawful or simply culturally unacceptable, most notably marriage between individuals of different races or marriages between individuals of the same gender.[6]) And there are, of course, committed couples who choose not to mark their partnership with a public event of any sort.

When contemporary couples begin to think about welcoming children, they face an array of options not widely available to previous generations. Heterosexual couples sometimes face fertility challenges that previous generations suffered in silence; many today join support groups to find others with whom they can negotiate this journey. Gay and lesbian couples who once felt parenthood was out of reach are now creating families. Once those children arrive, through birth or domestic or foreign adoption, Jewish families, some now enriched by family members of different races and ethnicities, welcome their children with a wide range of celebrations and performative words and rituals, choosing names from a wide range of options reflective of the children's rich and varied inheritance. Some parents choose circumcision for their sons, and others decide against it, while joyfully celebrating the entrance of their sons into the covenant. There are also couples who choose not to expand their families with children, as well as single men and women who extend their families by welcoming children, an option that was not widely spoken about even fifty years ago.

Many are reimagining family to include several generations of individuals, "related" to each other or not, in networks of support and care that benefit all. Today's Reform families are rich in diversity, and those who celebrate the bounty of insights, viewpoints, customs, and sensitivities that come with difference are rewarded. Congregations and communities that both see and embrace our multiracial, multiethnic, differently abled family members are enriched and deepened. Today's Reform communities are strongest when every individual, born in Brooklyn or Beijing, Karachi or Kalamazoo, Cincinnati or Cameroon, stands and proudly proclaims, "This is what a Jew looks like."

Many Reform congregations and communities welcome all who arrive at their doors, and some leaders and community organizers go out of their way to deepen the diversity of their reach by hiring staff members from diverse backgrounds and posting photographs on their websites and in their publications that reflect that the Jewish community is no longer only white and European. Wise Jewish leaders are comfortable with the realities that face many contemporary families, including but not limited to the challenges of two working parents and of single parents, the weight of caring for elderly or ill family members, a range of health-care challenges, the lack of universal affordable child care, and dealing with disability and mental illness. And at this time, some of our families are also facing a range of significant legal challenges: barriers to second parent adoption, complicated immigration issues, underemployment, and more. Additionally, many of our families have been through divorce, loss of jobs, or the death of a primary provider or are simply struggling with making ends meet in our grossly inequitable economy.

On those rare Sabbaths when I am blessed to gather three and sometimes four generations around my Shabbat table, I delight in the diversity of souls who make up my family. Some of us were born into Jewish families. Some of us grew up oceans away from where we sit today. We are a mixed multitude of genders and partners, of origins and options. We are making families with the gifts of generosity, open hearts, and advanced science. We share both diversity and uniqueness with the families of the world. Like many families with whom I've been privileged to work and pray, we are working on caring for one another with intention, patience, and humor.

At the end of his life, my father repeated his Sabbath prayer with a winking addition: "turning the hearts of the parents to the hearts of the children, wherever they may be." I believe that it is time for us to find words that fit today's Jewish families. Here is one suggestion: "May God's messenger of peace come and turn the hearts of the parents, wherever and whoever they are, to the hearts of children, wherever and whoever they are, and the hearts of the children to the parents, wherever, whoever, however they are. May each of us discover connections and sources of strength that help us to see and delight in this world on this Shabbat and on every day."

Each of us is born to fulfill a unique destiny. We may be born into Judaism, or we may find Judaism later in our lives. Or we may follow another path, and then, at some juncture, for a reason we may not ourselves understand, we find our way to a Sabbath table, to a Passover celebration, to a quiet, empty sanctuary, or into a synagogue resonant with joyful prayer. Jewish families, in all our diversity, are gatherings of contradictions and fierce loyalties, collections of souls who disagree with and fiercely defend one another. Our families frustrate and delight. And, when we are fortunate, our families welcome us home.

NOTES

1. "Every person born into this world represents something new, something that never existed before, something original and unique. 'It is the duty of every person to know and consider that she is unique in the world in her particular character and that there has never been someone like her in the world, for if there had been someone like her there would have been no need for her to be in the world. Every single person is a new thing in the world and is called upon to fulfill her particularity in the world.'" Adapted from Martin Buber, *The Way of Man* (New York: Citadel Press, 1964), 16.

2. Jenna Weissman Joselit, *The Wonders of America: Reinventing Jewish Culture, 1880–1950* (New York: Hill & Wang, 1994), 10.

3. Henry Berkowitz, *Kiddush or Sabbath Sentiment in the Home*, 2nd ed. (Philadelphia, 1921), 16.

4. Paula E. Hyman, "The Modern Jewish Family: Image and Reality," in *The Jewish Family: Metaphor and Memory*, ed. David Kraemer (New York: Oxford University Press, 1989), 179.

5. David Kraemer, "Family and Family Values: Mutable or Immutable?" (Berman Jewish Policy Archive), January 18, 2001, http://www.bjpa.org/Publications/details.cfm?PublicationID=835.

6. Loving v. Virginia, 388 U.S. 1 (1967), Obergefell v. Hodges, 567 U.S. (2015).

40

CONTEMPORARY JEWISH SEX ETHICS

RABBI DAVID A. TEUTSCH, PHD

When I was in college in the late 1960s, it was commonplace for Jewish couples who were living together to maintain two apartments because they knew that their parents would strongly disapprove. Such an arrangement is a rarity today, which is just one indication of how much sexual mores have changed in the Jewish community over the last fifty years. Given that change, how can we think with clarity about our sex lives today?

Traditional Jewish sex ethics reflects many values that most of us continue to affirm. These include pleasure, *b'riut*/health, *kavod*/human dignity, *mishpachah*/family, *ahavah*/love, *b'rit*/covenant, and *k'hilah*/community, to name a few.[1] Before we explore them, it is important to consider what has changed scientifically and historically since the basic strands of the halachah (Jewish law) regulating sexual expression developed in the biblical and Talmudic periods. Those changes help to explain the ways in which contemporary Jewish sex ethics differs from halachah.

Most Jews today live in countries with postmodern economies. Relatively few jobs require the kind of brawn that factory work or plowing behind an ox or horse did.[2] Women are employed in the same kinds of jobs as men. The patriarchy of earlier times has moved

413

steadily toward equal rights and opportunities for women. That trend is strongly supported by liberal Jews out of a commitment to justice. With the average human life span much longer than it once was, women also spend many more adult years not involved in child-rearing.

Given the male inheritance rights of an earlier time, men were anxious to establish that the children in their households were biologically their own, which is one reason they restricted women to having sex with their husbands but did not make the requirement mutual. Today, the existence of scientifically accurate paternity tests can eliminate that doubt. The privileges of patriarchy also played a role in that one-way restriction; egalitarianism, by contrast, requires that covenants about sexual exclusivity be mutual.

Science has allowed us to decouple sex and procreation in several ways. The advent of the contraceptive pill, intrauterine devices (IUDs), and other modes of contraception has made it possible to engage in sex with little worry about pregnancy. The availability of sperm banks and in vitro fertilization means that women can become pregnant without engaging in sex. The legalization of surrogacy for those unable to bear children—both men and infertile women—has opened new avenues for taking on the first mitzvah of the Book of Genesis, *p'ru ur'vu*, "be fruitful and multiply." The inevitability of the connection between sex and procreation has been broken: today there can be sex without pregnancy, and pregnancy without sex. This has far-reaching implications for the sex ethics of gay people and straight ones, for those who are single and those who are married. These changes are underlined by the fact that at this writing the birthrate among non-Orthodox Jews in North America is 1.9, which is below the zero population growth rate of 2.1, while the birthrate in the Orthodox world is 4.1, almost double the rate of ZPG.

In biblical and Talmudic times, no developmental stage equivalent to adolescence was recognized. Young people went to work early, acting as young adults. The advent of education that extends through the teen years changed all that, and adolescence emerged as a life stage. Today, most North American Jews are able to attend college, and many attend graduate or professional school as well. In affluent societies, the availability of scholarships and loans and lengthy educations has created prolonged adolescence. In earlier times, when teenagers often married and started families, an argument for abstinence until the wedding was much more plausible, though obviously not always heeded.

These social, scientific, and technological factors have combined to cause most Jews to make fundamental changes in contemporary sex ethics. Many of these have resulted in permission for previously forbidden actions, but some have done the reverse. To understand how that could be, it is important to remember that contemporary thinking about sexual ethics does not begin with norms—what one must or must not do. It generally begins with values and ideals.[3] Our sex lives do not occur in a vacuum. They are both a cause and an effect in our lives, communities, and cultures. Affirming certain values relevant to sexuality only makes sense if we affirm those values along with others in our broader social context as well.[4] One test of a sex ethic is whether, if everyone lived by it, the resulting changes in society would be for good or ill.

As the philosopher Alasdaire MacIntyre has pointed out,[5] human beings make their decisions in a moral thicket that includes ideals, virtues, values, norms, obligations, beliefs, and principles. They rely on inherited practice until something happens to disrupt that practice. In the face of disruption or new situations, they apply the elements of their moral thickets and make a decision that, they believe, is responsive to the changed situation and in harmony with the moral elements to which they are committed. Liberal Jewish sex ethics is responsive to many values and beliefs.[6] Among the most important are the following:

***Ahavah*/love** is present in the Divine-human partnership, in the relationships between family members, and among friends. It is also a key element binding life partners. It should not surprise us that sexual activity is often described as "making love." Sexual activity often plays a key role in creating and maintaining a couple's loving relationship.

***B'rit*/covenant** involves an agreement between the partners. One understanding of what happened at Mount Sinai is that a *b'rit* between God and Israel was created. Another kind of *b'rit* is the one that binds marital partners. Consciously made agreements also exist between couples who are not married. Forming such agreements and living up to them creates safety and trust.

***B'riut*/health** plays a critical role in living a good life. The obligation to heal extends in Jewish thought not only to others but also to oneself. Preserving health requires not engaging in dangerous sexual practices and taking reasonable precautions to avoid violence as well as sexually transmitted diseases (STDs).

***B'tzelem Elohim*/in the image of God** is a reference to Genesis 1:26, which proclaims that human beings are reflections of the divine image. We should treat each other not as objects but as subjects, for each individual is of infinite worth. This entails a profound concern with one's partner and his or her experience.

***Emet*/truth** is of vital importance in creating authentic relationships between a couple, in a family, and within a community. Healthy relationships need a high level of honesty and forbearance to flourish.

***Kavod*/human dignity**, a core value in shaping the relationship between parents and children, should be reflected in all human interactions. Because of the intimacy involved in shared sexual activity, mutually respectful treatment takes on particular importance.

***K'dushah*/holiness** can demarcate time, space, and actions. Sexual intimacy has the potential to shine a light onto the face of the other, bringing awareness of the divinity in a partner. Moments of shared transcendence are holy. Even more holy are such moments amidst a sustained, loving, and covenanted relationship.

***K'hilah*/community** is the very basis of the Jewish people. It is the mediating structure through which individual Jews relate not only to other Jews, but to others around them. The recognition that human beings are social animals means that we need to regulate ourselves so that community can flourish. Our sexual lives should strengthen the relationships that bind communities together.

Mishpachah/**family** provides not only the locus for child-rearing, but for most people the strongest, longest-lasting relationships of our lives. Sexual expression should take place in a way that strengthens relationships and protects vulnerable family members.

Sh'lom bayit/**peaceful home** is a value that grows out of the family being the social building block of Jewish civilization in general and of Jewish communities in particular. *Shalom* requires justice, caring, and having enough to live a dignified life. *Sh'lom bayit* thus speaks to shared life based on genuine mutuality.

Simchah/**joy** or pleasure is an essential part of the Jewish experience. Jewish tradition has always been sex-positive, and it gives attention to *onah*, the obligation to help one's partner become sexually satisfied. All forms of sexual expression between consenting adult partners are permitted as long as they do not inflict any kind of bodily or psychological harm, though most traditional Jews continue to affirm that spilling semen, "the sin of Onan," is a forbidden practice.

Tzedek/**fairness** is a standard applied not only to social justice but to commercial and individual relationships and transactions as well. Fair treatment includes accepting the constraints that a partner places on sexual activity and not imposing one's will on someone who cannot give free consent because of age, disability, social or economic pressure, or temporary incapacity.

Tz'niut/**modesty** has all too often been invoked by men in patriarchal societies to women's detriment, a reprehensible situation. However, there is an aspect to *tz'niut* that should not be lost. Keeping our sexual acts and the details of our sexual relationships private is a positive aspect of *tz'niut*. So is conducting oneself in speech, action, and dress in a way that is not intended to attract undue attention. *Tz'niut* is a wonderful personal quality when it emerges out of an inner sense of modesty rather than societal pressure or control.

While this is not an exhaustive list of values, it provides key vocabulary for considering our sex lives. Using all these values, it is easy to imagine the ideal sexual situation: a married couple, very much in love, taking great pleasure in making love together in a way that is mutually satisfying. Such a relationship would embody all the values listed above. But consider for a moment what proportion of all adult sex acts fulfill this ideal. Not those of people not yet married. Not of widows or divorcees. Not of those who never marry. And even among the married population, a considerable amount of sexual expression does not achieve the ideal. In short, ideals are aspirational. It is not reasonable to limit sexual activity to an ideal situation. It might never come along. This is a point made by Karen Carpenter and Rabbi Dana Evan Kaplan in a recent essay, where they argued that it is important for Reform ethics to see a much broader range of sexual conduct as licit.[7]

Yet there are norms that we all recognize as making some sex acts out of bounds. Seven examples follow.

While the writers of traditional Jewish texts did not understand the harmful nature of sex acts involving children, contemporary liberal Jews recognize their devastating psychological impact. We regard sexual contact with children as a very serious transgression. When adults exploit teenagers, this is no better. And of course someone who cannot or does not give unencumbered consent must also be left alone.

Another norm involves not bringing social or economic pressure to bear on someone to extract sexual favors. In these situations, too, unencumbered consent is impossible. This kind of exploitation is common across all age groups. It is particularly reprehensible when young women who are relatively inexperienced are subjected to this kind of pressure, which is a form of sexual harassment.

A third powerful norm is the taboo against incest, sexual activity between closely related relatives. This taboo helps sustain trust and nurture within the family, strengthens *sh'lom bayit*, and prevents exploitative relationships. There is no justification for incest.

A fourth norm recognizes that deception or intentional withholding of information prevents a partner from making an informed choice and that such manipulation is therefore forbidden. It falls into the category of *g'neivat daat*, theft through deception.

A fifth norm is that one should not violate the covenant with one's primary partner or a covenant that a potential sexual partner has with his or her primary partner. Violating promises or abetting another in the violation of promises is unethical unless special circumstances exist, such as advanced dementia on the part of the primary partner, which can be understood to nullify that portion of their covenant.

A sixth norm is that professionals such as rabbis, therapists, and physicians must not enter into sexual activity or romantic relationships with congregants, clients, and patients, because their professional relationship creates an imbalance that makes unencumbered consent impossible.

A seventh norm is the prohibition against all forms of bestiality. There is no way to obtain unconstrained consent from an animal.

While these norms exclude some conduct, there is a much broader range of activity that these norms do not exclude. Some of these are preferable to others, and some people will regard some of this activity as beyond the pale. About this people will differ. A look at some of these situations follows.[8]

Masturbation is one of the most common forms of sexual activity. While those in the traditional world consider it wrong for men to masturbate because it involves *hashchatat zera*, "spilling of seed," or semen, this never prohibited women from masturbating. Liberal Jews do not consider spilling semen a transgression. Masturbation need not affect anyone beyond the masturbator, so if it is pleasurable for an individual, there is no reason to abstain from it. While it does not build relationships, neither does it hurt them.

The ethics of all sexual relationships should be judged by the same standards. Applying the values and ideal discussed above, it is apparent that they can be applied equally to the relationships of heterosexuals, homosexuals, and bisexuals. The biblical understanding of homosexual acts as *to-eivah*, an unnatural "abomination," dissolves before the current scientific understanding that homosexuality regularly occurs in nature. Up to 10 percent of adults are gay or lesbian. Recent scientific research strongly supports that homosexuality is a natural phenomenon.[9] Artificial insemination, surrogacy, and adoption make child-rearing as plausible for a gay or lesbian couple as they are for a straight one.

When considering what sexual activity is appropriate when, numerous issues arise. More intimate sexual activities involve greater intensity and vulnerability. Maturity generally increases with age, so teenagers should be able to grow into more intimate sexual activity very slowly, over a period of years. Creating an environment that supports respect for boundaries and limits and that ensures sexual activity is limited to providing unpressured mutual pleasure requires ongoing education at home, in temples and schools, and throughout the community.

Even when a person is mature and sexually experienced, rushing into sexual intercourse very early in a relationship is usually unhelpful to the goal of gradually building emotional intimacy and mutual understanding. When a significant relationship has been built, sexual intimacy has a much more meaningful context. Thoughtful communication avoids misunderstandings and unnecessary conflicts. Knowing a partner well enough to comfortably discuss sexually transmitted diseases and contraception may be one good measure of whether a comfortable relationship has been established.

There may be circumstances in which a casual sexual relationship or even a one-night stand might be an activity of choice when no emotionally intimate, long-term relationship is available. Such a choice should not be tainted by use of drugs or excessive alcohol, as these substances prevent unencumbered consent. One should not enter into a one-night stand in the illusion that it will develop into a meaningful, long-term relationship. Furthermore, it should be kept in mind that such activities may later make it more difficult to connect emotional intimacy with sexual activity.

The desire for physical intimacy and pleasure need not diminish with age. At every stage of adult life, people are entitled to make their own decisions about this, and those around them should support their desire for privacy regardless of the nature of their residence.

Among Ashkenazic Jews, monogamy has been the norm for the last one thousand years. More recently, with greater affluence and longer average life spans, the rate of divorce has risen markedly, and serial monogamy (one marriage after another) has become common.

For a variety of reasons, including women's economic independence, prolonged education, and modern birth control, marriage is now often preceded by a prolonged period of cohabitation. Cohabitation and other forms of exclusive, long-term relationships that are shaped by mutual agreements are covenanted relationships.

In North American society, monogamy is entrenched in both law and custom. Nonetheless, there are those who manage multiple relationships both inside and outside marriage. If this is a violation of agreements a couple has made, it is unethical, but some people opt for one form or another of polyamory by mutual agreement. This raises several issues. What is the impact on children? Given how difficult it is to maintain one long-term relationship and the likelihood of jealousies and complexities, will this destabilize family units? Will it injure communities? How should the deviation from well-established custom (*minhag*) be taken into consideration? The Sephardic world never forbade polygamy, but it was not broadly practiced. It should be remembered that many factors beyond sexual pleasure and emotional intimacy deserve consideration when something as far outside common practice as polyamory is under consideration.

An almost infinite number of shades of difference exist in individuals' personal situations, emotional lives, personal tastes, orientation, and so on. Of course an essay such as this one cannot deal with every possible situation, but the approach outlined here should be able to provide guidance in almost any circumstances. Moving as close to the Jewish ideal as personal circumstances allow is a reasonable long-term goal. Meantime, striving for mutual understanding, emotional intimacy, spiritual connection, clear agreements, and mutual pleasure is the basis for a liberal Jewish sexual ethics.

NOTES

1. I have dealt with the subject of sexual and family ethics extensively in *A Guide to Jewish Practice: Everyday Living* (Wyncote, PA: Reconstructionist Rabbinical College Press, 2011), 161–236. This essay draws on that larger essay without duplicating it.

2. A fuller treatment of this historical argument can be found in Paul Wolpe and Janell Carroll, *Sexuality and Gender in Society* (New York: HarperCollins College, 1996).

3. This approach can be found in *Choosing a Sex Ethic*, an important and pioneering effort by Eugene Borowitz (New York: Schocken Books, 1969). A more recent example is the statement by the CCAR Ad Hoc Committee on Human Sexuality in *CCAR Journal* 48, no. 4 (Fall 2001): 9–13. See also my "Rethinking Jewish Sexual Ethics," *The Reconstructionist* 54, no. 8 (July–August 1989): 6–11, 22.

4. For a more comprehensive list, see that section in *A Guide to Jewish Practice: Everyday Living*, 565–78.

5. See Alasdaire MacIntyre's *After Virtue* (Notre Dame, IN: University of Notre Dame Press, 1981) and *A Short History of Ethics* (New York: Macmillan, 1966).

6. For a more complete list, see *A Guide to Jewish Practice: Everyday Living*, 565–78.

7. See Karen Carpenter and Dana Evan Kaplan, "Non-Marital Sex in Reform Judaism: Reconciling Theory with Reality," *Sexuality and Culture: An Interdisciplinary Quarterly* 19, no. 4 (2015): 916–27.

8. This essay does not deal with transgender issues because they are not directly about sexual expression, and they say nothing about a transgender person's sexual orientation. Suffice it to say that given the commitment to *emet*/truth described above, all people should attempt to present themselves to others in a way that mirrors their self-perception and understanding of their own identity.

9. For a summary of recent research on homosexuality, see William Yarber, Barbara Sayad, and Bryan Strong, *Human Sexuality: Diversity in Contemporary America*, 7th ed. (New York: McGraw-Hill, 2010), 172–73.

41

CONVERTING TO JUDAISM

RABBI DANA EVAN KAPLAN, PHD

Many people have the impression that Judaism is not a religion you can convert into or, at the very least, that most Jews would not be receptive to a convert in their midst. This is not the case, certainly not in Reform Judaism. Many of our leaders and thinkers have spoken out strongly in favor of encouraging individuals to convert, even organizing campaigns to make our welcoming policy known. Those interested in embracing the Jewish religion should do so in the expectation that people will be warm and welcoming.

I do have to add a caveat. As a reader who has gotten this far in this book, you have noticed by now that Judaism is not just a religion. What it is exactly is a bit of a mystery. It is certainly safe to say that it involves an element of what has been variously termed ethnicity, peoplehood, or even that much-maligned term race. The person becoming Jewish has to understand that he or she is not just converting into a religion but entering into a very large family. Jews feel that they are part of a people that has undergone a unique set of experiences covering many thousands of years. The concept of a distinctive entity called the Jewish people is already apparent in the Hebrew Bible. It uses several terms to refer to this people, including "congregation," "nation," and "kingdom." The words imply a spiritual and also a communal, family-like connection linking all these individuals one to another. And like all families, the Jewish family has its idiosyncrasies, peculiarities, and dysfunctions.

That said, Judaism is the purest manifestation of ethical monotheism. It can bring enlightenment and help the individual build a close and loving relationship with God. It can provide mechanisms to become a better person and to make a positive impact on the world. The Torah is a tree of life. We want to share its beauty and radiance with others, and we are commanded by God to do so.

Conversion, *giur* in Hebrew, is a formal process that a non-Jewish person undertakes in order to embrace the Jewish religion and become part of the Jewish community. Conversion to Judaism involves ceremonial procedures that are the culmination of educational and other preparation. Conversion is the end result of an informed decision to accept the beliefs of Judaism and adopt the associated practices. Specifics vary by denomination, however, meaning that what is required to convert in a Reform context will differ from what is required in a Conservative or Orthodox setting.

Even within Reform Judaism, there is no one uniform approach to conversion. Rabbis, congregations, and individual Jews are allowed a great deal of religious autonomy, which has fostered a variety of approaches to conversion and to every other aspect of religious belief and practice.

Conversion used to be different. In ancient times, converting to Judaism was a supremely organic process. One didn't need to go to a rabbi, fill out forms, take an Introduction to Judaism course, and complete a conversion ceremony. Conversion was just something that happened.

The very first mention of conversion to Judaism in the Bible involves tragic circumstances in the Book of Ruth. After Naomi's two sons die, she encourages her daughters-in-law to return to their tribes to rebuild their lives. "Turn back," she directs them, "each of you to [your] mother's house. May the Eternal deal kindly with you, as you have dealt with the dead and with me! May the Eternal grant that each of you find security in the house of a husband!" (Ruth 1:8–9). The women are crying as Naomi kisses them goodbye, but one of them, Orpah, nevertheless departs at this point. The other, Ruth, clings to Naomi, who ends up admonishing her, "See, your sister-in-law has returned to her people and her gods. Go follow your sister-in-law" (Ruth 1:15).

Now Ruth makes one of the Bible's most famous speeches—and one of history's clearest declarations of intent to embrace Judaism—saying, "Do not urge me to leave you, to turn back and not follow you. For wherever you go, I will go; wherever you lodge, I will lodge; your people shall be my people, and your God my god. Where you die, I will die, and there I will be buried." Here many people end the quote. I prefer to add one more sentence, because it emphasizes that God is the inspiration for her actions: "Thus and more may the Eternal do to me if anything but death parts me from you" (Ruth 1:16–17).

The medieval commentator Rashi held that Ruth's passionate declaration was the starting point, and the starting point only, of her conversion process. Upon hearing her daughter-in-law declare her love for Judaism, Naomi begins to shepherd Ruth through religious study, leading to formal conversion. But this could not have actually happened. There was no formal conversion process until Talmudic times, many hundreds of years after Ruth and Naomi lived. Despite the absence of a local Reform congregation, with no Reform rabbi anywhere in sight, without access to a Union for Reform Judaism (URJ) Introduction to Judaism course, with not even a conversion certificate available, Ruth, the story clearly shows, committed herself not only to joining the Jewish people in a communal sense, but to believing in their God and practicing their Jewish religion. We will never know exactly what Ruth understood these steps to mean—making Naomi's people and Naomi's God her own—but we can feel her sincerity and intent.

In throwing in her destiny with that of her mother-in-law in this way, Ruth signs on for a transformation of identity that goes far beyond strictly theological issues. Becoming a Jew by choice unequivocally involves assuming a new social identity to accompany a new religious identity; in a sense it requires the remodeling of the self. Embracing a new religion is not like buying a new winter coat. The choice needs to be felt deep down, and such deeply felt conviction holds implications for nearly every aspect of life.

Within Reform Judaism, the term "Jew-by-choice" has steadily replaced the term "convert to Judaism," because the latter tends to connote the kind of conversion experience associated with Christianity. Within Reform Judaism, becoming Jewish is typically viewed as a slow process of embracing a way of life and of growing into a way of looking at the world. A case can even be made that in a postmodern society, all Jews are Jews-by-choice. I am thus not terribly comfortable differentiating Jews-by-choice from the term's flip side, Jews-by-birth. Rather, I tend to stick with the terms "convert" and "conversion," although periodically I use the newer wording "Jews-by-choice." My term of preference is the Hebrew word *ger*. In the Bible, *ger* originally meant sojourner, a temporary inhabitant, a newcomer lacking inherited rights. Slowly, over centuries, the word *ger* took on the meaning of one who, although not born Jewish, embraced Judaism. *Gerut*, deriving from the root *ger*, began to be understood to mean the process of conversion to Judaism.

The Book of Exodus, composed at least twenty-five hundred years ago, refers to the Israelites themselves as *gerim*, or strangers, in Egypt. After the Israelites settled in the Holy Land, it was the non-Israelites who were referred to as "strangers." Strangers were expected to obey certain laws and in return were to be treated with kindness and respect. Clearly, the meaning of the term underwent a dramatic transformation over several hundred years. We know that religion can and must evolve and that people are going to understand things in their contemporary context.

Reform Judaism provides no single set of standards that all must adhere to concerning conversion. What one congregation does, others may not. Whatever the specific requirements, the most important thing is the potential convert's sincerity and enthusiasm. Typically, someone interested in converting to Judaism through the Reform

Movement will start attending services at a Reform synagogue. Because the Jewish religion is a belief system practiced in the context of a community, this is key. The person pursuing conversion will usually choose a synagogue where they can not only attend services but participate in adult education programs and be part of broader congregational life.

Sages in the Talmudic era believed that a person wanting to convert to Judaism should be motivated strictly out of love of God and the Jewish religion, having no lesser motives. Certain sages, though, understood that personal factors could not always be separated from altruistic religious commitment; they urged that each situation be evaluated independently. Today, we understand that it is often not possible or even desirable to completely distinguish altruistic from personal motivations. Altruistic factors might include belief in one God or perhaps the visceral feeling that Judaism "just feels right." Personal factors might include an impression that temple membership brings desired social status or can placate future in-laws. While personal factors alone aren't usually sufficient, we realize that they are always part of the equation for Jews-by-choice.

In recent years, however, non-Jewish spouses of Jews feel less pressure to convert. In part this change resulted from the Reform Movement's 1983 Patrilineal Descent Resolution, which stated that the children of a Jewish father and a non-Jewish mother would be considered Jewish if they were raised in the Jewish religion. Their upbringing would need to include significant public acts of religious identification: Jewish baby naming, bar or bat mitzvah, and confirmation. But non-Jewish women marrying into Jewish families were now free to decline to convert without risk to their ability to raise a Jewish family.

The Patrilineal Descent Resolution lowered rates of conversion, which in the long run was a good thing, making it easier for people to decide freely and authentically, without being pressured, to convert to Judaism. Today, a person converting to Judaism is likely to do so with a pure heart and without hesitation. The person who wants to convert, then, can expect to begin by attending services for a time and joining in activities at the synagogue, after which an Introduction to Judaism course is usually taken. Such a course may last sixteen to twenty-four weeks, teaching the fundamentals of Jewish thought and practice. It is usually designed with interfaith couples in mind, but also for those considering conversion apart from marriage and for adults who are already Jewish but feel a need to review basics of the religion. The Union for Reform Judaism has developed an introductory curriculum leading to a certificate of completion that some rabbis require as part of the conversion process.

Committing oneself to Reform Judaism's beliefs and the practices based on them requires knowing a considerable amount. Ideally, the knowledge will come not only from completing the introductory course and participating in temple life and talking with active members, but from studying independently. This used to mean reading books. Now, YouTube videos and the like provide additional means to deepen understanding of the Jewish religion.

Alternatively, conversion is viewed by some to be only the beginning. Extensive expertise is not expected of someone seeking to convert. Their knowledge can be expected to increase over the many coming years of their involvement in their new religion. Whatever its scope, the conversion process at some synagogues is overseen by the rabbi only, while at others a *beit din*, or court of three individuals (frequently rabbis) supervises it. The *beit din* may question the conversion candidate both about Judaism's substance and the candidate's educational preparation and religious experiences.

Talmudic requirements for conversion focus on ritual procedures rather than preparation for converting. These ritual requirements are circumcision for males and immersion for both males and females. Males are required to be circumcised, and previously circumcised males are required to undergo *hatafat dam brit*, the drawing of a drop of blood from the remnant of the foreskin. *Hatafat dam brit* is considered unnecessary by some Reform rabbis, who consequently do not require it, but would not object if a convert sought the ritual as an emblem of spiritual circumcision.

Talmudic guidelines require circumcision, called "the covenant of Abraham." Abraham was forty-eight years old, according to the midrash, when he began to believe in the one true God. Half a century later, despite his age, Abraham was commanded by God to circumcise himself—the whole procedure, on his own—when he was ninety-nine. The text suggests that one main reason was to hearten male proselytes who might fear themselves too old for circumcision and so abandon the idea of converting: Abraham got through it, and they will, too (Genesis 17:24). But in spite of rabbis' preference and Abraham's example, in the 1890s the Central Conference of American Rabbis voted not to require circumcision for conversion. Today, however, a growing number of Reform rabbis actually require circumcision for uncircumcised men converting to Judaism; a doctor performs the procedure.

Ritual immersion, or *t'vilah*, is the total submersion of the person becoming Jewish in a body of running water. In the time of the Jerusalem Temple, worshipers were required to purify themselves by immersing in a mikveh, a ritual bath, before entering the grounds of the sanctuary. Jews no longer need to purify themselves before entering the Temple; it was destroyed in 70 CE. The process was, however, applied by the sages to a new use. Immersion in running water became a symbolic process of connecting with God as well as a defining moment in the process of changing one's religious status—a rite of passage. The water must touch every part of the body; all jewelry and even makeup and nail polish—anything getting in the way of the water reaching every single pore—is removed, even contact lenses. The waters of the mikveh are said to spiritually elevate the individual.

Often before immersion, the person being converted recites two blessings. The first avers, "Our praise to You, Eternal our God, Sovereign of all, who, sanctifying us with divine commandments, has commanded us concerning immersion." The second, the *Shehecheyanu* blessing, is recited whenever a Jew experiences a particular joyous event or performs a joyous act, for the first time in a given year: "Our praise to You, Eternal our God, Sovereign of all: for giving us life, sustaining us, and enabling us to reach this season."

The state of immersion is transitory and intermediate. When we immerse, we cross the threshold from one status to another. Some have even described the mikveh as a spiritual womb. The convert is surrounded by water just like human fetuses are. As a child emerges from the womb into a world new to it, the convert emerges from the mikveh into a new spiritual life as a new person. A proselyte is like a newborn child.

Like other things, the mikveh ritual is not required in Reform Judaism, but it can be quite a moving spiritual experience for the person converting. For those invited along as witnesses, it can be inspiring to see how someone who was not raised as a Jew has come to love and cherish Judaism so much.

The beaches of Dauphin Island lie a short drive south of Mobile, Alabama, where I am a rabbi. When my congregation recently conducted a conversion ceremony, we chose the gulf waters surrounding the island as the place the conversion candidate would immerse himself three times. Traditional concerns for the water's free access had to yield to municipal law, so he wore swim trunks. I waded out with him, a measure against the undertow. Because the winter waters were chilly, the mikveh ended quickly, a dramatic contrast with the three years the candidate had spent preparing. The process of converting, as well as the immersion itself—and the witnessing of the immersion—invites emotional and spiritual catharsis.

When a person converts to Reform Judaism, most congregations conduct a conversion ceremony as part of religious services. At this time, the convert can take a Hebrew name. For those born Jewish, a Hebrew name is made up of one or two Hebrew first names followed by the words "son of" or "daughter of" and, finally, both parents' Hebrew first names. A Jew-by-choice has no Jewish birth parents, obviously, so by tradition he or she chooses a Hebrew first name, which is followed by the words meaning "son/daughter of Abraham and Sarah." Despite this tradition, I allow people I convert to use their birth parents' names, Hebraicized, if they prefer. A balance is desirable, I think, between seeing conversion as a new beginning and accepting that the person converting brings along prior relationships.

The Talmud advises a rabbi to turn away a potential proselyte three times. The advice reflects the three times Naomi tried to dissuade Ruth from coming with her. Only a person who perseveres should be received, for one should always discourage with the left hand and draw near with the right. Up to and even within the conversion ceremony, the Sages warned those seeking to convert that Jews not only assumed substantial religious obligations, they were hated by many, near and far. Reform rabbis are not, of course, required to follow this procedure, although we can understand why this approach was adopted two thousand years ago.

Interestingly, the Sages did not require proselytes to observe all of the commandments. What each would-be convert was required to accept was *ol malchut shamayim*, "the yoke of the kingdom of heaven"; that is, they needed to accept God's sovereignty in the world along with the obligatory nature of Jewish ritual. Then, they were taught several "heavier" commandments and several "lighter" ones and sent off to study further and observe further commandments as they matured into their new religion. Reform Judaism differs. It does not hold the commandments to be obligatory, instead charging each Jew to determine individually whether and in what way a commandment might be spiritually meaningful for them. The same autonomy is, of course, granted to someone converting to Reform.

Deciding to pursue conversion isn't always straightforward. An example is what to do when one spouse wants to convert while the other doesn't. It is beneficial to have partners convert together, mutually supporting each other's new belief system and related educational pursuits, ritual practices, and communal activities and obligations. Nevertheless, since the Reform Movement emphasizes individual religious decision-making, we will generally convert one partner without the other, unless doing so would create antagonism within their relationship.

But what of the case in which the non-Jewish spouse in an intermarriage converts to Judaism after the couple has been married? What usually would be recommended would be a second, Jewish wedding performed after the conversion. Now, both can place their commitment to each other within the broader context of God's loving relationship with the Children of Israel. A congregant at my student pulpit in Brisbane, Australia, said his little daughter got so used to seeing such religious weddings celebrated years after a civil ceremony that, attending the Jewish wedding of a very young couple, she wondered why they were marrying so soon!

A further example would be a request to convert a child to Judaism. Can minors be said to be choosing Judaism if they convert before reaching the legal age of consent, as when a family wants small children—even infants—converted to Judaism? In such situations, the converted will not understand the commitment they are making. Reform synagogues generally find the solution to be to go ahead with children's conversion ceremonies, anticipating that later bar or bat mitzvah and confirmation ceremonies will demonstrate that they have accepted the choice made for them earlier.

Conversion is important from an ideological standpoint, because it provides a litmus test for a whole series of issues. It is a chance to clarify what truly matters to us about Judaism. Given a relatively short period to teach someone what we think they really should know about Judaism, what will we choose? How will we present that material? Our choices say a lot about what we think is essential.

Conversion is also important in practical, organizational terms, to bring new members into the Jewish religion. Jewish identity is in fact connected to both a religion and an ethnicity. Most who convert to Judaism are attracted to the religion; but by converting, they in fact also join a tribe. In all likelihood they will feel less connected to the tribe than do people whose ancestors have belonged to it for thousands of years. Still, it is important they feel connected to the Jewish community, not just the Jewish religion.

The ultimate goal, however, is to help them to build a close relationship with God, as full members of the covenantal bond. We believe that the covenant between Jews and God is a relationship of loyalty and reciprocal love. It obligates us to try to live as God wants us to, something each of us must determine for ourselves, but typically comprising care and compassion for people we encounter as well as other behavior the Bible calls for, as elucidated by religious thinkers in each generation. There is room in this covenant, and in our faith communities, for people wanting to embrace our religion and join in its work promoting ethical, moral behavior reflecting the one true God.

42

A PERSONAL COMMENT BY A REFORM RABBI ON CONVERSION

Rabbi David Ellenson, PhD

A contemporary American Reform attitude toward conversion and outreach takes place against the backdrop of a modern setting where non-Orthodox Jews intermarry at a record rate. In this context, many if not most Reform rabbis and laypeople (including me) advocate an inclusive policy position on a broad range of personal status issues so that these intermarried Jews, their spouses, and their children will identify as Jews and participate in the life of the Jewish community. The issue does not center principally on whether conversion itself is permissible or desirable.

In adopting this stance, I feel that Reform Judaism wisely rejects the attitude in Jewish law that maintains that an individual who rejects even a single letter of Jewish law should be denied the right to convert (Babylonian Talmud, *B'chorot* 30b). Similarly, proponents of this attitude note that no gentile is allowed to convert to Judaism for an ulterior motive such as marriage (*Shulchan Aruch, Yoreh Dei-ah* 268:12). However, the bulk of individuals who seek conversion to Judaism during the modern era fully intend—in violation of the rule in *Yoreh Dei-ah* 268:12—to marry Jewish persons subsequent to their conversion. Furthermore, they generally have no intent—in opposition to the statement in *B'chorot* 30b—to be fully observant. Nevertheless, many of our contemporary Orthodox colleagues feel that the demands of Jewish law require adoption of this stringent position and would preclude acceptance of the overwhelming number of persons who would like to convert to Judaism at the present time. These rabbis in effect define a convert as a person who was formerly obligated to observe the Seven Noachide Laws that Jewish tradition asserts is incumbent upon all humanity. However, as a Jew, the convert would now be called upon to observe *taryag mizvot*—the 613 commandments that are binding upon every Jew. I believe this approach understands conversion to Judaism in terms that are far too narrow and constrained. It is an approach that does not reflect the broad spectrum of beliefs and practices—the pluralism—that marks modern Jewish life.

For these reasons, I and virtually all my Reform, Conservative, Reconstructionist, and Renewal rabbinic peers and a number of Modern Orthodox ones turn to other teachings and rulings in Jewish law and tradition for guidance on the issue of conversion. These precedents are fully anchored in Jewish tradition even as they run counter to the more stringent rules cited above. They allow for a Jewishly authentic yet broader and more lenient and welcoming approach to converts. For example, Talmudic narratives (*B'rachot* 31a and *M'nachot* 44a) concerning Rabbi Hillel and Rabbi Chiya, *Tannaim* of the first two centuries of the Common Era, indicate that these great authorities did accept converts who stated explicitly that ulterior motives prompted them to seek conversion to Judaism. Similarly, a passage in the Babylonian Talmud (*Sanhedrin* 99b) maintains that rabbinic courts that reject persons who desire to enter the covenant—even when they have ulterior motives—are guilty of inflicting great potential harm upon the Jewish people. Moreover, rabbis throughout Jewish history have frequently labeled children born of Jewish fathers and non-Jewish mothers as *zera Yisrael* (Jewish seed) or *zera kodesh* (holy seed) despite the ruling of traditional Jewish law that only children born of Jewish mothers are accorded Jewish status. These traditional rabbis have urged acceptance of such children into the Jewish fold through formal conversion even when it is unlikely that such children will grow up to be observant Jews.

Jewish law and tradition clearly contain ample precedents that justify a non-stringent stance on conversion.

Virtually all Reform, Conservative, Reconstructionist, and Renewal rabbis, and a number of Orthodox ones, employ these texts to justify their lenient approach to conversion. For them, formal membership in the Jewish people can be legitimated on the basis of these texts that display highly elastic considerations of what constitutes grounds for membership in Judaism. This approach to conversion best addresses the vast reality that is Jewish life today. It surely promotes a policy of welcome and inclusion that in my opinion and those of most other liberal Jews, rabbis and laypeople alike, is in the best interests of the Jewish people today.

The issue of ongoing discussion and sometimes contention that remains for many Reform Jews centers on questions of inclusion or outreach to persons who are not converted to Judaism but who, along with their children, dwell within the ambit of the Jewish community. After all, there have been significant rates of intermarriage in the American Jewish community since 1970, and the 2012 Pew Research Center's study of the American Jewish population reported that seven out of ten non-Orthodox Jews who were married between 2001 and 2011 married people who were born non-Jewish.[1] In the large majority of these intermarriages, the non-Jewish partner did not convert to Judaism. This means that the ethnic homogeneity that marked the Jewish community during the mid-twentieth century no longer exists. Simply put, most non-Orthodox Jews in North America born in the last third of the twentieth century and in the twenty-first century have grandparents, parents, aunts, uncles, and cousins who are not Jewish. The reality of intermarriage has combined with other factors (e.g., adoption of Asian children, the entrance of Jews of color into the community) to make the Jewish community more ethnically and racially heterogeneous than ever before in American Jewish history. In short, today there is a huge population of persons who are involved in some manner in the Jewish community who do not possess "official status" as Jews in a world where many persons comfortably hold multiple forms of identity.

In view of this, I believe that the policy of "audacious hospitality" that Rabbi Richard Jacobs, president of the Union for Reform Judaism, has articulated is the optimal policy option for the contemporary American Jewish community as it strives to retain and attract Jewish members and provide Jewish meaning for those who come within our ambit. In locales such as Boston and San Francisco where the Federation has taken the lead in offering programs welcoming interfaith couples into the Jewish community, the rate of Jewish identity and affiliation on the part of the offspring of these marriages has soared over the rates of disengagement that formerly marked the children of previous generations of intermarried Jews. Furthermore, a recent study by social scientist Leonard Saxe of Brandeis University has indicated that Jewish engagement among interfaith couples rose considerably where rabbis alone officiated at their weddings.[2] For all these reasons, I would argue that an attitude of embrace for the intermarried as well as all Jews is in the best interests of a diverse Jewish people today. This attitude, rooted in Jewish tradition and teaching, will promote our community as our people seek meaning and identity today and in the future.

NOTES

1. The Pew Study can be found under the title "A Portrait of Jewish Americans: Findings from a Pew Research Center Survey of U.S. Jews," October 1, 2013. The statistics on intermarriage can be found online at http://www.pewforum .org/2013/10/01/chapter-2-intermarriage-and-other-demographics/#intermarriage. For intermarriage statistics from 1970 and 1990, see National Jewish Population Study, "Intermarriage: Facts for Planning," http://www.jewishdatabank.org/Studies /downloadFile.cfm?FileID=1446, p. 10; and *Highlights of the CJF 1990 National Jewish Population Survey*, http://www.jewishdatabank.org/studies/downloadFile .cfm?FileID=3129, pp. 13–14.

2. Leonard Saxe, Fern Chertok, Graham Wright, and Shahar Hecht, *Under the Chuppah: Rabbinic Officiation and Intermarriage* (Waltham, MA: Brandeis University, Cohen Center for Modern Jewish Studies, October, 2016), https://www.brandeis .edu/cmjs/pdfs/jewish%20futures/RabbinicOfficiation102616.pdf, p. 1. For a report on the successful outreach efforts of the Boston and San Francisco Federations with intermarried couples, see Sue Fishkoff, "Boston Study Links Outreach, Jewish Choices," Jewish Telegraphic Agency, November 10, 2006, http://www.jta .org/2006/11/10/life-religion/features/boston-study-links-outreach-jewish-choices.

43

INTERFAITH FAMILIES

RABBI RACHEL GUREVITZ, PhD

The Reform Movement has been explicitly welcoming of interfaith families since the late 1970s. Today, the rate of intermarriage in the United States is nearly 60 percent. Much has been written about the challenges that come with our cultural and social success in fully integrating into U.S. society. But what we also know from those studies is that when the children of interfaith couples are given a formal Jewish education and access to Jewish social experiences, they are much more likely to identify as Jewish by religion and not simply as a cultural identity.

The Reform congregation has been the primary venue for interfaith families to make a synagogue their spiritual home. The result has been to enable interfaith families to make Jewish choices and to thrive and connect with Jewish community life. It has also created something new that may not have existed at any other time in Jewish history, or at least not in this way. While our congregations practice Judaism and celebrate Jewish holidays and life-cycle moments in deeply Jewish ways, many of the individuals who are practicing, observing, and celebrating with us are not Jewish.

Rabbi Reeve Brenner suggests that after decades of intentional outreach and welcoming of interfaith families into Reform congregations, we have inadvertently created a new category of individual in Jewish community life—the *toshav tzedek* (righteous resident). He defines such an individual as

> a non-Jew who has undergone or experienced Convergence not Conversion and does not claim or assert Jewish identity status. But of the four essential pillars of Jewish identity only self-affirmation, that is, claiming for self Jewish identity, is absent. After all the Toshav Zedek keeps mitzvot with family, consciously affirms (e.g., by shul membership) Torah (Judaism) as his/her foundational way of life and has filial (husband, child) belonging status.[1]

While the multitude of reasons why the non-Jewish member of a Jewish household may not choose to formally convert to Judaism is a topic for another chapter, as a congregational rabbi I can attest to the significant number of members in my community who are present and participating in Jewish learning, worship, volunteering, social justice, and life-cycle observances but who have not claimed Jewish identity for themselves as individuals. This is what convergence looks like. It is a wonderful and enriching facet of Reform congregational life today, but one that many communities have not fully grasped the impact of or the potential that lies in these contemporary realities.

We need to have a better understanding of what the identities, experiences, and hopes of the non-Jews in our midst really are. When they have chosen or affirmed that they will be part of a Jewish family and, further, make the synagogue their spiritual home, how do we honor and support that in the pursuit of creating engaged and meaningful Jewish communities? To explore some of these questions, I interviewed several non-Jewish members of Jewish families in my congregation. Among the interviewees were those, such as Kimberley, who continue to identify by another faith (and I would argue only in these instances is "interfaith" really the appropriate label). She continues to practice Catholicism as an individual but has been a dedicated and involved member of our congregation for almost thirty years. She raised her children only in the Jewish faith. Furthermore, she has found elements of Jewish observance and practice that she has experienced through her participation as part of a Jewish family to be deeply spiritual and supportive. Then there are those, such as Janice, Deborah, and Stephen, who grew up in another faith but no longer choose to identify by any particular faith (we might refer to such individuals as those of another heritage, as they often bring the cultural expressions of those traditions with them). Many of these members want to learn enough to be able utilize the spiritual tool box of Judaism. The synagogue is their only spiritual home, and they need support to be able to participate more fully. For some, that journey may one day lead to conversion, but not necessarily. A third category, which I did not interview, are those who are primarily disinterested in faith but are willing to be supportive of their Jewish spouse in raising their children with a Jewish identity. By deeply listening to my members without superimposing my own interpretations, I am becoming more attuned to the ways that I can truly respond to diverse families in my congregation and their desire for spiritually meaningful and engaged lives in the context of a Jewish community.

Sometimes one of the first interactions I have with a young interfaith family is when I receive a call to do a baby-naming ceremony. Whether in gesture, choice of readings, or taking the time to explain and offer choices around rituals, these interactions can create a touchstone moment in the lives of individuals who are trying to figure out whether there could be a shared spiritual communal home that would feel comfortable and nourishing to both parents. For some, a marriage ceremony, and the opportunity to work with a rabbi to create something deeply grounded in Jewish tradition yet responsive to the essence of the two souls being blessed, provides that first moment. Life-cycle rituals in general are deeply meaningful moments. In a community that is truly inclusive of non-Jews, less focus on what we will permit a non-Jew to do and more focus on how Jewish ritual enhances and enriches these moments in our lives will open doors to those who might choose to make the synagogue the spiritual home for their family.

Let us take the example of Jewish mourning rituals to illustrate this approach in practice. Of the individuals I interviewed for this chapter, all expressed a very high degree of feeling "at home" in our congregation. One area where I investigated a little further to see what the limits of "at home-ness" might be was the question of whether they would imagine reaching out to me as "their rabbi" if someone died. Would they feel that some of the post-burial practices of mourning in our congregation—having their loved one's name read during *sh'loshim* (the thirty days following the death) or even having a night of shivah (a gathering in their homes for visits and prayers during the first seven days of mourning)—would be available to them? And, if so, would they choose to access these opportunities within the synagogue context?

> One day [when] my mother or father passes, it would not have even occurred to me to reach out to the temple community to say that I had had a loss. . . . Any kind of a tradition—that is when people identify most with community and religion and that is a piece where, even though you are not Jewish, I think it would be great if we [the synagogue] still want you to know that you are part of our community and resources are available to you. . . . I think that would be a great thing . . . whether or not they [non-Jews in the congregation] avail themselves of it, you are continuously reaching out. . . . We want to feel part of the Jewish community because that is one of the reasons we sign up for this; not just for our husbands or our children. And I think that the more that you make those kinds of services known . . . they at least get the message on a consistent basis that we want you here and you are part of this community; whether or not you decide to make Judaism your chosen faith, you are still one of us. (Janice)

Janice recognizes that the instinctual thing to do at a time of loss is to go back to one's own traditions. Of course, in the case of a parent, a burial should be done according to the religious tradition observed by the parent. But what comes next for the individual who no longer identifies with that religious tradition and is an active participant, with their family, in a Jewish community? Janice is still learning about Jewish practices, so she identifies the job that the congregation could do in teaching and sharing some of our Jewish mourning traditions so that she would know what was available, so that she could potentially make that choice when the time came. Further, she ascribes great meaning and significance to the very act of a Jewish community offering this kind of support and making it available to her. She feels that even if a non-Jew in a Jewish congregation did not choose to avail themselves of the community practices and gatherings, being invited and included in this way would likely make someone feel truly "part of" the one spiritual community that they participate in.

Another congregant, Kimberley, who attends Shabbat services regularly and has been a member of the congregation for almost thirty years, is a practicing Catholic and still goes to church from time to time. When her father died, she initially allowed the congregation to add her father's name to the *sh'loshim* list because she recognized how it would help her children, both being raised Jewish, to mourn their grandfather. But after having had this experience, she reflected:

> But now I feel terrible if the name is read and I'm not there or someone from my family is not there for the service. I've become much more comfortable with that aspect of it and see how it's helpful and good. . . . I wouldn't have known that it was even available but they [the temple] called and asked, and I said "yes" but I just asked that it [the date] be on his English, Gregorian calendar—the *yahrzeit*—so it would be easy for me to remember.

Kimberley expressed her relationship to Judaism and our synagogue in more nuanced ways. She is very dedicated to our Jewish community and congregation, not only as the mother of Jewish children and wife of a Jewish man, but because, over time, she has found great meaning in Jewish ritual and Shabbat worship. At the same time, she shared with me that there are aspects of congregational ritual life and lay leadership where she has held back from involvement because, as she explains, "I don't want to lose myself totally." Note, this is not an individual who is trying to blend traditions or "be both." Her personal identity as a Catholic is very strong—she believes that Jesus is the Savior. But she has also found a spiritual home in our Jewish congregation as part of a Jewish family in a deeply authentic way, while recognizing why she is able to access an experience that her husband can't have in a Catholic church.

> I could see the Mass service . . . how someone Jewish would not feel comfortable at all at a Catholic Mass, especially at Easter and Good Friday. And yet, I went to [Shabbat] services and . . . nothing was offensive to me and it was all familiar because the foundation of Christianity and so-called Old Testament was, for the most part, familiar to me.

It is because of Kimberley's ability to access so much of Jewish community life and, through study and attendance, to gain familiarity and comfort with much of Jewish ritual that her family has been so present and integrated in the life of our congregation. Without that access, as the primary driver of her family's religious practice, it is unlikely that either her husband or her children would have had such an engaged Jewish congregational experience.

> Because I was practicing and my church is important to me and my relationship to God is important to me, I actually said to Ben [her husband] that if we're going to raise the kids Jewish they have to go to Hebrew school, we have to go to services regularly—we have to do all these things. He said, "OK," and that's what we did. . . . And it was my influence that we did that. And that's how we came to be.

Kimberley's Christian-influenced definition of what it means to be "practicing" a faith has informed what Jewish practice has looked like for her whole family. Her husband has and continues to be involved with several lay leadership roles, and her children are very Jewishly identified. I will return to this observation in a moment, in discussing how it can also shape the non-Jewish family member's understanding of conversion.

When a couple first visit a congregation, they often bring with them specific questions. When I interviewed some of my congregants, hearing what mattered to them and how they framed and interpreted what they heard was extremely enlightening; the words of a rabbi or lay leader may not always be received in the way that was intended, because we often make assumptions that the ones listening share our framework of understanding.

For example, I asked Deborah, another longtime member of the congregation who was born Catholic but one who does not personally identify by any particular faith of her own, "Do you recollect what made it feel 'this is right'—that this congregation would work not just for your kids but for you—a comfortable place for your whole family to be part of?" Deborah responded:

> One reason was we had a discussion [with the rabbi at the time]—I think I was pregnant at the time—about having a baby and having a bris [circumcision] and whether our kids would need to convert. And she was like, "Oh no, that's old school" or "Different sections of Judaism believe that but Reform don't"—and that was definitely a comfort. Because that was something that had seemed awfully strange to me—that you are "born" into a religion and that it matters if it is the mother or the father—that just seemed really strange, so it was comforting that she didn't feel that that was a factor. And I think she said, "Come to a service." And we happened to go to a women's service or a Sisterhood service or something. It was very feminist, so I was won over by that because that was what we just happened to go to.

Deborah wasn't sure if the rabbi had actually said, "That's old school," but it is informative that this is how she remembers it because it is indicative of her perception, her takeaway from that early conversation. Jewish identity is a complex matter, made more complex by denominational and national differences in how identity is recognized or confirmed. But to someone coming from a Christian background, faith is something you choose based on personal belief. In fact, Deborah still uses that frame to explain why, after so many years of participation in Jewish community and Jewish family life she has not converted:

> I think that I'd just have to be more religiously engaged in general to come to that point. But I do think that it's out there

somewhere. . . . [She mentions a relative who converted to Judaism but who doesn't engage much with Jewish practice.] Which is another of these strange things, where Jews don't always practice, whereas it is an important thing for Catholics. But often if there is any kind of discussion, I know way more about Judaism than she does. . . . I think I would have to be ready to be really engaged and practicing and understanding more of it a lot better to want to do that.

How might a rabbi respond? Some might clearly see an opportunity here to engage Deborah and help her reframe her understanding of choosing Judaism for her own, personal, identity. We might think we were doing her a service, but we might also be reacting with our own agenda to encourage conversion. There is a possibility that our words would be heard as "your understanding of why you have not yet chosen Judaism is incorrect, and let me give you my understanding." For me, having heard something similar voiced by several non-Jews who have been actively participating in Jewish congregational life for a long time and who have no other faith tradition that they identify by, my response is somewhat different. I am beginning to recognize that the Christian-influenced definition of a religious identity requires a degree of dogmatic certainty and an intensity of practice that is seldom a standard in Reform communities by which those born Jewish affirm their religious identity. A group conversation in which I can continue to listen to how my members grapple with these questions of belief and identity will help us consider, together, a plurality of choices that each of them may come to make over time.

Regardless of what may still lie ahead for Deborah, it is the interpretation she brought to that initial conversation with the rabbi that may have had some significant part in determining whether she would affirm and support her family's decision to join a Jewish congregation and engage in community life in the first place. Further, whether one agrees with her interpretation is less important than knowing that it exists and how crucial a role it might play in the choices that interfaith families make around engaging with Jewish congregational life.

Many congregations, including ours, explicitly welcome interfaith families in their marketing, whether on their websites or elsewhere.

That is an important first step to signal "there are families like you here." What happens next is equally important. Janice explains:

> We had the new member orientation and . . . a lot of the people we sat around with were interfaith. . . . It was always very welcoming to us. The whole way the temple is set up is very welcoming, with the couches and with the social hall . . . the building itself is very welcoming. It doesn't feel overwhelming.

We have learned that the more we make "relational Judaism" an integral part of everything we do, from the lobby furniture, to the integration of social opportunities as part of every Shabbat and festival celebration, to the website, to the creation of multiple intentional spaces for open, exploratory conversations with our members, the more we are also helping our interfaith families feel truly "at home."[2] Last year, in response to the conversations that began informally around a table as part of our three-part Kesher program to help new members connect with the congregation, we launched an Interfaith Family Advisory Group. Janice was a founding member of that group. The group met three times during the year, sometimes just to share experiences (both in the congregation and within their extended families), but also to give us input on ways we could help them connect further. While it is often difficult for younger, working parents to find the time to come to traditional adult education in the synagogue, many expressed a desire to be able to access learning that could help them become more familiar with Jewish ritual and practice.

> The fact is, when I'm in services its challenging because I don't know all the pieces of it, but people are very helpful, if I ask somebody. . . . For me personally, I'd like to learn more about Judaism and the time, obviously, is always the thing. (Janice)

We did run some one-off learning opportunities, such as a review of the choreography of a Shabbat service, in response to this input. We also decided to put together our first large-scale congregational seder, with the support of members of our Interfaith Family

Advisory Group, who expressed a particular need for experiencing a meaningful seder and wanted to create memories for their children when their own family members did not live close by. We also created a Facebook group, where questions could be asked at any time, and clergy post online videos and easy-to-absorb articles on how to make Shabbat in the home, how to prepare for an upcoming festival, and so on. The resources posted on ReformJudaism.org are often shared, as are the wonderful educational animated videos at bimbam.com. A colleague, Rabbi Ruth Gelfarb, runs a monthly family school at Har Hashem in Boulder, Colorado. The monthly experience, enabling learning and familiarity with Shabbat worship to grow incrementally over time, helps many parents gain both confidence and comfort in their participation in Jewish community life—a model that can go further than one-time programs.

> I think that the involvement that my daughter has had has been—I see that as a very good thing. I think that is also what helps to include me in everything. Seeing her involvement—seeing how she can help teach me as well as me teaching her. And everything that goes on in the temple with her things—a lot of what is getting me involved is getting the kids involved. (Stephen)

One of the ways in which we have helped the non-Jewish members of our Jewish families access Jewish education is through our family education programs. Each child's grade has one fall and one spring semester family education program. Parents arrive and have at least twenty minutes of informal, social time over coffee and bagels. They are introduced to the topic of the morning to give them a framework for the experience, and then they work in groups with their children. We have run social action education mornings, embedded in Jewish values, created resources to take home for upcoming festivals, and more. With our sixth graders, we have introduced programs where we work with parents only and with their children to help them find deeper meaning in the process of becoming bar or bat mitzvah. Of course, many congregations run programs like these for their families.

But taking the time to explicitly recognize and respond to some of the specific needs and questions of the non-Jewish parent in these Jewish families as part of these programs provides another opportunity to be truly inclusive and to help all of our members feel "at home" in our congregation.

In this chapter I have presented excerpts of narratives gleaned from conversations that I have had with individuals in my own congregation who I believe fit Brenner's definition of the *toshav tzedek*—one who has converged with a Jewish community but not converted to Judaism. Of utmost importance to me as a congregational rabbi is what I can learn about the meaning that the non-Jewish members of Jewish families in our congregations make of their experiences with us. In my own rabbinate, conversations like these have helped to shape my own responses to the needs of all of our members—responses that are still evolving as I become more aware and more sensitized to the opportunities we have to deepen Jewish engagement and practice among our members, as well as some of the relatively simple things I can do to help the non-Jewish members in our midst feel equipped to practice with us, to the degree that they choose.

In Jewish communal conversations we have often discussed our responses to interfaith families as a matter of Jewish continuity. I would invite us, instead, to focus on Judaism as a "public good." Rabbi Brad Hirschfield, explaining this concept, tells us that it is "making all things Jewish more accessible, more meaningful, more useable and more impactful in more ways to more people."[3] Understanding Judaism as "a public good," I see its rich potential to help all my congregants flourish, whether they be Jewish or those of another faith or heritage. The spiritual tool box of Judaism—life-cycle ritual, festival and Shabbat celebration, the practice of mitzvot, and the creation of deeply experienced and authentically felt community connections—is available to enable the spiritual flourishing of all who dwell among us.

NOTES

1. Reeve Robert Brenner, "The Toshav Tzedek," *Out of My Jewish Mind* (blog), February 23, 2017, https://outofmyjewishmind.wordpress.com.
2. Ron Wolfson, *Relational Judaism: Using the Power of Relationships to Transform the Jewish Community* (Woodstock, VT: Jewish Lights, 2013).
3. Maayan Jaffe, "The New Colors of CLAL: Organization Steps Forward to 'Make Jewish a Public Good,'" eJewish Philanthropy, December 1, 2015, http://ejewishphilanthropy.com/the-new-colors-of-clal-organization-steps-forward-to-make-jewish-a-public-good/.

SUGGESTED READING

T. Sasson, et al., *Millennial Children of Intermarriage: Touchpoints and Trajectories of Jewish Engagement* (Waltham, MA: Brandeis University, Cohen Center for Modern Jewish Studies, 2015).

44

MILLENNIALS: BUILDING THE FUTURE OF REFORM JUDAISM

Evan Traylor

In the past, as each new generation of Reform Jews in North America arrived and began to explore Judaism, they innovated and transformed the forms of institutions, organizations, and synagogues of the previous generation to create a Jewish life engaging to their generation. In the twentieth century, Reform Judaism's exploration and eventual acceptance of guitar music in *t'filah*, intermarried families, direct support of the State of Israel, and the LGBTQ community were directly connected to the changing interests and ideals of newer generations. In addition to holding different views of the world, newer generations allowed for a radical examination of the Jewish community and the ways in which it must shift to more effectively engage them and their peers in Jewish life.

Just as each new generation in the twentieth century reinvigorated Reform Jewish life, the millennial generation, less commonly known as generation Y, is the most primed generation to make an impact on the Reform Jewish community in the present and the future. Millennials are offering, and in some cases rightfully demanding, changes in the tenets of Reform Judaism and the Reform Jewish community to more eagerly pursue meaning, purpose, happiness, and success in their lives.

In addition to marrying later, owning homes at lower rates, and being the most educated generation ever, millennials are much more skeptical of institutional religious groups, believe less in an almighty God, and refute the concept of paying to be part of a religious community. Millennials are already making an impact on the Reform Jewish community to make it more diverse, inclusive, accessible, and ultimately successful in engaging the entire Reform Jewish community in the present and sustaining those changes for the future.

In 2013, a now infamous *Time* magazine cover named the millennial generation as the "Me, Me, Me" generation, labeling millennials as "lazy, entitled narcissists who still live with their parents."[1] As a millennial myself, I know that this claim could not be farther from the truth in understanding the millennial generation and our perspective on the world. We are smart, optimistic, determined, and ready to make our communities and world a better place. The characteristics of millennials, and specifically of Jewish millennials presented in this chapter, are trends that are currently shaping the structures within the Reform Jewish community and will continue to change and adapt these communities in the future. While not every trend represents a drastic break from previous generations, millennials have different needs and wants from every aspect of their lives, including families, career, religious beliefs, technology, and their overall perspective on the world. Approximately 95 percent of Jewish millennials are proud to be Jewish; however, many of us lack the adequate opportunities to engage in Jewish life in a way that is meaningful and special.[2]

Through an examination of the characteristics of the millennial generation and the ways in which Jewish millennials interact with Judaism and the Jewish community, I will demonstrate Jewish millennials' incredible ability to challenge the current status quo of the Jewish community and create the necessary changes to make Reform Judaism relevant, meaningful, and special for future generations of Reform Jews in the twenty-first century.

Who are the millennials? If you were to ask a group of ten people to describe the millennial generation in one word, you very well may receive ten different answers in response. The range of answers may include everything from "coddled" and "independent" to "narcissistic" and "world citizens"—and everything in between. From talk show hosts and magazines, to academics and business people, it feels like the millennials are quickly taking over our world. However, for a generation that has been talked about a lot throughout society, it's strange that many people don't know much about us and the way we interact with one another and the world. Before we explore the powerful and sustaining impact of millennials upon the Jewish community, it is necessary to examine the characteristics that make the millennial generation unique.

The basic demographic areas of the millennial generation demonstrate a generation drastically different from previous generations. While researchers are not definitive in their measurements, millennials are usually considered to have been born roughly between 1980 and 2000, making them approximately between the ages of seventeen and thirty-seven. Additionally, as of April 2016, millennials are the largest living generation in the United States; their seventy-five million members even make them bigger than the baby boomers. Millennials are also the most racially diverse generation in American history, with 43 percent of American millennials identifying as something other than exclusively white.[3]

While the demographic information for millennials already differentiates them from previous generations, the characteristics and trends of millennials are the ones that everyone is talking about (usually in a disparaging way). While millennials are the most educated generation ever (determined by percentage of people holding college degrees), two-thirds of them graduate with debt. This has an enormous impact on their optimism and persistence in the job market, often challenging themselves to seize every opportunity for advancement and progress in their careers. Millennials are also digital and technology natives; we either adapted quickly to technology or were born with it in our hands. In terms of relationships, millennials are marrying later, with only 26 percent of millennials ages eighteen to thirty-two being married, compared to 48 percent of baby boomers when they were that age. Regarding those people concerned with religious beliefs, the reports fail to give an accurate picture. It is true that one-third of millennials are not affiliated with any religion; however, 86 percent of us believe in some form of God or spiritual power. These trends are instrumental in understanding the unique and powerful perspective and actions of millennials today.

These demographics indicate that the millennial generation demonstrates the incredible characteristics needed for building the most inclusive, diverse, and thoughtful society in history. Additionally, understanding millennials requires some knowledge of the traumatic and memorable experiences that have ultimately shaped our unique perspectives of the world: the Columbine shooting, President Clinton being impeached, the terrorist attacks of September 11, 2001, the Great Recession, and the shooting at Newtown Elementary School. These experiences have crafted a generation that understands the preciousness of life and, for that, displays an optimism and confidence for making the necessary changes to make our Jewish community and world a better place.

Taking these demographics, characteristics, and trends into account, it is important to now focus specifically on Jewish millennials and how we do and do not interact with the Jewish community in order to explore their impact on Reform Judaism in the present and the future. Since the 2013 Pew Research Center's report *A Portrait of Jewish Americans*, much of the Jewish community has been celebrating, bemoaning, and fretting about Jewish millennials and their unique relationship with Judaism, Israel, and the Jewish community. Utilizing the findings of this Pew Research Center study as well as other sources from Pew, this chapter will explore the ways Jewish millennials understand and impact the Reform Jewish community through the following categories: marriage and families, career and lifestyle, religious beliefs, diversity, Israel, and technology.

The millennial generation has expanded the window of time between adolescence and full adulthood, significantly delaying the period in their life in which we marry and begin families. Only 26 percent of millennials between the ages of eighteen and thirty-two are married, compared to 48 percent of baby boomers during that age range.[4] As the millennial generation expands this time frame and chooses not to engage in the traditional form of involvement in the Jewish community (synagogue membership), Reform congregations have noticed the need to intentionally engage people in their twenties and thirties (an approximate range of millennials). Already, dozens of Reform congregations have created these programs to engage Jewish millennials, and more are excited for the opportunity to engage us in Jewish life and eventually, typically after we marry and begin our families, have us become members of their congregations. These congregations create attractive opportunities for Jewish millennials to connect to a community by holding innovative, meaningful, and fun programs (often outside the physical walls of a synagogue), restructuring their dues models to encourage millennials to join, and allowing for strong relationship building between the participants. The following examination of characteristics and trends among Jewish millennials all contribute to the creation and progression of these communities.

Among Jews marrying since 2000, 58 percent have married a non-Jewish spouse; this trend has seen a steady increase since before 1970, in which only 17 percent of Jews married a non-Jewish spouse. Additionally, while 96 percent of Jews married to a Jewish spouse intend to raise their children Jewish by religion, only 20 percent of Jews married to a non-Jewish spouse intend to do the same.[5] These trends have sparked some streams of Judaism to double-down on the importance of Jews marrying other Jews. However, the jury is in: the time for preaching that Jews should only marry other Jews is not working and must be over. Any community that continues this strategy is demonstrating their complete disregard for the enormous changes in North American Jewish life. All millennials, including non-Jewish spouses, are searching for meaning in their lives, and the Reform Jewish community, through its continued commitment toward full inclusion and empowerment of non-Jewish spouses, can serve as a valuable place of spirituality, learning, and community for millennials. As the opportunity to engage a wider number of non-Jewish spouses grows, the Reform Jewish community must continue adapting its liturgy, marketing language, and programming to ensure it is fully reflective of the people in our environment; anything less stands to alienate an enormous segment of the Jewish millennial population.

As the millennial generation delays marriage and the start of families, we fill this expanded time frame with experiences that fulfill our ambitious perspective on the world, especially for our education and careers. Known for our unwavering optimism and stemming from the coddling attitudes of our parents, millennials are go-getters, constantly striving to do more, see more, and be more in all aspects of our lives. Millennials value and believe in the power of education, and we are on track to be the most educated generation in history as determined by the percentage of people holding college degrees. According to Gallup, 21 percent of millennials say they've changed jobs within the past year, more than three times the number of other generations.[6] Many millennials do not begin jobs with the intention of leaving their workplace; however, if an organization or company does not have opportunities for quick advancement and growth, many millennials are not afraid to turn to other organizations to fulfill their ambitious worldview. An extreme desire for education and career advancement brings up several questions about the ways that millennials interact with the Jewish community: Why would millennials pay dues to a congregation if we are unsure we will be in that city next year? Why would millennials pay dues to a congregation if we are trying to pull ourselves out of student loan debt? Why pay for a Jewish community when we can find community at our work, fitness class, or book club? For those Reform congregations and communities searching to connect with Jewish millennials, put the needs and wants of millennials at the forefront of everything by giving us the tools, support, and space to connect with our peers in fun, exciting, meaningful, and accessible ways. Whether it's a happy hour, Shabbat experience, or networking session with Jewish leaders in various fields, giving us the opportunity to plan for and lead a community is crucial to successfully engaging this generation where we are.

Another important component of understanding Jewish millennials and the ways in which we interact with the Jewish community surrounds religious beliefs (and un-beliefs). Approximately 32 percent of Jewish millennials identify as one of the "nones," people who do not identify with any religion.[7] While this percentage has increased from previous generations, not all nones completely reject Judaism or the Jewish community; in fact, many still claim religious or spiritual beliefs as being important to their lives, and more than two-thirds of all millennials say they believe in God. In terms of religious or spiritual practice, there is not a very significant difference between Jewish millennials and previous generations in terms of celebration of holidays, connecting with Jewish culture more than with religion, remembering the Holocaust, observing Jewish law, and others. The large split between Jewish millennials and previous generations occurs in their involvement with Jewish organizations, in which Jewish millennials fall behind older generations in terms of synagogue membership, Jewish organization membership, and donations to Jewish organizations. Reform communities do not need to stray away from religious perspectives when engaging the millennial generation; however, if Jewish millennials are going to engage in the Jewish community, religious teachings and practices must be observed in a manner that is relevant to the present, pluralistic and diverse, inclusive of people from all backgrounds, and connected to society. Too many of Judaism's traditional practices and concepts—including liturgy depicting an all-knowing God, language that places Jews as the "chosen people," Jewish holidays removed from concepts of social justice, and services lacking spirituality—fail to provide Jewish millennials with the holistic lens that allows for many interpretations of the tenets of Judaism. These trends place Reform Judaism, the branch of Judaism rooted in contemporary interpretation and practice of Judaism and passionate about inclusion, accessibility, and making meaningful Jewish choices, at the forefront of opportunity to engage Jewish millennials in meaningful and relevant Jewish life.

Overall, millennials are the most diverse generation in U.S. history, with approximately 43 percent of millennials identifying as something other than only white. According to studies from Be'chol Lashon, a Jewish diversity organization that advocates for the complete inclusion of Jews of color into the Jewish community, approximately 10 to 20 percent of the Jewish community in the United States identifies as something other than exclusively white.[8] These statistics include Jews who identify as Asian, Native American, Latinx, black, biracial, and multiracial, as well as Mizrachi and Sephardic Jews. At a time in which both marriage between Jews and non-Jews is increasing and the marriage of people of different races and ethnicities in the U.S. population is also increasing, Jewish millennials are bringing diverse backgrounds, skin tones, and cultures into Judaism and the Jewish community. The Jewish community must explore Judaism through the eyes of the multiracial Jew who is a Black Lives Matter activist and loves the Saturday morning liturgy, the Jew who doesn't believe in God but loves the sweetness of a Rosh HaShanah–inspired cocktail, and the feminist Jew who questions the patriarchy of the Torah. As a Jew of color, I know how nerve-racking it can be to walk into a new Jewish space and wonder if the other people in the room will think that I am a legitimate Jew. Just as it is important for people of color to see people who look like them in various fields and institutions, Jews of color must see themselves in the Jewish community and feel confident they will not be alienated or ostracized through their involvement. Jewish millennials, and particularly young Jews of color, have brought more attention to the growing racial diversity of the Jewish community in recent years, and we will continue to shape the beliefs and operations of the Jewish community on this issue for decades to come.

The increase in globalization, ease in travel, and growth of information on different networks has created an environment in which millennials are naturally more connected and attuned to countries around the world. This trend also extends to Jewish millennials and our knowledge and connection, or non-connection, with Israel. Through Taglit-Birthright Israel, a once innovative, now commonplace organization that provides free trips to Israel for Jews between the ages of eighteen and twenty-six, more than five hundred thousand young Jews have traveled to Israel over the last sixteen years. However, while young Jews have gained more access to Israel, a significantly smaller percentage of Jewish millennials believe that caring about Israel is essential to being Jewish.[9] Several reasons could explain this decrease in the importance of Israel among Jewish millennials, including a generational separation from the Holocaust as the origin story of Israel, a frustration and disagreement with political decisions of the Israeli government (especially among an increasingly politically liberal generation), or a lack of understanding about Israel's place in the narrative of the Jewish people. Although not entirely different from previous generations, the diversity of opinions among Jewish millennials on Israel demonstrates the importance of the Reform Movement and Reform congregations in providing diverse and open opportunities to discuss and wrestle with all of the complexities of Israel, including politics, food, religions, environment, the military, history, and everything in between. The accomplishments of Birthright Israel should be celebrated throughout our community. However, it is one thing to send thousands of Jewish millennials to Israel, and it is another to provide them with the nuanced and comprehensive learning that allows us to see Israel as part of being Jewish.

One final trend among the millennial generation that must be explored to understand, connect with, and empower Jewish millennials is the enormous increase in technology and social media. Millennials are known as "technology natives," with much of the generation having grown up with computers, cell phones, the Internet, and social media. In addition to the growth of online search engines that have created an "answer now" culture among millennials, the rise of social media has provided platforms for millennials to constantly express our every thought and feeling to all of our networks of friends, families, and strangers. Through their experiences with and access to social media, millennials have their own personal brand, emphasize their adventures and experiences, and are conscious of how they are portraying themselves to the world. While the obvious implication for Reform congregations and leaders is the necessity of having a social media presence (e.g., Facebook, Twitter, Instagram, Snapchat, LinkedIn), Jewish millennials are also looking for the immediacy and "wow factor" that is the main feature of the technology and social media culture. Over the past ten years, as the world has been introduced to the modern forms of social media platforms, the Jewish community has struggled to keep up in terms of presence and engagement. The millennial generation's insistence on having immediate access to information and our constant search for fun and exciting content to share have challenged the Jewish community to upgrade its communication and programming methods; this shift will have a lasting impact on the ability for Jewish congregations and organizations to connect with a wider audience and move beyond its insider status.

I have seen the passion and commitment Jewish millennials, my peers and friends from summer camp and youth group, are applying to the Jewish community. Whether we are serving as new Jewish professionals, posting articles about Jewish topics or controversies, or creating our own Jewish experiences in our communities, Jewish millennials are seeking meaning, happiness, and community. Unfortunately, too much of our energy either is spent trying to shift and transform the priorities of organizations and synagogues or is spent outside of the organized Jewish sphere completely. While passionate about Judaism and the Jewish community, millennials have not been given the institutions and communities that wholly value our opinion or appreciate our efforts to make Judaism relevant and exciting for our generation. Millennials will continue impacting the trajectory of the Reform Jewish community for decades in the future through our examination of religious texts and communal norms, leadership as the next generation of rabbis, cantors, and educators, innovation to create new structures and organizations, and ultimately our involvement (or non-involvement) in the Reform Jewish community. The millennial generation represents new energy and optimism that will change our Jewish community, society, and world for the better. While it may be hard to let go of the keys, it's time to put us in the driver seat.

NOTES

1. Joel Stein, "Millennials: The Me, Me, Me Generation," *Time*, May 20, 2013, http://time.com/247/millennials-the-me-me-me-generation/.

2. Pew Research Center's Religion & Public Life Project, "Jewish Identity," chapter 3 in *A Portrait of Jewish Americans* (Washington, DC: Pew Research Center, 2013), http://www.pewforum.org/2013/10/01/chapter-3-jewish-identity/.

3. D'vera Cohn and Andrea Caumont, "10 Demographic Trends That Are Shaping the U.S. and the World," Fact Tank, March 31, 2016, http://www.pewresearch.org/fact-tank/2016/03/31/10-demographic-trends-that-are-shaping-the-u-s-and-the-world/.

4. Eileen Patten and Richard Fry, "How Millennials Today Compare with Their Grandparents 50 Years Ago," Fact Tank, March 19, 2015, http://www.pewresearch.org/fact-tank/2015/03/19/how-millennials-compare-with-their-grandparents/#!1.

5. Pew Research Center's Religion & Public Life Project, "Intermarriage and Other Demographics," chapter 2 in *A Portrait of Jewish Americans* (Washington, DC: Pew Research Center, 2013), http://www.pewforum.org/2013/10/01/chapter-2-intermarriage-and-other-demographics/.

6. Amy Adkins, "Millennials: The Job-Hopping Generation," Gallup Business Journal, May 12, 2016, http://www.gallup.com/businessjournal/191459/millennials-job-hopping-generation.aspx.

7. Pew Research Center's Religion & Public Life Project, "Overview," in *A Portrait of Jewish Americans* (Washington, DC: Pew Research Center, 2013), http://www.pewforum.org/2013/10/01/jewish-american-beliefs-attitudes-culture-survey/.

8. "Counting Jews of Color in the United States," Be'chol Lashon, http://www.bechollashon.org/population/north_america/na_color.php.

9. Pew Research Center's Religion & Public Life Project, "Connection with and Attitudes toward Israel," chapter 5 in *A Portrait of Jewish Americans* (Washington, DC: Pew Research Center, 2013). http://www.pewforum.org/2013/10/01/chapter-5-connection-with-and-attitudes-towards-israel/.

45

CREATING A LIFE OF MEANING BY CARING FOR OTHERS

Rabbi Neal Gold

The Rabbanit Bracha Kapach (1922–2013), recipient of the Israel Prize in 1999, was a giant of the human spirit. Her essence was providing for people in need and caring for those who were hurting, and she was one of my primary teachers in the art of Jewish giving.

She lived in the heart of Jerusalem, in the neighborhood appropriately called Shaarei Chesed (Gates of Loving-Kindness). To many people, she was known as the Wedding Dress Woman. Jews from around the world would bring her old wedding dresses, which she would repair, embroider, and deliver to poor brides. The dresses were just the tip of the iceberg; in fact, she would create entire weddings for brides and grooms who had nothing at all. She would provide the dress, the food, the musicians, and sometimes even the guests; after all, every daughter of Israel deserved a wedding of dignity and joy. But the iceberg was a lot bigger than that. Every year, she would coordinate the distribution of thousands of Passover food packages to people who otherwise wouldn't have been able to celebrate the Festival of Freedom. When she saw the number of poor children hanging out on the streets of Jerusalem in the summer, she created a summer camp for hundreds of them, a camp that did (and still does) everything that summer camps should do: sports, activities, hiking adventures, trips to the beach and to water parks. In other words, she looked carefully and sensitively at the great needs all around her—and then she acted to repair the brokenness that she observed. Small in stature, she created towering networks of caring and compassion.[1]

Most enlightening was the experience of simply sitting in her living room for a few hours. The conversation rarely would get far: telephone calls or knocks at the door provided a perpetual stream of interruptions. People with nowhere else to go were coming for her support—a perpetual stream of human beings living on the economic periphery of the Holy City, looking for assistance to get through the week. Other interruptions would be visitors from around the world bringing her money to distribute, just to be part of the pure and egoless network of caring that she created.

In 1993 I had the privilege not only to volunteer with the Passover food distribution, but also to spend a day with the Rabbanit making deliveries to homebound people all around Jerusalem. I watched her in action, the distillation of Jewish teachings about kindness and human dignity. She knew everyone by name. Before we would enter an aluminum-roofed home in Nachlaot, she would take me by the arm and, with tears in her eyes, say, "This is a very sad story . . ." It seemed like she personally knew every sorrowful, broken, and hurting soul in the city.

The Rabbanit Kapach, my hero, was the living exemplar of the fundamental Jewish values of *tzedakah* and *g'milut chasadim*. My goal in describing her is not that we should copy her, but that we should be inspired by her story to fix our own corners of the world.

Jewish tradition prescribes two distinct but related categories of mitzvot for doing the work of justice and kindness. *Tzedakah* refers to giving money away for the purpose of world repair. *G'milut chasadim* is an umbrella of mitzvot that involve giving time and energy—acts of thoughtful presence—in order to improve the world and care for others. Examples of *g'milut chasadim* include honoring parents, visiting sick people, caring for a dead body with dignity and honor, comforting mourners, raising orphans, dignifying elders, providing decent clothes for people without any, feeding hungry people, and many similar deeds.

In his great code of Jewish law, Maimonides describes the mitzvah of *tzedakah* this way:

> When a poor person comes asking, one should give to him according to what he lacks. And if the giver does not have the ability to do that, he should give what he is able.
>
> How much? Up to one-fifth of his resources: this is considered the mitzvah par excellence. One-tenth of his resources: this is considered average. Less than that is stingy [*ayin raah*].
>
> A person should never give less than a third of a shekel a year. One who gives less than this has not fulfilled the mitzvah.
>
> Even a poor person—who is sustained by *tzedakah*—is required to give *tzedakah* to another person.[2]

We can make a number of observations from this passage. First: the primary task of *tzedakah* is to fix undignified, even life-threatening, situations. The law reasonably understands that that is not always possible; still, the first principle of *tzedakah* is to give to the poor person "according to what he lacks." Second: for most of us, a 10 to 20 percent range of our income is expected to go to *tzedakah*. One who gives less than that is considered stingy—but we might interpret the phrase *ayin raah* to mean that the potential giver "just doesn't see." What doesn't she see? The great needs all around us, the potential to make the difference, the resources at hand . . . these are all symptoms of mitzvah myopia. Finally, the law states that even the poorest of the poor is required to give *tzedakah*. There are a variety of explanations for this unexpected statement. Perhaps it is a matter of belonging to the Jewish community: if we believe that giving is a fundamentally Jewish act, how can we deprive a person of essential Jewishness by saying, "You're too poor to help somebody else"? Or perhaps it is about being human: being able to help another person is an assertion of human worth and self-dignity.

Tzedakah entails money. It does not mean "giving of one's time," and it is not a synonym for "love." (It also does not mean "charity," and that is why teachers about *tzedakah* should shun the word. The etymology of "charity" is from the Latin root *caritas*, which entails compassion, mercy, and affection—often with Christian overtones. While these traits are also Jewish values, they are more appropriately linked with the definition of *chesed*—see below.) Of course *tzedakah* should be given with intention and kindness, but even devoid of "purest motivations," through the act of giving one still fulfills the commandment. In other words, all the love and compassionate feelings in the world will not build a cancer hospital, or rebuild a devastated village after an earthquake, or provide ten thousand anti-malarial nets to people in Africa. It takes money to accomplish these things.

It is no virtue in Judaism to impoverish ourselves; *tzedakah* is supposed to alleviate and transcend poverty. Therefore, halachah prescribes that 10 to 20 percent of a person's income rightfully belongs to *tzedakah*. Maimonides calls the 20 percent cap the "mitzvah par excellence." However, Jewish law waives this upper limit for people who are wealthy, for whom there is no risk of sinking into poverty by giving away more than 20 percent.

Money, therefore, is enormously important—but we should not exaggerate its power. Money is not love. It cannot hold the hand of a patient in the hospital, or provide comfort to a family sitting shivah, or provide companionship to a child who is alone. Judaism does not let off the hook anyone who merely says, "I wrote my check," when genuine human contact is what the situation demands. That is the realm of *g'milut chasadim* (acts of *chesed*/loving-kindness), which incorporates a wide rubric of Jewish acts, including visiting sick people, providing dignified burials for the dead, comforting mourners, honoring elders, providing dignified weddings for brides (the Rabbanit Kapach's specialty!), honoring parents, and many similar acts of compassion, kindness, and love.

Tzedakah and *g'milut chasadim* are, therefore, two different but intertwined types of Jewish action, and a Jew is expected to observe each of them. No one is exempt from doing acts of *chesed* by saying, "I gave at the office"; and, likewise, no one is exempt from giving *tzedakah* by saying, "I don't need to give money; I volunteer my time instead." They are two distinct items in the palette of 613 mitzvot. With this in mind, the Talmud discusses the relative strengths of giving with money (*tzedakah*) and giving with time and energy (*g'milut chasadim*):

Our Rabbis taught:

In three ways *g'milut chasadim* is superior to *tzedakah*:

Tzedakah can only be done with one's money, but *g'milut chasadim* can be done with one's person and with one's money;

Tzedakah can only be given to poor people, but *g'milut chasadim* can be done for both rich and poor people;

Tzedakah can only be given to the living, but *g'milut chasadim* can be done for both the living and the dead. (Babylonian Talmud, *Sukkah* 49b)

The Sages recognized that money is a powerful tool for improving the world in ways that boundless good intentions cannot. On the other hand, certain acts of *chesed* can impact the lives of others in ways that money never will. Therefore, both *tzedakah* and *g'milut chasadim* are parts of a spiritual regimen that puts our highest values into action.

Tzedakah should be an especially important category of study for Reform Jews, because the distribution of money (for most of us, a finite sum) reveals in a tangible way our most cherished values. In other words, paying lip service to certain beliefs and values is easy, but a ledger of a person's giving may tell a different story. The way we give *tzedakah* raises important questions: Am I living the values that I purport to hold? How have I determined my giving priorities? Which of my principles have I truly acted out? In no other realm of life can we so clearly measure whether our actions are in accordance with the values we purport to hold.

Since each of us has a finite sum of money to give away, we have to make hard decisions about which values are most important to us. Should our money go to disabled children, or to protect the environment, or to support Jewish education, or to house homeless people? Should we give locally, nationally, or overseas? Should we support specifically Jewish organizations or universal ones? What about political and social justice causes—are they more or less important than direct service to people in need? These are religious questions, which explicitly get played out in the mitzvah of *tzedakah*.[3]

For this reason, a healthy, ritualized *tzedakah* practice is vitally important for parents and for Hebrew schools. Parents are encouraged to collect *tzedakah* money with their children at ritualized times (e.g., at the beginning and end of Shabbat and holidays; to celebrate good news or milestones; to mark sad news or *yahrzeits*) and also at ad hoc times ("I found money in my pocket that I had forgotten about"; "I just feel like doing something good"). Most importantly, parents should involve their children in their *tzedakah*-distribution decisions, explaining, "This is a very important value to our family, and that is why we have chosen to support this *tzedakah* project." Similarly, Hebrew schools are encouraged not only to collect *tzedakah* from students, but also to invite students to help determine how the money should be distributed. (Surely I'm not the only child of the 1970s and '80s who remembers bringing Keren Ami money to Hebrew school. Only we never knew exactly where that money went—we joked that there was an old lady named Karen Amy in Israel to whom we were sending all that cash!)

Bar/bat mitzvah students have a special opportunity with the mitzvah of *tzedakah*. For many young people, bar/bat mitzvah is the first time that they will receive gifts of cash—often in substantial amounts. What happens to all that money? Often it gets put into savings, and some of it gets allotted for a special gift or set aside for a teenage trip to Israel. Yet all bar/bat mitzvah students should know that it is their right and privilege to take 10 to 20 percent of this money and use it for the purpose of doing good. For many, this is the first encounter with the real power of *tzedakah* money to make an impact on the world. It can be the moment of first awareness that with wealth comes an obligation to others—and that deep personal meaning can come from acting on this responsibility.

Another important inroad in Reform Jewish life is the formation of *tzedakah* collectives among friends, synagogues, and wider Jewish communities. Money, of course, is more powerful when it is pooled together from like-minded people. As with so many other contemporary forms of *tzedakah* and *g'milut chasadim*, the idea of grassroots *tzedakah* collectives was pioneered by the American Jewish educator Danny Siegel. His Ziv Tzedakah Fund (which closed in 2008, after giving away nearly $14 million over twenty-seven years) demonstrated how directed sums of money could achieve maximum impact. Indeed, a constant refrain in his teachings is that "there is no such thing as a small amount of *tzedakah*." Ziv's specialty was seeking out "Mitzvah Heroes" who performed profound acts of world repair, often in startlingly innovative ways, and Ziv's imprimatur on a *tzedakah* project was a guarantee of financial transparency and prudent use of the giver's money. Other *tzedakah* collectives have been directly inspired by Ziv's model of grassroots giving with minimal overhead, such as Kavod Tzedakah Collective (Omaha, Nebraska), the Good People Fund (Millburn, New Jersey), and Yad Chessed (Boston). Additional local *tzedakah* collectives would be a blessing to the Jewish community and the world. The power of joining with others to do good is invigorating; it infuses relationships with a sense of purpose and meaning. Reform Jewish communities—which strive to exemplify societies based on bedrock Jewish principles of justice, decency, and peace—should follow these examples of how groups of people can give Jewishly, together.

Ultimately, doing acts of *tzedakah* and *g'milut chasadim* is much more than "social action" or "philanthropy," which are bloodless and secular concepts. Instead, *tzedakah* and *g'milut chasadim* are gutsy, religious acts that channel godliness into the world:

> One who is generous to a poor person makes a loan to God; God will repay him his due (Proverbs 19:17).
> God considers this as if a person has dealt righteously with God directly; "God will repay him his due"—both in this world and in the world-to-come.
> Another interpretation: God says, "Lend me some *tzedakah* in this world, and I will repay you in the world-to-come."[4]

This midrash is audacious in the classic Rabbinic way: by giving *tzedakah* to a poor person, it is as if a person is giving God a loan. After all, goes this line of thought, God eventually would have saved the person from his suffering, but the *tzedakah*-giver got there first, pinch-hitting for God, so to speak! It is a bold description of the divine-human partnership that is needed to bring a fulfilled world into existence.

Does this mean that through the act of giving, people automatically will infuse their lives with meaning? Not necessarily. But Judaism does suggest that the covenantal relationship between God and people is expressed in this world by human kindness. If you love God, then you have to demonstrate love toward God's only image in the world—namely, other human beings.

Here is a dramatic illustration of this principle. Psalm 17:15 reads, "I, through *tzedek*, will look upon Your face." In the Talmud, Rabbi Elazar cites this verse as his justification for giving coins to a poor person before commencing his daily prayers. Thereafter the tradition arose to place a *tzedakah* box at the entrance to a synagogue's sanctuary, so that worshipers can give *tzedakah* before praying. And so, the tradition of giving at the entrance to the synagogue was established.

According to this passage, our acts of love and generosity toward others arouse God's love and generosity toward us, and qualify us, as it were, to step into God's presence. *Tzedakah* and *g'milut chasadim* make us partners with God, by bringing *sh'leimut*—wholeness—to people who remain hungry, hurting, or broken.

None of us needs to be a *tzadeket*—one of the truly righteous—on the level of the Rabbanit Kapach to discover the power of meaning-through-giving in our lives. But it is easy to observe that the most meaningful lives are often lived by those who regularly give to others. The pursuit of this ideal elevates human beings from the animal kingdom to something more, something "a little less than divine" (Psalm 8:6).

NOTES

1. Her biography is told in a beautiful Hebrew volume, *V'zot HaBracha*, Yael Shai (Jerusalem: *Ha-agudah l'tipuach chevrah v'tarbut*, 2005), and by Danny Siegel in his *Munbaz II and Other Mitzvah Heroes* (Pittsboro, North Carolina: Town House Press, 1988).

2. Maimonides, *Mishneh Torah, Hilchot Matanot Aniyim* 7:5.

3. Halachic sources wrestle with these questions and make certain priorities: one's household, for instance, takes precedence over the local community, and the local community takes precedence over far-off communities. However, there are many subtleties and nuances. In English, a fine anthology of Jewish legal sources on how to prioritize Tzedakah is Cyril Domb, ed., *Maaser Kesafim* (Spring Valley, NY/ Jerusalem, Israel: Feldheim Publishers, 1992). Less legalistic and more accessible is Danny Siegel, Giving Your Money Away: *How Much, How to, Why, Where and to Whom* (Pittsboro, North Carolina: Town House Press, 2006).

4. *Midrash Mishlei*, Chapter 19.

46

SACRED AGING

RABBI RICHARD F. ADDRESS, DMIN

The generation of baby boomers, that cohort born from the end of World War II through the beginning of the 1960s, has been one of the most studied population cohorts in American history. Living as they did through the explosion of suburbia, the political and social revolutions of the 1960s and 1970s, this generation, all of whom are over fifty years of age, is now rushing headlong into their own aging. A theme of this generation has been one of change, so it is no wonder that the boomers have had an impact on the Jewish community in terms of redefining ritual and affiliation patterns. While it is folly to try and put this "generation" into a neat, one-size-fits-all description, we can identify certain trends and characteristics of the Jewish element of this cohort.

Let me suggest that a way to conceptualize this emerging cohort is to see us as change agents—seekers, really, of meaning. The Hebrew letters *bet-kuf-shin* form the root of the word *m'vakshim*, or seekers. Have a serious conversation with our generation and you will almost always find that we are more aware of the passing of time, more aware of our own mortality, and thus increasingly concerned that we are searching for a means through which to live a life that has meaning—meaning not only for us, but for those who will remain after we die.

Professor Steven M. Cohen wrote of this emerging change within our community in a recent study:

> But not only are Jews (as others) living longer, they are living in an age of meaning-seeking, with the interest and wherewithal to make living a life of meaning an ultimate and reasonably obtainable objective for any point in their lives. As such, this aging yet largely healthy generation of American Jews poses a challenge (and opportunity) to a society and community that is yet unprepared for the totally new policy and planning possibilities that loom in the near future.[1]

This is, I believe, a major thrust of Jewish boomers. This is a generation that is seeking meaning, a search manifest through the blessing of longevity, which has raised the spiritual question of our own aging: what do I do with the time I have remaining?

For the most part, Jewish older adults have achieved a certain economic stability and security of station. As the first wave of boomers now reaches their seventies, issues associated with finding their own sense of meaning and purpose begin to emerge. Perhaps it is the realization of our own mortality or the awareness that we have seen friends and family deal with illness and death. Or perhaps it is the questions we ask: Who is that face we see in the mirror? Where has the time gone? And behind all of this is that basic spiritual question: what shall I do with the time I have left? This gift of time has allowed many to recalculate the focus on material issues. This recalculation of life's priorities was echoed by a contemporary scholar who noted that "people who are trying to develop themselves and find meaning in their lives are not engaging in secular pursuits; they are involved in spiritual quests."[2]

This generation also has begun to distance themselves from congregational life. Few congregations have a concentrated program of inreach to deal with the real-life issues that face this generation—new life stages and concerns that previously were rarely a part of the conversation. Now, this generation expects to live well into their nineties and, God willing, perhaps beyond. New life stages have emerged, and challenges—physical, fiscal, psycho-spiritual, and familial—find us looking to see how our faith and faith community can respond in meaningful ways. Too often we are met with communities that have yet to engage our issues from the perspective of Jewish texts and tradition. Issues such as caregiving, end-of-life issues, and loss demand responses that both engage and support this generation. As we confront so many new and challenging life changes, again, we seek meaningful answers to the spiritual question that underlies all of this: what shall I do with the time I am given?

Can our tradition provide a foundation of faith upon which to create a view of what may be called "sacred aging"? Let me suggest that there are several texts that can initiate that foundation. It is in Genesis 3:9 that we meet God's first question to us: *Ayekah*, "Where are you?" This is the question we spend our life trying to answer. It is not asking where we are physically, but rather spiritually, emotionally, and psychologically. It is a basic question because it reminds us that we are mortal, and this reality of our own mortality becomes slowly present in greater terms as we age. This *ayekah* introduces us to the questions of existence that are at the heart of our own individual search for meaning: why was I born, why must I die, and for what purpose am I alive? As we grow older, these questions become of greater importance as we become more aware of the scarcity of time. That horizon we looked out on when we were younger seemed endless. Now, we know that there is a finite limit to that horizon, and thus we begin to reevaluate how we allocate that gift of time.

Our second text, Genesis 37:15, emerges from the beginning of the Joseph cycle. Jacob instructs Joseph to go and find where his brothers are tending the flocks. Joseph sets out in his brightly colored coat and, by chance, meets a man (*ish*). This *ish* asks simply, *Mah t'vakeish?* This *ish*, who vanishes from the story after this brief encounter, does not ask, "Where are you going?" but "What are you seeking?" We are called in Genesis 3:9 to answer *ayekah*—where are we?—and now, by this *ish*, to answer what is it that we are seeking in the life before us? This powerful simple question is a message for us. What do we seek for our life? What changes do we desire? Look around at so many of the people we know who, at a certain age, transitioned into a new life, a new identity, often saying that in the time they have left they wish to do what they always wanted. Yes, there are "wild cards" that can impact our desire to follow our passion. The challenges of money and health are always present. Yet, Judaism, I suggest, gives us the permission, even the challenge, to have our own *lech l'cha* moment—to go forth into life without fear to seek our own passion in life. It may be risky, it may mean change, but we are free to answer, each in our own way, that question of *mah t'vakeish*?

Where are we in life? What do we seek? These questions lead us to a third text: Deuteronomy 30:19. This famous text reminds us of the eternal possibility of finding meaning in our life, and part of that process is understanding that we will have choices throughout our life and that we are told: *Uvacharta bachayim*, "Choose life!" Why is this so meaningful? In our desire to answer *ayekah*, we seek a sense of meaning and purpose, and in doing so, we need or are forced to make choices. Thus what we choose does determine the type of person we become. As we look forward in our life, the choices we need to make become more personal and, at times, more impactful to family. That is why the second part of the verse, "if you and your offspring would live," is so important, for we are bidden to make choices for life so that those who come after us may find blessing.

Our choices have an impact on the future. These choices that speak to the value of life remind us that as we seek to answer where we are and where we wish to be, we are part of something beyond our own self. We become aware of that as we age, and that is how we acquire a sense of wisdom. As we reflect on our life experience, we can gain the wisdom of knowing that what really counts in life is not the material, but the spiritual; not possessions, but relationships; not the corporate, but the caring. It is this realization that has given rise in so many congregations to a newfound understanding of the importance of legacy. What and how we choose can serve as a role model to those of our family who will survive us so we can come to understand that part of what we seek is the ability to create moments of meaning that will allow parts of us to be taken into our loved one's future, and in doing so, we transcend the now.

God's call "Where are you?"; that man's question "What do you seek?"; the charge of Moses to "choose life"—each are texts that can provide us with a foundation upon which to embrace the sacred as we grow and scan that ever-changing horizon that is our future.

NOTES

1. Steven M. Cohen, foreword to *Baby Boomers, Public Service and Minority Communities: A Case Study of the Jewish Community in the United States*, by David M. Elcott (New York: Research Center for Leadership in Action and Berman Jewish Policy Archive, NYU Robert G. Wagner Graduate School, 2010), 2.

2. Kenneth Pargament, *Spiritually Integrated Psychotherapy* (New York: Guilford, 2007), 41.

Part Six

DIGNITY OF THE OTHER

One of the most important insights of religion is that we must regard all relationships as sacred. Reform Judaism seeks to integrate this theology into every aspect of daily living. The essays in this section challenge us to look at this in new and expansive ways.

William Berkson, PhD, opens the book's final section with "Sacred Relationships," drawing on the Jewish wisdom tradition to explain how to bring God into personal relationships and tap those personal relationships to expand our capacity to experience religious insight.

In "Mussar and the Development of Spiritual Practices," Alan Morinis, DPhil, and Rabbi Barry Block discuss how Mussar, Jewish ethical teachings, can be character-strengthening.

Rabbi Jonah Dov Pesner and Rabbi David A. Saperstein write about the centrality of social justice in Reform Judaism. This is a mandate they themselves have lived as, respectively, the current director and the immediate past director of Washington DC's Religious Action Center of Reform Judaism, the social justice advocacy arm of the Reform Movement.

In "Integrating Our Stories: LGBTQ Folks in the Jewish Community," Rabbi Nikki Lyn DeBlosi, PhD, combines a personal narrative of her own spiritual autobiography with a discussion of Jewish law and thought as these can be brought to bear on LGBTQ+ matters.

In "Jews and Race," Rabbi Rachel S. Mikva, PhD, points out that although the civil rights movement has now achieved most of its basic aims, race is a construct that still confronts us. She explains how given texts in the Torah help us understand the issue, providing some provocative interpretations of those texts.

In "A Reform Jewish Response to Poverty," Rabbi Amy Schwartzman admits that responding to others' needs can be a daunting task but argues that it is of critical importance to aim high and work toward ending poverty.

Rabbi Shira Stern, DMin, BCC, in "Tending to the Sick," offers four precepts to create a spiritual framework for performing *bikur cholim*, "visiting the sick." This specific obligation reflects our religious commitment to comfort others in times of trouble.

Like Abraham, who opened his tent on all four sides to welcome guests, we too have an obligation to provide for others. In "Reform Judaism's Healing Tent," Rabbi Pearl Barlev, MAHL, BCC, tells the stories of a number of people who needed healing and explains how a religious response offered them comfort and peace.

Rabbi Lance J. Sussman, PhD, in "The Mission of Israel among Humanity," focuses on the religious injunction that Jews are obliged to serve as a "light unto the nations." This obligation to provide such a model is based on ethical monotheism, the belief that our ethical system grows out of our commitment to the one true God.

Rabbi Eric H. Yoffie concludes our collection with "The Importance of Reform Judaism," predicting that liberal religious groups will survive and even thrive. Yoffie writes passionately about the "middle way" of the Reform temple, emphasizing that Reform Judaism is "messy but spiritually serious," rooted in Torah but sensitive to changing cultural norms. Yoffie brings our volume to a close on an optimistic note, concluding that Reform Judaism's message is relevant right now for those seeking a synthesis of tradition and change.

47

SACRED RELATIONSHIPS

WILLIAM BERKSON, PHD

The usual critique of Reform by more traditional Jews is that it is Judaism "lite," a way for Jews to connect socially with their Jewish roots without ever being serious about religion. On the other side, atheists of Jewish heritage criticize Reform as not having the courage to follow its commitment to rationality and science to its logical conclusion. However, understood in depth, Reform Jewish piety is both more intellectually robust than the views of its traditionalist critics and more profound and life-enhancing than the shallow scientism of its atheist critics.

Reform piety is most obviously on display in life-cycle ceremonies, where Reform Jews pray with complete sincerity. Both the children and the families celebrating at a bar or bat mitzvah religious service are filled with emotion. The bar or bat mitzvah child feels that something momentous is happening. The families are flooded with memory and hope. Parents and grandparents remember their own *b'nei mitzvah* ceremonies, what happened before and since, and their own parents. And these emotions are often heightened by the treasured memory of a grandparent, now passed away, with whom the child grew up. At the bimah stand the memories of past generations and all the hopes for the generation now standing before the Torah for the first time. The mysteries of life and death, the cycle of generations, all are present to the worshipers.

Now a skeptic might argue that the emotion involved in life-cycle ceremonies is just love, and nothing specifically religious. Of course love is involved, but also more. To confirm the presence of specifically religious feelings, we need to understand them.

We human beings live not simply in response to what we are experiencing in the moment, but in a world of meaning, and this meaning is defined by our memories of the past and our imagination of what might yet come to pass. The way our lives are given meaning by our personal narratives can be seen in an old Yiddish saying: "When the father helps the son, both smile; when the son has to help the father, both cry." The actions of the father helping the son and the son the father may be the same. The big difference is in the stories that they both understand: the anticipation of the strength and joy that are to come for the son, in one case, and the concern about failing health and eventual death of the father, in the other. Meaning is constructed through personal narratives that go beyond the immediate place and time.[1]

Religious feelings are about the ultimate context of our lives, in particular our sense of what is most important in life. This ultimate context is of eternity, of the ultimate story that goes beyond all our individual lives. Science is limited in its power to tell us the key features of this ultimate context. Scientific explanations must be in words, in coherent sentences or equations. The paradigm of a scientific theory used to explain our world is Newton's famous law of motion: "$F = ma$"—force equals the product of mass and acceleration. This equation relates four different variables: force, mass, location in space, and time. Now we can always ask: Why is there time, why space, why mass, why force? And the question about time, in particular, raises issues of purpose in the universe. Science is inherently limited in answering these questions because any statement from which we can deduce diversity in the world must itself have many variables. And so we can always again ask "Why?" of these many variables. As a result, it is unlikely that science can ever answer ultimate questions of purpose and value in the universe.

The ultimate questions must, then, be a matter of faith. And because we are creatures guided by stories and meaning, we can't avoid the choice of what ends to value—of what to put our faith in. These choices of what to value are, as William James explained,[2] both unavoidable choices and ones where we don't have scientific evidence on which to base our judgments.

Ethics and Spirituality. The most important source of religious feelings today is loving relationships. If the love between parent and child is not sacred, then nothing is. In loving relationships, we sense that we are part of something larger than ourselves and to which something larger in the universe is giving a profound "yes." This is what Martin Buber recognized in identifying the intimacy of "I-Thou" relationships as our portal to experiencing the eternal Thou, God.

This feeling of ultimate value, of sacredness, is a matter of direct experience. It is not dependent on the traditional view of God as a personality who intervenes in the world to reward and punish, in this life or an afterlife. Nor are these religious feelings dependent on viewing the text of the *Tanach* as free of human error or its understanding of God as perfect. The independence of these religious feelings from the traditional beliefs is a necessity for Reform Jews, as many reject the traditional belief that God actively intervenes to reward and punish individuals.

Is it possible that our feeling of the transcendent value of loving relationships is just a functionally useful emotion, a result of evolution through random variation and the survival of the fittest—reflecting nothing transcendent? Yes, it is possible, but it is also possible that our feelings of the presence of Oneness also reflect reality, so that there is room for faith.

To understand the relationship of science and faith, we need to distinguish between a program of research inspired by a worldview that tries to answer ultimate questions and empirically testable scientific theories that may have been inspired by those worldviews. In evolutionary theory, the idea that evolution is the result of a random process, with no purpose in the universe, has been a worldview or untestable "metaphysics," which some researchers have used to guide research. These researchers have created testable theories of evolution involving random variation, and their success makes it clear that randomness plays some important role in evolution. But that does not mean that randomness is the whole story or that the metaphysics of a purposeless universe is either scientific or correct. We humans have purposes and long-term goals, and alternative explanations that do not assume pure randomness may be true. For example, the laws of nature may be structured so that evolution is possible or inevitable. Was there purpose behind the way the laws of nature are structured? Such ultimate questions are not decided on by current scientific theory alone, and more importantly can never be, because of the limitations of scientific explanation. Science constrains what form of faith is plausible but never removes the need for it.

The ultimate grounding of our experience of the sacred in loving relationships will ever remain shrouded in mystery. Our faith is ultimately a matter of the attitude we take to these ultimate mysteries. Einstein said:

> The most beautiful experience we can have is the feeling of the mysterious. It is the fundamental emotion which stands at the cradle of true art and true science. Whoever does not know it and can no longer wonder, no longer marvel, is as good as dead, and his eyes are dimmed. . . . A knowledge of the existence of something we cannot penetrate, our perceptions of the profoundest reason and the most radiant beauty, which only in their most primitive forms are accessible to our minds—it is this knowledge and this emotion that constitute true religiosity; in this sense, and this alone, I am a deeply religious man.[3]

Einstein, I think, identified the viable core of religious feelings that can survive a modern scientific sensibility: our awe and gratitude toward the mysterious causes of being. However, Einstein's own faith was unusual in that it was focused on feelings of awe of inanimate nature, rather than on the sacredness of intimate human relationships. As a result, he missed the importance of religious ethics, until later in life, when he was confronted by the horrors of the Nazi regime.[4]

The link between spirituality and moral conduct is a sense of the oneness of God and of our connectedness to the One. Our feeling that we are part of something greater, transcending my own life, and owe something to it is the key issue. Whether we believe that God is immanent or transcendent, or both, is not of the essence. What is critical is that we feel a sense of obligation beyond our own lives, which transcends "me, now," and that we set priorities for action accordingly. Thus, ethical conduct and religious feelings support one another.

The traditional sense of the Presence of Oneness in Judaism is not a full-blown mysticism in which the One is the only reality. In that kind of mysticism, our "selves" and the diverse and changing world of our conscious experience are illusions, unreal. To strongly support ethical conduct, our religious sensibility needs a sense both of the reality of the One and of the reality and value of individual selves, through time. Only with this dual sense of the reality of our world and of the transcendent oneness are our actions consequential and make a difference beyond our lives.

Ethics is in fact central to Jewish spirituality, because only when we act ethically do we lift our intimate relationships to the point that we experience their holiness. Ethical conduct and good character are the best way to engender deep trust, and trust promotes cooperation and intimacy. Trust has the capacity to free us from worry about the future of the relationship and enables us to savor, in the moment, the holiness of intimacy and love, including in Shabbat ceremonies. This experience of the sacred happens not only in marital relationships, but also in love between parents and children and for friends. Further, this appreciation of the sacredness in relationships can be transmitted most effectively to the next generation with the validation of a religious community—a religious community that explicitly states the values and supports and celebrates them in communal rituals. These same qualities can also lift the dignity of our work relationships and have us feel whole about our efforts. Unethical conduct, by contrast, sows mistrust, division, and eventually strife and violence. And relationships that are full of suspicion and conflict are not sacred and don't feel like a blessing.

Further, we directly experience moral values as sacred. This is something that even the great anti-religious English philosopher Bertrand Russell in effect conceded. His opponents argued that moral judgments are purely subjective, so the claim "that's wrong" actually has the same content as "I don't like it"; the only difference is verbiage that illegitimately tries to move the other person to your viewpoint. Russell's philosophy would not allow him to appeal to religious feelings to answer his opponents. However, being exceptionally honest, he admitted, "I cannot see how to refute the arguments for the subjectivity of ethical values, but I find myself incapable of believing that all that is wrong with wanton cruelty is that I don't like it."[5] And even though there is a great deal of variation throughout history on what exactly is kind or just, these values are common to all cultures, pointing to a deeper source. Just as we experience loving relationships as sacred, so too do we experience ethical conduct.

The Treasure of Jewish Spiritual Ethics. Judaism is, of course, not the only great religion to meld ethics and religiosity. However, it was the first, and still is the ethical tradition with the deepest insights. The Sages of the Talmud, in particular, developed Jewish ethics into the most powerful tool yet to promote cooperative and loving relationships. This power of Jewish values when lived is something that most Reform Jews sense from growing up in a Jewish family. However, the distinctive strength of Jewish spiritual ethics is not widely and well understood by Reform Jews. For while Reform Judaism has, to its great credit, emphasized the pursuit of social justice, it has relatively neglected the treasury of personal ethical guidelines that the Talmudic Sages developed.

The era from the founding Reform Pittsburgh Platform (1885) to after World War II was one of widespread anti-Semitism and little intermarriage, so the main concerns were communal. However, by the late 1960s, the challenges facing Jews in America had changed markedly. Concern about anti-Semitism was no longer a top priority, and many Jews intermarried. There was instead a new challenge. The increased security in the social position of Jews was paired with a reduced emotional security in modern work, marriage, and family. As a result, Jews began to look to organized religion less for communal defense and more for emotional and spiritual strength for themselves and their families. A deeper understanding of the Sages' guidelines for living would enable us better to put those guidelines into practice and so better lift our relationships to the sacred.

The foundation of the unique ethical approach of the Jewish Sages is Hillel's three questions: "If I am not for myself, who is for me? And being for myself, what am I? And if not now, when?" (*Pirkei Avot* 1:14). The first question legitimates pursuit of individual interest; the second appeals to obligations to others; the third anchors us in real time, with its risks and uncertainties. Hillel put these three as questions, I believe, because he intended them to be taken not only rhetorically, but also as questions actually to be answered at critical points in our lives. "Who is for me?" is a question about who I am in committed relationships with and who I can count on. The question "What am I?" looks to my roles in relationships. What are my obligations as a husband, father, co-worker? What specifically do I owe, and what do others owe me? As I seek both to serve my obligations in my roles and to enjoy life, answering "If not now, when?" reminds me to plan, to take into account the consequences of my actions, and to see which trade-offs between long and short term, self and others, are both most ethical and most desirable to me. This effort at answering the three questions is always a creative problem-solving process, guided by Jewish values, to find the best thing to do that serves both self and others, the present and the future.[6] The goal of balancing the interests of the individual and society, which is embedded in the whole tradition, is unique to Judaism.

A second key feature of Jewish wisdom is the system the Sages developed for growing and adapting the guidelines to meet new challenges. Embracing Socrates's idea that argument is a pathway to the truth, they established a critical tradition for developing and evaluating principles of both personal conduct and law. The key principle in creating and sustaining a critical tradition is "Every controversy for the sake of heaven will in the end be preserved" (*Pirkei Avot* 5:20).[7] True to this principle, the Talmud records debates and minority opinions, so that future generations can take up the ideas and perhaps learn from some insights that were missed by the majority. The critical tradition has given Judaism the strength to adapt to changing times and contributed to the miraculous preservation of Judaism through millennia. Those who follow this central stream of Jewish tradition are quite different from those called "fideists," who conclude from the necessity of faith that one must dogmatically commit to inerrant texts and unchanging traditions.[8] The tradition is both sacred and evolving.

A third distinctive feature of Jewish wisdom is its concern with resolving conflicts among values: choices of good versus good and between the lesser of evils. This focus was natural for the Sages, because the starting points of the discussions are the many diverse mitzvot in the Torah. An example is the discussion in the Babylonian Talmud, *Sanhedrin* 6b, of a conflict between justice and peace. When parties are in dispute in a civil lawsuit, strict justice can leave one party feeling aggrieved, leading to further strife between them. One rabbi suggests that arbitration is always preferable, because it can better promote peace, and another rabbi argues that strict justice should always rule, because that is what God demands. After debate, a third sage offers a resolution: judges should always first offer arbitration, but once one party turns to litigation, the parties should not be allowed to reverse the process.

Not only is the Jewish approach unique, but also the specific values that result are sometimes distinctive. Christian tradition, for example, emphasizes that a good person is self-sacrificing and tends to view pursuing your own happiness as selfish and sinful. Judaism is also different from Christianity in its focus on having a practical, doable ethic.[9] For example, instead of "turn the other cheek," Judaism permits self-defense and then discusses where it is permitted and where not.

Similarly, Christians such as the Catholic saint Thomas Aquinas and later the Protestant philosopher Immanuel Kant have the extreme view of forbidding lying even to save a life. In contrast, Judaism, recognizing it as a "lesser of evils" choice, commands lying to save a life. In line with its predominantly negative view of human desire, Christianity also has a strong ascetic tradition, including a valuing of celibacy, whereas Talmudic Judaism put strict limits on asceticism and rejects celibacy as sacred.

Similarly, there are fundamental differences with Buddhism. Buddhism is devoted to avoidance of suffering. It seeks to avoid suffering by achieving detachment from the "painted veil" of illusion of this world of our senses and our egos. Judaism, by contrast, is a religion of commitment. It accepts the world and our individual selves as real and as God's sacred creations and urges us to make the best of both. It embraces love, work, and family as activities that can both give us happiness and be lifted to a level of holiness through our actions. Buddhism has, like Christianity, favored the life of the monk, the ascetic, as an ideal, whereas Judaism has a life of engagement in love and work, as well as civic engagement, as the ideal. Notably, Buddhism also has no tradition of seeking social justice, whereas for the Hebrew prophets, from Moses onward, social justice is a central concern. This is not to deny that there is much overlap and also great wisdom in Christian and in Buddhist traditions. The Talmud itself enjoins us (*B'rachot* 58a) to say a blessing upon seeing a sage from other nations, and we should learn from and incorporate the best of this wisdom, just as the Sages did with Greek wisdom.

The Sages realized that while ethical values are necessary to achieve sacred relationships, they are not sufficient for successful relationships in love and work. The Sages called the subject of their guidelines *derech eretz*, "worldly wisdom" (literally, "way of the land"). "Worldly wisdom" includes not only what we now call ethical values, but also social skills, good manners, and an understanding of human psychology. Taken together, these lay out the path to success as a mentsh, the ethical path to sacred, enduring, and productive relationships. This wisdom is our precious legacy. But our legacy was developed in a different world and was not designed to meet the specific challenges of the new non-patriarchal family, nor of the hyper-competitive world of careers today.[10] As a consequence, today we need renewed and strengthened guidelines to help us better uplift and sustain our relationships as sacred relationships.

The Challenge to Judaism Today. Our changed world now challenges Judaism, just as it was challenged in the Talmudic era by a more urban community and by Greek wisdom. One of the key places creative development is needed today is in marriage and family, for we moderns have renounced the traditional acceptance of patriarchy and the subordination of women. In patriarchal marriage, the husband was given more power in decisions. For example, in Talmudic law, all properties of the wife before marriage and all earnings after marriage were controlled by the husband (Babylonian Talmud, *K'tubot* 46b), and only men, not women, could initiate divorce. In contrast, the modern ideal is "companionate marriage," in which husband and wife have an equal say in all decisions.

Modern companionate marriage fundamentally changes the decision process in marriage. It calls upon the couple to negotiate decisions on an equal footing and to come to agreement. Such discussion among equals where there is disagreement and high stakes is not easy to bring off. Modern psychology and its study of effective skills to foster good relationships have a lot to offer for meeting this challenge. However, scientific psychology has also had a key weakness: it has avoided discussing the impact of ethical conduct on relationships. The Sages, as we have seen, believed that moral qualities are central to good relationships. Indeed, the importance of ethical conduct to good relationships has been a part of every wisdom tradition, worldwide, for thousands of years. Thus what we need now is a synthesis of the strongest ethical tradition—our Jewish tradition—with the insights and social skills identified by modern psychology. Together these can become a tremendously powerful new *derech eretz*, wisdom on the conduct of personal life.

An illustration is what I have called "the *sh'lom bayit* discussion," which synthesizes basic Jewish values from Micah and social problem-solving skills from modern psychology—a synthesis that facilitates the kind of discussion most likely to lead to successful cooperation.[11] It can begin with a preliminary prayer, a reminder of how living the values that Micah celebrated can make a problem-solving discussion succeed:

> May it be your will, O Eternal our God, and God of our ancestors, that we have the humility to listen to one another, the kindness to seek mutually helpful solutions, and the sense of justice to make fair compromises. We ask for your blessing upon our home, that it may ever be a refuge of love and of peace.

Leading marriage researcher John Mordechai Gottman has found that starting softly is a key to successful outcomes. When people begin with language that attacks or blames the other person, it sets up a cycle of defensiveness and counterattack that rarely ends well. Raising an issue in language that successfully invites discussion is an art, and psychologists have important insights on this art.

Once an issue has been put on the table in a way that invites cooperative discussion, you should seek the other person's understanding of the problem and communicate yours. Seeking to understand the other person's point of view gains you information on what the other person is thinking and shows respect and empathy for the other person's point of view. Communicating your wants, needs, and understanding helps the other person to make his or her decisions.

The next step is to develop alternative plans of action, including compromises, and to evaluate them. Any debate on the merits of the options should be postponed until the very last part of this last step. By then, the ground is so well prepared that the best solution—including any compromise—is often already evident to both people.

This kind of new synthesis is something Reform is uniquely well suited to do, because of its belief in "Reform as a verb"—that we should grow Judaism, including through the insights of modern science. A valuable next step for the Reform Movement would be to establish an

Institute of Moral Psychology (Machon Derech Eretz) to incorporate the insights of modern psychology into Jewish worldly wisdom.[12] Then our community will be still better able to enlighten and support Reform Jews in uplifting our sacred relationships.

NOTES

1. McAdams, Dan P., *Stories We Live By* (Guilford Press, 1993).

2. James, William, 'The Will to Believe,' (1896)

3. Albert Einstein, "Mein Weltbild" (My Worldview), in *Ideas and Opinions* (New York: Crown, 1954), 11.

4. For more on Einstein's religiosity, see my article 'Einstein's Religious Awakening,' http://www.reformjudaism.org/einsteins-religious-awakening and Jammer, Max, *Einstein and Religion* (Princeton, 2002).

5. Russell, Bertrand, *Religion and Science* (Oxford University Press, 1935), 310–16.

6. See my commentary, *Pirke Avot: Timeless Wisdom for Modern Life* (Jewish Publication Society, 2010)

7. Popper Karl, *Conjectures and Refutations* (Basic Books, 1962), 149–50.

8. Bartley, W. W., *The Retreat To Commitment* (Knopf, 1962).

9. Silver, Abba Hillel, *Where Judaism Differed* (MacMillan, 1956).

10. For applying the value of generosity to the modern world, see: Grant, Adam, *Give and Take* (Penguin, 2014).

11. For more detail on the 'Shalom Bayit Discussion' see my article 'Guide for the Perplexed Parent,' in *Reform Judaism Magazine*, http://www.reformjudaismmag.net/302wb.html.

12. See the discussion forum for applying Jewish wisdom to modern life, www.mentsh.com.

48

MUSSAR AND THE DEVELOPMENT
OF SPIRITUAL PRACTICES

ALAN MORINIS, DPHIL, AND RABBI BARRY BLOCK

A workshop at the 2013 Biennial of the Union for Reform Judaism reported on the transformative role of Mussar in a variety of Reform congregations. Attendees were energized by lay and rabbinical presenters. As the question period began, one woman asked, "Has Mussar had any impact beyond Reform Judaism?"

We had to laugh. We are a practicing Orthodox Jew and a Reform rabbi. Alan, the Orthodox one, is founder and dean of the Mussar Institute. Barry is a Reform rabbi who has been eager to spread Mussar learning and practice in the Reform world. Together, we have experienced challenges in translating an eleven-hundred-year-old tradition for a modern, and particularly for a Reform, audience. For example, many of the texts are gender-bound in ways that trouble Reform Jews.[1] Often, Mussar teachings assume practices that are unfamiliar to most Reform Jews. Most vexing are conceptions of the Divine that many Reform Jews would reject.

Perhaps our Biennial questioner imagined Mussar to be uniquely Reform because of the Reform Movement's foundational emphasis on the individual.[2] Even as recent generations of rabbis have challenged the notion that the individual is the ultimate arbiter in matters of Jewish practice,[3] the movement has continued to emphasize the individual when addressing spiritual matters. Mussar is, at root, a spiritual discipline. In fact, our briefest translation of *mussar* is not the often used "Jewish ethics," but rather "Jewish ethical discipline." Mussar invites each individual to explore his or her own soul and to seek to repair that soul (*tikkun hanefesh*) in covenant with the Divine and with the community. Mussar, then, is uniquely suited, indeed desperately needed, to nourish the Reform Jewish *n'shamah* (soul) in the twenty-first century.

On the other hand, Reform Judaism has typically emphasized *tikkun olam*, the outward-facing social justice work of repairing the world, even to the exclusion of the inward-looking spiritual work of *tikkun hanefesh*.[4] Therefore, the significance of Jewish spiritual discipline to Reform Jews is less than obvious to many.

The origin of the Jewish spiritual tradition of Mussar can be dated to the writings of Saadyah Gaon in the tenth century, and books have continued to be added to the tradition right up to the present. The word *mussar* itself has several meanings, beyond our own described above. For example, *mussar* is translated as "correction, discipline, ethics, and instruction." Sometimes *mussar* can mean "rebuke" or "reproach." "Instruction" is the most inclusive definition, as in Proverbs 1:1, "The proverbs of Shlomo son of David, king of Israel, to have knowledge of wisdom and *mussar*." From the time of its inception through to the present, the concern of the Mussar masters has been to illuminate the path that a person can follow to achieve the highest purpose one can accomplish in life, which is to follow the Torah's injunction *K'doshim tih'yu*, "You shall be holy" (Leviticus 19:2). However we might define holiness—and there have been many attempts through the centuries—all agree that holiness refers to the highest level of spirituality possible for a human being.

Our spiritual ancestors recognized a paradox in the Torah's injunction to be holy: This verse directs us to become holy, and yet the description of the creation of humanity in Genesis 1 challenges that idea. Since we are made "in the image and likeness of God," whom we call the Holy Blessed One, aren't we already holy? That conundrum is underlined in the second half of the verse that directs us to become holy. In full, it says, "You shall be holy, for I, the Eternal your God, am holy" (Leviticus 19:2).

Made in the image of a holy God, human beings are, by definition and inherently, already holy. And yet we are told to "become holy." That paradox lies at the heart of Mussar: From a spiritual perspective, and in practice, how does a holy being become holy? How do you become what you already are?

The Mussar masters began to address this paradox by charting the inner life. Based on biblical sources but also observation, they concluded that the essential aspect of a human being is their soul-nature and that, while the soul is one and unified, it has three primary dimensions, represented by three words that all name dimensions of the unified "soul."

Two of these, *ruach* and *nefesh*, refer to more mundane and earthly aspects of the inner life. *Ruach* is that aspect of the soul that is the source of animation and vigor—no more, and no less, than the "spirit of life." *Nefesh* is the aspect of the soul that is most visible and accessible to us. Here we find all the human traits we see in others and ourselves, like the emotions and thought, desires and talents. This dimension of soul interfaces with this world and is the home of the personality, identity, and character.

The third aspect of the soul, the *n'shamah*, refers to the pure and holy essence of a person where the divine image resides, as Proverbs 20:27 identifies by saying that "the human soul [*nishmat adam*] is the candle of God" and the liturgy reinforces: "The soul [*n'shamah*] that You have given me is pure."

The task of becoming holy cannot demand that we acquire anything additional to the complete holiness already present in the *n'shamah*, which is the inner, heavenly dimension, said to be hewn from the Throne of Glory itself.[5] The Mussar masters of past centuries resolved the paradox by affirming that the radiant light of the *n'shamah* is holy and untainted, but that light can be obscured by obstructions situated at the level of the entirely earthly *ruach* and *nefesh*. In the Mussar view, becoming holy is not a matter of acquiring something we don't already have; rather, the work to become holy involves identifying and then eliminating the obstacles that occlude the light of holiness from shining brightly into our lives and, through us, into the world.

The Mussar masters focused primarily on the aspects of the *nefesh*-soul that are present in all of us—qualities like anger, envy, worry, laziness, miserliness, and the like—along with their "positive" counterparts—like calmness, contentedness, trust, alacrity, and generosity. Their conclusion is that all humans possess each of these traits, though their measure differs from person to person. Indeed, the collective term for the human inner qualities in Hebrew is *midot* (singular *midah*), which literally does mean "measure."

Any inner trait that tends in a habitual way toward one extreme or the other along a range creates, in effect, a barrier that obstructs the light of holiness from shining freely into the world. It's not that these traits tending to the extreme are "flaws"; rather, they are assignments, or rungs on the ladder of spiritual ascent. Those traits that tend toward either extreme make up an individual's personal soul curriculum, and it is that set of assignments that mark out that individual's personal path toward holiness.

The practice of Mussar is focused on identifying and then altering the measure of those extreme traits, as the impatient person works to become patient, the arrogant person (or, alternatively, the self-debasing person) to internalize humility, the angry person to cultivate inner calmness, and so on, according to whatever traits are to be found on each person's personal curriculum.

One can most easily identify the *midot* that make up one's personal spiritual curriculum by paying attention to those traits that play a role in the challenges or tests that show up repeatedly in one's life. The person who has an issue with truth will regularly trip over their lies—or, conversely, will hurt others by telling unnecessarily hurtful truths. The impatient person is annoyed by the long lines they encounter everywhere, while the overly patient person fails in the urgent work of addressing injustice. The arrogant person is forever encountering situations that challenge the ego. The self-debasing person is as trampled upon as a doormat. And so it goes for each of us, since it is a characteristic of human diversity that everyone is strong in some *midot* and weak in others. It is the weak traits, which we can also conceive of as the traits that have the greatest potential for growth, that turn ordinary situations into personal trials; and those very tests reveal a person's curriculum, which is their personal path to holiness.

And so, the pathway that Mussar lays out for becoming holy is by way of improving the qualities of the *nefesh*-soul. This insight defined the practical focus of Mussar. In order to purify and elevate the inner life and to release the light of holiness that is our inalienable birthright as human beings, one needs to undertake *tikkun hamidot*, rectifying the inner traits. Every inner trait tending to the extreme (in either direction) that is recalibrated toward the mean lifts one barrier that has been obscuring the radiance of one's inner holiness and releases more of that light to shine brightly in a life.

From the mid-nineteenth and into the early twentieth centuries, the teaching and practice of Mussar were the basis for a spiritual movement that took place in Eastern Europe, founded by Rabbi Yisrael Salanter and centered within the Lithuanian yeshivot. That movement has provided most of the techniques of practice through which a practitioner can accomplish *tikkun hamidot*. The Mussar teachers of that era realized, no doubt through observation, that change comes about more through experiential practice than through the acquisition of ideas. The first step in the practice of Mussar is to identify which *midot* are on one's personal curriculum. Practice begins with meditation and visualization but is most seriously undertaken through exercises in the real world of life, all of which are meant to generate specific experiences, since experience more than ideation does the work of "imprinting on the heart" the new behavior to which the practitioner aspires.

The European Mussar tradition was largely destroyed in the Holocaust that wiped out so many of its teachers. In the era following the Holocaust, Mussar met the fate of all Jewish spirituality. Despite its ancient origins and uninterrupted line of transmission, Mussar, marginalized throughout the Jewish world, was almost completely unknown in liberal Jewish circles, including Reform Judaism. Add the general neglect of the inner life as a Jewish concern in the late twentieth century, Reform Judaism's emphasis on rationality and social justice, and the postwar generation's pursuit of affluence and assimilation, and we can understand why the emergence of Mussar in the Reform world in the twenty-first century was an innovation.

Moreover, some of the teachings of classical Mussar are not easily embraced by most Reform Jews. Often, Mussar classics suggest perfection of a *midah* (soul trait) is best achieved by adhering to a particular practice of traditionally interpreted Jewish law that is not observed by most Reform Jews. To cite one example, Barry recalls the focus on the mitzvah (religious obligation) of hand-washing when he first encountered the *midah* of *z'rizut* (alacrity) in the Mussar Institute's introductory online course "Everyday Holiness."

Often more difficult are conceptions of the Divine. Classical Mussar texts assume a traditional conception of God as a transcendent Being. Reform Judaism is heavily influenced by twentieth-century God concepts, such as those of Martin Buber and Mordecai Kaplan, whose God concepts were anything but traditional. Many others proclaim themselves to be agnostic while retaining a steadfast Jewish identity and eagerness to learn from the tradition so long as it does not require acceptance of a God they do not recognize. Theology can be an issue in addressing any aspect of Mussar, but especially soul traits like *bitachon* (trust), *emunah* (faith), and *yirah* (awe).

Bitachon (trust), for example, is no less important in the twenty-first century than in earlier ages. Mussar teaches us to work toward the optimal outcome in any endeavor and then to trust that the result is God's will and therefore good, if perhaps in ways we cannot understand. For those liberal Jews who do not believe in a God who directs the events of this world, the *midah* must be reinterpreted. Therefore, Barry teaches that *bitachon* is not trust that any particularly desired result will be achieved, but that we will be "OK" even if it is not. Barry offers the possibility that God's will is at play, while also endorsing entirely non-theistic ways of viewing the ways of the world.

Mussar's first significant inroads into the Reform world were paved by the movement's twentieth-century thought leader Rabbi Eugene B. Borowitz, professor of Jewish religious thought at Hebrew Union College–Jewish Institute of Religion (HUC-JIR). In a 1999 collaboration with Frances Weinman Schwartz, Borowitz published *The Jewish Moral Virtues*, a comprehensive collection of Mussar teaching, solidly based on traditional sources but written in a modern, conversational style with contemporary applications.

Numerous Reform rabbis and educators taught the Borowitz and Schwartz book, which made the classical teachings of Mussar accessible to Reform readership, at least with skilled guidance. However, *The Jewish Moral Virtues* does not emphasize practice; more to the point, it does not suggest a specific approach to adopting Mussar as a way of life accessible to a wide variety of readers.

Two other books, *Jewish Spiritual Guidance: Finding Our Way to God*[6] and *Striving Toward Virtue: A Contemporary Guide for Jewish Ethical Behavior*,[7] were published and utilized by Reform rabbis and educators. However, it was not until the publication of *Everyday Holiness*,[8] the popularization of courses offered by the Mussar Institute, and the Institute for Jewish Spirituality's Mussar-based mindfulness leadership training programs that a system of learning and practice existed to facilitate widespread adoption. Since then, "Mussar," a word not spoken in the halls of HUC-JIR in decades past, has found a foothold in its curriculum.

This twenty-first-century embrace of Mussar by Reform Judaism may best be explained by the surfacing of a deep spiritual yearning among contemporary Jews, including Reform Jews, in ways that were not always compatible with Reform Judaism. Whereas classical Reform Judaism rejected any conception of the Divine deemed inconsistent with reason, our postmodern era invites individuals to seek spiritual answers to ultimate questions without necessarily subjecting those responses to rational examination. Reform Jews, no less than any other human beings, naturally ponder the purpose of human life and the nature of the afterlife. Postmodernity enables Reform Jews to embrace the possibility that each of us is a soul, perhaps not entirely coexistent with our physical bodies. Therefore, Mussar's guidance that we work to improve those souls is no longer foreign to Reform Jews. Moreover, modalities often suggested by the Mussar Institute and other twenty-first-century purveyors of Mussar discipline, such as chanting and meditation, are now widely accepted in Reform Judaism in ways they were not in the past.

At the same time, Mussar's focus on *tikkun hanefesh* and Reform Judaism's historically outward emphasis on *tikkun olam* are compellingly compatible. Ultimately, Mussar insists that each soul must learn to practice what it already knows,[9] bringing an enhanced purity of soul (which manifests as ethical strength and emotional maturity) to social justice work and advocacy.[10] Even mindfulness, while a worthy goal, is not sufficient. Mussar insists that we study and practice *chesed* (lovingkindness) in order to bring greater kindness into the world. Mussar requires us to learn *tzedek* (righteousness) so that we may strengthen our resolve to advocate for economic, racial, and environmental justice. Mussar calls on us to enhance our *z'rizut* (alacrity or zeal) to motivate ourselves off the sofa and into the streets and halls of Congress, to feed the hungry and to address the root causes of hunger in this broken world. And Mussar calls the activist's attention to personal inner qualities that may either facilitate or inhibit their social justice programs and campaigns.

Mussar reminds us that the Hebrew word for the *midah* of responsibility, *acharayut*, begins with three letters that also spell *acher*, meaning "other." Cultivating this soul trait, Mussar practitioners are called upon to examine the extent to which they have or have not taken ownership of the commandment to improve the lives of others. The *midah* of *n'davah* (generosity) asks us to consider whether we have given sufficiently of our time and money, while also calling upon Mussar students to ensure that they haven't been generous to an unhealthy degree, which could be damaging to self or other. Perhaps most challenging, the *midah* of *anavah* (humility) insists that the activist consider two possibilities, one more obvious than the other. First, of course, we must examine the extent to which the motivation for our social justice activities may be self-aggrandizement. Less apparent, but equally important, Mussar reminds us that one can have "too much humility," which isn't really humility at all, but rather a denial of one's responsibility and capability to step up to the challenge, in this case rationalizing inaction in the service of social justice.

Mussar practice, particularly through programs of the Mussar Institute, can also serve the critical community-building goals of Reform congregations.[11] Most Mussar Institute programs require forming and participating actively in a *vaad*, a word commonly used in Modern Hebrew to mean "committee." In a Mussar *vaad*, each member of the group is on the "committee" of all the other members, each of whom is working to perfect his or her individual soul. In a Mussar *vaad*, each participant helps others to identify the *midot* that may be stumbling blocks in reaching *k'dushah*, the holiness we are commanded to seek through our actions. At the same time, *vaad* participants also suggest *midot* that a given participant possesses in abundance, both contributing to that individual's journey toward holiness and available to that person as she or he seeks to do the ultimate work of Mussar, *tikkun hanefesh*, repairing the soul, through *tikkun midot*, repairing identified soul traits.

When a *vaad* functions optimally, the group builds a community that nurtures trust, fosters support, and bonds into an intimate spiritual fellowship within the congregation. As Dr. Ron Wolfson has taught us,[12] creating and sustaining relationships is the essential work required to sustain the synagogue and Jewish community in the twenty-first century.

In the years ahead, we anticipate that growing attention to the life of the spirit will turn increasing numbers of Reform Jews to Mussar study and practice, even as greater familiarity with Mussar will heal countless souls, enhancing their holiness and the holiness of their communities. We expect that *tikkun hanefesh* (repairing souls) will enrich and strengthen Reform Judaism's historic and ongoing commitment to *tikkun olam* (repairing the world). We are confident that the spread of Mussar *vaadim* (local "committees of souls") will serve the needs of individuals while simultaneously cultivating relationships that will strengthen synagogues and the communities they serve.

NOTES

1. Eugene B. Borowitz and Frances Weinman Schwartz, *Jewish Moral Virtues* (Philadelphia: Jewish Publication Society, 1999), 6.

2 Eugene B. Borowitz, *Reform Judaism Today* (New York: Behrman House, 1983), 94–95.

3. For example, the Central Conference of American Rabbis' 1999 "Statement of Principles" explicitly does not contain the phrase "individual autonomy" with reference to ritual decision-making.

4 Borowitz, *Reform Judaism Today*, 85–90.

5. *Zohar Chadash*, B'reishit 18b.

6. Carol Ochs and Kerry M. Olitzky, *Jewish Spiritual Guidance: Finding Our Way to God* (San Francisco: Jossey-Bass, 1997).

7. Kerry M. Olitzky and Rachel T. Sabath, *Striving toward Virtue: A Contemporary Guide for Jewish Ethical Behavior* (Hoboken, NJ: KTAV, 1996).

8. Alan Morinis, *Everyday Holiness* (Boston: Trumpeter, 2007).

9. This idea is best attributed to the recent Mussar teacher Rabbi Elya Lopian, who expresses this idea well by defining the practice of Mussar as "making the heart understand what the mind knows"; Eliyahu Lopian, *Lev Eliyahu*, trans. B. D. Klein (Jerusalem: K. Pinski, 1975).

10. Alan Morinis, *With Heart in Mind* (Boston: Trumpeter, 2014), 240–44.

11. No less is true in other communal settings.

12. Ron Wolfson, *Relational Judaism* (Woodstock, VT: Jewish Lights, 2013).

49

THE CENTRALITY OF SOCIAL JUSTICE IN REFORM JUDAISM

Rabbi Jonah Dov Pesner and
Rabbi David N. Saperstein

We met more than thirty years ago in the storied conference room of the Religious Action Center of Reform Judaism (RAC) in Washington, DC, at one of the earliest iterations of L'taken Seminars, which would, over the ensuing years, train over fifty thousand high school and college students in social justice awareness and skills. Rabbi Saperstein was a leader of the social justice agenda of the Reform Movement, Rabbi Pesner then a teenage student activist. Then, as now, we remain dedicated to enhancing the influence of the largest segment of American Jewry in making real our ancient mandate of *tzedek, tzedek tirdof,* "justice, justice shall you pursue" (Deuteronomy 16:20).

We are, of course, in no manner unique in our commitments as Reform Jews. Like so many others, we are a product of the convergence of 3,000 years of a Jewish prophetic tradition, 150 years of Reform Judaism in America with its emphasis on social justice, and a nation whose commitment to freedoms of speech, religion, and association and to the right to petition the government for redress of grievances welcomed us in our historical responsibility of preaching truth to power. Like countless rabbis, Jewish professionals and lay leaders, teens and adults, we have discovered in Reform Judaism the nexus between our love of Jewish text, wisdom, history, and ritual—and our passion to heal a broken world. Toward that goal, the Reform Movement engages Jews and non-Jews alike in campaigns to confront the systems of oppression that cause the most vulnerable among us to suffer. This essay focuses on our Reform Movement's work in the United States, but key to our social justice successes in the United States and Canada has been the countless contributions of our congregational rabbis and lay leaders as well as those of the members of our congregations who, as public officials, civic leaders, public intellectuals, academics, and activists, played such important roles in every cause for social justice in our nation's history.

American Reform Judaism has, from its beginnings, emphasized social justice as a pillar of our expression of Jewish living. The first American statement of our principles, drafted by the Central Conference of American Rabbis (CCAR) in Pittsburgh in 1885, references the Torah's goal of "regulating relations between rich and poor" and concludes, "We deem it our duty to participate in the great task of modern times, to solve, on the basis of justice and righteousness, the problems presented by the contrasts and evils of the present organization of society."[1]

In the second statement of our principles drafted in 1937 in Columbus, our rabbinic leaders expanded the themes of social and economic justice in a series of paragraphs related to ethical obligations, social justice, and the pursuit of peace, linking the latter to the biblical prophets. The rabbis affirmed, "Judaism seeks the attainment of a just society by the application of its teachings to the economic order, to industry and commerce, and to national and international affairs. It aims at the elimination of man-made misery and suffering, of poverty and degradation, of tyranny and slavery, of social inequality and prejudice, of ill-will and strife."[2]

In the most recent statement of principles, adopted in 1999, the theme of social justice continued to be emphasized.[3] In this more contemporary iteration, the statement grounds the Reform Movement's commitment in the notion of *tikkun olam* (literally "repairing the world"), arguing that our actions for justice and righteousness help bring about a better world. The 1999 statement deepens the Reform Jewish connection of social justice to the biblical prophets who demanded that ethical concerns be paramount in service to God. Perhaps the most important aspect of the centrality of social justice in Reform Judaism is that it was not really an innovation. Well before the meetings in Pittsburgh and Columbus, Judaism spoke with utter clarity about justice through the earliest writings, the Torah and the books of the prophets.

One of the Torah's first stories is the argument between God and Abraham, who challenges God to ensure that the innocents of Sodom and Gomorrah not be punished along with the guilty. The Exodus story, which is in many ways the master narrative of Judaism, is an archetypal telling of the Jewish people's experience of redemption, beginning with oppression, slavery, and genocidal efforts to destroy them (i.e., Pharaoh's command to kill the male children) and ending in freedom. Being commanded to tell the story, year after year, from generation to generation, in the synagogue and at home around the Passover seder table, helps explain Judaism's consistent emphases on social justice, on striving for the redemption of all. Relatedly, Torah repeatedly commands us to love, protect, and treat as ourselves the *ger*, "the stranger," because "you were strangers in the land Egypt." The injunctions to love and protect the *ger* are repeated in varied forms thirty-six times, more than any other commandment in the Torah, and remind us of our responsibilities to protect the weak and the vulnerable of our communities, even when they are not Jews themselves.

Many of the biblical prophets repeat the redemptive message of social and economic justice in their prophecies. A powerful example that plays a special role in our traditional liturgy and our Reform Jewish aesthetic is Isaiah's challenge to his society's elite during their worship:

Is this the fast I desire?
A day to afflict body and soul?
Bowing your head like a reed, covering yourself with sackcloth
    and ashes?
Do you call this a fast—a day worthy of the favor of Adonai?
Is not this the fast I desire—
to break the bonds of injustice and remove the heavy yoke;
to let the oppressed go free and release all those enslaved?
Is it not to share your bread with the hungry
and to take the homeless poor into your home,
and never to neglect your own flesh and blood?

(Isaiah 58:5–7)

Read on the holiest day of every year, Yom Kippur, Isaiah's prophecy (together with the Jonah story's message that God's call to justice is a universal one) serves as an agitational reminder to the assembled community of Jews of God's higher purpose in our fasting, repenting, and observing the rituals of the holiday.

There is more to Isaiah's message, however, which may be missed by most of us. It is in Isaiah's call to action, his demand that our observance lead us to feed the hungry, clothe the naked, and house the homeless. In saying that if we do all these things, we will be "the one who mends the breach and brings back the streets for dwelling" (Isaiah 58:12), Isaiah's message has messianic resonance, a vision that is echoed later by the Rabbis in the daily liturgy. At the conclusion of every worship service, Jews repeat these words contained in the *Aleinu* prayer: *L'takein olam d'malchut Shaddai*, best understood as reflecting our vision of a time when the world will be repaired under God's kingdom. For Reform Jews especially, this serves as a powerful metaphor for the underlying redemptive purpose of religious life: to tirelessly strive for a messianic time when the world as it is—parched with oppression and suffering—is transformed into the world as it should be—overflowing with justice and righteousness.

This traditional Jewish imperative for social justice was rooted in Judaism's distinctive concept of "ethical monotheism," of a God that calls the Jewish people to righteousness, justice, and peace—ideals that infused the prophetic voice of the Bible. In the eighteenth and nineteenth centuries, as much of the Western world altered its most foundational axioms from a God-oriented world to a logic-, science-, and rationality-centered one, this social justice emphasis of Judaism and other Western religions became intensified. A number of Age of Reason and Enlightenment era philosophers argued that the part of religion that was most rational and scientific was ethics. The faith traditions that emerged in this context elevated social justice to a centerpiece of religious expression. Out of this intellectual milieu arose the Social Gospel strands of Christianity as well as Reform Judaism's emphasis on the "prophetic tradition," expressed in the Reform Movement's focus on social justice. The synthesis of the traditional Jewish belief of being a "light to the nations" with rationalism strengthened the emphasis on social justice as an expression of authentic Judaism. This was true not only of Reform Judaism, but of Reconstructionist, Conservative, and strands of "modern" Orthodox Judaism. It has remained particularly true with Reform Judaism.

During the first several generations of Reform Judaism in the United States, many Jews participated in an array of social justice causes as individuals (think, for example, of the significantly disproportionate presence of Jews in the labor movement), and the communal commitment to social justice resided mostly in the preaching and public activities of the rabbis, who commanded religious and communal authority. To cite just a few representative examples across those early generations: Rabbi David Einhorn courageously denounced slavery and was forced to flee his congregation in Baltimore. His son-in-law, Rabbi Emil Hirsch, spoke repeatedly from his major pulpit in Chicago on social justice themes. From the turn of the century through the first couple of decades of the twentieth century, Hirsch supported and led various public causes for civil rights and economic justice and helped inspire the famous philanthropist Julies Rosenwald, who used his wealth from Sears, Roebuck to support similar causes. Over the first half of the twentieth century, Rabbi Stephen S. Wise became famous not only as one of America's greatest public orators and preachers, but for his zealous leadership of an array of social justice causes, domestic and international. And for each one of these famous voices, there were many scores of other Reform rabbis imbued with commitment to social justice as an expression of their Jewish values and identity. Indeed, the three ideological platforms that embraced social justice were all passed decisively by conventions of the Central Conference of American Rabbis, not by lay leaders.

In the aftermath of World War II, that began to change. The rabbis remained a mainstay of social justice work, but the move of the Union of American Hebrew Congregations (now the Union for Reform Judaism, and henceforth "URJ") from under the shadow of the Hebrew Union College in Cincinnati to the center of American Jewish life in New York City, led by Rabbi Maurice Eisendrath, himself a towering figure for social justice, helped move the URJ to a central role, alongside the rabbis, in building institutions of social justice at the local and national level. Eisendrath saw the synagogue as playing an indispensable role in social justice efforts. He hired prolific writers and creative programmers, Rabbi Eugene Lipman and Al Vorspan (as we write, Al remains, at ninety-five, one of American Jewry's most eloquent and brilliant expositors of Jewish social justice). Eisendrath charged them to spur the creation of synagogue social action committees and to develop educational, social service, and advocacy programs for congregations to do. In that postwar era, from the end of World War II through the McCarthy, civil rights, and Vietnam War eras, social action committees proliferated and became a norm, not just among Reform Jews but in synagogues of all streams.

A dramatic affirmation of the Reform Jewish commitment to *tikkun olam* was the founding of the Commission on Social Action and the Religious Action Center of Reform Judaism (the RAC). The former, a joint body of the CCAR and URJ, brings together representatives of the major institutions and affiliates of the Reform Movement, professional and voluntary, in establishing movement positions on critical issues of the day. In 1962, the URJ dedicated the RAC building in the heart of Washington, DC, so that the Reform Movement could directly advocate in Congress and the White House for social justice.

The RAC became a hub for the civil rights movement, housing for several decades the nation's largest umbrella civil rights organization, the Leadership Conference on Civil Rights. Dr. Martin Luther King, Jr., visited the RAC frequently and was invited by Rabbi Richard Hirsch, the RAC's first director, to use its facilities whenever he was in town. Parts of the Civil Rights Act of 1964 and the Voting Rights Act of 1965 were drafted there, and for thirty years much of the advocacy on behalf of civil rights legislation was shaped in the RAC's conference room. In those early decades, Eisendrath, Lipman, Vorspan, Hirsch, and Rabbi Balfour Brickner, together with leaders of the CCAR, played key roles in the battles on nuclear disarmament, civil rights, reproductive rights, the Great Society programs, separation of church and state, anti-apartheid efforts, the Soviet Jewry movement, and pro-Israel efforts. Those of us who succeeded that generation—Leonard Fein, Rabbis Eric Yoffie, Daniel Polish, Marla Feldman, Lynne Landsberg, Mark Pelavin, and Barbara Weinstein—have likewise played leadership roles in such coalition work, not only continuing key work on these causes, but adding environmental efforts, LGBTQ rights, international religious freedom—just as local rabbis and lay leaders have done throughout these past eighty years in communities across America. In these later decades, the RAC was the site where the mobilization to free Soviet Jewry was planned, the Dalai Lama attended his first Passover seder, and new coalitions crafted and advocated for the successful passage of the anti–human trafficking laws and the Sudan Peace Act.

In addition to advocacy work in Washington, the RAC has implemented social justice training programs for tens of thousands of students (in partnership with NFTY), as it has done for rabbis, lay leaders, synagogue social action committee chairs, Jewish and non-Jewish seminarians, and staffs of Washington, DC, denominational offices. At the local level, synagogues are increasingly engaged in interfaith coalitions on a range of issues and have built strong coalitions with the African American, Christian, and Muslim communities. Hundreds of our congregations have held public programs educating their own membership and the broader public on current affairs. Cooperation with local feeding programs for impoverished families, homeless shelters, literacy tutoring, and assistance to refugees were common programs involving hundreds of synagogues in a given year. The Reform Movement began to look at its own practices that needed reform—leading to the ordination of female and, later, LGBTQ rabbis and the push for *b'nei mitzvah* to engage in mitzvah programs. *Bikur cholim* and caring community programs deepened the engagement of our congregations in meeting the very real needs of our fellow congregants. Social justice programming has long been a mainstay of the programs of both our youth groups and our sisterhoods and complement the efforts of synagogue social action committees. Religious schools educate students using the tools of prophetic Judaism to convey relevance for modern themes. Holiday celebrations have increasingly incorporated social justice themes—Passover seders that elevate modern issues of racial injustice, Chanukah celebrated through a lens of religious freedom, Tu BiSh'vat celebrations that explore environmental concerns, and Purim understood through a lens of women empowerment—allowing Reform Jews to meaningfully engage with modern issues and continue the religious traditions of their ancestors.

Even the language and textual sources used to discuss Jewish social justice changed. While the voices of the prophets remained prominent, postbiblical sources were increasingly utilized. Rabbis and other leaders looked to Talmudic and medieval sources that discussed how to create equitable and just communities, and modern Jewish theologians like Leo Baeck, Martin Buber, Abraham Joshua Heschel, and Eugene Borowitz helped interpret Judaism through a twentieth-century framework that embodied themes including social justice. Contemporary American Jewry has framed the pursuit of justice in terms of *tikkun olam*, which has become the primary metaphor for the core Jewish concept that human beings have a sacred obligation to act to repair the vast brokenness in our world.

In this past generation, another sweeping change has impacted America's religious communities more broadly as well as the Reform Jewish community: the use of community organizing techniques to engage Jews more deeply in crafting social justice programs and advocacy. In the late 1990s, a handful of Jewish congregations became involved intensively with such community organizing, which heretofore had been largely Christian, and were empowered by its potential to effect social change at a local level. Congregations conduct "listening campaigns" in which they conduct conversations widely among members, study Jewish texts, and then identify issues that resonate with their Jewish values and social justice concerns. Through broad-based community organizations, they then reach across lines of race, class, and faith to act collectively on a range of local issues. Simultaneously, the congregations and their members formed meaningful relationships across lines of difference. The synagogues also became stronger because of the investment in relationship building within the congregation.

Together, we had the exciting experience of launching Just Congregations in 2006 to engage the entire Reform Movement in interfaith community organizing and seeing nearly three hundred congregations become involved at some level. Rabbi Stephanie Kolin joined the effort and expanded the Reform Movement's reach to the state level in launching Reform California and then Reform Ohio, which have, in 2015–17, already won victories on immigrant justice and criminal justice reform.

The shift toward engaging congregations through community organizing has helped move lay leaders, along with rabbis, to the center of the Reform Movement's social justice efforts. Our movement's greatest successes for social justice will be achieved when individuals work together to harness their power to create positive change.

The prominence of social justice in the Reform Movement has been among the chief reasons why it has succeeded and grown into, far and away, the largest segment of North American Jewry, despite the pull of secularism and fundamentalism that have vexed so many religious communities. Indeed, polling of the Jewish community has consistently affirmed that far more than ritual or worship, far more than support for Israel, commitment to or involvement in social justice is either one of or the most common way Jews express their Jewish identity. A Judaism that fails to embody these values, a Judaism that does not speak to the great moral issues of the lives of our children or the great moral issues of the world they will inherit from us, will not succeed in engaging the hearts and minds of the next generations of Jews.

This is an exciting era in the work of Jewish social justice. At a moment when so many of the extraordinary national and local achievements of the generations that have gone before are under attack, we are witnessing a remarkable resurgence of social justice activities throughout the Jewish community.

The Reform Movement has launched campaigns renewing our focus on racial justice, urging congregations to provide sanctuary to undocumented immigrants, and advocating for the rights and full inclusion of transgender and gender non-conforming people (the first major religious denomination to do so). The movement has engaged synagogue leaders across North America in a campaign called "The Urgency of Now" (drawing on the phrase from Dr. King's memorable 1967 Riverside Church sermon), through which the various institutions of Reform Judaism are organizing on a state, local, and federal level on these issues and more.

When we met more than thirty years ago, countless generations of prophets, rabbis, and leaders had articulated and fought for the Jewish vision of a world of justice. Generations of Reform Jewish leaders amplified that voice and animated that vision in the world, and we are proud to be part of a generation so effectively engaged in passing the commitment on to future generations of Reform Jews who will dedicate themselves to making real that ancient prayer *L'takein olam d'malchut Shaddai.*

NOTES

1. "The Pittsburgh Platform" (1885), http://ccarnet.org/rabbis-speak/platforms/declaration-principles/.

2. "The Guiding Principles of Reform Judaism" (1937), http://ccarnet.org/rabbis-speak/platforms/guiding-principles-reform-judaism/.

3. "A Statement of Principles for Reform Judaism" (1999), https://ccarnet.org/rabbis-speak/platforms/statement-principles-reform-judaism/.

50

INTEGRATING OUR STORIES: LGBTQ FOLKS IN THE JEWISH COMMUNITY

RABBI NIKKI LYN DEBLOSI, PHD

During my first year of college, I spent an awful lot of time in the Harvard Widener Library's stacks.[1] Venturing beyond the majestic Reading Room, I would slip into a dark hallway, list of call numbers in hand, and wander among utilitarian shelves past hundreds of leather-bound tomes. I skirted History and Philosophy, landing in rows of volumes covered in cheap cardstock, edges frayed: 1950s pulp novels, most of them with titles like *Odd Girl Out*.

I was looking for a story I wasn't sure existed but which I hoped desperately *did* exist, somewhere: a story that allowed a girl like me to be all of myself, without apology, a story that might comfort me with the knowledge that I was neither alone nor a freak. Terrified, I looked up "lesbian" in the card catalog and read every single book. From racy romance novels about butch lesbians "seducing" unsuspecting femmes (who inevitably affirmed their heterosexuality by the end) to historical and medical textbooks debating whether same-sex desire was a crime to be punished or a pathology to be cured, I read them all. The messages I received were often confusing, occasionally affirming, and in too many cases outright alarming. While today there are dozens (and counting) of novels for adolescents and emerging adults who identify as lesbian, gay, bisexual, transgender, gender-non-conforming, queer, and questioning—and plenty of other labels, as the lexicon expands—the 1990s Harvard library left me wondering what my life's story might be. Was I doomed to a life in the shadows? Would I be forced into a double life, closeted to those closest to me?

I didn't know it then, but I was engaging in a very Jewish project, one described vividly by Rabbi Lord Jonathan Sacks: "Imagine we are in a vast library." Suddenly, "you come across one book unlike the rest, which catches your eye because on its spine is written the name of your family. . . . It is the story each generation of your ancestors has told for the sake of the next. . . . As you turn the pages, you reach the last page which carries no entry but a heading. It bears your name."[2] As the poet Zelda evocatively writes, "Each of us has a name." Several, in fact. Those on our birth certificate and those labels we apply to ourselves as we try to categorize the world around us, trying to figure out where and how we belong. Newly arrived in college, I had several names, and I wanted to refine them. I wanted to shed some and acquire others. I had been Catholic. I had been "Nicole." I had been (presumably) straight. I had been a good girl—a goody-two-shoes. I eschewed my previous spiritual home, seeking a new one, and introduced myself to everyone as "Nikki." I tried really hard to embrace my nerdiness. And I spent an awful lot of time researching how I could authentically claim the label "lesbian."

Ultimately, labels may limit us, but they also help us navigate the world and find commonalities with others. You and I both call ourselves "Jewish," and that lets us know we are linked in some way. The label might not inform exactly how we each celebrate Shabbat (electronics or no electronics?) or what recipe we use for kugel (sweet or savory?), yet we know we belong to a community linked by tradition and values. We know we're not the only ones, which brings a sense of comfort and connection. While we might be happy to discuss what we have in common with our Christian, Muslim, Buddhist, atheist, and Hindu neighbors, when we call ourselves "Jewish," we are signaling that our community is distinct in ways we find important and valuable.

When queer folks seek, invent, and claim terms to describe our identities, genders, relationships, and families, we are engaging in a similar project: we are attempting to acknowledge what is distinct about us and, at the same time, establish a sense of connection, continuity, and belonging. We are seeking to know ourselves and to be known. Words help: naming is how God created the world, speaking each element and creature into existence. The words we in the queer community use have been changing, and they can be confusing, particularly to folks who are unfamiliar or who are trying hard to ally (many folks stress "allying" rather than "being an ally": allyship requires action, not labels). For example, the word "queer," long used as an insult, can still be used as an anti-LGBTQ invective, but it has also been taken up by many of us within the community as a term of pride. You think we're queer—meaning different in a negative way? Weird? Strange? Well, then, we'll take up the mantle and say: We're different and we're *proud of that difference*. We're not weird and strange; we're unique and beautiful!

As I wandered my university's library, I sought a new name. I was hoping that the book of my life would have enough room in its pages for the desire I was just beginning to vocalize. And, I couldn't articulate it then, but the label didn't matter so much as the shape of the story. A narrative has a beginning, a middle, an end. I wasn't sure whether the book of my life even had a plot, let alone a happily ever after.

When I was a girl, I would obsessively plan and picture my storybook wedding. I would design my white dress, the color scheme of the reception, even the pattern of china on which the tiered cake would be plated. But who would be my beloved, under the chuppah? A person in a suit, back turned to me. I could never picture the rest. I imagined my future as an extension of my present, me living in the top-floor apartment of a two-family house with my best friend, my parents in the apartment downstairs.

When I converted to Judaism, I sought the stories of the different movements. I searched for a narrative of welcome and possibility, and I learned that the Reform Movement's 1999 "Statement of Principles" explicitly invokes the term "inclusive." Here, then: a story to which I belonged, a story that could belong to me. Too many of the library books I had devoured so eagerly implied (or stated outright) that religion and same-sex desire were antithetical to one another. My Catholic upbringing, which rejected meaningful leadership roles for women and which condemned LGBTQ relationships, left no room for anything other than a "love the sinner, hate the sin" attitude. I thought Judaism was the answer. I thought I would emerge from the mikveh my full and true self—out, proud, religious, Jewishly committed, and embraced with open arms in every Reform Jewish setting I would encounter.

The relationship between Reform Judaism and LGBTQ inclusion has been more complex. At the heart of our challenge remains the mandate for storytelling. We can read about the long process of officially supporting anti-discrimination measures, civil rights, marriage equality, and inclusion for LGBTQ folks by the institutions of the Reform Movement. We can read the words "inclusive" and "welcoming" on URJ congregations' websites, not knowing for sure who is being addressed (Gays and lesbians? Interfaith families? Trans folks? Jews of color?). We can recall vividly or learn anew about Rabbi Alexander Schindler's 1989 call for an increase in visibility for gays and lesbians.[3] But we must ask ourselves whether we are committed to ensuring the visibility not only of folks who are brave enough to name their narrative and claim the words "lesbian," "gay," "bisexual," "transgender," or "queer"—but committed also to the visibility of *variety* in sexual orientation and gender identity as a positive value. Are we committed to telling more than one story about what constitutes a valuable and authentically Jewish life?

My coming-out experience began with a library search. Because I'm a nerd? Well, yes, but there's another reason: because I didn't know where else to search. I think about my trips to the Widener stacks every time I interact with students as part of my university job as Reform rabbi and senior Jewish educator. My calling has long been about amplifying the voices of the marginalized and increasing visibility for folks otherwise erased from our sacred texts. Together with my wife and our two sons, I model not only that it is possible to be Jewish and queer, but that the queer community can value our Judaism and the Jewish community can value our queerness. I model that we need not choose one over the other or compartmentalize the different parts of ourselves.

The well-intentioned focus on tolerance for the LGBTQ folks among us has limited our response to queer lives and stories.[4] Too often, the focus on tolerance sends the message that while it's technically acceptable to be gay, it's not ideal. It's a consolation prize, at best. It's a deviation not only from the norm in a statistical sense but from the norm in a moral sense. It's the knee-jerk reaction of parents whose children come out to them that makes them blurt, "But who will give me grandchildren?" So many assumptions lay buried in this question: that it's a child's duty to provide grandchildren to their own parents; that queer people cannot become parents; that our parents had expectations for our ideal futures and we have fallen short.

Tolerance looks very much like the classical Rabbinic logical structure *l'chat'chilah . . . b'diavad*, meaning "from the outset" and "after the fact."[5] Used to describe the way a person should fulfill a mitzvah (a commandment), these words teach a hierarchy for ideal ways to live according to Jewish law. Ideally, there is one way to fulfill Jewish values, "from the outset" (*l'chat'chilah*), but in extraordinary or exceptional cases, an alternative, less preferable way might suffice "after the fact" (*b'diavad*), at least technically. To choose a complex example, the sixteenth-century code of Jewish law the *Shulchan Aruch* argues that a man whose primary desire is for Torah study may, so long as his sexual drive does not lead him to otherwise sinful behavior, neglect the commandment to "be fruitful and multiply."[6] However, a seventeenth-century commentator is quick to correct, a person "in any event, does not, from the outset, behave this way."[7] In other words, while *acceptable* in Jewish tradition for a person not to have children, we would not permit a person, under Jewish law, to declare outright that they intend never to be a parent. Should they find themselves in a such a situation, we do not account it a sin, but we do not pretend to be proud or happy about it.[8]

520 · A LIFE OF MEANING

The reasoning and rhetoric of tolerance send those of us in the queer community a message: *l'chat'chilah*, a Jew achieves and embodies an ideal, valued, and valuable Jewish life by entering a heterosexual marriage, adhering to a binary view of gender that admits only "men" and "women" (no other categories, and no "switching" between or among categories); *b'diavad*, after the fact, if we cannot help it, our queer relationships—with or without children, with or without strict adherence to gender binaries, with or without a trans narrative—can suffice, in a pinch. Is this the message you would want young folks to hear when they come out as gay, lesbian, bisexual, transgender, or queer? *Your lives are less than ideal; to be out and queer is not what we want for you. But now that we know this truth about you, we'll deal with it.*

The Reform Movement, long a champion of inclusion, founded on the notion of gender equality (a notion that desperately needs expanding so that the entire community might embrace transgender lives and narratives), has an opportunity to ensure that all Jews—not *regardless of* but *because of, including, embracing* our gender and our sexuality—see ourselves celebrated in the unfolding story of the Jewish people. That scroll we remove from the ark each and every week, though it ostensibly has a beginning and an end, remains unfinished. The margins of the Talmud may seem filled with all the text they can hold, but there's so much more room left. Our story is an eternal one, and it is our job as Reform Jews to explore and to lift up as many versions of that story as we can. This is not merely a question of whether religious school registration forms continue to use the outdated language of "mother" and "father" rather than "parent 1" and "parent 2," but a question of whether we present to folks at all stages of their lives that being queer *and* Jewish is a possibility.

How crucial is this project? Literally, it is a matter of life and death: I recall sitting across from one young person who struggled with the self-knowledge of the same-sex desire they could not deny. At the beginning of their life, this young person declared desperately that they could see only two options for how their life would proceed: deny and ignore any trace of same-sex desire, lie to self and others, and enter a heterosexual marriage—or commit suicide. We cannot allow one more person to live under the illusion that queer Jews have just two choices and that each of them amounts to disappearance.

Each year on the second night of Passover, New York University's queer Jewish club hosts Exodus: NYU's Annual Queer Seder. Using the Haggadah I wrote and compiled,[9] the seder links the Exodus from Egypt (*y'tziat Mitzrayim*) to the ongoing experience of coming out of the closet (*y'tziah meihaaron*). We dedicate each of the four cups to the coming-out stories of our members (students, faculty, and staff, both Jewish and non-Jewish). Students speak about the struggle to understand their own desires and identities in the context of Jewish community.[10] They articulate the challenge to find models of ways to be both Jewish and gay. A cisgender,[11] gay man confidently attended wearing a skirt, his nails filed and polished to fabulousness. He acknowledged this as a formerly unimaginable, unimagined moment, but one that was central to his sense of himself as fully queer and fully Jewish. Another young person, who uses the pronouns "they/them," understands themselves in a broader historical context, acknowledging, "I am cautiously queer around my elders because I can hold simultaneous truths of liberation and deep pain held tight within the same word hurled like bricks or gleefully sewn on denim jackets."[12] Our Exodus community has witnessed tales of moms dropping the Thanksgiving turkey when a daughter declares she's a lesbian, of Jewish camp counselors who refuse to refer to transgender students with the correct name and pronouns,[13] of teachers who responded to tales of familial disappointment at a young person's coming out by saying, simply, "But I don't wish you were any other way, because then you wouldn't be you."

These students desperately need to integrate their Jewish selves with their queer selves. Too often, they've learned about one and they've learned about the other, but in separate contexts. They have heard few (if any) stories from Torah, *Tanach*, or Talmud that acknowledge same-sex desires or relationships; they have no notion that the Rabbis of our tradition have long acknowledged sexual and gender variation beyond the categories of "men" and "women."[14]

At Queer Havdalah events, I have watched students cry tears of joy and relief and disappointment, imagining what their childhoods might have been if only their communities had been proactive (rather than reactive) about queer identity, imaging what their futures might be as both out and Jewish. Why tears? Because we queer folks are too often expected to imagine ourselves into stories that leave little or no room for us. When our Hebrew school teaches us about the Jewish life cycle by staging a mock wedding between a *chatan* (groom) and a *kallah* (bride) but does not name the possibility of groom and groom or bride and bride (or, better yet, by occasionally also staging a mock same-sex Jewish wedding), we are expected to edit the picture in our minds to include ourselves, our futures. When our fellow congregants make innocent-seeming jokes about an infant at his *b'rit milah* about what a "ladies' man" he'll be some day, we have to correct the picture in our minds to include the possibility that this child may be a girl and that her gender identity might not have anything to do with how we might predict her sexuality to play out. It is rare that we have leaders (rabbis, educators, temple presidents, parents) who present queer Jewish lives as a valuable possibility before we've even begun to understand our own sexual or gender identities. But that's precisely what is needed.

If I could relive the experience of searching for those novels and medical texts and definitions of the word "lesbian"—I wouldn't. Because if I could relive the experience of coming out, I would relive the experience of coming to understand what human sexuality and gender identity are in a more organic and integrated way. I would not have had to look up the word "lesbian" and wonder what it might mean, because I would already have seen and heard and witnessed many stories about the value and the joy and the challenge of living a queer, Jewish life.

At the heart of every Reform congregation, beneath an eternal light, the Torah waits to be unrolled each and every Shabbat, each and every holiday. A scroll of black fire on white fire, the Torah is called a tree: a living entity that provides shade and fruit and clean air to breathe.

The Torah is composed of stories—and its unfolding continues to this very day. When we proclaim the stories of the Jewish people, we as Reform Jews must be expansive and generous in that reading. We must acknowledge the exclusions and violences done to and with Judaism against the queer community. We must present queer lives as equally valuable to straight, cisgender lives.

NOTES

1. I have previously and publicly discussed some of the stories in this essay, most notably at Brooklyn Heights Synagogue's Pride Shabbat on June 14, 2013.

2. Jonathan Sacks, *A Letter in the Scroll: Understanding Our Jewish Identity and Exploring the Legacy of the World's Oldest Religion* (Free Press, 2004), 43–44.

3. Cited in Denise L. Eger, "Embracing Lesbians and Gay Men: A Reform Jewish Innovation," in *The Sacred Encounter*, ed. Lisa Grushcow (New York: CCAR Press, 2013), 251.

4. For a more theoretically informed political analysis of the concept of tolerance, see Ann Pellegrini and Janet Jakobsen, *Love the Sin: Sexual Regulation and the Limits of Religious Tolerance* (Boston: Beacon Press, 2003).

5. Again, this concept is one about which I frequently speak and write, notably in a panel at New York City's Congregation Rodeph Shalom for the launch of *The Sacred Encounter*, in which my essay "Blessed Is the God Who Changes Us: Theological Que(e)ries" appears.

6. *Shulchan Aruch, Even HaEizer* 1:4 (4).

7. *Taz* to previous.

8. For more on the issue of childlessness in Jewish communities, see my Hebrew Union College–Jewish Institute of Religion (New York) rabbinic thesis, "*Yotzei Dofen*: Valuing Exceptional Jewish Lives."

9. Available on Keshet International's resource website, http://www.keshetonline .org.

10. I consulted students before including their stories here, unless they represent general patterns revealed in the stories over the past five years.

11. Meaning, the sex one was assigned at birth continues to match a person's interior sense of themselves as male or female.

12. Leah Miller, "Exodus," *Bronfman Center Blog*, April 20, 2017. Quoted with permission.

13. It is so painful for many transgender folks to be referred to by the names they were given at birth that some folks refer to this as their "deadname."

14. See, for example, the work of Rabbis Elliot Kukla and Reuben Zellman and organizations like TransTorah and ImmerseNYC.

51

JEWS AND RACE

RABBI RACHEL S. MIKVA, PhD

> At the first conference on religion and race, the main partici-
> pants were Pharaoh and Moses. Moses' words were: "Thus
> says the Lord, the God of Israel, let My people go that they
> may celebrate a feast to Me." While Pharaoh retorted: "Who
> is the Lord, that I should heed this voice and let Israel go? I
> do not know the Lord, and moreover I will not let Israel go"
> [Exodus 5:1–2]. The outcome of that summit meeting has not
> come to an end. Pharaoh is not ready to capitulate. The exo-
> dus began, but is far from having been completed.
>
> —*Abraham Joshua Heschel*

Heschel was speaking at the National Conference on Religion and
Race in 1963, in the thick of the struggle for African American civil
rights in the United States. Noting that "it was easier for the children
of Israel to cross the Red Sea than for a Negro to cross certain university campuses," he argued that the concept of race is antithetical
to religion: "To act in the spirit of religion is to unite what lies apart.
. . . To act in the spirit of race is to sunder, to slash, to dismember the
flesh of living humanity."[1]

Yet the construct of race still confronts us today, because racial
justice is not as simple as securing voting rights and access to public
facilities for people of all colors. Systemic racism plagues America in
criminal justice, local policing, employment discrimination, education,

health care and wealth disparities, daily microaggressions, and a host of other inequities. What does all this have to do with the Jews?

Jews were heavily involved in the fight for integration, voting rights, and an end to Jim Crow. They marched and lobbied and organized. Most people know about Andrew Goodman and Michael Schwerner, two white Jewish boys who were murdered alongside James Cheney in Mississippi 1964 as they tried to register African Americans to vote. Fewer people know about the seventeen white Reform rabbis who were arrested in St. Augustine, Florida, three days earlier, for the crimes of praying and eating with their black brothers and sisters. In jail their first night, they wrote about why they responded to Dr. King's call:

> We came because we could not stand silently by our brother's blood. We had done that too many times before. . . . Silence has become the unpardonable sin of our time. . . . We came as Jews who remember the millions of faceless people who stood quietly, watching the smoke rise from Hitler's crematoria. We came because we know that, second only to silence, the greatest danger to man is loss of faith in man's capacity to act.[2]

Jewish philanthropists gave heavily to historically black colleges and helped found or fund some of the pivotal organizations in the fight for racial equality: the NAACP, the Urban League, the Congress of Racial Equality. Rabbi Robert Marx, a Reform rabbi in Chicago, publicly called out other Jews who acted as slumlords or inner-city merchants who dealt unfairly with communities of color. He went on to found the Jewish Council on Urban Affairs, which continues to work in vital partnerships with diverse community organizations seeking social and economic equality.

Ideas about how to be effective activists and allies against systemic racism continue to evolve, and it has become increasingly evident how oppressions of race, class, gender, sexuality, and religion intersect in the perpetuation of injustice. Aware that historic participation in civil rights efforts is not sufficient, Jewish individuals and organizations remain active in the fight for racial justice in numerous ways and in disproportionate numbers. We find T'ruah, Bend the Arc, Jews for Racial and Economic Justice, HIAS, the Religious Action Center of Reform Judaism, and scores of others committed to the Black Lives Matter and Moral Monday movements, to criminal justice and immigration reforms, to living wage and migrant worker rights, to combatting police violence and Islamophobia.

It can require navigating complex spaces, especially as politics of the Israeli-Palestinian conflict intersect with anti-racist efforts. After the Movement for Black Lives issued a platform that included a plank labeling Israel as an apartheid state and claiming that U.S. support made it "complicit in the genocide committed against the Palestinian people," many Jewish anti-racist activists were caught in the middle.[3] Yet Rabbi Susan Talve insists on the transformative possibilities of remaining present to one another (*hineni*), of "listening deeply to each other's truths without becoming defensive. . . . I will keep showing up in uncomfortable and uninviting and messy places." She speaks of using her white privilege to "hold the space for those who are marginalized until their voices are heard and their children are safe in our streets."[4]

We also see Jews still willing to shine a light on bias within our community. In Israel, the Reform Movement has long been a leader in exposing and fighting racial prejudice against Palestinians, foreign workers, and non-Ashkenazi Jews. In the United States, the Jewish Multiracial Network and Be'chol Lashon (the latter organization's name means "in every tongue") confront the tendency to render millions of Jews of color invisible, imagining that they do not exist. Most books present Jewish diversity today by describing distinct religious movements; a few identify differences between Ashkenazic and Sephardic praxis. It is not surprising, then, that the majority of American Jews do not know that half of the Jews in Israel are not white, mostly from North Africa and Arabic-speaking countries (known as Mizrachi Jews). They may be vaguely aware of Latinx Jews who live or have roots in Central and South America, and they have heard of the Beta Yisrael from Ethiopia—but probably not the Lemba of southern Africa, the Abayudaya in Uganda, the Ibo in Nigeria, the B'nei Yisrael from India, or the Kaifeng Jews of China. They may not even know much about Black Hebrew and Israelite communities established in the United States or about the many Jews of color who have been part of majority-white congregations for generations.

Part of this erasure has to do with the unique history of Jews in the United States. Although the first Jews who came to these shores were Sephardic, arriving in the seventeenth century, the massive European immigration between 1880 and 1920 included over two million Ashkenazic Jews, overwhelming the existing communities and changing the racial balance. Like many ethnic (and non-Protestant) immigrant populations, these Jews were not considered white until after World War II, but now a significant majority of Jews in the United States identify as white and it has become the "norm." As Marla Brettschneider complains, "The very possibility of Black Jews is erased in the U.S. racial creation/coding of Jews and other groups in numerous subtle and insidious ways." She relates how she searched her university library catalogue for the subject heading "Black Jews." There was nothing listed, despite the fact that the library carries two books by women who are both black and Jewish, who use the words "black" and "Jewish" in their titles.[5]

Similarly when we talk about black-Jewish relations and the tensions that arose between the communities after the 1970s, there appears to be no room for a person who is both. Julius Lester talks about being sent to cover Louis Farrakhan's speech at Madison Square Garden in 1985; because Lester is a black man, no one there guessed he was also a Jew. The invisible clash of identities caused him to flee, frightened "like a *shtetl* Jew on Good Friday" by the anti-Semitic rhetoric and the cheers, at the same time that he knew the searing wound of racism's relentless heat.[6] Complexity of identity for individuals of mixed-race heritage can be even more challenging to navigate, as they sometimes encounter challenges to their authenticity when they try to celebrate their diverse parts.

White normativity prompts repeated marginalization for Jews of color. It can be as simple as walking into a synagogue where people presume you are not Jewish, or you must have converted, or you are adopted, or (if you are black) you must be from Ethiopia. If you are none of those things, you may become a creature of exotic fascination, which can be just as oppressive. White experience is centered in conversations about Jewish foods, names, hair, humor, neighborhoods, history, and culture. In "African American Jewish Women—Life Beyond the Hyphen," Yavilah McCoy comments:

> I find Grace when I can enjoy being "other" than the normative experience because I am valued as a contribution to the betterment of a whole. Sometimes it's difficult for me to hit up against cultures in people and organizations that manifest like walls—impermeable walls where difference feels like a reason to stay out and not engage. Grace, for me, comes when I can approach these encounters with compassion and love instead of anger. When I am able to reach deep within me to define myself within and hold on to that, while I share what I know . . . until eventually, what was seen as normative shifts.[7]

Ironically, erasure happens even in the way many white Jewish activists talk about fighting systemic racism, when they speak about how "we" need to reach out to the African American community—forgetting that they are also us. Social media is beginning to make Jewish diversity more visible, and 2016 saw the first national assembly for Jews of color in the United States, but there is a long way to go. Rabbi Ruth Abusch–Magder researched the growing discourse of white rabbis talking about systemic racism, affirming the acknowledgment of white privilege but also noting the need to complicate race beyond the binary of black and white, to recognize Jews of color, and to "complicate Blackness. . . . In addressing the harm of racism, we need beware of perpetuating the very stereotyping we abhor. White Jewish leaders should be careful not to talk about all Black people as in need of our help or rescue."[8]

The extensive history of anti-Semitism, and its transformation in the modern period from theological anti-Judaism to racial persecution, makes some white Jews resistant to acknowledging their white privilege. It can be difficult to recognize how the color of one's skin may bestow "an invisible package of unearned assets."[9] Despite the unparalleled integration of Jews into the fabric of America, many have also known physical and verbal violence, suffered social discrimination or subtle slights, or lost family members in the Shoah. They find anti-Semitic lies and hatred spewed about on the Internet, and they carry fears that any number of events in the world could be "bad for the Jews." It sometimes blinds white Jews to the skin privilege that they also bear.

Yet this history simultaneously helps to catalyze powerful empathy for marginalized individuals and communities. The Shoah illuminated the extent to which people could strip human identity from others, and many Jews feel compelled to resist the demonization or persecution of any group. The immigrant experience shaped American Jewish politics and a culture of concern. Making space for difference is good for the Jews, too.

Underlying these historical and sociological factors, Jews' ongoing commitment to racial justice springs from the religious tradition (even among secular Jews!), which is in turn shaped by texts. "Love the stranger as yourself, for you were strangers in the land of Egypt," it says in Leviticus 19:34—with similar admonitions in thirty-five other places in the Hebrew Bible, one of the most often repeated instructions we have. Empathy is presented as a foundational commandment. The idea of a just God committed to human liberation who will deliver the oppressed from bondage; the teaching that we are to experience Passover each year as if we ourselves were slaves in Egypt, newly redeemed; the command to pursue justice (*Tzedek, tzedek tirdof* [Deuteronomy 16:20])—economic justice, social justice, criminal justice, ecological justice, gender justice, racial justice—these flow from the books into which we have inscribed ourselves because they form the sacred story of our identity.

It is worth examining how Torah illuminates the conundrum of race today, even though we recognize that "race" is a modern construct; the idea that skin tone represents substantial social or biological difference was not present in ancient societies. Nonetheless, the Hebrew Bible has quite a lot to say about the good, the bad, and the ugly of how we form groups, establish boundaries, and evaluate difference. Space is too short for a thorough survey, but a few texts stand out.

In Genesis 1, humanity is created in the image of God—male and female, with no mention of race. We should not underestimate the radical power of this anti-racist teaching. Animals and plants are created according to their kinds, with different species, but there is no different breed of human. We are one species, all endowed with the immutable value inherent in a likeness of the Divine. At the same time, the Rabbis taught, there is absolute uniqueness to every human being. They imagined the remarkable difference between the way a human king mints coins in his likeness, every one the same, versus God's molding of each person a matchless creature, irreplaceable in the unfolding of history (*Mishnah Sanhedrin* 4:5).

Tanach also grapples with ways that human society fails to honor the divine image in the face of the other. In terse narratives, the text manages to reveal complexities that people often neglect. It teaches, for example, how difference is bound up with power. Just after Torah details the naturally increasing diversity of humanity, proliferating with peoples and languages after the Flood, it tells the story of Babel (Genesis 11). A powerful empire arises that imagines all the world the same; with everyone speaking the same language, nothing is beyond their reach, and they determine to build a tower with its top up in the heavens. We know of structures that might have inspired such a tale, ziggurats of the ancient Sumerian and Babylonian Empires.

Jewish tradition has discerned all kinds of potential problems with this project, such as trying to usurp the throne of God or caring more about the bricks than about the lives of those who fashion them.[10] Ultimately, however, the story is a critique of empire, of the notion that we maximize human greatness by privileging one language, one culture, one goal, one truth. Babel illuminates the path of tyranny and the legacy of racism. It is a mirror for Western colonialism and white privilege, where power has been confused with normativity, and "norm" has been confused with good.

At the end of the Babel story, God reestablishes difference, multiplying the languages and scattering the peoples across the earth. It is not a punishment, but a fulfillment of the divine command after the Flood: "Be fruitful and multiply; populate the earth and increase in it" (Genesis 9:7). Rabbi Jonathan Sacks teaches that Judaism begins with a theology of difference: the radical otherness of God should lead us to respect the radical otherness of diverse languages, nations, cultures, and races. He asserts that Babel is followed by the call to Abraham because God "turns to one people and commands it to be different *in order to teach humanity the dignity of difference.*"[11]

Other passages, however, highlight how easy it is to make difference appear as danger or as evidence of inequality. Pharaoh simply mentions that the Israelites could turn into a fifth column, and all of Egypt is ready to enslave them (Exodus 1:9–11). In the Book of Esther, Haman persuades King Ahasuerus to order the Jews' annihilation with a bribe and this insidious claim: "There is a certain people, scattered and dispersed among the other peoples in all the provinces of your realm; their laws are different from those of other people and they do not obey the king's laws. It is not in the king's interest to tolerate them" (Esther 3:8).

Sometimes we have to learn over against the text, as it is not innocent of polemic that poisons how we think about difference. In making the case against idolatry, *Tanach* goes beyond arguments that it violates the covenant and is an exercise in futility. It links practitioners to sexual immorality and child sacrifice (e.g., Hosea 4:13–14; Ezekiel 23:39) and sanctions violence against the sacred sites of the Canaanites: "Tear down their altars, smash their pillars, cut down their sacred posts, and consign their images to the fire. For you are a people consecrated to the Eternal your God: of all the peoples on earth the Eternal your God chose you to be God's treasured people" (Deuteronomy 7:5–6). We must recognize our own capacity to demonize difference when it suits our purposes.

Although some critics have identified Jewish chosenness with racism because chosenness is tied to a people rather than a faith, the argument does not fit the vast majority of biblical evidence. Jon Levenson asserts, "One of the hardest points of biblical thought to understand is the concept of peoplehood, which is familial and natural without being racial and biologistic."[12] Chosenness is *not* due to any innate superiority, racial or other. The biblical portrait of the people Israel includes not only descendants of Abraham and Sarah, but also a "mixed multitude" that emerges together out of Egypt (Exodus 12:38) and others who became part of the assembly (Deuteronomy 23:8–9). Rabbinic literature imagines that Abraham and Sarah gathered followers from among the surrounding populations at the very beginning (*B'reishit Rabbah* 39:14), and the Sages established a formal path for individuals not born to the community to join it. Over time, it grew even more multiethnic and multinational.

Parts of *Tanach* express concerns about intermarriage and formal treaties with polytheists who would then be in a position to lead the community toward idolatry (Exodus 34:15–16), but a desire to preserve the integrity of one's culture and praxis is not necessarily malevolent. Unfortunately the language of Ezra, when he rebukes the Jews for intermarrying and mixing "the holy seed" (Ezra 9:1), provides a glancing biblical foundation for those who want to read into chosenness a genetic foundation. While the Book of Ruth provides a compelling counter-voice (presenting the "House of David," elected by God to rule over Israel, as descended from a Moabite woman), the people of Israel is a "group," and with every group, from teenage cliques to nation-states, there is a risk of developing exclusivist strains.

Aware of this danger, the prophets teach in numerous ways that election does not provide exclusive title to divine concern. Amos wants the people to understand that God has a relationship with every nation: "'Children of Israel, are you not just like the Ethiopians to Me?' declares the Eternal. 'Did I not bring Israel up from the land of Egypt, but also the Philistines from Caphtor and the Arameans from Kir?'" (Amos 9:7). In calling the nation to account for its failures and warning that the consequences will be dire, he declares that chosenness entails not special privilege, but rather additional liability for falling short of God's call (Amos 3:1–2). The prophet conventionally identified as Third Isaiah is quite clear that foreigners who attach themselves to God and observe the covenant have equal status and equal claim to the spiritual inheritance; he presents the Temple as "a house of prayer for all peoples" (Isaiah 56:3–8). The Book of Jonah portrays a Hebrew prophet being sent to Nineveh, capital of the conquering Assyrian Empire, to save its residents from God's judgment; Jonah struggles with the mission, but God tries to teach him about divine compassion for the whole of creation.

These figures recognize the temptations of complacency, chauvinism, and parochialism that can accompany chosenness—and try to warn the people against them. The nation is reminded time and again that its election entails living in faithfulness with the covenant, including manifest concern for the marginalized within society, the widow, orphan, and stranger. Jeremy Cott calls the theology of the stranger an "anti-election" theology.[13] It might better be construed as the necessary corollary of election, a rule for how to conceive of and engage the "other" to prevent oppression and abuse.

There are a few biblical texts that talk about skin color or ethnicity in ways that get interpreted as race. Numbers 12 portrays Miriam and Aaron complaining about Moses's wife, "He married a Cushite woman!" God comes to the defense and strikes Miriam with snow-white scales on her skin. In fact, the complaint is just as much about Moses claiming a privileged relationship with the Most High even though God has spoken through his siblings as well; the comment about Moses's wife appears as a classic misdirection, one that likely has more to do with tribal identity than race. (Cushite is associated with African, sometimes more specifically translated as "Ethiopian.") Yet some rabbis read it as a racial reference and, following the ancient *Targum*, which translated the Hebrew word as "beautiful," asserted that she was in fact more beautiful in appearance and in deeds than all other women.[14] It is also suggested that Miriam is punished measure for measure, afflicted with skin "too white" for suggesting that Moses's wife has skin that is too dark.

The passage with the most problematic racial history has to do with Noah's son Ham, who "saw his father's nakedness" (Genesis 9:22). As a consequence, Ham's son Canaan is doomed to be the lowest of slaves to his brothers, and since Ham was the purported ancestor of African peoples, this narrative was deployed among the scriptural justifications for American slavery. There has been a great deal of discussion about Jewish attitudes and involvement in the colonial slave trade, much of it polemical, but the simple fact is that the relatively small number of Jews in the Americas tended to resemble their closest neighbors, with slave owners and abolitionists both citing Scripture to defend their point of view.[15]

The multivocality of the tradition traces back to its earliest layers of interpretation. Some Jewish exegesis suggested that Ham was "smitten in his skin." In the Talmud, it could easily be a reference to a skin disease, but several later interpretations linked it to the color of Ham's skin, commenting on physical traits like thick lips and kinky hair. In the twelfth century, the Spanish-Jewish commentator Abraham ibn Ezra specifically refuted the linkage of race and slavery: people are mistaken if they argue that Cushites are slaves on account of Noah's curse, because the very first king after the Flood was a Cushite (comment on Genesis 9:25). We also find a medieval midrash that identified the descendants of Noah's son Shem (namely Semites, including the Jews) as black and beautiful, with Ham's descendants also described as black—and all the children of Noah are blessed.[16]

The image of the Semites as black and beautiful likely drew on Song of Songs, in which the female protagonist declares, "I am dark and beautiful, O daughters of Jerusalem—like the tents of Kedar, like the pavilions of Solomon." She goes on to say, "Do not stare at me because I am swarthy, for the sun has beat down upon me" (Song 1:5–6), suggesting that darker skin within the ethnic group might have to do with working outside and reminding us how race and class are often linked. Of course the song also reflects the roots of Jewish history in the Levant, where "white" was likely not the default skin color.

While any selection and interpretation of biblical texts can communicate only a limited perspective, there is insight to be gleaned from the ancient words as they challenge us to grow in our capacity to navigate difference. They also reveal why modern issues of race are of intrinsic Jewish concern. Rabbi Ellen Lippmann tells the story of her congregation's journey, as they discerned a "Torah of Race" in their anti-racism efforts. They formed a task force, engaged in difficult conversations, undertook specialized training, ensured that people of color were hired as teachers and served as members of the board, and so on—all drawing upon the sacred times and sacred texts of Judaism to inform their efforts. "This is what we have learned: Working to undo racism is what we must do as Jews."[17]

In 1997, newly installed as the senior rabbi of a Reform congregation, I gave a Rosh HaShanah sermon on systemic racism. One furious member sent me a note afterward, demanding that I talk instead about something that "really matters to the Jews." I cannot think of anything that matters more. Heschel called racism an "eye disease," one that obviously infects the beholders as well as everyone and everything they see. We are all implicated in the enduring impact that conceptions of race have on our society.

FOR FURTHER READING

Alperson, Myra. *Dim Sum, Bagels and Grits: A Sourcebook for Multicultural Families.* New York: Farrar, Straus and Giroux, 2001.

Alpert, Rebecca. *Whose Torah? A Concise Guide to Progressive Judaism.* New York: New Press, 2008.

Azoulay, Katya Gibel. *Black, Jewish and Interracial: It's Not the Color of Your Skin, but the Race of Your Kin, and Other Myths of Identity.* Durham, NC: Duke University Press, 1997.

Brettschneider, Marla. *The Family Flamboyant: Race Politics, Queer Families, Jewish Lives.* Albany: State University of New York Press, 2012.

Brodkin, Karen. *How Jews Became White Folks and What That Says about Race in America.* New Brunswick, NJ: Rutgers University Press, 1998.

Carmi, Ruth. *Racism and Gender in Israel.* Jerusalem: Israel Religious Action Center / Israel Movement for Reform and Progressive Judaism, 2015.

Dorman, Jacob. *Chosen People: The Rise of American Black Israelite Religions.* Oxford: Oxford University Press, 2013.

Faber, Eli. *Jews, Slaves and the Slave Trade.* New York: New York University Press, 1998.

Goldstein, Eric. *The Price of Whiteness: Jews, Race and American Identity.* Princeton, NJ: Princeton University Press, 2008.

Greenberg, Cheryl Lynn. *Troubling the Waters: Black-Jewish Relations in the American Century.* Princeton, NJ: Princeton University Press, 2010.

Hurvitz, Einat, Leora Bechor, and Alona Lisitsa. *Love the Stranger as Yourself? Racism in the Name of Halacha.* Translated by Shaul Vardi. Jerusalem: Israel Religious Action Center / Israel Movement for Reform and Progressive Judaism, 2011.

Kaye/Kantrowitz, Melanie. *The Colors of Jews: Racial Politics and Radical Diasporism.* Bloomington: Indiana University Press, 2007.

Khazzoom, Loolwa. *The Flying Camel: Essays on Identity by North African and Middle Eastern Women of Jewish Heritage.* New York: Seal Press, 2003.

Lester, Julius. *Lovesong: Becoming a Jew.* New York: Arcade Books, 1988.

Parfitt, Tudor. *Black Jews in Africa and the Americas.* Cambridge, MA: Harvard University Press, 2013.

Pollack, Michael. *Mandarins, Jews and Missionaries: The Jewish Experience in the Chinese Empire.* New York: Weatherhill, 1998.

Sarna, Jonathan, and Adam Mendelsohn, eds. *Jews and the Civil War: A Reader.* Albany: New York University Press, 2011.

Schorsch, Jonathan. *Jews and Blacks in the Early Modern World.* Cambridge: Cambridge University Press, 2004.

Tobin, Diane, Gary Tobin, and Scott Rubin. *In Every Tongue: The Racial and Ethnic Diversity of the Jewish People.* San Francisco: Institute for Jewish and Community Research, 2005.

Walker, Rebecca. *Black, White and Jewish.* New York: Riverhead Books, 2005.

WEBSITES, VIDEOS, AND BLOGS

Be'chol Lashon, www.bechollashon.org

Jewish Multiracial Network, www.jewishmultiracialnetwork.org

Jews for Racial and Economic Justice, www.jfrej.org

Kulanu, www.kulanu.org

MaNishtana, https://manishtana.net

National Seed Project, nationalseedproject.org/white-privilege-unpacking-the-invisible-knapsack (including notes for facilitators)

Religious Action Center, www.rac.org/civil-rights

NOTES

1. Rabbi Abraham Joshua Heschel, "Religion and Race" (speech, National Conference on Religion and Race, Chicago, January 14, 1963), http://voicesofdemocracy.umd.edu/heschel-religion-and-race-speech-text/.

2. "Why We Went: A Joint Letter from the Rabbis Arrested in St. Augustine," June 19, 1964, http://jwa.org/media/why-we-went-joint-letter-from-rabbis-arrested-in-st-augustine.

3. See the Reform Movement's Religious Action Center statement critical of the plank while reaffirming its commitment to racial justice: http://www.rac.org/reform-movement-leaders-reaffirm-commitment-racial-justice-condemn-movement-black-lives-platform.

4. Susan Talve, "Here I Show Up, Across Political Divisions," *Sh'ma Now*, September 13, 2016, http://forward.com/shma-now/hineni/348849/here-i-show-up-across-political-divisions.

5. Marla Brettschneider, *The Family Flamboyant: Race Politics, Queer Families, Jewish Lives* (Albany: State University of New York Press, 2012), 20.

6. Julius Lester, *Lovesong* (New York: Arcade Books, 1988), 235–36.

7. Yavilah McCoy and Miri Hunter Haruach, "African American Jewish Women—Life Beyond the Hyphen," *Bridges* 16, no. 1 (Spring 2011): 183.

8. Abusch–Magder, "When White Rabbis Talk about Race," My Jewish Learning, September 21, 2015, http://www.myjewishlearning.com/rabbis-without-borders/when-white-rabbis-talk-about-race.

9. Peggy McIntosh, "White Privilege: Unpacking the Invisible Knapsack," *Peace and Freedom Magazine*, July/August 1989, 10–12.

10. See, e.g., *M'chilta Mishpatim; B'reishit Rabbah* 38:8; Babylonian Talmud, *Sanhedrin* 109a; *Pirkei D'Rabbi Eliezer* 24; and the commentaries of Rashi, Rashbam, etc.

11. Jonathan Sacks, *The Dignity of Difference* (London: Bloomsbury Academic, 2003), 53. See also the nineteenth-century Torah commentary on Babel by Rabbi Naphtali Tzvi Yehuda Berlin.

12. Jon D. Levenson, "The Universal Horizon of Biblical Particularism," in *Ethnicity in the Bible*, ed. Mark G. Brett (Boston: Brill, 1996), 160.

13. Jeremy Cott, "The Biblical Problem of Election," *Journal of Ecumenical Studies* 21, no. 2 (1984): 205–7. A portion of the preceding textual discussion is adapted from Rachel S. Mikva, *Dangerous Religious Ideas: A History of Scriptural Exegesis and Its Impact in Judaism, Christianity and Islam* (forthcoming); more extensive discussion of the significance of chosenness can be found there.

14. See, e.g., *Sifrei Numbers* 99; Babylonian Talmud, *Mo-eid Katan* 16b: *Midrash Psalms* 7:18.

15. See, for instance, the 1861 argument between Rabbi Dr. M. J. Raphall (http://www.jewish-history.com/civilwar/raphall.html) and Rabbi David Einhorn (http://www.jewish-history.com/civilwar/einhorn.html).

16. Babylonian Talmud, *Sanhedrin* 108b; *Tanchuma Noah* 13; *Me'am Lo'ez* (Rabbi Yaakov Culi, nineteenth century); *Pirkei D'Rabbi Eliezer* 23.

17. Ellen Lippmann, "A Jewish Congregation Tackles Racism" eJewish Philanthropy, September 6, 2016, http://ejewishphilanthropy.com/a-jewish-congregation

-tackles-racism; Lippmann, "Why Must We Work to Undo Racism as Jews?," Huffington Post, October 22, 2015, http://www.huffingtonpost.com/rabbi-ellen -lippmann/why-must-we-work-to-undo-racism-as-jews_b_8353772.html.

52

A REFORM JEWISH RESPONSE TO POVERTY

RABBI AMY SCHWARTZMAN

Judaism is replete with commandments, stories, comments, guidance, and concern for the poor. One might even say that Judaism expects us to be preoccupied with the work of ending poverty. From our earliest sacred books of the Torah, through the inspiring writings of the prophets and on to modern writings, Jewish texts provide insights, direction, and advice on how we should engage with those in need. If you have wondered how to respond to that person who asks you for money on the street; if you have debated which charity deserves your most significant contribution; if you are looking for guidance as you vote on a new tax plan—Judaism can help. Our tradition is deeply concerned with how we interact with the poor, including our attitude and our affect toward them. It provides direction about actual financial support from both individuals and communal organizations. For Reform Jews, who link ourselves to the prophetic call for social justice, it compels us to respond to the needs of those less fortunate in fulfillment of our most basic communal responsibility.

The Torah provides us with a foundational concept from which all commandments about the poor emanate. In Genesis 1:27 we read that each of us is created *b'tzelem Elohim*, "in the image of God." All people share this fundamental characteristic. The poor are no less connected to the Divine than the rich, and to diminish any human being is to offend the Creator, who instilled the same divinity in each one of us. This sense of equality and equity is also affirmed in the many texts that use the word *achicha*, meaning "your brother," to describe the one in need. He or she is not a stranger, not an unknown, but someone very close to you. Together these concepts demand that we treat the poor as our equal and even more as a member of our own family. Indeed if the person asking us for money on the street turned out to be our aunt or cousin, we would readily help them out. These small but significant words instruct us not only to respond to the poor because they are one of us but to do so with dignity and respect.

The Torah is not only concerned about our attitude to the poor; it also gives us some direction on practical ways in which we must respond to their needs. We are instructed to behave fairly to the poor, to be impartial when meting out justice (Leviticus 19:15). We are commanded to refrain from taking interest when lending money to those who need it (Exodus 22:24). The poor receive some of the tithes designated in the Torah, and they are allowed to take from the corners of the farmers' fields, thus providing them with food as well as a private and dignified way to attain it (Leviticus 19:10). While most of us are not farmers today, we can apply the idea that a portion of our yield be set aside in an accessible way to help others. It makes no difference how large or small our allegorical field is or how fruitful our crop; we are commanded to ensure that there is always a portion left for others.

When it comes to giving to the poor, perhaps the most compelling Torah text comes from Deuteronomy 15. First the text states that there will be no poor among us if we only follow all of God's commandments. After this aspirational line, Deuteronomy returns to a more realistic context and states in verses 7–8, "If . . . there is a needy person among you, one of your kin in any of your settlements in the land that the Eternal your God is giving you, do not harden your heart and shut your hand against your needy kin. Rather, you must open your hand and lend whatever is sufficient to meet the need." Both the attitude and the action demonstrate generosity. We are commanded to open our hearts and ours hands and to give.

As clear as Deuteronomy is in calling us to engage with the poor, our prophets speak with even more passion and commitment. Their call for social justice resonates in the ears of Reform Jews who are motivated by the message of moral decency. On Yom Kippur morning, in the congregations of the Reform Movement, we invoke the words of Isaiah, who rebukes the ancient Israelite community, telling them that fasting and bringing sacrifices while at the same time ignoring the needs of the poor and disenfranchised is an abomination to God. In response, Isaiah, invoking God, cries out, "Is not this the kind of fast that I have chosen: to loose the chains of injustice and untie the cords of the yoke, to set the oppressed free and break every yoke? Is it not to share your food with the hungry and provide the poor wanderer with shelter? When you see the naked, to clothe him and not to turn away from your own flesh and blood?" (Isaiah 58:6–7). Isaiah, Amos, Jeremiah, Ezekiel, and Zechariah continually speak of supporting the poor and chastise the Israelites for misuse of their own wealth and their abuse and neglect of those who live in poverty. There is no question that the highest concentration of appeals for just action for the poor can be found among the writings of the prophets.

While the Torah and the prophets paint a compelling picture of our requirement to support the needy, they fall short of answering many of the questions we regularly face in our day-to-day lives. Do I give money to a person who is in need even if she won't use that money wisely? Do I donate to a worthy organization when their executives are known to receive inflated salaries? Do I support a candidate whose policies on poverty are aligned with mine but whose beliefs about Israel are opposite from mine? As is so often the case, our later texts, such as the Mishnah and Talmud, bring more detail into our discussion of poverty. Likely this is a reflection of the fact that the laws compiled during biblical times reflected an agrarian society. We hear about leaving the corners of the fields for the poor and bringing a tithe from our flocks or crops. Once our community became more urban and industrial, the stratification of society became greater and more complex. More direction and guidance were needed to respond to the nuanced issues of economic security. While the Mishnah, the Talmud, and later works aren't able to address every dimension of support, they help us to drill further down so that we can better understand and respond to diverse needs. From them, we learn, for example, how to decide between providing a person with food versus shelter or responding to immediate needs versus planning for a sustainable financial future.

These later Rabbinic texts are engaged in two parallel conversations, both reflecting the core Jewish values of supporting the poor, not only financially but also emotionally and spiritually. The first conversation takes an objective approach to responding to those in need from a strictly financial lens. These discussions and debates, which begin as early as the Mishnah and continue through today, strive to establish a "poverty threshold" in order to prioritize resources. Three levels of need are determined in *Mishnah Pei-ah* 7:8, and all require a response from the community. Our texts state that a person who doesn't have enough food for a day, a person who is in critical straits, is entitled to receive support from a communal resource called the *tamchui*, which was likely a soup kitchen or food pantry. The person who doesn't have enough food for a week is eligible to receive support from the *kupah*, a type of community fund that distributed money or resources once a week. Finally there is a third category that resembles more of a poverty threshold. If an individual cannot sustain his or her household for a year, that person may receive *tzedakah*. *Tzedakah* here represents a larger group of community-supported donations and giving programs.

Whereas the first two levels of poverty reflect an immediate and urgent need, the third responds to a longer-term financial security. Jewish texts clearly state that to be financially stable everyone needs a home, cooking utensils, clothing, and enough money for a year (Jerusalem Talmud, *Pei-ah* 21a–b). In ancient times this was 200 *zuzim*. Our scholars were well aware that 200 *zuzim* in Jerusalem might not go as far as 200 *zuzim* in Beersheba, and they factored that into their equations as well.

In addition to trying to discern who is considered poor, our texts also make it clear who must respond. The Babylonian Talmud clearly states that a person who resides in a city for thirty days must contribute to the *tamchui*. If you live there for three months, then you must give to the *kupah*. After six months you must contribute to the clothing fund, and nine months to the burial fund (Babylonian Talmud, *Bava Batra* 8a). If you buy a house, indicating that you are there to stay, you have an obligation to all of the requirements of the third category of giving, *tzedakah*, along with the first and second category. From this we learn that we have obligations to help the poor on many levels related to how rooted you are in the place. We have to support those whose needs are immediate as well as contribute to organizations or systems that provide longer-term sustenance. It is not either-or; in our tradition it is both.

The Rabbis' second conversation is a much more subjective and detailed discussion of supporting others. In Deuteronomy 15:8 we are instructed to "open your hand . . . to meet the need." The Rabbis are also concerned with need beyond the basics. They consider an individual who is rich who suddenly loses his job. He doesn't have money to put gas in his expensive car. While we might be inclined to suggest that this person sell the car and start taking the bus, the Rabbis were sympathetic and believed that we actually had an obligation to be supportive even if in Talmudic days it meant providing "a servant to run in front of him and a horse for him to ride on" (Babylonian Talmud, *K'tubot* 67b). Need is not always measurable by hard facts. While later commentators would come to limit the type of support suggested above, the discussions and debates surrounding these ideas suggest that our job is to see the "need" in another person. A change in financial status may result in a need that others would consider an indulgence. But the Rabbis understood that the economic status of a person can influence his or her spiritual and mental health especially as he or she goes through difficult times, and even this is part of our responsibility.

There are numerous texts that suggest that giving emotional or spiritual support is even more valuable than giving in a material way.

Rabbi Isaac taught, "One who gives a coin to a poor person attains six blessings; but one who gives him a word of comfort attains eleven blessings" (Babylonian Talmud, *Bava Batra* 9b). These and other texts like it suggest that we cannot neglect the human side of the individual we are supporting. As important as it is to provide financial aid, we also have to find ways to provide our *achicha* with the intangible support he needs. It is not enough to fill the bowls at the soup kitchen if those who come for sustenance are suffering from isolation, anxiety, or depression. We can imagine that poverty can lead to a broken spirit. Judaism calls us to meet the needs of that spirit along with the needs of that body. We may do this ourselves by taking time to speak with the person who is in need, hear their story, and give them our time and attention. We also might do this by choosing organizations that deal with the whole person above and beyond the financial need. For this reason our tradition might encourage us to give to a clinic that provides wrap-around services over an organization that only gives out money for research.

Throughout the spectrum of discussions about poverty—those that are financial and those that go beyond material needs—Jewish texts clearly state that the best thing we can do for our neighbor in need is to help her to become fully self-sufficient once again. Poverty is not seen as a permanent state; it is not held up as an ideal or elevated way to live. Individuals should work to bring themselves out of poverty, and those who are receiving funds from others are even obligated to participate in *tzedakah* themselves. With this in mind, the biblical commandment to lend money without interest is considered one of the most meritorious forms of dispensing resources to the poor. Perhaps the most well-known text affirming this approach is Maimonides's treatise proposing eight levels of giving. The highest degree "is one who upholds the hand of a Jew reduced to poverty by handing him a gift or a loan, or entering into a partnership with him, or finding work for him, in order to strengthen his hand, so that he will have no need to beg from other people" (*Mishneh Torah, Hilchot Matanot Aniyim* 7:7). In many ways this captures the highest expectations of our engagement with the poor. It preserves dignity, self-respect, and privacy while providing an individual with the means to achieve self-sufficiency, all within an interpersonal relationship.

Responding to the needs of others can be a daunting task; thinking about combating poverty in our greater community, country, or world can be overwhelming. All Jews, no matter the movement with which they affiliate, must step up. It is clear that the commandments to support those in need are central to our tradition. Ending poverty may be an idealistic goal, but our sacred texts and the rabbis who interpreted them encourage us to do what we can to reach it. What we learn from the small portion of texts cited here is that we must become involved on both the small and big levels; we must give locally as well as nationally; we must provide for urgent support as well as helping with longer-term stability. That means being prepared to say yes when someone on the street asks you for money for food, or it may mean finding a local soup kitchen in which to volunteer. It also means working to change the larger issues surrounding economic need. That would include changing public policy or support of global efforts. Our tradition does not allow us to choose only one dimension—Judaism demands we fight against poverty on many levels at the same time.

No matter what choices you make in your personal *tzedakah* practice, one evident takeaway from these extensive discussions is that our involvement in combating poverty cannot be an afterthought. We shouldn't wait to assess our finances on December 31 and only then decide how much we have to give to others. Rather, to fulfill these mitzvot properly is to plan ahead and to make commitments in advance. We must commit to setting aside our resources at the beginning of the year—before we decide where we will go on vacation or if we will purchase a new car. We also must set aside time, especially time to be with others addressing non-material needs. The poor are as members of our families, and they need to feel emotionally and spiritually supported in addition to being financially sustained. We need this experience too. Through it we deepen our understanding and empathy for others. Through such personal encounters we fulfill our tradition's hope to preserve every human being's dignity and self-esteem.

Returning to our Torah, we must internalize and then actualize God's command to refrain from being hard-hearted or tightfisted toward the poor and instead open our hearts and our hands to provide for those in need. Each and every one of us must fulfill this mitzvah, but change will not come until all people take on this critical task. Alone our impact may be small, but together we can inch toward God's dream of a world without poverty.

53

TENDING TO THE SICK

Rabbi Shira Stern, DMin, BCC

We live in a world of instant access to our friends and families via social media, and yet we often feel isolated and alone. When community was central to our identity, we could rely on our neighbors and extended relatives to support us during times of need, just as we felt responsible to watch out for them when they were ill, bereft, or emotionally raw. Now we are lucky if we know our immediate neighbors, and more often than not, when we could benefit the most from their loving care, our needs are met instead by strangers in hospitals, subacute care facilities, long-term care facilities, long-term care housing, and hospices.

What can we do to transform this isolation into opportunity? We long for relationship, so we seek out new ways to connect and provide support for our immediate circle and then to an expanding circle of community. How do we learn that the theology of presence—showing up—impacts a broken soul? And how do we understand how to listen better, how to create sacred silence, and how to find the right prayers for healing to offer one another?

This chapter is intended as a guide for each of us who has struggled with helping those confronting illness of all kinds, be they physical, emotional, mental, or spiritual. As Reform Jews, we find new ways to interpret traditional texts, grappling with contradictions or solutions that are no longer useful to us. At the same time, we do not throw out the baby with the bathwater; much of what we know and what we believe is grounded in our biblical, Rabbinic, and post-Rabbinic literature.

We find in the Babylonian Talmud the following: "Rabbi Acha son of Rabbi Chanina said, 'He who visits an invalid takes away a sixtieth of his pain'" (*N'darim* 39b).

What does that mean, exactly, to those of us who require a rationale for our behavior? If visiting those who are sick indeed removes a sixtieth of their pain, does this mean that if we were to visit sixty times, they would have no pain at all? Or do we interpret the text to mean that no matter how helpless we feel when we are witness to intense physical or spiritual pain, every act, however small, makes a difference in the healing process of those we visit?

The Talmud provides us with two ways to respond to that question, both of which are deemed essential to the well-being of the patient.

First, we are required to attend to the person's physical needs:

> Rabbi Chelbo was sick. But none visited him. He rebuked them [sc. the scholars], saying, "Did it not once happen that one of Rabbi Akiva's disciples fell sick, and the Sages did not visit him? So Rabbi Akiva himself entered [his house] to visit him, and because they swept and sprinkled the ground before him, he recovered" (Babylonian Talmud, *N'darim* 40a)

Sometimes it is hard to find the right words to say to those who are ill. We find the temporary intimacy of a sickroom awkward. Do we discuss the diagnosis, keeping things on an intellectual level? What happens if patients tell us how they really feel? What then? Do we commiserate or distract them or change the subject? Do we sit close to the bed, hold their hand, and provide tissues for the tears?

Rabbi Akiva led by example, suggesting that doing small acts of compassion is even more important than words. Open a window, turn on a light, fluff a pillow, or follow the lead of the patient. When we do home visits, these might include providing prepared food, buying groceries, doing light housekeeping, or providing respite care for the primary caretakers. In an inpatient facility, it might mean communicating to the staff what the resident might not be able to articulate, securing an extra blanket, or feeding those unable to do so themselves.

This first responsibility seems both simple enough and accessible for everyone, and as it is incumbent on everyone, not even the rich and famous get a pass (*Shulchan Aruch, Yoreh Dei-ah* 335:2). Furthermore, this positive mitzvah answers the call we embrace as Reform Jews, repairing the world one person at a time.

To address these needs, we have to be present, actually or virtually. Patients need to know we are there, that we are fully present and are witness to their suffering. Literally showing up becomes the first step in establishing a theology of presence.

But even the Rabbis of the Talmud understood that doing is not enough. Formulating an appropriate prayer is also essential, so much so that they direct us not only *how* to pray but *when* to pray: not in the first three hours of the day, when the person looks fit, and not in the last three hours of the day, when the person looks so ill that the visitor would see prayer as hopeless (Babylonian Talmud, *N'darim* 40a). As long as one says a brief blessing, in any language (*Shulchan Aruch, Yoreh Dei-ah* 335:5), before ending the visit, the mitzvah of contributing to the recovery of the patient is fulfilled.

Prayer, however, is not always easy. In fact, for many it is the more difficult part of this Rabbinic formula. How exactly do we pray for healing? Do we follow a prescribed formula from traditional texts, or do we rely on more modern interpretations, accompanied by music, as in the various *Mi Shebeirach* prayers for healing now available to us? Do we teach ourselves how to create spontaneous prayers tailored to each individual we visit?

We may even think, "If I do not believe whether these prayers work, am I being inauthentic as a Jew and ineffectual as a visitor?"

There are scientists who claim that there is no rational explanation for how this kind of prayer might work, and others who believe in the possibility that the power of prayer can be answered by quantum physics, in which distant particles can affect the behavior of others in mysterious ways. This is something that puzzled Einstein in the 1930s: he referred to the phenomenon of entanglement as "spooky interactions between particles at a distance."

There some religious leaders, however, such as the Reverend Raymond J. Lawrence, who served as director of pastoral care at New York Presbyterian Hospital, who do not think that the idea of prayer and its power to intercede on a patient's behalf even belongs in the scientific realm. "Prayer can be and is helpful," Lawrence said. "But to think that you can research it is inconceivable to me. Prayer is presumably a way of addressing God, and there's no way to scientifically test God. God is not subject to scientific research."[1]

So what *do* we believe?

When I was newly ordained, I came to a tiny shul in New Jersey as their first full-time rabbi. Early on, I introduced the chanting of the *Mi Shebeirach* each time I read from Torah and at *Aleinu* when I did not. At first, very few people offered me the names of those for whom they were praying, but gradually the tradition became important enough for my congregants to stand and call out the names on their own. We learned about parents in the hospital, grandparents recuperating, children afflicted with diseases serious and less serious. I could see by the strength of their voices how well the patients were doing, or how poorly, and I was instantly reminded to call, to visit, or to send a note of support.

Why did they come? They were a group of loosely affiliated Jews, some with Orthodox backgrounds but secular practice, and others deeply committed Reform Jews who had never seen this ritual in their synagogues of origin. Why did they feel so strongly about our custom? Perhaps it was acknowledgment of their anxieties, or a public request for support, or a magical connection to God in their eyes. Maybe they thought praying for healing couldn't hurt, and surrounded as we were with large Catholic communities who regularly offered to light candles even for *our* sick relatives, it meant finding an appropriate Jewish corollary.

And yet, I struggled for years with providing my congregants a medium to deal with their fears for their loved ones at the same time as I questioned whether our *Mi Shebeirach* prayers were empty supplications.

I stood at my bimah solemnly receiving these gifts of names, watching the reactions of the families who, on hearing their pain and fear articulated and acknowledged, sat down in relief and visibly relaxed. I would wonder why such a simple act left them feeling transformed. I knew it was important to them, because if I neglected to read off a name they had requested, they would jump up to interrupt the service, so that my inadvertent mistake could be corrected immediately. What difference could this possibly make in the scheme of things? Did God personally hear my prayers—and theirs—and act upon them?

Twenty years later, after returning to chaplaincy as a full-time career, I began to see what had happened long before I acknowledged what was happening: chanting the *Mi Shebeirach* gave them something concrete to do when they felt helpless and impotent to "kiss it and make it better."

When I sat with patients of mine and held their hand and sang to them as they went to sleep, or prayed with families surrounding loved ones in the process of dying, or calmed a patient frightened of the uncertainty of prognosis, I felt a distinct change in the room. I have prayed that my patients find healing or release from constant pain, and I have seen changes in those for whom I have prayed. When I have sung at the bedside of a patient in ICU, monitored with machines that provide blood pressure, heartbeat, and oxygen levels, I have seen the pressure go down, the breathing become less labored, and the heartbeat slow to normal levels. And I have seen the tension and then the relief in neighboring patients who grab me as I leave a room and say, "Look, Rabbi, I don't know if I believe in God, but please, will you pray for me too?"

What do I believe or hope or intend that God will do when I pray on another's behalf? I believe that on some level I cannot yet fathom, God will hear my voice. I hope that God will open the gates of healing wide enough to let this person slip through, and I intend for those I pray that they be acknowledged and feel heard. I do not always pray for patients; many times, in the intensive care unit or the emergency room in the middle of the night, I have prayed for a family to find the strength to say goodbye before it is too late. I have prayed to feel the intense and overwhelming love of spouses who can't imagine a day without their partner after sixty years of marriage, so that I can use that palpable emotion to comfort them later. When this connection is made, when this prayer works, I believe—I hope, I expect—that it will pierce the atmosphere and God will hear. What God does with it is God's business. All I can do is open the door.

As a community of committed Reform Jews, we acknowledge the inherent value of petitionary prayers for healing. At the same time, many of us who want to build on this value are asking ourselves: What more can we do? How do we "pray with our hands and our feet," to paraphrase the famous quote of Rabbi Abraham Joshua Heschel on doing acts of social justice?[2]

We can concentrate on our families, our work, or ourselves and let others walk the hospital corridors or visit the housebound, or we can be on that frontline where the most mundane tasks become sacred ritual. When Moses collected offerings to build the Tabernacle, he was told, "Take from among you gifts to the Eternal; everyone whose heart is so moved [*n'div libo*] shall bring them" (Exodus 35:5). What more can we do when our hearts are moved to fulfill the mitzvah of *bikur cholim* (tending to the sick)?

Reform Jews have responded to the call of *bikur cholim* volunteer groups, which have become prevalent in synagogues, JCCs, and Jewish Federation outreach committees. Congregants give of their time by handing out flowers or prayer cards or offering challot and electronic candles for Shabbat. Seasoned volunteers might spend a few minutes with patients and their families, but many feel inadequate to the task and simply wish people a *r'fuah sh'leimah*—complete healing—before taking leave.

Many of us feel inadequate to find appropriate responses to the physical, emotional, and spiritual pain of those who are ill, whether they are loved ones or strangers. Now, *bikur cholim* volunteers crave better skills and more tools to bolster their repertoire, and we have resources to share.

We can help them help others by training them to listen differently, talk less, and be more present, even when they have a long list of people to visit. We can encourage them to bring their individual gifts to the bedside. Can they sing, or play an instrument, or knit a healing shawl?

Most of all, we can learn to hear the truth that lies in between the words, to pay attention when our loved ones ask this existential question from Psalm 22:2–3: "My God, my God, why have You forsaken me? Why are You so far from helping me, from the words of my groaning? O my God, I cry by day, but You do not answer; and by night, but find no rest."

We can offer them a theological formula that is the basis for clinical pastoral education,[3] the Torah for professional chaplains, crafted in Jewish language:

1. **Recognize that each person is a Living, Human Document:** Every person is sacred, as sacred as a Torah. We should be reverent in everyone's presence, not just those it is easy to visit. This requires setting aside all assumptions: find the holy spark in every one.

2. **Walk with the patient in their suffering:** Sit down and be with the patient. Allow them to dictate the conversation. If they need to unburden themselves, provide them the silence to do so. If they ask for strength, offer them support.

3. **Help them to articulate their truth:** Listen to both the words spoken and unspoken, and help them find the language that reflects their pain, their fear, their hopes, and their wishes.

4. **Help them to articulate their prayer:** Find the words that reflect the need. Is it a prayer of supplication, "Please, God, heal her/him/me"? Is it a prayer of gratitude? Is it a prayer of wonder

at the miracle in front of them or an agonized acknowledgment of the need to let go?

These four precepts create a spiritual framework for performing *bikur cholim*, so that the act becomes healing for both the receiver and the giver. Ultimately, all of our efforts to be present for those in need are healing to the world.

But the work, done correctly, is not easy. It is spiritual, uplifting, depressing, exhausting, exhilarating, life-affirming, awesome, sad, and joyful. To prepare to do this sacred work, when I wash my hands in preparation to enter the room, I do two things: I recite the prayer for the ritual washing of hands (*al n'tilat yadayim*), and then I stop to take a breath and say a prayer written by my teacher Rabbi Sheldon Zimmerman, called "A Prayer for Prayer."

In Your oneness, I find healing.
In the promise of Your love, I am soothed.
In Your wholeness, I too can become whole again.
Please listen to my call—
help me find the words
help me find the strength within
help me shape my mouth, my voice, my heart
so that I can direct my spirit and find You in prayer.[4]

NOTES

1. Rob Stein, "Prayer's Power to Heal Strangers Is Examined," *Washington Post*, July 15, 2005.
2. On the road from Selma to Montgomery, aside the Reverend Martin Luther King, 1965.
3. G. H. Asquith, "Anton T. Boisen and the Study of 'Living Human Documents,'" *Journal of Presbyterian History* 60, no. 3 (1982): 244–65.
4. Excerpted from Sheldon Zimmerman, "A Prayer for Prayer," in *Healing of Soul, Healing of Body*, ed. Simkha Y. Weintraub (Woodstock, VT: Jewish Lights, 1994), 101–2.

54

REFORM JUDAISM'S HEALING TENT

Rabbi Pearl Barlev, MAHL, BCC

Like the biblical patriarch Abraham, who opened his tent on all sides to welcome guests with hospitality and sustenance (Genesis 18:1–15), so does Reform Judaism. It is a modern home of this ancient tradition. Rabbi Rick Jacobs, president of the Union for Reform Judaism, explains that "nothing Jewish is alien to us. Reform Judaism is an evolving and profound expression of the Jewish tradition. Its essence is to respond to the call of God and to the imperatives of the day." Jacobs wants to create dynamic and inspiring places for people to encounter Judaism, including non-Jewish seekers. He says that "the key thing is to have the doorways open. Anyone who wants to be a part, they are welcome."[1]

And so too Reform Judaism's healing tent is such a place and is open to all who hope to discover their selves and aspirations among its contents and teachings. It is a place where Jewish expression can be a choice with an eye toward spirituality, community, and healing. Inspired by this view, this chapter brings together a collage of Jewish ideas, observances, and rituals portrayed through human stories. It is an invitation to look here to uncover "a Torah"—meaning a sacred life perspective—that can be new, personal, and meaningful and can help heal broken hearts and bodies.

In my role as rabbi/chaplain to medical and psychiatric patients,[2] both Jewish and interfaith, I have learned that healing is a complex, nuanced experience particular to each person and situation. Patients have expressed that healing is holy, explaining that it is filled with a godliness or an otherly quality that can be profoundly meaningful, beyond the intellect, and that mysteriously salves the soul. Thus healing can help transform difficult and seemingly intolerable situations. Healing can be measured in small moments or big strides. It can be an emotion from a kiss on the cheek or the remission documented in a doctor's report, and more. Examples of these in this chapter are relevant to people both in and out of hospitals who are in health crises and hard times. They tell of how individuals have understood and found respite when sickness or adversity has taken their strength and how, through that very sickness or adversity, some have come to find a new path toward themselves, God, or others, per their own need and capacity through ritual, prayer, and Jewish tradition.

We draw from Jewish wisdom as a guide to healing the spirit and also to honoring the medical aspects of healing the body. As Maimonides (twelfth century) articulated, "The physician should not treat the disease, but the patient who is suffering from it."[3] Likewise, Nancy Flam, a contemporary rabbi, explains:

> Jewish tradition has long recognized that there are two components of health, the body and the spirit. The *Mi Sheberach* prayer, traditionally recited for someone who is ill, asks God first for *refuah shleima*, or complete healing, and then specifies two aspects: *refuat hanefesh*, healing of the soul/spirit/whole person, and *refuat haguf*, cure of the body. To cure the body means to wipe out the tumor, clear up the infection, or regain mobility. To heal the spirit involves creating a pathway to sensing wholeness, depth, mystery, purpose, and peace. Cure may occur without healing, and healing without cure. Pastoral caregivers and family members of seriously ill people know that sometimes lives and relationships are healed even when there is no possibility of physical cure; in fact, serious illness often motivates people to seek healing of the spirit.[4]

Thus Maimonides and Rabbi Flam both direct us to pay attention to a person's essence or spirit, to understand that we are more than our bodies and that physical and spiritual healing are connected but different.

An illustration of this is found in one of the first references to healing in Torah, which is the swift transition from dark to light in the Creation story: "And God said, 'Let there be light!'—and there was light" (Genesis 1:3). Here we learn the optimistic lesson of how quickly things can change. We become aware that at any moment even a small light can appear in a dark place, which can help us see what the next steps can be.

I could see this in Josh, a twenty-five-year-old patient. He shared that after his bar mitzvah, his main Jewish spiritual practice was attending his family's Passover seder each year. Now he found himself in a hospital bed, depressed and in pain after a car accident. In the long and quiet hours he spent there, he ruminated over his life and longings. He felt lost and empty without all his pre-accident activities. Leaning back to his early Jewish education, he trained his attention on enriching his world with small gestures of goodness to others, like simply thanking the nursing staff for help, and the gratitude he noted when his pain lessened. These mindful behaviors began to light his way to make changes in himself as he discovered that these spiritual acts begat spiritual gratification, and he began to heal his world through benevolence, thankfulness, and spiritual practice.

One of the things that helped Josh do the work necessary for his healing was hope. Hope is fundamental to Judaism. At its core is the belief in the possibility of better times as depicted by Maimonides's famous Jewish declaration, "I believe with perfect faith in the coming of the Messiah and even though he tarries, I believe." This hope is expressed by Reform Judaism as a messianic time yet to be, brought by people's positive acts. So, whether by Messiah or a messianic time, Judaism holds that hope can be healing, and it is asserted by current medical standards too. "Hope is the expectancy of good in the future. It plays a role in the successful coping with illness and in improving the quality of a person's life. In the context of a terminal illness, hope can exist even when time is limited."[5]

The power of hope was evident, even as her death approached, in another patient. Sophie, a seventy-five-year-old widow and mother of adult son Dave, had the hospital rabbi called to her bedside. When I got there, she wanted to recite the Sh'ma, the final prayer said by Jews before dying. She spoke in a slow and loud voice, indicating to me the gravitas of this moment and her acceptance of her mortality, beginning, "Sh'ma Yisrael Adonai Eloheinu . . ." She stopped short of the last two words of the prayer. I thought she was too tired or perhaps had forgotten it. But she had a different reason. A long minute passed, then she continued, but instead of completing the prayer, she said defiantly, "And I am not finishing it until Dave comes!" She told me she had not seen Dave in three years, and her heart ached to see him again before she died. She had asked him to come now at the end of her life, to make peace and to hug him one more time. Sophie's hope to see her child and to mend their relationship somehow gave her strength to wait. When Dave came, they had two days together before she died. Dave told me that she died holding his hand and that in the end it was Dave who heard Sophie say the last words of the Sh'ma.

In this example, we see that even when all may seem hopeless, hope can still be present, as it was for Sophie. She held out on the hope that her son would come, that if she did not complete the Sh'ma her life would be extended long enough to see him, and that they would finally reconcile. In her words and as a result of her hope, "Now I can die with a smile on my face."

Sometimes relief for illness can come more symbolically. The tallit, or Jewish prayer shawl, provides an opportunity for this. Typically, this item worn by Jews during prayer is made of a soft fabric, has fringes on the corners that are knotted with sacred significance, and when pulled over the head can improvise as a private prayer or contemplative space.

An alternative take that uses the tallit as a healing resource helped another patient, Linda, a thirty-eight-year-old single mother whose life was splintered by a sickness that was to keep her in the hospital for many weeks. Her head spun with worry about what would happen to her two young children. She needed a plan but was so fearful and so sick that she could not bring her thoughts together. We created a ritual with an imaginary tallit. She imagined that she was wrapped in its protected and holy space, that she held each string in turn, and as she gathered each in her hand she named it per her haves ("I have savings, mom, neighbor . . .") and needs ("I need babysitters, strength, homework help . . .").

As she did this she blessed each string with her whispered prayer: "Please help me be strong and keep my life together. Please help me be strong and take care of my kids." Afterward, Linda remarked that this prayer shawl ritual, together with her own personal prayer, helped her to identify her needs and strengths and begin to pull a plan together, all of which were reassuring to her. She looked up at me and smiled: "I think God was in there with me."

But not all metaphors are so tied to specific worship items or ritual. Judaism teaches that Torah is the divine story of the Jewish people and encourages us to insert its wisdom into our own stories, for like Torah, which is constantly being revealed through interpretations, circumstances, and seasons, so too are our own narratives and innermost teachings.

It was such a season for Joanie, a fourteen-year-old girl who struggled with a sense of powerlessness that began after a bullying situation at school. Joanie loved superheroes and wished she could have their powers. She learned to retell her story, but a new version. Rather than through the lens of her pain, she told it through the dual lenses of Torah and of Wonder Woman's deflection bracelets! We took Torah guidance from the quote that Rabbi Akiva (d. 137 CE) is famous for saying is the most central concept in Torah: "Love your neighbor as you love yourself" (Leviticus 19:18). We focused on the "love yourself" part of the message. Joanie took to heart the directive to love herself and claimed superhero power by imagining she was wearing deflection bracelets that could protect her! She thus gradually began her healing by editing her story with self-love through the Torah insight and with the power of her favorite superhero, to help her reveal a new story sprung of her old one.

Sometimes, though, as Judaism teaches us, healing can be more hands-on, so to speak. A Talmudic story highlights the elegance and simplicity of the remedial potency of holding hands. When Rabbi Yochanan a great healer, became sick, his friend Rabbi Chanina came to visit him and held his hand, whereupon Rabbi Yochanan stood up. The question is asked: "Why, if Rabbi Yochanan was such a great healer, could he not raise himself?" The question is then answered: "Because the prisoner cannot free himself from prison" (Babylonian Talmud, *B'rachot* 5b). So because Rabbi Yochanan, a healer himself, needed another to help him heal, the teaching is that we can be strengthened by the touch or assistance of others. Whether this is a literal or figurative touch, the story attests to the curative power of friendship, assistance, and strength that can be exchanged in the mere holding of hands.

I got to see this in action with Leah, a forty-two-year-old woman on the adult psychiatric unit. She was sitting on the floor in the hallway of the unit and was holding a paper on which she had written in bold colored markers, "I am garbage." I sat down on the floor cross-legged and facing her as she stared at me. We sat quietly like that for a while, and then I opened my hands to invite her to hold them. And she did. There are times when words are not necessary. An invitation to hold hands can affirm support or ease fear, and even be a call to face or explore obstacles to well-being. This was the first of several meetings with Leah. It became our custom and even transformative modality to sit cross-legged on the floor facing each other and holding hands either in silence, prayer, or conversation. On the day Leah was discharged, she remembered us sitting on the floor on that first day and holding hands. "It was as if something was pulling me from a dark pit!"

Dr. Donald Friedman concurs and explains touch as "how empathy and compassion can be conveyed to a patient ... it does not have to be by grand gestures or calculated words. Sometimes ... all you need to do is extend a hand. This is certainly a testimony to the power of respectful touch ... and the possibility of connection and healing that it generates."[6]

Finally, we come to prayer. Honing prayer skills can be an odyssey of comfort and healing. The relationship between prayer and healing is noted in secular and Jewish references. Dr. Harold G. Koenig, director of the Duke University Center for Spirituality, Theology and Health, writes, "Studies have shown prayer can prevent people from getting sick and when they do get sick, prayer can help them get better faster."[7] The Maharal of Prague (sixteenth century) teaches that aside from helping prevent people from getting sick and helping them get better, prayer has the ability to replenish, refocus, refresh, and revive us from within our hardships.[8] I have divided my discussion of prayer into the personal and the liturgical.

Let's start with the personal. It is natural to desire or pray to pass through life unscathed and to banish bad things. We are reminded of the Torah story in which Moses "cried out" his soulful and singular plea for his sister, Miriam: "God please! Heal her! Please!" (Numbers 12:13). Like Moses's prayer, our prayer can be a call for help. We may come to learn that sometimes we get the answers we want, sometimes we do not. We might give up or be angry at a God who seems not to answer us, no matter our good deeds, prayers, or bargaining. However, ancient and conventional wisdoms guide us to involve ourselves with spiritual practice and teach that prayer from the heart can bring its own comfort to soothe pain. An example of this is in these poignant words I heard from a patient as she sat with eyes closed, on the edge of her hospital bed crying softly: "God, I am just a person in a hospital. Please help me." Then after a while in silence she whispered, "Thank you. Amen." After the prayer she appeared more peaceful. It seemed to have given her respite in her storm.

Liturgical prayer is also valuable in healing and has its own appeal, as it can bring us into a contemporary community of prayer and also sets us on the shoulders of the prayer-makers and petitioners throughout the Jewish ages. The following prayers, which can be found in any Jewish prayer book, can be powerful prescriptions for healing, whether used as prayer, contemplation, action, or discussion.

In the course of life, some of us experience feelings of guilt or shame. These emotions sometimes become the illness or can be piqued in response to an illness. A prayer that particularly addresses this focuses on purity:

Elohai, n'shamah shenatata bi t'horah hi.

My God, the soul You have given me is pure.

These words remind us that according to Judaism we are created as pure souls. This prayer focuses attention on that pureness and can help draw the mind away from destructive iterations to affirm and nourish a fractured heart.

This was evident in Mark, a sixty-four-year-old only child and medical decision-maker for his now deceased mother. Three years prior she had been in a coma, and doctors requested his consent to take her off life support due to her medical condition. Because she had left no advance directive, it was on his shoulders, and after much thought and soul-searching he gave his permission. The burden of the decision had plagued him with guilt since. "I basically gave the order to end my mother's life," he said to me. Like a medicine, he began to recite the words of the *Elohai N'shamah* prayer as needed whenever he felt waves of guilt coming over him. After time he found meaning and healing in intercepting the feeling with this prayer on pureness.

Another way to help with healing through prayer is to focus on daily blessings. Jewish tradition sets a goal to recite one hundred blessings per day. Each blessing, whether from Jewish or other sources or ad-libbed, can bring healing via attention to gratitude and godliness throughout the day.

An example from Jewish custom to consider is a blessing of gratitude for bread that also mandates us to be partners with God in our spiritual sustenance.

Baruch atah, Adonai Eloheinu, Melech haolam,
hamotzi lechem min haaretz.

Blessed are You, Adonai our God, Sovereign of the universe, who brings forth bread from the earth.

Even though the words say that God brings bread out of the earth, we know that actual bread does not grow directly from the ground. Rather, human effort turns grains into bread for physical sustenance. We can participate in our spiritual sustenance in the same way. Just as resources are supplied for us to make bread that feeds the body, resources are supplied for us to feed our spirits.

A Jewish spiritual resource not yet mentioned and with great potential to elevate the spirit is the acknowledgment of Shabbat as a day separate from others. Jewish tradition stresses the beauty and the holiness of the day and celebrates it with rituals like candles, wine, challah, and observing other Shabbat practices according to varying interpretations and adherences to Jewish law. Reform Jews may honor this day in these aforementioned and other ways, including disconnecting from electronics, observing family time, going to temple, festive meals, or other nurturing and renewing activities. This elegant resource of a sacred day of rest is a basic Jewish practice that inspires and uplifts us each week to seek holiness and recharging. How we choose to welcome Shabbat and its healing potential is an example of a resource that can provide us spiritual sustenance.

But this in itself does not necessarily assuage our feelings of being vulnerable. Here is a prayer that can offer peace of mind and a sense of protection at sleep and at weak times for people of all ages:

B'sheim Adonai Elohei Yisrael,
Mimini Michael,
Umis'moli Gavriel,
Umil'fanai Uriel,
Umei-achorai R'fael,
V'al roshi Sh'chinat El.

In the name of Adonai, God of Israel,
From my right, Michael,
And from my left, Gabriel,
And from in front of me, Uriel,

And from behind me, Rafael,
And at my head, the Divine Presence.

Each of the four angels' names above refers respectively to a godlike essence: amazement, strength, light, and healing.

Kaitlyn, a ten-year-old cancer patient, was scared of just about everything connected to being in the hospital—doctors, needles, pain—all frightening and not much fun at all. Kaitlyn was enthusiastic when her mom and I spoke to her about this prayer and imagining that these angels could come anytime to help her when she wanted. Mom bought four cute little angel dolls, and Kaitlyn quickly named them and sang her rhyme: "Awesome, Strong Girl, Light Girl, and Doc, please help me not be scared a lot!" She kept them close, especially at night, when she tucked them in right next to her. She had created a playful yet serious plan from the core of this prayer that in some way could offer her some healing relief in her situation.

Still, the most basic of liturgical prayers have to do with acknowledging the presence of and nurturing a relationship with God. A belief that there is a higher power or higher order in the universe can offer us comfort.

Sam, a fifty-two-year-old, self-described cultural Jew, was looking for that very solace. His sudden heart attack left him searching for a spiritual life that he had not previously cultivated. Together we used the words at the beginning of many Jewish prayers:

Baruch atah, Adonai Eloheinu, Melech haolam

Blessed are You, Adonai our God, Sovereign of the universe

And then he practiced adding his own personal expressions of awe, thanks, or yearning. For example:

For me getting that it's okay that I cannot even understand You for now.

For being around for my prayers, when I don't know what else to do.

Please help me get through this.

Like many of us, Sam was a seeker looking for spiritual relief and connection. The Jewish prayer language provided a platform to articulate his sacred thoughts and longings and an introduction to the healing potential of prayer and belief.

My wish is that from the broad swath of examples in this essay you will find entry points into the vast and varied gleanings of the Jewish experience in Reform Judaism's healing tent.

May you begin to find meaning and sustenance for your healing here.

B'ruchim habaim! Blessed are those who come! Welcome!

NOTES

1. Uriel Heilman, "For New Reform Leader Richard Jacobs, Big Tent Movement Is the Idea," Jewish Telegraphic Agency, March 22, 2011, http://www.jta.org/2011/03/22/life-religion/for-new-reform-leader-richard-jacobs-big-tent-movement-is-the-idea.

2. Names and identifying data have been changed for confidentiality.

3. Goodreads, http://www.goodreads.com/quotes/371714-the-physician-should-not-treat-the-disease-but-the-patient.

4. Nancy Flam, "The Jewish Way of Healing," *Reform Judaism*, Summer 1994, http://kalsman.huc.edu/articles/JewishWayOfHealing.pdf.

5. Paul Rousseau, "Hope in the Terminally Ill," *Western Journal of Medicine*, August 2000, http://www.ncbi.nlm.nih.gov/pmc/articles/PMC1071019/.

6. Donald M. Friedman, "Touch in Medicine," Jewish Sacred Aging, http://jewishsacredaging.com/touch-in-medicine.

7. "Science Proves the Healing Power of Prayer." NewsmaxHealth, March 31, 2015, http://www.newsmax.com/Health/Headline/prayer-health-faith-medicine/2015/03/31/id/635623/.

8. Maharal of Prague, *N'tivot Olam, Nativ HaAvodah* 2.

55

THE MISSION OF ISRAEL AMONG HUMANITY

Rabbi Lance J. Sussman, PhD

The Six-Day War had just ended when, in June 1967, I became a bar mitzvah at Temple Oheb Shalom in Baltimore, Maryland. Many years later, my memory of that Saturday morning is clear: walking up to the bimah as the *Union Prayer Book*'s "Reading of Scripture" began and, in my best teenage boy voice, commencing my part in the service with the stirring words of Isaiah II: "And it shall come to pass in the end of days that the mountain of the Lord's house shall be established . . . and all nations shall flow to it." It was my prophetic moment and I loved it.

At the time, I did not connect the Isaiah passage with the *UPB*'s "Adoration" and the establishment of "God's kingdom on earth" or Israel Zangwill's stirring, High Classical anthem "All the World Shall Come to Serve Thee" with one another as expressions of a specific, lofty, and challenging view of redemption and the role of the Jewish people in that universal process. But somehow, it made sense that my "religion" had a vision for the whole world. I was proud to be anchored in this Judaism and sensed that it had big plans for humanity. Many years later, I learned that the great radical Reform rabbi David Einhorn audaciously viewed Judaism as "truth uniting [all of] humanity."

Many years passed before I became aware of the concept of *the mission of Israel*, the belief that the ultimate purpose of Judaism in the eyes of the classical Reform tradition was for our group to lead all people to a belief in the one true God and to serve as *a light to the nations*. Like others of my generation, I went with Reform Judaism's flow from its confident universalism of old to its more particularistic view that was a function of the time. I did not understand that a theological shift was taking place. I did not see that Israel's historical role as the hope of humanity (as expressed at the theological peak moments of the Reform service of my youth) was to be dethroned by secularized Jewish survivalism, theological relativism, and a nearly total abandonment of belief in Judaism's role in redeeming humanity at large.

As a bar mitzvah, that had been my belief; we were more reasonable, more rational, more progressive, and more humanistic than any other faith, so eventually everybody else would join us. That is exactly what my prayer book said, and at that time I did not doubt it for a moment. As a friend said to me years later, "We had to stay Jewish until everybody else becomes Unitarian." The old Reform Judaism of the *Union Prayer Book*, from *Aleinu* to the "Final Benediction," affirmed that Judaism had a mission—the "mission of Israel"—that it was the juggernaut of salvation for all people. In the bold words of the 1885 Pittsburgh Platform, "We extend the hand of fellowship to all who cooperate with us in the establishment of the reign of truth and righteousness among men."

As a teenager, I was not aware that Reform's former universalism had something to do with its historical struggle with Zionism and, subsequently, its general lack of concern for rescuing Jews during the Holocaust. Reform, it seemed, was more for humanity than for the Jewish people. By the dawn of the 1970s, in the aftermath of the Six-Day War, a growing pride in Israel had already resulted in a significant re-ethnization of Reform Jewish identity.

In college I discovered Mordecai Kaplan's critique of the notion of the chosen people and tacitly agreed with Kaplan that it seemed a bit haughty. "Treasured people" made sense, but claims of racial superiority seemed liked a betrayal of my inherent American liberalism. The contemporary idea that all faiths were "chosen" and that the Jews were actually a "choosing people" went a long way to reassure me that our loftiest goals endured and could be shared with other religious traditions.

On the other hand, my first encounters with "other" religious traditions did not go very well. The truth is I grew up knowing virtually no non-Jews. My Sunday school once took a field trip to a Catholic cathedral in Baltimore's geographic center. I felt like I was in an army unit that had been cut off during a fierce battle and was now trapped behind the enemy's lines.

In a college class on world religions, I read in Hindu scripture and from the teachings of the Buddha; I even felt a bit inspired by them. But when it came time to read from the New Testament, I found I could not even open my study Bible until after I read the 1974 version of Dr. Samuel Sandmel's *A Jewish Understanding of the New Testament.* I read the assigned Gospel passages and discovered that "in the end of (my college) days," my early understanding of Isaiah II was still in place—although we no longer sang "All the World Shall Come to Serve Thee" on the High Holy Days.

I experienced an even greater intellectual crisis in my basic humanities course. My instructor, who was undeniably Jewish, stated that the Greeks were superior to the Hebrews and that Judaism was basically a fossilized faith *à la* British historian Arnold J. Toynbee. Luckily, through relatives I had a direct line of communication with Jacob B. Agus, a Conservative rabbi and Harvard-trained philosopher, who had tangled with Toynbee before me. In a brief exchange of letters, he reassured me that Judaism was neither fossilized nor inferior to any other religious or philosophical tradition. I felt a whole lot better, but I also knew my Jewish firewall had been damaged.

The potholes in my belief in the mission of Israel grew deeper when I became an instructor at the State University of New York at Binghamton. I taught the course on religion in America and became particularly interested in the study of modern religion. During this time I learned to see Reform Judaism as part of the larger landscape of religious modernism, with a preference for the rational and empirical over the spiritual and mystical and, most of all, an abiding belief in the philosophy of progress.

Progress—the intoxicating idea that because of scientific advancements, everything gets better as time wears on—seemed inevitable until the bloody savagery of World War I. No serious religious thinker took the philosophy of progress seriously after this, and the carnage of World War II solidified the opinion. Individual people may be good, but as for humanity as a whole, the evidence showed we are as beastlike as we are human. By 1945, America could at best hope to make half the world safe for democracy. As for Judaism, its mission was to build a tiny state on the Mediterranean Sea and to help black Americans break the legal and social chains of southern segregation. Reform Jews may have given social justice the mystical name of *tikkun olam*, but Reform's goals and methods became increasingly secular. Food drives became our road to salvation instead of leading the nations to Jerusalem.

What about the rest of humanity? What about being a "light to the nations"? As early as 1937, Reformers began to view the salvation of the world as a shared activity, a process we participated in but no longer led. The diminishment of Judaism's redemptive purpose was clearly expressed that same year in the Columbus Platform:

> Throughout the ages it has been Israel's mission to witness to the Divine in the face of every form of paganism and materialism. We regard it as our historic task to cooperate with all men in the establishment of the kingdom of God, of universal brotherhood, justice, truth and peace on earth. This is our Messianic goal.[1]

In the latter twentieth century, Judaism's capacity to participate in the shared redemption of the world was challenged from within by an ever-rising tide of mixed marriage. Fragmented by assimilation and diminishing Jewish identity, how would the Reform community lead the world to Jerusalem and a messianic era? Nothing seemed to stem the sociological tide, and no new theological claim of chosenness seemed available to rally the people. Instead, we learned of a 614th commandment: to commit ourselves to "sacred survival"—to not let Hitler win posthumously. By the end of the twentieth century, the prophetic challenge was no longer to save the world but to save the Jewish people.

To some extent, the nascent Reform Jewish Outreach, whose initial goal was the integration of non-Jews into Reform synagogues, sought to provide for a path toward limited salvation, its own way, recapturing Reform's old commitment to universalism by making Reform Judaism more inclusive of non-Jews. If we cannot transform the whole world, we can at least find a way to have part of the larger world join us in our march to redemption. Soft missionary work and acceptance of patrilineal descent repositioned Reform Judaism as once more a universally available faith.

But such outreach weakened as a denominational goal, as intermarriage in the aggregate became statistically normative in the American Jewish community and the urge to convert non-Jewish spouses diminished. Like the Exodus of old, a significant "mixed multitude" became part of Reform Jewish life. Calls to shrink the sociological tent of Reform Judaism waxed and waned. By the beginning of the twenty-first century, notions of Jewish peoplehood and Jewish personhood had clearly become more porous. The idea that a tribally defined Jewish people would lead humanity to salvation seemed more unlikely than ever.

The idea of the "mission of Israel," however, did not die. In declaring independence, the State of Israel claimed both prophetic and teleological purposes. Through science and democracy, it would, it said, become a new light to the nations. Israel's technological achievements continue to keep the light lit in the realm of science, but in the realm of global politics, on the other hand, Israel now finds itself painfully marginalized.

The Jewish group today most responsible for lighting the torch of Jewish messianism is Chabad. Aggressive and controversial, Chabad is not only animated by redemptive urgency, it believes its branch of Judaism to be the standard-bearer for redemption of the Jewish people and salvation of the world. In the worldview of Chabad, their emissaries are doing the authentic mystical work of *tikkun olam*, the repair of the world made possible by the gathering of the divine sparks of creation and the building of the pathway for the Messiah to lead the Jewish people back to Jerusalem and build the Third Temple. Then and only then, Chabad teaches, "will the nations flow" to the Holy City.

Importantly, Chabad seeks not only to redeem the Jewish people but to save the whole world, requiring that it wean the gentile nations from idolatrous ways, in favor of an ethical and monotheistic religion. Chabad's little known Bnai Noach program seeks to implement Isaiah's vision of the "end of days" for all non-Jews in addition to its "outreach" program to gather all the Jews of the world under its messianic canopy. In my opinion, Chabad's tremendous success is not only a function of its followers' belief in their rebbe and of incredibly effective marketing techniques; it is also a function of their sellable theology of redemption. Religion without a path to redemption is, it seems, narcissistic and uncompelling.

The latest challenge in Reform Judaism's long effort to define its understanding of redemption and the pursuit of the mission of Israel comes out of Buddhist tradition: JuBuism. The new Reform *machzor* (High Holy Day prayer book), *Mishkan HaNefesh*, published in 2015, offers an alternative reading to the classic passage "May the time not be distant." It has a clearly anti-Buddhist message, initially. The alternative passage begins, "The time may be distant and the outcome uncertain—for how could suffering, endemic to the human condition, ever come to an end?" Then, surprisingly, an Orthodox Buddhist response is offered: "Cessation of desire, relinquishing attachment, diminished expectations—all these might ease the pain of being alive." After that, the text sharply turns in the direction of traditional Jewish teleology, admonishing readers to "decide instead that you'll continue to dream, hope, remain fiercely attached to bringing a better day, even if the outcome's uncertain and time is very distant."[2]

The *machzor* editors, not willing to leave the anti-Buddhist response quite alone, also remind readers (commenting "below the line" on the phrase "the time may be distant") of the martyred Anne Frank. She wrote in her diary, "It's really a wonder I haven't dropped all my ideals, because they seem so absurd and impossible to carry out." But she then concluded, "I must uphold my ideals, for perhaps the time will come when I shall be able to carry them out," returning traditional Jewish optimism to her words. A historical redemption seems part of the religious DNA of the Jewish people and its ancient faith. If Reform Judaism could today offer a theological path to redemption for Jews and others, would it regain self-confidence and be able to offer more than an eclectic set of traditions and innovations spiritual nurture? Is there a way Reform Judaism can, with intellectual and religious integrity, renew its commitment to its founding principle of the mission of Israel and the redemption of humanity? And, most of all, what authentic answer will it give to its young people's penetrating question "Why be Jewish?"

Redemption implies an ultimately irresistible transformative force in the universe. God, as my teacher Alvin J. Reines explained to me, is the ontological precondition of existence but not the ultimate source for salvation. A living God, I learned from years of work as a pulpit rabbi, must be more than a theological proposition. A living God has to have a presence and message for humanity. Long before Mordecai Kaplan wrote of God as "the power that makes for salvation," God—the God of the prophets—was the God of moral urgency, who demanded we work for redemption through justice, not merely sacrifice on the altar of ritual to the sounds of psalms and other liturgical recitations.

Defining today's morality is not easy, but Reform Judaism still claims that task (despite endless philosophizing about the nature of ethics) and continues to tie redemptive justice to its fundamental mission. Fair labor practices, civil rights, feminism, LGBTQ rights, and more are causes Reform has collectively understood to be part of its sacred task. From early in its history, Reform has claimed it follows the path of revelation that is progressive in the sense of historical evolution, liberal values, and the redemption of humanity.

A Reform Judaism reconceptualized in the context of the mission of Israel as its redemptive goal would find in ritual not just individual spiritual endeavor, but a tool to inspire and transform. The end of the prayer service would not be a veritable fourth-period clock in a blowout game, ticking perfunctorily; it would be a crescendo of purpose and proclamation of intent. Memory and tradition would be harnessed to inspiration and hope; social justice would be not just policy debate but sacred cause, for the good of all.

If Reform Judaism were to redefine and embrace anew the mission of Israel—the purpose of being Jewish—perhaps it could also rethink its now atrophied Outreach program. Is Jewish survival the main reason we accept non-Jews in our midst as equal partners, or are we seeking partners in the sacred work of redemption? Do converts need to undergo sixteen weeks of Judaization and Jewish socialization, or do they need to embrace a basic commitment to help make the world a better place through Judaism?

Jewish identity is not enough. To survive, modern Judaism needs to rediscover Judaism's basic religious purpose. A Jewish creed may be helpful, but it too is insufficient unless it is purposeful. The purpose of Jewish life today cannot merely be to preserve itself, nor to re-create itself through new music and clever Jewish apps. To be meaningful is to be purposeful, and Judaism has long held that the redemption of humanity from indifference, injustice, and inequality is its purpose. Powerful prayers, effective programs and advocacy, and an explicit commitment to redeeming the world are our collective path. Spiritualizing our path is clearly part of our work, but we do not undertake it for spirituality's sake alone. Spirituality devoid of redemptive purpose is narcissism, and narcissism is vanity and a chasing after wind.

Can, today, a compelling theological argument be made for redemption? The great Jewish philosopher Franz Rosenzweig wrote passionately about redemption in his 1921 *Star of Redemption*. He understood redemption as the theological core of the Jewish tradition and all of existence:

> For God is not only the redeemer, but also the redeemed. In this redemption God redeems the world by way of man and redeems man by the way of the world. For then true unity is

created—God-man-world. Eternity enters into being and death is pushed off and the living become immortals in eternal praise of redemption.[3]

Redemption, Rosenzweig boldly asserts, is the power that completes God.

At Passover—Judaism's paradigm of redemption—one of the things I ask my congregation to do is to write their own Four Questions. Not just any Four Questions, but their most important Jewish questions. I once received a very powerful response to my challenge. A woman in my synagogue wrote to me explaining that she had only one question. She explained that she loves Judaism and regularly attends synagogue. However, unlike her Quaker and Catholic friends, her Judaism did not inform her core as a person. She likes our songs and our customs but never turned to Judaism to answer her deepest questions. Why, she asked, didn't her Judaism address the core of her being?

A Judaism that is primarily made of ritual, as beautiful and lyrical as many ritual practices can be, is incomplete. It addresses the need for community and spirituality. But it is not yet a Judaism with a transcendent purpose, a redemptive goal. The transcendent purpose of Judaism is to teach the Jewish people, and then share with all humanity, the Jewish way of love and kindness, the redemptive path of *chesed*, transcendent loving-kindness.

Chesed is Judaism's foremost value. When we practice it, we are at our most godlike. When we teach it, we make it our ethic. When we pursue it, we help establish justice as the standard for society. *Chesed* is the path to redemption, and redemption is why we exist as a people. Our mission as Reform Jews, our mission of Israel, is to raise the banner of *chesed* for all; only when we have raised it can we sing with fullness of heart that "all the world" will come to serve the God whose name will finally "become One."

NOTES

1. "The Guiding Principles of Reform Judaism" (1937), http://ccarnet
.org/rabbis-speak/platforms/guiding-principles-reform-judaism/.

2. Edwin Goldberg, Janet Marder, Sheldon Marder, and Leon Morris, eds.,
Mishkan HaNefesh: Machzor for the Days of Awe, vol. 1, *Rosh HaShanah* (New York:
CCAR Press, 2015), 85.

3. Franz Rosenzweig, *Star of Redemption*.

56

THE IMPORTANCE OF REFORM JUDAISM

RABBI ERIC H. YOFFIE

Reform Judaism is, and will remain, the dominant form of Judaism in North America. And slowly, it will become a significant Jewish force in the State of Israel, although for the foreseeable future its adherents there will be modest in number.

Those who predict decline or even disaster for Reform Judaism tend to be those who predict collapse for all types of modern liberal religion. The world is moving toward secularization, they claim. They see evidence of such "decline" everywhere, and particularly so in the West. In this view, only rigorous traditionalism can survive. Religious systems not rooted in some form of fundamentalism will fail to hold their own against modernity and the culture of autonomy that follows in its wake. Purity of faith, unquestioning belief, deferring to the mandates of authoritative religious leaders, and isolation from the temptations of modern society are the necessary ingredients for a functioning religious community. All other expressions of religion, including liberal religions of every variety, are doomed.

This view is widely held but clearly wrong. As noted by the late Peter Berger, the secularization theory has been empirically disproved.[1] Religion is a powerful force in human consciousness; it is indeed growing in most parts of the world. Secular ideologies cannot in the long run satisfy the craving of human beings to give meaning to personal experience. The search for meaning and the need to find significance in our lives are eternal human concerns to which only religion can respond.

It is Berger's view that the secularization of Europe is the exception rather than the rule of modern history, while in the United States, secularization affects certain elites but not the majority of average citizens. Religion remains robust in America. Here, and in other modern societies as well, one finds what Berger calls "cognitive contamination"—which means that the relationship between religion and modernity is not a matter of either/or, but rather of both/and.[2] Secularity and religion coexist, in society and in the minds of individuals.

Acknowledging this enables us to understand both the complexity of America's religious situation and the attraction, staying power, and promising prospects of Reform Judaism there. On the one hand, America is home to a rapidly changing religious landscape. Approximately 20 percent of Americans assert that they have no religious identity at all.[3] Among those ages eighteen to twenty-nine, 32 percent are "nones," not identifying with any particular religious institution or denomination. Never since modern polling began have such numbers of Americans distanced themselves from formal religious identification.

On the other hand, lack of affiliation is related to many things, including the transience of the workforce, diminishing ethnic ties, and the later age of marriage. Almost 70 percent of the unaffiliated say they believe in God; clearly, then, unaffiliated does not mean "without religion" and does not preclude affiliation at a later time. It is true that young people do not like institutions, are skeptical of hierarchies, and are reluctant to "join" anything. But in an era of information overload, virtual rather than face-to-face relationships, and dramatically shifting cultural norms, they also crave community and in-person connection. They yearn for the narratives, rituals, and practices that will help them deal with the economic pressures and the cultural chaos of their society. And many of them acknowledge that they need, or at least are open to, God, prayer, and a place that accepts them for who they are, because they can no longer make it alone.

In short, the same people who immerse themselves in social networks and embrace market-based consumerism do not want to abandon religion; they want to reconfigure it. They do not want to discard all religious authority but to rethink it. In a restless, changing America, most Americans, it turns out, are creatures of balance who need points of fixity in their world. They want a new synthesis between tradition and modernity and between tradition and change. As modern life showers them with seemingly endless choices, which they find both reassuring and unsettling, they want not to give up on religion and spirituality, but to experiment with new and unconventional ways to express them.

And it is precisely in cultural climates of turmoil and change that Reform Judaism has thrived and will continue to thrive. Reform Judaism might not prosper everywhere, but America has provided a welcoming environment for the Torah-centered and synagogue-centered liberal Judaism that Reform has produced.

Why is America so hospitable to Reform? The answer is far from simple. Judaism is a complex religious system that has sustained the Jewish people for three millennia. It offers elaborate norms of ritual and ethical behavior and a vast compendium of legal deliberation and philosophical speculation.

Reform Judaism, only slightly more than two hundred years old, is the most modern version of this ancient religion. It was born in Germany in 1810 as a revolutionary religious movement and soon made its way to America. Here, it quickly discarded the theological certainties of what we now call Orthodox Judaism and, in the process, set aside the heavy obligations of personal religious observance that flow from traditional belief. Committed to modernity, rational thought, and the fundamental congruence of religion and science, Reform embraced the principle of progressive revelation. This embrace turned out to be a complicated matter. A revelation that is more ongoing than fixed is liberating for both the individual and the community, but it is also disconcerting. It makes the Reform revolution permanent and imposes the onerous burden of informed choice on every Reform Jew in every era.

But the burden of choice proved to be bearable. Some Jews want, and believe in, a binding religious law, given at Sinai. In America, however, most Jews do not. They refuse to see Torah as God's immutable word and insist that autonomy and pluralism are essential elements of Judaism. It turns out that the principles of choice and freedom, rooted in classical liberalism, have shaped not only America's political ideals but the religious outlook of America's Jews as well.

And Reform leaders have not been troubled that this is so. From Reform's earliest days, its American rabbis and teachers have promoted an open, choice-driven, evolving Jewish tradition and have seen it as consistent with Judaism's ancient teaching.

At the same time, pluralism and choice have not led, as some feared, to a Reform Judaism in which "anything goes." Touches of the radical and the bizarre inevitably appear in Reform settings from time to time; after all, America's religious marketplace is the most diverse on earth. And it is true that a pronounced anti-Zionism flourished in Reform's earlier days. Still, as a mature movement, Reform has remained firmly theistic, text-centered, grounded in Jewish peoplehood, and organized around the traditional categories of God, Torah, and Israel. While individual Reform Jews may or may not believe in God, Reform as a collective has rejected a purely humanistic foundation for Reform belief. And generally speaking, Jewish atheists have looked outside of Reform Judaism for their religious home. So too have radical syncretists, who mix Judaism together indiscriminately with other religious traditions; antinomian elements, who emphasize faith while setting aside Jewish practice and moral law; and neo-Chasidic spiritualists, who present simplistic and often phony versions of Jewish mysticism as the heart of Jewish tradition. Reform Judaism, happily, has mostly avoided these plagues.

What has emerged from Reform's pluralism is a Judaism that is open but restrained; that is new and evolving but framed by the language and the values of Torah. This Judaism speaks to Jews who are thoroughly American and in search of a religious middle way. The idea of Reform Judaism as a near-crazy movement of religious extremists is a comfortable stereotype for those who find Reform distasteful, but it is laughably inaccurate in today's America.

And who are these "middle way" Jews of Reform Judaism? They are broadly liberal and do not believe in unreflective adherence to tradition. Embracing the view of the Reform founders, they repudiate the idea that halachah (the code of Jewish law) is the foundation of Judaism, a principle at the heart of Orthodoxy and, at least in a formal sense, at the heart of Conservative Judaism as well. They are also tired of religious fanatics of all kinds and of all traditions, including their own; as a result, they have absolutely no use for Israel's settler rabbis and coercive religious establishment. They are equally tired of the silly spirituality of celebrities, quasi-kabbalists, and so-called spiritual seekers who want feel-good religion that doesn't involve any actual commitment, inconvenience, or work. They see themselves as Jews of the synagogue, partners in a sacred odyssey of a sacred people. They know that effort is required to do Judaism right, and they look to their congregations to find the support of others who share their devotion.

What is perhaps most interesting about the "middle way" Jews of the Reform synagogue in America is how well they are doing. There is much talk of the "crisis" of the Reform synagogue, and it is true that there is a crisis of sorts; change is happening rapidly, and financial pressures are widely felt. But the fact is that American Reform synagogues have always been in crisis of one kind or another. Fresh winds of change are never absent from the American religious scene, and Reform synagogues are always rethinking and readjusting. But this, of course, is a good thing. And on balance, Reform synagogues are healthy and optimistic places. As sociologist Steven M. Cohen has reported, the membership of Reform congregations grew by more than 20 percent between 1990 and 2013.[4]

Reform rabbis and synagogue leaders have been particularly adept at reading the needs of their "middle way" Jews and at reconfiguring

584 · A LIFE OF MEANING

the purpose and program of their congregations accordingly. In a community yearning for structure and holiness, Reform has offered both a revival of worship and study and a commitment to "re-ritualization," which involves embracing rituals and traditions once discarded as obsolete. In a community with large numbers of converts and non-Jews, Reform has opened its door and made them feel at home. In a community with liberal political instincts and a strong sense of communal obligation, Reform has insisted that the quest for justice in America and in the world is a central part of our religious mission. In a community that expects inclusion, Reform has welcomed the full participation of women without equivocation. In a community respectful of scholarship but resistant to hierarchy, Reform has created a partnership that is rare in Jewish life, one between rabbinate and laypeople.

Not all of these things happened at precisely the same time, of course. In its two-century history, Reform Judaism has flourished in some periods and stagnated in others and has emphasized different themes and values in different eras. In its earliest days, it promoted modest liturgical reform. As it began to take shape as a movement, it separated itself from Europe's Orthodox rabbinical establishment with the radical step of jettisoning its commitment to Jewish law, substituting a focus on ethical action. Once it had moved to America, ethics, both personal and communal, remained central, and Reform retained a strong ethical thrust throughout the civil rights era in the mid-twentieth century. The last half century has arguably been Reform's most creative and tumultuous period, as social justice has shared the agenda with new thinking on a range of spirituality and outreach concerns.

In the current era, it is safe to say that Reform Judaism has become a rather messy big tent movement, with a larger range of belief and practice than at any other time in its history. Always brash and forward-looking, Reform in recent decades has trampled taboos and crossed categories in a particularly imaginative way, becoming more "traditional" and more "radical" at the same time.

On the traditional side, Reform Jews are no longer afraid of religious feeling. While committed to a rational mind-set and to a Judaism of study and contemplation, they want to open themselves up to the mystical without surrendering more inductive ways of thinking.

This means that Reform prayer on Shabbat has, in less than two decades, shifted dramatically from what it was, shocking Reform Jews who grew up with the formal, well-ordered religious services of the classical Reform tradition. Shabbat worship in the overwhelming majority of Reform synagogues today is filled with elements of passion and religious fervor. Reform Jews have returned exuberance and ecstasy to their prayers, along with greater use of Hebrew, the chanting of Torah, and, for some, wearing prayer shawls and head coverings.

"Re-ritualization" means a greater openness to rituals of every sort, including a wide range of holiday and life-cycle rituals and various types of Reform kashrut. Practices once universally dismissed in Reform circles as obstructing "modern spiritual elevation" are now seen by many Reform Jews as helping to give structure to the holy in everyday life.[5]

Is this ritual reawakening in reality mindless traditionalism, a form of "neo-*frumkeit*"—that is, quasi-Orthodoxy—that violates basic Reform values? Hardly. There is no inclination in the Reform Movement to submit to the discipline of Jewish law in its entirety, a step that would render Reform Judaism meaningless. What has been happening instead is a welcome expansion of religious doing, carried out by rethinking and experimenting with every element of the ritual tradition. But the system, while eclectic, is not indiscriminate. Those practices broadly embraced in Reform ranks generally meet the criteria that one would expect from a liberal movement: They are rituals that not only cultivate a sense of the sacred but are, or are adjusted to be, inclusive, egalitarian, and ethically centered, and thus can be seen as authentically Reform.

At the same time, alongside this reintegration of some traditional ritual into Reform practice, Reform Judaism over the last quarter century has demonstrated extraordinary theological radicalism. This is most evident in its reconsidering of the status of gays and lesbians in Judaism and its redefinition of who is a Jew. In a radical break with what had been seen as normative Jewish belief, the Reform Movement now ordains gay, lesbian, and transgendered Jews as rabbis and encourages full equality for them in all areas of synagogue life. No less dramatic, the movement grants the children of Jewish fathers raised as Jews the same Jewish status as that enjoyed by the children of Jewish mothers.

These steps have won near universal acceptance in Reform ranks; indeed, most Reform Jews see them as Reform Judaism at its very best. Younger members, and the majority of older members as well, are absolutely committed to an inclusive Reform Judaism. They are appalled that in other places in the Jewish world, gay Jews, non-Jewish spouses, Jews of color, and Jews with disabilities are not always welcomed with open arms and often are not welcomed at all. Young Reform Jews are supportive, to be sure, of increasing use of ritual, Hebrew, ecstatic prayer, and study of Torah; such things are consistent with their religious inclinations and adventurous spirit. But, for most of them, it is the fearless openness of Reform that is its greatest asset. And they applaud the gusto, optimism, and risk-taking that have inspired Reform leaders to take this radical path, brushing aside counsels of timidity in the process.

Of course, none of this means that social justice, long central to Reform thinking and practice, has disappeared from the movement's agenda. It has perhaps retreated a bit in Reform consciousness, mostly because the Reform agenda has become more crowded with multiple Jewish concerns. Still, the odds are good that the next decade will see a jump in the importance of Reform Jewish social action. As inequality grows and class divisions become more pronounced, liberal religion in America will expect its religious leaders and institutions to offer a role for religion in making society more just. And Reform Jews, who see the struggle for justice as a natural extension of their religious commitments, will be in the forefront of these voices.

Reform Judaism, therefore, is something of a paradox. Is it flourishing? Yes. Is it fragmenting? Yes. Is it more Torah-centered, traditional, and ritual-oriented? Yes. Is it chaotic, revolutionary, and constantly groundbreaking? Yes. In short, it is a modern Jewish movement built on liberal principles—messy but spiritually serious, rooted in Torah but always sensitive to the quick drift of history.

The challenges that it faces are many, of course. The local synagogue is the building block of Reform Judaism, but the structure of the synagogue is in a state of upheaval. New membership models are coming into being, with partial and fee-for-service membership systems competing with the "family memberships" that have been standard for most of the last century. Millennials in particular, who resist long-term membership commitments, prefer a system in which meaningful fees are expected for all synagogue classes and events other than worship. In addition, large and expensive infrastructures are giving way to simpler and shared physical facilities, and a mostly suburban movement is beginning to develop a significant urban component. These developments, still in their early stages, are all positive ones and likely to make the synagogue stronger and more resilient.

The absence of a coherent Reform theology is another challenge, and potentially a more serious one. Without a common belief system, one might reasonably argue, a movement inevitably lacks the religious integrity essential for its success.[6] Nonetheless, Americans, practical and utilitarian in outlook, are not a theologically-minded religious people. Neither are Jews of any denomination, and this is true of Reform Jews as well. The Reform Movement has produced theologians, but nothing approaching a consensus theology. According to many Reform leaders and thinkers, theology is not essential; it is far more important to unite around shared practices than shared beliefs. For modern Reform Jews, in this view, God is often not the first step but the last. If Reform Jews are committed to Jewish community and Jewish doing, it is that commitment, rather than a set of theological principles, that will ultimately point them in the direction of God and belief.

Of course, if Jewish doing is important, then promoting a consistent pattern of Reform observance is essential. And this may be the greatest challenge of all. Since Reform Judaism is grounded in the principles of autonomy and pluralism, there is not a single way to be an observant Reform Jew. For some, prayer and Torah study are given priority; for some, repair of the world; and for some, devotion to Jewish people-hood. But the fact that individual Reform Jews decide this for themselves does not mean that Reform rabbis and teachers cannot guide their members in fashioning a liberal, modern, Torah-inspired Jewish life. One of the triumphs of Reform Judaism today is the number of Reform Jews who have become impressive exemplars of Jewish living, making space for serious Judaism in their day-to-day lives. And the task ahead is to increase the number of these Jews, creating, with the synagogue's help, praying and studying communities to support them and share in their struggle.

One final challenge must be confronted: there is a desperate need to extend the reach of Reform Judaism to the State of Israel. Two major centers, the United States and Israel, dominate the Jewish world. Their domination will increase in the future, as the non-American Diaspora continues to dwindle. But while Reform is the largest Jewish movement on American soil, it has struggled to find its place in Israel. The reasons for this are many. Reform, which came late to the Zionist cause, had its origins in Central Europe. The Eastern European Jews who founded Israel, though, and the Jews from Arab lands who make up half of her population knew nothing of progressive Judaism in any form. Israel also has an Orthodox establishment, a remnant of British imperial rule, which uses coercive legislation to suppress Reform Judaism and all challengers to its monopolistic position in Israeli society.

It may be less than readily apparent, but the reality is that this dispiriting dominance of the official Orthodox rabbinate in Israel is already collapsing. Ossified religious establishments always collapse, of course, particularly those dependent on artificially imposed government structures. The increasingly hysterical tone of the Orthodox rabbinate's attacks on Reform Judaism are a sign of desperation and weakness, not of strength. And it is by now clear what should have been clear all along: Israeli Jews are not different in any fundamental way from Jews elsewhere, in other places and periods. Claims that most

Israelis are secular are no more valid than claims that most American Jews are secular. Israelis too search for meaning that only Jewish tradition and Jewish texts can provide. They too yearn for the holy, the transcendent, and the fire of faith, even if they cannot precisely articulate what their Judaism means to them.

Many Israelis will find what they are looking for in some form of Israeli Orthodoxy. But with a Reform infrastructure finally in place in Israel, and with Israelis showing increasing interest in progressive alternatives to Orthodoxy, it is only a matter of time until American Reform has a significant sister movement in Israel. And as they spread together the message of liberal, enlightened Judaism, the interaction of these two movements will strengthen both.

On balance, then, Reform Jews are filled with optimism about their faith. They reject the sense of despair that is so endemic in our society today. To be sure, they know that in our very complicated, technologically sophisticated world, many people feel lost and diminished. They can be realistic, but they reject the kind of realism that involves relinquishing age-old spiritual traditions that, leavened by progress and change, offer a forward-looking reading of Torah and a new way to conceive the future.

And of one thing they are certain: they believe that Reform provides a better way, which includes a yearning for justice and the hope for a richer spiritual life. They believe that through Reform Judaism, the unthinkable slowly becomes thinkable. And since hoping and dreaming are a collective activity, they see their task as carrying Reform Judaism's message from the Reform synagogue into the lives of Jews everywhere, and from there into the world.

NOTES

1. Peter Berger, "Urbanity as a Vortex of Pluralism," *American Interest*, February 3, 2016, https://www.the-american-interest.com/2016/02/03/urbanity-as-a-vortex-of-pluralism/.

2. Berger, "Urbanity as a Vortex of Pluralism."

3. Pew Research Center's Forum on Religion and Public Life, *"Nones" on the Rise* (Washington, DC: Pew Research Center, 2012), 1–16, http://www.pewforum.org/2012/10/09/nones-on-the-rise/.

4. Steven M. Cohen, "For Reform Jews, Some Good News on Engagement," Jewish Telegraphic Agency, November 5, 2015, http://www.jta.org/2015/11/05/life-religion/op-ed-for-reform-jews-some-good-news-on-engagement.

5. Michael A. Meyer, *Response to Modernity: A History of the Reform Movement in Judaism* (New York: Oxford University Press, 1988), 388.

6. Dana Evan Kaplan, "The Theological Roots of Reform Judaism's Woes," *The Forward*, February 25, 2011. http://forward.com/opinion/135476/the-theological-roots-of-reform-judaism-s-woes/.

Acknowledgments

Rabbi Dana Evan Kaplan, PhD

I would like to thank, first of all, each of the wonderful contributing authors. They brought to us their hearts and souls and went on to condense a lifetime of learning as well as a lifetime of experiences into short essays—much shorter than they or we would have liked. Their intellectual depth, combined with their deep concern and commitment, make what they have to say here important.

Thank you to Rabbi Hara Person, chief strategy officer of the Central Conference of American Rabbis and publisher of the CCAR Press, who listened to my book idea and encouraged me to develop it. She advised me and discussed its development with me for years over the course of its evolution. Thanks to Rabbi Steven Fox, chief executive of the Central Conference of American Rabbis, for preparing the foreword to the collection, thereby giving it his blessing. I value that. I owe special thanks to three scholars—Rabbi Fred Greenspahn, PhD, Rabbi Geoff Dennis, and William Berkson, PhD—for their guidance during the earliest stages of the book and its development. Their feedback concerning my vision for the book and on the structuring of its contents was crucial.

I would especially like to express my appreciation to Rabbi Beth Lieberman, CCAR Press executive editor, who deftly and with a strong hand guided this project to the finish line, as well as Sasha Smith, the CCAR Press's miracle worker/editorial assistant, astute rabbinic intern Shira Gluck, brilliant copy editor Debra Hirsch Corman, and the superbly talented CCAR team of press operations manager Debbie Smilow, communications manager Carly Linden, marketing and sales manager Ortal Bensky, and digital media manager Rabbi Dan Medwin.

At Springhill Avenue Temple in Mobile, Alabama, thanks to staff members Susie Broos and Susan Herring for the completion of a great deal of supportive work; and as well to Michael Pereira, current president and lover of antique aeroplanes, and Alan Hirsch, past president, who Rolls with the Tide. Thanks to my whole congregation for the wonderful interactions we enjoy that create the congenial atmosphere required for work of this sort. I learn new things from them all the time, about myself, about Reform Judaism, and about living meaningfully.

The people who come to services week after week deserve special acknowledgment, for caring so obviously about Reform Judaism, praying together as a community every Shabbat, and providing the sense of religious community that makes the difference for me. My Wednesday night Torah study group has challenged me intellectually with enthusiastic questions and ideas. Our discussions have been continually inspiring and helpful, and I look forward to studying this book with them soon. Thanks to Jamie Novetsky, our director of music, for responding enthusiastically to my requests for feedback. Thanks to Jonathan Fratkin, MD, for his wise counsel, and to Jeanine Watson for spectacular editorial assistance in Mobile, Alabama, helping me productively analyze my own writing and that of the other contributors, improving the quality of this collection throughout.

Everyone who has helped in my own Jewish and humanistic education and the institutions that have molded me over the years are remembered with gratitude, including the Stephen Wise Free Synagogue, the Jewish Center, and Congregation Rodeph Shalom, all three houses of worship my family attended as I was growing up in New York City; Ramaz School; Camp Dark Waters; Congregation B'nai Shalom, Temple Israel, and the Chase Collegiate School, in Waterbury, Connecticut, attended during my high school years; Yeshiva University, the University at Albany, Plymouth State University, Tel Aviv University, and finally the Hebrew Union College–Jewish Institute of Religion, which gave me the training to be a rabbi.

I want to remember my late mother, Meriel Kaplan, who was an aspiring writer who tragically died very young of breast cancer. I want to remember my late father, Norman Kaplan, DDS, who after reading the third of my books delicately commented that they all covered similar ground! I want to remember my aunt Ruth Moskowitz, who was instrumental in giving me a love of writing, also spending countless hours discussing the contemporary Jewish situation with me. I want to remember my uncle Herman Moskowitz, who was a devoted tennis player and played hours each day in Connecticut, rain or shine, summer or winter, until shortly before passing away at age ninety-seven. I am still in touch with his friends Evelyn and Jackie Marshak, who keep me up to date on what is happening in Waterbury, Connecticut.

Finally, much love to Joan "Samantha" Ewan, soon of Tel Aviv University, a whole new chapter. Mazel tov! I am so appreciative of your encouragement, your insight, your support, and your spiritual wisdom. May God bless you and nurture you. My appreciation for your gift of Skinny, the furry little Jamaican who brought out my emotional side, though he never seems to want to debate contemporary religious controversies. One Love, One Heart.

As we discourse and debate and disagree, may we all try to live up to the words of Micah 6:8: "What does God demand of you? Do justly, love mercy, and walk humbly before your God."

About the Authors

Rabbi Richard F. Address, DMin, is founder and director of Jewish Sacred Aging®, LLC and the website www.jewishsacredaging.com. He has served congregations in California and New Jersey and served on the staff of the Union for Reform Judaism for over three decades, as regional director and as director of the Department of Jewish Family Concerns. He was ordained by Hebrew Union College–Jewish Institute of Religion in 1972.

Rabbi Stephanie M. Alexander is the senior rabbi at Kahal Kadosh Beth Elohim in Charleston, South Carolina, where, in partnership with KKBE's lay leadership, she has worked to expand adult education offerings, deepen connections to Israel, welcome dynamic scholars and artists, and expand involvement in social justice. Rabbi Alexander is a past-president and founding member of CAJM, the Charleston Area Justice Ministry, a faith-based social justice organization of twenty-nine diverse congregations. She and her husband, Rabbi Aaron Sherman, and their son have lived in Charleston since 2010.

Rabbi Carole B. Balin, PhD is professor emerita of history at Hebrew Union College–Jewish Institute of Religion and senior director of special projects at Auburn Seminary. She has written and lectured extensively on the history of Reform Judaism.

Rabbi Pearl Barlev, MAHL, BCC, is a mentor, writer, musician, lover of life, rabbipreneur, and spiritual teacher for wholeness and happiness. Ordained by Hebrew Union College–Jewish Institute of Religion in 2007, she has served for ten years as rabbi/Jewish staff chaplain and an interfaith chaplain for medical and psychiatric patients at Ronald

Reagan UCLA Medical Center and Santa Monica UCLA Hospital and concurrently served as part-time pulpit rabbi to Santa Ynez Valley Jewish Community for six years. Rabbi Barlev brings to her rabbinate an intimate understanding and respect for the breadth of Jewish observance and culture and a passion for the ideal of *am echad lev echad*, "one people one heart." She draws on the ideals of Reform Judaism and the wisdom of traditional Jewish teachings as a path to the possibilities of peace, meaning, and healing for the individual, the Jewish community, and the interfaith community at large.

William Berkson, PhD, earned his doctorate in philosophy under the late Sir Karl Popper, at the London School of Economics. Since 1995, he has been a Jewish educator and director of the Jewish Institute for Youth and Family, which developed the *Becoming a Mentsh* curriculum on Jewish values. His most recent book is *Pirke Avot: Timeless Wisdom for Modern Life*, and he manages a forum on Jewish wisdom, Mentsh.com.

Rabbi Barry Block serves Congregation B'nai Israel in Little Rock, Arkansas. A Houston native and graduate of Amherst College, he was ordained by Hebrew Union College–Jewish Institute of Religion in New York in 1991. A member of the CCAR Board, he has contributed to CCAR Press publications, including *The Sacred Encounter* and *Navigating the Journey*. A Mussar Institute Board member and facilitator, Rabbi Block draws inspiration from Alan Morinis and relishes every opportunity to collaborate with him.

Cantor Rosalie Boxt is the director of worship for the Union for Reform Judaism, working with congregations, clergy, and worship teams on music and worship issues, as well as coordinating national events and all Biennial worship. She is a Synagogue 3000 fellow, a partner in the Kalsman Institute on Judaism and Health, and a past vice president for member relations of the American Conference of Cantors (ACC). She was a songleader for the URJ Kutz and Goldman Union Camps for many years, has served on faculty of the URJ's songleading program Hava Nashira for almost twenty years, and continues to teach young adult songleaders across the country. She served as the cantor of Temple Emanuel in Kensington, Maryland, from 2001 to 2017 and was ordained by the Debbie Friedman School of Sacred Music of Hebrew Union College–Jewish Institute of Religion.

Rabbi Mike Comins is founding director of the Jewish, online education center Lev Learning (LevLearning.com), teaches the Making

Prayer Real course and curriculum he created (www.makingPrayerReal .com), and directs the TorahTrek Center for Jewish Wilderness Spirituality (www.TorahTrek.org). A yeshivah-trained, Israeli-ordained Reform rabbi and a licensed Israeli desert guide, he holds an MA in Jewish education (Hebrew University), with an emphasis in contemporary philosophy. He is the author of *Making Prayer Real: Leading Jewish Spiritual Voices on Why Prayer Is Difficult and What to Do about It* and *A Wild Faith: Jewish Ways into Wilderness, Wilderness Ways into Judaism.*

Rabbi Shoshanah Conover serves as the associate rabbi at Temple Sholom of Chicago. She is a senior rabbinic fellow of the Shalom Hartman Institute and a vice chair of Chicago's Jewish Community Relations Council. She serves on the Executive Committee of the Chicago Board of Rabbis as well as the Union of Reform Judaism's Commission on Social Action. She received AVODAH's Partner in Tzedek Award and enjoys co-hosting the podcast *The Chosen Films.*

Rabbi Stanley M. Davids received his BA magna cum laude from Case Western Reserve University, where he was elected to Phi Beta Kappa. He was ordained by Hebrew Union College–Jewish Institute of Religion in 1965 and was subsequently awarded his doctor of divinity from HUC-JIR. A past national president of the Association of Reform Zionists of America (ARZA), Rabbi Davids has served on the Board of Governors of the Jewish Agency, on the Executive of the World Zionist Organization, as international president of the Alpha Epsilon Pi Fraternity, and as a member of the Board of Overseers of HUC-JIR.

Rabbi Nikki Lyn DeBlosi, PhD, serves as Reform rabbi and senior Jewish educator at New York University's Bronfman Center for Jewish Student Life. Ordained in 2013 by Hebrew Union College–Jewish Institute of Religion, she holds a BA summa cum laude in women's studies from Harvard University and an MA and PhD in performance studies from New York University. The *Forward* named her one of "America's Most Inspiring Rabbis" in 2015. She lives in Brooklyn with her wife and two sons.

Rabbi Geoffrey W. Dennis, ordained by Hebrew Union College–Jewish Institute of Religion in 1996, is rabbi of Congregation Kol Ami in Flower Mound, Texas, and teaches in the Jewish and Israel Studies Program of the University of North Texas. A Schusterman Israel Fellow of Brandeis University and a Brickner Fellow of the Reform Religious Action Center, he is the author of over thirty academic articles, encyclopedia entries, and essays, as well as two books, the most recent *Sefer ha-Bahir: Selections from the Book of Brilliance, the Classic Text of Early Kabbalah.*

Rabbi Lisa Edwards, PhD, has been a Jewish lesbian activist from the pulpit, on the page and on the Web, in the classroom, and in the streets of Los Angeles for over two decades. Since 1994, she has been rabbi (now senior rabbi) of Los Angeles congregation Beth Chayim Chadashim (BCC), "House of New Life." The first synagogue in the world founded by gays and lesbians (1972), BCC joined the Union for Reform Judaism in 1974 and today serves an all-inclusive, progressive, diverse community celebrating Jewish faith, values, and culture.

Rabbi David Ellenson, PhD is chancellor emeritus and former president of Hebrew Union College–Jewish Institute of Religion. Ordained by HUC-JIR, New York, in 1977, he received his PhD in religion at Columbia University in 1981. He currently serves as director of the Schusterman Center for Israel Studies and visiting professor in the Department of Near Eastern and Judaic Studies at Brandeis University. Rabbi Ellenson and Rabbi Michael Marmur are now completing an anthology on American Jewish thought.

Rabbi Sue Levi Elwell, PhD, is the founding director of the Los Angeles Jewish Feminist Center and first rabbinic director of Ma'yan. She has spent her career working toward creating and sustaining healthy, inclusive, vibrant, and open-hearted communities and congregations. She has served as a congregational rabbi, congregational consultant, and college teacher. She edited and contributed to *Lesbian Rabbis: The First Generation* and *The Open Door*, the CCAR Haggadah; served as the poetry editor of *The Torah: A Women's Commentary*; and edited and contributed to *Chapters of the Heart: Jewish Women Sharing the Torah of Our Lives*, which was a finalist for the 2014 National Jewish Book Award. Rabbi Elwell currently serves as spiritual director at Hebrew Union College–Jewish Institute of Religion in New York.

Rabbi Ted Falcon, PhD, is a Reform rabbi with a doctorate in professional psychology who explores the frontiers of a universal spirituality in his work as spiritual therapist, teacher, and writer. He founded meditative synagogues in Los Angeles in 1978 and in Seattle in 1993. His books include *Judaism For Dummies* and *A Journey of Awakening*. With a pastor and an imam, Rabbi Falcon is one of the Interfaith Amigos, supporting more effective interfaith cooperation. They have written *Getting to the Heart of Interfaith*, *Religion Gone Astray*, and *Finding Peace through Spiritual Practice*. Rabbi Falcon lives in the Pacific Northwest.

Rabbi Steven A. Fox is the chief executive of the Central Conference of American Rabbis (CCAR), the rabbinic leadership organization of Reform Judaism in North America and worldwide. Since joining the CCAR in 2006, Rabbi Fox has led the transformation of the CCAR into a twenty-first-century organization, working to sustain and enrich the Jewish community to ensure a vibrant Jewish future. His first publication on Reform Judaism was "On the Road to Unity: The UAHC and American Jewry, 1873–1903," *American Jewish Archives Journal*, Vol. xxxii No. 2 (1980).

Rabbi Joan S. Friedman, PhD, was ordained by Hebrew Union College–Jewish Institute of Religion in 1980 and has served as a congregational rabbi and as a college chaplain. She was a longtime member of the CCAR Responsa Committee. In 2003 she received her PhD in Jewish history from Columbia University and is currently associate professor of history and religious studies at the College of Wooster, where she chairs the program in Middle Eastern and North African Studies. She is the author of *"Guidance, Not Governance": Rabbi Solomon B. Freehof and Reform Responsa*, a 2013 National Jewish Book Award finalist.

Rabbi Hillel Gamoran was ordained by Hebrew Union College–Jewish Institute of Religion and received his doctorate at the College of Jewish Studies in Chicago. He served as the spiritual leader of Beth Tikvah Congregation in Hoffman Estates, Illinois, for thirty-four years. He was an active member of the Central Conference of American Rabbis and, for five years, was chairman of its Task Force on Hebrew Literacy. He is the author of *Jewish Law in Transition: How Economic Forces Overcame the Prohibition against Lending on Interest* and has published numerous scholarly articles.

Rabbi Neal Gold is a teacher and student based in Massachusetts, where he is pursuing graduate work in Near Eastern and Judaic studies at Brandeis University. He has worked as director of content and programming for ARZA, the Association of Reform Zionists of America, and for over eighteen years he served congregations in New Jersey and Massachusetts. In October 2016 he was a delegate for ARZENU, the international Reform Jewish movement, at the Thirty-Seventh World Zionist Congress in Jerusalem.

Rabbi Elyse Goldstein was ordained in 1983 and received her doctor of divinity, honoris causis, in 2008. She is currently the rabbi at City Shul, a synagogue she founded in Toronto in 2012. She is one of seven women featured in the Canadian National Film Board documentary *Half the Kingdom* and author of *ReVisions: Seeing Torah through a Feminist*

Lens and editor of *The Women's Torah Commentary*, *The Women's Haftarah Commentary*, and *New Jewish Feminism: Probing the Past, Forging the Future*.

Rabbi Lisa L. Goldstein is the executive director of the Institute for Jewish Spirituality. Previously, she was the executive director of Hillel of San Diego and an assistant rabbi at Congregation Shaare Emeth in St Louis, Missouri. She has also served as a group leader for American Jewish World Service and, as a Mandel Jerusalem Fellow, developed an innovative approach to integrating contemplative practice and justice work.

Rabbi Paul Golomb, ordained by Hebrew Union College–Jewish Institute of Religion in New York in 1975, is the rabbi emeritus and senior scholar at the Vassar Temple in Poughkeepsie, New York. He has published articles on modern Jewish thought, Reform Zionism, and interfaith relations. Rabbi Golomb served as editor-in-chief of *CCAR Journal: The Reform Jewish Quarterly* from 2013 to 2018.

Rabbi Rachel Gurevitz, PhD, is rabbi at Congregation B'nai Shalom, Westborough, Massachusetts, where she serves a diverse congregation that draws its membership from over fifteen surrounding towns. A PhD in cultural geography has enabled her to bring insights from sociology and cultural studies to better understand the needs of her community, while her grounding in Jewish mysticism infuses the ways she seeks to enrich the spiritual lives of her congregation. She is a fellow of CLAL's Rabbis Without Borders, blogs for My Jewish Learning, and is married to Rabbi Suri Krieger, with whom she is blessed to have four adult stepchildren.

Named among New York's "Most Influential Religious Leaders" by the *New York Observer*, **Rabbi Ammiel Hirsch, LLB** is the senior rabbi of Stephen Wise Free Synagogue in New York City. *City & State New York* magazine named him "the borough's most influential voice" for Manhattan's more than three hundred thousand Jews. He previously served as executive director of the Association of Reform Zionists of America. An accomplished teacher and public speaker, Rabbi Hirsch is also the coauthor of the acclaimed *One People Two Worlds: A Reform Rabbi and an Orthodox Rabbi Explore the Issues That Divide Them*.

Joel M. Hoffman, PhD, lectures widely to religious and community groups around the world. He holds a PhD from the University of Maryland in College Park and has served on the faculties of Hebrew Union College–Jewish Institute of Religion in New York City and Brandeis University in Waltham, Massachusetts. He is the author of four books about Hebrew and the Bible, most recently *The Bible Doesn't Say That: 40 Biblical Mistranslations, Misconceptions, and Other Misunderstandings*.

Joshua Holo, PhD, is associate professor of Jewish history and the dean at the Hebrew Union College–Jewish Institute of Religion's Jack H. Skirball Campus in Los Angeles. He specializes in medieval Jewish history and has published on the Jews of the Christian Mediterranean.

Rabbi Dana Evan Kaplan, PhD (EDITOR) is the rabbi of the Springhill Avenue Temple and teaches Judaism at Springhill College, both in Mobile, Alabama. Before that, he led the United Congregation of Israelites in Kingston, Jamaica, and Temple B'nai Israel in Albany, Georgia. He has had an adventurous career in the United States, as well as abroad, including extensive experience in the South. His rabbinic ordination is from Hebrew Union College–Jewish Institute of Religion in Jerusalem, and he holds a PhD in American Jewish history from Tel Aviv University. His works include *The New Reform Judaism*; *Contemporary American Judaism: Transformation and Renewal*; *The Cambridge Companion to American Judaism*; *American Reform Judaism: An Introduction*; *Platforms and Prayer Books*; and *Contemporary Debates in American Reform Judaism*. In his spare time, he enjoys scuba diving with whale sharks, hiking up to Blue Mountain Peak, and biking (at a leisurely pace) in Kerala.

Rabbi Gilad Kariv is the president and CEO of the Israel Movement for Reform and Progressive Judaism (IMPJ). For the last seventeen years, he has been an active and committed member in the IMPJ. He previously served as the associate director of the Israel Religious Action Center, the legal and public policy arm of the IMPJ. He has written numerous articles and position papers on Judaism, religion and state, and community empowerment. His articles appear in leading Israeli newspapers, and his opinions are frequently quoted in articles on legal issues, public policy, and social action. Recently Rabbi Kariv led the negotiations on the Kotel issue together with leaders of the Conservative Movement, the Reform Movement, the Jewish Agency for Israel, and the Jewish Federations of North America, which resulted in a historic decision to create a pluralistic section of the wall. Rabbi Kariv lives in Ramat Gan with his wife, Noa, and their three children.

Rabbi Jan Katzew, PhD, serves as associate professor of education and Jewish thought and as director of service-learning at Hebrew Union College–Jewish Institute of Religion in Cincinnati. He has published essays and articles in popular as well as scholarly journals, given lectures, facilitated workshops, and served as a scholar-in-residence at scores of congregations, conferences, and seminars on Jewish thought,

Israel education, interfaith relations, and Mussar literature. He has also served as an educational consultant to congregations and day schools throughout North America. Rabbi Katzew is married to Cantor Alane Katzew.

Rabbi Peter S. Knobel, PhD is rabbi emeritus of Beth Emet The Free Synagogue, Evanston, Illinois. He is a past president of the Central Conference of American Rabbis and served as the chair of the Ad Hoc New Siddur Committee, which produced *Mishkan T'filah: A Reform Siddur* (CCAR Press). He is the editor of *Mishkan Moeid: A Guide to the Jewish Year* (CCAR Press). He currently serves on the faculty of the Spertus Institute in Chicago, Illinois.

Rabbi Charles A. Kroloff, a past president of the Central Conference of American Rabbis, is rabbi emeritus of Temple Emanu-El, Westfield, New Jersey, which he served for thirty-six years. He is currently vice president for special projects at Hebrew Union College–Jewish Institute of Religion, where he teaches rabbinical students. A past president of ARZA, the Association of Reform Zionists of America, he is certified as a marital and family therapist. A graduate of Yale University, he is the author of *When Elijah Knocks: A Religious Response to Homelessness*; *54 Ways You Can Help the Homeless*; *Reform Judaism: A Jewish Way of Life*; and numerous essays and articles.

Rabbi Michael Marmur, PhD, is the Jack, Joseph, and Morton Mandel Provost of Hebrew Union College–Jewish Institute of Religion. He writes and teaches in the field of homiletics and Jewish thought, and is the aurhot of *Abraham Joshua Heschel and the Sources of Wonder* (University of Toronto Press, 2016). He has lived in Israel since 1984.

Rabbi Dalia Marx, PhD, a tenth-generation Jerusalemite, earned her doctorate at the Hebrew University and her rabbinic ordination from Hebrew Union College–Jewish Institute of Religion in Jerusalem and Cincinnati. She is currently a professor of liturgy and midrash at the Jerusalem campus of HUC-JIR and teaches in various academic and nonacademic institutions. Rabbi Marx writes for a number of publications and is active in promoting liberal Judaism in Israel. She is the author of *When I Sleep and When I Wake: On Prayers between Dusk and Dawn* (in Hebrew) and *A Feminist Commentary of the Babylonian Talmud (Tractates Tamid, Middot and Qinnim)* and has coedited or contributed to a number of books.

Michael A. Meyer, PhD, is the Adolph S. Ochs Professor of Jewish History emeritus at Hebrew Union College–Jewish Institute of Religion in Cincinnati. He is the author, among other works, of *The Origins of the Modern Jew: Jewish Identity and European Culture in Germany 1749–1824* and *Response to Modernity: A History of the Reform Movement in Judaism.* He has edited *German-Jewish History in Modern Times* (4 volumes) and, with W. Gunther Plaut, *The Reform Judaism Reader: North American Documents.* His books have won three Jewish book awards.

Rabbi Dr. Rachel S. Mikva serves as the Herman Schaalman Chair in Jewish Studies and Senior Faculty Fellow for the InterReligious Institute at Chicago Theological Seminary. The institute and the seminary work at the cutting edge of theological education, training religious leaders who build bridges across cultural and religious difference for the critical work of social transformation. She is the author of *Broken Tablets* (2000), *Midrash vaYosha* (2012), and *Dangerous Religious Ideas* (forthcoming).

Rabbi Geoffrey A. Mitelman is the founding director of Sinai and Synapses, an organization that bridges the scientific and religious worlds, and is being incubated at CLAL—The National Jewish Center for Learning and Leadership. His work has been supported by the John Templeton Foundation, Emanuel J. Friedman Philanthropies, and the Lucius N. Littauer Foundation, and his writings about the intersection of religion and science have appeared on the homepages of several sites, including the Huffington Post, Nautilus, Science and Religion Today, Jewish Telegraphic Agency, and My Jewish Learning. He has been an adjunct professor at both the Hebrew Union College–Jewish Institute of Religion and the Academy for Jewish Religion and is a sought-out teacher, presenter, and scholar-in-residence throughout the country. For seven years, he served as assistant and then associate rabbi of Temple Beth El of Northern Westchester, and he appeared on *Jeopardy!* in March 2016. He lives in Westchester County with his wife Heather Stoltz, a fiber artist, with their daughter and son.

Alan Morinis, DPhil, is founder and dean of the Mussar Institute and an active interpreter of the teachings and practices of the Mussar tradition. Born and raised in a culturally Jewish but non-observant home, he studied anthropology at Oxford University on a Rhodes Scholarship. Since 1997, the nearly lost Jewish spiritual discipline of Mussar has been his passion, a journey recorded in his book *Climbing Jacob's Ladder.* He is the author of *Everyday Holiness: The Jewish Spiritual Path of Mussar,* his guide to Mussar practice; and *With Heart in Mind: Mussar Teachings to Transform Your Life*.

Rabbi David W. Nelson, PhD, is a visiting associate professor of religion and campus rabbi at Bard College in Annandale on Hudson, New York. For fifteen years he was a senior teaching fellow at CLAL—The National Jewish Center for Learning and Leadership. He is the author of *Judaism, Physics and God: Searching for Sacred Metaphors in a Post-Einstein World* and *The Emergence of God: A Rationalist Jewish Exploration of Divine Consciousness*.

Rabbi Jonah Dov Pesner serves as the director of the Religious Action Center of Reform Judaism. He has led the Religious Action Center since 2015. He also serves as senior vice president of the Union for Reform Judaism. Named one of the most influential rabbis in America by *Newsweek* magazine, he is an inspirational leader, creative entrepreneur, and tireless advocate for social justice. Ordained at Hebrew Union College–Jewish Institute of Religion in 1997, he was a congregational rabbi at Temple Israel in Boston and at Temple Israel in Westport, Connecticut. A graduate of Wesleyan University and the Bronx High School of Science, Rabbi Pesner is married to Dana S. Gershon, an attorney. They have four daughters: Juliet, Noa, Bobbie, and Cate.

Rabbi Rachel Sabath Beit-Halachmi, PhD, serves the Hebrew Union College–Jewish Institute of Religion as President's Scholar and the National Director of Recruitment and Admissions. Former Vice President of the Shalom Hartman Institute and instructor of liturgy and theology at HUC-JIR in Jerusalem, Rabbi Sabath was ordained at HUC-JIR in New York, and earned a PhD in Jewish philosophy from the Jewish Theological Seminary. For several years, Rabbi Sabath wrote a monthly column in the *Jerusalem Post* and writes regularly for the Times of Israel, the Huffington Post, and other publications. She coauthored two books and published numerous articles including "Radically Free and Radically Claimed" in *Jewish Theology in Our Time*. Rabbi Sabath teaches and mentors students of HUC-JIR and speaks throughout North America on leadership, Israel, gender, and theology. For more than a decade she also served as the rabbi of Congregation Shirat HaYam on Nantucket Island. She is married to Rabbi Ofer Sabath Beit-Halachmi, and they have three children.

Rabbi David N. Saperstein served for forty years as the director of the Religious Action Center of Reform Judaism, after which he served, through January 2017, as the U.S. Ambassador-at-Large for International Religious Freedom. An attorney as well as a rabbi, he taught courses on church-state law and Jewish law for thirty-five years at Georgetown University Law Center. Currently, he serves as the senior advisor on policy and strategy for the Union for Reform Judaism, as well as senior fellow both at Georgetown University's Berkley Center for Religion, Peace, and World Affairs' Religious Freedom Research Project and at Georgetown's School of Foreign Service's Center for Jewish Civilization.

Rabbi Richard S. Sarason, PhD, is director of the Pines School of Graduate Studies and the Deutsch Professor of Rabbinics and Liturgy at Hebrew Union College–Jewish Institute of Religion in Cincinnati. His academic publications are in the areas of early Rabbinic literature and thought as well as the history of Jewish liturgy. He is the author of *Divrei Mishkan T'filah: Delving into the Siddur* (CCAR Press), his commentary on the current North American Reform prayer book. He serves as vice chair, for HUC-JIR, on the Joint Commission on Worship, Music, and Religious Living and has taught at many Reform congregations and Reform Movement programs.

Rabbi Amy Scheinerman is a hospice chaplain, writer, and teacher. She travels widely as a scholar-in-residence, teaching Talmud. Her forthcoming book *The Talmud of Relationships* will be published in two volumes by the Jewish Publication Society. Rabbi Scheinerman has served in the pulpits of Reform, Conservative, and unaffiliated congregations. She maintains a Torah commentary blog at http://taste-of-torah.blogspot.com and a Talmud blog at http://tenminutesoftalmud.blogspot.com. She lives in Maryland with her husband Ed, a mathematics professor and dean at the Johns Hopkins University; together, they have four children and three grandchildren.

Rabbi Amy Schwartzman is the senior rabbi of Temple Rodef Shalom in Falls Church, Virginia, where she has worked since her ordination from Hebrew Union College–Jewish Institute of Religion in 1990. In addition to serving a dynamic congregation, she is involved in leadership roles for her community as well as the Reform Movement. She is especially active in housing issues, mental health initiatives, and supporting those on the fringes of our society. Within the Reform Movement she serves in a number of leadership roles for the Central Conference of American Rabbis, as well as HUC-JIR. Rabbi Schwartzman and her husband, Kevin Moss, live in McLean, Virginia, with their two daughters.

Rabbi Robert M. Seltzer, PhD, is professor emeritus of Hunter College and the Graduate School of the City University of New York, where he has taught Jewish history and directed the interdisciplinary Jewish Studies Program for almost fifty years. He received his BA from Washington University in St. Louis, MA from Yale, master of arts in Hebrew letters and rabbinic ordination from HUC-JIR, and PhD in Jewish history from Columbia University. Many years ago he was president of the National Federation of Temple Youth (NFTY), much later president of the Association for Jewish Studies (the AJS), and more recently the honoree of *Reappraisals and New Studies of the Modern Jewish Experience: Essays in Honor of Robert M. Seltzer.* He is author of *Jewish People, Jewish Thought: The Jewish Experience in History; Simon Dubnow's "New Judaism": Diaspora Nationalism and the World History of the Jews;* and many articles and edited books on aspects of Jewish history from ancient to recent times.

Rabbi Mark Dov Shapiro, ordained by HUC-JIR in 1977, is rabbi emeritus of Sinai Temple, Springfield, Massachusetts. He is also editor of the CCAR Press volume *Gates of Shabbat.* His interest in faith, literature, and history have shaped his learning and teaching. He created "The God Survey," which was documented in *Reform Judaism* magazine; he has written as well about the prophets Isaiah and Jeremiah. His commitments to social justice and interfaith work are central to his community involvement.

Rabbi Suzanne Singer has served as the rabbi of Temple Beth El in Riverside, California, since 2008, where she also served as educator for eight years. Previously, she served as a rabbi of Temple Sinai in Oakland, California, where she launched a Fain Award–winning social justice conference. She received a Master's in Journalism from the University of California, Berkeley, in 1975, and a Master's of Judaic Studies and Master's of Hebrew Letters from Hebrew Union College–Jewish Institute of Religion in 2000 and 2002, respectively. She was ordained at HUC-JIR in 2003, where she won awards in Bible, liturgy, Rabbinic literature, and ethics. Before becoming a rabbi, she was a producer and programming executive for PBS, for which she won two national Emmys.

Rabbi Shira Stern, DMin, BCC, was ordained by Hebrew Union College–Jewish Institute of Religion in 1983 and received her doctor of ministry in 2004. She has been a pulpit rabbi and director of the northeastern region of MAZON: A Jewish Response to Hunger. She is a board-certified Jewish chaplain and has served in hospitals, hospices, and long-term care facilities, as well as working as the director of the

Joint Chaplaincy Program in Middlesex, New Jersey; the director of the Jewish Institute for Pastoral Care in New York City; and now the director of the Center for Pastoral Care and Counseling in Marlboro, New Jersey, specializing in bereavement. She continues to serve as a disaster spiritual care lead for both the Red Cross and the Office of Emergency Management for the State of New Jersey.

Rabbi Lance J. Sussman, PhD, eighth senior rabbi of Keneseth Israel (KI), Elkins Park, Pennsylvania, is an affable, scholarly rabbi who revolutionized worship in his 167-year-old Reform synagogue, introducing visual *t'filot*, illustrated sermons, and for KI children, the "KI Puppets." As chair of the CCAR Press, he helped launch the Reform Movement's latest *Mishkan* prayer-book series. Rabbi Sussman has taught at Princeton University, Temple University, and Hunter College, among others, and has authored several books and numerous articles in the field of American Jewish history. His research on the *"t'reifah* banquet" was featured in the PBS series *God in America*. He founded the Cheltenham Area Multifaith Council and is involved in Jewish-Muslim dialogue.

Rabbi David A. Teutsch, PhD, is the Wiener Professor Emeritus of the Reconstructionist Rabbinical College, where he previously served as president for a decade. He is the editor of the seven-volume *Kol Haneshamah* prayer-book series and the three-volume *Guide to Jewish Practice*, which won the National Jewish Book Council Kraft Award for Contemporary Jewish Practice, as well as author of many other books and articles. A past president of the Society of Jewish Ethics and of the Academic Coalition for Jewish Bioethics, he serves on the editorial board of the *Journal of Jewish Ethics*. A renowned consultant and trainer, he earned his AB with honors at Harvard University, his MA and MHL from Hebrew Union College–Jewish Institute of Religion in New York, and his PhD from the Wharton School, where his dissertation focused on organizational ethics.

Rabbi Rachel Timoner is the senior rabbi of Congregation Beth Elohim in Park Slope, Brooklyn, where her leadership centers on spiritual life and social justice. She previously served as associate rabbi of Leo Baeck Temple in Los Angeles, and was ordained by Hebrew Union College–Institute of Religion in 2009. Her chapter is adapted from her book *Breath of Life: God as Spirit in Judaism.*

Evan Traylor, originally from Oklahoma City, Oklahoma, is serving as the inaugural Presidential Fellow for Millennial Engagement at the Union for Reform Judaism (URJ). He graduated from the University of

Kansas in 2016, where he studied political science, Jewish studies, and leadership studies. An alumnus of NFTY, Greene Family Camp, and Kutz Camp, Evan has held many leadership roles in the Jewish community, including serving as the North American president of NFTY, trustee for the URJ Board, and student member of the Hillel International Board of Directors.

Rabbi Kari Hofmaister Tuling, PhD, received rabbinic ordination in 2004 and earned her PhD in Jewish thought in 2013, both from the Hebrew Union College–Jewish Institute of Religion in Cincinnati. She has served congregations in Connecticut, Indiana, New York, and Ohio and has taught Jewish studies courses at the University of Cincinnati and the State University of New York, Plattsburgh. She currently serves as the rabbi of Congregation Kol Haverim in Glastonbury, Connecticut.

Rabbi Mark Washofsky, PhD, is the Solomon B. Freehof Professor of Jewish Law and Practice at Hebrew Union College–Jewish Institute of Religion in Cincinnati, where he teaches Talmud and halachic literature. His publications focus on the relationships between halachah, contemporary legal theory, and Reform Judaism. He is the author of *Jewish Living: A Guide to Contemporary Reform Practice* and the editor of *Reform Responsa for the Twenty-First Century* (CCAR Press). He served as chair of the Responsa Committee of the Central Conference of American Rabbis from 1996 to 2017.

Rabbi Dvora Weisberg, PhD, is professor of Rabbinics and the director of the Rabbinical Program at Hebrew Union College–Jewish Institute of Religion in Los Angeles. She received her PhD in Talmud and Rabbinics from the Jewish Theological Seminary of America and was ordained by HUC-JIR. Her research focuses on gender and the family in Rabbinic literature. Dvora's passion is engaging her students, at HUC-JIR and beyond, in the study of Talmud.

Rabbi Eric H. Yoffie served as president of the Union for Reform Judaism from 1996 to 2012. He writes and lectures on American Judaism, interfaith relations, and Israel and the Middle East, and he writes a regular opinion column for the Israeli daily *Haaretz*. His articles may be found at ericyoffie.com.

Rabbi Mary L. Zamore currently serves as the executive director of the Women's Rabbinic Network. She is also the editor of and a contributing author to *The Sacred Table: Creating a Jewish Food Ethic* (CCAR Press), which was designated a finalist by the National Jewish

Book Awards. Ordained by Hebrew Union College–Jewish Institute of Religion in New York in 1997, she graduated from Columbia College and also studied at Yad Vashem and Machon Pardes. Rabbi Zamore is an active contributor to the Huffington Post, scholar-in-residence, and writer.

Rabbi Ben Zeidman grew up in Columbus, Ohio, before earning a BA in international relations from James Madison College at Michigan State University, with a specialization in Jewish studies. He was ordained by Hebrew Union College–Jewish Institute of Religion in 2010 and then served as a rabbi at Temple Emanu-El in New York City until 2015. He was the developmental editor of the *The New Union Haggadah, Revised Edition* and a contributing author for *Lights in the Forest: Rabbis Respond to Twelve Essential Jewish Questions* (both CCAR Press). Rabbi Zeidman, his wife, Katie, and his children, Oliver and Isabel, now live in El Paso, Texas, where he proudly serves as rabbi at Temple Mount Sinai.

Classical Sources Cited

Bible (*Tanach*)

Five Books of Moses (Torah)

Genesis (*B'reishit*)

1	137, 531
1:1	8, 81
1:3	559
1:26	15, 416
1:27	36, 213, 313, 541
1:28	199
1:31	220
2:7	132n2
3:9	473
9	87
9:7	532
9:8–11	199
9:22	535
9:25	536
11	531
12:1	261
12:1–2	397
12:1–3	90
12:2	81
15:18	91
17:1–9	90
17:4	91
17:5	91
17:24	429
18:1–15	557
18:19	87
22:12	25
37:15	473

Exodus (*Sh'mot*)

1:9–11	532
3:13–14	18
4:23	124
5:1–2	525
7:3	125
7:16	124
12:38	533
14–21	91
16:23	229
19	381–82
19: 4–6	82
19:5	92, 382
19: 5–6	xxvi, 10, 92
19:6	199, 352
19:8	82

Midrashic Works

Mishnah

Talmuds

Babylonian Talmud (*Talmud Bavli*)

Jerusalem Talmud
(*Talmud Yerushalmi*)

Pei-ah
21a–b   544

Yoma
6:4   63

Codes

Shulchan Aruch
Joseph Karo

Even HaEizer
1:4 (4)   523n6

Yoreh Dei-ah
268:12   435
335:2   551
335:5   551
402:12   61

Mishneh Torah
Moses Maimonides

Hilchot Matanot Aniyim
7:5   465
7:7   546

Hilchot M'lachim
6:10   137

Yesodei HaTorah
1   16

Other Classical Sources

Guide of the Perplexed
(*Moreh Nevuchim*)
Moses Maimonides
1:40   106

Zohar
Bamidbar, B'haalot'cha
58–64
307–8

Index

faith and, 483–84
morality and, 58
prayer and, 552
religion and, 57–66
science of Judaism. See *Wissenschaft des Judentums*
scientific approach, 185
secularization, 175–76, 579–80
self-control, 63–64
the self/selfhood, 50, 62, 99–100, 257–58
Seligmann, Caesar, 353–54
semen, 417, 419
separation of milk and meat, 214
sermons, rabbinical, 351
Sex, Murder and the Meaning of Life (Kenrick), 62
sex ethics, 413–22
sexual harassment, 418
sexual identification/sexuality, 35–36, 63, 415–19, 515–23. *See also* gay/lesbian communities/couples/rights; transgender people/issues
sexual relationships, 420–21. *See also* gay/lesbian communities/couples/rights
Shabbat, 208, 217–25, 227–35, 230, 237–40, 271–73, 404–5
activities, 221–25, 230. *See also* candles, lighting; prayer/prayer services; rest
in community/with family, 222–23, 234, 405–6
healing power of, 565
intentionality and, 217–20, 224
meals, 224, 233
prohibitions, 218, 228–30, 284–85
sounding shofar on, 323–24
study and, 223, 234–35
synagogue and, 233–34
unconditional acceptance and, 264–65
Shammai, 221, 294–95, 322–23
Shapira, Kalonymus Kalman, 219, 224
Shavuot, 396
Shimon ben Yochai, 279
the *Shiviti*, 264
sh'lom bayit, 417–18, 491. *See also* Jewish home
Shlomo Ephraim of Lunschitz (rabbi), 293
Shlomo HaLevi (rabbi), 280
Sh'ma, 255–56, 367n25, 560
sh'mirat haguf. See health preservation

sh'mirat hateva. See the environment/environmentalism
the Shoah. *See* Holocaust
shofar, sounding and hearing of, 323–24
Shulchan Aruch, 113
the sick, 549–56. *See also* healing
siddurim (s. siddur). *See* prayer books
Siegel, Danny, 469
Silent Spring (Rachel Carson), 137
Silver, Abba Hillel (rabbi), 83
simchat chochmah, 397
Simlai (rabbi), 200
Sisterhoods, 33
social action/justice, 24, 489, 503–13, 572, 579–90, 586. *See also* fair trade; fair treatment; justice/injustice; sacred action; *tikkun olam*
sod, 306
Sofer, Moses (rabbi), 282
Soloveitchik, Joseph (rabbi), 106–7
Song of Songs (book), 535–36
Sorin, Gerald, 382–83
the soul, 17, 219–20, 494–95
immortality of, 47–48, 52–53
improvement of, 499–500
Spinoza, Baruch (Benedict), 68
on divine authority, 127, 133n4, 156
expulsion from the community, 184
on free will and determinism, 127
on God, 26
spirit (*ruach*), 17–18, 495–96
spiritual expression/practices, xviii–xix, 168, 186, 255–65, 499–500
interpretation, 292
prayers and, 364
seeking, 472–75
spiritual revolutions, 283. *See also* exile
Star of Redemption (Rosenzweig), 576–77
"Statement of Principles for Reform Judaism" (1999). *See* 1999 Pittsburgh Platform
Stone, Warren (rabbi), 144–45
the stranger, 108–10, 205, 391, 426, 505, 530, 534
s'udah sh'lishit, 224
summer camps, 142–43
sustainability, 142, 144–45. *See also* the environment/environmentalism
synagogues. *See also* prayer/prayer services; religion: formal/traditional/institutional; under individual names
distancing from, 472